READING THE OLD TESTAMENT

An Introduction to the Hebrew Bible

READING THE OLD TESTAMENT

An Introduction to the Hebrew Bible

BARRY L. BANDSTRA

HOPE COLLEGE

Wadsworth Publishing Company

I(T)P™ An International Thomson Publishing Company

Belmont • Albany • Bonn • Boston • Cincinnati • Detroit • London • Madrid • Melbourne
Mexico City • New York • Paris • San Francisco • Singapore • Tokyo • Toronto • Washington

Religion Editor: Tammy Goldfeld
Editorial Assistant: Kelly Zavislak
Production Editor: Michelle Filippini
Managing Designer: Stephen Rapley
Print Buyer: Diana Spence
Permissions Editor: Bob Kauser

Text and Cover Designer: Lisa Berman
Copy Editor: Cheryl Ferguson
Photo Researcher: Bobbie Broyer
Signing Representative: Thor McMillen
Compositor: Joan Olson, Wadsworth Digital Productions
Printer: Malloy Lithographing, Inc.

Poem on page 470 from *The Poetry of Robert Frost*. Copyright © 1956 by Robert Frost. Copyright © 1928, 1969 by Henry Holt & Co., Inc. Reprinted by permission of Henry Holt & Co., Inc.

For more information, contact Wadsworth Publishing Company.

Wadsworth Publishing Company
10 Davis Drive
Belmont, California 94002, USA

International Thomson Editores
Campos Eliseos 385, Piso 7
Col. Polanco
11560 México D.F. México

International Thomson Publishing Europe
Berkshire House 168–173
High Holborn
London, WC1V 7AA, England

International Thomson Publishing GmbH
Königswinterer Strasse 418
53227 Bonn, Germany

Thomas Nelson Australia
102 Dodds Street
South Melbourne 3205
Victoria, Australia

International Thomson Publishing Asia
221 Henderson Road
#05–10 Henderson Building
Singapore 0315

Nelson Canada
1120 Birchmount Road
Scarborough, Ontario
Canada M1K 5G4

International Thomson Publishing Japan
Hirakawacho Kyowa Building, 3F
2-2-1 Hirakawacho
Chiyoda-ku, Tokyo 102, Japan

Library of Congress Cataloging-in-Publication Data

Bandstra, Barry L.
    Reading the Old Testament : an introduction to
the Hebrew Bible / Barry L. Bandstra
          p.   cm.
    Includes bibliographical references and indexes.
    ISBN 0-534-21354-5 (alk. paper)
    1. Bible. O.T. — Introductions. I. Title.
BS1140.2.B32   1995
221.6'1—dc20
                            94–13210

To former students in my Introduction to Biblical Literature *course at Hope College who helped me shape this book*

and

To future students who may better understand and appreciate the Old Testament Scriptures with the help of this book.

CONTENTS

PREFACE

To Students of the Old Testament

This textbook was written for you. Inspired by my former students, it has been informed by fifteen years of teaching a college-level introductory course in biblical literature. Here are some suggestions for getting the most out of it.

Because this textbook examines the text of the Old Testament, it quotes passages from the Bible and then interprets them. Maps, historical explanations, illustrations, and textual commentary were designed to aid you in comprehending specific texts of the Hebrew Bible.

Each chapter incorporates the following components, all specifically designed to aid you in studying the Old Testament.

Names and Terms to Remember. Near the beginning of each chapter is a list of key names and terms for that chapter. If you look over this list before you read the chapter, you will be alert to the main characters and concepts you should end up knowing. Each term is in boldface when it is defined in the chapter. The list would also be useful for study purposes before tests and quizzes. Review the list and make sure you can identify each of the names and terms along with its historical and literary context. Near the end of the book is a complete glossary of all of these names and terms with their definitions.

Questions for Review. Each chapter includes a short set of questions to help you identify and review some of the main themes of that chapter.

For Further Study. At the end of each chapter is a list of books that can be used to study the material in more depth. The resources included in these sections were chosen because they are especially understandable to students at your level of study.

To Teachers of the Old Testament

This textbook was designed first and foremost to teach students how to read the biblical text. Although it treats literary issues throughout, it is not a "Bible as Literature" textbook. Although it utilizes historical research and reconstructs Israelite history, it is not a "History of Israelite Religion" textbook.

The overall approach of the textbook is this: beginning with actual biblical passages, it teaches how to draw out meaning by doing close readings of texts right in the textbook. Significant, sometimes lengthy, portions of the biblical text are included in the body of the textbook. This is done for two reasons. First, by including biblical texts in the textbook, it is easier to follow the textual commentaries. Second, by including biblical texts right in the textbook, it is more likely that students will actually read portions of the primary text, the Old Testament. In the past using other textbooks I have found that students often read the textbook but not the assigned Old Testament readings, because it was more difficult to read the Bible itself, and the textbook summarized the main points anyhow.

As the textbook develops the meaning of specific texts, it draws from history, archaeology, and literature, not in isolation, but in order to explain something in the biblical text. My intention is to show how the ancillary disciplines of history, archaeology, literary criticism, and linguistics can be used to inform our reading of the text. In sum, this approach intends to teach students how to interpret biblical texts properly by modeling how it should be done. Its long-term goal is to equip students to handle the Bible correctly, so once they are out of the course they can evaluate how others read the text and can apply appropriate methods in their own reading.

This textbook introduces modern critical methodologies by way of interpreting texts, rather than by describing the methodologies theoretically. Through using the textbook by the end of the course students will have practiced source analysis, form-critical analysis, reader-response criticism, canonical interpretation, and more.

This textbook is appropriate for beginning students of the Old Testament and is targeted at the freshman–sophomore university level. It can be used in Old Testament/Hebrew Bible courses whether they are organized by literature or history. If by literature, you would assign chapters as you cover specific books of the Bible. If by history, you would probably assign chapters out of their order in the table of contents as they correspond to the period of history you are covering.

This textbook is organized into three main sections according to how the books of the Old Testament have been grouped in the Jewish tradition. Each of the three sections has a preface, called the prologue, and a summarizing epilogue to help focus issues. Special pedagogical components of the textbook are as follows:

Chapter Introductions. The introductions to each chapter attempt to establish functional and thematic parallels between the world of the biblical text and the modern world. These parallels draw students into the material and suggest ways in which the ancient biblical text provides perspectives and articulates values that may be of service today.

Maps. Maps are generously distributed throughout the textbook. They are customized to illustrate specific moments in biblical history.

Time Lines. These, too, are frequently supplied, because special efforts are needed to correlate literature, history, and text.

Questions for Review and Questions for Discussion. The Questions for Review may be helpful to test students' comprehension of the chapter, and would be especially useful for review before tests. The Questions for Discussion are intended to push student thinking beyond the bounds of the chapter by suggesting ways the material may relate to issues with which they can identify. In addition to their use in a review or discussion setting, these questions may be useful as starters for term papers.

For Further Study. Appended to each chapter is a short bibliography of reading material pertinent to topics within that chapter. The works are briefly described, and were deliberately chosen because they are understandable to students in the beginning to intermediate level. The chapter bibliographies are not intended to be comprehensive.

Resources for Old Testament Study. A classified bibliography of additional scholar's resources is in an appendix. In addition to providing bibliography on individual books of the Old Testament, it could be used as an introduction to biblical research in general because it explains the various types of study tools available to students.

Acknowledgments

My thanks go first to my students at Hope College who gave me encouragement and, most importantly, feedback and advice. They used this textbook while it was in its formative stages.

Hope College, in general, provided a wonderfully supportive environment for this project. The administration provided funding for a sabbatical leave and summers freed up for research, without which I could not have carried on. Departmental colleagues were unflagging in their encouragement. Allen Verhey read some early chapters and gave perceptive commentary. Elton Bruins imparted constant encouragement, and Dennis Voskuil agreed to use the manuscript in his classes even when it was only half-baked. Out of all of this collegial contact came much helpful critique and not a little moral support.

The project could not have happened without the ever-present support of Karen Michmerhuizen, who directs the Religion Department at Hope College (especially its professors) like a maestro. The following students also deserve special credit: Karla Van Huysen for her artistic contributions; Rob Harrison, Craig Stapert, and Michael Theune for helping with the manuscript at various stages of its development.

I also wish to thank the staff of the Cook Theological Research Center at Western Theological Seminary for the generous use of their collection, and especially for the use of a wonderful sixth-floor office during my sabbatical leave. The staff of the Gordon and Margaret Van Wylen Library at Hope College was also most cooperative, especially when it came to securing interlibrary loan materials.

The outside readers were very helpful in shaping the book, and they are as follows: Bernard F. Batto, DePauw University; Rosalie Beck, Baylor University; Peter J. Haas, Vanderbilt University; Ralph Neall, Union College; John Priest, Florida State University; Sharon Pace Jeansonne, Marquette University.

The editorial staff at Wadsworth Publishing Company was supportive throughout. I am appreciative of Sheryl Fullerton, who gave me the initial encouragement to pursue the project. Special thanks to the ever-kind Tammy Goldfeld, religion editor at Wadsworth; Michelle Filippini, the textbook's production editor; and Cheryl Ferguson, the text's copyeditor. For what might be laudable, they get the credit; for its shortcomings, I take the blame.

Lastly but especially my family—I am eternally grateful to my wife, Debra, and our three sons, Adam, Jonathan, and Daniel, for their endurance and long suffering. What I've done is done for them. Thanks also to my parents and mother-in-law for the loving environment they foster, with special thanks to my father-in-law, John Rosier, for his active and sustaining interest in the project from beginning to end.

READING THE OLD TESTAMENT

An Introduction to the Hebrew Bible

INTRODUCTION

The focus of our study is the Old Testament. As sacred scripture for three of the world's great religions, Judaism, Christianity, and Islam, it has been revered for thousands of years. Full of rich tales and colorful heroes, it has inspired some of the world's greatest works of art, music, and literature. Not least of all, it is a fascinating and spiritually moving book.

READING THE OLD TESTAMENT

Reading the Old Testament is intended for students who wish to learn about the Bible by reading the Bible. It works through the Old Testament book by book, explaining the meaning of the text and making connections between yesterday and today. Along the way it draws from some of the best thinking of modern biblical scholarship in order to explain the literary shape of the text and the history behind it. Do not let the mention of history and literature put you off. After all, the Old Testament is an ancient book, some portions as old as 3,000 years, and we need help to recover its original meaning. Rest assured, all of our historical and literary research will be relevant and will help us read and understand the biblical text.

WHAT IS THE OLD TESTAMENT?

What exactly is this book we call the **Old Testament**? The Old Testament can be many different things, depending on who you are.

It is a collection of sacred writings from ancient Israel, what Judaism refers to as the **Hebrew Bible,** the Hebrew Scriptures, or the Written Torah (to distinguish it from the Oral Torah of the rabbis).

The same book is called the Old Testament by Christians—*old* because Christians view it as the indispensable prologue to the New Testament. Some suggest *Older* Testament would be a better title in order to avoid any suggestion that it is outmoded.

The Old Testament can be many different things, depending on why and how you are reading it. Viewed as literature, the Old Testament is a rich and varied collection of poetry, drama, story, and legal prose. Viewed linguistically, it is an ancient text written in foreign tongues, mostly Hebrew, but also containing some Aramaic. Viewed as history, it provides a wealth of information about the culture and times of ancient Israel. Viewed as theology, it reveals Israel's concept of God and communicates deep spiritual truths. Although there are many ways in which the Old Testament can be viewed, all make reference to the same body of writings.

For the most part, the terms Old Testament and Hebrew Bible refer to the same writings. You will find them used interchangeably in the textbook. The difference between the two terms is relevant when making reference to the arrangement of books in the Bible. As the table on pages 5 and 6 displays, the Hebrew Bible organizes the books differently from the Old Testament of Christianity, though they contain the same books. Only the Old Testament of the Roman Catholic and Orthodox traditions includes additional books.

The preference for one term over the other may imply something about the religious perspective of the user. Notably for Christians, using the term Old Testament implies that the content of this book must be seen in relation to its fulfillment in the New Testament. A Jew could not be expected to use the phrase Old Testament with that same connotation. The field of biblical studies is moving in the direction of referring to the Old Testament as the Hebrew Bible in order to be more inclusive of differing faith communities. For Christians this does not imply a weakening of commitment to both testaments, just a sensitivity to persons of other faiths. Another term for the Old Testament that is gaining recognition and acceptance is *First Testament*.

The next observation is potentially confusing. The Hebrew Bible is one book, judging by the fact that it is typically bound as a single volume. At the same time, it is an anthology of books—a virtual library of twenty-four originally separate works. The individual books came from a variety of authors writing over a span of one thousand years or more. They were gathered together and included in a single work we call the Hebrew Bible because early God-fearing Jews judged this particular collection of writings to contain an authoritative record of God's torah for them.

The Jewish community that gave rise to the Hebrew Bible divided the various books into three collections, called the Law, the Prophets, and the Writings. The Hebrew names of these collections are **Torah**, **Nevi'im**, and **Ketuvim**. Taking the first letter of each of these three words, and inserting the vowel "a," the Jewish community gave the name **Tanak** (sometimes also spelled Tanakh) to their Bible. Our textbook takes its basic structure from these three main collections of the Hebrew Bible, and it uses the labels Torah, Prophets, and Writings.

The final collection is called the canon. The term canon, as applied to the anthology of books constituting the Hebrew Bible, implies that it is the authorized collection of books recognized by the Jewish community. Calling it the authorized collection of books implies that there were other books as well and that choices had been made. There were, in fact, many more Jewish writings, written in both Hebrew and Greek, circulating within the Jewish community in those days. But the Jewish community came to accept only a certain number of books as the ones through which they believed God spoke. Those they believed God used to communicate his will for the community, they treated as the divinely inspired books.

But not all Jews accepted the limits of this particular collection we are calling the Hebrew Bible. There were many Jews living outside the territory of Palestine in what were largely Greek-speaking areas. The sum of Jews living outside Palestine is called the **Dispersion**, sometimes also the **Diaspora**. The Jewish communities of the Diaspora, especially the one in Alexandria, Egypt, were literarily productive and had their own ideas of what should be included in the canon. They had come to revere other books in addition to those included in the canon recognized in Palestine.

The additional materials, some full books, others just appendices, are known as the **Apocrypha**. They are accepted as Scripture today by the Roman Catholic and Orthodox churches. The Greek canon that includes the Apocrypha is called the **Septuagint** (often abbreviated by Roman numeral LXX). Protestant churches, along with the Jewish community, deny their authority and instead accept the more restricted Hebrew Bible of Palestinian Judaism.

The specific books of the Hebrew Bible found in each of the three main divisions of the Tanak are found in the left column of the following table. The middle and right columns provide the order of books in the Protestant and Roman Catholic/Orthodox versions of the Old Testament. Although they are ordered differently, the Hebrew Bible and Protestant Old Testament contain exactly the same books. The Roman Catholic/Orthodox Old Testament contains additional books called the Apocrypha, also called the Deutero-Canonical books, which are identified by italics in the table.

Traditionally Jews and Christians have traced the origin of the Bible to God. The doctrine of biblical inspiration affirms that the very words of the biblical text in some significant way come directly from God. Using human agents, God "inscripturated" his word for humankind. Whatever one's view of the inspiration of the biblical text, all students of the text would agree that the text was delivered through human agency.

It would be a gross oversimplification to imagine that one person sat down to write the entire Hebrew Bible. Many groups and individuals were responsible for handing down the material contained in the Old Testament and for giving the individual books their final shape. Most remain nameless to this day. Even the books of identifiable prophets such as Isaiah and Amos were not entirely written by those men. The books are collections of their sayings, which anonymous editors gathered together and annotated.

Much of the material that eventually was included in the Hebrew Bible started out as folktales, songs, and religious liturgies. The common people inherited these stories and passed them on from one generation to the next by word of mouth. Oral tradition, as it is called, was the source of many of the stories that have survived about the ancestors and Israel's early history. Priests and highly trained scribes, typically employed by the king, were virtually the only ones able to read and write. They were responsible for gathering materials from oral and written sources, organizing them, and compiling them into books. Probably the earliest that any books were written down was around 950 B.C.E. during the reign of Solomon, the king of Israel at its Golden Age.

The Hebrew Bible took centuries to shape. After individual books were completed, they were joined into collections of books. The earliest collection was the Torah. It was given its overall shape sometime during the Babylonian exile and was accepted as authoritative by 400 B.C.E. The Torah was followed by the Prophets, which were closed around 200 B.C.E. After the Writings were added, the Tanak was completed around 100 C.E. as reflected in a conference of rabbis meeting at Jamnia. Though the process was in fact much more complicated than the above summary implies, the Hebrew Bible as we know it today became a fixed collection after a long period of growth and development.

Having basically defined the anthology called the Old Testament, we can ask, why is this textbook called *Reading the Old Testament*?

First, the title should communicate that we will give attention to the reading process. We will learn the right way to read the text, paying attention to proper methods and reading practices.

Second, the title means to suggest that we focus our energies on reading the *text* of the Old Testament.

BOOKS OF THE HEBREW BIBLE/OLD TESTAMENT

Hebrew Bible—Tanak (Judaism)	Old Testament (Protestant Christianity)	Old Testament (Roman Catholic Christianity)
I. Law (Torah)	Genesis	Genesis
Genesis	Exodus	Exodus
Exodus	Leviticus	Leviticus
Leviticus	Numbers	Numbers
Numbers	Deuteronomy	Deuteronomy
Deuteronomy	Joshua	Joshua
	Judges	Judges
II. Prophets (Nevi'im)		
A. Former Prophets	Ruth	1 Samuel
Joshua	1 Samuel	2 Samuel
Judges	2 Samuel	1 Kings
1 Samuel	1 Kings	2 Kings
2 Samuel	2 Kings	1 Chronicles
1 Kings	1 Chronicles	2 Chronicles
2 Kings	2 Chronicles	Ezra
	Ezra	Nehemiah
B. Latter Prophets		
Isaiah	Nehemiah	*Tobit*
Jeremiah	Esther	*Judith*
Ezekiel	Job	Esther and *Additions*
The Twelve:	Psalms	Job
Hosea	Proverbs	Psalms
Joel	Ecclesiastes	Proverbs
Amos	Song of Solomon	Ecclesiastes
Obadiah	Isaiah	Song of Solomon
Jonah	Jeremiah	*Wisdom of Solomon*

(continued)

Hebrew Bible—Tanak (Judaism)	Old Testament (Protestant Christianity)	Old Testament (Roman Catholic Christianity)
Micah	Lamentations	*Ecclesiasticus*
Nahum	Ezekiel	Isaiah
Habakkuk	Daniel	Jeremiah
Zephaniah	Hosea	Lamentations
Haggai	Joel	*Baruch and Letter of Jeremiah*
Zechariah	Amos	Ezekiel
Malachi	Obadiah	Daniel and *Additions*:
III. *Writings (Ketuvim)*	Jonah	*Susanna*
Psalms	Micah	*Song of the Young Men*
Proverbs	Nahum	*Bel and the Dragon*
Job	Habakkuk	Hosea
The Song of Songs	Zephaniah	Joel
Ruth	Haggai	Amos
Lamentations	Zechariah	Obadiah
Ecclesiastes	Malachi	Jonah
Esther		Micah
Daniel		Nahum
Ezra		Habakkuk
Nehemiah		Zephaniah
1 Chronicles		Haggai
2 Chronicles		Zechariah
		Malachi
		1 Maccabees
		2 Maccabees

You might ask, what else could be the focus of our attention? Well, we could use the Old Testament as a source book to learn more about the history of the Israelites. Or we could use it to learn about their religion and theology. But if these were our goals, we would be using the Old Testament as a resource to get at something else.

Instead, we have chosen to treat the Old Testament text as the object of our study, rather than to treat the Old Testament as a tool to write history or theology. Our intention is to discover the meaning of the Bible inductively, by reading it.

Actually, though, setting up our study as an either/or is a false dichotomy. As a matter of fact, we will be studying history and religion and much more in the process of reading. We do this because we want to study the text appropriately, and this is done best by putting it in literary and historical context.

Furthermore, we will focus on the text because the text of the Old Testament is the lasting expression of the faith of Israel. It is through the biblical text, and only through the text, that we come to understand the early community of that faith that serves as the foundation of three great religious traditions, Judaism, Christianity, and Islam. As we will see, there is a fundamental relationship between the text of the Hebrew Bible and the community that produced it.

The Old Testament has many "personalities," depending on how we approach it. If we were studying it as literature, we would find a collection of well-crafted world-class literature. If we were studying it for history, we would find the record of a group of people called the Israelites, later the Jews, who lived in ancient times. If we were studying it for theology, we would discover Israel's concept of God and how they organized communal life to reflect their relationship to him.

Each of the above descriptions of what the Bible is "about" presupposes an approach to reading it; each has its own particular method and tools. Each of these ways of approaching the text is valid in its own right and even necessary for reading the Old Testament.

READING THE OLD TESTAMENT AS LITERATURE

Though the literary material of the Hebrew Bible is ancient compared to the Western literary tradition, this does not mean it is primitive or artless. The Hebrew tradition utilized a rich repertoire of literary techniques. The stylistic techniques and literary strategies we will notice in the text include hyperbole, metaphor, symbolism, allegory, personification, irony, wordplay, and parallelism.

[1] John Bright, *A History of Israel*, 3d ed. Philadelphia: Westminster Press, 1981.

We will become sensitive to the different types of writing that we will encounter. Conventions differ for different types of literature. For example, writing styles and reader expectations for historical narrative differ considerably from those of poetic hymns, and these are in turn different from the conventions of apocalyptic literature. Types of literature, such as those just mentioned, are called **genres**. The major genres found in the Hebrew Bible include narrative, prophecy, law, hymn, proverb, chronicle, and genealogy. We have to be alert to the conventions of these genres, and we will have to become "literarily literate." Reading the Hebrew Bible in our role as literary critics, we will learn the literary conventions of the ancient writers.

READING THE OLD TESTAMENT AS HISTORY

The place and time of the Old Testament are far distant from us. We will have to recover the original historical and geographical setting of the Hebrew Bible in order to understand and appreciate it. We must try to see the world as David, Isaiah, and Ezra saw it, at least to the best of our ability. Though not an easy job, it is a rewarding one. To do so we will draw from the discoveries of generations of historians, archaeologists, and biblical scholars.

The history of Israel is intertwined with the histories of many ancient nations. In Mesopotamia, the Sumerians pioneered civilization and were followed by Babylonians, Assyrians, Hurrians, Amorites, and Arameans. In addition, the Egyptians, Hittites, Phoenicians, and Philistines interacted with Israel and were significant factors in determining the directions Israel's history was to take. Historians, on the basis of ancient documents and archaeological discoveries, have been able to reconstruct the histories of these peoples, sometimes in remarkable detail.

Some of the most amazing discoveries have been textual ones. The Rosetta stone, discovered in 1801, provided the key to deciphering hieroglyphics. This opened up for interpretation the vast library of inscriptions, letters, and texts from Egypt. The Ebla tablets from Syria, dating as early as the third millennium B.C.E., are even now being translated and published. They increase our knowledge of Semitic civilization in western Mesopotamia and Syria. Other texts, artifacts, and building structures from Ugarit, Mari, Nuzi, Nippur, and many other sites enable us to reconstruct a context for the Hebrew Bible. Some of these discoveries will be described in more detail as they are relevant to the interpretation of specific texts.

The Hebrew Bible is itself the major source for the writing of Israelite history. It contains most of the information we have available concerning the kingdoms of Israel and Judah. It has virtually the only information available about the ancestors of Israel. But we have to remember that we cannot read the Hebrew Bible as a straight record of events. It is first and foremost a literary and theological creation that was profoundly shaped by the religious and social world of the writers. While it contains records of certain events, it is not first of all historiography. In other words, it was not intended to be a chronicle of events as they happened, such as modern scientifically researched works of history are. Consequently, it can provide some historical information, but it is not, strictly speaking, history.

Reading the Hebrew Bible literarily and in historical context are fundamental. Last, but not least, there is a third dimension to the text that we will investigate.

READING THE OLD TESTAMENT AS THEOLOGY

The text of the Old Testament contains the record of Israel's faith journey and its application of tradition to life. The literature of the Hebrew Bible is the product of a God-fearing community. The people who wrote the books of the Old Testament composed them as the expression of their faith and because they believed these writings might inspire faith, courage, and understanding.

Most of the books arose at important turning points in Israel's growth as a nation. The community grounded its experience of God in their history and believed that his commitment to them provided a certain measure of security in a threatening world. But their world never stayed the same. Empires rose and empires fell. Israel had to adapt to the changing political and social environment. Part of the adaptation was applying the traditional guarantees of God to an uncertain future. From Torah to Writings, the history of the text's composition reveals the community's record of how they heard God speaking to them.

The Old Testament is the record of a creative tension between religious tradition and the need for change. Earlier forms of tradition were embodied in early documents, and these can be reconstructed and examined by us. These earlier documents defined truth to the early community that produced them. They provided the people with religious and ideological stability, a way to understand God and his way with humankind. But as history moved on, new interpretations and applications were needed.

These texts encapsulate a long and lively dance of interpretation and reinterpretation. The text of the Hebrew Bible is the written expression of an extended conversation that took place over a thousand-year period of time. Political and social changes within the community inspired the need for new interpretations and applications of the older authoritative texts. The older texts provided the foundation for the life of the community and allowed for stability in the midst of changed circumstances.

Part of what we mean by "reading the Old Testament theologically" is to read the text as the record of the faith of a community that was defined by its theological traditions and that took its traditions seriously. It considered its traditions authoritative and leaned on those traditions as it faced the future.

Old and new, stability and change, tradition and innovation, text and reinterpretation—these are the parameters that will order our reading of the theology of the Hebrew Bible. We will be "tradition archaeologists" as we peel away the strata of this dynamic process of tradition and change.

WHERE SHOULD WE START?

One of the toughest questions we face as we approach our study of the Old Testament is this—Where should we start reading? The answer is not as obvious as it may seem. Should we start at the very beginning? If so, the beginning of what? Should we start with the narratives that deal with the earliest events, such as creation and the flood? Or should we start with the narratives that were written first? Note that these are not necessarily one and the same.

The problem of starting point exists because of the complexity of the Old Testament's literary history. The basic problem is this: the time at which the traditions were written down is not the same as the time of the events themselves. Most of the written accounts of biblical events come from a time much later than the events themselves. The Old Testament is not a journal of the events as they happened.

As we read the Old Testament we will have to make a special effort to stay aware of this distinction between chronological history (the original moment in time of the reported event) and literary history (when the account of the event was written down). Some textbooks organize the study of the Hebrew Bible on historical grounds. They establish a basic historical framework and the literature of the Old Testament is inserted into this framework. In contrast to this literary–historical approach, *Reading the Old Testament* is organized canonically. This is to say, we deal with the biblical books in sequential order as they are found in the Hebrew Bible.

Still, this book is amenable to either the literary–historical or the canonical approach. No matter how we might approach the Old Testament, or for whatever reason, we have to start at the same place, namely, with the text. That is where every interpretation must begin. Our textbook is above all a text-centered introduction, because it recognizes that the biblical text is the fundamental starting point for any type of reading.

To this end, *Reading the Old Testament* contains substantial selections of the actual text of the Hebrew Bible—in translation of course.[2] The only way to understand the Old Testament is to read it! Basic historical and literary information is provided as needed for interpreting the texts. We will draw upon political history, archaeology, literary criticism, linguistics, sociology, and theology to explain the text and develop its meaning.

SURVEY OF OLD TESTAMENT HISTORY

At the beginning of our study it is important to get a sense of the scope and flow of Israelite history. In many cases, the books of the Old Testament were written hundreds of years after the events they relate. It is always a good idea to get a sense of the historical context of the writer to determine why he or she told the story in that particular way. Often what they were writing was to them already ancient history. Then-current circumstances profoundly affected the way they told the story.

To an extent, this makes our study a circular undertaking. We need to understand the end point of Israelite history in order to understand why they described the beginning and middle in the way they did. So we will survey the beginning, middle, and end to be in a position to put it all together. The following survey of

---

[2] The translations of the Hebrew Bible found in this textbook were done from the original Hebrew text by the author of the textbook. They try to be colloquial and reflective of the original wording of the text without being slavishly literal.

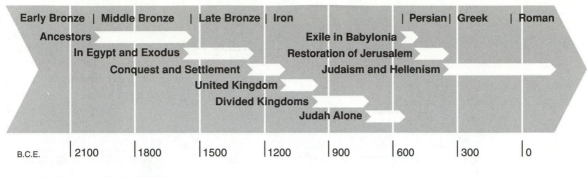

Early Bronze	Middle Bronze	Late Bronze	Iron			Persian	Greek	Roman	

Ancestors

In Egypt and Exodus

Conquest and Settlement

United Kingdom

Divided Kingdoms

Judah Alone

Exile in Babylonia

Restoration of Jerusalem

Judaism and Hellenism

B.C.E.   2100   1800   1500   1200   900   600   300   0

FIGURE 1 TIME LINE: SURVEY OF OLD TESTAMENT HISTORY

Israelite history divides it up into its major periods (see Figure 1). It covers Israelite history with broad strokes. The details will, of course, come out when we deal with these events within the Old Testament books.

PRE-ISRAELITE HISTORY (THIRD MILLENNIUM B.C.E.)

Civilization, at least in the ancient Middle East, began with the Sumerians. The Sumerians came from the mountains of what is today Iran. They were the first to build cities and to practice irrigation agriculture. They invented writing, produced a literature, and even developed law codes.

Sumerian government took the form of city–states. Each city–state was independent and controlled its surrounding countryside. The city–state was governed by a council of elders, and all landholders had a say in decision making—an early form of democracy. But because the governing council type of organization was unable to cope effectively with military crises, it gave way to dynastic kingship.

The Sumerians controlled the southern part of **Mesopotamia**, the land between the Tigris and Euphrates Rivers, until about 2400 B.C.E. At that time the Akkadians, led by Sargon of Akkad, established a Semitic[3] empire. The Akkadians borrowed much of their culture from the Sumerians. Except for a resurgence of Sumerian rule for a hundred years beginning in 2050 B.C.E., the Semitic Akkadians, Babylonians, or Assyrians ruled Mesopotamia until Cyrus the Persian established the Medo-Persian empire in the sixth century B.C.E.

The term **Fertile Crescent** is used to refer to the half-moon-shaped inhabitable area of the ancient Middle East where civilizations thrived (see Figure 2). This general area, in which Israel was located, has a rich and venerable history. It generated extensive literary and religious traditions. The Sumerians and their successors the Babylonians and Assyrians wrote law books, collected proverbs and wisdom sayings, wrote religious myths and heroic epics, and composed hymns. The Egyptians also developed a rich culture. Many artifacts and texts

---

[3]The term *Semitic* designates a race of people originating in Southwestern Asia. Semites include Akkadians, Babylonians, Assyrians, Hebrews, and Arabs. The terms *Semite* and *Semitic* derive from the name of the biblical figure Shem, the son of Noah, who, according to the genealogy of Genesis 10, sired population groups in the areas occupied by these peoples.

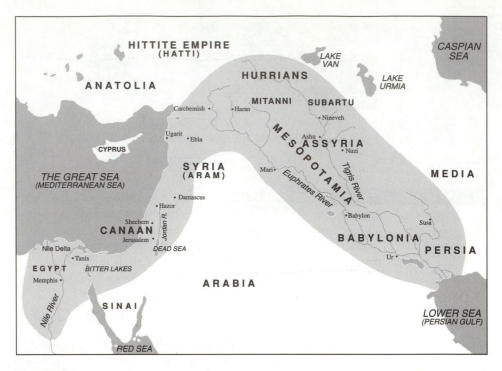

FIGURE 2   ANCIENT MIDDLE EAST AND FERTILE CRESCENT

have survived to this day and have been unearthed by archaeologists. This cultural and literary material is essential background for understanding the world view within which Israel developed its own identity.

ANCESTRAL PERIOD (ROUGHLY 2000–1550 B.C.E.)

Abraham was not an Israelite. It would be chronologically skewed to say that he was. Biblical tradition records that he came from Ur, and Ur was in the heart of lower Mesopotamia, which would have made Abraham some sort of Mesopotamian.

A NOTE ON TERMS FOR ISRAELITES

Speaking of chronology, it is important to use terms referring to the Israelites appropriately. Before Israel became a nation, its ancestors would not have been called Israelites. Properly speaking, they were Hebrews. Nor should people from either the ancestral period or the time of the monarchy be called Jews. That term is reserved for the descendants of the Israelites after the Babylonian exile of the sixth century B.C.E.

It is difficult to determine an exact date for the period of Israel's ancestors. The best guess is that Abraham and Sarah, Isaac and Rebekah, and Jacob's family lived sometime between 2000 and 1550 B.C.E. From what we know about these ancestors they appear to have been a transient seminomadic people. For example, Abraham traveled from lower Mesopotamia to upper Mesopotamia, on to Canaan, and even as far as Egypt.

The God who was later identified with the God of Israel encountered Abraham. This God made a covenant with Abraham that included promises of future well-being, including the inheritance of Canaan as a family homeland and the growth of the family into an international empire. The stories about Abraham and Sarah, Isaac and Rebekah, and Jacob and Rachel detail how those promises began to find fulfillment.

The Joseph story relates that the ancestral clan moved to Egypt because of a prolonged famine in Canaan. They were warmly received there because Joseph, the son of Jacob, held a high position within the Egyptian government. The family grew in number while in Egypt and ended up staying there for generations.

IN EGYPT AND THE EXODUS (1550–1280 B.C.E.)

After a change in government the attitude of the Egyptians toward the Hebrews turned sour, and they enslaved them. God raised up Moses to lead the people back to the ancestral homeland of Canaan. The Egyptians were at first reluctant to allow the Hebrews to leave but were convinced by a succession of devastating plagues sent by God. The escape from Egypt, called the exodus, is celebrated yearly in the Passover.

The Hebrews left Egypt around 1280 B.C.E., pursued by the Egyptian army. At one point it looked as if they were doomed, trapped between the chariots of Pharaoh and the deep Red Sea. But God opened up a pathway through the sea and they escaped, leaving the Egyptian army to drown when they tried to follow.

The Hebrews traveled on to Mt. Sinai, where God appeared to Moses and the people. God entered into an arrangement with them, termed the Mosaic covenant, whereby he committed himself to them, and they in turn agreed to obey the Ten Commandments. Israel came into existence as a nation as a result of the set of events surrounding the exodus from Egypt and covenant-making on Mt. Sinai.

CONQUEST AND SETTLEMENT (1280–1020 B.C.E.)

The Israelites remained in the Sinai wilderness for forty years, a generation. Then, under the leadership of Moses' successor Joshua, twelve tribes entered Canaan and began the long process of settling in. Loosely organized into a federation of tribes, there was no centralized government at this time and, after Joshua died, no overall leader. Each tribe was driven by its own interests.

Occasionally certain gifted leaders came to the forefront, typically when there was a problem with other groups in the area. Although the name is somewhat misleading, these leaders were called *judges* and included Deborah, Gideon, and Samson. While certain judges did hear legal cases, more typically they were military captains who organized and inspired Israelite tribal groups to defeat their enemies.

A Note on the Name of God

The treatment of the divine name in English translations of the Hebrew Bible and in this textbook needs to be explained. The God of Israel was referred to in various ways. Sometimes God was just "God"—in Hebrew, *Elohim*. When you see *God* in the text, this stands for *Elohim*.

Other times God is referred to by his personal name, YHWH. It is rendered Yahweh in some versions, and "the LORD" in others. Notice that the letters "ORD" in LORD are in smaller-sized capital letters. This is to distinguish it from the divine title "the Lord." Most modern translations of the Hebrew Bible employ this typographic convention to indicate when YHWH is in the underlying Hebrew text.

The four-consonant divine name YHWH is referred to as the *tetragrammaton*. When the Hebrew text refers to Yahweh it uses the four consonants YHWH with a special configuration of vowels. This signals it was not pronounced out loud. The name *Yahweh*, or *Jehovah* in its older pronunciation, is never spoken out loud in Judaic contexts. In Jewish tradition the words "the LORD," *adonay* in Hebrew, are substituted for YHWH.

The convention we use in *Reading the Old Testament* is to reproduce YHWH in translated biblical quotations and to use the scholar's Yahweh in explanatory notes.

In addition to judges, priests directed the spiritual life of the people. They were usually from the tribe of Levi. They managed various sacred sites throughout the land and presided over religious ceremonies, most of which involved animal sacrifices. There were rival priestly factions in Israel, and the tension among these factions gave rise to alternate interpretations of Israel's history. These alternate interpretations are reflected in the different sources we find underlying the Torah.

The most famous priest, who also happened to be a judge, was Samuel (after whom two books of the Old Testament are designated). He was the most effective leader of his time. As a youth he lived in Shiloh, which was the major religious center of the federation. There a tent shrine housed the ark of the covenant, the sacred chest that stored the federation's covenant documents.

The major national threat at the time of Samuel was the territorial expansion of the Philistines. Around 1200 B.C.E. they settled on the coastal plain of Canaan. As they tried to expand westward toward the Jordan River they put pressure on the Israelites living there. In time, Philistine pressure became too much for tribal captains and regional judges to handle. Israel needed a centralized government and national leader capable of meeting the Philistine threat. The nation was on the verge of extinction until Israel found a king.

UNITED KINGDOM (1020–922 B.C.E.)

In response to this Philistine crisis, the twelve tribes accepted the institution of the monarchy. Samuel, the most influential priest and prophet at that time, designated Saul from the tribe of Benjamin to be Israel's first king. He began his reign around 1020 B.C.E.

The notion of having a king was not altogether well received. There were many in Israel who felt that charismatic, *ad hoc* leadership was the godly way to go. The move to monarchy, this transition from judge to king, came about only with great difficulty. And some people never really did accept it.

Saul at first demonstrated leadership ability. He was able to muster the troops to face Israel's enemies. But he lost the crucial support of Samuel when he offered a sacrifice before a battle—something only a priest was allowed to do. Samuel disowned Saul and anointed David to be king in his place.

Saul continued to reign until his death at the hands of the Philistines. After Saul died, his son Ishbosheth assumed the throne and the northern tribes accepted his authority. But all the while, David was gathering support. David was acclaimed king by those who lived in the southern tribe of **Judah, which was** David's home territory. Ishbosheth was ineffective, and after he was assassinated by men from his own court, David became king of all twelve tribes.

David was a remarkable leader and an astute politician. In order to appeal to the broadest constituency, he moved his headquarters from Hebron in Judah to the neutral site of Jerusalem. Previously belonging to the Canaanites, David captured it and made "the City of David" the administrative center of his kingdom. He also brought the ark of the covenant there, effectively transforming Jerusalem into the religious capital of the nation.

In a move designed to unite the northern and southern components of his now United Kingdom, he appointed a chief priest from each region. Zadok was the chief priest from Judah, tracing his lineage back to Aaron, the brother of Moses. Abiathar was the chief priest from the north, descended from the priests of Shiloh where the ark of the covenant was once kept. The conflict between these two priestly traditions influenced the formation of certain books of the Hebrew Bible.

David was effective in neutralizing those enemies that had given Saul resistance. He effectively contained Philistia and brought Syria, Ammon, Moab, and Edom under Israelite control. His empire stretched from the El–Arish wadi on the Sinai–Mediterranean coast to the Euphrates River in the north. The kingdom of David represents the era of Israel's glory. During the reign of David, the territory and power of Israel were at their greatest extent ever.

But at home, David's sons were maneuvering to assume control, even before his death. A fight over succession to the throne broke out. Amnon and Absalom, two influential princes, died in the process. Then Adonijah, being one of the older remaining sons, made his move. He gained the support of David's general, Joab, and Abiathar, a chief priest.

However, Solomon was David's personal choice. Supported by Bathsheba, David's favorite wife (and, not incidentally, mother of Solomon), by Nathan, the court prophet, and by Zadok, the other chief priest, Solomon won. Upon assuming the throne he had Adonijah and Joab executed. He exiled Abiathar to Anathoth, a small town just a few miles north of Jerusalem.

Solomon inherited an extensive empire. He set about upgrading it to world-class standards by constructing monumental buildings and through international diplomacy. He constructed a finely adorned temple for Yahweh in Jerusalem. He built an even larger palace for himself. To protect his kingdom he built fortress cities around the country. In order to forge international diplomatic ties, he married 700 foreign princesses.

To get the work done and pay the bills, he forced citizens of Israel to work as slaves on his projects and imposed a heavy burden of taxation on the country. This created considerable dissatisfaction among his constituency, especially those who lived in the north, who were unsure about the Davidic dynasty to begin with.

DIVIDED KINGDOMS (922–721 B.C.E.)

The United Kingdom lasted for the rule of three kings, Saul, David, and Solomon. During that time it was magnificent, but to achieve that greatness Solomon mortgaged the nation's future. Solomon may have died in peace, but he left behind a precarious kingdom and a legacy of resentment.

After Solomon died and his son Rehoboam took the throne, the northern leadership held a conference with him. They wanted to find out whether or not Rehoboam had decided to continue Solomon's oppressive policies. When Rehoboam refused to back down, they rebelled and pulled out of the Davidic empire. Rehoboam was powerless to stop them.

In these events we see the old, fiercely independent spirit of the tribes reasserting itself. The kingdom reverted back to what it had earlier been, a southern faction and a northern faction. Biblical historians talk of a "United Kingdom," but while it lasted it was an unnatural alliance. It was only due to the military savvy and political genius of David that the two groupings of tribes ever overcame their regional identities, put aside parochial differences, and became one kingdom.

The **Northern Kingdom**, now called **Israel**, choose Jeroboam to be its king. Jeroboam chose the city of Shechem to be his capital. It was the place of covenant renewal under Joshua and a city strongly associated with the tribal federation of the judges period. But Jeroboam had a serious problem. Israel, though politically independent of Judah, still worshiped Yahweh, the same god Judah worshiped. The religious practices of Yahwism were still associated with Jerusalem, the home base of the Davidic family. That was where the ark was housed, where the temple was located, and where the chief priest officiated. If the people had no choice but to go to Jerusalem to fulfill their religious duties, Jeroboam feared the people might develop divided loyalties.

To counter this threat he developed a version of Yahwism for Israel. He instituted alternate feast days, a new set of priests, and new religious centers. These religious centers, one at Bethel near the Judean border and one at Dan near the northern border, housed golden bull statues, which became the new symbols of divinity in Israel.

The powerful empire that once was David's no longer existed. In its place were two relatively small states, certainly insignificant compared to the empires of their day. They shared many of the same traditions, were similar in religion, and both still worshiped Yahweh. But they were different in other ways.

Throughout its history, Judah was ruled by the Davidic family. It lasted as an independent nation until 587 B.C.E. Not so Israel. The Northern Kingdom never had a stable monarchy. Instead, one dynasty after another tried to establish itself, resulting in political instability. As an independent nation Israel lasted only two hundred years. In 721 B.C.E. it was conquered by the Assyrian empire. Much of its population was dispersed throughout Assyrian territory. Some Israelites were able to escape south to Judah.

JUDAH ALONE (721–587 B.C.E.)

After 721 B.C.E. Judah was the only kingdom of "Israelites" left. The territory north of Judah was now an Assyrian province.

Ahaz, who was the Judean king at the time of the demise of Israel, remained loyal to Assyria after 721 B.C.E. His son Hezekiah, however, established alliances with Egypt and Babylon as a hedge against Assyria. This roused Sennacherib, king of Assyria, to mount an attack on Jerusalem in 701 B.C.E. Under mysterious circumstances Sennacherib withdrew his troops before achieving the surrender of the city.

Manasseh, the next king of Judah, ruled for 45 years, content to submit to the Assyrians and benefit from the international peace that came from the arrangement. Toward the end of his reign Assyria was on the decline, and Babylonia was gaining strength and territory. By the mid-seventh century B.C.E. things were astir in the ancient Middle East, and even Egypt was reasserting influence in Canaan.

In this volatile situation Josiah assumed the throne in Judah. He was greeted as David "reborn." He won back some territory in the north. He also backed a major religious reform in Judah—a reform that is intimately associated with the book of Deuteronomy.

In 622 B.C.E., during the reign of Josiah, a scroll was found in the Jerusalem temple in the course of cleaning up the sanctuary for a return to authentic Yahwistic worship. The scroll contained a collection of laws that had its origin in the Northern Kingdom. This scroll has been identified as the core of the present book of Deuteronomy. Called the "book of the covenant," it inspired serious Yahwistic revival in Judah, entailing sweeping political and religious changes.

Nebuchadnezzar, meanwhile, was extending Babylonian influence westward. Defeating the combined forces of Assyria and Egypt at Carchemish in 605 B.C.E., he now had access to Canaan, including Judah.

Nebuchadnezzar captured Jerusalem in 597 B.C.E. He deported its king Jehoiachin to Babylon, along with Jerusalem's influential citizens. Nebuchadnezzar placed Zedekiah on the throne, fully expecting him to be cooperative. When Zedekiah made an alliance with Egypt, Nebuchadnezzar felt compelled to return to Jerusalem. In July of 587 B.C.E. he thoroughly destroyed Jerusalem, including its temple. Zedekiah was blinded and taken away captive. In a second deportation, Nebuchadnezzar took even more of Jerusalem's citizenry to Babylon, and rendered Judah incapable of ever again affronting him.

EXILE IN BABYLONIA (587–539 B.C.E.)

The leaders of Judah were now refugees living in Babylonia. This was the most trying time in Israelite history, religiously and politically. The people lost everything that previously had defined them. They lost:

1. *political independence*. Judea was now a backwater province of the Babylonian empire. It would not regain national sovereignty until the time of the Maccabees in the second century B.C.E.

2. *their king.* The leadership of the Davidic dynasty was incapable of leading. Previously God had channeled national blessing through the house of David. Now the Davidic king, Jehoiachin, was in a Babylonian prison.

3. *the temple*. This was the focus of their religious life, and now the temple, along with the royal palace and the entire city of Jerusalem, lay in ruins. The sacrifices that kept them right with God could not be offered.

4. *the land*. The Promised Land had been the preeminent evidence of God's favor, and now it was no longer in their hands. Many of those who survived the war of 587 B.C.E. had been taken captive to Babylonia, and those who remained had no resources or leadership.

But this tragedy was more than just a national defeat. In the religious outlook of this period, each nation was protected by its patron god. Yahweh was the God of Israel. Yahweh was the real power behind the national fighting force. The victory of Nebuchadnezzar could only imply, as many thought, that Marduk, the patron god of Babylon, was supreme. The military defeat became a crisis of faith.

The great miracle of the Babylonian exile was that faith in Yahweh did survive. Prophets were instrumental in interpreting the disaster and revealing Yahweh's intention in allowing it to happen. Priests rekindled Israel's faith out of the ashes. Temple service and animal sacrifices, no longer performed in exile, gave way to Sabbath worship and study of the Torah as important religious activities. A Davidic king no longer ruled, but a new sense of the kingship of Yahweh took hold. The land was lost, but circumcision became a symbol of transformed hearts whereby the faithful could enter a new spiritual kingdom.

RESTORATION OF JERUSALEM (539–400 B.C.E.)

After Nebuchadnezzar died, the Babylonian empire quickly disintegrated. On October 29, 539 B.C.E., Cyrus of Media captured Babylon without a fight. Soon afterward Cyrus signed an edict allowing Judeans to go home if they wished. He even supported the rebuilding of their religious center in Jerusalem with royal funds. Many chose to return to Jerusalem.

The first group of refugees returned in 538 B.C.E., led by Sheshbazzar. This group was successful in laying the foundations for a rebuilt temple. But life was hard, and they soon abandoned the project. The second group returned in 520

B.C.E., led by Zerubbabel and the high priest Jeshua. They managed to finish a temple building by 515 B.C.E. Called by scholars the "Second Temple," this structure became the focus of religious devotion again. But the nature of religion had fundamentally changed from what it was before the exile. The new style of faith and practice in the Second Temple period is the beginning of what comes to be called Judaism.

The fifth century was a crucial time in the development of this emerging Judaism. The two missions of Nehemiah in 445 and 432 B.C.E. reestablished the viability of Jerusalem, still the holy city of faith. Nehemiah managed to rebuild its walls and secure it against threats and attacks from its rivals in Samaria to the north—old Israel, the Northern Kingdom (old feuds die hard).

Ezra was perhaps even more important because of the way in which he redefined the identity of God's people. Having the authority of the Persian crown, he dissolved any marriages involving Judeans and non-Judeans and sent the odd party packing. He also applied the law of Moses as state law. Ezra was severe, but he deemed this necessary since times were tough and the identity of the community was at stake.

JUDAISM AND HELLENISM (400 B.C.E.–70 C.E.)

Judea remained a Persian province until Alexander the Great's invasion of the Middle East in 333 B.C.E. With his victory at Issus he secured control of the area and spread Greek culture, government, and language throughout that region. The Hellenistic period had begun.

The major challenge to Jewish culture and religion was Hellenism. The Greek language displaced Aramaic as the language of the civilized world. Greek literature, philosophy, and institutions such as the gymnasium, polis (city), and theater fundamentally affected society. Hebrew culture and traditions were sorely threatened.

The Maccabean uprising was one attempt to reverse the progress of Hellenization. Led by Judas the Maccabee, the Jews were able for a time to reestablish home rule. It was effective to the point that an independent Jewish state was created, lasting almost eighty years, from 142 to 63 B.C.E. Beginning in 63 B.C.E. the Romans took control of the Middle East, including Palestine.

Jewish society was anything but homogeneous at this time. The Sadducees, one religious–political party, were not opposed to accommodating the Greek spirit of the age. But the Pharisees, another party, remained devoted to the Mosaic definition of Jewishness and sought to apply it consistently to national life.

The Essenes, with whom many scholars associate the Qumran Dead Sea Scrolls, were the most conservative. They led a monastic existence in the wilderness, withdrawn from the Jewish religious establishment in Jerusalem that they believed was corrupt. They devoted themselves to the Torah, and in that way prepared themselves for the eagerly expected Messiah. Christians, another group arising out of Jewish society, believed they had found the Messiah in Jesus of Nazareth.

The Jewish group called the Zealots sought to rid Judea of Roman occupation. They precipitated a rebellion, called the First Jewish Revolt, which resulted in the complete destruction of Jerusalem in 70 C.E.

Turning now to the Old Testament itself, we first study the Torah. The Torah lays the foundations of Israelite faith and practice.

TORAH

1

PROLOGUE TO THE TORAH

Names and Terms to Remember

anthropomorphism	Elohim	Priestly source
D	Elohist source	Torah
Deuteronomy	J	tradition history
documentary hypothesis	P	Yahweh/YHWH
E	Pentateuch	Yahwist source

The Hebrew Bible consists of three main sections, the Torah, the Prophets and the Writings. The Torah consists of five books: Genesis, Exodus, Leviticus, Numbers, and Deuteronomy. After explaining some terms, this chapter introduces general issues in the study of the Torah.

TERMS FOR TORAH

The term *Torah* has many meanings and connotations in a Hebrew Bible/Old Testament setting. It can refer to the "T" section of the Tanak (the Jewish name for the Hebrew Bible), which consists of the first five books of the Bible. It also has a much broader meaning. In Jewish tradition, *torah* designates "the revelation of God." As the revelation of God's will given to humankind for their benefit, *torah* also means "instruction," and is another word for the teachings of the Bible. Torah was Israel's constitution, the foundation of its spiritual and community life.

Although Torah is the traditional name for the set of books Genesis, Exodus, Leviticus, Numbers, and Deuteronomy, modern scholars tend to call it the Pentateuch, a term derived from the Greek word for "five scrolls."[1] You will find the term *Pentateuch* most often used in academic settings and *Torah* most often in religious ones.

The Torah is the most intensely studied section of the Hebrew Bible. Consequently, there is a wealth of scholarship attempting to sort out where it came from and what it means. A good deal of modern pentateuchal scholarship wrestles with the issues of authorship and literary composition.

TORAH AUTHORSHIP AND COMPOSITION

Ancient views of authorship and book publication differed quite a bit from those of today. In biblical culture authors did not sign their books. In fact, the shaping of what we now call biblical "books" probably came about through the collaboration of many individuals.

In any case, none of the books in the Hebrew Bible have unambiguous indications of authorship. Determinations of authorship must be made by inference from clues in the texts themselves. The origin and authorship of many books, especially the books of the Torah, remain under discussion in current scholarship.

---

[1] *Penta* means five, and *teuchos* means scroll. Literally, the Greek word *teuchos* refers to a jar in which a scroll was stored.

MOSAIC AUTHORSHIP

Traditionally, Jewish and Christian communities have held that Moses wrote all of the Torah. Moses was the religious leader of the Hebrew people who directed them out of Egypt and on to Canaan in the thirteenth century B.C.E. In this traditional view the books of the Torah are referred to as the Five Books of Moses.

A number of texts associate the Torah with Moses. Ezra read from "the book of the *torah* of Moses, which the Lord had given to Israel" (Nehemiah 8:1). About that same time the Chronicler (see chapter 18) referred to a passage from Deuteronomy as being from "the book of Moses" (2 Chronicles 25:4). The Jewish philosopher Philo, the Jewish historian Josephus, and New Testament writers (see Matthew 19:7–8 and Acts 15:2) assumed the Torah's Mosaic authorship, as did the Babylonian Talmud (see Baba Bathra 14b).

A close study of the Torah reveals that the issue of authorship is more complex than that. Common sense informed scholars as early as the Middle Ages that Moses could not have written the account of his own death, contained in Deuteronomy 34:5–12. Some then suggested that Joshua, Moses' assistant and successor, might have appended it.

Other features of the text suggest non-Mosaic authorship and a complex process of development. Often the text refers to Moses in the third person, rather than with the first-person pronoun "I," suggesting someone other than Moses wrote those sections. In three distinct places Genesis contains the ploy of a patriarch lying about his wife's marital status to save his own skin, twice with Abraham and Sarah (12:10–20 and chapter 20) and once with Isaac and Rebekah (26:6–11). This suggests to some scholars that one basic story circulated in variant forms in different documents, and all were included in the final text.

Some modern biblical scholars still affirm the Mosaic authorship of the Pentateuch. Yet most scholars are convinced that the Torah was given its final shape much later than the lifetime of Moses. While differing considerably in how they reconstruct the underlying sources and the process of composition, most believe the Torah was composed from a variety of materials over a long period of time. The following discussion summarizes the major views.

DOCUMENTARY HYPOTHESIS

The study of ancient languages and literatures blossomed during the Renaissance and Reformation. This prompted a new look at the Hebrew Bible. The existence of similar stories in Genesis (as just mentioned) prompted Richard Simon (1638–1712) to develop a theory that the Pentateuch had been compiled from a number of sources, some of which may have derived from Moses. He claimed the final Pentateuch was produced by Ezra in the postexilic period (fifth century B.C.E.).

A variation in the way pentateuchal texts refer to God, either as **Elohim** (translated God) or **YHWH** (pronounced **Yahweh**, and rendered the LORD in most English translations), prompted Jean Astruc (1684–1766) to argue that Moses compiled the Pentateuch from two different written documents and other minor materials. Ironically, Astruc defended Moses' role as compiler and author. Yet the approach he advocated gave birth to the **documentary hypothesis,** which ultimately took the Pentateuch out of the hands of Moses.

Over the course of the next two centuries the documentary hypothesis developed into the dominant explanation of the authorship and composition of the Pentateuch. The documentary hypothesis deconstructed the Pentateuch into four primary underlying documentary sources. A **Yahwist source** was dated to the tenth or ninth century B.C.E., an **Elohist source** to the eighth century, **Deuteronomy** to the seventh century, and a **Priestly source** to the sixth or fifth century.

The classical documentary hypothesis used five literary identifiers to sort out the sources: (1) duplication and repetition of material; (2) variation in the way God was referred to; (3) contrasting author perspectives; (4) variation in vocabulary and literary style; and (5) evidence of editorial activity.

Variations on the documentary hypothesis have been proposed. The supplement hypothesis accepts the notion of written source documents. In its reconstruction of the composition process it claims one of the documents was the backbone of the Pentateuch and others were added to fill out the story. The Priestly source is usually identified as the backbone.

The fragment hypothesis was inspired by the difficulties scholars had in firmly identifying documents that served as sources. It denies that they actually existed as identifiable written works. Instead, this hypothesis argues that the Pentateuch was composed of a great variety of originally independent oral and written traditions, none of which was a dominant source.

A major reconstruction of the Pentateuch was developed by Noth (1948). He revised and supplemented the documentary hypothesis with a study of **tradition history**. Tradition history starts with the oral traditions that lie behind small textual units and traces how these units were combined into more comprehensive tradition blocks.

Noth (1948) identified a small number of core Israelite beliefs about God's direction of Israelite history. The earliest beliefs were guidance out of Egypt and guidance into the Promised Land. To these were later added the themes of God's promises to the ancestors, guidance through the wilderness, and divine revelation at Sinai. These core beliefs attracted illustrative stories and clusters of episodes, or tradition blocks, accumulated around those beliefs. After these tradition blocks combined, they became the foundational narrative about Israel's past. From this narrative the Yahwist, Elohist, and Priestly written sources derived.

Noth saw the evolution of the written sources as a dynamic process of reworking and expansion as the tradition developed in conversation with the ongoing history of the Israelite people. He identified the Priestly source as the backbone of the Pentateuch to which the Yahwist and Elohist sources were added.

FOUR MAJOR SOURCES

If the multiple-source view of the Pentateuch is generally correct, the Torah developed over a long period of time. None of the actual writers of the sources have been identified by name, but we can piece together some general features of the individuals and groups responsible. Each of the sources has a distinctive style, vocabulary, and theology. Each came out of a particular period in Israel's history, and each reflects the attitude and perspective of a particular constituency within Israel.

A short summary of each literary source follows. A fuller explanation of each source can be found in the "Epilogue to the Torah." The explanations there will make more sense after we have had a chance to study the text of the Pentateuch and read the sources themselves.

Yahwist Source (J)

The earliest written source of the Torah is the Yahwist source. It got this name because the entire source uses the divine name Yahweh to designate God. It is sometimes called an epic because in grand epic style it tells the story of how humankind developed and how one branch became the people of God. It frequently makes use of anthropomorphism; that is, it often describes God as having human characteristics, such as when he walked in the Garden of Eden.

The Yahwist source is referred to as J in scholarly literature, because German scholars first formulated this source analysis, and Yahweh begins with a "J" in German. It appears to contain the first account of where Israel had come from, and why the nation was so special to God. This national story provided a common identity for all the people united under the rule of the Davidic dynasty. The Yahwist composed his story sometime during the reign of Solomon (961–922 B.C.E.), though some scholars would date it as much as a century later. Remembering it was written at the time of the early monarchy in Judah is one way to remember to associate the Yahwist, or J source, with Judah—both begin with J.

The Yahwist source was written out of a love of the royal house, providing a sense of history and a sense of destiny for the grand new kingdom of David. The Solomonic era was most conducive to such a historical project. This golden age had the resources and provided the opportunity to write a national epic. Royally sponsored scribal schools provided the training, royal income supported the work, and the increased international contact afforded by the new international status of Israel stimulated reflection, and perhaps even prompted in some measure the need for a national story.

The Yahwist was especially interested in those traditions that supported the legitimacy of Davidic rule and the centrality of the tribe of Judah. He believed that God's plan was working itself out in the rule of David and Solomon. The Yahwist came from Judah, so he naturally thought highly of King David. David was originally from Bethlehem in Judah, and ruled from Hebron, a major city in Judah, for many years (see Figure 1).

The Judah connection is evident in the Yahwist's interest in Abraham. The bulk of the Abraham traditions are associated with locations in and around Judah. For example, several Yahwist stories of Abraham have him living in Hebron (Genesis 13:18; 23:2). On the other hand, the Jacob stories are generally located in the north or in Transjordan.

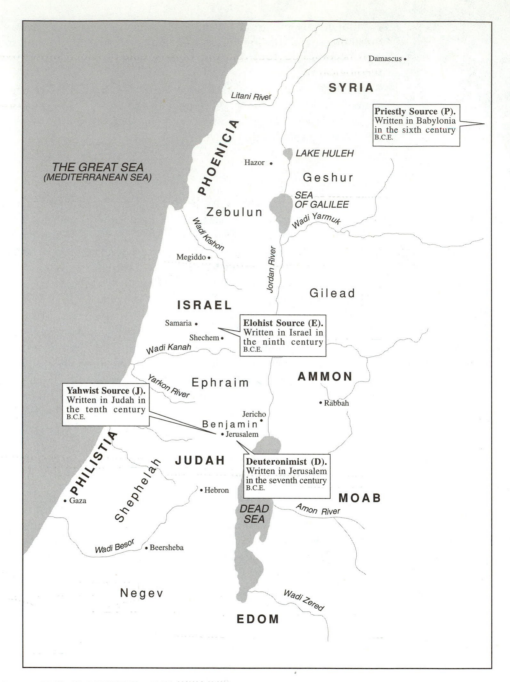

Labels within the map:

Damascus

SYRIA

Litani River

Priestly Source (P). Written in Babylonia in the sixth century B.C.E.

PHOENICIA

LAKE HULEH

Hazor

Geshur

THE GREAT SEA (MEDITERRANEAN SEA)

SEA OF GALILEE

Zebulun

Wadi Yarmuk

Wadi Krishon

Jordan River

Gilead

Megiddo

ISRAEL

Samaria

Elohist Source (E). Written in Israel in the ninth century B.C.E.

Shechem

Wadi Kanah

AMMON

Yarkon River

Ephraim

Yahwist Source (J). Written in Judah in the tenth century B.C.E.

• Rabbah

Jericho

Benjamin

• Jerusalem

Deuteronimist (D). Written in Jerusalem in the seventh century B.C.E.

PHILISTIA

JUDAH

MOAB

Shephelah

• Hebron

• Gaza

DEAD SEA

Amon River

Wadi Besor

• Beersheba

Negev

Wadi Zered

EDOM

FIGURE 1 SOURCES OF THE TORAH BY LOCATION

There are other obvious connections between the patriarch Abraham and the kingdom of David. The covenant God made with Abraham promised that his descendants would possess the land "from the river of Egypt to the . . . river Euphrates" (Genesis 15:18–21). Not coincidentally, these turn out to be the borders of the nation under King David.[2]

It becomes obvious that the Yahwist epic provided supportive history and a theological foundation for the new empire of David. Going back to its primeval stories, it first exposed the need for an enlightened empire by painting a picture of human sin and natural rebellion. Then, by unfolding the groundwork of the empire in Yahweh's promises to Abraham, it revealed the plan of Yahweh. The empire of David was its culmination.

The Yahwist is bold and honest in his portrayal of Israel's early history. He does not overly glorify the role of Yahweh's chosen ones, but has a keen eye for human failing. Yet his eye is always on the promises of Yahweh, which wend their way to fulfillment within the crucible of human history.

Watch for these features of the Yahwist source in the Pentateuch:

- divine promises
- geographical locations in Judah
- use of anthropomorphic imagery (God in the form of a human)

Elohist Source (E)

The Elohist source gets its name from the Hebrew word *Elohim*, which it uses to refer to God. *Elohim* is the general word for God, as opposed to the personal divine name Yahweh. The Elohist source has survived only as fragments that had been inserted into the Yahwist Epic. It is not nearly as extensive, at least in its recoverable form, as the other sources.

Fragments of the Elohist source are found in Genesis, Exodus, and Numbers, and maybe even in Joshua and Judges. The Elohist source appears for the first time at Genesis 20. Here God appeared in a dream, rather than directly to individuals as we tend to find in the Yahwist Epic. The Elohist source favors a distant God who comes in dreams or in the form of an angel. In contrast to the Yahwist Epic, the Elohist source refers to Sinai as Horeb, and refers to the Canaanites as Amorites.

The Elohist author lived in the Northern Kingdom shortly after the breakup of the Davidic kingdom, sometime in the period 900–850 B.C.E. The Northern Kingdom was ruled by a succession of dynasties. The largest tribal territory in the Northern Kingdom, called Israel after the breakup, was Ephraim. Because the tribe of Ephraim was immense and was politically dominant, the whole northern territory was sometimes just called Ephraim. It is easy to remember that E is from the north—both Elohist and Ephraim begin with E.

The Elohist was a thinker and theologian and was probably a Levite. Based on his attitudes, he probably did not hold a position in the royal court, but we cannot be much more precise than that. Whoever he was, his perspective was conditioned by the theological and political difficulties of Israel in the ninth and eighth centuries B.C.E.

---

[2] See R. E. Clements, *Abraham and David* (London: SCM Press, 1967) for a detailed development of the connection between Abraham and David.

While the Yahwist believed God would overcome the problem of sin and extend blessing to all the families of the earth through the agency of the Davidic empire, the Elohist lived at a different time, and the national mood was somber. Israel was struggling with its identity. God seemed distant. There was spiritual drifting. The Levites had something to say about this, and drew upon stories that reinforced Israel's special relationship with God.

Watch for these features of the Elohist source in the Pentateuch:

- concern with moral and ethical issues
- "fear of God"
- God revealing himself in dreams
- great heroes of faith portrayed as prophets
- importance of locations in Israel (Ephraim, the Northern Kingdom)

Combined Yahwist–Elohist Version (JE)

The Elohist source eventually found its way south to Judah, where it merged with the Yahwist source. It is understandable that the two sources would be joined together. Both had the same basic scope, though the Elohist did not have any preancestral stories. Both the Yahwist and Elohist sources shared the fundamental conviction that Yahweh is the God of the Israelites and that he must be worshiped by the people.

The joining of the two sources into JE, what some scholars call the "Old Epic" tradition and others the "Jehovistic source," took place shortly after the fall of Israel in 721 B.C.E. The northern Levite author of the Elohist source fled south to Judah after the Assyrian invasion, taking his writings with him. He ended up in Jerusalem, and king Hezekiah used the Elohist material, combined with the Yahwist material, as the manifesto for a national religious revival. Putting these two traditions together supported the legitimacy of the Davidic line, of which Hezekiah was a part, and also promoted the religious and moral devotion that was at the heart of the Elohist tradition.

Perhaps the combination of these two national stories, one from the north and one from the south, also served to promote a sense of unity among the people. Those from the north who fled to the south and found a home there after 721 B.C.E. now also had a voice in the national story.

Deuteronomy (D)

Deuteronomy (D) follows chronologically the Yahwist and Elohist sources. It differs significantly in that it was not combined with those sources into a larger work. While the Yahwist, Elohist, and Priestly sources were combined together to create Genesis, Exodus, Leviticus, and Numbers, the book of Deuteronomy stands apart from these four books.

The book of Deuteronomy is somewhat different from the preceding four books of the Pentateuch in another way. It is not so much an account of events as it is a collection of Moses' sermons delivered to the Israelites just before they entered the Promised Land. It has a style quite different from that of the preceding books. Most of it is a direct address to the Israelites.

Deuteronomy contains traditions that can be traced all the way back to Israel's tribal origins. Levites living in the north are the ones who shaped the material and preserved it. It has certain affinities with the Elohist source. Details of the style and theology of Deuteronomy will be dealt with in chapter 5, which is devoted exclusively to that book. It is not crucial at this point to go into detail, because, unlike the other sources, we do not have to know about Deuteronomy in order to identify the sources of Genesis through Numbers.

Priestly Source (P)

Judah was conquered by the Babylonians in the sixth century B.C.E. and many survivors of the disaster were taken to Babylonia as refugees. The trauma of this exile prompted the survivors to conclude that the tragedy happened because they had forsaken the covenant. In exile they were at risk of losing their social and religious identity. Priests took the initiative to sustain the faith of the refugees and rebuild their identity. They gave traditional religious practices new significance, particularly the observance of the Sabbath day and the covenant ritual of circumcision.

The Priestly source (P) came into existence out of this context. The Priestly source is usually dated to the period of the Babylonian exile (587–539 B.C.E.) or to the postexilic period immediately after that. The priests recovered and recorded religious traditions so that the identity of the community would not be lost. They sought to reinforce covenant practices in repentance for past neglect and to avert a subsequent and possibly worse tragedy.

The Priestly source also developed to deal with the problem of defining Judean faith in contrast to Babylonian religion. What is the place of other nations and empires in our God's plan? How can we affirm the power of our God, when we live in a world dominated by Babylonians who trumpet the power of their god Marduk? Why is our God silent as we suffer? Priestly theology sought to adapt Israelite faith to the changed circumstance of the Israelites in the sixth century B.C.E.

Watch for these features of the Priestly source in the Pentateuch:

- thematic importance of blessing and curse
- covenants with God that mark important moments
- genealogies that establish connections among people and events
- social and religious role of priests
- Word of God as a driving force in history

CHALLENGES TO SOURCE ANALYSIS

Theories of pentateuchal sources continue to be revised and refined in modern scholarship (see Figure 2). From some quarters the whole enterprise of source analysis has come under challenge.

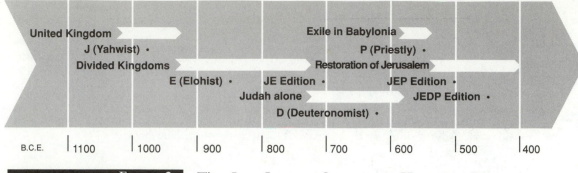

FIGURE 2   Time Line: Literary Sources and Historical Periods

Priestly Editing, No Priestly Source

Cross (1973) argues that a combination of Yahwist and Elohist sources is the core of the Pentateuch. He argues that a Priestly source never existed independently. Rather, Priestly writing consisted of editing the other two sources and adding comments and other material as needed.

Late Date for the Yahwist Source

Schmid (1976) argues that the Yahwist source, usually dated to the reign of Solomon in the tenth century B.C.E., should instead be dated to the time of the exile in the sixth century B.C.E. He claims the Yahwist source must have come later because preexilic classical prophecy (eighth and seventh centuries B.C.E.) makes virtually no reference to the stories contained in the Yahwist source.

Van Seters (1975) examines the Abraham stories in Genesis and concludes that they reflect names, customs, and institutions of the exilic period of Israel's history, and not the time of a supposed Yahwist in Solomon's kingdom. Consequently, he argues that it arose in the exilic period.

Rejection of Source Theories

Rendtorff (1990) rejects the tradition historical reconstruction of Noth by arguing that there was no early foundational narrative. He concludes that the glue holding together pentateuchal themes is very late, coming from the Deuteronomic school. He argues against the whole enterprise of source analysis and claims that there were no Yahwist or Elohist sources, only late tradition complexes.

Whybray (1987) accepts the existence of preexisting traditional material, yet argues that the process of composition was a literary process. Supported by insights from literary critics such as Alter (1982), Whybray suggests that repetition, the use of different divine names, and inconsistencies in the text were deliberate literary devices used to create texture. He claims such phenomena should not be used to reconstruct underlying documents.

As we can see from this review of pentateuchal theories, there are many proposals and counterproposals in the study of the Torah. Older source theories continue to be revised and new perspectives and theories continue to emerge. Some scholars reject source analysis entirely, claiming it compromises the literary integrity of the Pentateuch. Still others challenge the whole enterprise because it is inconsistent with their view of how God spoke through Moses. The field of pentateuchal studies is more unsettled today than it ever was.

Still, there seems to be a general consensus that the Torah is many-layered. Underlying sources did exist. Whether they were oral or written, or a combination of both, is not entirely clear. When they arose is not entirely clear, either. Yet for many students of the Torah, thinking about it as having arisen from a combination of four basic sources is the most productive way to begin thinking about the shape of the literature and the theology of the writers. Furthermore, references to these sources and their implied background is found throughout scholarship on the Torah today. We cannot begin to understand scholarly conversation on the Pentateuch without a knowledge of this approach.

So, without fully endorsing any particular theory of source analysis, and realizing that scholarship is open-ended, we will use the four-source theory—sometimes called JEDP—to provide the framework for our reading of the Torah.

FOR FURTHER STUDY

Treatments of the Pentateuch as a Whole The following books treat all of the books of the Pentateuch.

Blenkinsopp, Joseph (1992). *The Pentateuch. An Introduction to the First Five Books of the Bible.* Anchor Bible Reference Library. New York: Doubleday. Accepts the basic source theory but incorporates newer literary observations into his analysis.

Hamilton, Victor P. (1982). *Handbook on the Pentateuch*. Grand Rapids, Mich.: Baker. A content summary and analysis of each of the main sections of the Pentateuch with extensive bibliographies.

Mann, Thomas W. (1988). *The Book of the Torah. The Narrative Integrity of the Pentateuch*. Atlanta: John Knox Press. A literary and thematic treatment of the Pentateuch that does not deal with sources.

Sailhamer, John H. (1992). *The Pentateuch as Narrative. A Biblical-Theological Commentary*. Library of Biblical Interpretation. Grand Rapids, Mich.: Zondervan. Focuses on the narrative and literary continuity of the Pentateuch as a whole.

Introductions to Source Theories Summary explanations of source theories can be found in most modern introductions to the Old Testament, including the following.

Fohrer, Georg (1968). *Introduction to the Old Testament*. Nashville, Tenn.: Abingdon.

Hayes, John (1979). *An Introduction to Old Testament Study*. Nashville, Tenn.: Abingdon.

Schmidt, Werner H. (1984). *Old Testament Introduction*. New York: Crossroad.

The following books are useful for detailed study of the Pentateuch and scholarship on it.

Campbell, Anthony F., and Mark A. O'Brien (1993). *Sources of the Pentateuch. Texts, Introductions, Annotations*. Minneapolis, Minn.: Fortress Press. Collects the texts of the Priestly, Yahwist, and Elohist sources in separate chapters, with notes and explanation; a convenient way to view the source texts as continuous narratives.

De Vries, Simon J. (1987). "A Review of Recent Research in the Tradition History of the Pentateuch." In *Society of Biblical Literature Seminar Papers*, ed. K. H. Richards. Atlanta: Scholars Press. An extensive review of recent pentateuchal research.

Criticism of Source Analysis Introductions to the Old Testament from conservative religious traditions typically contain systematic critiques of source analysis approaches. See the following introductions.

Archer, Gleason L. (1974). *A Survey of Old Testament Introduction*. Chicago: Moody Press.

Harrison, R. K. (1969). *Introduction to the Old Testament*. Grand Rapids, Mich.: Eerdmans).

In addition to the critical assessments of the documentary hypothesis mentioned in the previous discussion (with their citations given in "Works Cited" below), the following books analyze the source theory approach to the Pentateuch.

Cassuto, Umberto (1961; original Hebrew edition, 1941). *The Documentary Hypothesis and the Composition of the Pentateuch*. Jerusalem: Magnes Press. Argues against a source theory of the Pentateuch.

Kikawada, Isaac M., and Arthur Quinn (1985). *Before Abraham Was. The Unity of Genesis 1–11*. Nashville: Abingdon. Argues that Genesis 1–11 has an essential literary unity which refutes the theory of underlying literary sources.

Segal, M. H. (1967). *The Pentateuch. Its Composition and its Authorship*. Jerusalem: Magnes Press. Argues against a source theory from a conservative Jewish position.

Tigay, Jeffrey (1985). "The Evolution of the Pentateuchal Narratives in the Light of the Evolution of the Gilgamesh Epic." In *Empirical Models for Biblical Criticism*, ed. Jeffrey Tigay. Philadelphia: University of Pennsylvania Press. In the title essay of this collection, based on extrabiblical texts, Tigay presents an alternate model for the growth of the Pentateuch as opposed to the theory of sources.

WORKS CITED

Alter, Robert (1982). *The Art of Biblical Narrative*. New York: Basic Books.

Cross, Frank Moore (1973). *Canaanite Myth and Hebrew Epic. Essays in the History of the Religion of Israel*. Cambridge, Mass.: Harvard University Press.

Friedman, Richard Elliott (1987). *Who Wrote the Bible?* Englewood Cliffs, N.J.: Prentice–Hall.

Noth, Martin (1948; English edition 1972). *A History of Pentateuchal Traditions*. Englewood Cliffs, N.J.: Prentice–Hall.

Rendtorff, Rolf (1990). *The Problem of the Process of Transmission in the Pentateuch*. Sheffield: JSOT Press.

Schmid, H. H. (1976). *Der sogenannte Jahwist: Beobachtungen und Fragen zur Pentateuchforschung*. Zürich: Theologischer Verlag.

Van Seters, John (1975). *Abraham in History and Tradition*. New Haven, Conn., and London: Yale University Press.

Whybray, R. N. (1987). *The Making of the Pentateuch: A Methodological Study*. Sheffield: JSOT Press.

GENESIS 1–11: PRIMEVAL STORY

Names and Terms to Remember

Abel	creation	Gilgamesh Epic
Adam	Divine Council	image of God
Babel, Tower of Babel	Eden	Marduk
Cain	Eve	Noah
chaos	flood	Primeval Story
cosmology	genealogy	ziggurat

The book of Genesis, fifty chapters in length, is a foundational book. It is the first book of the Hebrew Bible and, not coincidentally, speaks of origins. It gives account of the creation of the world. As it does so, it establishes fundamental truths about the nature of God, humankind, and the universe. It also gives account of the origin of the nation of Israel by telling stories of its ancestors. It is such an important book that we will devote two chapters to it. This chapter will cover Genesis 1–11, the world-in-general origin stories. Chapter 2 will cover Genesis 12–50, Israel's origin stories.

We call the origin stories of Genesis 1–11 the **Primeval Story**; *primeval* refers to the earliest ages of human culture. The Primeval Story is a unified account of earliest events, from the creation of the world to the dispersal of humankind over the face of the earth. The Primeval Story is not history as we ordinarily use that term. Even a moment's reflection would indicate that the earliest events of creation had no human eyewitnesses. What has been passed down through the text could hardly have been based on firsthand reports. These stories are mostly legends and sagas.

The Yahwist, to whom we referred in the Prologue to the Torah, seems especially fascinated with this early period. His stories make up a large part of Genesis 1–11. The Yahwist probably wrote during the time of the Davidic monarchy. He was interested in recording stories of "universal" history contained in Genesis 1–11 because it was during the Davidic monarchy period that Israel became a world-class empire due to David's territorial conquests. The growth of the kingdom and the development of cultural contacts with other nations prompted the Yahwist and other intellectuals to turn their attention to the larger world in order to understand their place in it and other nations' relationship to Israel's God.

The other literary source found in the Primeval Story is the Priestly source. The Priestly source contributed its own versions of the creation and flood stories, along with some other material. The Elohist source is not present at all. We will first read the portions of the Primeval Story that derive from the core epic shaped by the Yahwist. Then we will read those portions attributed to the Priestly source. Finally, we will make some observations concerning how the entire Primeval Story was put together.

YAHWIST CORE PRIMEVAL STORY

The stories of Genesis 1–11 contributed by the Yahwist establish the basic plot of the Primeval Story. These stories primarily focus on the growth of the human race, and they demonstrate how sin dogged that development.

CREATION (2:4B–25)

The story of the **creation** of the first man and the first woman opens the Yahwist core epic. The story is told by learned court scribes who wanted to account for the big issues. Where did we come from? Where did sin come from? Why do we have to die? It does not tell the story in a scientific way. Providing a reasoned scientific account is obviously not its purpose.

The **Adam** and **Eve** described in this story are the first couple, and at the same time they are "everyman" and "everywoman." If we were to render their Hebrew names with English equivalents literally, they would be "Mr. Man" and "Ms. Life," respectively.

> *2:4b On the day YHWH Elohim made the earth and the heavens, 5 no vegetation yet being on the earth, no plant yet springing up (for YHWH Elohim had not caused it to rain on the earth and there was no man to till the ground; 6 only a mist rose from the earth and watered the surface of the ground), 7 then YHWH Elohim fashioned some dust of the ground into a man. He breathed the breath of life into his nostrils and he became a living being.*

Notice how many times the words "earth" and "ground" are used. The "earthiness" of the story suggests it comes out of a peasant, agricultural setting. This story makes a connection between earth and humanness by a linguistic pun in the Hebrew text: ground is *adamah* and man is *adam*. Word play occurs frequently in the Hebrew Bible and was often used to make a serious point. We could duplicate the pun with *humus* and *human*; that is, if we did not think puns were silly in our culture.

Yahweh God is described as a potter when he fashions the man out of earth. One can almost picture God on his knees in the clay, working over the body of the first man, manually shaping the physical form. The image of the potter is a good example of the Yahwist's use of anthropomorphic language; that is, he describes God as if God had human characteristics. Note also how life resulted only after God infused the body with his own breath. The Yahwist seems to be telling us that a human person consists of both physical body and divine life-breath.

The next few verses describe the place called **Eden.**[1] The text clearly implies that Eden lay somewhere in the vicinity of the Tigris and Euphrates rivers. These two rivers define Mesopotamia, a term that literally means the land "between the rivers." Eden has never been located, nor should we expect to find it. The name signifies a place of primeval harmony and self-sufficient abundance that supposedly once existed but no longer does.

The ancient Sumerians of Mesopotamia had their own story of origins in a primeval wonderland. Enki and Ninhursag were two gods, a husband and wife, who enjoyed goodness as long as they stayed near the tree of life. They lived in a

---

[1]The term "eden" is related to the Sumerian word *edin*, which refers to the fertile steppe region in the Mesopotamian basin, which later became barren. The Babylonian word *edinu* then came to mean "plain, desert." Eden in the Hebrew Bible was translated *paradeisos* in the Septuagint, which became "paradise" in English.

place called Dilmun, which was located in what is now called the Persian Gulf, in roughly the same place Eden was thought to have been (Pritchard 1969: 37–41). Figure 1.1 details this area.

The garden of Eden had a tree of life. In fact, Eden was well-populated with trees. All the trees were available for human use except the tree of knowledge.

> *15 YHWH Elohim took the man and placed him in the garden of Eden to till it and oversee it. 16 And YHWH Elohim commanded the man, "You may eat from any tree of the garden; 17 except you shall not eat from the tree of good and bad knowledge. On the day you eat from it you shall die."*

The man was placed in the garden to care for it. He was not placed in the garden simply to enjoy it, but also to tend it. The text implies that even from the beginning humankind was assigned to be keeper of the earth. That task was part of humankind's essential identity and responsibility.

Of all the good things in the garden, God only prohibited the man from eating from the tree of knowledge. The punishment for disobedience was death. As we will see, the tree of knowledge plays a crucial role in Genesis 3, where eating from it becomes the symbol of disobedience. The significance of the tree of knowledge and the prohibition of eating its fruit is much debated (Barr 1993).

God was concerned for the first man's welfare and feared he might get lonely.

> *18 Then YHWH Elohim said, "It is not good that the man should be alone. I will make him a helper matched to him." 19 So out of the ground YHWH Elohim formed every beast of the field and every bird of the air, and brought them to the man to see what he would name them. Whatever the man named each living creature, that became its name. 20 The man named all the beasts, birds, and living things. But the man had no helper matched to him.*

God recognized that the man had no companion, so animals were formed. Naming the animals demonstrated the man's superiority over them. In the ancient world the authority to give names implied mastery. Some see in the man's naming the animals an early form of scientific classification and an attempt to order the world in which he lived. This kind of "scientific" activity marked the heady, enlightenment mentality of the Davidic court in Jerusalem.

But the animals were not his equal. They did not satisfy his deeper longing. The newly formed man still lacked a suitable companion. Yahweh, as is typical of this epic, was sensitive to innate human needs and wanted to provide genuine fulfillment for the human creature he had made.

> *21 YHWH Elohim cast a deep sleep upon the man. While he slept he took one of his ribs and closed up with flesh the place where it had been. 22 YHWH Elohim built a woman from the rib he had taken out of the man. He brought her to the man.*

A woman was created out of the body of the man so that they would be of the same substance. The choice of the rib was no doubt deliberate. The Hebrew word

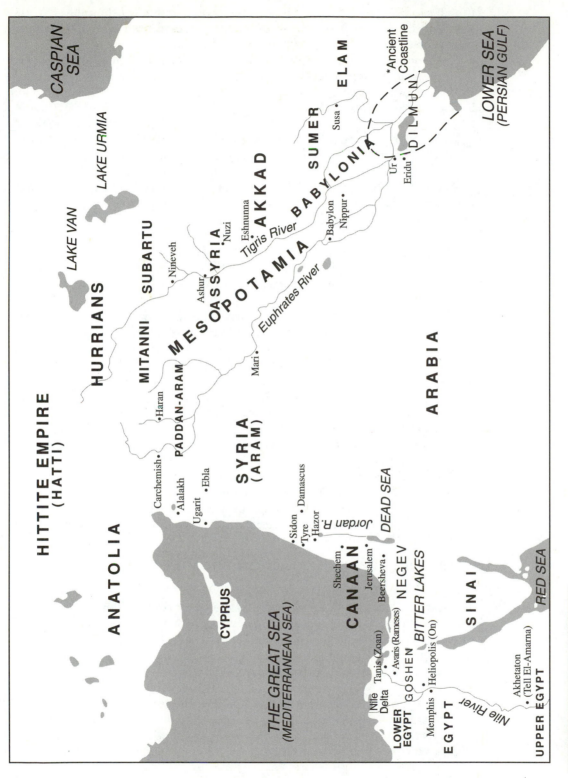

FIGURE 1.1   Early Civilizations in Mesopotamia, Egypt, and Asia Minor

for rib can also mean "side." Perhaps the choice of this word implies that the man and the woman were meant to be side by side, in other words, to complement each other.

The woman is now the one who is "a helper matched to him," according to the Hebrew text. Note that the term *helper* does not imply a position of inferiority. In support we need only cite Exodus 18:4, where, using the same term, God is described as a *helper* to Moses.

23 Then the man said, "Finally this is bone of my bones, flesh of my flesh. Let her be called 'woman' because she was taken out of 'man.'"

Another pun is used in the original text and it is similar to the pun in English: man is *ish* and woman is *ishah*. This is yet another of the writer's ways of affirming the essential relatedness of man and woman.

24 Therefore a man leaves his father and his mother and adheres to his wife, and they become one flesh. 25 And the man and the woman were both naked, but they were not ashamed.

These words are comments of the narrator from a time when marriage had become an established social practice—obviously from a much later time than the implied setting of creation. They are a commentary on the oneness of man and woman in the marriage institution. The primary allegiance will be to the marriage partner, rather than to father and mother.

Becoming one flesh denotes the spiritual, emotional, and sexual union that characterizes marriage. Though without clothes, the original couple were unabashed at their nakedness. They felt no need to shield themselves from the other's gaze. Their relationship was characterized by an almost childlike innocence and naiveté.

Overall, this account stresses God's involvement with the creatures he had fashioned. He lived in intimate association with them in the Garden of Eden. The next story provides an explanation of why humankind no longer lives in the immediate presence of God in a perfect world. It is because they chose to disobey a divine directive.

DISOBEDIENCE AND EXPULSION FROM EDEN (3:1–24)

The story of the origin of sin in Genesis 3 is a direct continuation of the creation story of Genesis 2. The disobedience of Eve and Adam described here is referred to as the *fall* in some theological communities. It is the occasion when humankind rejected the authority of Yahweh. The essential temptation to the woman and man was to become like gods (or like God—Elohim can be translated either way).

3:1 The serpent was craftier than any other wild creature that YHWH Elohim had made. It said to the woman, "Did Elohim say, 'You shall not eat of any tree of the garden'?" 2 And the woman said to the serpent, "We may eat of the fruit of the trees of the garden, 3 but Elohim did say, 'You cannot eat of the fruit of the tree which is in the middle of the garden, nor can you touch it, or you will die.'" 4 But the serpent said to the woman, "You would not die. 5 Elohim said that because he knows that when you eat from it your eyes will be opened, and you will be like Elohim (gods/God), knowing good and evil."

There is a subtle connection between chapters 2 and 3 in the Hebrew text. Whereas the primeval couple were "naked" (Hebrew *arom*), the serpent was "crafty" (Hebrew *arum*). This is a literary signal that these two chapters form a unified story. Another signal is the continuation of the name YHWH Elohim to refer to God. This is a relatively rare designation, and is found only in the Yahwist.[2]

Who was this serpent and where did it come from? Apparently, it was one of the creatures God had made. Only in later interpretations is the serpent identified with Satan and the Devil (see, for example, Revelation 12 in the New Testament). Ancient mythological texts, however, suggest that more is involved here than just snakes. The serpent is akin to the dragons and monsters of ancient creation myths, creatures such as Lotan (Leviathan) in the Baal texts from Ugarit and the water god Apsu in the Enuma Elish from Mesopotamia.

The serpent was able to entice the woman by suggesting that maybe God did not have humankind's best interests in mind. Maybe God was trying to keep something from them in order to protect his own power. The serpent never did tell a lie. It only planted the seed of doubt in the woman's mind by suggesting that God was trying to hide something.

6 So when the woman saw that the tree was a good food source and that it was pleasant to look at and desirable for gaining wisdom, she took some of its fruit and ate. She also gave some to her husband and he ate. 7 The eyes of both of them were opened and they knew that they were naked. They sewed fig leaves together and made themselves loin cloths.

The woman, then the man, ate the fruit of the tree, because in their judgment it looked good.[3] Their choice to pursue a course of action contrary to God's revealed command, "Do not eat!," was the assertion of human independence and autonomy, and a denial of humankind's subordination to God.

Contrary to what God seemed to be implying in the warning "on the day you eat of it you shall die," they did not die on the spot. Death as threatened in Genesis 2 apparently implied much more than just the cessation of physical life. Death signified alienation from God and became evident first of all as interpersonal disharmony and shame.

[2] The name YHWH Elohim is perhaps a deliberate literary and theological way of combining the name for God used by the Priestly source (Elohim), with its connotations of power, with the personal name of God used throughout the Yahwist source (YHWH).

[3] Common lore has it that the original couple ate an apple. But note that the text says nothing about apples here. The fruit was probably something native to the ancient Mesopotamian world, perhaps a pomegranate, date, or fig.

8 They heard the sound of YHWH Elohim walking in the garden in the cool of the day. The man and his wife hid from YHWH Elohim among the trees of the garden. 9 YHWH Elohim called to the man and said to him, "Where are you?" 10 He said, "I heard you in the garden and I got afraid, because I'm naked. So I hid." 11 He said, "Who told you that you were naked? Did you eat from the tree from which I commanded you not to eat?" 12 The man said, "The woman you gave me, she gave me something from the tree and I ate." 13 Then YHWH Elohim said to the woman, "What did you do?" And the woman said, "The serpent tricked me and I ate."

The couple felt vulnerable and defensive and made clothes to cover their nakedness. Each was unable to bear the penetrating stare of the other. In addition, they felt estranged from God and became fearful. So they hid in the garden.

When God finally confronted them, both tried to disown responsibility for their actions. The man blamed the breach on the woman, and she on the serpent. Denying personal responsibility, the text suggests, is a primal human impulse.

Each of the three received a suitable punishment. The punishment took the form of a specific curse placed upon each. God's curse is the opposite of God's blessing. It establishes and assures that a bad thing will happen to the object of the curse.

14 Then YHWH Elohim said to the serpent, "Because you did this, cursed are you more than any beast or creature of the field. On your belly you will go, and dust you will eat all the days of your life. 15 Enmity I will create between you and the woman, and between your offspring and her offspring. He will bruise your head and you will bruise his heel."

The serpent was made the lowliest of God's creatures. The curse on the serpent is somewhat cryptic. But God seems to be saying that the temptation to evil, as represented by the serpent, will not dominate humankind. The couple's offspring will be bruised by the serpent's evil but will not be overcome. Perhaps by this the text suggests that, at the very least, there is a ray of hope.

16 To the woman he said, "I will greatly increase your pregnancy pain: in pain you will bear children. Yet you will long for your husband and he will dominate you."

The woman was cursed in her relationship to her husband and in her essential role of continuing the race. They were created for a relationship of mutuality, but now the husband would dominate. The text states unambiguously that the subordination of woman to man follows the break with God and is a result of the curse. Subordination of female to male is not part of the created order. In addition to interpersonal dysfunction, the woman would have great pain in the course of childbirth and child rearing.

17 And to the man he said, "Because you heeded your wife and ate from the tree I commanded you not to, cursed is the ground on account of you:

you will eat with pain all the days of your life. 18 Thorn and thistle will
sprout for you when you want to eat the plants of the field: 19 by the sweat
of your forehead you will eat bread until you return to the ground (for from
it you were taken)—for dust you are and to dust you will return."

The man was created to care for the ground and till it. His curse related to
this essential function. From then on food production would be accomplished
only with great difficulty. Although he was intimately tied to the ground (remember the pun on his name), it would resist him as he tried to draw subsistence from
it. Furthermore, when he died, he would return to the soil out of which he was
formed.

As a whole, these curses set the stage for the blessing that would be voiced by
God in Genesis 12. That blessing would be the beginning of God's program to
overcome the broken relationship of the garden. In the meantime the couple was
clothed by God. Then they were expelled from the garden, according to God, because "the man has become like one of us, knowing good and evil." (3:22) A
cherub guard was placed at the entrance to the garden to keep the man away
from the tree of life.[4]

Here we will step back from the text and consider the more general issue of
how we should understand the sin this original couple committed. There are
three basic interpretations.

1. *Ethical Interpretation.* By eating from the tree of knowledge, humankind
made a choice to discriminate between what is good and what is bad on the
basis of their own judgment, rather than by automatically accepting God's
definition. By acting on their own, the couple irrevocably separated themselves
from God, and their relationship to God was forever afterward changed.

2. *Knowledge Interpretation.* The Hebrew phrase "good and evil" can
sometimes designate the totality of knowledge (see Deuteronomy 1:39 and
2 Samuel 19:35). Eating the fruit of that tree was an act of human pride
and an attempt to know everything God knows. God would not tolerate
any such challenge to his preeminence, and expelled the original couple
from the garden lest they eat from the tree of life and become invulnerable.

3. *Sexual Interpretation.* The story in Genesis 2–3 deals quite a bit with
sexual matters. The couple is naked and not ashamed. Later they experience
shame because of their nakedness. Even the serpent has been interpreted by
psychoanalytic interpreters as a sexual symbol. The Hebrew term for knowledge can have sexual associations, as when, in Genesis 4:1 "Adam knew
Eve"—clearly a euphemism for sexual intercourse. The sexual interpretation
suggests that coming to knowledge, symbolized by eating the forbidden fruit,
signifies the passage from childhood through puberty to adulthood. Sexual
experience involves the pains and alienations of coming to know oneself and
the other in new ways. Discovering the sexual impulse means one cannot go
back to the innocence of the garden ever again.

---

[4] A cherub was not a cherry-cheeked child, such as we might imagine Cupid with his bow and
arrow. In the ancient Middle East a cherub (*cherubim* in the plural) was a man-headed bull with eagles' wings that stood guard outside Mesopotamian temples.

All three interpretations have hints of truth in them. Yet the big affront to Yahweh seems to be humankind's desire to become like gods, to be independent, self-sufficient entities. By focusing on this dimension, perhaps the first interpretation contains the most truth. By their act of self-determination, the original couple expressed their intent to live by their own authority, not by God's. God would not abide this direct challenge. He expelled them and denied them access to perpetual life, symbolized by the tree of life.

This concern with self-determination versus divine determination appears to be the key to the Yahwist's interest in this story. Would the prosperity of the Davidic empire lead the Israelites into an attitude of self-sufficiency? Would they forget about Yahweh? Would they try to grasp greatness on their own, or would they wait for God's blessing? The Yahwist recalls the story of the first ancestors as a warning against self-determination.

Although the notion of a "once for all fall" is not found in the Hebrew Bible, this story became the basis for the Christian notion of "original sin." It appears first in 2 Esdras 7:118, and was developed by Paul in the New Testament, who said, "Sin came into the world through one man," and "One man's trespass led to condemnation for all" (Romans 5:12,18 NRSV). Mainstream Judaism never accepted the notion of original sin. Instead, it held that one is subject to an evil impulse (*yetser hara*), which can be controlled by the good impulse (*yetser hatov*). This good impulse is cultivated by doing godly deeds and observing the commandments.

Pre-Flood Generations (4:1–26)

Once kicked out of the garden, Adam and Eve had sexual relations (for the first time?) and their first son, **Cain**, was born. He was followed shortly afterward by **Abel**. Cain was a farmer and Abel a shepherd. Each offered a gift to God from his respective produce. Abel's offering was accepted by God but Cain's was not. Out of jealousy Cain impulsively killed Abel. Cain was alienated from the ground and was forced to become a wanderer.

A similar conflict story is found in Sumerian literature. In Dumuzi and Enkimdu the shepherd-god Dumuzi vied with the farmer-god Enkimdu for the favors of the goddess Inanna. Dumuzi quarreled with Enkimdu and won the prize of Inanna's attention (Pritchard 1969:41–2). Both the biblical and Sumerian stories reflect the early conflict over use of the precious arable land: would it be used for agriculture or for grazing? Who has a right to the land, shepherd or farmer?

The story of Cain and Abel in its Genesis setting means more than this, though. Its immediate effect is to demonstrate the snowballing effect of sin. Adam and Eve sinned against God and were cursed. The curse was passed on to their children. With the second generation death was no longer just a spiritual condition of alienation from God, but also a physical reality.

The escalation of violence continued. Cain's offspring included Lamech, who was the prototype of violent attackers (4:17–24). He boasted to his two wives that he took revenge on a man by killing him, although he himself had only been slightly wounded.

But even while violence was increasing, there was a parallel development. Culture and technology rapidly developed. Cain's son Enoch built the first city. And Lamech's three sons were credited with various first-time achievements: Jabal for domestication of animals, Jubal for music, and Tubal-cain for copper and iron industries.[5] Is it possible that in associating these developments with the notoriously sinful line of Cain the writer was making a negative judgment on these so-called advances? There was a tradition in Israel that a patriarchal seminomadic and unurbanized lifestyle kept one closest to God. The Yahwist writer may have been implicitly criticizing the cultural advancements of the Davidic monarchy by associating them with the line of Cain and Lamech.

Certainly such momentous human achievements were not the work of single men, certainly not all from the same family. The text is telescoping into a brief span developments that took many, many generations. But interestingly, the text does evidence the importance of these developments and places them in early prehistory. Archaeologists and anthropologists have confirmed the importance of these developments for the progress of civilization, and they say that these developments occurred first in the Middle East.

DIVINE–HUMAN INTERMARRIAGE (6:1–4)

The Yahwist exposed the limitless human capacity for wickedness. Sin grew in extent and intensity, from sibling murder to the blood feud of Lamech (4:23–24). The growth of sin culminated in the encounter between the sons of God and the daughters of men.

> 6:1 *When humankind began to multiply on the face of the ground, and daughters were born to them, 2 the sons of Elohim saw that the daughters of humankind were good. They took wives for themselves from them as they chose. 3 And YHWH said, "My spirit shall no longer remain with humankind forever, because they are flesh. His life span will be 120 years. 4 The fallen ones were on the earth in those days (and also afterward) when the sons of Elohim had intercourse with the daughters of humankind and gave birth for them. They are the warriors, from eternity called the men of a name.*

Certainly one question is, "Who are the sons of God?" Some interpreters have suggested they are the offspring of Cain, and that this story records the interbreeding of the lines of Cain and Seth. A mixture of the good and the bad genes resulted in the flood. This view is mistaken. Parallels to the phrase in biblical and extrabiblical literature prove that these "sons of God" are divine creatures, commonly identified as angels (for example, see Job 1:6). They appear to have been errant members of the **Divine Council**, the body of angels who rule the universe with God. They were sexually attracted to human women and sired a race of giants.

---

[5] Mesopotamian tradition likewise traces these arts and accomplishments back to primeval times. It recalls a line of seven *apkallus*, wise men who lived before the flood. They taught humanity the arts and crafts of civilization. A reflection of this tradition may be what we have in chapter 4, which also contains seven generations in the Cain genealogy.

The possibility of such interbreeding defies human conceiving. Were it in fact possible, presumably such interbreeding would have resulted in humans acquiring the immortality of divine creatures. Probably for this reason God took steps to limit the longevity of humankind to a maximum of 120 years.

Most scholars see in this story the survival of an early myth about the gods and humanity. Fantastic and strange as the incident may seem, it plays an important role in the narrative scheme. The incident was used by the Yahwist to explain why God was finally moved to action. Sin had evolved so far as to infect the relationship between the divine and the human realms. The proper distinction between heaven and earth was no longer being maintained.

Yahweh sent a **flood** to wipe out humankind because it had become so evil. The flood story of Genesis 6–9 is a composite of J and P elements. The Yahwist contribution focuses on the elimination of humankind. We will postpone a full treatment of the flood story until later, when we examine the Priestly contributions to the Primeval Story. There we will study the Priestly flood story and set it next to the Yahwist version.

Summarizing the Yahwist version for now, **Noah** got in a boat along with his family and a representative sample of the creatures Yahweh had made. God personally closed the door on the ark. Then the flood came. It lasted forty days. After those days Noah sent out a dove to test how much the waters had dried up. When on the third try the dove did not come back, Noah opened the covering of the boat and everyone got out. Noah offered sacrifices to Yahweh, who then vowed never again to curse the earth in such a way:

> 8:20 Noah built an altar to YHWH. He took one of every clean animal and one of every clean bird, and offered whole burnt offerings on the altar. 21 When YHWH smelled the pleasant aroma, YHWH said in his heart, "I will never curse the ground again on account of humankind. The deviousness of the human heart is corrupt from youth on up. I will never again destroy every living thing as I have just done. 22 As long as the earth exists, seed-time and harvest, cold and heat, summer and winter, day and night, will not cease."

Again the Yahwist uses the language of curse, reinforcing the danger to which humankind is always subject. God as much as admits that human nature is such that sin will always be around. But this will never again be cause for God to wreak mass destruction. God pledges never to destroy the earth on account of humankind. Presumably God would devise another plan to deal with the effects of sin. Certainly the Yahwist is anticipating the blessing God will articulate to Abraham, which will forever overcome the curse.

NOAH'S INSOBRIETY (9:18–27)

After the flood, Noah and his three sons began to repopulate the earth. Noah settled down and became a farmer, much in the tradition of Adam and Cain before him. In the process, Noah, "a righteous man, upright in his generation" (6:9), fell prey to what appears to be unseemly behavior. God's judgment on humankind in the flood obviously had not improved human nature.

9:20 Noah became a man of the ground. He planted a vineyard, 21 drank wine, and got drunk. He was uncovered in his tent. 22 Ham, the father of Canaan, saw the nakedness of his father and told his two brothers outside. 23 Shem and Japheth took a cloak, placed it on their shoulders, walked backward, and covered the nakedness of their father. Their faces were turned away so they did not see the nakedness of their father.

The text is not direct in its negative judgment on Noah, but from other biblical passages we can assume that drunkenness was not approved.[6]

24 When Noah awoke from his insobriety, he knew what his youngest son had done to him. 25 He said, "Cursed is Canaan! The most lowly servant will he be for his brothers." 26 He also said, "Blessed is YHWH Elohim of Shem. May Canaan be his servant. 27 May God enlarge Japheth. He will dwell in the tents of Shem. May Canaan be his servant."

Note the special interest in Canaan. The action of cursing Canaan is especially difficult to justify. Why should Ham's son and not Ham himself suffer the consequences? Perhaps the "Ham to Canaan" direction of cursing reinforces the biblical rule that later generations suffer the consequences of the sins of previous generations.

Additionally, there may have been a political agenda in this story. Living in the tenth century and connected to the royal court, the Yahwist was interested in justifying the elimination of the Canaanite inhabitants of Palestine who were Israel's enemies. This story gives Israel religious warrant for dispossessing the Canaanites and possessing the land.[7]

But whatever the underlying political motivation for the cursing of Canaan, the Yahwist placed this story here to prove that sin was still around after the flood. Not even Noah was perfectly righteous after all.

TOWER OF BABEL (11:1–9)

The **Tower of Babel** episode continues the story of rebellion against God and depicts the overreach of human aspirations.

11:1 The whole earth had one language and the same vocabulary. 2 When they left the east they found a valley in the land of Shinar and settled there. 3 They said to each other, "Let us make bricks and bake them thoroughly." So they had bricks for building blocks and tar for mortar. 4 Then they said, "Let us build a city, and a tower with its top in the heavens. Let us make a name for ourselves so we will not be scattered around the earth."

---

[6] We cannot be sure exactly what made Noah so distraught. Bassett (1971) suggests that Ham committed incest with Noah's wife, arguing that uncovered nakedness is equated with sexual intercourse. Cohen (1974) suggests that Ham acquired Noah's sexual potency by the act of seeing him naked. Such interpretations go beyond what is given. The text is not specific enough to tell exactly what Ham's offense was, beyond the fact that he dishonored his father.

[7] Other places where the Yahwist shows special interest in neighboring peoples include Genesis 26 on the Philistines (this is especially anachronistic—the Philistines did not establish a presence in Palestine until the 13th century; presumably, Abraham is much before that); Genesis 29–31 on the Arameans; and the Book of Numbers' wilderness stories on Ammon, Moab, and Edom.

The locale of this story is the broad plain of lower Mesopotamia called Shinar. Humankind was a unified community. The people had plans to secure their own greatness, "to make a name for themselves." They were intent on creating their own city and culture—do we have more Yahwistic negative commentary on urban life here? Building a tower that would reach heaven itself was their goal. Yahweh, however, took considerable offense at this.

> *5 YHWH[8] came down to see the city and the tower which the men had built. 6 YHWH said, "If as one people with one language this is the beginning of what they can do, then nothing they plan will be impossible for them. 7 Let us[9] go down and confuse their language there so no one can understand the other's language."*

Why should Yahweh get so upset? What could be the threat? Surely the ancient people were incapable of building a skyscraper that could come anywhere near a Sears Tower or World Trade Center! Surely they could never physically enter heaven to challenge God!

Whether or not they could actually do it, God took their activity as yet another attempt to grasp greatness rather than waiting for God's blessing. God took offense at their plan because it seemed as if they were trying to become gods themselves by reaching heaven on their own.

> *8 And YHWH scattered them from there around the earth. They quit building the city. 9 For that reason he called its name Babel because there YHWH confused the language of the entire earth, and from there YHWH scattered them around the earth.*

God confounded their ability to communicate effectively. They could no longer cooperate and their building plans had to be scrapped. The result was human disunity. The word *confuse* used here is the seed of another pun in the original text. "Confuse," *balal* in Hebrew, contains a word play on **Babel**.

Perhaps there is an additional level of meaning in the text. Babel is also the way the Hebrew language writes *Babylon*. With this story we may be learning how and why Israel's great nemesis later in history, the Babylonian Empire, got its name. This story characterizes the great Babylon, even at the very beginning of history, as an evil city that by its primeval activities demonstrated its defiance of God.

The Tower of Babel story is a good example of how thematic analysis can be supported through literary analysis. Literary criticism[10] focuses on the structure

---

[8] Notice how the name of God in this episode is now simply YHWH, and not YHWH Elohim as in the earlier Yahwist stories.

[9] Who is the "us" in "Let us go down" (verse 7)? Possibly, the Divine Council again. This is discussed in greater detail under the "Priestly Creation Story—Day Six."

[10] This literary criticism is sometimes called the New Literary Criticism to distinguish it from source analysis of the Pentateuch, the research that uncovered the JEPD traditions. That enterprise was also called Literary Criticism in its day. One recent collection of New Literary Critical readings, including a treatment of the book of Genesis, can be found in Robert Alter and Frank Kermode's *The Literary Guide to the Bible* (1987).

and plot development of stories. This approach has been especially productive of late and is one of the most promising fields of research. One such literary analysis of the Tower of Babel story has revealed its artistry (Fokkelmann 1975). Upon close reading, it has well-formed and symmetrical structures, defined by repeated words and phrases. One study of the narrative reveals it consists of parallel action sets. Table 1.1 displays the literary parallels.

TABLE 1.1 LITERARY PARALLELS IN TOWER OF BABEL STORY

Human Plans (1–4)	*Divine Action (5–9)*
One language, same vocabulary (1)	One people, one language (6)
Settled there (2)	Confuse language there (7)
Let us make bricks (3)	Let us go down (7)
Let us build a city (4)	Quit building the city (8)
Make a name (4)	Called its name (9)
Lest we be scattered around the earth (4)	YHWH scattered them around the earth (9)

The point of observing the literary structure of the story is this. The attempted ascent of humankind is placed alongside the going down of God. The language of the text highlights the nature of God's actions as a response in kind to human efforts. For everything that humankind tried to do, God had a countermeasure. This reactive nature of God seems to characterize the Yahwist epic. It portrays God as especially ready to respond to the problem of human sin, both negatively (curse) and positively (blessing).

In addition to thematic and literary analysis, archaeology and cultural analysis can further increase our understanding of the text. The "tower with its top in the heavens" was a *ziggurat*, to use the Babylonian term that designated such structures. A Babylonian ziggurat was a stepped, pyramid-shaped structure that typically had a temple on top. Remains of ziggurats have been found at the sites of ancient Mesopotamian cities, including Ur and Babylon (see Figure 1.2).

The reason ancient Mesopotamians built ziggurats derives from their understanding of religion and the gods. In ancient times mountains were often considered to be holy places where gods were thought to dwell. For example, Zeus dwelt on Mt. Olympus, Baal on Mt. Saphon, and Yahweh on Mt. Sinai. Such mountains were contact points between heaven and earth.

On the Mesopotamian plain there were no mountains. To remedy this lack, the inhabitants constructed artificial ones, ziggurats. One of the most famous ancient ziggurats was Etemenanki in Babylon, completed by Nebuchadnezzar around 600 B.C.E. According to Babylonian religion, Babylon was built by the gods and was the dwelling of **Marduk**. From there people could meet the gods. This is reflected in the authentic Akkadian name for Babylon. Derived from the Babylonian phrase *bab-ilu*, it literally means "gate of the gods." The Hebrew folk derivation of the name from "confuse" does not correctly reflect this true native meaning of the name Babylon.

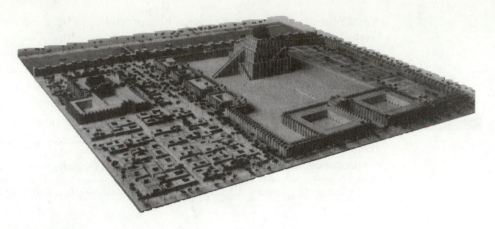

FIGURE 1.2 A ziggurat is a temple tower. Babylonians built terraced pyramids out of mud bricks with each story smaller than the one below it. This is a photograph of a model of the tower of Babylon called Etemenanki.

The Babylonians believed their capital city, through its ziggurat, gave them access to the heavens, as the name Babylon suggests. It was this presumption, this affront to the true God, that at some level lies behind Israel's Tower of Babel story.

The Tower of Babel story closes the Yahwist primeval story on a sad note. As a collection, the primeval story of the Yahwist deals with the relationship of God and humankind. Originally the relationship was close and pure. Then humans willfully began to desire to be gods themselves. This demolished the intimacy of the divine–human relationship and had long-range ill effects on humankind and the larger created world. In sum, the episodes of the Yahwist primeval story demonstrate the disastrous effects of human sin.

PRIESTLY PRIMEVAL ADDITIONS

The Priestly writer has a different agenda in his primeval stories. His creation and flood stories do not deal with the problem of sin but present the gift of divine blessing.

PRIESTLY CREATION STORY (1:1–2:3)

The Priestly source also contains a story of creation. Because this story of creation deals more comprehensively with God's creation of the world as a whole, it was logically placed first.

The book of Genesis got its name from the first phrase, "in the beginning." Indeed, Genesis begins at the very beginning as related by the Priestly source. In rather broad strokes it paints a picture of the big components of the universe as they come into being: sky, land, sun, moon, animals, humankind. It does not go into a whole lot of detail.

While it specifies how the world came into being, it simply assumes the existence of God and gives no explanation of where God came from. The reference to God used in this account of creation is Elohim. It is Israel's most neutral and general way of referring to God and suggests a powerful and stately divine being.

Remember that the order of the individual stories in the Pentateuch does not necessarily correspond to the order in which they were written. This first account of creation (Genesis 1) was actually composed later than the second one (Genesis 2). This first account is the product of the Priestly writer and reflects his intense concern with the right order of things.

Priests were the overseers of society, the bureaucrats if you will, who made sure the community adhered to the guidelines established by God. They were concerned with things sacred, including Sabbath worship and Sabbath regulations. All of these concerns can be seen in one way or another here. In fact, the worship orientation is so strong that some have actually classified Genesis 1 as a liturgy, that is, a text used in formal temple worship. While certainly reflecting a stately "holy" language, calling Genesis 1 a liturgy perhaps overstates the case.

DAY 0: WATERS OF CHAOS

Day Zero

Often, ancient texts are difficult to interpret, either for linguistic or cultural reasons. This is evident, for example, when we try to understand the first verse of Genesis chapter 1.

1:1 In the beginning Elohim created heaven and earth.

The first verse can be translated either of two ways. Both are linguistically acceptable. The first option, "In the beginning God created heaven and earth," implies that the writer was interested in positing an absolute beginning to the world.

1:1 When Elohim began to create heaven and earth,

This translation, "When God began to create heaven and earth, the earth was untamed and shapeless," suggests that the writer was more interested in the condition of the world when God started his creating work, rather than in an absolute beginning to it all.

The issue might seem of little significance, but it bears directly on the question of whether God created the world out of nothing, called creation *ex nihilo*, or whether there was an already-existing substance that God shaped into a structured world. The second option seems more consistent with the rest of the account and is the one we follow here.

> *2 the earth was untamed and shapeless, and darkness was on the surface of the deep water. And the wind /or spirit of Elohim hovered over the surface of the water.*

The text describes the state of the world as dark, messy, and very soggy. Water is twice mentioned. It seems that everything was just a mass of water "stuff." The term *deep water* signifies not just bottomless oceans, but the threatening waters of Mesopotamian lore that the ancient peoples always feared would be their undoing.[11] These are the waters of **chaos**.

These first two verses describe the preexisting state of things at the time God started creating. In other words, the text tells us that God did not start with a clean slate, with nothingness. There was something there to begin with, an unruly, threatening, dark mass of chaotic "water stuff." God's work of creating things does not begin at verse one but at verse three.

God's creating mechanism turns out not to be manual labor but speaking. When God speaks things take shape. This suggests that God was intentionally pictured here as a royal figure, a king—for kings are the only beings whose word is law and at whose mere utterance things happen.

 Day 1: Light

Day One

> *3 Elohim said, "Let there be light!" And there was light. 4 Elohim saw that the light was good, and he separated the light from the darkness. 5 Elohim*

---

[11] The Hebrew word behind "deep water" is the equivalent of the Akkadian word *Tiamat*, which stands for the ocean goddess we will read about in the Mesopotamian version of the creation story called the Enuma Elish.

called the light day and the darkness he called night. So evening and morning of the first day came about.

Light is essential for all life. Nothing can live without it. It is the precondition of all life. The first thing God created was light. Light also has connotations of goodness and safety, especially when contrasted with the darkness of chaos.

The creating activity of this day is curious, at least from our modern scientific perspective. Only later did God create the sun. We would think that the order should be reversed or that the two events should be simultaneous. Light comes from a sun and does not exist by itself. So how can there be evening and morning of the first day when there is no sun to regulate day and night?

These are just two of many indications that the creation story does not meet our standards of scientific accuracy, and we should not expect it to. Rather, the writer had another intention. He created a somewhat artificial symmetry, as we will see, which highlights the order of God at the expense of modern-day scientific explanation.

DAY 2: WATER BARRIER / DOME

Day Two

6 Elohim said, "Let there be a barrier in the middle of the water, a separator between water and water." 7 Elohim made the barrier and separated the water under the barrier from the water above the barrier. And it happened. 8 Elohim called the barrier heavens. So evening and morning of the second day came about.

God created a barrier to separate water. The barrier is called "firmament" and "dome" in other translations. To understand what God was accomplishing here we must visualize the **cosmology** of the biblical world, that is, their mental picture of the universe. They believed that the inhabited earth existed as an island of sorts, surrounded completely by water. Its existence was precarious at best. The waters that surrounded the inhabited earth always threatened to break the dams and come flooding down on top of it. God was responsible for keeping the water at bay.

A visual reconstruction of ancient cosmology will help us understand the creation story (see Figure 1.3).

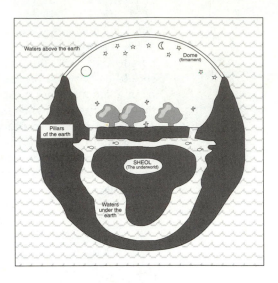

FIGURE 1.3 The ancient view of the structure of the physical world identifies three regions: a body of water above the earth held back by the dome of heaven, the earth itself, and a body of water below the earth. Life exists in the space between the two vast bodies of water. All three general regions are mentioned in passing in Exodus 20:4, "You shall not make for yourself an idol in the form of anything that is in heaven above, or on the earth beneath, or in the water under the earth."

There were two great bodies of water: one above the sky, the source of rain and snow, and one below the sky, the source of oceans, lakes, rivers, and wells. While strange to us, this design made perfect sense to the prescientific ancient Mesopotamians. It is not difficult to see why. Beyond the sky on a clear day there is a vast blueness, in hue very close to that of the ocean. Looking over the horizon of the Persian Gulf or the Mediterranean Sea, water blended into sky, suggesting that they were made out of the same material. It is not surprising that they thought water lay beyond the sky in the heavens. And they no doubt asked, Where do rain and snow come from? Well, God opens the windows of heaven and releases water in measured amounts. Knowing nothing about the cycle of evaporation, condensation, and precipitation, this they could understand.

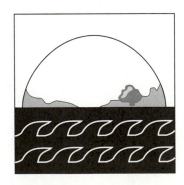

DAY 3: DRY LAND AND VEGETATION

Day Three

9 Elohim said, "Let the water under the heavens be gathered to one place and let dry land appear." And it happened. 10 Elohim called the dry ground earth and the waters gathered to one place he called seas. Elohim saw that it was good. 11 Elohim said, "Let the earth sprout greenery on the earth, seed-producing plants, fruit trees producing fruit according to their type. And it happened. 12 The earth brought forth greenery, seed-producing plants according to their type, and trees producing fruit which have their seed in it. Elohim saw that it was good. 13 So evening and morning of the third day came about.

The water under the barrier was still mixed with what was to become dry land. These two elements were separated on the third day. The dry land was called *earth* and the water was called *sea*. As a second act on Day Three the ground sprouted with plants that could propagate themselves. Thus, on the first three days God created the basic environment: light, the heavens, and the earth.

DAY 4: SUN, MOON, AND STARS

Day Four

14 Elohim said, "Let there be lights in the barrier of the heavens to separate day and night, and let them be used for signs, seasons, days and years. 15 Let there be lights in the barrier of the heavens to light the earth." And it happened. 16 Elohim made the two great lights, the great light to govern day and the small light to govern night, and the stars. 17 Elohim put them in the barrier of the heavens to light the earth: 18 to govern day and night and to separate light and darkness. Elohim saw that it was good. 19 So evening and morning of the fourth day came about.

The work of creation continued to happen through separating and dividing. On Day Three water was separated from water, and land was separated out of the "chaotic waters." On Day Four the lights in the sky separated day from night. Perhaps a Priestly concern with structure and "everything in its right place" is reflected here.

Certainly in the overall structure of creation Day Four is related to Day One. On Day One light "in general" was created. On Day Four the phenomenon of light is actualized by light-giving entities.

The language of ruling is introduced into the account at this point and becomes an important factor in Days Four and Six. Here, these bodies of light have a ruling and regulating function. They determine the calendar and the seasons. We see here further evidence of the interest of the Priestly writer in the orderliness of the created world. Religious life was organized around a cyclic series of holy days and festivals, all determined by the course of the sun and moon. The priests were the caretakers of religious life, and it was important for them to point out that the regularity of life was established by God at creation.

DAY 5: BIRDS AND FISH

Day Five

20 Elohim said, "Let the waters swarm with swarms of living creatures, and let birds fly over the earth up against the barrier of the heavens." 21 Elohim created the great sea monsters and every teeming living creature which swarms the waters according to their type, and every flying bird according to its type. Elohim saw that it was good. 22 Elohim blessed them by saying, "Be fruitful and increase in number and fill the waters in the seas, and birds, increase in number on the earth. 23 So evening and morning of the fifth day came about.

Creatures to inhabit the sky and sea were created on this day. The literary scheme the writer used is becoming clearer. Day Five corresponds to Day Two. The living areas, sky and sea, that appeared as a result of the creation of the barrier on Day Two were filled with inhabiting creatures on Day Five.

These living creatures were given God's verbal blessing to be fruitful and increase. Such a word of blessing expressed God's intention for the future welfare of these creatures. This is the first mention of what is to become a very important theme in Genesis—blessing. Growth and living space are blessings from God and express his desire for the welfare of his creatures.

DAY 6: ANIMALS AND HUMANKIND

Day Six

24 Elohim said, "Let the earth produce living creatures according to their type: beast and swarmer and land animal according to its type. And it happened. 25 Elohim made the land animal according to its type, and the beast according to its type, and the swarmer of the ground according to its type. Elohim saw that it was good. 26 Elohim said, "Let us make humankind as our image, according to our likeness. And let them rule over the fish of the sea, the bird of the heavens, the beast, the whole earth, and all the swarmers which swarm on the earth.

There were two distinct creative acts on this day, as there were on Day Three. First, God created the types of animals that live on land. Then, in a separate act, God created humankind. The description of this last act differs from the preceding. Instead of "Let there be . . ." God said, "Let US make. . . ." To whom was God speaking when he said this? There are three possible solutions to this question.

1. God was simply thinking out loud, talking to himself. Supporters of this position point to the fact that Elohim, the word for God, is grammatically plural. This might account for the plural "us." A variation is to call this the "plural of majesty," which high authorities prefer others use when addressing them—something like "your Highness."

2. Especially those trained in Christian theology prefer to see a reflection of the Trinity here. God the Father was conferring with God the Son and God the Holy Spirit. This option is remote, however. Certainly the early writer of this passage had no conception of a Trinity. That doctrine is only a much later theological development. The first control on our interpretation is this—what could the original writer have meant?

3. The most likely reading is that "us" refers to the Divine Council. The Divine Council was thought to be the governing assembly of angelic divine beings that supervised the world with God. The angels, called "sons of God" in other texts, were the parliament of heaven. A good example of this notion is in Job 1–2, where the "sons of God" met in session with Yahweh and the accuser (the satan) to evaluate the sincerity of Job's piety.

An implication of this last option is that the act of creating humankind was so momentous that God thought it best to seek the approval and cooperation of the Divine Council. It underscores the importance of humankind. In addition, it implies that the **image of God**, which humankind was about to share, was something common to God and angels alike. God said, "Let us make humankind in OUR image."

27 And God created humankind as his image: as the image of God he created him, male and female he created them. 28 And God blessed them and God said to them, "Be fruitful and increase in number and fill the earth and dominate it and rule the fish of the sea, bird of the heavens, and every swarming creature on the earth."

A couple of important points should be noted with regard to the image of God. Male and female alike share in the image, whatever it is. Furthermore, God's blessing is somehow attached to being created in God's image. That blessing has something to do with growth and fertility as well as power and rulership.

The image of God idea mentioned in this text has become very important for a biblical–theological understanding of the nature of humankind. It defines, according to the Hebrew tradition, who and what we are. It suggests that in some fundamental way we are like God. But what exactly is meant by the phrase "image of God"? Many theologians have made suggestions. Clines (1968) reviews many of the proposals.

Some suggest the image of God has to do with the spiritual qualities of God that humans originally shared with God, qualities such as wisdom and righteousness. Others suggest that the image of God has to do in some way with a physical shape or form that we have in common with God. This view, which implies that God has arms and legs, is usually rejected.

Still others, including the theologian Karl Barth, note how being made as the image of God is followed immediately by the words, "male and female he created them." This, they say, means that in God, as in humankind, there is relationship within unity. Having been made in the image of God, therefore, means that interpersonal relationship is the essential characteristic of humankind, as it also is with God. Giving it another twist, others suggest the mention of male and female makes explicit that both males and females "image" or reflect God, or that God has both male and female components. Being so concise and without elaboration, the text can only be suggestive. So how can we decide what it means?

As always, the text itself must provide the essential clues. Notice that the primary textual connection of the image of God is to the mandate to rule and have dominion. When *image* is mentioned in verses 26–30, it is followed by a call to action: "Let them have dominion." This in itself suggests that the image of God is not something we have, but it is something we do. Humankind was created to model God's (and the Divine Council's) ruling function on the new earth God had created. Humankind was created *as* God's image rather than *in* it.

This interpretation can be corroborated by comparative ancient material. In Mesopotamia a conquering monarch would install statues of himself in the territories subject to his rule. These statues would be visible evidence of his claim to authority. It would remind the subject people that he was in charge. In a similar way, according to Genesis 1, humankind was to represent the rule of God on the earth and put that rule into effect. They functioned as walking, talking images of God, created by God's authority, and designed to rule the earth on his behalf.

An archeological discovery from 1979, the Tell-Fekheriyeh statue of Adad-iti, provides an analogy of the Genesis 1 image of God notion (Millard and Bordreuil 1982). The statue of king Adad-iti contains an Assyrian inscription dedicating the statue to the god Adad. It also contains a translation of the inscription into Aramaic. The Aramaic translation contains the two words *statue* and *image,* which are linguistically equivalent to the Hebrew *likeness* and *image* found in Genesis 1:26. This suggests that Genesis 1 may have deliberately used the "statue" notion to describe humankind.

In the inscription the king acknowledged that the god Adad was his lord and was the one who had blessed him. The statue was set up by Adad-iti to acknowledge Adad's blessing. It also memorialized the king's rule over the territory of Guzan in Assyria and, in the words of the text, was to function "for perpetuating his throne, for the length of his rule."

In the case of the biblical text, God created humankind as his image on earth with the authority to rule. We are not to infer anything about the physical shape of God from the fact that humankind is God's "statue." Rather, the text is saying that humankind was created to perform a unique function, to be a reminder of God's rule—moreover, to rule the earth as God's agents.

Day Seven

> 2:1 *The heavens and the earth and all their host were complete. 2 Elohim finished the work he had done on the seventh day, and he ceased on the seventh day from all the work he had done. 3 Elohim blessed the seventh day and made it holy, because on it he ceased from all his work of creating that he had done.*

These last verses round out the week. God was finished. This implies that creation was perfect. No more work was needed, no tinkering necessary to fine-tune the product. So he could stop working. The Hebrew verb for "to stop, cease" is *shabbat.* From this derives the word for the special Jewish weekly holy day, Sabbath.

The seventh day was given special status. It was the only day blessed by God. A priestly concern surfaces clearly here. In the very story of creation the writers find hard and fast warrant for the holiness of the Sabbath day.

THE STRUCTURE OF GENESIS 1

The distribution of the separate creative acts into six 24-hour days was a deliberate scheme imposed by the Priestly writer. Organizing the activities in this way suggests that there was a rhythm and intentionality to God's design. It wasn't off the cuff. The world that humankind inherited was a highly structured one.

We noticed hints of the symmetry when we examined the text. Table 1.2 makes the structure clear.

TABLE 1.2   LITERARY SYMMETRY OF GENESIS 1

Day	Environment	Day	Inhabitant
1	Light	4	Sun, moon, stars
2	Sky and sea	5	Birds and fish
3a	Dry land	6a	Land animals
3b	Vegetation	6b	Humankind

Each and every living being had its place within the structure, with humankind at the apex. The creation of humankind was the culmination of God's efforts. After that he ceased making new things. God saw that everything he had created was complete and without flaw.

MESOPOTAMIAN CREATION STORIES

The Priestly writer certainly drew from notions, stories, and literary material that were part of the larger ancient Middle Eastern cultural environment when he constructed his account of creation. The **Enuma Elish** is the most well-known Babylonian creation composition. It exists in various copies, the oldest dating to at least 1700 B.C.E. Originally it was written on six tablets, to which was added a seventh containing a hymn to the god Marduk. The Enuma Elish reveals a great deal about the Babylonian realm of the gods and how the people imagined creation. But the overall intention of the piece is to extol the strength and superiority of Marduk, the patron god of Babylon. The work has obvious affinities with the biblical text (Heidel 1963a). The following are excerpts from the Enuma Elish (Pritchard 1969).

Tablet 1

> When on high the heaven had not been named,
> Firm ground below had not been called by name,
> Naught but primordial Apsu, their begetter,
> And Mummu-Tiamat, she who bore them all,
> Their waters commingling as a single body;
> No reed hut had been matted, no marsh land had appeared,
> When no gods whatever had been brought into being,
> Uncalled by name, their destinies undetermined—
> Then it was that the gods were formed within them.

The name of the document, Enuma Elish, is the Akkadian language original of the first phrase "when on high." Most ancient works were titled by their first word or phrase.

Before heaven and earth were formed there were two vast bodies of water. The male sweetwater ocean was called Apsu, and the female saltwater ocean was called Tiamat. Through the fusion of their waters, successive generations of gods came into being.

As seems to be the case with Genesis, water is the primeval element in the Enuma Elish. But here water is identified with the gods, and the gods have unmistakable gender. The creation of the younger gods takes place through sexual union.

In contrast to Genesis, the Enuma Elish is intensely interested in the realm of the gods. While the first divine beings Apsu and Tiamat are not accounted for, the successive generations are.

Tablet 2

Tiamat prepared for battle against the gods, her offspring.
To avenge Apsu, Tiamat wrought evil.

The younger, noisy gods disturbed the tranquility of Apsu. When Apsu devised a plan to dispose of the younger gods, their wisest one, Ea, found out about it. He killed Apsu. Tiamat was very angry that they had killed her husband. She decided finally to do away with the younger gods with the help of her henchman Kingu.

Tablet 4

They erected for Marduk a princely throne.
Facing his fathers, he sat down, presiding. . . .
"We have granted thee kingship over the universe entire.
When in the Assembly thou sittest, thy word shall be supreme."

When the younger gods heard about this, they found a champion in the god Marduk. He agreed to defend them only if they would make him king. After he passed a test of his powers, they did so.

One of the big concerns of this text is explaining how Marduk came to be the supreme god of Babylonia. He became king because he defended the other gods and subdued the threat of Tiamat, the great threatening ocean goddess.

Then joined issue Tiamat and Marduk, wisest of gods.
They strove in single combat, locked in battle.
The lord spread out his net to enfold her,
The Evil Wind, which followed behind, he let loose in her face.
When Tiamat opened her mouth to consume him,
He drove the Evil Wind that she close not her lips.
As the fierce winds charged her belly,
Her body was distended and her mouth was wide open.
He released the arrow, it tore her belly,
It cut through her insides, splitting the heart.
Having thus subdued her, he extinguished her life.

When finally they met on the field of battle, Tiamat opened her considerable mouth as if to swallow Marduk and plunge him into the immeasurable deeps.

Marduk rallied and cast one of the winds into her body, expanding her like a balloon. Marduk took his bow and shot an arrow into her belly. It split her in half and killed her.

Notice how the winds were the friends and weapons of Marduk. With them he achieved victory over Tiamat. Genesis also records the importance of the wind of God, which hovered over the untamed waters before creation.

> *He split her like a shellfish into two parts:*
> *Half of her he set up and ceiled it as sky,*
> *Pulled down the bar and posted guards.*
> *He bade them to allow not her waters to escape.*

Marduk split her in two like a clam. Out of her carcass he made the heavens. The "clamshell" of heaven became a barrier to keep the waters from escaping—a parallel to the Genesis notion of a barrier or firmament. The victory over Tiamat is associated with keeping the primeval waters under control.

The text follows with a description of Marduk fixing the stellar constellations in the heavens. And they, along with the moon, established the course of day and night and the seasons.

Tablet 6

> *"Blood I will mass and cause bones to be.*
> *I will establish a savage, 'man' shall be his name.*
> *Verily, savage-man I will create.*
> *He shall be charged with the service of the gods*
> *That they might be at ease!"*
> *They bound Kingu . . .*
> *They imposed on him his guilt and severed his blood vessels.*
> *Out of his blood they fashioned mankind.*

Thus, Marduk devised a plan to relieve the drudgery of the gods. They were tired of laboring to meet their daily needs. Marduk created humankind out of the blood of Kingu to be the servants of the gods. So, humankind had a divine origin insofar as Kingu was from the Divine Council. But the creation of humankind was the result of revenge against Kingu and Tiamat. Humankind does not have the high sense of purpose that is present in Genesis 1.

In appreciation for their deliverance, the gods built Marduk a palace in Babylon. Called *Esagila*, it meant "house with its head in heaven." There Marduk sat enthroned.

Chaos and Cosmos

The similarities and differences between Genesis 1 and the Enuma Elish are intriguing. One of the most striking features of Genesis that the Enuma Elish helps to bring to light is the struggle between order and chaos that lies just under the surface of the Genesis text. Marduk's battle with Tiamat reveals that the effort to create the world, in Mesopotamian lore, took the form of a battle. The victory secured Marduk's position as king over creation. The comparison may help to explain the claims of Yahweh's kingship over creation in such places as Psalms 29 and 93, where he is proclaimed to sit enthroned over the floods.

The water imagery of Genesis 1 suggests that we are in the same realm of water ideas as the Enuma Elish. Struggle for supremacy dominates the Enuma Elish. While little of the struggle is outwardly evident, the creation of the world by way of creating order dominates the text of Genesis 1.

The notion of struggle is, however, by no means absent in other texts of the Hebrew Bible. They reveal that God battled a dragonlike creature and secured his people against the threat of the waters of chaos. The monster of chaos was variously called Leviathan (Psalm 74:14), Rahab (Psalm 89:10), Dragon (Isaiah 27:1), and Sea (Job 7:12).

The historical enemies of Israel are frequently pictured as manifestations of the forces of chaos, as when Egypt is called Rahab, and the crossing of the Red Sea is equated with God's cutting the primeval water monster in pieces (Isaiah 51:9–10). An appreciation of creation imagery is necessary for understanding texts such as these (see Day 1985).

Comparison of the biblical account of creation and the Enuma Elish suggests that Genesis 1 was intended to refute claims made about Marduk in Babylonia. Remember that the creation story of Genesis 1 probably took final shape during the Babylonian exile, at which time the Israelites were most certainly exposed to the creation myths of the Babylonians. The biblical account asserts that Israel's God, and by implication not Marduk, brought the world into being.

These comments about the Babylonian stories of creation and water imagery help clarify other biblical texts. The following story of the flood cannot be understood apart from issues of creation and chaos.

THE FLOOD (6:5–8:22)

The story of the flood is a composite of material from the Yahwist and Priestly writers. The immediately preceding Yahwist story of the Sons of God and the daughters of men in Genesis 6:1–4 provides the paradigm illustration of the disintegration of the structures of right and wrong in the world. Following this episode, both the Yahwist writer and the Priestly writer give their analysis of the state of the world and why God decided to "uncreate" it.

Yahwist Version (6:5–8)

And YHWH saw that the evil of humankind on the earth was great; every willful plan of its mind was only evil every day. YHWH regretted that he had made humankind on the earth, and he was pained to his heart. YHWH said, "I will wipe out humankind which I had created from the face of the ground, from humankind to beast to reptile to bird of the sky. For I regret that I had made them. And Noah found favor in the eyes of YHWH.

Priestly Version (6:9–13)

This is the account (Heb. toledot) of Noah: Noah was a righteous man, upright was he in his generation. Noah walked with Elohim. Noah sired three sons: Shem, Ham and Japheth. And the earth was corrupt before Elohim, and the earth was full of violence. And Elohim saw the earth: it was corrupt. For all flesh corrupted its way on the earth. And Elohim said to Noah, "The end of all flesh before me is coming. For the earth is full of their violence. I am destroying them with the earth."

In the Yahwist version, humankind is primarily at fault, and it becomes the focus of Yahweh's wrath. The Priestly version is introduced by P's characteristic "these are the generations" *toledot* notice (for more on *toledot* see chapter 2). In the Priestly version, there is greater interest in how humankind had corrupted the earth that God had made. Its orientation is more global. This difference in outlook is consistent with what we saw in the creation accounts. The P account in Genesis 1 was global compared to the J account in Genesis 2, which focused on humankind.

The following story of the flood is separated into its two versions for easy comparison. We include the entire flood story in translation here because it is a superb case study of a story in double tradition. As you read the two versions side by side, be attentive to the differences as well as the similarities.

Yahwist	Priestly
	6:14 "Make an ark out of gopher wood; make it an ark with rooms; cover it inside and out with pitch. 15 This is what you should make it: an ark 300 cubits long, 50 cubits wide, and 30 cubits high. 16 Make an opening for the ark, a cubit from the top; put a door in the side of the ark; give it a bottom deck, a second and a third floor. 17 Now I am bringing a flood, water, upon the earth, to wipe out all flesh under heaven in which there is the breath of life. Everything on the earth will die. 18 I will establish my covenant with you. You will enter the ark, you and your sons and your wife and your sons' wives with you, 19 as well as every living thing—two of each kind, a male and a female, you should bring into the ark to live with you; 20 birds according to their kind, animals according to their kind, reptiles according to their kind, two of each will come to you to stay alive. 21 Take every type of food which would be eaten, and store it so you and they have food." 22 Noah did everything God had commanded him. He did it.

7:1 YHWH said to Noah, "You and your household enter the ark, for I have seen that of all this generation you are the only righteous one according to my standards. 2 Of all the clean animals, take seven male and mate pairs. Of all the unclean animals, take one male–mate pair; 3 of the birds of the sky seven male–female pairs to preserve seed over all the earth. 4 For in seven days I will start it raining on the earth and it will rain forty days and forty nights. I will wipe out from the face of the ground all the life I created. 5 Noah did everything YHWH commanded him to do.

> 6 Noah was 600 years old at the time of the flood, the water upon the earth. 7 Noah and his sons and his wife and the wives of his sons entered the ark with him, away from the waters of the flood.

8 Of the clean animals, of the unclean animals, of the birds and everything that creeps on the ground, 9 two by two they came to Noah in the ark,

> a male–female pair, as God had commanded Noah.

10 After seven days the waters of the flood inundated the earth.

> 11 In the six-hundredth year of Noah's life, in the second month, on the seventeenth day of the month, on that very day, all the sources of the great deeps burst forth, and the windows of the heavens were opened.

12 And the rain was on the earth forty days and forty nights.

> 13 On that same day Noah entered the ark, along with Shem, Ham and Japheth, the sons of Noah, and Noah's wife, and the three wives of his sons with them, 14 they and all animals according to their kind, and beasts according to their kind, and reptiles who swarm on the earth according to their kind, and birds according to their kind, every bird, every winged creature. 15 They came to Noah in the ark, two by two from all flesh in which there is the breath of life. 16 Those entering were male and female from all flesh, as God had commanded him.

And YHWH closed him in. 17 And the flood lasted forty days and forty nights on the earth. The waters increased and lifted the ark so it rose above the earth.

> 18 The waters surged and increased greatly over the earth and the ark drifted over the surface of the waters. 19 The waters continued to surge over the earth. They covered all the highest mountains under heaven. 20 The waters swelled fifteen cubits more, covering the mountains. 21 All flesh traversing the earth died, bird, beast, animal, everything swarming on the earth, and all humankind.

22 Everything which had the breath of life in its nostrils, everything on dry land, died. 23 He wiped out all life which was on the surface of the ground, man, animal, reptile, bird of the sky. They were wiped off the earth. Only Noah in the ark remained.

> 24 The waters surged over the earth 150 days. 8:1 Then God remembered Noah and all the animals and all the beasts which were in the ark with him. God caused a wind to blow over the earth and the waters subsided. 2 He stopped up the sources of the great deeps and the windows of heaven.

The rain stopped falling from heaven. 3 The water retreated rapidly from the earth.

> At the end of 150 days the waters began to diminish. 4 On the seventeenth day of the seventh month the ark rested on the

mountains of Ararat. 5 The waters kept on diminishing until the tenth month. On the first day of the tenth month the tops of the mountains became visible.

6 At the end of forty days Noah opened the window of the ark which he had constructed.

7 He sent out the raven. It left and went back and forth until the water dried up from the earth.

8 He sent the dove out to see if the waters had decreased from off the surface of the ground. 9 But the dove couldn't find a place to rest its feet, so it returned to him in the ark. For the water was on the face of the earth. He extended his hand and took it in, and it returned to him in the ark. 10 At the end of seven more days he sent the dove out from the ark again. 11 The dove came to him in the evening with a plucked off olive twig in its beak. Then Noah knew that the water had further diminished from off the earth. 12 After seven more days he sent the dove out again and it did not come back to him again.

13 On the first day of the first month of the six-hundred-and-first year the waters began drying up from the earth.

Noah removed the covering of the ark and now saw that the ground had dried up.

14 By the seventeenth day of the second month, the earth was dry. 15 God spoke to Noah, 16 "Leave the ark, you and your wife and your sons and your sons' wives, 17 all the animals which were with you: bird, beast, all reptiles which swarm on the earth. Take them out with you and let them swarm on the earth and be fruitful and increase on the earth." 18 So Noah left the ark with his sons and his wife and his sons' wives, 19 all the animals, all reptiles, all birds, all earth swarmers; according to their families they left the ark.

20 Noah built an altar to YHWH and he took one of each of the clean animals and one of each of the clean birds and offered a whole burnt offering on the altar. 21 YHWH smelled the sweet savor and YHWH said to himself, "Never again will I curse the ground on account of humankind. The impulse of their heart is evil from their youth on. I will never again destroy all life as I have done. 22 As long as the earth lasts, planting time and harvest time, cold and heat, summer and winter, day and night, none will cease.

The Priestly rendition was artfully interwoven into the Yahwist core version. But the vocabulary of each is so distinctive that, for the most part, the two sources can be easily distinguished. Read separately, we notice the following things. The Yahwist version has no telling of the building of the ark, though perhaps it was eliminated in favor of the Priestly description. In the Yahwist version the flood waters are the result of a torrential downpour lasting forty days, later receding in seven-day periods. In the Priestly version the flood is supernatural, inundating the earth from above the firmament (the windows of heaven) and from below the surface of the ground (the sources of the great deep). It prevails for 150 days, and takes 220 days to finally disappear.

In the Yahwist version the animals are gathered in sevens for the clean and only by twos for the unclean. The excess clean animals were presumably the ones used for Noah's sacrifice after leaving the ark. Only clean animals would be accepted by YHWH. The Priestly writer is content with one pair of each species of animal, and Noah does not offer a sacrifice, presumably because the proper rules for sacrifice have not yet been established. That would happen only beginning with the Mosaic period.

Again, the two sources reveal their distinctive themes. The Yahwist source is more interested in Yahweh's feelings, and it focuses on the male in his relationship to the ground. On the other hand, the Priestly source is more interested in the torah of God and the structure of the created world. Interested in fine details, it is the textual source that reports God's specific instructions for building the boat.

MESOPOTAMIAN FLOOD STORIES

Flood stories are found in many cultures around the world. The stories that come closest to the Genesis flood story were found, not surprisingly, in Mesopotamia.

The Deluge Tablet

The hero of the story, Ziusudra, heard the decision of the Divine Council to destroy humankind. He survived the flood by building a boat. The following excerpt is from the fragmentary Sumerian deluge tablet (Pritchard 1969: 44).

> *All the windstorms, exceedingly powerful, attacked as one,*
> *At the same time, the flood swept over the cult-centers.*
> *After, for seven days (and) nights,*
> *The flood had swept over the land,*
> *(And) the huge boat had been tossed about by the windstorms on the great waters,*
> *Utu came forth, who sheds light on heaven (and) earth.*
> *Ziusudra opened a window of the huge boat,*
> *The hero Utu brought his rays into the giant boat.*

The mention of the great waters, the boat, and the window on the boat all have biblical parallels.

Gilgamesh Epic

The most detailed story about a flood is found in the eleventh tablet of the **Gilgamesh Epic**.[12] Gilgamesh was a famous post-flood king of Uruk. He went to Utnapishtim to learn the secret of eternal life. Utnapishtim was a pre-flood hero

[12] Of all the Mesopotamian flood stories, the Gilgamesh Epic contains the closest parallels to the biblical story (Heidel 1963b). The story has a long literary history (Tigay 1982). It goes back as early as 2,000 B.C.E. and may be based on the flood story found in the Atrahasis Epic (Lambert 1969). The version we quote dates to around 650 B.C.E.

who survived the flood and was granted eternal life by the gods. The following is the recollection given by Utnapishtim (Pritchard 1969: 93–97). In order to survive the coming flood, the gods advised him as follows:

> *Tear down (this) house, build a ship!*
> *Give up possessions, seek thou life.*
> *Forswear (worldly) goods and keep the soul alive!*
> *Aboard the ship take thou the seed of all living things.*
> ...
> *Six days and [six] nights*
> *Blows the flood wind, as the south-storm sweeps the land.*
> *When the seventh day arrived,*
> *The flood(-carrying) south-storm subsided in the battle,*
> *Which it had fought like an army.*
> *The sea grew quiet, the tempest was still, the flood ceased.*
> ...
> *When the seventh day arrived,*
> *I sent forth and set free a dove.*
> *The dove went forth, but came back;*
> ...
> *Then I sent forth and set free a raven.*
> *The raven went forth and, seeing that the waters had diminished,*
> *He eats, circles, caws, and turns not round.*
> *Then I let out (all) to the four winds and offered a sacrifice.*
> ...
> *The gods smelled the sweet savor,*
> *The gods crowded like flies about the sacrificer.*

The text has clear parallels to the biblical flood story, from the waters that come, to the boat, even to the birds that Utnapishtim sent out the window to look for dry land. And as did Noah, Utnapishtim sacrificed to the divine after he abandoned the boat.

GENEALOGIES

An additional contribution of the Priestly source to the Primeval Story is genealogies. A **genealogy** is a record or table of the descent of a person, family, or group from an ancestor or ancestors; in other words, a family tree. Most readers would probably rather ignore genealogies completely. They tend to be boring, yet they are very important to the overall scheme of things. Wilson (1977) did one of the best studies of the social and theological function of genealogies.

The genealogies of Genesis 1–11 do a number of things. First, they give evidence that humankind did in fact multiply and fill the earth, as God had mandated them to do. This is evidence of blessing. Second, they draw the connection from Adam to Abraham, so that the lines of continuity between Israel and its origin are traced all the way back to creation. Third, the genealogies structure the account into two main segments. The genealogy of Genesis 5 contains ten generations between Adam and Noah. The genealogy of Genesis 11 contains ten generations between Noah and Abraham. The significance of this structure will be evident in Table 1.3 and will be further explained in the next chapter.

OVERALL SHAPE OF GENESIS 1–11

The Primeval Story seems to have been composed out of two sets of stories, one from the Yahwist source and the other from the Priestly source. The basic theologically charged story and plot were contributed by the Yahwist, to which the Priestly writer added stories and genealogies.

These two sources had some stories in common. When we focus on the account holistically we see that there are pervasive themes and structures uniting Genesis 1–11 that extend through the whole of Genesis.

THEMES OF THE PRIMEVAL STORY

Genesis 1–11 answers many of those questions that every thinking Israelite must have had at one time or another. Where did our world come from? Who made it? Where did sin come from? Who are our ancestors?

The Primeval Story is a theological interpretation of how the world came into being. In it we have an account of creation, not because a record of creation events was somehow passed down through the ages from the very beginning of time, but because at some point Israel's theologians came to recognize that their God, to be the best God, must be the most powerful being in the universe. They wanted to profess that their God was the one responsible for the very existence of the world. That affirmation was especially important to them when they faced personal and national crises. They believed that because their God was powerful enough to create the world, he was also powerful enough to rescue them.

What is the overall intent of these stories when seen together as a unit? The Primeval Story as a whole gives us the following account. God created the world a perfect place. The creation, however, was distorted and corrupted by humankind's efforts to achieve autonomy from God. God's first response to the growing problem of sin was to wipe the slate clean with a flood and begin again with righteous and upright Noah.

But even after the earth was un-created and then re-created, sin was still present. Noah's drunkenness, perhaps a sin in itself, brought out the worst in his son Ham. And just as before the flood, sin continued to spread and increase in perversity. The immensity of sin was evident in the monstrous city and tower-building project conceived by humankind. God was outraged by this project. But he did not repeat his prior attempted solution. He did not send another flood. Indeed, he could not. He had made a covenant through Noah that he would never again eliminate the life he had created just because of sin. Instead, at that point, he narrowed the focus of his attention and concentrated on the line of Shem. Out of that line he took Abram and created a people called Israel.

PARALLEL DEVELOPMENTS IN GENESIS 1–11

The Yahwist ordering of primeval events established the basic outline for the Primeval Story. To it were added elaborations from the Priestly source. The overall structure of the Primeval Story demonstrates that after each new beginning humankind sinned.

The true nature of sin, from first to last, was to try to become like God in some way: by knowing good and evil (Adam and Eve), or through divine marriage (Sons of God and human women), or by ascending into heaven through the tower (Tower of Babel). The first time, God responded with destruction. The second time, because of his covenant commitment through Noah, God acted to overcome the sin of humankind.

Table 1.3 summarizes the parallel thematic development of the text. Specific parallels and similarities between equivalent stories are suggested by the arrangement of elements in the table.

The parallels are remarkable in some cases. In column one Eve and Adam ate fruit and sinned; in column two Noah drank from the fruit and occasioned sin. In column one Cain sinned and was cursed; in column two Ham sinned and Canaan (which in Hebrew, as in English, sounds much like Cain) was cursed. Genealogies stand in parallel positions across the columns.

The keyword *shem*, "name," appears to have some significance as a signal of structure. The essential failure of humankind was trying to make a name for itself. In each parallel series of events, the culminating sin was humankind's at-

TABLE 1.3   **PARALLEL STRUCTURE OF GENESIS 1–11**

Creation to Noah (10 generations)	*Flood to Abram (10 generations)*
A. Creation (1–2)	A. Re-creation (8:1–9:17)
1. Deeps (1:2)	1. Deeps (8:2)
2. Blessing (1:22)	2. Blessing (8:17)
3. Mandate (1:28)	3. Mandate (9:1–2,7)
4. Food (1:29–30)	4. Food (9:3)
5. Adam worked the ground (2:15)	5. Noah worked the ground (9:20)
B. Adam and Eve ate fruit of the tree (3)	B. Noah drank fruit of the vine (9:18–28)
1. Fruit of the tree (3:1–7)	1. Wine (9:20–21)
2. Nakedness exposed (3:7)	2. Nakedness viewed (9:21–23)
C. Cain sinned and was cursed (4)	C. Ham sinned and Canaan was cursed (9:25–27)
D. Genealogy: Adam to Noah (5)	D. Genealogy: Sons of Noah (10)
E. Sons of God (6:1–4)	E. Tower of Babel (11:1–9)
1. Divine–human mix (6:1–2)	1. Reach heaven (11:4)
2. Men of a name [Heb. *shem*] (6:4)	2. Make a name [Heb. *shem*] (11:4)
F. Flood (6:5–7:24)	F. Genealogy of Shem (11:10–26)
Result: Undoing of creation	Result: God focuses on Abram and makes his name (Heb. *shem*) great (12:2)

tempt to become like God. Be it marriage with divine beings or a building project that would give them access to heaven, they were misguided and ultimately frustrated by God.

The first attempt resulted in the flood, a destructive cleansing of the world that had become corrupted. After the second attempt, the Tower of Babel, God turned his attention to Shem, whose name means *name*. From his line God took Abram and made a special covenant with him. God promised to make his name great and to make him a great nation. The lesson: The human race would achieve blessing and distinction only through the initiative of God, and not through its own engineering and scheming.

SUMMARY OF LITERARY SOURCES IN GENESIS 1–11

The Yahwist source contributed the core of the Primeval Story. The Priestly source contributed its own versions of the creation and flood stories as well as genealogical material. The Elohist source, found elsewhere in Genesis through Numbers, is not present here at all. The exilic Priestly editor skillfully combined the Yahwist and Priestly sources and used genealogical material to give the chain of stories historical connectedness. Table 1.4 specifies the distribution of source material.

TABLE 1.4 SOURCES OF THE PRIMEVAL STORY

	Yahwist (J)	*Priestly (P)*	*Editor*
Creation	2:4b–25	1:1–2:3	
Generations			2:4a
Garden of Eden	3:1–24		
Cain and Abel	4:1–16		
Cain genealogy	4:17–26		
Adam genealogy	5:29	5:1b–28, 30–32	5:1a
Sons of God	6:1–4		
Flood	6:5–8; 7:1–5, 10, 12, 16b–17, 22–23; 8:2b–3a, 6, 8–12, 13b, 20–22	6:9–22; 7:6–9, 11, 13–16a, 18–21, 24; 8:1–2a, 3b–5, 7, 13a, 14–19; 9:1–17	
Noah's insobriety	9:18–27		
Noah's age			7:6; 9:28–29
Sons of Noah genealogy	10:8–19, 21, 24–30	10:1b–7, 20, 22–23, 31, 32	10:1a
Tower of Babel	11:1–9		
Shem genealogy		11:10b–26	11:10a
Terah genealogy		11:27b–32	11:27a

Notice that the Yahwist supplies the bulk of the narrative material—almost everything except for the first creation story and parts of the flood story. For these, the Priestly writer had his own traditions, which he added to those of the Yahwist. The editor arranged the material and inserted transitional phrases and sentences.

The Ancestral Story continues the story line of the Primeval Story. It shows how God developed his plan to bless humankind. We will examine it in the next chapter.

QUESTIONS FOR REVIEW

1. Compare and contrast the Israelite understanding of God as implied in Genesis 1:1–2:4a with the understanding of God implied in 2:4b–25.

2. What does the story of disobedience in Eden (Genesis 3) tell us about the Israelite understanding of sin?

3. What are the similarities and differences between the Enuma Elish and the biblical stories of creation?

4. What is the theological and thematic importance of the biblical flood story in relation to the entire Primeval Story?

5. How is the Tower of Babel story related to previous stories of sin in Genesis 3–10? Why is it a fitting conclusion to the overall tale of disobedience told in the Primeval Story?

QUESTIONS FOR DISCUSSION

1. We have seen that the Primeval Story is a composite literary product with identifiable original sources, including the Yahwist epic core and later Priestly additions. In what ways does the epic core of the Primeval Story reflect the historical context of its writer? Likewise, how do the Priestly additions reflect their exilic context? Along these same lines, our modern origin stories, whether stories of cosmology (the "Big Bang") or of national origin, reflect to a certain degree our own understanding of ourselves (or how we would like to be). Think about the similarities and the differences.

2. Compare and contrast the various creation stories described in this chapter: the Yahwist account in Genesis 2–3, the Priestly account in Genesis 1, and the Mesopotamian account of the Enuma Elish. What does each account communicate concerning the nature of the divine realm? What does each imply about the nature of humankind? In much the same way, our modern world tries to account for origins, and these accounts imply something about values. What does a modern scientific account of the origin of human beings, such as would be found in the disciplines of physical anthropology and modern medicine, imply about human nature?

3. The Primeval Story as a whole implies that God created the world by subduing and shaping the waters of chaos. Later, humankind rebelled against God and contaminated the world. After an attempt to start over, even the "reborn" world of Noah was sinful. What does it say about God that God kept starting over, yet never gave up trying to fashion a perfect world? What does this imply about humankind?

FOR FURTHER STUDY

In addition to the following monographs, consult commentaries on the Book of Genesis. For a list of such commentaries, see the bibliography in the appendix. The following books are close readings of the Primeval Story.

Blocher, Henri (1984). *In the Beginning. The Opening Chapters of Genesis*. Downers Grove: Inter-Varsity Press. A detailed examination of the first three chapters of Genesis from an evangelical Christian perspective.

Coote, Robert B. (1991). *In the Beginning: Creation and the Priestly History*. Philadelphia: Fortress Press. Interprets the creation narrative against its Priestly background.

Miller, Patrick D., Jr. (1978). *Genesis 1–11. Studies in Structure and Theme*. JSOT Supplement Series 8. Sheffield: JSOT Press. A thematic study containing three treatments: the Divine World and the Human World, the Correspondence of Sin and Judgment, and the *adamah* motif.

WORKS CITED

Alter, Robert, and Frank Kermode (1987). *The Literary Guide to the Bible*. Cambridge, Mass.: Harvard University Press.

Barr, James (1993). *The Garden of Eden and the Hope of Immortality*. Philadelphia: Fortress Press.

Bassett, F. W. (1971). "Noah's Nakedness and the Curse of Canaan: A Case of Incest?" *Vetus Testamentum* 21: 232–37.

Clines, David J. A. (1968). "The Image of God in Man." *Tyndale Bulletin* 19: 53–103.

Cohen, H. Hirsch (1974). *The Drunkenness of Noah*. University: University of Alabama Press.

Day, John (1985). *God's Conflict with the Dragon and the Sea*. Cambridge: Cambridge University Press.

Fokkelman, J. P. (1975). *Narrative Art in Genesis. Specimens of Stylistic and Structural Analysis*. Assen: Van Gorcum.

Heidel, A. (1963a). *The Babylonian Genesis*. 2d ed. Chicago: University of Chicago Press.

Heidel, A. (1963b). *The Gilgamesh Epic and Old Testament Parallels*. 2d ed. Chicago: University of Chicago Press.

Lambert, W. G., and A. R. Millard (1969). *Atrahasis*. Oxford: Clarendon Press.

Millard, A. R., and P. Bordreuil (1982). "A Statue from Syria with Assyrian and Aramaic Inscriptions." *Biblical Archeologist* Summer 1982: 135–41.

Pritchard, James B. (1969). *Ancient Near Eastern Texts Relating to the Old Testament*. 3d ed. with supplement. Princeton, N.J.: Princeton University Press.

Tigay, Jeffrey H. (1982). *The Evolution of the Gilgamesh Epic*. Philadelphia: University of Pennsylvania Press.

Wilson, Robert R. (1977). *Genealogy and History in the Biblical World*. New Haven, Conn., and London: Yale University Press.

GENESIS 12–50: ANCESTRAL STORY

2

Names and Terms to Remember

Abimelek	Hagar	primogeniture
Abraham (Abram)	Isaac	Rachel
Abraham cycle	Ishmael	Rebekah
Abrahamic covenant	Jacob	royal grant covenant
Ancestral Story	Jacob cycle	Sabbath
circumcision	Joseph	Sarah (Sarai)
covenant	Joseph cycle	suzerainty covenant
cycle	Mosaic covenant	theophany
Esau	Noahic covenant	toledot
Goshen	Pharaoh	

The environment in which a person is reared significantly affects what that person will become. Each person is likewise affected by genetics. How much we are products of environment and how much we are products of parentage is the nurture versus nature debate and is for philosophers and psychologists to work out. Nonetheless, almost everyone would agree that we tend to mirror our mothers and fathers, and knowing how they came to be who they are can tell us a lot about ourselves.

The **Ancestral Story**, which is the subject of this chapter, is the account of the forebears of the nation of Israel. The great Hebrew storytellers instinctively knew that Israel's grandparents could teach the Israelites a great deal about their national character. The stories in Genesis 12–50 deal primarily with the great patriarchs and matriarchs of Israel, namely **Abraham** and **Sarah**, **Isaac** and **Rebekah**, **Jacob** and **Rachel**, and **Joseph**. These stories are the prehistory of the nation, the cultural genetics of the people (see Figure 2.1).

The three narrative sources of the Torah—the Yahwist epic, the Elohist source, and the Priestly source—interweave to create the Ancestral Story. The Elohist source appears here for the first time in our studies. All three sources are well attested in Genesis 12–50 and make significant contributions. Table 2.3 at the end of this chapter displays the distribution of ancestral material among the various literary sources.

Note that we cannot treat equally all the episodes of the Ancestral Story in this chapter. We will closely read only a few episodes; the others we will summarize. Our approach is to take selected episodes from each of the narrative sources to illustrate the perspective of each source on the ancestors. Then we will relate how the material was organized to form the canonical Ancestral Story we have today.

YAHWIST ANCESTRAL STORIES

The Tower of Babel story was the last Yahwist episode of the Primeval Story. The Yahwist source had traced the course of humankind's sinning against God. In addition, it related the response of God: confrontation and expulsion from Eden, the flood, scattering humankind, all the nations falling under the curse of God. The Yahwist's portrayal of human activity suggests that all human efforts are nothing if they are an attempt to grasp rather than to receive greatness.

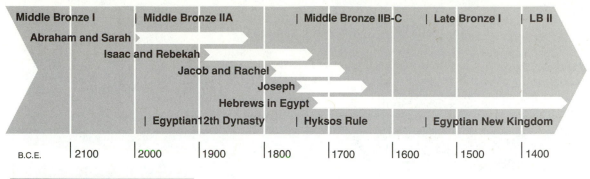

| Middle Bronze I | Middle Bronze IIA | Middle Bronze IIB-C | Late Bronze I | LB II |

Abraham and Sarah

Isaac and Rebekah

Jacob and Rachel

Joseph

Hebrews in Egypt

| Egyptian 12th Dynasty | Hyksos Rule | Egyptian New Kingdom |

B.C.E. | 2100 | 2000 | 1900 | 1800 | 1700 | 1600 | 1500 | 1400

FIGURE 2.1   TIME LINE: THE ANCESTORS

The result of human history to that point was that humankind had distanced itself from God. Yet, it was in dire need of help, which could only come from God. The Ancestral Story relates how help came when Yahweh turned his attention to Abraham. The first episode is Genesis 12:1–3, which marks the end of the primeval era and the beginning of the Ancestral Story.

PROMISE TO ABRAHAM (12:1–3)

The blessing speech in 12:1–3 is crucial for understanding the theological intention of the Yahwist source. Abraham[1] was commanded to leave home and family to follow Yahweh's leading to a new land (see Figure 2.2).

God promised Abraham a homeland and offspring. The new start hereby initiated for Abraham was a new start for the human race as a whole.

> *12:1 Now YHWH said to Abram, "Go from the land of your birth and your kin and your father's house to the land that I will show you. 2 And I will make you into a great nation, and I will bless you, and make your name great, so that you will be a blessing. 3 I will bless those who bless you, and him who curses you I will curse; and through you all the families of the earth shall bless themselves/or be blessed."*

Take note of the phrases "great nation" and "make your name great" in Yahweh's statement. It is God who would secure the future greatness of Abraham. Recall the earlier significance of "name" in Genesis 6:4 ("men of a name") and 11:4 ("make a name for ourselves"). The "name" (Hebrew *shem*) God would make for Abraham now overcomes and actualizes the earlier misguided aspirations of humankind.

The prominence of the term blessing in this text (used five times) indicates that God has something special in store for Abraham. But not only for him; the

---

[1] There may be some confusion over the name *Abram*. Genesis refers to the first patriarch as Abram from the time of his departure from Ur until the covenant of circumcision. At that point his name was changed to Abraham (Genesis 17:5). In an attempt to avoid confusion, we will consistently refer to him as Abraham in our text interpretations, even if such use is textually inaccurate at first.

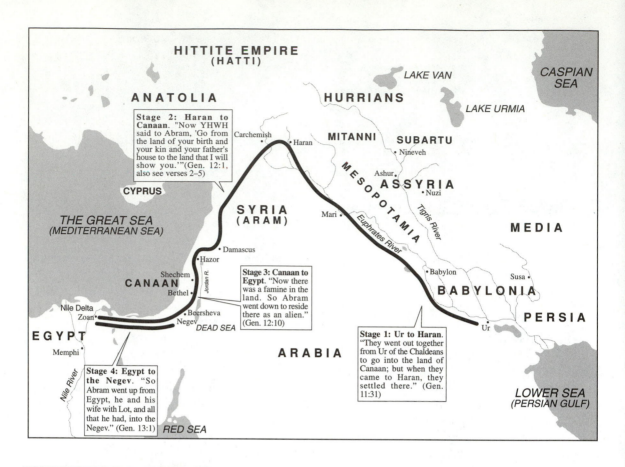

FIGURE 2.2 ABRAHAM'S JOURNEYS Abraham was originally from Ur in Mesopotamia. He and his extended family first traveled to Haran, where they stayed for quite a while. Prompted by God to leave, Abraham took Sarah and Lot with him and journeyed on to Canaan.

whole human race would find blessing and move out from under Yahweh's curse through Abraham. This is as close as we come to an overall theological theme of the Yahwist epic. No doubt the Yahwist writer, living at the Davidic court, believed that God's blessings had been given to David, especially through the gift of empire. He saw this as the beginning of the renewal of society—perhaps even a new world order.

COVENANT WITH ABRAHAM (15:1–21)[2]

The Yahwist contains accounts of all the ancestors, including Abraham and Sarah, Isaac and Rebekah, Jacob, Rachel, and Jacob's twelve sons. Many of the

---

[2] Chapter 15 is assigned to the Yahwist because of its style and theme, but we should note that it contains some inconsistencies that suggest it has elements from elsewhere, probably from the Elohist source. Verses 3, 5, and 13–16 are usually assigned to the Elohist because revelations in visions are typically an Elohistic characteristic.

stories of the ancestors are concerned with the continuity of blessing from one generation to the next, and often specifically which son would inherit the promises first given to Abraham.

Although Yahweh had promised that Abraham would become a great nation, at an advanced age he and Sarah still had no children. In a highly significant passage Yahweh approaches Abraham and with a **covenant** confirms the promises he earlier had made. A covenant defines the expectations and obligations of a relationship. We could say that at this point Yahweh formalizes his relationship with Abraham.

1 After these events, the word of YHWH came to Abram in a vision, "Don't be afraid, Abram.

God came to Abraham in a vision, indicating Abraham's special relationship with God. The phrase "The word of YHWH came" typically introduces revelation to a prophet (see 1 Sam. 15:10, Hosea 1:1). Fear was a natural reaction when in the presence of God. "Don't be afraid" is a phrase frequently used to introduce an announcement of salvation (see Isaiah 7:14 and 10:24, as well as Genesis 21:17, 26:24, and 35:17).

I am your shield. Your reward will be very great."

God declared himself to be Abraham's shield, that is, his protector. The reward here is not an earned prize but a gift of special recognition for a faithful servant of the king.

2 Abram said, "My Lord YHWH, what of lasting significance can you give me since I continue to be childless, with Eliezer of Damascus, a servant, standing to inherit my estate!" 3 Abram further stated, "You have not given me offspring. One of my servants stands as my heir." 4 Then there was a word of YHWH for him, "That one shall not be your heir! One who comes from your own loins—he will be your heir." 5 He took him outside and said, "Look at the heavens and count the stars if you can. So will your offspring be." 6 He placed his trust in YHWH, and he (YHWH) considered that a righteous act.

Abraham did not have a natural-born son, and his inheritance was due to go to his servant, Eliezer of Damascus. This story demonstrates that concern over descendants is central to the plot line, and this will be a continuing interest of the Yahwist Ancestral Story. Lacking a son, Abraham was insecure, not sure that God's promise would ever be realized. After God reassured him that he would have numerous offspring—even more than the stars—Abraham committed his future to God, even though he saw no concrete evidence of fulfillment. God took this blind faith as evidence that Abraham wanted to stand in a relationship of living trust with him.

The term *righteous* is a significant theological term here. Righteousness in the Torah applies to human activity. Righteous acts are God-approved ones, whereby the doer demonstrates he intends to stand in a relationship of dependence on God. Here Abraham's faith is reckoned as a righteous act.

The next part of the story (verses 7–12, not given here) describes a rather strange ceremony. Abraham slaughtered a heifer, she-goat, ram, turtledove, and pigeon. He placed the animal halves in two rows. After he was cast into a deep sleep, Yahweh appeared to him and symbolically passed between the animals in parallel rows.

This ritual ceremony drew Abraham into a formal relationship with God. In the ritual God demonstrated to Abraham the seriousness of his promise. In a ceremonial way God staked his life on the promise of offspring.

17 When the sun set and it was dark, a smoking oven and a flaming torch passed between these pieces.

The narrative says that God took the form of a smoking oven pot and torch for the purposes of the ceremony. God has no physical form in the Hebrew Bible, but when he does appear, typically he is represented by smoke and fire. Such a symbolic appearance of God is called a **theophany.** The most notable such appearance was his descent onto Mt. Sinai in Exodus 19, when he appeared to the Israelites and delivered the Mosaic covenant.

The ceremony took the form of a ritual of self-condemnation. By passing between the dissected animals, God was ritually calling down upon himself the same fate the animals suffered, should he be unfaithful to the covenant promise.[3]

The entire encounter between Abraham and Yahweh in this passage is summarized in the statement, "Yahweh cut a covenant with Abram." In biblical language, "to cut a covenant" refers to the animals that were ceremonially cut in half. The cutting of the animals and passing between the pieces is the ritualized self-condemnation referred to above, invoking self-mutilation and death if one is disloyal to the covenant. This business of the covenant is central to biblical theology.

A covenant is a framework for a relationship that finds its origin in the realm of politics and international law. In the ancient world, kings would formalize relationships with individuals and with entire nations by means of covenants. Even today the same thing is done among nations. We call them treaties or alliances, such as the North Atlantic Treaty Organization (NATO), but they amount to much the same thing.

There were two types of covenant in the ancient Middle East, suzerainty covenants and royal grant covenants. A **suzerainty covenant** was a treaty imposed on a people to define mutual political obligations. A suzerain was a sovereign ruler who controlled vassal or client states. The sovereign king typically demanded total loyalty and in return promised to provide protection and support as long as the vassal remained faithful. Later we will see that the covenant God made with Israel through Moses at Mt. Sinai was a suzerainty covenant. The Elohist source profiles the suzerainty covenant as the paradigm of God's relationship to Israel, as we will see in the next chapter.

A **royal grant covenant** consisted of a grant of property or rights. The grant was usually made as a reward for faithfulness or loyal service. For example, kings

[3] A similar ceremony is attested in Jeremiah 34:18 and in an eighth century B.C.E. treaty where an ass is cut in half as a ceremonial condemnation (Pritchard, 1969: 532).

would bestow land on loyal military officers after a campaign. The Yahwist in this passage uses the form of the royal grant covenant.

> *18 On that day YHWH cut a covenant with Abram: "To your offspring I give this land: from the River of Egypt to the Great River, the Euphrates."*

Land boundaries were typically specified in royal grant covenants. Such is the case here. Not accidentally, these borders correspond with the much later established limits of the Davidic–Solomonic kingdom (see 1 Kings 4:21). The point is that Israel's claim to the land, even to the definition of the borders, was traced back by them to the covenant promise Yahweh made to Abraham.

The Yahwist used the royal grant covenant to define the essential structure of the relationship between God and Abraham. Yahweh made a royal grant–type covenant with Abraham because Abraham demonstrated his faith. So, God granted Abraham the land of Canaan.

GROWTH OF THE CLAN

The Yahwist tells many stories about the ancestors. He is especially interested in the realization of Yahweh's promise to Abraham. Abraham and Sarah were unable to have children for a long time. They grew impatient and arranged for a surrogate wife for Abraham, named **Hagar**, who bore a son, **Ishmael**. After a long wait, Abraham and Sarah had a son of their own named Isaac. This son, Isaac, married Rebekah, and they had two sons, Jacob and Esau.

Jacob inherited the promises of Abraham from Isaac. He, in turn, had twelve sons. By now a large family, they were forced to move to Egypt when there was a famine in Canaan. Joseph, Jacob's favorite son, being a high government official there, made the arrangements. We will come back to the Joseph story later in this chapter.

ELOHIST ANCESTRAL STORIES

The Primeval Story contains no material from the Elohist source. The first Elohist stories we can find in Genesis have to do with the ancestors. Genesis 15 seems to bear some of the characteristics of the Elohist source, but chapter 20 is the first full-blown Elohist episode.

ABRAHAM, SARAH, AND ABIMELEK (20:1–18)

In chapter 20 Abraham and Sarah encounter **Abimelek**, and Abraham again seems threatened. It is an instructive, as well as interesting, story to read, because it contains many of the central themes of the Elohist.

> *20:1 Abraham traveled from there to the area of the Negev and made his home between Kadesh and Shur. When he was staying in Gerar 2 Abraham claimed about his wife Sarah, "She is my sister." So Abimelek, king of Gerar, had someone get Sarah.*

It is not clear where "there" was. It probably refers to Mamre-Hebron, the last known home of Abraham. From "there," Abraham and Sarah moved to the area around Gerar. Its powerful king, Abimelek, took Sarah to wife.

Abimelek desired Sarah—strange, at least according to Genesis 17:17, which places her at ninety years of age. Remember, though, these seemingly contradictory points arise because of the combination of stories from different sources, and we may just have to accept the fact that certain inconsistencies like this may be present in the final text.

> *3 Elohim came to Abimelek in a dream at night and said to him, "You are a dead man on account of the woman you have taken. She is married." 4 Now, Abimelek had not made any sexual advances. He said, "My Lord, would you kill people even though they were innocent? 5 Did he not say to me, 'She is my sister'? And she is the one who said, 'He is my brother.' With a pure heart and clean hands I did this."*

Characteristic of the Elohist, God does not appear directly, but communicates in dreams or visions. Also, this story contains a first for Genesis: in a dream God comes to Abimelek, a foreigner. This opens up an intriguing possibility—that Israel's God could be in relationship with a foreigner, and that a righteous Gentile could exist. As a whole, the Torah implies that God stands related only to Israel. This story itself leaves room for discussion.

The question of Abimelek's guilt is thorny. He is guilty of wrong because he took someone else's wife. But he is innocent insofar as he had been deceived by Abraham. On top of it, Abimelek never even touched Sarah. So why should he be found guilty?

> *6 Elohim said to him in the dream, "I, too, know that you did this with a pure heart. It was I that kept you from sinning against me; for that reason I did not let you touch her. 7 Now then, return the man's wife. He is a prophet—he will pray for you, and you will live. But if you do not return her, you should know that you will die, you, and everything that belongs to you."*

God came to Abimelek a second time in a dream and revealed he had been working in Abimelek's life to prevent him from doing anything wrong. Is the Elohist telling us God providentially attends to the behavior of even non-Israelites?

Note also the language used to describe Abraham. God calls him a *prophet*. This is the first time the term *prophet* is used in the Hebrew Bible. The term here refers to someone who is able to intercede between God and other people. The Elohist source as a whole appears to be intimately associated with prophetic circles in the North and so would naturally be interested in prophetic models and in tracing the prophetic calling to Israel's earliest history.

> *8 So Abimelek rose early in the morning, and called all his servants, and told them everything; and the men were very afraid. 9 Then Abimelek called Abraham, and said to him, "What did you do to us? What did I do to you,*

that you should bring on me and my kingdom this problem? You did things to me that shouldn't have been done." 10 Abimelek also said to Abraham, "What were you thinking when you did this thing?"

Abimelek took the whole matter very seriously. He called together his servants and they talked about it. Had they known that Sarah was Abraham's wife? If they had, then maybe he was guilty. But they had not.

Abimelek turned the tables and blamed the situation on Abraham. Abraham's guilt now became the issue. He really was the guilty one because he let Abimelek get into trouble with his deception.

11 Abraham said, "I did it because I thought, 'There is no fear of Elohim at all in this place. They will kill me because of my wife. 12 Besides, she is my sister anyway, the daughter of my father (though not the daughter of my mother), and she became my wife.' 13 When Elohim made me leave my father's house, I said to her, 'This is how you should show your loyalty to me: everywhere we go, say of me, 'He is my brother.'"

The reason Abraham acted the way he did is now made clear. He was concerned that there was no "fear of God" in Gerar. In fact, Abimelek and his men seemed to have had a very healthy respect for God, confirmed by the way in which God came to Abimelek directly, warned him, and saved him from disaster. The story seems to suggest that Abraham had underestimated the moral character of these foreigners. Apparently "fear of God"—a big interest of the Elohist— is not found exclusively in Israel.

14 Then Abimelek took sheep and oxen, and male and female slaves, and gave them to Abraham, and returned his wife Sarah to him. 15 And Abimelek said, "Now, my land is open to you; live where you want to." 16 To Sarah he said, "See, I have given your brother a thousand pieces of silver; it is your vindication in the eyes of all who are with you; and it proves to everyone that you are in the right." 17 Then Abraham prayed to Elohim; and Elohim healed Abimelek, and also healed his wife and female slaves so that they could bear children. 18 For YHWH had closed all the wombs of the house of Abimelek because of Sarah, Abraham's wife.[4]

Abimelek graciously gave gifts to Abraham to make a public acknowledgment of responsibility. Furthermore, he gave an open invitation to Abraham to settle anywhere he wanted to. Then Abraham interceded prophetically and Abimelek and his people were made whole again. Even though Abraham was the one at fault, curiously he is also the one who can remedy the situation. He is a prophet and hence is capable of mediating healing to Abimelek and his people.

The plot motif of this story, the patriarch claiming that his wife is his sister, is also found in Genesis 12:10–20 and in 26:6–11, both by the Yahwist. Having

---

[4] Verse 18 appears to be a later addition. It uses the divine name Yahweh and appears merely to be an explanation of why these people needed to be healed.

this particular motif in three separate stories is one of the supporting reasons for a multiple literary source theory of the Pentateuch.

TESTING OF ABRAHAM (22:1–19)

This story is one of the most profound tales of the Torah. It conveys a deep lesson of testing and faith. Not only is it one of the most poignant tales in the Hebrew Bible, it is one of the best crafted.

Applying the perspective of the newer literary criticism to look for structure, we see that it is segmented into three units on the basis of repeated phrases. The repeated phrases are indicated by bold type in the translation. Each of the three units is introduced with a summons, each time addressed to Abraham. In each unit Abraham responds the same way.

1. God summons Abraham (1–2)
    God: "Abraham!"
    Abraham: "I am right here."
    Command: "Take your son."
2. Isaac summons Abraham (7–8)
    Isaac: "Father!"
    Abraham: "I am right here."
    Question: "Where is the lamb?"
    Abraham: "God will provide."
3. Angel summons Abraham (11–12)
    Angel: "Abraham, Abraham!"
    Abraham: "I am right here."
    Command: "Do not harm the boy."

The following discussion of Genesis 22 examines the account by units. The words in boldface are the elements of the outline that reveal the structure.

1. God summons Abraham

> 1 After these events, Elohim tested Abraham. He said to him, "**Abraham!**" He answered, "**I am right here.**" 2 He said, "**Take your son**, your only one, he whom you love, Isaac, and go to the land of Moriah, and sacrifice him there as a whole burnt offering on one of the mountains, the one I will tell you."

The first sentence of this unit is a theme statement. "Elohim tested Abraham" gives us the purpose of the story right at the beginning. God was testing Abraham's faith. Many Elohist stories have to do with faith and faithfulness. An interest in this theme can be explained partially by conditions at the time the Elohist source was written. It was a time of severe testing in Israel, and a story like this assured the people that God could be behind such testing and that it could serve a purpose.

Unit 1 contains God's command to sacrifice Isaac. Moriah is impossible to locate geographically. The later tradition of 2 Chronicles 3:1 identifies Mount Moriah with the site of Solomon's temple. The connection this story draws between Abraham and Solomon's temple through the interpretation of the Chronicles tradition gives the site of the temple an ancestral connection, hence the site acquires greater venerability.

3 Abraham got up early in the morning and saddled his donkey and took two of his servants with him, and Isaac his son. He cut offering wood and journeyed to the place Elohim told him. 4 On the third day Abraham glanced up and saw the place in the distance. 5 Abraham said to his servants, "Stay here with the donkey. I and the boy will go there. We will worship and we will return to you." 6 Abraham took the offering wood and put it on his son Isaac. He took in his own hand the fire and the knife. And the two of them walked together.

Unit 1 contains emotionally charged narrative. Abraham and his dear son together traveled to the mountain. They ascended the mountain, Isaac carrying in his own arms the wood that was intended to ignite himself as a whole burnt offering to God. The notice that "the two of them walked together" is touching in its simplicity.

2. Isaac summons Abraham

*7 Isaac said to Abraham his father, "**Father!**" And he said, "**I am right here, my son.**" And he said, "The fire's here, and the wood. **Where is the sacrificial lamb?**" 8 Abraham said, "**Elohim himself will provide a lamb for the offering, my son.**" And the two of them walked together. 9 They came to the place Elohim told him and Abraham built there the altar and arranged the wood and bound Isaac, his son, and put him on top of the wood. 10 Abraham reached out his hand and took the knife to slaughter his son.*

Unit 2 is distinctive among the three units. Only here Abraham replies a second time. He says, "God himself will provide a lamb for the offering, my son." By the way, catch the double intent in the phrase, "God will provide a lamb, my son." "My son" is both the one addressed and the lamb. Certainly, it is at this point that Abraham makes his most profound statement of faith: "God will provide." Note how the story centralizes Abraham's profession of faith by placing it in the middle of the three-unit literary structure.

Note also how Abraham went all the way and bound Isaac on the altar. This story is called the *akedah* in the Jewish tradition, the word for "binding" in the original Hebrew text of verse 9.

3. Angel summons Abraham

*11 The Angel of YHWH called to him from heaven, "**Abraham, Abraham!**" And he said, "**I am right here.**" 12 And he said, "**Do not reach out your hand to the boy** and do not do anything to him. For now I know that you fear Elohim. You have not held back your son, your only one, from* *me." 13 Abraham raised his eyes and saw a ram right there, with one of its horns caught in a thicket. Abraham went and took the ram and sacrificed it as a whole burnt offering in place of his son.*

Note the introduction of the name of God, "YHWH," at this point in the story. Verses 11–18 have certain characteristics of the Yahwist, especially the mention of blessing. Perhaps this indicates that the Elohist used an earlier form of the story from the Yahwist source that he reshaped to develop his own version.

In the nick of time, the angel of Yahweh stopped Abraham. The sacrifice was halted because God felt assured that Abraham truly feared God. Note that in this paragraph YHWH substitutes for Elohim. Presumably, the editor is putting his own stamp on the story at this point, probably the Priestly writer, who was interested in the sacrificial dimensions of this story.

Units 1 and 3 are tightly linked. Verses 2 and 12 are linked by the phrase "your son, your only one." Verse 2 establishes the test: take your son. Verse 12 records passing the test: you have not withheld your son.

14 Abraham called the name of that place "YHWH provides." To this day it is said, "On YHWH's mountain it will be provided."

Tradition apparently invested this place with great significance, even though today we do not know exactly what place is being referred to. In the editor's own day, it was still an important place of worship. It gets its name *provided* from the ram God made available as a substitute for Isaac.

15 The Angel of YHWH called to Abraham a second time from heaven 16 and said, "I swear by myself (YHWH's oracle) that because you did this, you did not withhold your son, your only one, 17 I will richly bless you and greatly increase your offspring—like the stars of heaven and the sand of the sea shore. And your offspring will inherit the gate of their enemies. 18 All the nations of the earth will bless themselves through your offspring, because you obeyed my voice."

Having passed the test of faith, God repeated the promise of blessing. Abraham's offspring would increase and he would be richly blessed. This reaffirms the Yahwist principle that blessing follows obedience.

The analogies of *sand* and *stars* recall the covenant promises found in Genesis 13:16 and 15:5, respectively. The phrase "sand of the seashore" also creates a link to 1 Kings 4:20, where this promise was seen to be fulfilled in the Solomonic kingdom. This further reinforces the theological understanding that the blessings of the later monarchy were founded on the promises to the ancestors.

19 And Abraham returned to the servants and they journeyed to Beersheba together. And Abraham lived in Beersheba.

Abraham traveled to the southern part of Palestine, called the Negev, where he established himself. Curiously, no mention is made here of Isaac, only Abraham and the servants. One might think Isaac would be explicitly mentioned after having survived a close encounter with the knife.

Yet the focus of this episode is surely on Abraham. In this remarkable story we see a changed man, one radically different from the early Abraham of chapter 12. Then, he was afraid of losing his own life, he was insecure, and he deceived the Pharaoh of Egypt to save his own skin. He did not trust God to protect him even though God had promised that he would.

The later Abraham of this episode declined to cling to what, humanly speaking, must have been his last hope for a future. He did not take Isaac and run from God. Instead, willing to sacrifice Isaac, he obeyed God. In so doing he demonstrated his deep and secure faith in the promises of God. The testing of Abraham episode within the overall account of Abraham displays his maturation in the faith.

Maybe this story had a different meaning before it found its way into the Ancestral Story. It is probable that this Abraham–Isaac story originally existed independently before the Elohist or any other source existed. Using the procedures of form criticism to recover the original setting of the isolated tale, some scholars have suggested that the original intent of this story was to displace child sacrifice as a form of worship and replace it with animal sacrifice. Perhaps this is the story the Elohist found.

Reconstructing the course of its inclusion into the book of Genesis, the Elohist took the core story and supplemented it with the promise of blessing and other details from the Yahwist source. He was interested in the story for his own reasons and reshaped it to show how God may test one's faith, yet ultimately provide. This story is a likely example of an early tale that meant one thing, then was taken up by a later writer and given new meaning in connection with his themes and interests.

There are indications in the overall account of Abraham, roughly chapters 12–25, that in fact we should see the Abraham of chapter 22, the "late" Abraham, in relation to the "early" Abraham. In particular, there is point–counterpoint between Genesis 12 and 22 drawn by verbal and thematic parallels. The following is a list of explicit parallels between them:

> 12:1 Go from your land
> 22:2 Go to the land
>
> 12:6 Moreh
> 22:2 Moriah
>
> 12:3 All peoples on earth will be blessed or/ bless themselves through you
> 22:18 Through your offspring all the nations on the earth will bless themselves

These correspondences suggest that these two stories are to be seen in juxtaposition, as a kind of framework perhaps, around the Abraham collection of stories. What is the point of these connections? The editor who brought J and E together urges us to see the testing of Abraham as the last step toward the realization of the promises stated in 12:1–7. As a result of his willingness to sacrifice his son Isaac, Abraham finally demonstrated that he relied implicitly on the promises of God. He staked his future on God, not on the life of his son. So, the account of Abraham finds satisfying resolution.

JACOB WRESTLES WITH GOD (32:22–32)

The Elohist has no further major contribution to the Abraham stories. In fact, he seems to be more interested in Jacob than in Abraham or Isaac. This should not be surprising because many of the Jacob stories have Ephraimite or Transjordanian locations, precisely the places dear to the Elohist.

The story of wrestling with God in chapter 32 demonstrates the persistence of the patriarch Jacob in trying to secure a blessing, even under the most trying circumstances. The setting is his return to Canaan after having lived with his uncle Laban in Paddan-Aram[5] for many years. He was fearful of meeting his brother **Esau**, whom he had alienated by stealing the family blessing.

> *22 That same night he got up and took his two wives, his two maids, and his eleven children, and crossed the ford of the Jabbok. 23 He took them and sent them across the wadi, along with everything he owned. 24 Jacob was left alone; and a man wrestled with him until the break of the day.*

Verses 22–24 are usually attributed to the Yahwist writer. They are part of the Yahwist's account of Jacob's trip back to Canaan. The story of the wrestling (25–32) is itself actually quite self-contained. These introductory verses meld the wrestling into the larger Jacob narrative by giving it a context.

The Jabbok River runs through Transjordan and into the Jordan River. Jacob and company had to travel through that territory on their way back to Canaan.

> *25 When the man saw that he could not gain the advantage over Jacob, he touched his hip socket; that put Jacob's hip out of joint as he wrestled with him. 26 Then he said, "Let me go, for day is breaking." But Jacob said, "I will not let you go, unless you bless me." 27 And he said to him, "What is your name?" And he said, "Jacob." 28 Then he said, "Your name will no longer be called Jacob, but instead Israel, for you have wrestled with Elohim and with men, and have prevailed."*

The assailant is called a *man* here, but as the story develops it becomes clear that it is Elohim himself. Jacob, whose name means "heel-grabber," hence "trickster," undergoes a name change to Israel, which means "wrestles with God." By giving an account of his dual name Jacob/Israel, the Elohist identifies Jacob here as the patriarch of the nation of Israel. This is consistent with the story because Jacob/Israel had twelve sons (one of them, Joseph, had two of his own sons who became tribes), who were the tribal fathers who in turn sired the twelve tribes of Israel.

---

[5] This is the term the Elohist and the Priestly writer use to refer to Aram, modern-day Syria. The Yahwist uses the term Aram-Naharaim.

29 Then Jacob asked him, "Please tell me your name." But he said, "Why are you asking for my name?" And there he blessed him. 30 So Jacob called the name of the place Peniel, saying, "I have seen Elohim face to face, and I am still alive." 31 The sun rose upon him as he passed Penuel, he was limping because of his thigh. 32 Therefore to this day the Israelites do not eat the muscle of the hip which is part of the hip socket, because he touched Jacob's hip socket on the muscle of the hip.

Peniel (with an alternate spelling Penuel) literally means "face of God," getting this name because Jacob saw God directly here. A recurring theme in the Elohist is that one cannot look at God and live (see also Moses at the burning bush in Exodus 3). This reinforces the utter powerfulness of Elohim. Yet Jacob saw the face of God and lived, a sign that indeed he was blessed.

The final note in verse 32 is introduced by "Therefore to this day," an unmistakable indicator that this version of the story was written down at a time later than the event itself, namely, when Israelites were around. Apparently this story, however old the core of it may have been, was appropriated at a later time and was used to explain the Jewish avoidance of eating the thigh muscle, identified in Jewish tradition with the sciatic nerve. But determining earlier meanings of the episode is more difficult.

Again working with the methodology called form-criticism, scholars have for a long time reasoned that this story contains the remains of a very early mythic tale of a river-spirit or demon. In many cultures rivers were thought to possess a power that tried to thwart a crossing unless the river-spirit was appeased. This element may have been present at a very early stage. Although a primitive motif may have been behind this story at one time, those notions of demonic spirits have been sublimated in this version. The one trying to stop Jacob is identified with Elohim.

The meaning of the story is elusive. Yet at the very least it serves to characterize Jacob as persistent, even relentless, in his pursuit for blessing. Taken together with the other Jacob stories, this story says Jacob would stop at nothing to secure a personal advantage. Recognizing that Jacob here in some way stands for all Israel, the story must also be saying something about the nation. Is it saying that Israel also worked hard to secure a blessing, sometimes too aggressively? Is it saying that all along it was wrestling with God? Yet the story also seems to be suggesting that Jacob's persistence paid off, and that in spite of his sometimes questionable tactics, he gained a blessing . . . perhaps even because of them.

PRIESTLY ANCESTRAL MATERIAL

Most of the contributions of the Priestly source to the Ancestral Story are genealogies and assorted editorial comments. Perhaps the most significant extended narrative is the covenant of circumcision in chapter 17. In order to provide a theological context for understanding it, we should look more broadly at Priestly covenant theology.

COVENANT THEOLOGY

The Priestly writer developed a theologic organization of history. In his view, God revealed himself progressively through history in various ways. The general schema of history developed by the Priestly writer is worked out in three covenants. Each covenant is marked by a distinctive sign that would be evidence that it was still in force.

Noahic Covenant and the Rainbow

God made the first covenant with Noah after the flood.[6] The Priestly source's record of the **Noahic covenant** (Genesis 9:1–17) contained the promise that the earth would never again be destroyed with a flood. The following excerpt from Genesis 9 contains God's words instituting the covenant.

> 9 *"Now I am establishing my covenant with you and with your offspring after you 10 and with every living creature which was with you: bird, beast and land animal which was with you, all those leaving the ark, all life on earth. 11 I will establish my covenant with all of you: Never again will all flesh be cut off by the waters of the flood. Never again will there be a flood to wipe out the earth." 12 And Elohim said, "This is the sign of the covenant which I am making between myself and all of you, and with every living creature which is with you, for generations forever: 13 the rainbow which I have put in the sky will be a sign of the covenant between myself and the earth."*

This is the first recorded covenant in the Hebrew Bible. It establishes a binding relationship between God and the earth. Note that only God makes a commitment here. There is no reciprocity—no return pledge of loyalty from humankind or any other creature. All living things are the gracious recipient of his promise to preserve life indefinitely.

Note that the covenant was made with all living things, not just humankind. This is characteristic of the Priestly writer who, as also revealed in the Genesis 1 creation story, is more global in scope and interest, more so than the Yahwist writer, who focused intently on humankind.

The ageless quality of this covenant is marked by the Priestly vocabulary: "established," "never again," "forever." A rainbow appears against the clouds after the sun returns following a rain—a natural sign of hope after a torrential downpour. The rainbow was appropriated as the sign of God's eternal commitment to this covenant.

In the biblical world a covenant was a basic structure, a legal metaphor, whereby God guaranteed his abiding relationship. The Noahic covenant was initiated by God and stood as an eternal sign of hope and promise. While traditionally bearing the name of Noah, this covenant was established with all living things, indeed, the entire world. The covenant with Abraham, which we treat next, is more restricted, being national in scope.

---

[6] For a discussion of Noah and the flood, see chapter 1.

Abrahamic Covenant and Circumcision

Covenant theology, which is central to the thought of the Priestly writer, is found clearly laid out in Genesis 17. As Genesis 12:1–3 was central to Yahwist theology, Genesis 17 is foundational to Priestly theology.

In the **Abrahamic covenant** there is a clear movement from the initial declaration of the covenant to the promises attached to the covenant, and on to the response of Abraham to God's covenant initiative.

> *17:1 Abram was ninety-nine years old. YHWH appeared to Abram and said to him, "I am El Shaddai. Live in my presence and be perfect. 2 So I will put my covenant between me and you: I will multiply you greatly." 3 Abram fell on his face. Then Elohim spoke with him: 4 "My covenant now is with you; you will be the father of a multitude of nations. 5 And your name will no longer be Abram, but your name shall be Abraham, for I will make you the father of a multitude of nations. 6 I will make you very prolific, and I will make you nations, and kings will come from you. 7 I will solidify my covenant between me and you and your offspring after you, for generations, as a long-lasting covenant as your Elohim and your offspring's Elohim after you. 8 And I will make the land of your sojournings, the land of Canaan, your and your offspring's long-lasting possession. And I will be their Elohim." 9 Elohim said to Abraham, "You will keep my covenant—you and your offspring after you. 10 This is the covenant you will keep, the one between me and you and your offspring after you: Circumcise every male."*

Notice how three different designations of God (YHWH, El Shaddai, Elohim) are used in this passage. God revealed himself to Abraham and the other ancestors as El Shaddai. The ancestors never knew his name to be Yahweh. Here, in one of his rare uses of the name Yahweh, the Priestly writer makes explicit the identification between Yahweh and El Shaddai so his readers will not be confused. In the Priestly historical record, God did not clarify that he was one and the same—Yahweh and El Shaddai—until he spoke to Moses (see Exodus 6:3). In 17:3 the writer reverts to his normal pre-Exodus designation for God, "Elohim."

The language of multitudes and multiplying used throughout this passage recalls the promise placed on humankind in Genesis 1:28. Abraham was viewed by the Priestly writer as the one who would fulfill the promise given at creation. "Father of a multitude of nations" is the Priestly equivalent of the Yahwistic promise of becoming a great nation, spoken by God to Abraham in Genesis 12:2.

The imminent fulfillment of the promise of offspring was signaled by a name change. *Abram*, meaning "Exalted Father," was changed to *Abraham*, "Father of a Multitude," affirming that the promise of offspring was still intact.

Immediately after God's reaffirmation of the promises, **circumcision** was introduced as the ceremony and perpetual sign of the commitment of Abraham and his offspring to God. Circumcision is the surgical removal of the foreskin of the penis. In fact, circumcision is still practiced today in many hospitals. For parents who choose to have their sons circumcised, it usually takes place a day or two after birth. In the Jewish community it happens with great ceremony in the synagogue eight days after a son is born.

Dear Ann Landers: My wife and I were both in our mid-30s when we married four years ago. We did not plan on having a family, but when she discovered she was pregnant at the age of 40, we were thrilled.

We learned through amniocentesis that the baby she is carrying is a boy. We are terribly excited. Now comes the problem:

Should the baby be circumcised? I say yes. My wife says no. According to what she has read, the practice is no longer necessary, and she sees no reason to put the infant through all that pain.

Our family physician and my wife's obstetrician are both in favor of circumcision, but they say the decision must be made by the parents. Since my wife and I hold opposite views, we'd like yours.
—**Mr. Pro and Mrs. Con in Baltimore**

Dear P. and C.: Some highly respected physicians can be found on both sides of this issue.

Circumcision of newborns was considered a routine procedure until 1971, when the American Academy of Pediatrics said there might be religious reasons for circumcision, but it had no medical benefits whatsoever.

Years later, after a survey was taken at several hospitals, it was discovered that the babies who were NOT circumcised were 10 times more likely to suffer from urinary tract problems and kidney infections than those who had gone through the procedure.

Dr. Thomas E. Wiswell, chief of neonatology at Walter Reed Army Medical Center, who previously had opposed circumcision, changed his mind when he read studies that indicated circumcision affords a high degree of protection against cancer of the penis. Of the 50,000 cases of penile cancer reviewed, only 10 occurred in men who were circumcised.

Have I told you more than you wanted to know? Perhaps, but the statistics make a strong case for circumcision. (February 21, 1993)

Chapter 17 on circumcision is theologically important because, as part of the covenant arrangement, God requires Abraham to do something to demonstrate his good faith. Abraham must perform the ritual of circumcision. Abraham carried it out, and he, Ishmael, and all the males in his household were circumcised. Abraham vowed to live deliberately in such a way that he would please God—live "perfectly," the text says.

By practicing the rite from generation to generation, the Israelites demonstrated their solidarity with God in covenant. Contrast the Yahwist perspective, in which covenant was primarily a mechanism whereby Yahweh granted blessing in perpetuity. For the Yahwist, covenant took the form of a royal grant covenant given to Abraham with no action required in return.

There are three additional restatements of the Abrahamic covenant in the Priestly source. Each has thematic and literary similarities to Genesis 17. In the first one, Genesis 28:1–4, Isaac passes on the blessing to Jacob immediately before he travels to Paddan-aram, the Priestly term for the region of Syria.

1 Isaac called Jacob and blessed him and commanded him, "Do not take a Canaanite to wife. 2 Get up and go to Paddan-aram, to the household of Bethuel your mother's father, and take a wife from there, from one of the daughters of Laban, your uncle. 3 May El Shaddai bless you, make you fruitful and multiply you. May you become a horde of people. 4 May he give you as well as your offspring the blessing of Abraham so you will inherit the land of your sojourn, which Elohim gave to Abraham."

In the Yahwist account of this blessing (Genesis 27), Jacob took it from Isaac by deceit. In this account, Isaac gives it to Jacob deliberately and intentionally. Furthermore, in contrast with the Yahwist version, where Jacob hastily fled from angry Esau, here Jacob deliberately heads for Paddan-aram to find a wife from the clan.

The phrases "blessed him and commanded him," "El Shaddai bless you, make you fruitful and multiply you," "you and your offspring," and "the land of your sojourn" are all found in Genesis 17 as well. They ultimately go all the way back to the program of prosperity for all of creation, stated in the Priestly version of creation in Genesis 1.

This covenant promise of blessing had special relevance to the Priestly writer's earliest audience. The promise that Jacob would return to the land of Canaan, even though he would be gone for many years, must have inspired hope in the hearts of the Priestly writer's refugee colleagues. They too, like Jacob, could claim possession of the land, even though absent from it.

The second Priestly restatement of the covenant blessing is found in Genesis 35:9–12, stated within the context of Jacob's return to Canaan. The vocabulary of blessing dominates this short passage, including the characteristic Priestly key phrase "be fruitful and multiply."

9 And Elohim appeared to Jacob again, this time when he returned from Paddan-aram, and he blessed him. 10 Elohim said to him, "Your name is Jacob, but no longer will you be called Jacob. Rather, Israel will be your name." So He called his name Israel. 11 Elohim said to him, "I am El Shaddai. Be fruitful and multiply. A nation, indeed a horde of nations, will come from you. You will produce kings. 12 The land which I gave to Abraham and Isaac I am also giving to you. To your offspring after you I give the land."

The Yahwist version of Jacob's return to Canaan developed it as a series of confrontations. First, Jacob wrestled with God at the Jabbok River (Genesis 32:22–32). In the course of the wrestling match God changed Jacob's name to Israel. Then, Jacob/Israel had an uneasy meeting with Esau, after which they each went their separate ways.

Here in the Priestly version the meeting is nonconfrontational. When Jacob returned to Canaan after all those years away, God simply appeared to him to confirm the promises, not to challenge him. Also notice that here we find the Priestly version of Jacob's name change.

The third Priestly restatement of the covenant blessing is found in Genesis 48:3–7. Here, the promise given to Abraham, Isaac, and Jacob is passed on to the next generation. This time God does not speak directly, but father speaks to son.

3 Jacob said to Joseph, "El Shaddai appeared to me at Luz in the land of Canaan, and blessed me. 4 He said to me, 'I am about to make you fruitful. I will multiply you and make you a horde of people. I will give this land to your offspring after you as a long-lasting possession.'"

The Priestly writer reiterates the two basic covenant promises: numerous offspring and possession of a homeland. The promise was given to the ancestors going down into Egypt, an exile of sorts, analogous to the Babylonian experience of a much later age.

These covenant promises were realized gradually. The promise of numerous offspring was the first to bear fruit. In Exodus 1:7, the narrator notes that even though they were in Egypt, the "offspring of Israel were fruitful and swarmed; they multiplied so bountifully that the land was filled with them." They would not regain the land until the conquest led by Joshua.

After all these restatements, the realization of the Genesis 17 promises begins to find fulfillment in Exodus 6:2–8. Here, the El Shaddai of the Ancestral period reveals himself as the Yahweh of Israel. In connection with this revelation of his name, Yahweh reaffirms the promise that they would inherit a land and drives it toward fulfillment. Here we find the quintessential formula of covenant: "I will take you to myself as a people, and I will be your God." (Exodus 6:7)

Mosaic Covenant and the Sabbath

The third of three great Priestly covenants is the **Mosaic covenant**. It is called the Mosaic covenant because it was mediated to Israel through Moses. Given at Mt. Sinai, it marks the last great stage in the Priestly history of salvation. This covenant, now a covenant with all the people of Israel, was regulated by an extensive set of laws and regulations that can be found in the books of Exodus, Leviticus, Numbers, and Deuteronomy. The people express their solidarity with God in this covenant by observing the **Sabbath** day, called in Exodus 31:12–18 the "sign of the covenant," and by keeping the other laws. The Mosaic covenant will be treated in more detail in the next chapter.

COVENANTS AND THE EXILE

Each of the three covenants marks a significant moment in the development of God's covenantal relationship. Each covenant has a specific sign attached to it whereby the continuation of the covenant would be evident.

God made the Noahic covenant with the entire world. Its sign, the rainbow, was passive in the sense that it was not up to the people. This covenant was unilateral, calling only for God to keep his promise.

This was not the case with the second and third covenants. Both were prime moments in God's relationship with Israel, and both called for a response by the people. The Abrahamic covenant was marked by circumcision and the Mosaic covenant by the Sabbath. By faithfully practicing these two rituals, the people demonstrated their solidarity with God in the covenant.

The importance of these last two signs is clear in the context of the composition history of the Priestly source. The signs of circumcision and Sabbath observance became the primary identifying symbols of the covenant community of the exilic and postexilic periods. During those times the religious identity of God's people was threatened. These rituals became primary identifiers because they could be practiced anywhere. Even though the people were not in Jerusalem, the only place temple rituals and sacrifices could be practiced, they could still perform circumcisions and observe the Sabbath. Through this analysis we can see how the religious needs of a later day influenced the recording of earlier history.

ANCESTRAL CYCLES

Our analysis of the ancestral narratives in terms of the major literary sources has revealed that each source shapes its telling of ancestral stories from an identifiable perspective. Each particular episode of each source bears marks of the personality of its source.

We move now to a survey of the last level of composition in the book of Genesis. To form the Ancestral Story as we have it in Genesis, stories from each of the sources were artfully combined. A study of how they were combined reveals the organization of the major ancestral story complexes.

The Ancestral Story does not have the same kind of structure as the Primeval Story. The Primeval Story was organized into two series of parallel developments. The Ancestral Story is organized into three story collections, each called a **cycle** of stories because it revolves around a major figure. The three cycles treat Abraham, Jacob, and Joseph. These three cycles are separated from each other by two brief genealogical notices that treat the two ancestral offspring, Ishmael and Esau, who were not considered part of the direct lineage of Israel.

The overall structure of the Ancestral Story is provided by the repeated use of the Hebrew term *toledot*. The word **toledot** means "generations" and comes from the Hebrew word for giving birth. It is rendered in various ways by different English translations, as you can see from the options available for handling Genesis 2:4.

> *New Revised Standard Version: "These are the **generations** of the heavens and the earth when they were created."*
> *New International Version: "This is the **account** of the heavens and the earth when they were created."*
> *New Jewish Publication Society Version: "Such is the **story** of heaven and earth when they were created."*

Toledot has to do with "developments," for lack of a better word. When found in the phrase "These are the generations of," it introduces an account of what next happens to the offspring.

The term is found eleven times in Genesis. Ten of those times it is found at important break points in the narrative. Virtually every time it is found it has a transitional function. It draws the preceding section to a conclusion and introduces the next section.

TABLE 2.1   ANCESTRAL CYCLES OF TOLEDOT

	Toledot . . .	Ancestral Text Unit
1	of Terah	Abraham Cycle (11:27–25:11)
2	of Ishmael	Ishmael Genealogy (25:12–18)
3	of Isaac	Jacob Cycle (25:19–35:29)
4	of Esau	Esau Genealogy (36:1–43)
5	of Jacob	Joseph Cycle (37–50)

The Ancestral Story consists of five toledot sections: three major ones (1, 3, and 5) and two minor ones (2 and 4). The major ones contain many stories and the minor ones consist merely of descendant lists, as shown in Table 2.1.

The cycles centering on Abraham and Jacob could be called albums. The individual tales within each cycle are not tightly connected, seemingly not ordered by a clear plot structure. The stories are more in the nature of snapshots in a picture book. Yet, in these two cycles we can recognize certain thematic and theological continuities.

On the other hand, the stories in the Joseph cycle are dramatically related in what may be the world's earliest short novel. The Joseph cycle is replete with consistent characterization, dramatic tension, and suspense, as befitting any good tale.

The following three sections summarize the story lines of each of the three ancestral cycles. Numbers in parentheses are chapter numbers in the book of Genesis.

ABRAHAM CYCLE (11:27–25:18)

Abraham migrated from Ur in southern Mesopotamia to Palestine (12–13); (see Figure 2.2). He received promises of land and a large family. Because of a famine he sought refuge in Egypt for a time. God made a covenant with Abraham promising that he would have offspring (15). When a son did not arrive, Abraham and Sarah arranged to have a surrogate son, Ishmael, through Sarah's servant, Hagar (16). God reaffirmed the covenant promise of offspring and instituted the ritual of circumcision (17). God announced to Abraham and Sarah that a genuine son was on his way (18–19). After the promised son Isaac was born, Ishmael and his mother Hagar came into conflict with Sarah and were driven away (21). Then God tested Abraham's faith by commanding him to slaughter and sacrifice Isaac. At the last moment God stopped Abraham from killing Isaac (22). Sarah died shortly thereafter and was buried in a plot purchased by Abraham (23). Abraham arranged for a wife for Isaac, Rebekah, who was from their clan back in Aram (24). The promise having been realized, Abraham passed away (25).

A moment's reflection would confirm that the **Abraham cycle** does not give us a biography of Abraham. Such was not its purpose. It does not contain any stories about his birth or his youth. In fact, most of the stories have to do with his

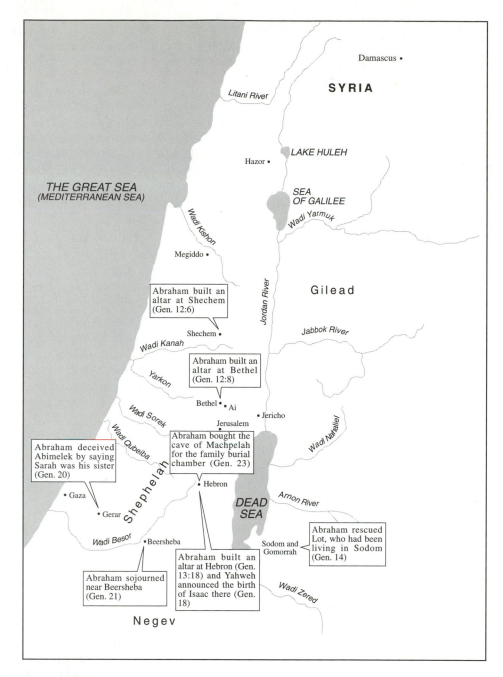

The map contains the following labels:

Damascus

SYRIA

Litani River

LAKE HULEH

Hazor

SEA OF GALILEE

THE GREAT SEA (MEDITERRANEAN SEA)

Wadi Kishon

Wadi Yarmuk

Megiddo

Jordan River

Gilead

Abraham built an altar at Shechem (Gen. 12:6)

Shechem

Jabbok River

Wadi Kanah

Abraham built an altar at Bethel (Gen. 12:8)

Yarkon

Bethel • Ai

Wadi Sorek

Jerusalem

Jericho

Wadi Qubeiba

Abraham bought the cave of Machpelah for the family burial chamber (Gen. 23)

Wadi Nahaliel

Abraham deceived Abimelek by saying Sarah was his sister (Gen. 20)

Shephelah

• Gaza

Hebron

• Gerar

DEAD SEA

Arnon River

Abraham rescued Lot, who had been living in Sodom (Gen. 14)

Sodom and Gomorrah

Wadi Besor

Beersheba

Abraham built an altar at Hebron (Gen. 13:18) and Yahweh announced the birth of Isaac there (Gen. 18)

Abraham sojourned near Beersheba (Gen. 21)

Wadi Zered

Negev

FIGURE 2.3   ABRAHAM IN CANAAN

relationship to God and how that relationship determined the future course of his life. The Abraham cycle is something we could call theological history.

Three literary–theological issues weave their way through the Abraham cycle and serve to give it unity. Identifying them will help us see the larger harmony of the cycle. These issues are so prominent in the cycle not only because of their overall theological significance, but also because they were relevant to later generations who faced situations similar to those Abraham faced.

1. *Offspring.* Israel saw itself descending from Abraham in a line of succession miraculously engineered by God. The Abraham cycle concentrates many of its stories on the question of family succession: having children, ensuring the continuity of the family line, determining which child will enjoy the family inheritance, guaranteeing the future. Many times in Israel's history, the people needed assurance that God was interested in keeping their people alive, and their faith was bolstered by these stories.

2. *Relationship with God.* God was the one who determined and guided Abraham's future. And Abraham learned to depend on him more and more as time went on. God's relationship with Abraham defined how Israel should stand with God: their present status before God as his chosen people was a consequence of God's faithfulness to Abraham, and their future depended on God's promise, as did Abraham's. The Abraham cycle describes how God defined the shape of covenant relationship with such instruments as the giving of blessing and the requirement of circumcision.

3. *Land.* Israel was interested in its claim that the land of Canaan was its heritage and homeland. The people found justification for that claim in the promise made to Abraham and in the fact that he actually lived in Canaan for many years. Their claim to the land, therefore, goes back to the early days, long before the conquest under Joshua in the thirteenth century B.C.E.

These three themes are not only foundational to the Abraham cycle, but also find resonance in the Jacob and Joseph cycles. In fact, they could be considered the fundamental issues of the whole Torah.

JACOB CYCLE (25:19–35:29)

Twin sons, Esau and Jacob, were born to Isaac and Rebekah. Esau, the firstborn, sold his birthright to Jacob (25). Later Jacob stole the family blessing from Esau (27). Esau despised his birthright and married foreign women, demonstrating why he was unworthy of the blessing. Jacob fled from his brother (28) and lived for an extended period of time with his uncle Laban in Haran. Jacob eventually married Rachel and Leah, the daughters of Laban, and had many children (29–31). Rachel became the dominant wife. Laban grew jealous of Jacob because God caused Jacob's flocks to increase at Laban's expense. So Jacob was forced to leave Paddan-aram with his family and his considerable belongings. Returning to Palestine he wrestled with God (32) and met Esau (33). He and his family settled in Palestine but tried to remain separate and distinct from the Canaanites who lived in the land (34). This is detailed in Figure 2.4.

The **Jacob cycle** continues many of the themes of the earlier parts of Genesis, including the themes of blessing, offspring, and land—but gives each theme a different twist. The Abraham cycle dealt primarily with fertility and offspring, especially how the promises were passed on from father to son through the inter-

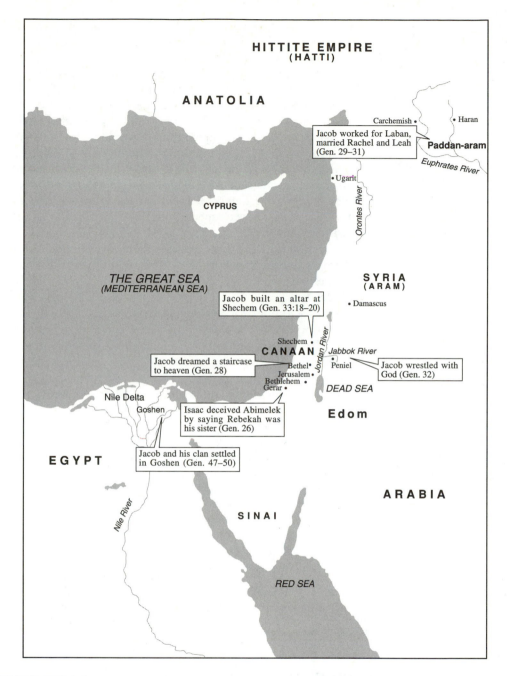

HITTITE EMPIRE
(HATTI)

ANATOLIA

Carchemish •   • Haran

Jacob worked for Laban,
married Rachel and Leah
(Gen. 29–31)

Paddan-aram

Euphrates River

• Ugarit

CYPRUS

Orontes River

THE GREAT SEA
(MEDITERRANEAN SEA)

SYRIA
(ARAM)

Jacob built an altar at
Shechem (Gen. 33:18–20)

• Damascus

Shechem •

Jordan River

Jabbok River

CANAAN

Jacob dreamed a staircase
to heaven (Gen. 28)

Bethel•
Jerusalem •
Bethlehem •
Gerar •

Peniel

Jacob wrestled with
God (Gen. 32)

DEAD SEA

Nile Delta

Goshen

Isaac deceived Abimelek
by saying Rebekah was
his sister (Gen. 26)

Edom

Jacob and his clan settled
in Goshen (Gen. 47–50)

EGYPT

ARABIA

SINAI

Nile River

RED SEA

FIGURE 2.4   JACOB'S TRAVELS

vention of God. The Jacob cycle is concerned with a somewhat different problem. If there is more than one son, how should God's promises and the family inheritance be passed on? Stated another way, the Jacob cycle is concerned with the brother-to-brother relationship within the promise, rather than the father-to-son relationship. The theme of these stories, still concerning offspring, is sibling rivalry and reaching for the blessing.

Jacob, driven largely by his own (and sometimes his mother's) scheming and trickiness, fought to win the blessing. The Jacob cycle tells us in great detail how he did that. It contains stories of human deviousness, played out against the backdrop of divine determination. The irony of the cycle is that God, even while Jacob was in the uterus, had determined that he would be the divinely favored one.

The Jacob cycle reveals an interesting quality about our storytellers. As much as they revered their patriarchs and matriarchs, the biblical writers harbored no illusions. They knew that Abraham, Isaac, and Jacob—indeed the whole lot—had serious character defects. Israel's stories about its forerunners are remarkable for their honesty, seen especially in this cycle. Insofar as the nation identified itself with its forebears (remember, Jacob IS Israel), Israel had an amazing capacity for self-criticism. The Israelites saw themselves in their parentage, and it was not always a flattering picture. For example, both Abraham and Isaac so struggled in their faith that they hid their true relationship to their wives to save their own skins. And Jacob did everything he could to deny his twin brother his rightful inheritance and instead grabbed it for himself.

In addition to thematic unity, the Jacob cycle betrays a symmetrical literary structure. The following outline displays the broad narrative scheme that takes its shape from corresponding notions.

> A *Birth of Jacob and Esau: Jacob gets the birthright (25)*
>   B *Isaac and Abimelek: conflict over land (26)*
>   C *Jacob flees from Esau with the blessing (27)*
>   D *Jacob at Bethel: "house of God" (28)*
>   E *Jacob stays with Laban (29–31)*
>   D' *Jacob at Peniel: "face of God" (32)*
>   C' *Jacob and Esau reconciled (33)*
>   B' *Jacob and Shechem: conflict over marriage (34)*
> A' *Return to Canaan and death of Isaac (35)*

As the outline illustrates, the stories have a remarkable symmetry, with A corresponding to A', B to B', and so on. Chapters 26 and 34 often seem out of place to interpreters because they break up the flow of Jacob events. But these otherwise isolated and incongruous B episodes have a place in the overall literary scheme. In both literary and structural ways, the Jacob cycle has an amazing wholeness.

JOSEPH CYCLE (37–50)

The **Joseph cycle** is a marvelous piece of storytelling. It is one of the most artfully written pieces of Hebrew literature. Some call it a short story, others a novella. It is remarkable in the way it sustains a story line over many chapters, whereas most other Hebrew stories are only a few paragraphs long. The Joseph cycle is a mixture of elements from three Pentateuchal sources, the Yahwist, Elohist, and Priestly.

In spite of the variety of its sources, the Joseph cycle is a tightly told tale of family rivalry and providential deliverance. Joseph was the favored son of Jacob's twelve. In the story, Joseph's brothers came to dislike him immensely. They decided to kill him. In the Yahwist version his brother Judah tried to save him, but in the Elohist version it is Reuben. Reuben was the oldest son, the firstborn of Leah. Out of spite Joseph's brothers sold him into slavery. He ended up being a servant to Potiphar, an Egyptian official (37). An interlude describes Judah and Tamar's conflict over marriage rights and offspring (38).[7] Going back to the main story, Joseph faithfully served Potiphar, but wound up in jail after Potiphar's wife tried to seduce him. While in jail Joseph distinguished himself by his trustworthiness and his ability to interpret dreams (39–40). After **Pharaoh** had a series of dreams he could not understand, Joseph was brought in to interpret the dreams and came to a high governmental position (41). Joseph rose from slave and prisoner to minister of agriculture.

This set the stage for Joseph to pay his brothers back for their nastiness. Under his leadership Egypt prepared for a famine, which, in turn, provided the occasion for a reunion with his brothers (see Figure 2.5). When they came to buy grain he gave them fits of anxiety. He accused them of espionage and imprisoned one of his brothers, inflicting on Simeon the ordeal he himself had suffered because of them.

He eventually revealed his identity to them, forgave them, and brought the entire family to live in the **Goshen** region of Egypt (see Figure 2.6). Goshen is a fertile area in the eastern Nile delta. There they weathered the famine together and settled down (42–47). Finding life comfortable there, they grew into a sizable clan under the care of Jacob. In his old age Jacob passed on the family blessing to his grandchildren Ephraim and Manasseh (48) and his sons (49). Shortly afterward he died and was taken back to Canaan for burial (50).

In like manner Joseph, before he died in Egypt, extracted a promise from his family that they would not bury him in Egypt but would carry his bones back to Canaan. When after the Exodus the Israelites returned, he was buried in Shechem, the capital of Israel in the Northern Kingdom. This story, obviously of special interest to the Ephraimites, derives from the Elohist source.

In a sense it is curious that Joseph should get so much press. Joseph is not the most significant of Jacob/Israel's sons, judged on the basis of later tribal history. Of all Jacob's sons, we might expect Judah to get the most attention. His tribe is the focus of so much later history and was the home of the Davidic monarchy. We are justified in asking why so much time is given to Joseph in the book of Genesis. Perhaps this is part of it. Ephraim was the core of the Northern Kingdom, and Joseph was the father of Ephraim and Manasseh, the two largest tribes of the ten northern tribes. Certainly this is reason enough for at least the Elohist writer to be interested.

Furthermore, we should remember that the Joseph cycle is really the toledot of Jacob. In other words, it is the account of what happened to all of Jacob's offspring, not just to Joseph. In fact, all the sons of Jacob are treated in this material.

---

[7] Robert Alter (1982; see chapter 1) gives a plausible explanation of the placement of the Judah–Tamar story here. He suggests positioning it next to the story of Joseph with Potiphar's wife provides counterpoint to the character of Joseph, and the figures are mutually illuminating as they are set side by side.

FIGURE 2.5 Foreigners implore an Egyptian royal servant on this relief from the tomb of Horemheb at Memphis. No doubt in a similar manner Joseph's brothers begged him for food and, later, mercy.

True, one gets short treatment (Judah) and another gets major coverage (Joseph); still all get at least some mention, if only in the ancestral blessing (Genesis 49). The story focusing on Joseph simply became the occasion to reflect on the most serious threat to the promise to date; namely, the exit of the chosen people from the Promised Land. In a lesser way, even the Judah–Tamar story (Genesis 38) reflects on threats to the promise, in this case by loss of offspring. The continuity of the promise is threatened, indeed, if the patriarch neglects his duty.

A subtheme of the Joseph cycle is the issue of **primogeniture**, the right of the firstborn son to inherit his father's estate. This continues an interest found in both the Abraham and Jacob cycles. Joseph was the son who received the greatest attention, though as the firstborn of Rachel, he was not the firstborn overall. The firstborn overall, Reuben, was denied preeminence because he slept with one of Jacob's wives. Judah was one of the youngest sons of Jacob and Leah, yet he became one of the premier tribes of Israel. The intentionality of this subtheme in the Joseph cycle is confirmed by the switch of blessings on Manasseh and Ephraim. Ephraim received the blessing of the firstborn even though he was the younger of the two (Genesis 48).

FIGURE 2.6   This painting on the wall of a tomb at Beni-hasan depicts people from Asia arriving in Egypt. In a similar manner, the clan of Jacob traveled from Canaan and settled in the Goshen region of the Nile Delta.

All of this business about inheritance and the firstborn, an issue that keeps re-curring in the Ancestral Story, is partially an explanation of geographical and so-cial realities. It is the writers' way of explaining the later preeminence of the tribes of Judah and Ephraim, even though they were not firstborn sons.

There may also have been an interest in the issue of primogeniture in relation to the establishment of the Davidic monarchy. Remember that much of this Gen-esis material probably was written down during the time of David and Solomon. King David, Israel's greatest king, was himself the youngest son of Jesse, not the oldest. Likewise Solomon, David's son, was not first in line for the throne. Per-haps the writer was providing historical precedent in these ancestral stories in order to legitimize the throne of David.

Theologically speaking, the Joseph cycle is perhaps the most difficult cycle to comprehend. It contains the smallest amount of God-talk. Yet there is a theolog-ical message, which was not lost on the ancient reader.

One of the theological lessons Israel learned from the Joseph cycle or, for that matter, from all three cycles, is that God does not follow human convention when he decides whom he will bless. He is unpredictable and likely as not will choose the younger over the older. As a further indication of the sovereignty of God, the younger son predestined for greatness was in almost every case conceived through the help of God after an extended period of barrenness (Isaac to Sarah, Jacob and Esau to Rebekah, Joseph to Rachel, Perez to Tamar—though more through Tamar's initiative than God's help). In sum, the continuity of the promise was God-determined in every way.

Lastly, we should note that the Joseph cycle is important because it gave the explanation of how and why the Israelites ended up in Egypt. Looking ahead to the book of Exodus, where the Israelites are in bondage, we need to know how they got there. The Joseph cycle explains this and anticipates how God will rescue his people in the great exodus from Egypt.

OVERALL SHAPE OF GENESIS

The all-pervasive interest of Genesis is the wonder of human life. Virtually every story in Genesis has something to do with the theme complex of blessing–fertility–offspring–continuity–survival–life. From Eden to the Promised Land, human history was driven by God's command to be prolific and prosperous. And, as the story has it, that is just what happened.

This overriding concern of Genesis, the continuity of blessing from Eden to Israel, is reflected in the very structure of the book. The structure shows how one stage of blessing continued into the next. This structure was the work of the final compiler of the Torah, the Priestly editor, and was organized by toledot. Earlier we saw how it provided the structure of the Ancestral Story. In fact, toledot statements extend throughout the entire book of Genesis.

Dividing the book into two main sections, the Primeval Story (1–11) and the Ancestral Story (12–50), the toledot of Genesis give structure to the entire book. The ten toledot are divided into two units of five and five according to their subject matter. Table 2.2 gives the organization of Genesis by toledot.

| TABLE 2.2 | TOLEDOT OF GENESIS |

Primeval Story	*Ancestral Story*
1. Heavens and Earth (2:4)	6. Terah (11:27)
2. Adam (5:1)	7. Ishmael (25:12)
3. Noah (6:9)	8. Isaac (25:19)
4. Shem, Ham, Japheth (10:1)	9. Esau (36:1,9)
5. Shem (11:10)	10. Jacob (37:2)

The ten toledot of Genesis start the book off with the widest possible scope, the universe, and gradually constrict the purview of the book until it ends with Jacob, the eponymous ancestor of the nation of Israel. Figure 2.7 further illustrates this narrowing by indicating how the toledot progress, while some family branches are given account and are then dropped from further consideration because they are no longer the main interest of the editor.

Toledot Number	Toledot Name	
		Primeval Story
1	Heaven and Earth	
2	Adam	
3	Noah	
4	Shem–Ham–Japheth	
5	Shem	
		Ancestral Story
6	Terah	*=Abraham Cycle*
7	Ishmael	
8	Isaac	*=Jacob Cycle*
9	Esau	
10	Jacob	*=Joseph Cycle*

FIGURE 2.7   NARROWING THE SCOPE OF GENESIS

Table 2.3 is a reference for readers who wish to return to the text of the Ancestral Story and examine it with a view to each story's origin. The table lists the specific episodes of the Ancestral Story and assigns each to its probable sources.[8]

[8]The information in Table 2.3 follows Friedman (1987), pp. 247–49.

TABLE 2.3   LITERARY SOURCES OF GENESIS 12–50

Episode	Yahwist (J)	Elohist (E)	Priestly (P)	Editor
Toledot of Terah				11:27a, 32
Abraham's journey	12:1–4a		11:27b–31; 12:4b–5	
Promise to Abraham	12:6–9			
Wife–sister	12:10–20			
Abraham and Lot	13:1–5, 7–11a, 12b–18; 14:1–24		13:6, 11b–12a	
Abrahamic Covenant	15:1–21		17:1–27	
Hagar and Ishmael	16:1–2, 4–14		16:3, 15–16	
Three visitors	18:1–33			
Sodom and Gomorrah	19:1–28, 30–38		19:29	
Wife–sister		20:1–18		
Birth of Isaac	21:1a, 2a, 7	21:6	21:1b, 2b–5	
Hagar and Ishmael		21:8–21		
Abraham and Abimelek		21:22–24		
Sacrifice of Isaac		22:1–10, 16b–19		22:11–16a
Abraham's kin	22:20–24			
Cave of Machpelah			23:1–10	
Rebekah	24:1–67		25:20	
Sons of Keturah	25:5–6	25:1–4		
Death of Abraham			25:7–11a	
Toledot of Ishmael			25:13–18	25:12
Toledot of Isaac				25:19
Jacob and Esau	25:11b, 21–34; 27:1–45		26:34–35; 27:46; 28:1–9	
Wife–sister	26:1–11			
Isaac and Abimelek	26:12–33			

Episode	Yahwist (J)	Elohist (E)	Priestly (P)	Editor
Jacob at Bethel	28:10–11a, 13–16, 19	28:11b–12, 17–18, 20–22		
Jacob, Leah, and Rachel	29:1–30			
Jacob's children	29:31–35; 30:24b	30:1–24a	35:23–26	
Jacob and Laban	30:25–43	31:1–2, 4–16, 19–54; 32:1–3		
Jacob's return	31:3, 17, 18a; 32:14–24	32:4–13; 33:1–17	31:18b; 35:27	
Jacob to Israel		32:25–33	35:9–15	
Shechem	34:1–31	33:18–20		33:18
Return to Bethel		35:1–8		
Death of Rachel		35:16–20		
Reuben's sin	35:21–22			
Death of Isaac			35:28–29	
Toledot of Esau	36:31–43		36:2–30	36:1
Joseph and his brothers	37:2b, 3b, 5–11, 19–20, 23, 25b–27, 28b, 31–35	37:3a, 4, 12–18, 21–22, 24, 25a, 28a, 29, 36	37:1	37:2a
Judah and Tamar	38:1–30			
Joseph and Potiphar's wife	39:1–23			
Butler and Baker		40:1–23		
Joseph and Pharaoh		41:2–45a, 46b–57	41:45b–46a	
Jacob's sons in Egypt	42:1–4, 8–20, 26–34, 38; 43:1–13, 15–34; 44:1–34; 45:1–2, 4–28	42:5–7, 21–25, 35–37; 43:14; 45:3		
Jacob in Egypt	46:5b, 28–34; 47:1–27a, 29–31; 49:1–27; 50:1–11, 14–23	46:1–5a; 48:1–2, 8–22; 50:23–26	46:6–27; 47:27b, 28; 48:3–6; 49:29–33; 50:12–13	48:7; 49:28

In sum, though constructed out of a great variety of stories, genealogies, and explanatory notes, the various formal and thematic features of the book of Genesis serve to give it a remarkable literary and theological unity. And the ending, leaving Jacob's family in Egypt yet awaiting return to the Promised Land for the burial of Joseph's bones, thrusts us onward to the book of Exodus.

QUESTIONS FOR REVIEW

1. Compare the accounts of God's covenant with Abraham in 13:14–17, 15:17–21, and 17:1–21. How are they alike and how are they different?

2. Define the term *theophany* and list the episodes where God appeared to people in the Ancestral Story. List the various ways in which God appeared. Identify the typical ways God appeared to people in each of the three literary sources.

3. What changes did Abraham and Sarah undergo from the beginning of their cycle to the end? What about Jacob?

4. Trace the theme of blessing and curse through the Jacob cycle. What is the significance of blessing in the Ancestral Story?

5. How can we account for the similarities among the stories about Sarah and the pharaoh (Genesis 12:14–20), Sarah and Abimelek (Genesis 20:10–20), and Rebekah and Abimelek (Genesis 26:6–11)?

6. How does the Joseph cycle differ from the other two cycles? How is it similar to them?

QUESTIONS FOR DISCUSSION

1. Abraham, Isaac, and Jacob are considered the fathers of the nation of Israel. In a way, telling their stories is telling the story of the Israelites. What episodes in the Ancestral Story can you identify as revealing especially clearly the character of the nation of Israel? Also, in a more specific way, what episodes may have reinforced a northern Israelite identity? What episodes may have reinforced a southern Judean identity? How do we use stories to clarify our personal identities? Our national identities?

2. Which ancestral stories relate to the issue of faith in God? List some specific episodes that stand out in

your mind that have to do with issues of belief, trust, and faith. What developments can you trace in the growth and quality of the ancestors' faith? What may the Ancestral Story as a whole be saying about the nature of faith and relationship to God?

3. What do the stories of the matriarchs reveal about the social role of women in the ancestral period? How does the sociology of women in that time, insofar as you have been able to glean it from the texts, compare with your understanding of the role of women in society today?

FOR FURTHER STUDY

Ancestral Story issues. Millard, A. R., and D. J. Wiseman, eds. (1980). *Essays on the Patriarchal Narratives.* Winona Lake, Ind.: Eisenbrauns. Contains chapters on the patriarchs in scripture and history, methods of studying the patriarchal narratives as ancient texts, archaeological data and the dating of the patriarchs, comparative customs and the patriarchal age, the religion of the patriarchs, and the literary structure of Genesis.

Moberley, Robert W. (1992). *Genesis 12–50.* Old Testament Guides. Sheffield: JSOT Press. Discusses all the major issues of interpretation, including composition, historicity of the ancestral figures, ancestral religion, and hermeneutical questions. A special section is devoted to Genesis 22.

Steinberg, Naomi (1993). *Kinship and Marriage in Genesis. A Household Economics Perspective.* Philadelphia: Fortress Press. Examines Genesis 12–50 with a focus on inheritance, marriage, and land ownership. Argues that maternity and marriage partner are crucial factors in determining the choice of Isaac and Jacob as heirs.

Thompson, Thomas L. (1974). *The Historicity of the Patriarchal Narratives.* ZAW Supplement 133; Berlin: Walter De Gruyter. Argues that the ancestral stories contain no authentic history, but are fictional stories created very late in Israel's history.

Van Seters, John. (1975). *Abraham in History and Tradition.* New Haven, Conn., and London: Yale University Press. This book, along with the preceding one by Thompson, challenges the authenticity of the Genesis portrayal of the ancestors as early figures, instead arguing that they have no historical basis in fact.

Westermann, Claus (1976). *The Promises to the Fathers. Studies on the Patriarchal Narratives.* Philadelphia: Fortress Press. A close reading of the crime–punishment narratives of Genesis 1–11, the Abraham cycle, and the Jacob cycle.

Unity of Genesis. Brisman, Leslie (1990). *The Voice of Jacob. On the Composition of Genesis.* Bloomington and Indianapolis: University of Indiana Press. Using newer literary methods, argues that Genesis arose as a conversation between a pious traditionalist writer and a revisionist writer.

Clines, David J. A. (1978). *The Theme of the Pentateuch.* Supplement Series, 10. Sheffield: JSOT Press. Identifies literary and theological themes that bind together the diversity of Genesis.

Cohn, R. (1983). "Narrative Structure and Canonical Perspective in Genesis." *Journal for the Study of the Old Testament* 25: 3–16.

Dahlberg, B. (1982). "The Unity of Genesis" in *Literary Interpretation of Biblical Narrative, Volume 2.* Ed. K. Gros Louis. Nashville, Tenn.: Abingdon. A literary reading of Genesis.

Rendsburg, Gary (1986). *The Redaction of Genesis.* Winona Lake, Ind.: Eisenbrauns. Identifies editorial features of the text that serve to give it unity.

WORKS CITED

Alter, Robert (1982). *The Art of Biblical Narrative.* New York: Basic Books.

Friedman, Richard Elliott (1987). *Who Wrote the Bible?* Englewood Cliffs, N.J.: Prentice-Hall.

Exodus: Deliverance and Covenant

3

Names and Terms to Remember

Aaron	Decalogue	Moses
absolute law	Exodus	Passover
Book of the Covenant/	golden calf	Pharaoh
Covenant Code	Horeb	Sinai/Mt. Sinai
burning bush	Hyksos	Tabernacle
case law	Jethro/Reuel	Ten Commandments
Code of Hammurapi	Miriam	

The book of Exodus gets its name from the central event of the book. The **Exodus** from Egypt was the set of events whereby Moses led the Hebrew people out of Egypt to begin their journey to the Promised Land.

The book of Exodus follows the book of Genesis. It can be divided into two main parts on the basis of subject matter. Part 1 contains the traditions of the Hebrews' exit from Egypt (chapters 1–18). Part 2 contains traditions centering on the Sinai revelation of Yahweh (chapters 19–40). See the time line in Figure 3.1.

In summary fashion, this is the story line. The introduction (Exodus 1) establishes a connection with Genesis and the ancestors and goes on to describe the way the Egyptians oppressed the Hebrews. The Egyptians forced the Hebrews into slavery. When this did not stop their growth, they killed male Hebrew infants. **Moses** was born under these conditions (2). As an infant his parents hid him for a while and then put him in a basket and set him afloat in the Nile River. Pharaoh's daughter found him, had compassion on him, and raised him at the royal court.

After Moses prematurely attempted to rescue some fellow Hebrews by killing their Egyptian slave master, he fled Egypt and went to live in the Sinai wilderness. There he married Zipporah and raised a family. While shepherding the flocks of his father-in-law **Jethro**, he met Yahweh at the **burning bush** (3–4), who told him to return to Egypt. In Egypt he mediated the Hebrews' deliverance from slavery and oppression. With a series of natural and supernatural disasters, Yahweh demonstrated his power, and the Hebrews escaped into the Sinai wilderness (5–12).

The Egyptians pursued them, and just when it looked like the Hebrews were doomed, God opened a pathway through the Red Sea. The Hebrews passed through safely, but the Egyptian army drowned (13–15). Then Moses led the people to Mt. Sinai, the location of the burning bush where earlier he had met Yahweh (16–18).

At Mt. Sinai, Yahweh revealed himself to the Hebrews and established a covenant relationship with them (19–24). In addition to making the covenant, he gave them instructions for implementing structures of worship (25–31). Immediately after the people agreed to the terms of the covenant they broke it by worshiping an idol associated with a foreign god (32–34). Though they deserved total destruction, God reestablished covenant with the Hebrews. Then, while still encamped at the base of Mt. Sinai, the Hebrews built the **Tabernacle**, an elaborate yet portable sanctuary, as a dwelling for their God (35–40).

Middle Bronze IIA	Middle Bronze IIB-C		Late Bronze I		Late Bronze IIA-B		Iron

Hyksos

Egyptian 18th Dynasty

Egyptian 19th Dynasty

Hebrews in Egypt

Jacob and Joseph to Egypt •

Hebrew Exodus from Egypt •

Israelite Conquest of Canaan

B.C.E.	1800	1700	1600	1500	1400	1300	1200	1100

FIGURE 3.1   TIME LINE: EXODUS FROM EGYPT

EXODUS DELIVERANCE TRADITIONS (CHAPTERS 1–18)

The first half, roughly, of the book of Exodus is a narrative account of the Hebrews' escape from Egyptian bondage and their journey to Mt. Sinai.

ISRAEL IN EGYPT (1)

The book of Exodus begins by drawing a connection to the Joseph cycle of Genesis to show how the Hebrews found themselves to be in Egypt in the first place. Chapter 1 recalls the family of Jacob and mentions all twelve sons by name. The writer calls them the sons of Israel, which is appropriate because Jacob's name was changed to Israel and he was the eponymous ancestor of the nation. Drawing a connection to the ancestral blessing[1] and going even further back to the creation blessing,[2] the writer states that Israel was fruitful and multiplied.

The Hebrews had lived in Egypt for many generations when the government changed and the Egyptian **Pharaoh**, or king of Egypt, enslaved these Hebrews. Notice how their covenant blessing became their curse; they had become so numerous the new government began to see them as a threat.

> 1:8 A new king rose to power over Egypt, who did not know about Joseph. 9 He said to his people, "Now, the Israelites are more numerous and powerful than we are. 10 Come on, let us deal shrewdly with them, or they will become even more numerous. If war breaks out they would join our enemies, fight against us, and leave the land." 11 They put slave masters over them to inflict hard labor on them. They built the store cities Pithom and Rameses for Pharaoh.

Moses was one of the Hebrews, but he escaped enslavement and instead grew up in the royal palace. Still, he identified with the Hebrews and took up their cause. When he killed the Egyptian slave master, he fled Egypt and found refuge

---

[1] See Genesis 28:3, 35:11, and the explanation of the Abrahamic covenant in chapter 2.
[2] See Genesis 1:28, 9:1, and the explanation of the Priestly creation blessings in chapter 1.

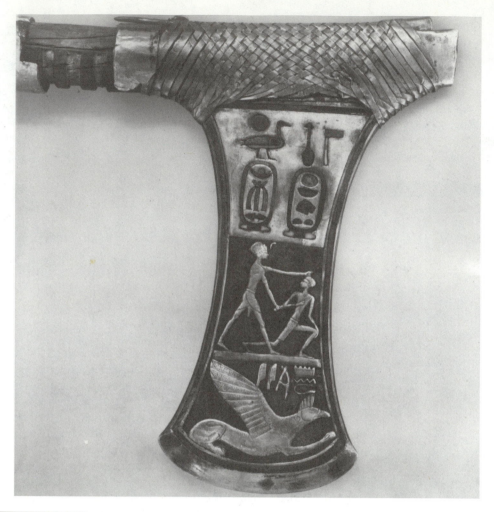

The picture on this ceremonial ax depicts the Egyptian Pharaoh Ahmose smiting an enemy. Ahmose was credited with expelling the Hyksos, who were foreign invaders of Egypt. Jacob, Joseph, and all the Hebrews were likely considered part of the Hyksos group and thus were disliked by indigenous Egyptians.

in Midian. There he met the God who later would engineer the escape of the Hebrews from Egypt.

Egyptian history provides a context for understanding the changed attitude of the Egyptians toward the Hebrews implied in verse 8: "a new king rose to power over Egypt, who did not know about Joseph." A group of non-Egyptians ruled northern Egypt from 1750 to 1550 B.C.E., a break in the flow of indigenous Egyptian government called the Second Intermediate Period. Called the **Hyksos**, they came from Syria and Palestine—the same general area the ancestors of the Hebrews called home (Figure 3.2). If Joseph was part of the foreign influx of the Hyksos, this would explain how he could come to such prominence and power in Egypt.

For obvious reasons these Hyksos were not appreciated or well liked by indigenous Egyptians. They began to dominate and expel the Hyksos under Pharaoh Ahmose I (1552–1527 B.C.E.), when the eighteenth dynasty of Egyptian rule was inaugurated. If the traditional date of the Exodus early in the thirteenth century B.C.E. is accepted, the Pharaoh at the time of the Exodus was Rameses II (1290–1224 B.C.E.), the great empire builder of the nineteenth dynasty. The length of Hebrew oppression and captivity in Egypt may have been more than 200 years. The precise identity of the "new king...who did not know about Joseph" is impossible to discern, although he was presumably someone from the eighteenth or nineteenth Egyptian dynasty.

The Hebrews were made the slaves of the Egyptians. They were set to work on Egyptian building projects. Two sites are given by name, Pithom and Rameses. These have been identified as two Egyptian fortress cities in the eastern Nile delta region that were strategic in defending Egypt from Asian attack (see Figure 3.3).

EARLY MOSES (2–3)

Moses' encounter with God at the burning bush marks a turning point in Israel's history. It tells how Moses first met the God of Israel and was persuaded to go back to Egypt to engineer the release of the Israelites. It tells how he learned the identity of the God who would deliver the Hebrew people from bondage. The account is a mixture of Yahwist and Elohist material, with the Elohist predominating.

1 Moses was tending the flock of his father-in-law, Jethro, the priest of Midian; and he led his flock to the west side of the wilderness, and came to Horeb, the mountain of Elohim.

Jethro is the name of Moses' father-in-law in the Elohist source, **Reuel** in the Yahwist source. **Horeb** is the name the Elohist (as well as Deuteronomist) applies to the mountain of God, whereas in the Yahwist and Priestly sources it is called **Sinai**. Some scholars have suggested that Horeb and Sinai are not the same place. According to this view, Horeb would be located somewhere in Midian, and Mt. Sinai in the Sinai peninsula.

2 The angel of YHWH appeared to him in a flaming fire out of the middle of a bush. As Moses watched, the bush burned but it didn't burn up. 3 Moses said to himself, "I'm going to stop and observe this amazing thing! Why doesn't the bush burn up?" 4 When YHWH saw that Moses stopped to observe, Elohim called to him out of the middle of the bush and said, "Moses! Moses!" He replied, "Yes, I'm here." 5 He said, "Don't get any closer. Take your sandals off your feet. The place where you are standing is holy ground."

Verses 2–4a come from the Yahwist. Verse 2a serves as a summary statement for the story. Probably added later, it gives the story an explanatory framework so that we will understand that Yahweh did not appear directly to Moses (as implied

FIGURE 3.3 **BRICKMAKING IN EGYPT** From an Egyptian tomb painting dating to the eighteenth dynasty, laborers are shown processing the raw mud and forming the bricks that were used to construct walls and buildings.

in the body of the story) but indirectly in the form of an angel or messenger. The word translated *angel* can also mean messenger.

The "flaming fire" that is so prominently a part of this story is typical of the way God appears to the Israelites. In Genesis 15 he appeared to Abraham in a smoking fire pot. In the wilderness he will appear in a pillar of fire, as on Mt. Sinai.

Whereas God is referenced as Yahweh in verse 4a, note that in 4b the reference changes to Elohim, indicating the return of the Elohist form of the story.

> *6 He said, "I am the Elohim of your father, the Elohim of Abraham, the Elohim of Isaac, and the Elohim of Jacob." Then Moses hid his face, because he was afraid to look at Elohim.*

This verse explicitly associates the God of the Exodus with the God of the ancestors. Note also how the Elohist protects Moses from looking directly at God. Facing God directly is not allowed in Elohist theology. The fear of God is a powerful motif in the Elohist source.

The source switches back to the Yahwist in verses 7–8.

7 YHWH said, "I have seen the hardship of my people in Egypt. I have heard their cry for relief from their oppressors. I know of their suffering. 8 I have come down to deliver them from the grip of Egypt and bring them up out of that land to a good and spacious land, a land flowing with milk and honey, to the place of the Canaanites, the Hittites, the Amorites, the Perizzites, the Hivites and the Jebusites.

As always in this source, Yahweh is a caring and compassionate God. He hates to see his people suffer. He intends to remedy the situation by bringing the people to the land he had promised to give to Abraham's descendants. That is why these verses are here.

This land is described as "flowing with milk and honey." Obviously milk did not flow through the streams or honey ooze down the wadis. This is a picture of the wealth of the land. It supports cattle and all those flowering plants that support life.

The six nations listed here are often cited as inhabiting Palestine (for example, see Genesis 15:18–21, where these and more are listed).

The following verses, 9–15, come from the Elohist source.

9 The cry of the people of Israel has now reached me. I have seen the oppression with which the Egyptians mistreat them. 10 Go, I will send you to Pharaoh so that you can bring my people, the sons of Israel, out of Egypt."

Characteristic of the Elohist, God acts through an intermediary, in this case, Moses. The focus here is on the wrong of the Egyptians rather than on the suffering of the Israelites.

11 But Moses said to Elohim, "Who am I that I should go to Pharaoh and bring the sons of Israel out of Egypt?" 12 He said, "But I will be with you. This shall be the sign for you to know that I have sent you: when you have brought the people out of Egypt, you shall worship Elohim on this mountain."

Moses revealed his deep-seated feelings of inadequacy in serving as mediator. Humility is a sign of genuine godliness in God's prophets. The Yahwist source, which is not quite so adoring of Moses as the Elohist, portrays him as putting up more resistance. The sign God gave him was not something that would give him assurance right then and there, but would be a later confirmation of his calling.

13 Then Moses said to Elohim, "If I come to the people of Israel and say to them, 'The Elohim of your fathers has sent me to you,' and they ask me, 'What is his name?' what shall I say to them?" 14 Elohim said to Moses, "Ehyeh-asher-ehyeh." And he said, "Say this to the people of Israel, 'Ehyeh has sent me to you.'" 15 Elohim also said to Moses, "Say this to the people of Israel, 'YHWH, the Elohim of your fathers, the Elohim of Abraham, the

Elohim of Isaac, and the Elohim of Jacob, has sent me to you': this is my name forever, and thus I am to be remembered throughout all generations."

Moses asked God for his identification. Who are you, really? Which God are you?

God identified himself as the God of the fathers, later specified as the patriarchs Abraham, Isaac, and Jacob. Then God in a cryptic manner said, "Ehyeh-asher-ehyeh" is my name. This revelation of the divine name has given rise to reams of research and all kinds of speculation.

Most scholars acknowledge that *ehyeh* is a Hebrew verbal form meaning "I am." The whole phrase means "I am who I am," or "I will be who I will be." When the first-person verbal form *ehyeh* is transformed into the third-person form it becomes *yahweh*, which can be translated "he is." It has also been translated "he causes to be." But what this name really signifies is another question.

The name of God remains a mystery, maybe even deliberately so. At the same time God revealed it, he concealed its precise meaning. We can only speculate what "I am" means. Perhaps God was suggesting he was the only self-existing one. Others, relating the name to the verb "to be" in a causal sense, have said it is a statement about God's creative power: "I am the one who calls into being."

Whatever the deeper meaning of the divine name Yahweh, it is the name by which all the textual sources identify the God of Israel from this point on. It is the name of Israel's patron deity, a name that is specifically associated with the covenant. From this point on, even the Elohist uses YHWH instead of Elohim for the divine name, though not to the exclusion of the name Elohim.

The change of divine name is also noted in the Priestly source at Exodus 6:2–5. This account adds that the ancestors knew God by the name El Shaddai (probably meaning "God Almighty"), but through Moses and the Exodus he made himself known as Yahweh.

Having received acquaintance of the divine name, as well as of his mission, Moses went back to Egypt and presented Yahweh's demand to Pharaoh that Israel be allowed to leave. Pharaoh refused to budge. Only after a devastating series of disasters did he allow them to go.

PLAGUES (4–11)

Moses was commissioned by God to go to the ruler of Egypt and demand the release of the Israelites. The actual commissioning just occurred at the burning bush, a story told mostly by the Elohist. Going to Pharaoh, Moses functioned as a prophet, that is to say, as a messenger delivering a message in the name of God:

4:21 YHWH said to Moses, "When you return to Egypt, make sure you perform before Pharaoh all the miracles I have given you the ability to do. Yet, I will harden his heart so that he will not allow the people to leave. 22 You must say to Pharaoh: 'This is what YHWH says: Israel is my first-born son, 23 I command you, "Let my son leave so that he may worship me"; if you refuse to let him leave, I will slay your first-born son.'"

After Pharaoh refused to honor God's command, God sent a series of disasters against Egypt, the plagues. These were intended to give evidence of Yahweh's power and force Pharaoh to let the Hebrews go.

Apparently there were two different traditions of the plagues. The core plague narrative comes from the Yahwist source. The Yahwist provides evidence of eight plagues[3] and focuses on the role of Moses. The Priestly additions highlight the role of Aaron. The final text of the plagues narrative has ten plagues. Table 3.1 compares the core Yahwist version of the plagues with the Priestly edition, which added two plagues. An asterisk marks the plagues added by the Priestly edition.

TABLE 3.1 THE J AND P VERSIONS OF THE PLAGUES

Yahwist	Completed Priestly Edition
1. Water to blood 7:14–18, 20b–21a	1. Water to blood 7:19–20a, 21b–22
2. Frogs 7:25, 8:1–4, 8–15	2. Frogs 8:5–7
	*3. Gnats 8:16–19
3. Flies 8:20–32	4. Flies (J)
4. Cattle plague 9:1–7	5. Cattle plague (J)
	*6. Boils on humans and animals 9:8–12
5. Hail 9:13–35	7. Hail (J)
6. Locusts 10:1–20	8. Locusts (J)
7. Darkness 10:21–29	9. Darkness (J)
8. Death of firstborn 11:1–8	10. Death of firstborn (J)

The plagues of gnats and boils were added to the original series by the Priestly editor who was responsible for the final edition. The last plague was the death of the firstborn human and beast among the Egyptians. This was the last straw. It impelled Pharaoh to drive the Israelites out of his land.

EXODUS FROM EGYPT (12–15)

The Israelites did not experience the devastating tenth plague. Moses instructed each Israelite family to kill a lamb as a substitute for its firstborn. They must paint blood from the slaughtered lamb on the door frames of their homes. When God saw this evidence of the sacrifice on a house, he would "pass over" that house, sparing its firstborn son.

This means of avoiding the tenth plague developed into a ceremonial meal called the **Passover**. During this meal the lamb, which had been roasted, was

---

[3] Compare Psalm 78:43–51, which also lists eight.

eaten along with unleavened bread, that is, bread made without yeast. The yearly celebration of the Passover developed into one of Israel's most important festivals. It stood as a memorial to freedom and God's compassion on his people. Called the Passover seder, it is still celebrated each year in the spring by Jews around the world. A form of the Passover also still survives in the Christian Eucharist, or Lord's Supper.

Expelled from Egypt, the Israelites fled into the Sinai peninsula. Pharaoh had second thoughts about allowing the Israelites to leave. He mustered his troops and chariots and chased after the Israelites. After a short time, the Israelites were caught between the army of Pharaoh and the waters of the Red Sea. The Israelites escaped through the sea while the army of Pharaoh drowned.

All three sources, the Yahwist, Elohist, and Priestly, contribute to the story of the Exodus and the crossing of the Red Sea. It is the most important event in Israel's historical experience, the culmination of the great work of God in delivering the Israelites from oppression and bondage. It would forever be remembered as the event that revealed the great love, compassion, and power of Israel's God. Its significance to the religious faith of Israel can hardly be overestimated.

The exit from Egypt and deliverance at the Red Sea is the salvation high point in Israel's history. It became the paradigm saving event. When at a later time Israel was alienated from the land and oppressed by foreign overlords, especially the Babylonian exile, they recalled the great Exodus from Egypt and this gave them hope.

Being the core salvation event that it is, it should not be surprising to find out that each major source tradition has something to say about it. The text given below indicates the sources by a change in indentation. First read the entire story, then go back and read each of the sources separately. The Elohist is less extensive here. You will see how the Yahwist and Priestly sources tell the story coherently if read on their own.

Yahwist	Elohist	Priestly	Editor

13:17 When Pharaoh sent the people away, Elohim did not lead them by way of the Philistine's land, though that was near. For Elohim said, "The people might change their mind when they meet opposition, and return to Egypt." 18 So Elohim brought the people around via the wilderness Red Sea route. The sons of Israel went up from the land of Egypt in battle formation. 19 Moses took the bones of Joseph with him. He had made the Israelites swear, "When Elohim visits you, take my bones with you from there."

20 They traveled from Sukkoth and encamped in Etam, on the edge of the desert.

21 And YHWH was going ahead of them by day in a pillar of cloud to lead them in the right direction, and at night by a pillar of fire to illumine them, so they could travel day and night. 22 The pillar of cloud did not disappear during

Yahwist	Elohist	Priestly	Editor

the day, nor the pillar of fire at night. 14:1 And YHWH spoke to Moses, 2 "Tell the sons of Israel to return and encamp in front of Pi-hahirot, between Migdal and the sea, in front of Baal-zephon; you shall camp facing it, by the sea. 3 And Pharaoh will say of the sons of Israel, 'They are wandering aimlessly in the area. The wilderness has shut them in.' 4 I will harden Pharaoh's heart, and he will chase them. In that way I will get glory for myself over Pharaoh and his entire army. The Egyptians will know that I am YHWH." They did so.

5 When the king of Egypt was told that the people had escaped, Pharaoh and his officials changed their minds concerning the people. They said, "What have we done, letting Israel abandon our work?" 6 So he got his chariot ready and took his army with him: 7 six hundred elite chariots and all the other chariots of Egypt with officers commanding all of them.

8 YHWH hardened the heart of Pharaoh king of Egypt and he chased the Israelites, who boldly had just left.

9 The Egyptians pursued them, all Pharaoh's horses and chariots, his charioteers and his army.

They overtook them where they were encamped by the sea, by Pi-hahirot, in front of Baal-zephon.

10 As Pharaoh drew near, the Israelites looked back. The Egyptians were catching up to them. Being terribly afraid they cried out to YHWH.

11 They said to Moses, "Was it because there weren't enough graves in Egypt that you took us out to die in the wilderness? What are you trying to do to us by bringing us out of Egypt? 12 Didn't we tell you this back in Egypt, 'Leave us alone and let us serve the Egyptians'? It would have been better for us to serve the Egyptians than to die in the wilderness."

13 Moses said to the people, "Don't be afraid. Have faith. Witness the deliverance that YHWH will accomplish for you today. The Egyptians you see today you will never see again. 14 YHWH will fight for you. You don't have to do anything."

15 YHWH said to Moses, "Why are you crying out to me? Tell the Israelites to go forward. 16 Lift up your staff and stretch out your hand over the sea and divide it so that the Israelites can go into the sea on dry ground. 17 I will harden the hearts of the Egyptians so that they will go in after them. In that way I will get glory for myself over Pharaoh and his entire army, his chariots and his charioteers. 18 Then the Egyptians will know that I am YHWH, after I

have gotten glory for myself over Pharaoh, his chariots and his charioteers."

19 The angel of Elohim who was going ahead of the Israelite army moved and went behind them.

The pillar of cloud moved from in front of them and stood behind them.

20 It came between the Egyptian army and the Israelite army.

The cloud and the darkness were there. It lit up the night. Neither came near the other all night.

21 Moses stretched out his hand over the sea.

YHWH drove back the sea with a strong east wind all night and turned the sea into dry land.

And the waters were divided. 22 The Israelites went into the sea on dry ground. The waters formed a wall on their right and on their left. 23 The Egyptians pursued them, going into the sea right after them, all of Pharaoh's horses, chariots and charioteers.

24 At the morning watch YHWH looked down from the pillar of fire and cloud upon the Egyptian army. He threw the Egyptian army into a panic. 25 He clogged their chariot wheels so that they maneuvered clumsily. The Egyptians said, "Let's get away from the Israelites, for YHWH is fighting for them against Egypt."

26 YHWH said to Moses, "Stretch your hand out over the sea so that the water will come back upon the Egyptians, upon their chariots and charioteers." 27 So Moses stretched out his hand over the sea.

The sea returned to its normal depth by dawn. The Egyptians fled from it, but YHWH tossed the Egyptians into the sea.

28 The waters returned and covered the chariots and the charioteers, the entire army of Pharaoh that had followed them into the sea. Not one of them survived. 29 But the Israelites had walked through the sea on dry ground. The waters had formed a wall on their right and on their left.

30 Thus YHWH saved Israel from the Egyptians that day. Israel saw the Egyptians dead on the seashore. 31 Israel saw the marvelous work that YHWH did against the Egyptians. The people feared YHWH, and put their faith in YHWH and in his servant Moses.

Compare the two accounts closely and you will see notable differences in emphasis. In particular, note that the Yahwist and the Priestly versions seem to tell the story of the miracle somewhat differently.

Yahwist source: 14:21b

YHWH drove the sea back with a strong east wind all night and turned the sea into dry land.

According to the Yahwist, the people were saved when God sent a wind to drive back the sea. In this version God acted directly. In the Priestly version, the miracle is more spectacular, with the water rising up on either side of the traveling Israelites.

Priestly source: 14:21a, 22–23
Moses stretched his hand over the sea, and the waters were divided. The Israelites went into the sea on dry ground. The waters formed a wall on their right and on their left.

Compare God's role in the accounts. Notice how God acted indirectly through Moses in the Priestly version. In the Yahwist version, Yahweh alone is credited with the feat.

Overall, the Red Sea tradition of the Yahwist places primary focus on Yahweh and his activity. He was the one who saved Israel. He was present in the cloud. Moses' only role was to reassure the people that they would be saved. The Yahwist strand concentrates less on the details of the miracle and more on the faith response of the people. The Israelites moved from fear to faith as they stood back and saw what Yahweh had done.

On the other hand, the Red Sea tradition of the Priestly source has much more interaction between Yahweh and Moses. Yahweh mostly speaks to Moses. And rather than God acting directly, Moses mediated the deliverance in this story as he stretched out his hand to separate the sea. As additional evidence of indirect approach, note that Yahweh instigated the Exodus crisis in the first place by hardening Pharaoh's heart so that his glory would be revealed in the miraculous deliverance (see Figure 3.4).

Chapter 15 celebrates the victory over Pharaoh in a poetic song of triumph. Moses and his sister **Miriam** led the people in thanksgiving to God: "I will sing to YHWH, for he has triumphed gloriously; horse and rider he has thrown into the sea." Moving on from the shore of the Red Sea, the Israelites traveled to Mt. Sinai, where Yahweh would make a covenant with them.

WILDERNESS JOURNEY (16–18)

After the escape from Egypt, Moses led the Israelites to the place of the burning bush so that they could meet Yahweh. Figure 3.5 shows the probable route of the Exodus.

On the way to Mt. Sinai Moses led the people to Rephidim in the wilderness, expecting to find much-needed water there. But the water turned out to be undrinkable. The people turned on Moses and blamed him for their predicament. God instructed Moses to strike the rock (the location is called Horeb). Water flowed out of the rock and the people drank.

Then the Amalekites fought with the Israelites. Joshua led the counterattack, and the Israelites prevailed as long as Moses' arms were raised to God. This episode is notable because it introduces the Amalekites, who are a persistent Israelite enemy. By being the first ones to attack the new nation, the Amalekites get the honor of being the prototype of the enemy of God's people. Always attentive to the worship dimension of Israel's experience, the Elohist notes that

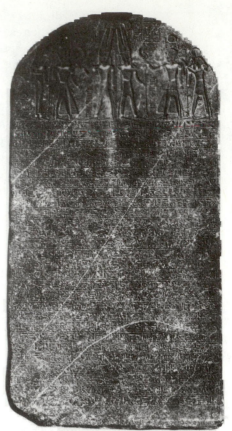

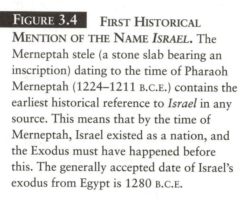

FIGURE 3.4 **FIRST HISTORICAL MENTION OF THE NAME *ISRAEL*.** The Merneptah stele (a stone slab bearing an inscription) dating to the time of Pharaoh Merneptah (1224–1211 B.C.E.) contains the earliest historical reference to *Israel* in any source. This means that by the time of Merneptah, Israel existed as a nation, and the Exodus must have happened before this. The generally accepted date of Israel's exodus from Egypt is 1280 B.C.E.

Moses built an altar there in commemoration of the event and called it "Yahweh is my banner."

Jethro, Moses' father-in-law, met the people in the wilderness. Observing that Moses was exhausting himself with the administration of the community, he convinced Moses to delegate all but the most difficult cases to subordinates. Jethro, called the priest of Midian, also made a most remarkable confession. He acknowledged that Yahweh was greater than any other god because he delivered the people from Egyptian oppression. Then Jethro offered sacrifices to God. The Elohist is showing how outsiders, too, can perceive the greatness of Israel's God and worship him.

SINAI COVENANT TRADITIONS (CHAPTERS 19–40)

The second half of the book of Exodus, as well as the entire book of Leviticus and a portion of Numbers, takes Mt. Sinai as its geographical setting. Here at Mt. Sinai the Hebrews received the definitive revelation from Yahweh.

The distinctive identifiers of the J and E sources are not apparent in Exodus 19–24 and 32–34, so it is difficult to assign specific passages to either of these sources with a great deal of confidence. The lack of identifying characteristics

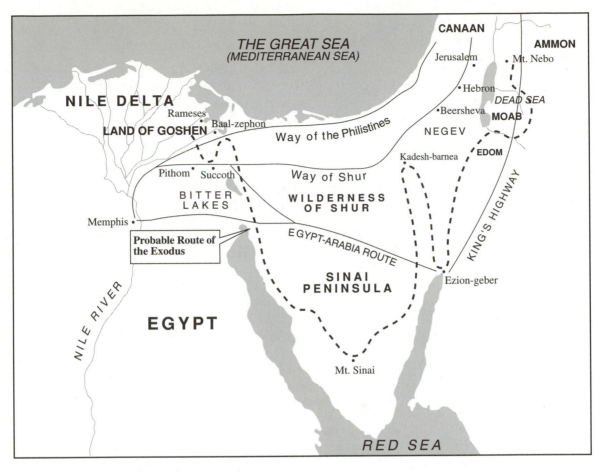

FIGURE 3.5   MAP OF EGYPT, THE SINAI, AND CANAAN SHOWING THE POSSIBLE
ROUTES TAKEN BY THE HEBREWS

may be due to the origin of these materials. They may have come from diverse
sources and were appropriated by J or E with minimal reworking.

THEOPHANY ON THE MOUNTAIN (19)

Moses brought the Hebrews to the mountain in the wilderness where earlier he
had met God. Upon arrival God first met with Moses, then he appeared to all
the people. In our examination of chapter 19 we will segment it into paragraphs
by literary source.

Introduction (P)

*1 On the third new moon after the people of Israel had gone forth out of
the land of Egypt, on that day they came into the wilderness of Sinai. 2*

And when they set out from Rephidim and came into the wilderness of
Sinai, they encamped in the wilderness;

Verses 1–2a are attributed to the Priestly source, which typically tracks the itinerary of the Israelites as they traveled from Egypt to the Promised Land. The connection between the Exodus event and the giving of the covenant is drawn explicitly by this passage.

God to Moses (E)

and there Israel encamped before the mountain. 3 And Moses went up to
Elohim, and YHWH called to him out of the mountain, saying, "Thus you
shall say to the house of Jacob, and tell the people of Israel: 4 'You have
seen what I did to the Egyptians, and how I bore you on eagles' wings and
brought you to myself. 5 Now then, if you will obey my voice and keep my
covenant, you shall be my own possession among all peoples (though all
the earth is mine), 6 and you shall be my kingdom of priests and holy na-
tion.' These are the words which you shall speak to the children of Israel."

Verses 2b–9 are exclusively the work of the Elohist. The destination of the people was the mountain of God, as the Elohist refers to it; here, mountain for short. God's statement is a well-formed literary unit with an introduction ("Thus you shall say") and a conclusion ("These are the words which you shall speak"). Here, Israel is called the house of Jacob. You may recall that the Elohist hails from the north, and that Jacob was most closely associated with the northern territories, including the city Bethel.

The Elohist stresses the conditional character of covenant. The people will remain God's adopted people if they demonstrate obedience as defined in the covenant. They were separated from the rest of the nations to become God's special possession. Yet, the Elohist also knows of Israel's broader responsibilities. They will minister to the remainder of humanity as a kingdom of priests.

Moses to the Elders (E)

7 So Moses came and called the elders of the people, and set before them
all these words which YHWH had commanded him. 8 And all the people
answered together and said, "All that YHWH has spoken we will do." And
Moses reported the words of the people to YHWH. 9 And YHWH said to
Moses, "Now I am coming to you in a thick cloud, so that the people may
hear when I speak with you, and may also believe you forever." Then
Moses told the words of the people to YHWH.

Moses presented God's program to Israel's leadership. They agreed to the general terms of the meeting, which designated Moses as the intermediary between God and the people. The Elohist portrays Moses as the prototypical prophet, standing between God and Israel to mediate the covenant. The people could not view God directly, but when they saw the luminescent cloud they were assured of God's presence and knew he was conferring with Moses. Here, as throughout Israel's history, a glowing cloud was evidence of God's presence.

In the next section, largely attributable to the Yahwist, God tells Moses how to prepare the people for their meeting.

Yahweh to Moses (J)

> *10 And YHWH said to Moses, "Go to the people and consecrate them today and tomorrow, and let them wash their garments, 11 and be ready by the third day; for on the third day YHWH will come down upon Mt. Sinai in the sight of all the people. 12 And you shall set bounds for the people round about, saying, 'Take heed that you do not go up into the mountain or touch the border of it; whoever touches the mountain shall be put to death; 13 no hand shall touch him, but he shall be stoned or shot; whether beast or man, he shall not live.' When the trumpet sounds a long blast, they shall come up to the mountain." 14 So Moses went down from the mountain to the people, and consecrated the people; and they washed their garments. 15 And he said to the people, "Be ready by the third day; do not have intercourse with a woman."*

This version implies that God will appear directly to the people. Consequently, the people had to prepare themselves ritually in order to meet Yahweh. Here in the Yahwist version the people meet God directly, contrasting with the Elohist version where Moses is the intermediary between God and the people.

The people made themselves ritually clean, a process called *consecration*. The instructions in verse 15 were obviously directed at the male population. Note the directive: Do not have intercourse with a woman. Laws of ritual purity demanded refraining from sexual intercourse.

Theophany on the Mountain (J and E)

> *16 On the morning of the third day <u>there were thunders and lightnings, and a thick cloud upon the mountain, and a very loud trumpet blast. All the people in the camp trembled.</u> 17 <u>Then Moses brought the people out of the camp to meet Elohim; and they took their stand at the foot of the mountain</u>. 18 And Mt. Sinai was wrapped in smoke, because YHWH descended upon it in fire; and the smoke of it went up like the smoke of a kiln, and the whole mountain quaked greatly. 19 <u>And as the sound of the trumpet grew louder and louder, Moses spoke, and Elohim answered him in thunder</u>. 20 YHWH came down onto Mt. Sinai, on the top of the mountain. YHWH called Moses to the top of the mountain and Moses went up.*

Verses 16a, 18, and 20 belong to the Yahwist; 16b–17 and 19 belong to the Elohist (here underlined). The Elohist has God reveal himself on the mountain in meteorological phenomena: thunder and lightning and a thick cloud. These signs are all associated with the thunderstorm. In this portrayal Yahweh appears as a storm God. Baal of Canaanite religion was also associated with these features.

The people were fearful of God and trembled—the "fear of God" is one of the characteristic themes of the Elohist.

In verse 18, which bears the marks of the Yahwist source, the appearance of Yahweh is more like a volcanic eruption than a thunderstorm. Smoke ascended in a column, and there was an earthquake. This is evidence that we might have two different theophany traditions in Exodus 19, an Elohist–Horeb one and a Yahwist–Mt. Sinai one.

Verse 20 returns us to the Yahwist version. God came down upon the mountain, and Moses went up—yet another time. Moses is in communication with God, but, according to the Yahwist, it must take place on the mountain. The Elohist makes things easier. A meeting tent would be constructed, which would be a place Moses could go to confer with God.

A paradigm of divine communication is established in the theophany passages of Exodus 19. It was on the mountain of God, called Mt. Sinai by the Yahwist and Horeb by the Elohist, that direct revelation from God was delivered. This narrative lays down the foundation of all the laws that follow in Exodus, Leviticus, and Numbers. All of the moral and ritual legislation articulated in those books is presented as having been delivered to the people by God through Moses. All laws, to be authoritative, must be associated with Moses and God's revelation on the mountain.

SINAI COVENANT (20–24)

Although the Elohist source contains some ancestral material, the heart of this source is the Exodus from Egypt and covenant making on the mountain. The Elohist contains one of our best records of the nature of the covenant relationship God established with his people.

Covenant traditions were stronger in the northern territories of Israel than in Judah to the south. The covenant accounts of the Elohist provide a direct link to these covenant traditions going all the way back to the time before the monarchy. Before becoming a nation, the tribes had formed a federation headquartered at Shechem. There they periodically engaged in covenant renewal ceremonies that affirmed their solidarity and confirmed their faith in Yahweh. The ceremony led by Joshua in Joshua 24 is the most elaborately described of these ceremonies.

It is probable that the Elohist was associated in some way with prophetic circles in Israel, most likely with an Elijah group. Moses' activities on the mountain of God are very much like those of the northern prophet Elijah who came after him.[4] Points of similarity include the following. Moses, like Elijah, was the champion of God confronting a difficult and contentious Israelite people. Each had a loyal disciple, Joshua and Elisha, respectively. And both Moses and Elijah traveled to Horeb (see 1 Kings 19).

The covenant making that takes place in Exodus was a response to the miraculous escape from Egypt that God had arranged. In this covenant God formalized his relationship with the Hebrews by, in effect, putting it down in a contract—what governments would call a treaty.

---

[4] The story of Elijah is summarized in chapter 9.

Ten Commandments (20:1–17)

God devised a set of basic moral mandates that, once put into effect, defined Israel's relationship to him and to each other. Delivered to the Israelites through Moses, they are commonly called the **Ten Commandments**, also called the **Decalogue**.[5] The core commandments appear to come from the Elohist, with elaborations to some of the commandments coming from later Priestly additions.[6]

All of these commands are addressed in the second-person plural to all the people of Israel. The ambiguity of "you" in English (is it singular or plural?) is not present in the Hebrew text.[7] The commandments are introduced in the following way.

1 And Elohim spoke all these words, saying, 2 "I am YHWH your Elohim, who brought you out of the land of Egypt, out of the house of enslavement.

This contains the prologue to the commandments that emphasizes the loving character and concern of God in rescuing the Israelites from slavery. Because he delivered them from slavery he comes to them with a covenant. The implication of this prologue is that obedience to these commands would be Israel's expression of appreciation, and not an onerous imposition from a distant and demanding God.

3 "You may not have any other Elohim (gods/God) except me.

This command prohibits devotion to any God but Yahweh. Perhaps to your surprise, it does not categorically deny the reality of other gods.

4 "You may not make for yourself a sculpted image, or any representation of anything that is in heaven above, or on the earth below, or in the water under the earth. 5 You may not bow down to them or serve them; for I YHWH your Elohim am a possessive god, visiting the guilt of the fathers upon the children, upon the third and the fourth generations of those who disown me, 6 but showing loyalty to the thousandth generations of those who love me and keep my commandments.

This command prohibits using any physical form to represent Yahweh. Nothing that God has created could ever adequately represent him. The only thing that bears a likeness to God is humankind, which was created in his image, "after

---

[5] This Exodus 20 set of Ten Commandments is sometimes called the ethical decalogue to distinguish it from the ritual decalogue of Exodus 34 that comes from the Yahwist source.

[6] A virtual duplicate of these Ten Commandments can be found in Deuteronomy 5.

[7] Different religious traditions number the commandments differently. The traditional Jewish division finds the first commandment in verse 2: "I am YHWH your Elohim" and joins verses 3 and 4 into the second commandment. Some Christian traditions begin numbering the commandments with verse 3, so the first commandment is "You may not have any other gods except me." The Roman Catholic and Lutheran branches of Christianity combine the "no other gods" and "no images" statements into one commandment and divide the coveting commandment into two parts: commandment 9 is "you shall not desire your neighbor's house" and commandment 10 is "you shall not covet your neighbor's wife."

his likeness," according to Genesis 1. This command to appropriately honor God stresses the seriousness with which God treated loyalty and disloyalty.

The reference to heaven above, earth below, and water under the earth in the formulation of this command suggests that the Israelites had a tri-level concept of the cosmos. This was also evident in the creation narrative of the Priestly source.

> 7 *"You may not take the name of YHWH your Elohim in vain; for YHWH will not hold him guiltless who takes his name in vain.*

This command originally intended to prohibit taking false oaths. But more than that, it also forbade disrespect shown to God by using his name wrongly or frivolously. God's name was special. It was the nearest the Israelites came to possessing any part of God, and had to be treated with the utmost care. Later Jewish practice takes this prohibition so seriously that the name of God, and even the word *God*, was never spoken, with phrases such as "the Lord" and "the Name" used in its place, and G_d used in print.

> 8 *"Remember to keep the Sabbath day holy. 9 Six days you may work, and do all your jobs; 10 but the seventh day is a Sabbath to YHWH your Elohim; in it you shall not do any work, you, or your son, or your daughter, your male servant, or your female servant, or your cattle, or the resident alien who lives with you; 11 for in six days YHWH made heaven and earth, the sea, and everything in them, and ceased from work on the seventh day; by doing this YHWH blessed the Sabbath day and made it a holy day.*

The sabbath command institutionalizes a periodic cessation of typical daily work. The term *sabbath* literally means "to cease, to stop, to rest." The warrant for such a time of inactivity is the pattern of creation in which God completed his efforts in six days and ceased work by the seventh. The explanation from creation was added by the Priestly writer to provide the reason for the institution.[8]

> 12 *"Honor your father and your mother, so that your days in the land which YHWH your Elohim gives you may be numerous.*

Respect must be shown to ancestors and especially parents. A high social value was obviously placed on children's duty to care for parents. Note that this is the only command that has the promise of blessing attached to its observance.

> 13 *"You must not murder.*

This is a prohibition of murder, and not of killing generally. Certainly capital punishment was mandated for many offenses in the Hebrew Bible.

---

[8]The Deuteronomy 5 restatement of this command warrants Sabbath rest by recalling Israel's period of slavery in Egypt and God's deliverance. In that light, Sabbath rest commemorates Israel's freedom.

14 *"You must not commit adultery.*

In its original setting this command primarily prohibited sexual relations with another man's wife. This prohibition against the sexual promiscuity of married persons is aimed to protect the blood line of offspring. This was a crucial issue in matters of inheritance where the father wants to be sure he has sired his heir.

15 *"You must not steal.*

Stealing in the first instance probably applied to persons rather than property in the biblical world. Kidnapping was a common ancient practice (see Exodus 21:16) and this commandment was intended to provide for personal security. Later it was extended to material property.

16 *"You must not bear false witness against your neighbor.*

Deceitfulness and perjury are in view, perhaps first of all in a legal setting. But the commandment extends to a general protection of personal reputation that is crucial for maintaining social order.

17 *"You must not covet your neighbor's estate: that is, you must not covet your neighbor's wife, or his male servant, or his female servant, or his ox, or his ass, or anything that belongs to your neighbor."*

This is the only command that was intended to regulate attitude rather than behavior. The reason is clear. Coveting, or deeply desiring what is not one's own, is a state of mind that often leads to breaches of the other prohibited behaviors. By implication its opposite, a contentment with what God had already provided, was commanded.

The commands naturally divide into two general categories. The first commands define behaviors that apply to the people's relationship to God. They define that relationship as an exclusive one demanding their total loyalty. The latter commands define behaviors that apply to relationships within the community. Together, these categories constitute the essence of covenant. Put positively they command this: Love God and your neighbor as yourself.

Most of the Ten Commandments have the form of **absolute law**, also termed *apodictic law*. The commands, in other words, are unconditional. They apply with no "ifs, ands, or buts." Even though most of these commands are negative in form ("do not do this"), this does not imply that God's requirements were oppressively restrictive. Instead, they merely place certain general types of actions and attitudes out of bounds, but beyond that leave a rather wide latitude for freedom of action. They were certainly not perceived as oppressive by the Israelites, who found delight in God's law (see, for example, Psalms 1 and 119). Although cast in the negative, they can be considered general policy statements that were intended to shape the broader religious and moral character of the nation.

The Book of the Covenant (20:18–23:33)

The **Book of the Covenant**, also called the **Covenant Code**, is the earliest biblical set of covenant laws and is found in Exodus 20:22–23:19. Probably going back to premonarchic traditions, it seems to have been an independent collection predating the Elohist, but preserved by the Elohist. Supporting a premonarchic setting is the observation that the material of this law code reflects a livestock economy rather than a settled agricultural or urbanized economy.

The Book of the Covenant is introduced with a narrative describing the theophany and the people's reaction to it.

> *20:18 Now when all the people witnessed the thunder and the lightning and the sound of the trumpet and the mountain smoking, the people were afraid and trembled; and they stood far away. 19 They said to Moses, "You speak to us, and we will listen; but do not let Elohim speak to us, otherwise we will die." 20 Moses said to the people, "Do not be afraid. Elohim has come to test you, and so that you may be aware of his fearfulness. Then maybe you will not sin."*

After he gave the Ten Commandments, God again appeared in the phenomena of the storm theophany, heralded by a trumpet. The people were terrified of the appearing of God. "Fear of Elohim" is very important in this narrative, as in the Elohist source as a whole. Out of fear of being too close to God the people again enlisted Moses as their intermediary. Moses assumed the role of the prophet and explained that God was putting them through this experience so they would be impressed with his power and think twice before sinning.

> *21 The people stood far away, while Moses drew near to the thick cloud where Elohim was. 22 And YHWH said to Moses, "This is what you should tell the people of Israel: 'You have seen for yourselves that I have spoken with all of you from heaven. 23 You must not make me into a god of silver, and you must not make for yourselves gods of gold.'"*

Moses approached God, who was in the form of a thick dark cloud. The cloud was the visible evidence of God's presence. The Covenant Code proper begins with verse 22. Note that a change from the preceding verse is evident; the divine name changes from Elohim to Yahweh.

Yahweh impressed upon them that they were encountering the God of heaven. The prime directive was the absolute prohibition of making statuary representations of God. The God of heaven cannot be represented by metal images as the god of the Canaanites could.[9]

This general prohibition of idols and the prescription concerning the type of altar that could be used (verses 23–26) precede the main body of laws, which is introduced with the preface, "These are the ordinances which you

---

[9] The statement prohibiting "gods of gold" no doubt has the golden calves of Jeroboam in view. He is the king who set up golden calves in cult centers in Dan and Bethel in the tenth century B.C.E. This act of idolatry became the epitome of wickedness to the Deuteronomic historian of the monarchy. See chapter 9.

must place in front of them." (21:1). The typical form of these ordinances in the Book of the Covenant differs from the form of the Ten Commandments. The Book of the Covenant contains **case law**, also called *casuistic law*. This type of law has the form "If . . . then." An example of case law follows: the law of the goring ox.

> 21:28 *"If an ox gores a man or a woman to death, the ox must be stoned, and its flesh may not be eaten; but the owner of the ox will not be liable. 29 But if the ox has had the habit of goring in the past, and its owner had been warned but had not kept it restricted, and it kills a man or a woman, then the ox must be stoned, and its owner also must be put to death."*

Typical of case law, a condition is specified, in this case, an ox that gores a person. The consequence is then specified: the ox must be killed, but the owner may not benefit from it by eating the meat. In this case, the owner is not held responsible.

In this case, a subcategory that would result in a much harsher punishment is specified. If the ox had the habit of terrorizing the community and the owner did nothing to prevent it, and it kills someone, the owner will be held directly responsible and must be put to death along with the animal. In addition to injury laws, the Book of the Covenant contains laws regarding slaves, death sentences, bodily injuries, a calendar of feasts, and other religious duties.

Covenant Confirmation (24:1–15)

After the content of the covenant had been revealed, the covenant relationship was ceremonially initiated. Chapter 24 contains two traditions relating to the covenant ratification ceremony. In the first tradition, only representatives of the people approach God, and only Moses gets close.

> 1 And he said to Moses, *"Come up to YHWH, you and Aaron, Nadab, and Abihu, and the seventy elders of Israel, and worship at a distance. 2 Moses alone shall come near to YHWH; but the others shall not come near, and the people shall not come up with him."*

This tradition is continued in verses 9–11, which describe the meal Moses, Aaron, Nadab, Abihu, and the elders ate with God in a covenant confirmation ceremony. In this version the people take part in the covenant ceremony only indirectly, through their leaders.

> 9 Then Moses and Aaron, Nadab, and Abihu, and the seventy elders of Israel went up, 10 and they saw the Elohim of Israel; and there was under his feet what looked like a sapphire stone street, like the heaven itself for clarity. 11 And he did not lay his hand on the leaders of the people of Israel; they saw Elohim, and ate and drank.

All in all this is a remarkable story, quite uncharacteristic of the Elohist's theology, which guards people from seeing God. Perhaps this is a story from a different source than the Elohist. Here Israel's leadership actually sees God. And even though they saw God, they did not die.[10]

In the second version all the people gathered together for sacrifices and directly took part in the covenant ceremony.

> *3 Moses came and told the people all the words of YHWH and all the ordinances; and all the people answered with one voice, and said, "All the words which YHWH has spoken we will do." 4 And Moses wrote down all the words of YHWH. And he got up early in the morning, and built an altar at the foot of the mountain, along with twelve pillars, matching the twelve tribes of Israel. 5 And he sent young men of the people of Israel, who offered burnt offerings and sacrificed peace offerings of oxen to YHWH. 6 And Moses took half of the blood and put it in basins, and half of the blood he threw against the altar. 7 Then he took the book of the covenant, and read it in the hearing of the people; and they said, "All that YHWH has spoken we will do, and we will be obedient." 8 And Moses took the blood and threw it upon the people, and said, "Here is the blood of the covenant which YHWH has made with you, in agreement with all these words."*

In this ceremony the altar represents God. When Moses took blood from the sacrifices and sprinkled it on the altar and on the people, the two parties were bound together in the covenant. Blood represents life in the Hebrew Bible. This ceremony symbolically states that both parties were pledging their lives to the endurance of the covenant relationship.

Note how the people agreed to the covenant with full knowledge of its requirements. The Book of the Covenant[11] was read directly to them and the people knowingly accepted the covenant requirements. The covenant would remain in effect as long as they were obedient. As with Exodus 19:3b–6, here too the Elohist covenant has a condition attached to it, the condition of the people's obedience.

After the covenant ratification ceremonies, God called Moses up to the mountain to receive copies of the law.

> *12 YHWH said to Moses, "Come up to me on the mountain, and wait there. I will give you the stone tablets containing the law and the commandment, which I have written for their instruction." 13 So Moses got up with his servant Joshua, and Moses went up into the mountain of Elohim. 14 And he said to the leaders, "Wait here for us, until we return. For now, Aaron and Hur are with you; whoever has a problem, let him go to them." 15 Then Moses went up onto the mountain, and the cloud covered the mountain.*

---

[10] Eating such a meal at the conclusion of a covenant is also found in Genesis 31:46, 54. Eating a ceremonial meal in the presence of God is an important component in later sacramental meals such as the Eucharist or Lord's Supper.

[11] The book of the covenant mentioned in verse 7 is usually understood to refer to the Book of the Covenant (Exodus 20:22–23:33) we just examined.

These verses record yet another trip up the mountain and seem to contain yet another tradition of meeting God. Joshua and Hur are introduced in this account, while Nadab and Abihu are absent.

Moses received the stone tablets containing "the law and the commandments." This seems to be a reference to the Ten Commandments, but one cannot be sure. Moses already had something written down, according to 24:17 (the Book of the Covenant). In any case, these stone tablets are the ones Moses smashes in Exodus 32.

Reading through these chapters we might get exhausted for Moses—he has been going up and down, up and down. It is really difficult to sort out how many trips he has actually taken. Apparently, these chapters have a very complicated editorial history. Each tradition has Moses going up the mountain, and they were all retained in the final version.

COVENANT BREAKING AND REMAKING (32–34)

No sooner was the covenant made and ratified by the people than the Israelites demonstrated their willingness, even eagerness, to disregard it.

The material between chapters 24 and 32 is a collection of Priestly legislation on the Tabernacle, the ark, and the priesthood. When we get back to the narrative following this ritual legislation, we come to the dramatic and sad affair of Israel's covenant breaking.

The Golden Calf (32–33)

Moses took longer on the mountain than the people had expected. Thinking that they had lost Moses and thus their contact with God, they demanded that **Aaron** provide a substitute means to approach the deity. Responding to their urging, Aaron solicited gifts from the people and proceeded to make a **golden calf**:

32:4 He took the gold from them, cast it in a mold, and made a calf image. They said, "These are your gods, Israel, who brought you up out of the land of Egypt." 5 When Aaron saw it, he built an altar before it and made a proclamation, "Tomorrow there will be a feast to YHWH."

At least two things are obvious from this brief excerpt. First, the Israelites were committing idolatry, and that idolatry was centered on a golden calf. The golden calf unmistakably echoes the golden calves that Jeroboam set up in Dan and Bethel when he established religious centers in the Northern Kingdom of Israel in the tenth century B.C.E. The negative way in which the golden calf is viewed in Exodus is a veiled prophetic condemnation of Jeroboam's golden calf centers. The statement, "These are your gods," in the plural, when only one calf was molded, evokes the multiple calves of Jeroboam. In fact, these words are the same as the words of Jeroboam in 1 Kings 12:28.

Second, the Elohist was not an admirer of Aaron. His story directly implicated Aaron the high priest in this act of idolatry and turning away from Yahweh. Why would the Elohist want to put Aaron in a bad light? Because the Elohist and his group had migrated to Jerusalem after the fall of Israel in 722

B.C.E. They were unable to practice their livelihood in Jerusalem, even though they were Levites, because the family of Aaron, also of the tribe of Levi, had the priestly craft locked up tight. The privilege of serving as a priest was inherited, and one had to be from the family of Aaron of the tribe of Levi to qualify. Aaron, understandably, came under their severest criticism.

Turning back to the story, we see that God was extremely angry and resolved to destroy the people and begin building a nation from Moses. Moses argued with God, suggesting that if all the Israelites died, the Egyptians would have triumphed. He urged God, "Turn from your fierce anger, change your mind, and do not bring catastrophe on your people." God responded to Moses' plea and voided his threatened punishment.

God instructed Moses to return. Going down the mountain he saw the pagan revelry of the people. In anger he smashed the two tablets containing the record and testimony of the covenant. This effectively signaled that the covenant had been broken because the people had compromised their loyalty by worshiping another god.

The people had gone wild in celebration, and Aaron was held to blame.

32:25 When Moses saw that the people were out of control (for Aaron had let them get out of control, to the point that they were a menace to anyone opposed to them), 26 Moses stood at the entrance to the camp and said, "Who is on YHWH's side? Come over to me!" 27 He said to them, "This is what YHWH, the Elohim of Israel, says: 'Each of you, strap your sword to your side. Go back and forth through the camp, from gate to gate. Each of you kill your brother, your friend, and your neighbor.'" 28 The Levites did what Moses commanded, and about three thousand people fell on that day. 29 Moses said, "Today you have dedicated yourselves to YHWH, each at the cost of a son or a brother. You have earned a blessing today."

This incident demonstrated the loyalty of the Levites to the cause of Yahweh. They were the only ones who had not succumbed to the lawlessness of golden calf worship. The story, again, pictures the Levites in a very favorable light; not surprisingly, for the Elohist was a Levite.

Yahweh then told Moses to take the people and head on to the Promised Land without their God. But Moses refused to go on alone. He met with Yahweh in the tent of meeting, where Yahweh appeared in the pillar of cloud. Again, Yahweh changed his mind and decided to continue on with the Israelites. As proof of his commitment, the glory of Yahweh passed by Moses, and Moses caught a glimpse of the backside of Yahweh.

The tent of meeting is the symbol of Yahweh's dwelling among the people in the Elohist story. He never mentions the ark of the covenant, only the tent of meeting. Perhaps this is because the Elohist was from the north, where Shiloh was situated. Shiloh was the home of the tent shrine during the days of the tribal federation. The Yahwist never mentions the tent of meeting. The ark ended up in Jerusalem, and that was the focus of worship there. That was of interest to the Yahwist, who was from Judah, but the Elohist ignored it, because he was not allowed to minister in Jerusalem.

Ritual Decalogue (34)

Exodus 34 contains ten commandments (a decalogue) that appear to be earlier than the ten commandments found in Exodus 20—the famous Ten Commandments. It is called the ritual decalogue because the laws relate to worship practices. Yahweh placed these covenant obligations upon the people in order for them to remain in a favorable relationship with him. Various schemes have been devised to come up with the exact ten suggested by 34:28. This is one possible enumeration.

1. You may not worship any other god, because YHWH, whose name is Jealous One, is a jealous God. (14a)
2. You may not make molten gods for yourselves. (17)
3. Every firstborn human or animal belongs to God. (19a)
4. No one may appear before God without an offering. (20c)
5. You can work six days, but on the seventh day you may not work. (21a)
6. You must observe the feast of weeks, the first fruits of the wheat harvest, and the feast of ingathering. (23)
7. You may not offer the blood of my sacrifice with anything leavened. (25a)
8. The Passover sacrifice must not remain until the morning. (25b)
9. You must bring the best of the first fruits of the soil to the house of Yahweh your God. (26a)
10. You may not boil a kid in its mother's milk. (26b)

Most of these laws concern the duties of individual nonpriestly Israelites regarding proper worship of God and ritual obligations. The Yahwist is concerned primarily with the people's relationship to Yahweh in a religious context, and especially that they honor him exclusively and in the proper manner.

The Yahwist had little else to contribute to Israel's story from the time the people left Sinai to their encampment on the edge of the Promised Land.

Mesopotamian Law Collections

The legal traditions of Israel stand within a well-developed context of legally ordered societies in the ancient Middle East and Egypt. There are many points of contact with other ancient law codes. Many ancient Middle Eastern cities have yielded texts through the work of archaeologists. At least seven law codes have been found. The earliest one is the Sumerian code of Ur-Nammu, dating to the twenty-second century B.C.E.

The most famous collection is the **Code of Hammurapi**. Hammurapi was a Babylonian ruler from the eighteenth century B.C.E. (see Figure 3.6).

The code begins with Hammurapi's calling "to promote the welfare of the people . . . to cause justice to prevail in the land, to destroy the wicked and the evil that the strong might not oppress the weak." (Pritchard 1969:164). It is important to note that Israel shared with her neighbors an ideal of justice that would be administered by a righteous king. David and Solomon were thought to epitomize this ideal.

FIGURE 3.6 **THE HAMMURAPI STELE** The Code of Hammurapi contains 282 laws chiseled onto a slab of basalt rock. On the top there is a picture of Hammurapi kneeling in prayer before the sun god Shamash, the god of justice. This stele was obviously a monument of some type, and not first of all a reference manual for the use of judges at court. Perhaps it served to give public testimony to the character of Babylonia's king as a promoter of justice and right.

There are strong similarities between the Code of Hammurapi and certain Israelite legal material, especially the Book of the Covenant. For instance, as with the Israelite laws, the Code of Hammurapi contains the law of retaliation (*lex talionis*), which prescribes punishment in kind.

Code of Hammurapi (§§196–197)
   If a man has destroyed the eye of another man, they shall destroy his eye. If he has broken another man's bone, they shall break his bone.

Book of the Covenant (Ex 21:23–25)

If any injury occurs, you shall take life for life, eye for eye, tooth for tooth, hand for hand, foot for foot, burn for burn, wound for wound, beating for beating.

While such physical retaliation may seem brutal, in fact, it was humane in its day. Specifying restitution in kind prevented resort to harsher means, typically the death penalty, for such offenses.

TABERNACLE DESIGN AND CONSTRUCTION (25–31, 35–40)

Certainly, for the Priestly writer, the covenant established with Israel from Mt. Sinai was essential. But for this writer, the most important aspect of the Sinai experience was receiving the gift of the Tabernacle. The Tabernacle was the portable tent shrine that served as God's place of residence among his people throughout their wilderness travels.

A great deal of text is spent on the Tabernacle shrine, first detailing the plans for the worship center (Exodus 25–31) and then describing its construction (Exodus 35–40) (see Figure 3.7). The Tabernacle assured the Israelites that God would be present with them throughout their history. So much time was spent on the Tabernacle because the main duty of the priesthood was to facilitate the meeting of Yahweh and his people.

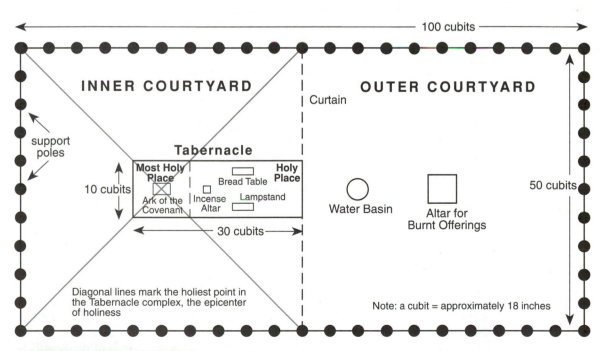

FIGURE 3.7   LAYOUT OF THE TABERNACLE COMPLEX

In addition to the portable tent shrine, the Israelites constructed the many implements, utensils, and articles of ceremonial clothing they would need to perform their ritual service. Included in the list are the ark of the covenant to store the covenant documents, the table for the bread of the presence, the lampstand (*menorah* in Hebrew), and the altars of incense and burnt offering.

OVERALL SHAPE OF EXODUS

As with Genesis, the book of Exodus contains material from the Yahwist, Elohist, and Priestly sources (see Table 3.2 for the distribution of sources). They have been integrated in such a way as to tell a profound story. At its most basic level, the canonical form of Exodus—especially the way the story of the Exodus was placed before the Sinai traditions—conveys a deep truth concerning the relationship of God's salvation and Israel's life. The flow of the story says that God gave special treatment to the Israelites because of his love for them and out of faithfulness to the ancestral promises. Only after delivering them from slavery did he formalize the relationship with a covenant. Only then did he expect commitment from them. In other words, obedience to Torah, as defined by the Sinai covenant, was expected, but only as the response to the deliverance of the Exodus and not as a precondition of experiencing God's care and salvation.

Furthermore, the book of Exodus helps us to place the phenomenon of biblical law in perspective. Law plays an unmistakably important role in the Torah. The books of Exodus, Leviticus, and Numbers contain a large percentage of legal material and ritual regulation. In spite of its bulk, we must note that all this technical material is embedded within historical narrative. Biblical laws do not stand isolated but are associated with the historical experience of Israel. This provides them with a grounding in Israel's experience with Yahweh and comes with his authority.

This helps us to understand the overall purpose of law in its setting within the Hebrew Bible. Law was not given as a set of conditions to be met in order to establish a relationship with God. The narrative demonstrates that the relationship, by the time of the Exodus, was already a long-standing one. Rather, the purpose of covenant law structures was to preserve an already-established bond between God and his people. In this perspective, law served to define the shape Israel's obedience would need to take in order to sustain that relationship.

If we closely examine Exodus, Leviticus, Numbers, and Deuteronomy, we find that they contain many collections of legislation, including the Ten Commandments (in two versions, Exodus 20 and Deuteronomy 5), the Covenant Code (Exodus 20:22–23:33), the Ritual Decalogue (Exodus 34), Ritual Laws (Leviticus 1–16), the Holiness Code (Leviticus 17–26), and most of the book of Deuteronomy. Viewed with an eye to each collection's source and historical context, we would see that they come from different settings, some of them no doubt later than the time of Moses. Yet all of them are in one way or another associated in these narratives with the figure of Moses. This molding was deliberate, as Moses was considered the prime lawgiver of Israel. For any legal tradition to have full legitimacy it would have to be associated with him.

TABLE 3.2   LITERARY SOURCES OF THE BOOK OF EXODUS[12]

	Yahwist (J)	Elohist (E)	Priestly (P)	Editor
Transition				1:1–5
New Generation			1:6–7	
Enslavement		1:8–12	1:13–14	
Infanticide	1:22	1:15–21		
Moses' birth and early years	2:1–23a			
Israel's cry			2:23b–25	
Moses' call	3:1–8, 16–22; 4:1–31	3:9–15	6:2–25; 7:1–9	6:26–30
Plagues: Moses versus Pharaoh	5:1–6:1; 7:14–29; 8:1–28; 9:1–7, 13–34; 10:1–29; 11:1–9		7:10–13; 9:8–12	11:9–10
Exodus	12:21–23	12:24–39; 13:1–16	12:1–20, 40–49	12:50–51
Red Sea crossing	14:5–7, 10b, 13–14, 19b, 20b, 21b, 24, 27b, 30–31; 15:1–18	13:17–19; 14:11–12, 19a, 20a, 25a; 15:20–21	13:21–22; 14:1–4, 8, 9b, 10a, 10c, 15–18, 21a, 21c, 22–23, 26–27a, 28–29	13:20; 15:19
Marah	15:22b–25a			15:22a, 27
Commands		15:25b–26		
Food			16:2–36	16:1
Water		17:2–7		17:1
Amalekites		17:8–16		
Jethro		18:1–27		
Horeb/Sinai	19:10–25	19:2–9; 20:18–21	19:1	
Decalogue		20:1–17	additions	
Covenant Code		20:22–23:33		
Horeb/Sinai		24:1–18		
Tabernacle design			25:1–31:11	
Sabbath command			31:12–18	
Golden calf		32:1–33:11		
Theophany	34:1–13	33:12–23		
Decalogue	34:14–28			
Moses' face aglow			34:29–35	
Tabernacle construction			35–40	

[12] This is a condensed version of the table found in Friedman (1987), pp. 250–52.

Table 3.2 categorizes the legal collections and narratives of the book of Exodus according to their reputed literary sources.

QUESTIONS FOR REVIEW

1. Summarize the Egyptian historical context for the Exodus.
2. Where and when did God reveal his name to Moses, and how was this related to the Exodus?
3. What is the Passover, and how is it related to the Exodus from Egypt?
4. What different collections of biblical law are found in the book of Exodus, and how do they differ?
5. What was the Tabernacle and what was its function?

QUESTIONS FOR DISCUSSION

1. The book of Exodus brings together two great human themes, namely, freedom from oppression and rule by law. What is the relationship between these two themes? Why was it important, and what effect did it have, that both are associated with Israel's deity and, in fact, became realities through his initiative?
2. Why was it important for Israel to associate its legal tradition with Moses and with God's appearing on Mt. Sinai? What effect did this have on the nature and authority of law in Israel? How does this compare with the foundation of law and the grounding of authority in modern nation–states?
3. Describe the various ways God revealed his presence and made himself known in the book of Exodus. In what ways was God visible, and in what ways invisible? What does this imply about Israel's understanding of the nature of its God and its life in his presence?

FOR FURTHER STUDY

General studies. Childs, Brevard H. (1974). *The Book of Exodus*. Old Testament Library. Philadelphia: Westminster Press. A commentary on the text of Exodus, with detailed notes and bibliography.

Sarna, Nahum (1986). *Exploring Exodus. The Heritage of Biblical Israel*. New York: Schocken Books. A narrative exposition of the book of Exodus.

Topical studies. Baltzer, Klaus (1971). *The Covenant Formulary in Old Testament, Jewish, and Early Christian Writings*. Philadelphia: Fortress Press.

Harrelson, Walter (1980). *The Ten Commandments and Human Rights*. Overtures to Biblical Theology. Philadelphia: Fortress Press. The core of the book is an exposition of the Decalogue; it views the Ten Commandments as a charter of human freedom.

McCarthy, Dennis J. (1978). *Treaty and Covenant*. Analecta Biblical 21a. Rome: Biblical Institute Press.

Redford, Donald (1992). *Egypt, Canaan and Israel in Ancient Times*. Princeton, N.J.: Princeton University Press. Uses textual and archaeological evidence to explain the relationship between Egypt and Israel from early history to the destruction of Jerusalem.

WORKS CITED

Friedman, Richard Elliott (1987). *Who Wrote the Bible?* Englewood Cliffs, N.J.: Prentice-Hall.

Pritchard, James B. (1969). *Ancient Near Eastern Texts Relating to the Old Testament*. 3d ed. with supplement. Princeton, N.J.: Princeton University Press.

Leviticus and Numbers: Ritual and Holiness

Names and Terms to Remember

Aaron	Holiness Code	Phineas
atonement	holy/holiness	Priestly Code
Balaam	kosher	sacrifice
Balak	Levites	
Day of Atonement/Yom Kippur	manna	

The book of Leviticus immediately follows the book of Exodus and continues the story of the Hebrews in the wilderness of Sinai. In this chapter we treat the books of Leviticus and Numbers together because they are similar in many ways. Both contain a good deal of religious legislation, all of it God's revelation to Moses at Mt. Sinai. Both are predominantly concerned with matters of ritual, sacrifice, and priesthood. And both books have their setting in the Sinai wilderness between Egypt and the Promised Land.

The content of these books is a departure from the types of material we have been studying in Genesis and Exodus. There is no drama to relate because nothing really "happens" to the Hebrews in Leviticus and the first part of Numbers. For the most part, the material is a record of laws. The story of the journey to the Promised Land resumes only in the latter half of the book of Numbers. We turn first to the book of Leviticus.

BOOK OF LEVITICUS

At this point, the writer of a Hebrew Bible textbook might offer an apology for having to deal at all with the book of Leviticus. Most readers think that Leviticus is boring and dull. After all, it deals with such things as sacrifices, worship rules, priests, and purity. What could be more uninteresting?

Well, maybe the text and its subject matter are not all that gripping. But what is important is the vision of Israel's ideal relationship with God that this material conveys. Leviticus deals with this fundamental question—How can God and humankind meaningfully relate to one another and live together in harmony?

STRUCTURE OF LEVITICUS

Leviticus in its entirety belongs to the Priestly tradition of the Pentateuch. The last verse of the book gives Leviticus a historical and geographical setting at Sinai during Israel's sojourn in the wilderness. Thus, as it stands, the book is a continuation of the story of God's revelation to Moses that began in the book of Exodus. The complete Mt. Sinai revelation actually runs through the entire book of Leviticus and continues until Numbers 10:10. This collection of moral and ritual laws can be referred to as the **Priestly Code**. It constitutes the bulk of the Priestly source of the Pentateuch that we began examining in Genesis and Exodus.

The book of Leviticus consists of various collections of religious laws. The main sections of Leviticus are as follows:

1–7	Laws of sacrifices
8–10	Ordination rites of the priests
11–16	Laws of Purity
17–26	Holiness Code
27	Appendix on religious vows

A close examination of the language style and presumed sociological setting of the laws suggests that in their current form they have come from the exilic period or later. Other books of the Hebrew Bible, Ezekiel, Ezra, and Chronicles, have a close affinity with the Priestly Code, and they are all postexilic. But the traditions behind many of the Levitical laws go back as early as the premonarchic period. Some of the laws even have analogies to early Mesopotamian legal material. Though some of the individual laws and collections were preexilic, they were given their final shape by a priestly group in the exilic period.

The **Holiness Code,** found in chapters 17–26, is the most distinctive subcollection of the Priestly Code. While the issue of the dating of the Priestly writings as a whole is still under discussion, it is quite likely that the Holiness Code comes from the period of the late Israelite monarchy. It appears to have been composed in Jerusalem not long before the Babylonian exile. As its name suggests, it is preoccupied with matters of holiness, and the constant refrain is "you (Israel) must be **holy** for I (Yahweh) am holy."

Given the highly detailed and monotonous nature of the priestly legislation, it is easy to get lost in minutiae. An overall framework is needed for understanding the meaning of the laws. There are three general approaches to the biblical system of clean and unclean things. The hygiene theory claims that the laws were intended to keep Israelites from things that had a high likelihood of doing bodily harm, such as pork and contagious skin diseases. The cultic theory argues that objects and actions that were associated with forbidden pagan cults were forbidden to Israelites, and so were declared unclean.

The structuralist theory discerns in the system of regulations an ordered world view that defined things as either normal or abnormal. Deviations from normalcy were classified as unclean. The structuralist approach is followed by Wenham (1979) and Jenson (1992).

PRIESTLY WORLD VIEW

Leviticus, along with the rest of the Priestly Code, employs a distinctive way of looking at the world in relation to God. Everything in the world is graded in **holiness,** to use Jenson's terminology, in relation to Yahweh. The result is that everything in the world has a set place in the divine order, and everything derives its meaning from its relationship to God.

In particular, the major religious dilemma facing the Israelites was this: How could a perfectly holy and righteous God ever be in direct contact with a sinful people? The rituals and regulations laid out in all their detail in Leviticus explain how. In essence it comes down to this. The Israelites must become a holy people, sometimes also called a holy nation: "You must be holy, for I am holy."

The terms that are critical to this world view and that need explanation are *holy* and *clean*, and their opposites, *profane* and *unclean*. According to Leviticus 10:10, the Aaronic priesthood is "to distinguish between the holy and the profane, and between the unclean and the clean."

Holiness is a difficult notion to grasp. Holiness has to do with the qualitative difference and total otherness of God. He is of a fundamentally different category than human beings. Because he is totally different from humankind, especially in regard to his absolute power and perfection, humans need to respect his total otherness and stand in awe of him. Though the analogy is woefully imperfect, the awesomeness of God is like the awe ordinary citizens feel when they stand in the presence of the president of the United States, or better yet perhaps, in the presence of a sports superstar, renowned actor, or famous rock musician.

The priestly rituals of Leviticus were intended to distance humans from their imperfect world so they could assume a measure of the holiness that belongs to God. In order for the Israelites to become holy they must refrain from sin and stay away from uncleanness. In the priestly world view, sin was closely associated with uncleanness. Leviticus categorizes the world into clean and unclean things and describes procedures that can move one from the state of uncleanness to cleanness. Some of the most important rituals involve animal sacrifices and reconcile penitent Israelites to God if sin and uncleanness have separated them. In short, Leviticus defines the procedural means by which God and humankind can dwell together in harmony.

The normal or natural state of objects and persons is to be clean, and a clean thing can be elevated to the status of holiness through the process of sanctification (literally, making holy). Clean things can become unclean through contact with other unclean things, such as dead bodies. In order for an unclean person or thing to get back to the state of cleanness, it must be purified. Once clean, it could then be sanctified through an additional procedure. Once made holy, it was devoted exclusively to divine service.

Holy persons and things can be rendered profane, or unholy, through ritual procedures of decommissioning or by contact with something unclean. A profane thing may be clean or unclean, but in either case, it cannot be in direct contact with Yahweh.

The notions of clean and unclean are related to the way the priestly group understood the created world and was the expression of a comprehensive world view in which everything had its proper place. The process of putting things in their places began with creation as told in the Priestly version (Genesis 1). On the second and third days of creation the three elements of sky, earth, and sea were delimited through a process of separation. Then, God fashioned living creatures for each environment, and each environment's creatures received standard habits and means of locomotion that defined them. In particular, the sky was populated by noncarnivorous winged creatures. The earth was inhabited by four-legged creatures that chewed the cud and had cloven hooves. The sea was inhabited by creatures with scales and fins.

Creatures that did not fit the standard profile were considered unclean, for example, crabs and lobsters. Although they live in the sea, they have legs rather than fins. Thus, cleanness was related to a notion of "normalness," and cleanness was protected by keeping things separate and in their proper environment.

TABLE 4.1   HOLINESS CONTINUUM[1]

	Very Holy	*Holy*	*Clean*	*Unclean*	*Very Unclean*
Places	holy of holies	holy place	court	camp	outside the camp
People	high priest	priest	Levites, clean Israelites	minor impurities	major impurities, the dead
Rituals	sacrifice (not eaten)	sacrifice (priests eat)	sacrifice (nonpriests eat)	purification (1 day)	purification (7 days)
Times	Day of Atonement	festivals, Sabbath	common days		

Food sources that did not meet the priestly definitions of normalcy were unclean and therefore unfit for human consumption. The definitions of clean and unclean are also called the laws of **kosher**.

Definitions of normalcy and laws for maintaining separations apply to many things besides food. For example, they dictate which kinds of thread can and cannot be woven together to make fabric, and which kinds of people can and cannot marry. As a whole, priestly legislation defined a total lifestyle regulating diet, hygiene, social activity, and the calendar.

Table 4.1 is an attempt to synthesize the priestly world view. It relates the basic areas of life to the notions of holiness and cleanness.

The following discussion is a survey of the particular areas of existence and reality (derived from the left vertical column of Table 4.1) as they are defined by the range of holiness (the top horizontal row).

Holy Places

A fundamental concern of the priestly code was the creation of a place where Israel could dwell in the presence of God. Throughout the Hebrew Bible a key to Israel's welfare is living in proximity to the presence of God.

The place where Yahweh lived was the holiest place imaginable. The tabernacle complex, whose structure, service, and construction are described in Exodus 25–31 and 35–40, was the portable temple of the Israelites. Leviticus and Numbers contain many references to the structure and implements of the tabernacle.

Haran (1978) and Jenson (1992) explain the significance of the details of the structure. The tabernacle complex, as with the other symbols of Israel's ritual system, had zones of holiness. The direction of holiness moved from outside the

---

[1] This table derives from Jenson (1992: 37). Jenson develops a notion called the "holiness spectrum" and has a separate chapter on each dimension: spatial, personal, ritual, and temporal.

camp to the holy of holies. For each zone the priestly code defined who is allowed to be there, ending up with only the high priest in the holy of holies, and that on only one day each year. Gradations of holiness are evident also in the construction materials of the tabernacle complex, with fabrics and metals increasing in value moving with each level of holiness.

The symbolism of the tabernacle expresses two important themes of priestly theology. The first is the theme of the continuity of life. The floral designs on the walls of the tabernacle and implements suggest the "tree of life" artistic motif. The untarnishable gold of the implements and holiest room suggest the unchangeableness of God. The daily lamp-lighting ceremony symbolizes the light of God that never ceases.

The second is the theme of the presence of God. The tabernacle was considered to be the dwelling place of God. The tabernacle structure, as well as all the rituals, allows for God to be present among his people.

The portable feature of the tent of dwelling indicates that God was not sedentary but would be with his people wherever they went. This notion may have been especially important to the priests of the exilic period who shaped these texts, giving expression to their conviction, similar to Ezekiel's, that God was present to them even in exile away from the Promised Land.

Holy People

The priestly code defined the social and ritual roles of all people within Israel, and an examination of these roles reveals a hierarchy of holiness. Membership in social groups was based on family lineage, and roles were assigned accordingly. The tribe of Levi provided the officials who were authorized to perform religious functions. Both Moses and his brother **Aaron** were from this tribe.

Only direct descendants of Aaron could function as priests or become the high priest (see Figure 4.1). Priests were the only ones allowed to offer sacrifices and enter the sanctuary. The high priest could consult with God directly in the cloud and by means of divination dice called the Urim and Thummim. Other members of the tribe of Levi, those not of the family of Aaron, had duties outside the sanctuary itself, and in general assisted the Aaronic priests. This included guarding the sanctuary and dismantling and erecting it when it was moved. Israelites belonging to the other eleven tribes could not themselves perform religious rituals but had them done by priests.

A number of ritual descriptions and camp narratives serve to define the status and role of the tribe of Levi and of groups within it. Leviticus 8–9 describes the process of the ordination of Aaron and his sons. Leviticus 10 describes the deaths of Nadab and Abihu, two sons of Aaron, who illegally performed certain rituals. Numbers 8 describes the process of the ordination of the Levites. Numbers 16–17 narrates the rebellion of Korah and his followers (Levites, but not from the family of Aaron), who presumed to perform priestly rituals and were executed by God for it. This narrative also contains the story of the blossoming of Aaron's rod, which demonstrated the God-given authority of the tribe of Levi over the other eleven tribes. And Numbers 18 defines the responsibilities of Aaronic priests and other Levites.

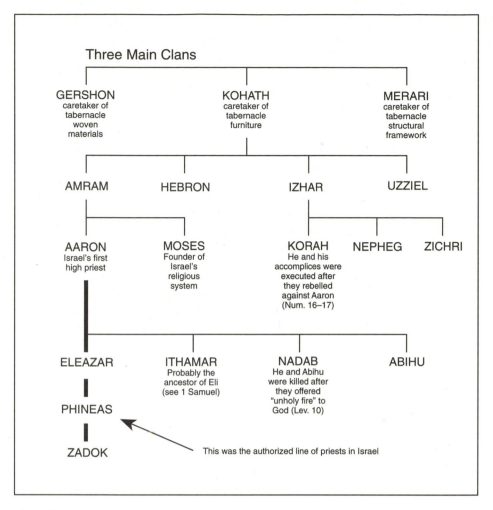

Three Main Clans

GERSHON
caretaker of
tabernacle
woven
materials

KOHATH
caretaker of
tabernacle
furniture

MERARI
caretaker of
tabernacle
structural
framework

AMRAM   HEBRON   IZHAR   UZZIEL

AARON
Israel's first
high priest

MOSES
Founder of
Israel's
religious
system

KORAH
He and his
accomplices were
executed after
they rebelled
against Aaron
(Num. 16–17)

NEPHEG   ZICHRI

ELEAZAR

ITHAMAR
Probably the
ancestor of Eli
(see 1 Samuel)

NADAB
He and Abihu
were killed after
they offered
"unholy fire" to
God (Lev. 10)

ABIHU

PHINEAS

ZADOK

This was the authorized line of priests in Israel

FIGURE 4.1   **THE TRIBE OF LEVI AND RITUAL ROLES** This diagram illustrates the structure of the tribe of Levi in relation to the roles assigned to particular members and families.

Sacrificial Rituals

The primary religious rituals of Israelite religion involved sacrifices and offerings. The priestly ritual system was complex, and the meaning of procedures was rarely explained. In most respects it is quite foreign to our way of thinking. Consequently, the precise theological significance of **sacrifice** is still open to debate.[2]

The rules of the priestly sacrificial system are laid out in Leviticus 1–7. There are five main types of sacrifice: whole burnt offering, grain offering, peace offer-

[2] Levine (1974, 1989) and Milgrom (1983, 1990) are two of today's most prominent interpreters of ancient Israelite ritual practice.

ing, purification offering, and reparation offering. Any given priestly ritual usually incorporated several different types of sacrifice.

The whole burnt offering may be considered the preeminent sacrifice. It gets this name because the entire animal was consumed by the fire on the altar. Such a sacrifice was made daily to Yahweh. The purpose of the sacrifice was to give something pleasing to God. It was not used for atonement for sins.

The purification offering, sometimes called sin offering, was used to purify a person after he or she had incurred an impurity of some kind, such as through childbirth, a skin disease, or contact with something dead. This offering was also used to secure forgiveness after a deliberate sin.

The reparation offering involved an offering of restitution; that is, if an action involved economic loss to someone else, reparation must be made to cover the loss, with an additional portion as punitive damages.

The grain offering indicates that not all sacrifices were bloody sacrifices of animals. Offerings of agricultural produce were given as gifts to God, and a portion of such sacrifices was used to support the priests.

The last category of offering is the peace offering. A portion of the meat of this sacrificed animal was retained for the food use of the person making the offering. This offering, sometimes called the fellowship sacrifice, drew the parties together, including God, in a festive meal. Meat was not often eaten in biblical times, so when it was, it was a time of celebration, and it was done in the presence of God.

The overall significance of sacrificial rituals may have been this. Various types of impurities and deliberate sins disturbed God's ordered universe. Sacrificial rituals were the mechanism by which disruptions within God's world were acknowledged and made right. The various rituals of purification brought one closer to the state of holiness so that one could live in proximity to God. This is the purification model of sacrifice that is argued by Milgrom (1983) and Jenson (1992).

Within this system sacrifice seems to play a significant role in the process of atonement. **Atonement**, reconciliation or "making at one," brings a person back into fellowship with God after a disruption in the relationship. In the priestly system, this could only be achieved through a blood sacrifice. Leviticus 17:11 is often taken as a key to priestly atonement theology.

> *For the life of the flesh is in the blood; and I have given it to you for making atonement for your lives on the altar; for, as life, it is the blood that makes atonement. (NRSV)*

Being the substance of life, blood was held in particular reverence. The blood of the sacrificed animal substituted for the life of the offending person and functioned to return that person back to fellowship with God.

Holy Times

Just as space was sacred or profane, so was time. The year defined the basic cycle of larger events and organized the cultic calendar. The year was defined by the solar calendar, but because months were defined by the cycle of the moon, there was a need to adjust the shorter twelve-month lunar year (354 days) to the solar year (365 days) by occasionally adding a thirteenth month.

There were longer periods of time, including the sabbatical year cycle (every seventh year was sacred) and the year of Jubilee (the year after seven sabbatical year cycles, that is, the fiftieth year). But the most important units of repeated time were the day, the week, and the month (which was defined by the moon). Months were labeled by number, with the year beginning in the spring.

The Sabbath, the seventh day of the week, was a day set apart from the others. Special rules governed activity on that day, mainly restricting what could be done.

Special yearly sacred days were also defined. There were five primary sacred times, all of which are still observed within Jewish communities (see Table 4.2); some of these correspond to calendrical moments in the Western world. Note, for example, that the spring equinox, Passover, and Easter all converge, and not by accident.

Israelites were required to be in Jerusalem for the observance of these festivals. They were worship occasions, and in the rabbinic period were marked by the reading of books from the Five Scrolls of the Hebrew Bible. For example, the Song of Songs was read on Passover, and the book of Ruth was read during the Feast of Weeks.

In addition to these festivals, other feasts and fasts were instituted later during the postexilic periods. Purim celebrates the deliverance of the Jews during the Persian period, as told in the book of Esther. The story of the rededication of the temple during the Greek period is told in the book of 1 Maccabees and is celebrated at Hanukkah, the Festival of Lights, which comes at the winter solstice. Fasts were instituted to memorialize tragic historical events, including the fall of Jerusalem and the destruction of the temple in 587 B.C.E.

TABLE 4.2   FEASTS AND HOLY TIMES

Sacred Time	Hebrew Name	Agricultural Occasion	Historical Association	Biblical Reference
Feast of Passover (Feast of Unleavened Bread)	Pesach	Spring barley harvest	The Exodus: deliverance from bondage and freedom	Exod. 12:6, Lev. 23:5–8, Num. 28:16–25, Deut. 16:1–8
Feast of Weeks (Pentecost)	Shavuot	Summer wheat harvest		Exod. 34:26, Lev. 23:9–21, Num. 28:26–31
Trumpets	Teruah		God's revelation at Sinai (?)	Lev. 23:23–25, Num. 29:1–6
Day of Atonement	Yom Kippur			Lev. 16, 23:26–32, Num. 29:7–11
Feast of Booths (Feast of Ingathering)	Sukkot	Autumn harvest	Wilderness wandering, harvest	Exod. 23:16, Lev. 23:33–36, Deut. 16:13–15

Features of holy place, holy people, holy time, and sacred ritual all come together in Leviticus 16, where the **Day of Atonement** ritual, in Hebrew called *Yom Kippur*, is described. Of all the sacred times, the Day of Atonement was considered the holiest. It was only on this day that anyone entered the Holy of Holies of the tabernacle, and later, the temple.

On the Day of Atonement the High Priest, here Aaron, offers a bull as a purification offering. Then he takes two goats. He slaughters one of them, collects its blood, and sprinkles it on the mercy seat, a term designating the lid of the ark of the covenant. After exiting the tabernacle, he places his hands on the head of the other goat, thereby transferring the sins of the people to this animal. Called the goat for Azazel in Hebrew (where *Azazel* may designate the underworld), this goat has come to be called the scapegoat. It was sent away into the wilderness to disappear, taking with it the sins of the people.

The book of Numbers, which follows Leviticus, also contains a collection of ritual laws.

BOOK OF NUMBERS

Numbers divides into three sections on the basis of content and geographical setting:

1:1–10:10	Priestly code (continued)
10:11–22:1	Journey from Sinai to Kadesh to Moab
22:2–36:13	Events in Transjordan

A short description of each of these sections follows.

PRIESTLY WORLD VIEW (CONTINUED)

Numbers 1:1–10:10 is a continuation of the priestly code. It is the final section of the Sinai legal tradition complex that extends all the way back to Exodus 19.

Chapters 1–4 describe the organization of the **Levites** and the arrangement of the camp. At the center stood the tabernacle. Closest to it were the Levites, and then came the other tribes. This layout is a component of the holiness continuum, where priests and Levites were the holiest class of people, as shown in Figure 4.2.

The priestly code defined a social hierarchy within Israel, not surprisingly putting the priests of the family of Aaron at the top of the scale. Next in descending order came the other families of the tribe of Levi. Of the remaining tribes, Judah was placed in a position of preeminence directly to the east, right near the entrance of the tabernacle compound. Lowest on the scale were resident aliens; that is, people not belonging to any tribe but living among the Hebrews. Farthest out were the foreign nations, by implication also furthest from God.

Additional laws of cleanness are given in following chapters, as well as regulations concerning the firstborn and the Nazirite vow. The common thread uniting all this material is a concern with the holiness of the people. They must be holy in order for Yahweh to remain in their midst.

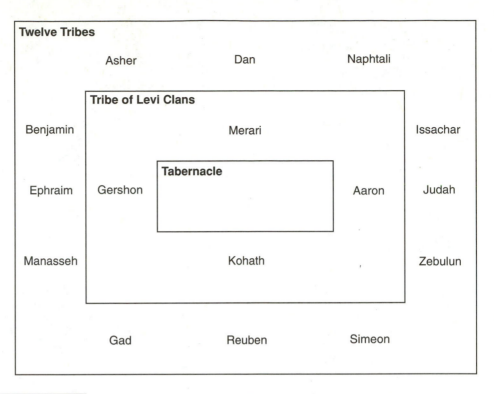

Twelve Tribes

Asher   Dan   Naphtali

Tribe of Levi Clans

Benjamin   Merari   Issachar

Tabernacle

Ephraim   Gershon   Aaron   Judah

Manasseh   Kohath   Zebulun

Gad   Reuben   Simeon

FIGURE 4.2 LAYOUT OF THE ISRAELITE CAMP The configuration of the Israelite camp shows how the clans and tribes were arrayed around the tabernacle in concentric regions of holiness.

JOURNEY FROM SINAI TO KADESH TO MOAB

With Numbers 10:11–22:1 we are back to material deriving from the three Pentateuchal sources, the Yahwist, Elohist, and Priestly. This block of material is historical narrative and describes the journey from Sinai to Kadesh, the long stay at Kadesh, and the journey to Moab (see Figure 4.3).

About a year after they had arrived in the Sinai wilderness, the cloud of God's presence lifted and signaled that Israel must move on to the Promised Land. The Israelites had a number of experiences in the wilderness, many at Kadesh, before they reached the edge of Canaan.

The people complained about the monotony of daily **manna** meals. Manna was the substance the people had been gathering as food, perhaps the sweet secretion of a certain insect on tamarisk bushes in the Sinai region. The people demanded meat. The strain of handling the complaints and demands of the people wearied Moses. In response, Yahweh instructed Moses to appoint seventy elders as assistants. Similar to Exodus 18, Moses commissioned officers of tens, fifties, hundreds, and thousands at Jethro's advice. Moses arranged the seventy men around the tent of meeting to receive their commission.

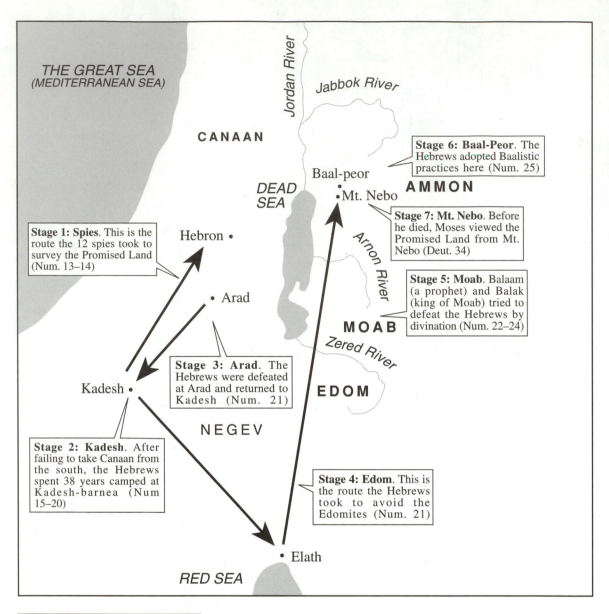

THE GREAT SEA
(MEDITERRANEAN SEA)

Jordan River

Jabbok River

CANAAN

DEAD
SEA

Baal-peor

Stage 6: Baal-Peor. The Hebrews adopted Baalistic practices here (Num. 25)

Mt. Nebo

AMMON

Stage 1: Spies. This is the route the 12 spies took to survey the Promised Land (Num. 13–14)

Hebron •

Stage 7: Mt. Nebo. Before he died, Moses viewed the Promised Land from Mt. Nebo (Deut. 34)

Arnon River

Stage 5: Moab. Balaam (a prophet) and Balak (king of Moab) tried to defeat the Hebrews by divination (Num. 22–24)

• Arad

Stage 3: Arad. The Hebrews were defeated at Arad and returned to Kadesh (Num. 21)

MOAB

Zered River

EDOM

Kadesh •

NEGEV

Stage 2: Kadesh. After failing to take Canaan from the south, the Hebrews spent 38 years camped at Kadesh-barnea (Num 15–20)

Stage 4: Edom. This is the route the Hebrews took to avoid the Edomites (Num. 21)

• Elath

RED SEA

FIGURE 4.3   THE JOURNEY FROM KADESH TO TRANSJORDAN

11:25 Then YHWH came down in the cloud and spoke to him, and took some of the spirit that was on him and placed it on the seventy elders. When the spirit took possession of them they prophesied, but did not keep doing it.

Two men who had been designated for leadership, Eldad and Medad, were not present at the tent. Nonetheless, they too received the spirit and prophesied in the middle of the camp. Joshua was upset over this, but Moses said, "Why are you upset? It would be good if all Yahweh's people prophesied." Yahweh had put his spirit on all of them.

Here the Elohist expresses his ideal of prophecy, that all the people would be inspired by God as were Moses and the other leaders. Moses is portrayed as the good and enlightened leader who is not trying to exalt himself. Rather, he wishes all the people would be close to God.

The special position of Moses is nonetheless reinforced in Numbers 12. Aaron and Miriam (Moses' brother and sister) challenged Moses after he married a foreigner. They claimed that Yahweh could also speak through them. The three of them went to the tent of meeting, where Yahweh appeared in the pillar of cloud and spoke to Aaron and Miriam:

> 12:6 *"Hear my words: If you have a prophet among you, I, YHWH, reveal myself to him in a vision, I speak with him in a dream. 7 With my servant Moses it is different. He is entrusted with my entire estate. 8 I talk with him mouth to mouth, plainly and not in riddles. He beholds the shape of YHWH. 9 Why are you not afraid to challenge my servant Moses?"*

Miriam was afflicted with a skin disease for seven days and remained outside of camp. Aaron was spared, but probably only because he was the high priest.

This story tells us many things. It reflects once again the disdain the Elohist had for Aaron because he had the audacity to challenge Moses. The Elohist had a special contempt for the Aaronid priesthood in Jerusalem. The story also demonstrates the high regard the Elohist had for Moses. Throughout the Elohist source, Moses is pictured as central to the purposes of God. Here we learn why. Moses was closest to God. He was not an ordinary leader but a prophet, and even more than just a prophet—God had put him in charge of the entire project.

A curious feature of the story told in Numbers is that many of these episodes, all of which take place after the giving of the covenant at Sinai, are duplicates of experiences they had on the first leg of the wilderness journey traveling from Egypt to Sinai. Table 4.3 indicates some of the duplications.

Presumably, the duplicate versions were retained because the independent sources each had the stories. Perhaps the retention of the duplications by the

| TABLE 4.3 | STAGES OF THE WILDERNESS JOURNEY |

Egypt to Sinai (Exodus)	Sinai to Canaan (Numbers)
1. Moses and his father-in-law: 18:1–27 (E)	1. Moses and his father-in-law: 10:29–32 (J)
2. Murmuring of the people: 16:1–12 (P)	2. Murmuring of the people: 11:1–6 (E)
3. Quails and manna: 16:13–35 (P)	3. Quails and manna: 11:4–35 (E)
4. Water from rock at Meribah: 17:1–7 (J and E)	4. Water from rock at Meribah: 20:2–13 (E)

editor signals that the character of the people had not changed from before Sinai to after.

The Numbers account of those wilderness experiences highlights the dissatisfaction of the people. They complained about the food, and God at the same time both fed them and punished them (chapter 11). Aaron and Miriam complained about Moses' leadership and God vindicated him (chapter 12).

Moses sent twelve spies into Canaan from Kadesh in order to survey its fortifications. Ten spies counseled the people not to invade Canaan; only Joshua and Caleb supported the attack that Yahweh commanded. Because the people refused to follow God's leading, God punished them by decreeing that they would die in the wilderness, and only their offspring, the second generation, would gain possession of Canaan (chapters 13–14).

Following this reversal, Korah, Dathan, and Abiram complained about the leadership of Moses and Aaron, and God destroyed them; then all the tribes took exception to the special privileges of the Levites, and God vindicated them (chapters 16–17). When Moses reacted arrogantly to the murmuring of the people, God punished him (chapter 20). When finally the people left Kadesh to go to their invasion staging area, the entire first generation had passed away. There was certainly a lesson here for that exilic generation looking to return home after Babylonian captivity.

Interspersed among these narrative accounts of Israel's wilderness experiences are chapters containing priestly regulations. Chapter 15 prescribes offerings that atone for inadvertent sins. Chapter 18 prescribes the portions of the offerings that can rightfully be claimed by priests. The red heifer ceremony of chapter 19 provides for cleansing and the restoration of holiness.

The logic of this cultic material intertwined with the narrative is understandable. The narratives all have to do with complaints and privileges: various groups complained that other groups or individuals received preferential treatment. The priestly cultic legislation settles matters of priestly privilege and provides the means to restore holiness after the kinds of sins that got the Israelites in trouble in the wilderness.

These same sins would plague the Israelites though their history. Thus, the historical material also becomes the occasion to illustrate the characteristic attitude of the Israelites, one of intermittent complaining and faithfulness. It also provides the means to overcome alienation from God and restore holiness.

EVENTS IN TRANSJORDAN

The third major section, Numbers 22:2–36:13, contains a variety of materials all set in Transjordan. Arriving in Transjordan, the Hebrews faced two significant threats. First, a Mesopotamian prophet named **Balaam** was hired by **Balak**, the king of the Moabites, to curse the Hebrews and thereby achieve victory for the Moabites (22–24). This is one of the most remarkable stories in the Hebrew

Bible. In it, Balaam's donkey talked to him and warned him about an angry angel that was ready to stop him from completing his mission.

When Balaam finally arrived in Moab to curse the Hebrews, he ended up blessing them each time he opened his mouth. Consequently, the Hebrews prevailed. The story reinforces the destiny of these people. Nothing could stop them, neither the mighty warriors of the Transjordan, nor supernatural divination. Directed and defended by Yahweh, they would surely enter the Promised Land.

The second threat in Transjordan was local religion. A local Baal shrine at Peor near the Hebrew camp attracted a number of Hebrew worshipers. Hebrew males were found engaging in ritualized prostitution in this Baal temple. But Aaron's grandson **Phineas** stood up for Yahweh and put an end to this particularly heinous form of false worship.

Following these narratives the last chapters of Numbers deal with inheritance laws, practices concerning the spoils of conquest, land boundaries, and tribal allotments. Clearly attention turned to those issues the Israelites would soon face as they entered the Promise Land west of the Jordan River. This third section of Numbers thus looks forward to and prepares Israel for the conquest of the land.

OVERALL SHAPE OF LEVITICUS AND NUMBERS

The priestly code of cultic legislation makes up the bulk of the books of Leviticus and Numbers. It consists of a variety of materials, some early and some late. It was edited into its final form in the exilic period.

But the material is not presented as a code book or simply as a list of laws. The editors made the deliberate move of framing all of the legislation as the revelation of Yahweh to Moses on Mt. Sinai. All of the laws are embedded in historical narrative.

Furthermore, the laws are consistently introduced with the phrase, "YHWH spoke to Moses saying." The priestly editors no doubt did this to give greater authority to their formulation of law and to legitimize their contemporary religious institutions. But it was also their way of affirming that they stood in the Mosaic tradition and that the whole of God's revelation came in a supernatural way on Mt. Sinai.

The book that follows Numbers is Deuteronomy. Deuteronomy is geographically and temporally continuous with the end of Numbers. While Deuteronomy is a completely different kind of material than Genesis through Numbers, it picks up the story line appropriately. Numbers ends with Israel in Moab, poised to enter Palestine. In Deuteronomy Moses tells the Israelites, by then the second generation, to remain faithful to Yahweh so that they could continue the work of conquest, enter the Promised Land, and maintain possession of it.

QUESTIONS FOR REVIEW

1. Who were Israel's leaders during the wilderness period? What stories dealt with issues of religious leadership?
2. Summarize the basic world view of the priestly code.
3. What were the functions of sacrifice?

4. How did the organization of Israel's camp reflect the priestly world view?
5. The Israelites often complained to Moses and to God about conditions in the wilderness. What stories dealt with the murmuring of the people and God's miraculous caring for the people?

QUESTIONS FOR DISCUSSION

1. Reflect on offices of leadership in Israel, as defined in the laws and reinforced in various stories. How did one qualify to be a religious leader in those days, and how does that compare to the ways in which leaders are chosen today?
2. Israel's laws and rituals prescribed and prohibited behaviors in all areas of life. What does this imply about their view of what religion is? Do you think they would have understood the distinction between

sacred and *secular* that we easily draw today?
3. Ponder the stories that reflect negatively on the Israelites. Why were these stories told? What were they implying about the character and faith of that first generation of Israelites that left Egypt? How might these stories about the faithless first generation be related to the apparent biblical preference (refer to firstborn son stories in Genesis) for the younger son over the older?

FOR FURTHER STUDY

deVaux, Roland (1961). *Ancient Israel: Its Life and Institutions*, trans. John McHugh. New York: McGraw-Hill. A collection and distillation of the historical, legal, and sociological data of the Hebrew Bible into a description of Israelite religious and social institutions.

Gammie, John G. (1989). *Holiness in Israel*. OBT. Minneapolis: Augsburg Fortress Press. A theological study of the notion of holiness in the Hebrew

Bible, explaining the particular emphases of the complementary views of priests, prophets, and sages.

The following are two of the best commentaries.
Levine, Baruch (1989). *Leviticus*. TC. Philadelphia: Jewish Publication Society.
Milgrom, Jacob (1990). *Numbers*. TC. Philadelphia: Jewish Publication Society.

WORKS CITED

Haran, Menahem (1978). *Temples and Temple-Ser-vice in Ancient Israel. An Inquiry into the Char-acter of Cult Phenomena and the Historical Setting of the Priestly School*. Oxford: Clarendon Press.

Jenson, Philip Peter (1992). *Graded Holiness. A Key to the Priestly Conception of the World*. JSOT Supplement Series, 106. Sheffield: Sheffield Academic Press.

Levine, Baruch (1974). *In the Presence of the Lord*. SJLA, 5. Leiden: E. J. Brill.

Levine, Baruch (1989). *Leviticus*. TC. Philadelphia: Jewish Publication Society.

Milgrom, Jacob (1983). *Studies in Cultic Theology and Terminology*. SJLA, 36. Leiden: E. J. Brill.

Milgrom, Jacob (1990). *Numbers*. TC. Philadelphia: Jewish Publication Society.

Wenham, Gordon (1979). *Leviticus*. NICOT. Grand Rapids, Mich.: Eerdmans.

DEUTERONOMY: THE TORAH OF MOSES

Names and Terms to Remember

centralization of worship	shalom
covenant	Shema/Great Commandment
Deuteronomist	suzerainty treaty
Deuteronomistic Historian	syncretism
Deuteronomistic History (DH)	theocracy
Josiah's reform	

Deuteronomy is the key that unlocks the Torah and the Prophets. Such is the claim of modern students of the Hebrew Bible. Close study of the book of Deuteronomy inspired a revolution within biblical studies that opened new ways of understanding the theology of the Pentateuch and narrative historical books.

CONTENT OF DEUTERONOMY

Deuteronomy has a different character compared to the preceding four books of the Torah. It consists of speeches Moses delivered to the Israelites in Transjordan while they prepared themselves to enter the Promised Land.

GREAT TEXTS

We will begin our study of Deuteronomy by doing a close reading of some great texts. These texts will give us the flavor of the book and introduce us to some of its main ideas.

Great Commandment (6:4–9)

The core of the book of Deuteronomy is a law code contained in chapters 12–26. This law code is introduced by two speeches of Moses. The first introductory speech (1:1–4:40) is a review of Israel's history from the time God spoke to them at Mt. Sinai (called Horeb in Deuteronomy) up to that point.

Moses highlighted two features of their history. First, the wilderness generation had been unfaithful time and again. They had constantly complained, mumbled, and grumbled. Second, the Lord had demonstrated his faithfulness by giving them all they had needed and by giving them victory over all their enemies. Moses was conveying a warning to these Israelites. "Do not be unfaithful, as was that first generation, or you will not reach your goal."

The second introductory speech (4:44–11:32) contains a rehearsal and elaboration of the Decalogue from Exodus 20, with a few changes. This generation needed to hear the commandments afresh. If they did not hear and obey them, they were as doomed as the first generation.

Immediately preceding the decalogue in its Deuteronomic version is the following charge.

Michelangelo's Moses

5:1 Moses called all Israel and said to them, "Hear, Israel, the laws and rules I speak in your hearing today! Learn them and make sure you do them. 2 YHWH our God made a covenant with us on Horeb. 3 It was not with our fathers that YHWH made this covenant but with us, those of us living here today."

Notice the sense of earnestness in Moses' preaching style. This is entirely characteristic of the addresses of Moses in Deuteronomy. There is no mistaking that Moses wanted to impress on the people the crucial importance of the covenant. It is not ancient history, nor did it apply just to their forebears. The covenant applies directly to them. Moses spoke in such a way that the obligation of the covenant falls on each generation, not just on the generation that actually heard the original words at Horeb.

After stating the Ten Commandments, Moses encapsulated the essence of this torah in one of the most notable passages in the Hebrew Bible, Deuteronomy 6:4–5. The Jewish community calls it the **Shema**, from this passage's first word. Along with Deuteronomy 11:13–21 and Numbers 15:37–41 it is the prime prayer of Judaism, recited daily by observant Jews. Jesus identified it as the **Great Commandment** in Mark 12:29–30.

6:4 Hear, Israel: YHWH is our God, only YHWH. 5 You shall love YHWH your God with all your heart, and with all your soul, and with all your strength. 6 These words which I command you today—take them to heart. 7 Repeat them to your children. Say them when you are sitting in your house, when you are walking on the road, when you lie down and when you get up. 8 Tie them as a sign on your hand. Let them be headbands above your eyes. 9 Write them on the door frames of your houses.

The first few words of our text offer many possibilities in translation, all equally allowable given the rules of the Hebrew language, yet each having a different twist.

- YHWH is our God, YHWH alone
- YHWH our God—YHWH—is one
- YHWH is our God; YHWH is one

Is the Hebrew statement an affirmation of the oneness of God—a profession of monotheism in the face of the pantheon of gods the Israelites knew from their Canaanite, Egyptian, and Mesopotamian neighbors? Or is it primarily the affirmation that Israel's God is YHWH and that they may have no other?

It is difficult to be sure what those first words really mean. An affirmation of monotheism seems a bit too abstractly philosophical for those times, although it is conceivable that the statement was intended to deny the many Baal and Asherah gods the Canaanites recognized.

Moses and the Deuteronomist were probably not interested in affirming the unitary nature of God so much as impressing upon Israel that there is only one God *for them*. His name is Yahweh. He had been faithful to them in the past.

And they must be loyal to him now. There may be other so-called gods among the other nations. But Yahweh is certainly the only God that deserves and demands Israel's love. The command to love Yahweh is central to the book of Deuteronomy.

Only in Jerusalem (12:2–7)

The Deuteronomist promoted loyalty to Yahweh by advocating **centralization of worship**. Yahweh could only be worshiped in one place.

> 2 You must completely eradicate all the places where the nations you are dispossessing used to worship their gods, places on the high mountains, on the hills, and those under lush trees. 3 Break down their altars, smash their pillars, burn their sacred poles with fire, and cut down the idols of their gods. Eradicate their name from that place. 4 Do not worship YHWH your God in the same way as they did theirs. 5 Rather, you shall seek out the place that YHWH your God will choose out of all your tribes to put his name, where he will dwell. You should go there. 6 Bring your burnt offerings and your sacrifices, your tithes and donations, your pledges and contributions, and the firstborn of your herds and flocks. 7 There you shall eat in the presence of YHWH your God, you and your household, rejoicing in everything you undertake, in whatever YHWH your God has blessed you.

The phrase "the place YHWH your God will choose" is an oblique way of referring to Jerusalem. The exact place could not be named because the surface setting of Deuteronomy is a time before Jerusalem had been founded by that name as an Israelite city. The various types of sacrifices and offerings in this passage indicate that all forms of worship and the payment of all dues were to be made at this central sanctuary.

Worship centers traditionally were located on hills or other high places, frequently in forests and groves. That goes for the Canaanites and other inhabitants of Palestine ("the nations you are dispossessing") as well as for the Israelites. Both of the places Israel's God revealed himself were mountains. Mt. Sinai was where the covenant was given, and Israel's chief sanctuary was located on Mt. Zion in Jerusalem.

The Israelites were warned away from using traditional Canaanite high places because of the danger of **syncretism**—blending Yahwism with Baalism or some other foreign religious element, maybe in unintentional ways.

The experience of the Northern Kingdom suggested that a variety of worship centers could be very dangerous to the faith life of the people. In the north before its destruction many cities contained shrines. Usually they were located in places where Baal and Asherah used to be worshiped, and aspects of the worship of Baal were frequently assimilated to worship of Yahweh at those places. Sometimes it was difficult to tell the difference between worship of Yahweh and worship of Baal. Prophets frequently condemned such worship places (Hosea 8:11; Jeremiah 11:13). The attraction of such shrines was one of the major reasons for the fall of the Northern Kingdom.

The writer responsible for the book of Deuteronomy, called the **Deuterono-mist**, knew too well the price of such disloyalty. Probably a Levite from the north, after its destruction in 721 B.C.E. he fled south and brought a message of warning to Judah in the hope that its people might avoid a fate similar to that of Israel.

The centralization of worship in Jerusalem mandated in this text was initiated during the reign of Hezekiah. He abolished the offering of sacrifices anywhere but in the capital. Josiah went even further. He abolished all sanctuaries and temples throughout the land, except for the Solomonic temple in Jerusalem. In this way stricter control over the religious practices of the people could be maintained.

Archaeological excavations at Arad, a Judean city in the south of Palestine, support the biblical description of these religious reforms. Arad contains remains of a temple structure and altars, all built according to the specifications of the Jerusalem temple and its altars. Such a temple was found dating to before the time of Hezekiah. It was destroyed during Hezekiah's reign and rebuilt, but without an altar for burnt offerings. When later the Hezekiah-age city of Arad was destroyed, it was rebuilt during the time of Josiah, but the temple itself was not redone. These changes at Arad are consistent with the centralization efforts of Josiah, as mandated in Deuteronomy.[1]

A Prophet Like Me (18:15–22)

One of the central themes of Deuteronomy is the exclusive relationship between Yahweh and Israel. Yahweh was their God and he demanded total loyalty. The Deuteronomist set Israel apart from the other nations in many ways, including how they would maintain contact with God. Whereas other people employed diviners, sorcerers, and soothsayers to hear a divine voice, Israel was not allowed to use such means. Instead, Israel would hear God through a prophet. Moses addressed the people:

> *18:15 "YHWH your God will raise up a prophet from among your own people, one like me. To him you shall listen, 16 just as you requested of YHWH your God at Horeb in the assembly when you said 'If I hear the voice of YHWH my God and see this great fire again, I will die.' 17 So YHWH said to me, 'They are right in what they said. 18 A prophet I will raise up from among their own people, one like you. I will put my words in his mouth and he will speak to them what I command him. 19 Everyone who does not listen to my words which he speaks in my name—I will hold him responsible. 20 But, the prophet who presumes to speak a word in my name which I did not command him to speak, and which he speaks in the name of other gods, that prophet will die.' 21 You might ask yourself 'How can we recognize the word which YHWH did not speak?' 22 What the prophet speaks in the name of YHWH and which does not happen or come about is not a word YHWH spoke. Presumptuously the prophet spoke it. Do not be afraid of him."*

[1] For a description of the excavations at Arad, see Herzog (1987).

God would raise up a prophet like Moses. The need for a prophet was revealed by the fear of the people as they stood before Yahweh at Horeb. They could not stand up under the intensity of direct contact with God. They thought they would die. It is a truism of the Hebrew Bible that one cannot look upon God directly and live.

Moses mediated between God and Israel. He became the enduring Deuteronomic model for prophetic communication between God and his people. A true prophet receives his words directly from God. A true prophet is distinguished by his access to the Divine Council, where he receives God's words directly from his mouth.

The test of authentic Yahwistic prophecy is how well prediction coincides with fulfillment. In Deuteronomic perspective, prophecy is predicting future events.[2] The criterion for true and false prophecy was the "wait-and-see" test. If a prophecy was genuine, it would come to pass. But this was not very helpful to contemporaries of the prophets who were trying to figure out right now who was genuine. This test really only works for later generations. They can evaluate the prophetic message in terms of the events predicted. Have they or have they not taken place? And it only works for past prophets (probably ones already long gone) whose words have been recorded and written down.

The Deuteronomist is really providing a test for his seventh-century contemporaries. They were able to evaluate past claimants to prophetic office—men such as Isaiah, Amos, and Hosea. Having passed the test, these men would have been authenticated as true prophets. Listen to them and learn from their writings. All others are false. As one test for canonization, this would help decide which writings would have authority within the community and which would not.

The Earliest Creed (26:5–9)

The last chapter of the central law code mandates a ceremony of first fruits. This ceremony is one of the three big yearly festivals established in Israel according to Deutonomy 16:16. It was called the Festival of Weeks because it occurs seven weeks after Passover. Later it was also called Pentecost, from the Greek word for fiftieth (the fiftieth day after Passover).

As proof that they had actually entered the Promised Land, and as proof that it was a good and productive place, each Israelite had to take the first produce of the harvest and bring it to the sanctuary. This was authentication that Yahweh's promise to the ancestors had come true. As part of the ceremony, the one offering the harvest gift would recite the following historical summary.

26:5 "A wandering Aramean was my father. He went down into Egypt and lived there as a resident alien with only a small group. He became a great nation, strong and numerous. 6 The Egyptians treated us badly and persecuted us. They imposed hard labor on us. 7 We cried out to YHWH, the

[2] We will see that this is a somewhat restricted notion of prophecy when we study the prophetic book

God of our ancestors. He heard our voice and saw our persecution, our toil and our oppression. 8 YHWH brought us out of Egypt with a strong hand and an outstretched arm, with awesome power, with signs and with wonders. 9 He brought us to this place and gave us this land, a land flowing with milk and honey."

Three major historical moments are evoked in this sketch of Israel's early history. The first is the patriarchs, or at least one patriarch. The description "wandering Aramean" best fits Jacob, whose name was changed to Israel. He is the one who brought his family to Egypt to join Joseph. The second event is Israel's experience of slavery in Egypt, along with the plagues and the miraculous Exodus.

The third event is the conquest of Canaan. The gifts of produce taken from that land were proof that they were now in the Promised Land, the "land flowing with milk and honey." This description can be found throughout the Pentateuch to describe Canaan. It not only contrasts Canaan with the wilderness out of which Israel came, but also captures in a phrase the lush bountifulness of the land God gave his people.

Von Rad (1966) proposed that these verses contain the earliest digest of Israel's faith. He suggested that the events summarized here are the core of Israel's salvation history. He claimed the outline of events contained in this creed formed the basic historical outline of what came to be Genesis through Joshua.

Carmichael (1969) has called into question the antiquity of this statement, suggesting instead that it was composed for the occasion of the first fruits festival by the Deuteronomist himself and is not an ancient independent creed. Whatever its origin, it is a powerful expression of the essence of Israelite faith, one that each Israelite could own. The statement expresses a faith grounded in historical events, in the history where Yahweh encountered his people.

Choose Life! (30:15–20)

This is the concluding section of the last address of Moses. These verses bring together the big covenant themes of the book: commandment, obedience, blessing and curse, promise and fulfillment. Moses demands a decision from each member of the community. "Choose life or death, but you must choose!"

30:15 "See, I have put before you today life and good, death and bad. 16 This is what I am commanding you today: to love YHWH your God, to walk in his ways, and to keep his commandments, laws and rules. Then you will live and increase, and YHWH your God will bless you in the land you are entering in order to possess it. 17 If your heart turns and you do not listen, but you go astray and worship other gods and serve them, 18 I tell you this very day that you will perish. You will not have a long life in the land you are crossing the Jordan to enter and possess. 19 I call as witnesses against you today heaven and earth. Life and death I set before you, blessing and curse. Choose life so that you and your offspring may live, 20 loving YHWH your God, heeding his voice, clinging to him. For he is your life, your longevity, so you may settle in the land which YHWH swore to give to your ancestors, to Abraham, to Isaac, and to Jacob."

This final entreaty reveals more clearly than anything else that Deuteronomy is more than just theological instruction. It is a covenant document that demands a commitment from the people of God.

The choice is laid out in all its simplicity. Choosing to keep Yahweh's covenant entails life and prosperity; breaking covenant entails death. This black-and-white set of options is characteristic of Deuteronomic theology generally and also finds expression in wisdom literature. The life of obedience leads to **shalom**, the Hebrew notion of complete blessing. A life of disregard for God is foolishness and leads to death. Blessing and curse are, respectively, the outcomes of obedience and disobedience.

The focus of the Deuteronomist is transparent in passages such as this. By framing the message as the speech of Moses directed to the people in the second-person singular, "you," he succeeds in merging the generation that was about to enter the land with the reader/hearer of Deuteronomy in the seventh century B.C.E., when the people were threatened with the loss of their homeland by foreign invasion. It did not take great spiritual insight on the part of seventh-century Judeans to see the connection between the call to faithfulness addressed to the generation of Moses (so that the people could cross the Jordan to enter the land and keep it) and the call to their own faithfulness (so that Judah would not lose the land they already possessed).

Certainly these words became even more meaningful when, after 587 B.C.E., the Judeans were in fact exiled from their homeland. If the people renewed their faithfulness, perhaps Yahweh would bring them back to the Promised Land. Indeed, Moses' call to faithfulness becomes timeless. His injunction to obey the covenant *today* becomes a call to faithfulness in every age.

GREAT THEMES

Deuteronomy is perhaps the most obviously theological book in the Hebrew Bible, if by *theological* we mean spelling out in a clear teaching style what the nature of God is and what faith entails. The theological teaching of Deuteronomy can be distilled into three phrases.

One God

The Deuteronomist affirms a "practical" monotheism. He was not interested in abstract theological formulations. He stated that there was only one God who was interested in Israel. God demonstrated that by his care in the past. He demands their undivided loyalty in the present. He is the one and only God for them.

The people are bound to Yahweh by means of a legal contract, called the **covenant**. This covenant defines the shape of their loyalty and specifies how they would remain in God's good graces.

One People

Deuteronomy is addressed to the people of God as a whole. No distinction is made between southern and northern kingdoms. There are no tribal distinctions.

This presumes a unity to the people of God. This is affirmed in the covenant formula, "Yahweh is the God of Israel, and Israel is the people of God."

The oneness of the people transcends generations. The book is addressed perpetually to the "now" generation. References to *today* and *this day* abound. The covenant is made "not with our fathers but with us alive today."

The unity of the people is not based on genetic commonality but on the belief that God called them to be his people. They alone are the people of God, set apart from the rest of the nations and held together because Yahweh, in love, chose them. Sometimes called the "election" of Israel, this notion affirms that these people were singled out by God at his own initiative. That is what makes them special—Yahweh's "treasured possession" in Deuteronomy's language (7:6; see also Exodus 19:5 where the same term is used).

One Faith

Israel got in trouble because it lost religious focus. Local variations in religious practices and the tendency to drift in the direction of Baalism resulted in unorthodox worship. The Deuteronomist demanded uniformity in worship. This could only be enforced if one central sanctuary was officially designated. "The place Yahweh will choose" became the only worship center. Although left unspecified in the text, the Deuteronomist no doubt had Jerusalem in mind.

FORM OF DEUTERONOMY

Deuteronomy is a different kind of book compared to the rest of the Pentateuch. It has a consistent style unmatched in Genesis through Numbers. It consists of the sermons Moses delivered to the Hebrews before they entered the Promised Land. Characterized by a certain preachiness (but do not let that put you off), it contains spiritually challenging material.

Deuteronomy got its name from Deuteronomy 17:18, which states that the king was to receive a "copy of the Torah" to guide him. This was mistakenly translated "a second law" in the Septuagint, *deuteronomion* in Greek. Deuteronomy is not a "second law" but a retelling and reapplication of the law given at Sinai. The Hebrew name for the book is *Words*, taken from the first phrase of the book, "These are the words that Moses spoke to all Israel beyond the Jordan."

AUTHORSHIP

The authorship of the book of Deuteronomy is a two-level issue, involving the surface setting of the book (what the book portrays itself to be) and the actual setting (when it was actually written).

The *surface* setting of Deuteronomy is this. What little action there is took place in Transjordan (the modern Hashemite Kingdom of Jordan) just before the people crossed the Jordan River and entered Palestine. The best current estimate is that it would have happened around 1250 B.C.E.

Moses addressed all the people of Israel, urging them to be faithful to the Lord. In so doing they would ensure prosperity and peace in the new land they were poised to enter. The speeches contain a reapplication of the Mosaic Torah to these people, updated for a settled-down life in the homeland Yahweh had promised them. Most of the book is made up of speeches by Moses, addressed directly to the Israelites. At the very end of the book the manner of speaking changes and becomes a narrative description of the death of Moses. The leadership role then shifts to Joshua, who becomes Moses' successor.

But the *actual* setting of the book, that is, when it was written down, differs from its surface setting. The core of Deuteronomy was written sometime during the Israelite monarchy, perhaps as early as the reign of Hezekiah (715–687 B.C.E.), or as late as the reign of Josiah (640–609 B.C.E.).

Deuteronomy in some form (probably only the inner core of laws) was the "book of the Torah" that was found in 622 B.C.E. during the religious revival of King Josiah. The similarities between **Josiah's reform** (told in 2 Kings 22–23) and the prescriptions of Deuteronomy are too close to be coincidental. Both involved centralizing worship in one place, celebrating Passover in a particular way, and prohibiting certain specific pagan practices. Furthermore, the phrase "book of the Torah," found in 2 Kings 22:8, is found in other places where it can only refer to Deuteronomy (for example, Deuteronomy 30:10, Joshua 1:8 and 8:31–35).

Thus, Deuteronomy exists in two worlds, and both settings must be understood to fully appreciate the book. Set at the time of Moses, it was given its shape during the time of Josiah some five centuries later. While the core traditions may go back to the Moses of the Exodus, the book as we have it today was shaped some 600 years later. Who, during the reign of Josiah, was responsible for giving the book its shape?

It is hard to pin down Deuteronomy's author, called the Deuteronomist by scholars. Evidence from the book suggests that the author came from the Northern Kingdom and reflects its traditions. This is indicated by the terms he uses, which are consistent with other known northern traditions, for example, Horeb for Sinai and Amorites for Canaanites. Also, many of Deuteronomy's laws seem to derive from the Covenant Code (Exodus 20:22–23:33), which is from the Elohist source and embodies northern perspectives.

Beyond this the specific social background of the author is difficult to determine. The preaching style of Deuteronomy suggests that the book might have been written by northern Levites, who warned and encouraged their congregations in periodic covenant renewal ceremonies at the great northern worship centers such as Shechem and Bethel (von Rad 1938). Friedman (1987) thinks he can be quite specific. He believes the Deuteronomist was a Levitic priest from Shiloh, and he argues that Jeremiah was in fact this Deuteronomist.

According to the Levitic priestly theory, when the Northern Kingdom was destroyed by the Assyrians in 721 B.C.E. these Levites fled south, taking with them their oral and written traditions. These then formed the foundation of their preaching in Judah. The Deuteronomist drew on this material for his book.

But there are other considerations as well. The close connection between Deuteronomy and the religious reforms supported by Josiah might suggest that the writer was close to the royal court in Jerusalem. The description of the discovery of the law book, as described in 2 Kings 22–23, associates the find with Shaphan the royal secretary and Hilkiah the high priest. Both were trusted associates of King Josiah.

A variation of this setting of Deuteronomy's authorship suggests that Deuteronomy came from administrative circles. In Israel, administrators and middle-level politicians tended to arise from scribal circles. Weinfeld (1972) studied what he felt were connections in Deuteronomy to Israel's wisdom tradition, and suggested that Deuteronomy is the product of an ancient Israelite civil service interest. Deuteronomy, he says, is the expression of a governmental group interested in shaping the structure and life of the nation.

There is yet another theory. Nicholson (1967) suggests that the writer was deeply influenced by prophets and prophetic movements, especially those in Israel. The book of Deuteronomy certainly does hold a high opinion of prophets. Moses is portrayed as the model of all prophets.

As we can see, Deuteronomy has elements consistent with priestly, prophetic, royal, and wisdom connections. But what do we do with this?

The multitude of authorship options suggests at the very least that we should be cautious about identifying Deuteronomy with any one social or political interest group in Israel. We can certainly say this much, though. The writer was deeply committed to revitalizing the faith and practice of Israel. And he viewed himself as standing solidly in the tradition of Moses. Indeed, virtually the entire book is framed as the very words of Moses!

Rather than arguing for one interest group as opposed to some other, perhaps these multiple connections are best taken as an indication of the wide range of interests of the Deuteronomist. He succeeded in constructing a holistic vision of the Israelite community that accounted for all the major participants.

The critical issues of precisely when and where the book was written should not overcloud the overall impression of the book, that it embodies a genuine testimony of Mosaic faith. Admittedly, the seventh-century writer shaped that testimony, being sensitive to the issues of faith and life in the Judah of his time. But nonetheless, he felt he was presenting the essential thrust of Moses' message. While shaping the words he put in Moses' mouth, he certainly felt he was representing the Mosaic tradition faithfully.

STYLE AND STRUCTURE

The content of Deuteronomy is presented as an anthology of speeches given by Moses to the Israelites just before they were to take possession of the Promised Land. He counseled and cajoled them, "Be faithful to YHWH and you will be blessed." More obviously than any other material in the Hebrew Bible, this material is sermonic . . . "preachy," if you will.

Deuteronomy is permeated with phrases such as "with all your heart and soul," "in order that it may go well with you," "be thankful," and "if only you obey the voice of Yahweh your God." It contains both a call to faithfulness and a call to social responsibility.

Deuteronomy was designed to appeal to the hearts and minds of its listeners. The bulk of the book is framed not as a narrative but as a direct address to the people. Although not noticeable in English translation (because *you* can be either singular or plural), the book vacillates, apparently indiscriminately, between address to individuals, *you*, and to the people as a whole, *all of you*. With this "shotgun" approach, the Deuteronomist targets each person, and—virtually at the same time—the group, suggesting that they are in this together as the one people of God.

The book of Deuteronomy as we have it is the result of a long process of development and deliberate shaping. That should be no surprise. Almost every book of the Hebrew Bible was!

The editor of Deuteronomy left us some helpful clues to the shape of the book. The main textual units are easily recognizable because what turns out to be a formula introduces them. The words *this is* or *these are*, in boldface in Table 5.1, stand as a title at the head of all but one major section.

The nucleus of Deuteronomy is the set of laws in chapters 12–26. If we visually diagram the book, we see this central set of laws surrounded by concentric sets of material. This material reinforces those laws and gives them context. Simplifying matters somewhat, the inner circle of speeches by Moses (5–11 and 27–28) bracket the core laws (12–26) and are themselves surrounded by a prologue (1–4) and an epilogue (33–34) containing the farewell of Moses and various appendices. The covenant renewal section (29–32) is the only section that breaks the symmetry. Figure 5.1 illustrates the basic arrangement.

To a degree, this diagram coincides with the composition history of the book. The book was written in stages. The central law code was probably written first, no later than the reform of Josiah. The historical prologue was added to the book when Deuteronomy became the prologue to the **Deuteronomistic History**. More about that later.

TABLE 5.1	TEXTUAL UNITS IN DEUTERONOMY
1:1–4:43	"**These are** the words that Moses spoke to all Israel beyond the Jordan"
4:44–11:32	"**This is** the torah that Moses put before the Israelites"
12:1–26:19	"**These are** the laws and rules that you must diligently keep"
27:1–28:68	"Then Moses and the elders of Israel charged all the people as follows"
29:1–32:52	"**These are** the words of the covenant that the Lord commanded Moses to make with the Israelites"
33:1–34:12	"**This is** the blessing with which Moses, the man of God, blessed the Israelites before his death"

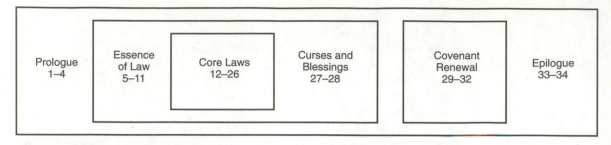

| Prologue 1–4 | Essence of Law 5–11 | Core Laws 12–26 | Curses and Blessings 27–28 | Covenant Renewal 29–32 | Epilogue 33–34 |

FIGURE 5.1   STRUCTURE OF DEUTERONOMY

ISSUES IN DEUTERONOMY

The book of Deuteronomy has attracted a great deal of scholarly discussion on two issues: the nature of Israel's covenant in relation to extrabiblical covenants; and the relationship between Deuteronomy and the books of Joshua, Judges, Samuel, and Kings.

TREATY AND COVENANT

Given the shape of Deuteronomy as a call to covenant faithfulness, it is not surprising to find that major components of Deuteronomy have parallels in ancient treaty ceremonies. Ancient treaty ceremonies initiated covenant relationships between two parties. Treaty documents associated with such ceremonies were a permanent record of the conditions of the relationship. The term *covenant* can be used for both the type of relationship between the parties and the document that defines that relationship.

Certain parallels between Deuteronomy and ancient treaty documents are so close that some scholars have argued that Deuteronomy is explicitly a treaty document such as was used in Hittite and Assyrian covenant ceremonies (Mendenhall 1955; Kline 1963). Today this view is considered a bit of an overstatement. Deuteronomy is not itself a treaty document, though most certainly it contains covenant language and major elements of such ancient treaty texts. Better understood, Deuteronomy is an anthology of sermons based on the covenant concept.

Ancient treaty documents such as we know them from the Hittites and the Assyrians were legal texts used in the administration of conquered kingdoms. Using somewhat antiquated terminology, such an administrative document is usually called a **suzerainty treaty**, a suzerain being a feudal lord who controlled a vassal state.

The most extensive body of suzerainty treaties comes from the Hittite empire of the Late Bronze Age (ca. 1400–1200 B.C.E.). Equally important and closer in time to the Deuteronomist are legal documents from the Neo-Assyrian empire (935–612 B.C.E.) that make extensive use of the treaty form. These empires are identified in Figure 5.2.

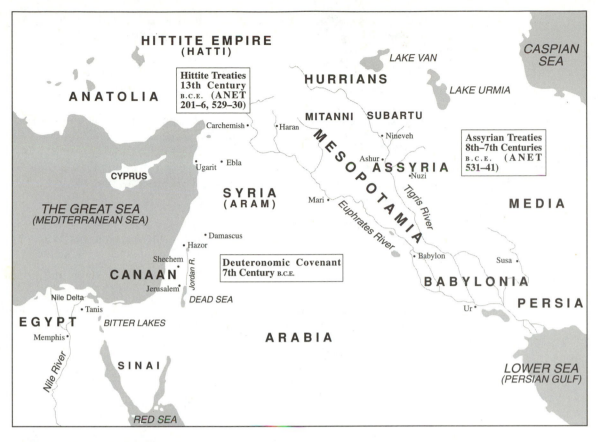

FIGURE 5.2 ANCIENT MIDDLE EAST, HIGHLIGHTING HITTITE AND NEO-ASSYRIAN EMPIRES

Close study of these Hittite and Neo-Assyrian treaty documents has revealed that they have a number of components in common. A complete treaty document would contain the following elements.

1. *Introduction.* Sometimes called the *preamble*, this introduces and identifies the parties to the treaty.

2. *Historical Background.* This details the history of the relationship between the parties to the treaty.

3. *Conditions.* These conditions, sometimes called *stipulations*, are the terms of the treaty. Among other things, the suzerain places upon the vassal the demand for total loyalty.

4. *Publication.* This describes where the treaty document would be stored and when it would be recited in public.

5. *Divine Witnesses*. This specifies the gods who would be called on to witness the making of the treaty (equivalent to a notary public today) and who would also enforce any breach of the treaty.

6. *Blessing and Curse*. This was a list of the good and bad things that would happen to the vassal if the treaty was kept or broken.

The book of Deuteronomy contains remarkable parallels to the components of ancient treaty documents, as the following list suggests.

1. *Introduction*. 4:44–49. Moses speaking for Yahweh. "This is the law that Moses set before the Israelites" (4:44). This provides the setting for the covenant addresses.

2. *Historical Background*. 5–11. This contains recollection of Israel's experience at Horeb and in the wilderness, which is the occasion for Moses to warn the people to be obedient.

3. *Conditions*. 12–26. The central law code. "These are the laws and rules that you must diligently keep" (12:1).

4. *Publication*. 27:1–10. Covenant ceremony. "Write on the stones all the words of this law" (27:8). Covenant renewal every seven years with public reading is specified in 31:10–13.

5. *Divine Witnesses*. "I call as witnesses against you today heaven and earth" (30:19). Yahweh himself would guard the covenant and enforce it.

6. *Blessing and Cursing*. 28. "If you obey Yahweh your God, . . . all these blessings will come upon you." (28:1–2); later chapter 28 spells out the curses.

The profound similarities between Deuteronomy and the ancient treaty form suggest that the Deuteronomist intentionally framed Yahweh's relationship with Israel in treaty terms. Clearly, the Deuteronomist was influenced by broader ancient Middle Eastern legal traditions and utilized them to give shape to the relationship Yahweh established with his people Israel. He used the political metaphor of treaty and covenant to conceptualize the spiritual relationship between Yahweh and Israel.

If Deuteronomy was intentionally framed, at least in part, on the analogy of a suzerainty treaty, the theological effect may be this. Yahweh is given the role of the suzerain, and Israel is his vassal. On analogy with other nations, they had their suzerain (a king), but Israel had Yahweh. In other words, Deuteronomy as suzerainty treaty presents Yahweh as the Great King of Israel. Israel was not supposed to have a human king because Yahweh was its king. The term that signifies the rule of God is **theocracy**, and this was the preferred form of government for Israel.[3]

---

[3]Deuteronomy 17:14-20 deals with the office of king, but emphasizes that he must be subject to the torah given to him by the levitical priests.

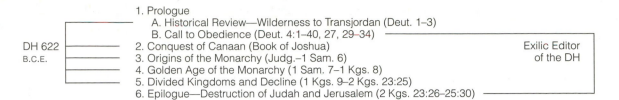

1. Prologue
   A. Historical Review—Wilderness to Transjordan (Deut. 1–3)
   B. Call to Obedience (Deut. 4:1–40, 27, 29–34)
2. Conquest of Canaan (Book of Joshua)
3. Origins of the Monarchy (Judg.–1 Sam. 6)
4. Golden Age of the Monarchy (1 Sam. 7–1 Kgs. 8)
5. Divided Kingdoms and Decline (1 Kgs. 9–2 Kgs. 23:25)
6. Epilogue—Destruction of Judah and Jerusalem (2 Kgs. 23:26–25:30)

DH 622
B.C.E.

Exilic Editor
of the DH

FIGURE 5.3   THE DEUTERONOMISTIC HISTORY

DEUTERONOMISTIC HISTORY

The content of Deuteronomy is important well beyond the book itself. Deuteronomy represents a theological tradition that is reflected in many other books of the Hebrew Bible. It is the theological "lens" through which Israel's greatest historian focuses attention on the national epic.

Deuteronomy stands in an interesting relationship to the rest of the Pentateuch. Deuteronomy is really self-contained and can be understood apart from Genesis through Numbers. It is identified as a literary source separate from the Yahwist, Elohist, and Priestly sources that created Genesis through Numbers. Although it does not tell the story in the same way, it is connected to those books and is, narratively speaking, a continuation of the history they began.

On the other side of Deuteronomy in the canon are the narrative historical books. The history of Israel's monarchy, including the events leading up to the formation of the nation, are contained in Joshua, Judges, Samuel, and Kings. This material is not historiography in a social–scientific sense, but then it never intended to be. It tells the story of the nation from the theological perspective that Israel prospered or suffered in relation to how obedient or disobedient they were to the covenant. As went their faith, so went their national standard of living. The writer is called the **Deuteronomistic Historian** because he derived his basic theology from Deuteronomy.

Closely examining the book of Deuteronomy, scholars have suggested that most of the prologue, chapters 1–3, are in fact the work of the Deuteronomistic Historian and not the Deuteronomist himself. Here's how the theory goes. The Deuteronomistic Historian, writing at the time of Josiah, took Deuteronomy (which probably only consisted of chapters 5–26 and 28) and prefaced it with his own historical introduction (what is now chapters 1–3). He then used all that material as the first part of his *magnum opus*, the **Deuteronomistic History** (or **DH** for short). Many scholars think that the DH was edited later by an exilic theologian who added Deuteronomy 4:1–40, chapter 27, and chapters 29–34. Figure 5.3 displays the shape of the DH by this theory.

The Deuteronomistic Historian really set out to answer significant questions concerning Israel's national destiny. First, by writing theological history he attempted to answer the question, "Why did Israel, the Northern Kingdom, fall to the Assyrians?" Second, he attempted to shed light on the question, "Why is Josiah trying to reform the religious practices of Judah?" We will examine his answers in the Former Prophets section of Part Two: Prophets of our textbook.

QUESTIONS FOR REVIEW

1. What is unique about Deuteronomy compared to the other books in the Pentateuch?
2. What are the major themes of Deuteronomy?

3. What are the similarities between Deuteronomy and ancient Middle Eastern suzerainty treaties?

QUESTIONS FOR DISCUSSION

1. What themes of Deuteronomy reinforce the major themes of Genesis through Numbers?
2. God used the covenant, a notion coming out of the realm of politics and international relations, to define his relationship with Israel. What is the effect and meaning of using this notion to define the God–human relationship, instead of using another metaphor such as parent–child?

FOR FURTHER STUDY

Craigie, Peter (1976). *The Book of Deuteronomy*. NICOT. Grand Rapids, Mich.: Eerdmans. A widely respected conservative commentary on the book of Deuteronomy.

Hillers, Delbert (1969). *Covenant. The History of a Biblical Idea*. Baltimore: Johns Hopkins Press. An account of the development of the covenant theme, tracing the influence of ancient treaty forms.

McConville, J. Gordon (1993). *Grace in the End. A Study of Deuteronomic Theology*. Grand Rapids, Mich.: Zondervan. Examines Deuteronomic theology from a conservative perspective.

Wolff, Hans Walter (1975). "The Kerygma of the Deuteronomic Work." In *The Vitality of Old Testament Traditions*, ed. Walter Brueggemann and Hans Walter Wolff. Philadelphia: John Knox Press. An essay that explains the theology of Deuteronomic literature.

WORKS CITED

Carmichael, Calum M. (1969). "The Deuteronomic Credo." *Vetus Testamentum* 19: 284–89.

Friedman, Richard Elliott (1987). *Who Wrote the Bible?* Englewood Cliffs, N.J.: Prentice-Hall.

Herzog, Ze'ev (1987). "Arad: An Ancient Israelite Fortress with a Temple to Yahweh." *Biblical Archaeology Review* 13/2: 16–35.

Kline, Meredith (1963). *Treaty of the Great King. The Covenant Structure of Deuteronomy*. Grand Rapids, Mich.: Eerdmans.

Mendenhall, G. E. (1955). *Law and Covenant in Israel and the Ancient Near East*. Pittsburgh: Biblical Colloquium.

Nicholson, Ernest W. (1967). *Deuteronomy and Tradition*. Philadelphia: Fortress.

von Rad, Gerhard (1938; trans. 1966). *The Problem of the Hexateuch and other essays*. New York: McGraw-Hill.

Weinfeld, Moshe (1972). *Deuteronomy and the Deuteronomic School*. Oxford: Oxford University Press.

EPILOGUE TO THE TORAH

Names and Terms to Remember

Pentateuch
Tetrateuch

The Torah contains a fascinating kaleidoscope of material—stories about extraordinary characters such as Sarah and Jacob, laws that were intended to shape Israel into a just and God-fearing society, poetic deathbed testaments from the likes of Moses, and much more. The Torah comes from a variety of different sources: oral traditions as early as the ancestors themselves, written materials from various periods of the monarchy, and who knows what else or from where.

But we must not lose sight of the proverbial forest because we see only the trees. The Torah, complex though it is because of the variety of its sources and their sociohistory, still tells a coherent and unified story. The Torah has direction, it has flow. This epilogue explains how the pieces of the Torah were joined together to tell Israel's early story.

TORAH SOURCES

The "Prologue to the Torah" explained in general terms that the Torah was shaped from sources. As we looked at the books of the Torah we took note of which sources contributed what portions of the Torah. Now, having had the experience of reading the Torah, we step back to synthesize what we have learned about these materials.

YAHWIST

The Yahwist source is the earliest written source. Its story line was the foundation of the story told in the Torah, and the other sources built on it.

Story Line

The Yahwist source begins at Genesis 2:4 and continues through the book of Numbers. When the individual episodes are gleaned out of Genesis, Exodus, and Numbers and viewed together in isolation, the Yahwist epic tells a story of marvelous scope and deep human interest. The Yahwist epic extends from the creation of humankind, through the age of the ancestors, to the deliverance from Egypt and the journey through the Sinai wilderness. Some scholars even argue that the Yahwist source continues into the books of Joshua and Judges, incorporating accounts of the conquest and settlement.

Table 1 lists the major episodes of the Torah that most scholars credit either entirely or in large part to the Yahwist writer:

TABLE 1   MAJOR EPISODES OF THE YAHWIST SOURCE

Story Complex	Episode	Reference
Primeval Story		
	Creation	Genesis 2:4b–25
	Garden of Eden	Genesis 3:1–24
	Cain and Abel	Genesis 4:1–16
	Sons of God	Genesis 6:1–4
	Flood	Genesis 6–9 (with P)
	Tower of Babel	Genesis 11:1–9
Ancestral Story		
	Abraham: Ur to Canaan	Genesis 12:1–13:18
	Hagar and Ishmael	Genesis 16
	Sodom and Gomorrah	Genesis 18–19
	Wife for Isaac	Genesis 24
	Sarah as Sister	Genesis 26
	Jacob, Leah, and Rachel	Genesis 29
	Dinah and Shechem	Genesis 34
	Joseph Story	Genesis 37–50 (with E and P)
Exodus and Sinai		
	Plagues and Exodus	Exodus 1–17 (with E and P)
	Ritual Decalogue	Exodus 34 (with E)
Wilderness Experiences		
	Spies	Numbers 13–14 (with P)
	Rebellion of Korah	Numbers 16 (with P)

The overall plot of the Torah was shaped by the historical sequence of events in the Yahwist source. By the stories it contains, it established the seven major event complexes that constitute the structure of pre-Israelite history.

1. Stories of human origins.
2. A covenant with the ancestors.
3. Persecution in Egypt.

4. Exit from Egypt.
5. Wandering in the Sinai wilderness.
6. A covenant made at Mt. Sinai.
7. Temporary encampment in Transjordan.

The later sources added additional stories to these topics but did not essentially change this direction of development or the itinerary.

Style

The Yahwist was a gifted storyteller who was especially interested in the human side of things. The following are some of the stylistic features of the Yahwist.

Yahweh is often represented with humanlike qualities. He is alternately a potter, a gardener, a "man"—the literary technique called *anthropomorphism*. Yahweh walks with Adam and Eve, seals the door of the ark, has a meal with Abraham, bargains with Abraham over Sodom and Gomorrah, and actually changes his mind about destroying Israel because of the golden calves. Yahweh appears directly to people and expects a childlike faith and obedience.

Yahweh is intent on working out events so that the objects of his attention will be blessed. Yet he is a God who is absolutely opposed to sin. After it happens, he confronts the offenders and does not let a challenge to his authority go unpunished, as in the Garden of Eden and the Tower of Babel stories.

The Yahwist has his own characteristic vocabulary. Some examples:

- "to bless" is the characteristic way Yahweh deals kindly with others
- "to know" is a euphemism for sexual intercourse
- "to find favor" for pleasing someone
- Canaanites for the inhabitants of Palestine, whereas the Elohist uses Amorites
- Reuel or Hobab for Moses' father-in-law, whereas the Elohist uses Jethro
- Sinai for the residence of Yahweh, whereas the Elohist calls it Horeb
- Israel rather than the name Jacob for the third patriarch.

The Yahwist is also very fond of word play, often using it to make a theological point or to provide a suggestion of the origin of someone or something—called an *etiology:*

- Eve, the mother of all living, from *hawwah*, "life" (Genesis 3:20)
- Babel, the place where language was confused, from *balal*, "to confuse" (Genesis 11:9)
- Edom, an alternate name for Esau, from *edom*, "red," the color of Esau's complexion, the color of the stew he ate in lieu of his birthright, and the color of the mountains of the territory called Edom
- Israel, "one who strives with God," the name for Jacob after he wrestled with God at the Jabbok (Genesis 32:27).

The Yahwist is refreshingly honest when he deals with the character flaws, even sometimes blatant sins, of the main characters. He is not interested in whitewashing them or making them squeaky clean "heroes of the faith." He exposes:

- the lie of Abraham when he tells Pharaoh that Sarah is his sister (Genesis 12:10–20)
- the underhanded deceit of Jacob in tricking Esau and Laban (Genesis 27; 30–31)
- the dastardly trick of Simeon and Levi in killing the Shechemites (Genesis 34).

The Yahwist writer tends to express his theology through speeches of Yahweh placed at decisive transition points in the epic. The following divine speeches occur in Genesis:

- 2:16–17, the prohibition of eating from the tree, "lest you die"
- 3:14–19, the curses on the serpent, woman, and man
- 4:6–7, 11ff., to Cain, "if you do well you will be acceptable"
- 6:3, 5–8, before the flood, "I am sorry that I have made them"
- 8:21–22, after the flood, "I will never again curse the ground"
- 11:6–7, Tower of Babel, "this is only the beginning of what they will do"
- 13:14–17, to Abraham after Lot separated
- 18:17–19, about Sodom and Gomorrah

Such theologizing in speech typifies the Yahwist's literary–theological perspective that God was immediately present to these people and spoke with them directly.

Theology

The core of the Yahwist epic is the divine promise to Abraham in Genesis 12:1–3. The groundwork justifying the need for divine help and promise was laid in the stories of the growth of sin in the primeval era. Humankind tried to become great on its own, to be like God. But it resulted in utter failure.

Greatness would come only through Yahweh's initiative. Yahweh took that initiative with Abraham. Israel's history is interpreted as illustration and fulfillment of the promises made to him. "I will make your name great" (12:2) becomes the prefiguring of the great name of David and Israel (2 Samuel 7:9–16).

The unconditional promise made to Abraham, from the perspective of the Yahwist at the Davidic court, echoes the promise Yahweh made to David. The promises were made without demands, as a gift from the divine king to his favored "son." Even when the recipient demonstrates himself unworthy, the promise is not withdrawn.

The promise, however, was not intended to be a merit badge worn with self-satisfaction. It was unearned. But it was to be worn as a reminder of responsibility. Abraham, and hence David and all Israel, were chosen to be an instrument of blessing: "Through you all families of the earth shall bless themselves/be blessed." This universal intent was certainly reinforced and justified when the Yahwist prefaced the national story with the "all-world" Primeval History, Genesis 2–11.

The optimism of the royal court is certainly communicated in this vision of national destiny. Yahweh was working out his universal plan through Israel. The Yahwist never flagged in his zeal for this mission: to extend the blessings of Yahweh to the other nations. Only later, when the shortcomings of the Davidic dynasty became evident and competing theologies demanded a hearing, was there a challenge to this vision. The first to offer a counterview was the Elohist writer.

ELOHIST

The Elohist source was written after the Yahwist source and comes out of the Northern Kingdom in the ninth or eighth century B.C.E.

Story Line

The Elohist source is the most difficult source to handle. It is certainly more fragmentary than the Yahwist source, probably because where it duplicated the Yahwist source its version was dropped. It was perhaps designed to be a corrective supplement to the Yahwist source. In any case, there is more controversy about the Elohist than about any other source in the Pentateuch. Some scholars dispute that it ever existed. They suggest that the Elohist was not a continuous source but only the residue of some editing done by a group of priests from northern Israel who supplemented the Yahwist. Westermann (1976) claims that the so-called Elohist material does not come from a common source but is a potpourri from a variety of different places.

Nonetheless, there may be enough evidence to suggest that an Elohist source once did exist. For instance, doublets of certain basic story plots are found, and the duplicates evidence the characteristic vocabulary of the sources. The patriarch who tells a prominent foreigner that his wife is his sister so that he would not be killed for her is found in both Yahwist (Genesis 12:10–20 and 26:7–11) and Elohist (Genesis 20:1–18) versions. Also, certain narratives contain a combination of both Yahwist and Elohist material, suggesting that both traditions had the same story and were later combined. Examples of this are Jacob's dream (Genesis 28:10–22), Moses's calling (Exodus 3), and the theophany at Sinai (Exodus 19).

Table 2 contains the major Elohist passages recognized by most scholars.

As we know, the Yahwist uses the divine name Yahweh from the very beginning. In contrast, the Elohist is more historically accurate. In his account (as also in the Priestly account), the name Yahweh was first revealed to Moses just before the Exodus. So in his stories before the time of Moses he uses the divine name Elohim, the more generic Hebrew way of referring to God.

Beginning with Exodus 3, however, it is especially difficult to tell the difference between Yahwist material and Elohist material. Beginning at that point both use the divine name Yahweh. Usually, though, we can still identify them by their characteristic vocabularies, styles, and themes.

TABLE 2   MAJOR EPISODES OF THE ELOHIST SOURCE

Story Complex	Episode	Reference
Ancestral Story		
	Sarah as Sister	Gen. 20:1–18
	Sacrifice of Isaac	Gen. 22:1–10, 16b–19
	Jacob Wrestles with God	Gen. 32:22–32
	Joseph Short Story	Gen. 37–50 (with J and P)
Exodus and Sinai		
	Midwives	Exod. 1:15–21
	Burning Bush	Exod. 3:1–15 (with J)
	Exodus from Egypt	Exod. 13
	Wilderness Incidents	Exod. 17–18
	Theophany	Exod. 19:1–9
	Ten Commandments	Exod. 20:1–17 (with P)
	Book of the Covenant	Exod. 20:18–23:33
	Covenant Ceremony	Exod. 24:1–18 (with P)
	Golden Calf	Exod. 32–33
Wilderness Experiences		
	Complaints and Disputes	Num. 11–12
	Balaam and the Moabites	Num. 22–24

Style

The distinguishing vocabulary of the Elohist writer includes using Jethro to refer to Moses' father-in-law (Reuel or Hobab in the Yahwist). Instead of Sinai as the place of covenant making (as in the Yahwist and in the Priestly source), the Elohist calls it the mountain of Elohim or Horeb.

The Elohist is fond of using repetitions when God is calling someone, for example, "Abraham, Abraham" (Genesis 22) and "Moses, Moses" (Exodus 3). And the preferred response is "I'm here."

The Elohist source does not have any preancestral stories: no stories of creation or the universal origins of humankind. Perhaps this indicates that the Elohist was more narrowly focused on Israel as the people of God. The Yahwist, in contrast, had a universal interest. Abraham was called to be a blessing to the nations. According to the Elohist, Israel was called to be God's people, exclusively devoted to him.

The Elohist is hesitant to criticize the ancestors and leaders (except Aaron). The story of Abraham and Sarah (Genesis 20) is instructive in this regard. The Elohist implies that Abraham is at least technically correct, if not entirely candid, when he says to Abimelek that Sarah is his sister. When the Yahwist tells basically the same story in Genesis 12 he does not leave Abraham any room for doubt, like the Elohist, but instead implies his guilt.

Coming to faith and living the life of faith were not easy in the view of the Elohist. God initiated trials and tests to hone the faith of God's people. Abraham was tried, Israel was tested. But God always provided, in the end. The Elohist had a special interest in the faith and obedience of the covenant people. He was concerned that the people be obedient first of all to God. That obedience is crystallized in the phrase "the fear of God" in the Elohist stories. Virtually every story has a moral about fearing God. No doubt it recommends the attitude of fearing God because of the propensity, especially of people in the north, to offend the God of Israel by worshiping Baal of the Canaanites.

Theology

The Elohist emphasized the transcendent nature of God. There are no direct encounters between God and the people, as in the Yahwist account. When God does come to people, he typically does so in dreams, visions, or by messengers, and always from a distance. When God appears, it is in the form of a cloud or a flame. And even when he appears personally to Moses (Exodus 33), Moses sees only God's back. Consistent with this fear of the presence of God, it is the Elohist who tells us that no one can look at God and live (Exodus 33:20).

Another distinctive feature of the Elohist is his concern with prophecy and hearing God. The premonarchic heroes of the faith, Abraham, Joseph, and Moses, are portrayed as prophets. They show tremendous respect for God and "fear" him. When they approach God, they do so by using the appropriate ritual forms. The Elohist's interest in prophets and prophecy suggests that he might have had significant contact with the prophetic circles in Israel, probably the circles associated with Elijah and Elisha, who were prophets in northern Israel in the ninth century B.C.E.

The Elohist highlights Moses as the spiritual leader of the people. Moses had an indispensable role in mediating the covenant. The Elohist does not talk at all about a covenant with Abraham as the basis of God's future relationship with the Israelites. Rather, the Mosaic covenant established at Horeb (the Elohist way of referring to Mt. Sinai) is the basis of the people's bond with God.

The Elohist pays particular attention to Israel's special covenantal relationship with God. He stresses that the covenant community God formed with Israel at Horeb in Moses' day is more fundamental than the ruling arrangement with the Davidic dynasty in Judah, or the newly shaped dynasties in the Northern Kingdom. The Elohist was not awed by powerful governmental structures, as was the Yahwist of the Davidic court. He was more critical of the establishment and the powers that be.

The Elohist points out God's special interest in Israel. He tells how God acted decisively to preserve his people at critical junctures in their history. In the Elohist portion of the Joseph story, Joseph remarked to his brothers that what they had done to him was part of God's plan to preserve a remnant during the devastating famine (Genesis 45:5–7). The story of the faithful midwives Shiphrah and

Puah "who feared God" (Exodus 1:15–21) tells how they helped to preserve the family of Jacob during hard times in Egypt.

In summary, the Elohist suggests that Israel must fear God and be obedient. That obedience must be shaped by the covenant. God is present to his people, but at a distance and in a veiled way because he is so terrifying.

DEUTERONOMIST

Deuteronomy is chronologically the next of the pentateuchal sources, dated to the late seventh century B.C.E. The Deuteronomist was responsible for the book of Deuteronomy and for articulating the theological perspective of the Deuteronomistic History. There is no need to summarize the theology of the Deuteronomist here. That was done in chapter 5.

PRIESTLY

The last of the great pentateuchal traditions, the Priestly source, comes out of the circle of priests who tried to put Israel back together again, theologically speaking, after the tragedy of Babylonian exile.

Story Line

The Priestly writer contributed a great deal of material to the Pentateuch. Priestly material is found throughout the first four books, from the primeval story of Genesis to the book of Numbers. Table 3 outlines the main contributions of the Priestly source.

Priests who survived the destruction of Jerusalem in 587 B.C.E. were concerned that the story of God and his people not disappear. They also wanted to preserve and even revive traditional religious practices. They felt that neglect of such religious practices was the major reason God punished Israel with the Babylonian exile. Maybe if they were diligent, they reasoned, it would not happen again.

Instead of concentrating on Israel's historical traditions, P deals more with formal religion and worship, the priesthood and its regulations, genealogies, and sacrificial practices; in short, everything that enabled the community to maintain a right relationship with God and retain its identity in the face of changing times.

Style

Not the storyteller that the Yahwist was, the Priestly writer is more interested in discerning order and structure in God's plan for the world. This concern for order extends all the way from his story of creation, through the genealogies, into the categories of sacred and profane, pure and impure, clean and unclean.

The Priestly writer did have a sense of history and was very attentive to historical progression. This can be seen, for example, in his designations for God. God reveals himself progressively in history, and each major stage of the Priestly source is marked by a self-consciously appropriate divine name. The first stage is creation. Elohim is used to refer to God. Elohim is the generic name for God and

TABLE 3 | MAJOR EPISODES OF THE PRIESTLY SOURCE

Story Complex	Episode	Reference
Primeval Story		
	Creation	Gen. 1:1–2:4
	Genealogy of Seth	Gen. 5:1–28, 30–32
	Flood	Gen. 6–9 (with J)
	Table of Nations	Gen. 10
	Genealogy of Shem	Gen. 11:10–27
Ancestral Story		
	Covenant of Circumcision	Gen. 17
	Abraham buys Machpelah	Gen. 23
	Joseph Story	Gen. 37–50 (with J and E)
Exodus and Sinai		
	Call of Moses	Exod. 6–7 (with J)
	Exodus	Exod. 12–14 (with J and E)
	Tabernacle design	Exod. 25–31
	Tabernacle construction	Exod. 35–40
	Cultic regulations	Lev. 1-27
	Sinai wrap-up, departure	Num. 1–10
Wilderness Experiences		
	Spies	Num. 13–14 (with J)
	Rebellion of Korah	Num. 16 (with J)
	Levites	Num. 17–18
	Red Heifer	Num. 19
	Baal Peor sin	Num. 25 (with J)
	Appendices	Num. 26–36

has connotations of power and distance, consistent with P's rendition of creation.

The second stage is the ancestral period. Elohim revealed himself to Abraham as El Shaddai (Genesis 17:1ff.). We are not sure what this name means. It could be "God of the mountain" or "Mighty God," but it was used uniquely in this age, and uniquely by P. The third stage is the Mosaic era, when Elohim revealed his personal name Yahweh to Israel through Moses (Exodus 6:2ff.).

The Priestly writer has a set of stock phrases that distinguish his writing. Some of them are as follows:

- "to be fruitful and multiply"
- "throughout your generations"
- "this very day"
- "to establish a covenant," as opposed to "to cut a covenant" in JE
- "this is the thing that YHWH commanded"

In addition, the Priestly writer uses different technical vocabulary from the Yahwist or Elohist writers—for example, the words for person, congregation, tribe, and words for different types of property.

Theology

One of the emphases of the Priestly source is the continuity of God's care for Israel as demonstrated in its history. This is evident in certain pervasive themes:

1. *Blessing*. Blessing is something God does for the world. It is an expression of his favor. There are four epochs of blessing in the Priestly History. Each epoch of blessing is a stage in the development of God's interaction with his creation, culminating in blessing to Israel.

Humankind
"And God blessed them, and God said to them, 'Be fruitful and multiply, and fill the earth and subdue it; and have dominion over the fish of the sea and over the birds of the air and over every living thing that moves upon the earth.'" (Genesis 1:28)

Noah
"And God blessed Noah and his sons, and said to them, 'Be fruitful and multiply, and fill the earth. The fear of you and the dread of you shall be upon every beast of the earth.'" (Genesis 9:1–2)

Abraham
"I will give to you, and to your descendants after you, the land of your sojourning, all the land of Canaan, for an everlasting possession; and I will be their God." (Genesis 17:8)

Israel
"Your name is Jacob; no longer shall your name be called Jacob, but Israel shall be your name....I am God Almighty: Be fruitful and multiply; a nation and a group of nations will come from you; kings will come from your virility." (Genesis 35:10–11)

2. *Word of God*. Each of these stages of God's involvement with his world was driven by the spoken word of God. God's word brought the world into being (Genesis 1), it made a covenant with Noah after the flood

(Genesis 9) and later with Abraham (Genesis 17), and it finally drew up the national covenant with Israel (Exodus 20).

3. *Presence of God*. The Priestly source added a great deal of material relating to the presence of God among his people. It described in great detail the design and making of the ark of the covenant and the religious rites that would ensure that God would remain among his people.

What was the theological vision of this writer? What did he believe about God and the world? He envisioned a world ordered and controlled by God. Israel's history progressed according to a plan predetermined by God. God was in total control, and the world was secure and stable. The relationship between God and Israel was ordered by covenant.

Even if for some reason Israel alienated itself from God, there were sacrifices and rituals whereby a proper relationship could be reestablished. While on the one hand Yahweh was a demanding God, on the other hand he really only wanted to bless Israel. These assurances inspired hope in the hearts of an exilic Israel struggling to keep hope alive.

OVERALL SHAPE OF THE TORAH

Many issues concerning the literary analysis of the Pentateuch which are still open to discussion. One of them concerns the very nature of the Priestly contribution. Far from being a peripheral issue, this gets at the heart of the intent and purpose of the entire Pentateuch, because the Priestly writer was the last to work on this material.

Is there, in fact, such as thing as a Priestly source? Was the Priestly writer's work an independent literary source or was it just editorial work? Noth (1948) identified a Priestly narrative source that he claims existed independent of any other sources. The Priestly writer then took JE and wove it into his backbone source. Cross (1973) argued that the Priestly writer did not construct an independent narrative source, but only performed editorial work on preexisting material. The basis was JE, to which the Priestly editor added certain stories and legal materials in an attempt to reaffirm the traditions of Sinai.

Without taking sides, we would suggest that there are two dimensions to the Priestly tradition. First, there are the many stories that have a consistent style and focus when viewed as a group, the so-called Priestly source. Second, there are many features of Genesis through Numbers that suggest a deliberate overall structure due to editorial organizing and transition statements. The theology we can discern in this structuring is consistent with the views of the Priestly source, and so we naturally associate the two.

The exact date of the Priestly source has been debated. Kaufmann (1960) considers it preexilic, and even pre-Deuteronomic, because it does not reflect the centralization of religion in Jerusalem, which began only with Hezekiah. Hurvitz

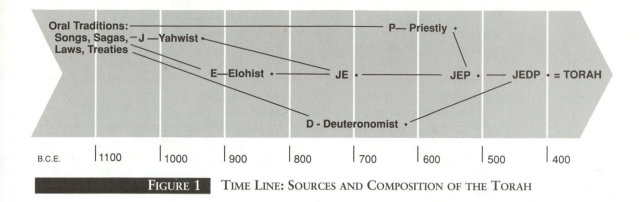

Oral Traditions: ────────────────────────────────── P— Priestly •
Songs, Sagas, — J —Yahwist •
Laws, Treaties

E—Elohist •──────── JE •──────── JEP • ──── JEDP • = TORAH

D - Deuteronomist •

B.C.E. |1100 |1000 |900 |800 |700 |600 |500 |400

FIGURE 1   TIME LINE: SOURCES AND COMPOSITION OF THE TORAH

(1974) compares the language of the Priestly source with known exilic and post-exilic writings and concludes that it does not necessarily fit best there. But the majority of scholars agree that it should be dated around 550–450 B.C.E.

Whether by writer or editor, the final shape of Genesis, Exodus, Leviticus, and Numbers was established through the efforts of the Priestly circle, and seems to have stabilized around the time of Ezra in the fifth century B.C.E. As a result of the Babylonian exile and Israel's later incorporation into the Persian empire, the Jews were no longer an independent nation. They had been absorbed into a larger dominating empire. But they still retained a large measure of religious and cultural freedom. The community, unable to define itself by political borders, articulated its sense of self by identifying with its ancestors. An important link with the past was forged by recovering, organizing, and editing those ancestral traditions that had survived the exile. The work that the Priestly circle put together, JEP, was then combined with Deuteronomy to form JEPD. Figure 1 illustrates the growth of the Torah through its various stages.

The editorial work of combining the various sources took place in stages. The editor (sometimes called a redactor by scholars) who joined the Yahwist (J) and Elohist (E) sources into JE put them together shortly after 721 B.C.E. The editor (a different one now) who added material from a Priestly source (P) did so around 500 B.C.E., giving rise to JEP. Deuteronomy was added around 400 B.C.E., and the Torah as we now have it became complete.

An issue that bears on the overall meaning of the Torah concerns the relationship of the book of Deuteronomy to the preceding three books. By the end of the fifth century B.C.E. there were two major collections of books. The first was Genesis through Numbers—a **Tetrateuch,** or set of four books. The second was Deuteronomy through Kings—the Deuteronomistic History. The first covered the early history of the nation, from creation to conquest. The second told the story of the rise and fall of the nation, from conquest to exile. Each collection has its own consistent voice and perspective.

But the Hebrew Bible did not divide the material along those lines. The major break in the canon of the Hebrew Bible comes *after* Deuteronomy, not before it.

The big question is this: Why do we have a **Pentateuch** instead of a Tetrateuch? Going by theological perspective, a Tetrateuch would be more natural, sharing as those books do the three sources J, E, and P.[1]

So why did the early Jewish community of faith structure the early books of the Hebrew Bible as a Pentateuch and not a Tetrateuch? The answer has a great deal to do with when and where the Torah took shape.

The Torah was formed in an exilic setting to provide a theological framework for a postexilic Jewish community. Above all, the exilic community needed a narrative and legal tradition that could provide direction to national life. The priests naturally turned to Moses as the great lawgiver. Since, in addition to Exodus through Numbers, Deuteronomy provided legal material attributed to Moses, it was included in this basic community document, thus creating a Pentateuch.

But more importantly, the Torah took shape as a document for a people "on the road," a people exiled and not yet home. In positing a Pentateuch, with a major break between Deuteronomy and Joshua, the community of faith was affirming this basic historical and theological fact. The people of God are continually moving from promise to fulfillment. The people of God have never "arrived." Like Moses, the exilic community viewed the Promised Land from a distance. By not including the conquest recorded in Joshua, the hope of the people resonated with that of their forebears. Like their ancestors, they too would gain possession of the land . . . someday. The structure of the Pentateuch affirms that the exilic community is essentially a community of hope.

---

[1] Von Rad (1938) argued that the tale of conquest in Joshua belongs with Genesis through Deuteronomy, resulting in a Hexateuch—a collection of six books. Joshua is the realization of the pentateuchal promises. The promises of land and offspring naturally culminate in the conquest.

FOR FURTHER STUDY

For material on source analysis and the structure of the Pentateuch, see the bibliography at the end of the Prologue to the Torah.

Yahwist. Bloom, Harold (1990). *The Book of J.* Translated from the Hebrew by David Rosenberg, interpreted by Harold Bloom. New York: Grove Weidenfeld. A modern deconstructionist's reading of the Yahwist document, which argues that J was a female.

Brueggemann, Walter. (1968). "David and His Theologian." *Catholic Biblical Quarterly* 30: 156–181. A summary of Yahwist theology.

Coote, Robert B., and David Robert Ord (1989). *The Bible's First History. From Eden to the Court of David with the Yahwist.* Philadelphia: Fortress Press.

Ellis, Peter (1968). *The Yahwist: The Bible's First Theologian.* Notre Dame, Ind.: University of Notre Dame Press.

Ollenburger, Ben (1987). *Zion, The City of the Great King: A Theological Symbol of the Jerusalem Cult.* Sheffield: JSOT Press A comprehensive treatment of Zion theology, which is another way of construing the Yahwist tradition.

Rendtorff, Rolf (1977). "The 'Yahwist' as Theologian? The Dilemma of Pentateuchal Criticism." *Journal for the Study of the Old Testament* 3: 2–10. In critique of the theory of literary sources.

Van Seters, John (1992). *Prologue to History: The Yahwist as Historian in Genesis.* Louisville, Ky.: Westminster/John Knox Press. Argues that the Yahwist was a historian in the period of the Babylonian exile.

Wolff, Hans Walter (1975). "The Kerygma of the Yahwist." In *The Vitality of Old Testament Traditions,* ed. Walter Brueggemann and Hans Walter Wolff, pp. 41–66. Atlanta: John Knox Press.

Elohist. Coote, Robert B. (1991). *In Defense of Revolution: The Elohist History.* Minneapolis, Minn.: Fortress Press.

Craghan, J. F. (1977). "The Elohist in Recent Literature." *Biblical Theology Bulletin* 7: 23–35.

Jenks, Alan W. (1977). *The Elohist and North Israelite Traditions.* SBL Monograph Series, 22. Missoula, Mont.: Scholars Press.

Wolff, Hans Walter (1982). "The Elohistic Fragments in the Pentateuch." *The Vitality of Old Testament Traditions.* 2d ed.; Atlanta: John Knox Press.

Priestly. Cross, Frank Moore (1973). "The Priestly Work," in *Canaanite Myth and Hebrew Epic.* Cambridge: Harvard University Press, pp. 293–352.

McEvenue, Sean E. (1971). *The Narrative Style of the Priestly Writer.* Analecta Biblica 50. Rome: Biblical Institute Press.

Patrick, Dale (1985). *Old Testament Law. An Introduction.* Atlanta: John Knox Press.

Tetrateuch–Pentateuch–Hexateuch. Auld, Graeme A. (1980). *Joshua, Moses and the Land: Tetrateuch–Pentateuch–Hexateuch in a Generation since 1938.* Edinburgh: T. & T. Clark.

Rad, Gerhard von (1938; trans. 1966). "The Form-Critical Problem of the Hexateuch," in *The Problem of the Hexateuch and Other Essays.* New York: McGraw-Hill.

WORKS CITED

Cross, Frank Moore (1973). "The Priestly Work," in *Canaanite Myth and Hebrew Epic*. Cambridge: Harvard University Press, pp. 293–352.

Hurvitz, Avi (1974). "The Evidence of Language in Dating the Priestly Code." *Revue Biblique* 81: 24–56.

Kaufmann, Yehezkel (1960). *The Religion of Israel: From Its Beginnings to the Babylonian Exile*. New York: Schocken.

Noth, Martin (1948; trans. 1972). *A History of Pentateuchal Traditions*. Englewood Cliffs, N.J.: Prentice-Hall.

von Rad, Gerhard (1938; trans. 1966). "The Form-Critical Problem of the Hexateuch," in *The Problem of the Hexateuch and Other Essays*. New York: McGraw-Hill.

Westermann, Claus (1976; trans. 1980). *The Promises to the Fathers: Studies on the Patriarchal Narratives*. Philadelphia: Fortress.

PROPHETS

2

PROLOGUE TO THE FORMER PROPHETS

FORMER AND LATTER PROPHETS

DEUTERONOMIC HISTORY

Names and Terms to Remember

Deuteronomic History (DH)
Former Prophets
Latter Prophets

FORMER AND LATTER PROPHETS

The second major section of the Hebrew Bible is the Prophets and follows the Torah. The basic division in the Hebrew Bible between Torah and Prophets goes back as early as the Hellenistic Period as attested by the book of Sirach. In the Hebrew Bible the section called the Prophets includes the narrative historical books Joshua, Judges, Samuel, and Kings (sometimes called the historical books in the Christian community), as well as the books more traditionally associated with the prophetic office, namely Isaiah, Jeremiah, Ezekiel, and the twelve so-called minor prophets.

The Prophets as a collection of books was further subdivided into two parts. The narrative historical books came to be called the **Former Prophets**, and the remainder were called the **Latter Prophets**. The distinction between Former and Latter in reference to the prophets does not refer to the chronology of the books but simply their placement in the Bible, as indicated here.

Former Prophets

Joshua	1, 2 Samuel
Judges	1, 2 Kings

Latter Prophets

Isaiah	Jonah
Jeremiah	Micah
Ezekiel	Nahum
Book of the Twelve:	Habakkuk
Hosea	Zephaniah
Joel	Haggai
Amos	Zechariah
Obadiah	Malachi

Our treatment of the prophets is divided into two parts corresponding to this division into Former and Latter Prophets. This prologue introduces the Former Prophets. A separate prologue will introduce the Latter Prophets, because the literature of the Latter Prophets presents different kinds of issues.

The narrative record of Joshua through Kings tells the story of Israel beginning with the conquest of Canaan under the leadership of Joshua. Then it recounts the process of settling the land and defending it against various enemies, told in Judges. The books of Samuel and Kings relate the rise of kingship in Israel and the development of Israel into two kingdoms. The story concludes with Judah's destruction at the hands of the Babylonians and the captivity of its leading citizens.

We will track two main issues through the Former Prophets. One issue is the theological perspective of the writers and compilers of this account. If we recognize the outlook governing its composition, we can better understand the intent of the story. The theological perspective of the Former Prophets is defined by Deuteronomy.

The other issue, not unrelated to the first, is the relationship between this theological literature and history. The account recorded in the Former Prophets may be termed *history*, but we must be aware of how we use that term. The writers should not be judged by our standards of scientific, objective historiography. They were believers in Yahweh, and it was their conviction that Yahweh was active in Israel's history.

It is significant that the Jewish community included the books Joshua through Kings in a section called "The Prophets." The intent of these narrative records was not to chronicle history for its own sake, but to bear witness to the work of Yahweh in the realm of human events. In this sense they are *prophetic*. Among other things, prophets were spiritually attuned individuals who were able to discern God's presence and work in the realm of human affairs.

DEUTERONOMIC HISTORY

Scholars sometimes refer to the Former Prophets as the **Deuteronomic History** (or **DH** for short) because the books in this collection were shaped by the theological perspective of the book of Deuteronomy. In some scholarly literature it is called the Deuteronomistic History; for our purposes this is equivalent to the DH.

The book of Deuteronomy is the narrative bridge between the Torah and the Prophets. It does double duty in the sense that it concludes the Torah and also sets the stage for the Prophets. As the conclusion of the Torah, it wraps up the early history of Israel, and does so sounding a note of anticipation. Moses had brought the Israelites to the edge of the Promised Land, but he himself died there. The great promises of land and nationhood still awaited fulfillment. The people were not yet in their promised homeland. Concluding the Torah with the book of Deuteronomy creates a feeling of expectancy, with the promises being fulfilled, at least almost so, in the book of Joshua (Figure 1).

Some scholars believe that the book of Deuteronomy was once attached to the Former Prophets, Joshua through Kings. The writer responsible for compiling this history added Deuteronomy 1:1–4:40 and chapters 29–34 to an earlier core Deuteronomy, once Deuteronomy came to be used as the preface to the entire Deuteronomic History. According to this view, the Deuteronomic History was completed shortly after the latest event mentioned in the book of Kings. That event was the Babylonians' release of Judah's king, Jehoiachin, from prison, which we can date to 561 B.C.E.

A good deal of scholarly research has focused on the theological perspective and integrating theme of the Deuteronomic History. Noth (1943) was the first scholar to develop the theory of a Deuteronomic History. He argued that the DH was composed to explain why the nation of Israel came to destruction by the Babylonians in the sixth century B.C.E. The story, he claims, focuses on the idolatry of Israel's kings and people, and explains why Yahweh allowed judgment to

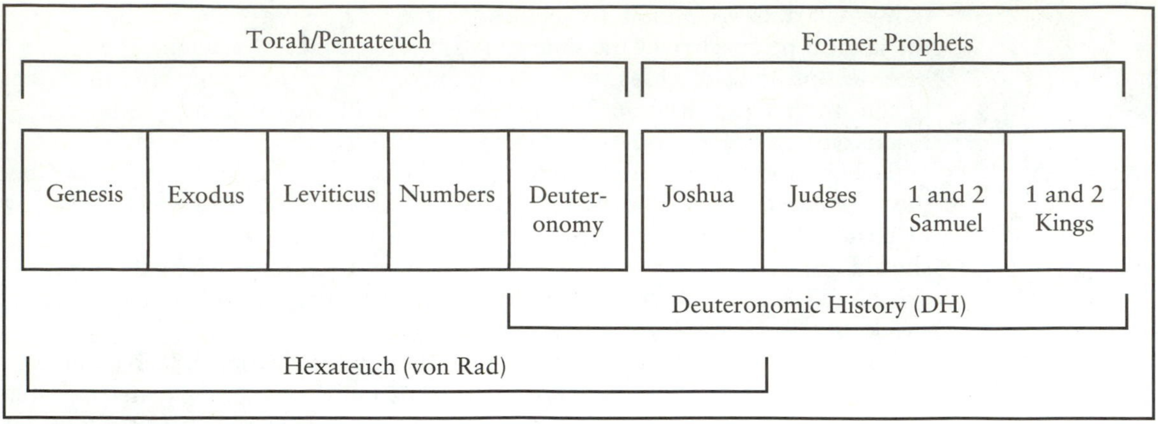

Torah/Pentateuch					Former Prophets			
Genesis	Exodus	Leviticus	Numbers	Deuter-onomy	Joshua	Judges	1 and 2 Samuel	1 and 2 Kings

Deuteronomic History (DH)

Hexateuch (von Rad)

FIGURE 1   GROUPINGS OF THE BOOKS

come upon them. Written to the Judean refugees of the Babylonian exile, the DH justified God and at least provided the assurance to the exiles that what happened, happened for a reason.

Von Rad (1962) found a more positive motivation behind the DH. In addition to the theme of judgment, which is most definitely there in the DH, von Rad suggested that grace was also present. Hope for the future was based on the covenant Yahweh had made with the house of David. That hope was still alive in the person of Jehoiachin. Von Rad argued that the release of Jehoiachin from prison, the note on which the book ends, was intended to provide inspiration to the exiles.

Wolff (1982) suggested that there is more to the purpose of the DH than justifying God's judgment or providing hope based on the Davidic covenant. He argued that the DH is essentially a call to repentance. It urges the exiles to turn from their disregard of God and repent. Only in this way would God restore his people to the covenant.

It is unrealistic to try to reduce such a complex work as the DH to one or two overarching themes. What these scholars have done is demonstrate the presence of certain significant themes that interweave the books of the DH. As you read the DH, be alert to the themes of God's judgment on apostasy, God's commitment to the house of David, and God's call to repentance.

The presence of multiple themes reflects that there was a complex history of composition to the DH. Its writers drew from many different sources and blocks of tradition. Within the books of the DH there are references to source books such as the "Book of the Chronicles of the Kings of Israel." And the individual books vary in tone, further evidencing development. A comparison of Joshua and Judges, for example, demonstrates how different in character and outlook they are, while both still contain Deuteronomic characteristics.

Cross (1973) has attempted to give account of the complexity of the editing of the DH. He has developed the theory that there were two editions of the DH. The first one took shape during the reign of Josiah (640–609 B.C.E.). Its governing themes were the effects of the sin of Jeroboam, who authorized Baal worship in the Northern Kingdom, and Yahweh's commitment to the house of David in the Southern Kingdom. It was written to be the inspiration for the reform program of Josiah.

The second and final edition, done during the exile around 550 B.C.E., consisted of a modest rewriting of the first edition. It reflects a more sober assessment of the future. It updated the earlier edition by adding the events that followed the reign of Josiah. The telling of the history of Israel and Judah thus becomes the occasion to enjoin the exiles to faithful living.

While the Deuteronomic History evidences an overall theological wholeness, each of the four books constituting it has its own literary unity, historical interest, stylistical character, and theological insight. We will now begin examining each of these four books of the Former Prophets, starting with the book of Joshua.

FOR FURTHER STUDY

Brueggemann, Walter (1968). "The Kerygma of the Deuteronomistic Historian: Gospel for Exiles." *Interpretation* 22: 387–402. Examines the term *good* in the DH to focus on how something good can come out of the exile.

Fretheim, Terence E. (1983). *Deuteronomic History*. Interpreting Biblical Texts Series. Nashville, Tenn.: Abingdon. Examines the DH by providing commentaries to specific texts.

Friedman, Richard Elliott (1981). *The Exile and Biblical Narrative: The Formation of the Deuteronomistic and Priestly Works*. Harvard Semitic Monograph Series, 22. Chico, Calif.: Scholars Press. The first chapter discusses Cross's two editions of the Deuteronomistic history, with special attention given to the editorial work of the exilic period.

Polzin, Robert (1980). *Moses and the Deuteronomist. A Literary Study of the Deuteronomic History—Part One: Deuteronomy, Joshua, Judges*. New York: Seabury Press. In this and the following two books Polzin writes a commentary on the DH, viewing it as a unified historiography artfully composed by literary minds.

Polzin, Robert (1989). *Samuel and the Deuteronomist. A Literary Study of the Deuteronomic History—Part Two: 1 Samuel*. San Francisco: Harper & Row.

Polzin, Robert (1993). *David and the Deuteronomist. A Literary Study of the Deuteronomic History—Part Three: 2 Samuel*. Indiana Studies in Biblical Literature. Bloomington: Indiana University Press.

WORKS CITED

Cross, Frank Moore (1973). "The Themes of the Book of Kings and the Structure of the Deuteronomistic History." In *Canaanite Myth and Hebrew Epic*. Cambridge, Mass.: Harvard University Press, pp. 274–89.

Noth, Martin (1943; English edition 1981). *The Deuteronomic History*. Sheffield: JSOT Press. This ground-breaking book first exposed the theological continuity of the Deuteronomic history. It is a translation of the first part of Noth's (1943)

Überlieferungsgeschichtliche Studien. Tübingen: Niemeyer.

von Rad, Gerhard (1962). *Old Testament Theology*. Vol. I. New York: Harper & Row, pp. 334–47.

Wolff, Hans Walter (1982). "The Kerygma of the Deuteronomic Historical Work." In *The Vitality of Old Testament Traditions*, ed. W. Brueggemann and H. W. Wolff, pp. 83–100. 2d ed. Atlanta: John Knox Press.

Joshua: Conquest of Canaan

6

Names and Terms to Remember

Ai	Gilgal	Jericho
ark of the covenant	Habiru / 'Apiru	Joshua
etiological tale	Hazor	lots / casting lots
Gibeon	holy war	Shechem

The book of Joshua contains the story of how the Israelites entered the land of Canaan and began to create a homeland. Under the leadership of Joshua the descendants of Jacob, now called the Israelites, entered Canaan and began to settle down there.

The book of Joshua picks up the story at exactly the same place Deuteronomy left it—with the death of Moses. The book of Joshua exhibits not only historical continuity but thematic continuity as well. One of the central themes of the Pentateuch was the promise of land. The book of Joshua details the actualization of this promise (see Figure 6.1).

The book of Joshua consists of three major sections. Chapters 1–12 contain stories of military confrontations with Canaanites resulting in victory for the Israelites. Chapters 13–21 contain delineations of Canaanite territories that were distributed among the twelve tribes of Israel. Chapters 22–24 wrap up the book with Joshua bidding farewell to the Israelites.

MILITARY CAMPAIGNS (1–12)

A straightforward reading of the book of Joshua suggests that all the Israelite tribes were united in one mighty fighting force. Led by **Joshua**, they stormed into Canaan and settled there. But be alert to hints that it may not have been quite so simple. A close reading of the books of Joshua and Judges suggests that the settlement was a long and complex process.

JOSHUA'S COMMISSION

After Moses died on Mt. Nebo (see Deuteronomy 34), Yahweh designated Joshua to take over as leader of the Israelites. Besides maintaining a connection with Deuteronomy by its references to Moses, see how the introduction to the book of Joshua in chapter 1 stresses the qualities of leadership Joshua must possess in order to lead the Israelites into the Promised Land.

1:1 After YHWH's servant Moses died, YHWH spoke to Joshua son of Nun, Moses's assistant, 2 "My servant Moses is dead. Get up now and cross over the Jordan, you and all this people, into the land I am giving to them, the Israelites. I have granted every place on which the soles of all your feet tread, just as I told Moses I would do. 4 These will be your boundaries: from the wilderness and the Lebanon as far as the great river, the Euphrates—the land of the Hittites all the way to the Great Sea in the west. 5 No one will be able to resist you as long as you are alive. Just as I was with Moses, I will be with you. I will not fail you. I will not abandon you. 6 Be

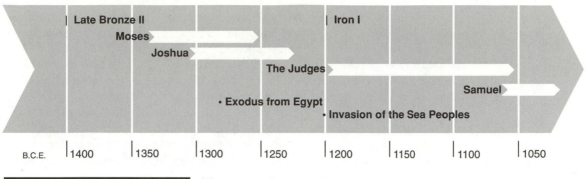

Late Bronze II

Moses

Joshua

Iron I

The Judges

Samuel

• Exodus from Egypt

• Invasion of the Sea Peoples

1400   1350   1300   1250   1200   1150   1100   1050

FIGURE 6.1   TIME LINE: BOOK OF JOSHUA

strong and courageous, for you will enable this people to inherit the land which I swore to their fathers I would give them. 7 Just be very strong and courageous. Make sure you do all the Torah which my servant Moses commanded you. Do not veer from it right or left. In that way you will succeed wherever you go. 8 Do not let this book of the Torah be missing from your mouth. Recite it day and night, so you are sure to do what is written in it. Then your way will prosper and you will succeed. 9 Have I not commanded you?—Be strong and courageous. Do not be terrified or frightened. YHWH your God will be with you wherever you go."

This passage contains Yahweh's speech commissioning Joshua as the new leader of his people. Yahweh does three things here: he encourages Joshua, he defines his responsibilities, and he assures him of God's continued presence. The vocabulary and sermonic style of this passage clearly mark it as Deuteronomic. Many of the same phrases are found, for example, in Deuteronomy 31:1–8, where Joshua received his first commissioning—phrases such as "Be strong and courageous," and "Do not be terrified or frightened." Note also the following features of this passage.

Moses is repeatedly called "YHWH's servant." This is a title of honor and reflects that Moses was dedicated to God's service. The title "Servant of YHWH" is a favorite Deuteronomic description of holy men and was applied primarily to kings and prophets in Deuteronomic literature.

The death of Moses signaled the start of the occupation of Canaan. Moses was not allowed to enter the land himself because he disobeyed God at Kadesh (see Numbers 20:1–13 and Deuteronomy 32:48–52). The death of Moses marks a major transition in Israel's history.

Notice the geographical markers in the text. The Jordan River is the eastern boundary of Canaan. The land lying to the east of the Jordan River was called Transjordan by the Israelites. Such a term obviously presupposes a position within Canaan in order for that land to be called the "across the Jordan" land. Still, certain Israelite tribes did claim territory in Transjordan at various times, including Reuben, Gad, and Manasseh. The reference to "the wilderness" is ambiguous. It could mean the eastern Arabian desert or the Sinai/Negev to the south.

The boundaries of the Promised Land here laid out define the northern and western borders in an expansive way. The territory promised to the Israelites extended as far north as the Euphrates River. The Abrahamic Covenant (see Genesis 15:18) and the Mosaic Covenant (see Deuteronomy 1:7) also extended the Promised Land to the Euphrates River. Not coincidentally the boundaries specified here in Joshua appear to coincide with the territorial extension of the Davidic kingdom.[1] The point is that the eventual Davidic kingdom was viewed as a fulfillment of God's design going back to Joshua, Moses, and Abraham.

Chapter 1 ends with Joshua instructing his helpers to prepare the people for crossing the Jordan River. They accepted his leadership and obeyed him, thereby demonstrating the effectiveness of his authority.

FIRST CAMPAIGN: JERICHO AND AI

In preparation for the invasion, Joshua sent an advance team of two men across the Jordan River to infiltrate **Jericho** and discover its weaknesses. The two spies found an accomplice in Rahab, a Jericho prostitute. She hid them from the king of the city–state of Jericho and in return extracted a pledge of protection from them: When they attacked Jericho, she and her family must be spared.

Before the spies left, Rahab uttered an amazing profession of faith, given the fact that she was Canaanite (2:8–13). She expressed her belief that Yahweh had providentially given the land of Canaan to the Israelites. The spies brought back an encouraging report (no doubt intentionally in contrast with the report of the ten cynical spies in the wilderness, see Numbers 13–14). Israel was ready to attack.

The priests picked up the ark and left Shittim, heading for the Jordan River. When their feet touched the waters of the Jordan, it stopped flowing, and the people crossed over on dry ground. This miracle of the crossing parallels the miracle of crossing the Red Sea (see Exodus 14), and by association with Moses and his miracle, the leadership of Joshua is again validated. Furthermore, these two crossings bracket the early history of the Hebrews: Yahweh gave them deliverance from oppression when they crossed the Red Sea on dry ground; he brought them into the Promised Land across the Jordan River on dry ground.

Once the entire group had crossed over, a representative from each tribe picked up a stone from the river bottom and carried it to **Gilgal**. Together they erected a twelve-stone monument to the crossing. One of the historical–theological motifs of the book of Joshua is remembering. The events to be remembered include this miraculous crossing Yahweh engineered, the victory over Jericho, and especially the making of the covenant. As you read the book of Joshua, note how the Israelites were to remember the work of Yahweh, and note how each event was marked with a physical memorial, usually a heap of stones in some distinctive formation. This twelve-stone monument is just the first of many memorials.

Also at Gilgal, Joshua had all the male Israelites circumcised. The core of this circumcision story appears to be an **etiological tale**, that is, a story meant to ex-

---

[1] See 2 Sam. 8:3, which extends David's reach far into Syria, if not all the way to the Euphrates River itself.

plain a phenomenon well-known to the writer and his original readers. In this case, the pile of foreskins left over after the mass circumcision (notice that this is another "heap," hence a memorial) was used to explain the place name Gibeath–haaraloth (5:3), a place presumably in the vicinity of the crossing. The name literally means *Hill of Foreskins*. This etiological tale was then taken up by the writer and incorporated into the narrative to make a significant point about the disposition of the Israelites. Those who were circumcised were, of course, the second generation of Israelites since the departure from Egypt. That they were uncircumcised implies that the first generation was unfaithful in yet another way. They had failed to perpetuate the essential sign of the covenant (see Genesis 17).

Gilgal, the first stopping place in the Promised Land, had additional significance. There the Israelites kept the Passover celebration for the first time since its founding in Egypt the night of the Exodus. This was to be a yearly celebration, yet this was the first time it had been observed. The text again suggests that the second generation was faithful whereas the first had not been.

Finally, with an unmistakable sign, Yahweh signaled that the Israelites had finally arrived in the land of promise. The manna that had sustained them for forty years in the wilderness ceased. Why? The Israelites no longer needed miraculous feeding because the produce of the "land flowing with milk and honey" would amply provide for them (see Figure 6.2).

Commander of Yahweh's Army

In a curious encounter between Joshua and a supernatural being prior to the battle for Jericho, Joshua's understanding of Yahweh's role in the conquest became clear.

> 5:13 *When Joshua was near Jericho, he looked up and was surprised to see a man standing right in front of him. His sword was unsheathed in his hand. Joshua walked up to him and said to him, "Are you on our side or are you against us?" 14 He said to him, "Neither. I am the commander of the army of YHWH. Now I have come." Joshua fell face down on the ground and did obeisance. He said to him, "What does my Lord have to say to your servant?" 15 The commander of YHWH's army said, "Take off your sandal from your foot, for the place on which you are standing is holy." And Joshua did so.*

On first meeting this "man" Joshua thought he was just another soldier. He innocently asked him if he would be joining the Israelite cause, or was he on the Canaanite side? When his identity as a representative of Yahweh became clear, Joshua immediately humbled himself by falling spread-eagle to the ground. This "commander" is probably to be identified with the "angel of YHWH," who appears elsewhere in the Hebrew Bible, most notably in the ancestors' encounters with God. As commander of the army of Yahweh, the army elsewhere called "the host of heaven," he was in charge of leading the conquest.

The meaning of this story is elusive and questions remain because the account is so sketchy. One possible interpretation is that this encounter would teach Joshua who was fighting for whom. This meeting clarified that Yahweh does not

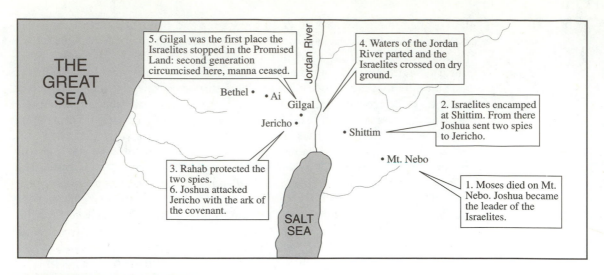

FIGURE 6.2   **CROSSING THE JORDAN RIVER**

fight for Joshua, as if Yahweh was at Joshua's command. Yahweh's army retains its independence, with Joshua fighting for Yahweh.

The command to take off his sandals is a quotation you might recognize from Moses' encounter with God at the burning bush (see Exodus 3). This experience of Joshua paralleling that of Moses further reinforces the legitimate succession of Joshua.

The statement that "this is holy ground" originally marked the site of this encounter as a holy place. Used now within the context of the Israelite movement into Canaan, it confirms that this was the "holy land," perhaps implying that Yahweh dwells here.

Cryptic though this story is, it is of signal importance, much as the other events at Gilgal were. Such a meeting with God's representative, a theophany, indicates that Yahweh is now present and accessible in the Promised Land. The fight for the holy land can now begin. The first battle is over Jericho.

Jericho's Walls Fall Down

The story of the famous fight against Jericho does not detail the military side of things. It does not describe the armor of the Israelites or any siege devices. Rather, the account describes the battle as a sacred event. Notice the central role of the **ark of the covenant,** the sacred storage box for the covenant documents, which doubles as God's throne and marks the location of his presence.

> 6:1 *Jericho was closed and inaccessible because of the Israelites. No one came out and no one went in. 2 YHWH said to Joshua, "See, I have given you control of Jericho, including its king and soldiers. 3 Have all the men of the camp walk around the city. Circle the city one time. Do this for six days. 4 Seven priests will carry seven ram's horn trumpets before the ark. On the seventh day you will circle the city seven times, and the priests will*

blow the trumpets. 5 When the ram's horn sounds, when you hear the sound of the trumpet, let the people shout loudly. Then the wall of the city will fall down, and each person can go straight in."

Did you notice the repeated use of the number seven? This stamps the event as priestly and holy. The number seven is associated with the divinely ordained structure of the week. Remember the priestly account of creation in Genesis 1:1–2:4. The seventh day, the day the walls fell, would naturally be associated with the Sabbath, although this is not stated in so many words. The fall of the city, taking place on the seventh day, Israel's holy day, marks the victory as the work of Yahweh. Remember that this story would have taken its final shape in the exilic community for whom circumcision and the Sabbath were central to the sense of identity.

Holy War

The army followed Yahweh's instructions and the city walls collapsed. Entering the city was now possible through breaches in the fortifications, so each soldier went straight in.

> *6:21 They devoted to destruction by the sword the entire city: man and woman, young and old, cow and sheep.*

The phrase "devoted to destruction," sometimes called "the ban," refers to the Israelite practice of destroying the entire population of a city along with all its material goods. This is the practice of **holy war**. In the religious perspective of holy war, Yahweh alone fights the battle and wins the victory, therefore to him alone belongs the booty. By killing and then burning the entire city, everything was given over to God. One of the implications of holy war for Israel is that making war was a not-for-profit enterprise. The Israelites were not allowed to benefit personally or materially from the spoils of this victory.

The instruction to totally eliminate the Canaanite enemy was given to effect a complete separation between the incoming Israelites and the native Canaanite inhabitants. As the account of the book of Joshua goes on to describe, this instruction was not carried out to the letter. The result was that many Canaanites were left in the land, and the eventual spiritual problems of the Israelites were traced to this shortcoming. The Canaanites kept luring the Israelites to follow after foreign gods.

The notion of Israelite holy war continues to be a problem among those who hold the Hebrew Bible dear. For many modern readers, it is a scandal that Israel's God should have mandated the complete destruction of a group of human beings. Can the same rationale be used in the postbiblical age to justify war against "heathens," as happened during the Crusades and at other times? How should we deal with the warfare ideology of the book of Joshua?

There is no easy answer. But certain issues should be considered. First, the narrative may be an idealization. That is, perhaps the Israelites never consistently enforced the ban or completely destroyed a resident population. That they did not is in hindsight the Hebrew Bible's own theological explanation of why a pure Yahwism never took hold.

Second, we must remember that this period in Israel's history was unique. What may have been demanded at that time in holy war does not necessarily apply to later periods. Holy war was instituted only to give Israel a homeland in Canaan and cannot be generalized as a religious principle for all time.

Third, the results of archaeological investigations are inconclusive, but they do suggest that there was no complete destruction of Jericho at the time of Joshua's incursion. In other words, the archaeological record suggests that the ban was never in fact completely carried out. See the box about the archaeology of Jericho for some details.

Jericho was a pile of burned rubble after the Israelites were done with it—another memorial heap. It was never to be rebuilt (though Hiel of Bethel later tried, see 1 Kings 16:34), as a reminder of the power of Yahweh and the Israelites over the Canaanites.

After the victory at Jericho the Israelites attacked **Ai**. Expecting only minimal resistance, Joshua sent a small raiding party against the city, yet the Israelite fighters were soundly defeated. This defeat was a signal that God was displeased with the Israelites. By **casting lots** an Israelite named Achan was identified as the culprit. Casting lots was the mechanical means whereby God revealed his decisions. The **lots** were small objects made of clay, wood, or stone, like dice. After being thrown, their configuration provided answers. Because Achan had stolen goods from Jericho, God was displeased with all the Israelites. Only after the offender was purged from their midst would God's favor be restored.

Achan and his entire family were taken outside the camp, where they were executed by stoning. Stoning usually took the form of throwing the guilty party off a precipice. Only if the offender did not die from the fall would he be pelted with rocks until dead. While the punishment seems severe—not just Achan himself but also his entire family were killed—it has a certain logic. The act of disobedience was considered so serious that Achan needed to be deprived of any future life in Israel. By eliminating all his offspring his family name was forever erased

Ai in Hebrew means ruin (today it is called et-Tell, which in Arabic also means ruin). There may very well be another etiological tale, along with a clever pun, here. The Israelites of the monarchic and exilic periods would have known this site as a ruins, and this story told them how it happened.

Ai was a massive fortified city of some twenty-seven acres through much of the Early Bronze Age (3300–2000 B.C.E.). From then until the beginning of the Iron I Age it lay in ruins. If the conquest is to be dated around 1250 B.C.E., there was no occupation at Ai at the time of Joshua. The Iron Age occupation began around 1125 B.C.E., covering only about two acres and consisting of an unfortified village. Perhaps a later Israelite capture of Ai was credited to Joshua.

from among the Israelites. It is ironic that nonetheless we still remember him through the narrative. And the pile of rocks heaped over Achan and his family were a reminder to Israel of the need for strict obedience to Yahweh.

Having been purged of the sinner, the Israelites again attacked Ai. Joshua was more deliberate in his plans the second time around. He set an ambush, drawing the soldiers of Ai outside the city walls. He surrounded them with his men and completely burned the city and its inhabitants. The account ends with Joshua covering the city of Ai with stones "which stand there to this day" (8:29). It seems that Joshua and the Israelites were intent on leaving stone memorials wherever they went, and they all remain "to this day." They did it at Gilgal after crossing the river, Jericho's walls fell in a heap of stones, Achan and family were buried under stones, and here is yet another stone memorial. Note where else in following chapters of Joshua you find piles of stones, and try to determine why they are mentioned and their significance.

Altar at Shechem

God instructed Joshua to build an altar on Mt. Ebal. Mt. Ebal, along with Mt. Gerazim, flanks the important site of **Shechem** in central Canaan. Here Joshua paused with the people to recall to their memory the torah of Moses.

8:30 Then Joshua built an altar to YHWH the God of Israel on Mt. Ebal, 31 just as Moses YHWH's Servant commanded the Israelites, as it is written in the book of the torah of Moses: "an altar of untrimmed stones on which no iron tool has worked." They offered burnt offerings to YHWH on it, and sacrificed peace offerings. 32 He wrote on the stones there a copy of the torah of Moses. He wrote it in front of the Israelites. 33 All Israel (that is, the elders, the officers and the judges), foreigners as well as citizens, were standing on either side of the ark facing the levitical priests who carry the ark of the covenant of YHWH. Half of them were in front of Mt. Gerazim and half of them were in front of Mt. Ebal, just as Moses, YHWH's Servant, had commanded earlier, so that the people of Israel could get blessing. 34 Then he called out the words of the torah, blessing and curse, according to all that was written in the book of the torah. 35 There was not one word which Moses commanded that Joshua did not call out before the congregation of Israel, including women and children and the foreigners who lived among them.

It did not take long for us to come across another rock memorial. In this passage we find yet another pile of rough stones, this time forming an altar to Yahweh. The altar was erected in connection with the ceremony of remembering the torah of Moses, that is, the covenant God made with Israel through Moses.

You may have noticed that this passage has strong Deuteronomic overtones. It is, in fact, a passage with many parallels to Deuteronomy 27:1–8, which calls for a time of remembering the covenant once the people reach the Promised Land. The event recorded here marks a milestone in the Joshua stories of conquest. This story seems to imply that after taking Jericho and Ai the Israelites were secure enough in the land that they could do what Moses had commanded them in Deuteronomy. Perhaps it also hints of their faithfulness.

A further note of fulfillment echoes in this passage. Although Shechem is not itself mentioned, every Israelite would have known that it lay between Mt. Ebal and Mt. Gerazim. Shechem had significant associations. It was the first stopping place of Abraham when he entered Canaan. There Abraham built an altar, and there God first gave him the promise of possession of Canaan (see Genesis 12:6–7).

Shechem also has important federation associations. As we will see in Joshua 24, it was where Joshua bound the tribes together in a covenant. And it was the site where the Northern Kingdom rallied and found unity under Jeroboam when it broke away from Judah.

After this Shechem interlude, the narrative returns to the business of securing the land. The first campaign in the central hill country established the Israelite presence. New territory must now be taken—first south, then north, in two additional campaigns.

SECOND CAMPAIGN: FIVE SOUTHERN CITY-STATES

The presence of the Israelites in Canaan was viewed increasingly as a threat by most of the indigenous Canaanites. But apparently isolated villages decided it would be to their advantage to make peace with the Israelites. One such village was **Gibeon**.

The problem for them, however, was that they knew that the Israelites were not in the practice of making peace but were under holy war orders of blanket extermination. But the Gibeonites were clever in getting around this. Although they lived only a short distance away from Gilgal where the Israelites encamped, they disguised themselves as foreigners. They figured that if they were foreigners who presumably held no claim to Canaan, then the Israelites might make a treaty with them.

The Israelites were tricked by this deceit and entered into formal treaty arrangements with the Gibeonites, which included a pledge of mutual protection. When the Israelites found out that these people lived only a short distance away they were furious, but they could not dissolve the treaty and still be deemed honorable. In retaliation for their trickery, the Israelites enslaved the Gibeonites, making them "hewers of wood and drawers of water," but stopped short of killing them.

When the larger Canaanite city–states of the area heard of the Gibeonites' accommodation to the Israelites, they in turn were furious and attacked Gibeon. The Israelites were bound by treaty to come to their aid. In the process of rescuing the Gibeonites, Joshua and the Israelites defeated the kings of five important southern city–states: Jerusalem, Hebron, Jarmuth, Lachish, and Eglon. This secured the territory of what would become Judah for the Israelites.

THIRD CAMPAIGN: HAZOR

A coalition of city–states in the region of the Sea of Galilee was organized by Jabin, king of **Hazor**. They fought against the Israelites at Merom. Joshua and the Israelites won a great victory and burned Hazor to the ground.

This was a tremendous victory. Hazor was the dominant urban center in northern Canaan in the Middle Bronze Age. Its principal investigator, Yadin (1972), has called it "the New York City of Canaan." It was smaller in the Late Bronze Age, yet still significant. Being able to dispose of Hazor, the Israelites must have been a considerable fighting force.

ARCHAEOLOGY OF HAZOR

Hazor is a massive site that has been extensively unearthed. It was occupied during the Late Bronze Age (1550–1200 B.C.E.). The site contains unmistakable evidence of destruction by fire in the second half of the thirteenth century B.C.E. This destruction is credited to Joshua by most scholars. Hazor was resettled after this devastation and the material remains suggest it was by a less sophisticated people, usually identified with the Israelites. These people lived in tents and huts. The site was refortified and developed in the time of Solomon.

The narrator asserts that the conquest was now complete (see Figure 6.3). Note the finality of his summary statements:

- "Joshua left nothing undone of all that YHWH had commanded Moses" (11:15)
- "Joshua took all that land, just as YHWH told Moses. Joshua gave it as an inheritance to Israel. Each tribe got its allotment. The land had rest from war." (11:23)

The wars of conquest now at an end, Joshua set about dividing up the land among the tribes.

TRIBAL TERRITORIES (13–21)

Chapters 13–21 consist of lists of tribal boundaries and settlements and, frankly, make for boring reading. Nonetheless, they do provide a more nuanced picture of the occupation. In addition to tallying the territory taken by the Israelites, there are accounts of failures to expel the Canaanites.

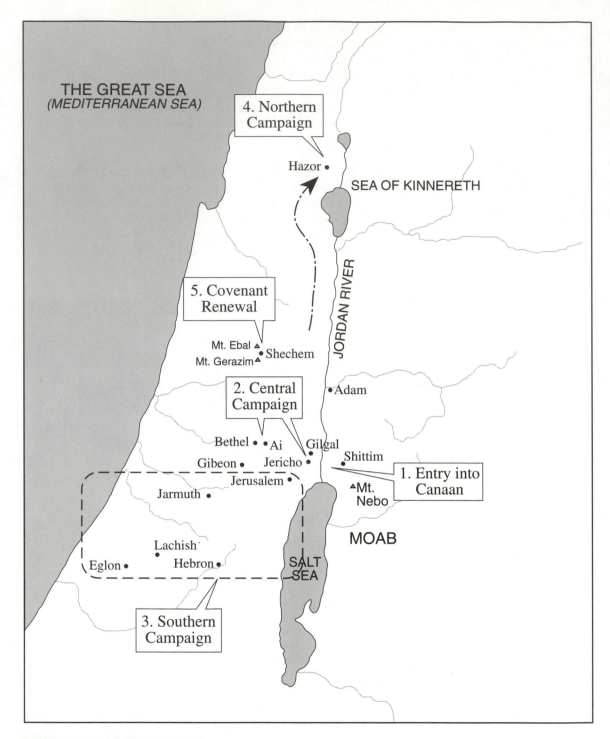

THE GREAT SEA
(MEDITERRANEAN SEA)

4. Northern Campaign

Hazor

SEA OF KINNERETH

JORDAN RIVER

5. Covenant Renewal

Mt. Ebal ▲ • Shechem
Mt. Gerazim ▲

• Adam

2. Central Campaign

Bethel • • Ai   Gilgal
Gibeon • Jericho • • Shittim

Jerusalem •

1. Entry into Canaan

Jarmuth •

▲ Mt. Nebo

MOAB

Lachish •

Eglon •   Hebron •

SALT SEA

3. Southern Campaign

FIGURE 6.3   CAMPAIGNS OF THE CONQUEST

Theologically, the narrative makes a point about possession of the land. Joshua apportioned the territories on the basis of lots, the same method used to determine Achan's guilt. Distributing the land by this means reinforced the belief that Canaan belonged ultimately to Yahweh, and God distributed it according to divine wishes.

Also notable was the establishment of cities of refuge. These were six cities to which a person could flee and find protection in case he accidentally killed another person. The intention of this provision was to call a halt to the clan feuds that would otherwise result when such accidents happened.

The Levites were given forty-eight cities throughout the land. The Levites did not have an extended tribal territory as such. Instead, they were scattered throughout all the other tribes and lived in these levitical cities. An examination of the cities and their histories of occupation suggests that this list better reflects a network of levitical cities in the eighth century B.C.E. rather than the twelfth century. These sites appear to have been centers for Torah instruction by the Levites. The Levites appear to be responsible for the Deuteronomic History, so naturally they would be concerned to suggest that their special cities had authorization going back to the earliest period of the settlement, the time of Joshua.

As with the account of military occupation, so with the account of territorial allotments: the account ends with a neat summary suggesting finality and completeness.

> 21:43 So YHWH gave to Israel all the land which he had sworn to give to their fathers. They took possession of it and settled in it. 44 YHWH gave them rest on every front just as he had sworn to their fathers. Not one of their enemies remained facing them. YHWH gave them power over all their enemies. 45 Not one promise of all the good promises which YHWH spoke to the house of Israel remained unfulfilled. Everything came true.

In no uncertain terms this summary reinforces the fulfillment dimension of the occupation. Everything happened just as God had promised to the ancestors God was with the people, giving them complete victory and perfect shalom.

The phrase *house of Israel* is used only here in Joshua. It encapsulates the notion of the unity of Israel and suggests that they are now a family living in a home of their own.

When we considered the archaeology of Jericho and Ai we saw that the material evidence at times seemed to clash with the biblical narrative. Textual scholars and archaeologists have been wrestling with the historical and material evidence to reconstruct how the Israelites came to occupy Canaan. As we will see, the reconstruction of how the conquest occurred, if we can even call it a conquest, has implications for the question of the ethnic and sociological identity of the nation of Israel.

The stories of military conquest in Joshua 2–12 account for only a small number of Canaanite cities. Conquering Jericho, Hazor, and a handful of other places does not constitute a sweeping military subjugation of the entire land of Canaan. Joshua 13 mentions certain territories that remained unconquered during the

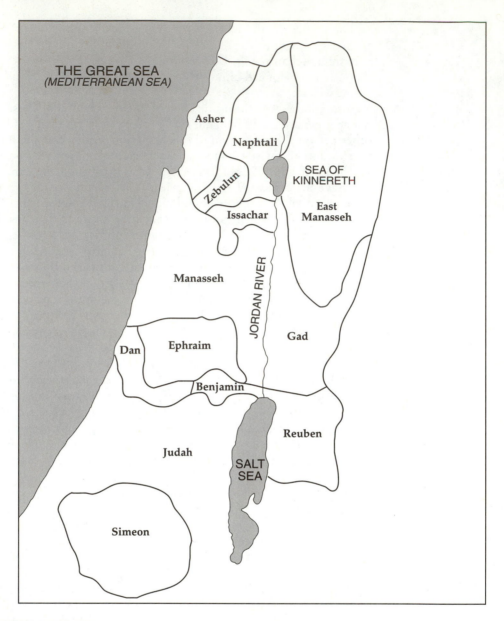

THE GREAT SEA
(MEDITERRANEAN SEA)

Asher

Naphtali

SEA OF
KINNERETH

Zebulun

Issachar

East
Manasseh

Manasseh

JORDAN RIVER

Dan

Ephraim

Gad

Benjamin

Reuben

Judah

SALT
SEA

Simeon

FIGURE 6.4   TRIBAL TERRITORIES

lifetime of Joshua. The incompleteness of the occupation under Joshua becomes even clearer when reading the book of Judges. The first chapters contain extensive inventories of land not taken, indicating that the Israelites were a minority in Canaan, subsisting primarily in the hill country. The cities and the plains were still controlled by Canaanites.

How, then, did the Israelites eventually come to dominate the area? All of the indications point to a complicated and gradual process of Israelite settlement and control. This issue is the subject of vigorous debate, and the issue will not be resolved for some time to come. On the basis of archaeological and sociohistorical data, there are three basic models of the occupation.

1. *Migration Model.* Formulated by Noth (1960) and refined by Weippert (1971), this theory denies that there was any significant military action, apart perhaps from a few minor skirmishes. Instead, over a span of centuries, groups of seminomadic herdsmen began to settle down in those regions of Canaan that were capable of sustaining a sedentary agricultural way of life.

The entity called Israel took shape when such groups settled down after a period of peaceful infiltration. They derived their unity not from shared ancestry but from a common sociotheological perspective. Each group took with them stories of their past, including their religious traditions. The stories were combined, unified, and harmonized to suggest that the entire history was from the beginning owned by the entire group. Thus, the final story, contained in Genesis through Joshua, is an idealization based on a composite of many histories.

2. *Military Conquest Model.* This approach, associated with Albright (1949) and Wright (1962), tends to accept and support the essential historical accuracy of the Joshua account by relating it to modern archaeological findings. It suggests that Joshua led a core group into Transjordan and Canaan and secured their presence in the land. Evidence of a sudden violent destruction in the thirteenth century B.C.E. can be found at several city sites. Some of these cities were subsequently rebuilt, but in a manner suggesting a lower level of skill and resources. They correlate this change in technique and level of material culture with the transition from sophisticated Canaanite occupation to a less-developed Israelite takeover. One of the problems with this theory, however, is that the key sites of Jericho and Ai do not evidence destruction at the expected time.

3. *Internal Revolt Model.* First articulated by Mendenhall (1962) and now closely associated with Gottwald (1979), this theory holds that there was minimal incursion of foreign groups from outside of Canaan. Rather, the birth of Israel was the result of internal political upheaval and social revolution. In the thirteenth century B.C.E. Canaan was controlled by numerous city–states, and these in turn were controlled by kings and aristocrats who oppressed the rural farmers and herdsmen. The latter became increasingly disaffected with the autocratic control of the urban establishment. These disenfranchised people banded together and wrestled control away from the oppressing upper class. Joshua and a small group of Hebrews were the catalyst for the insurrection.

Mendenhall finds support for this theory in a known group of marginalized citizens called the **Habiru**, sometimes transliterated as **'Apiru**. Attested in Canaanite-related documents called the Amarna letters, the Habiru were indigenous Canaanites of inferior social status who were pressuring the ruling establishment. The Hebrews may have been this kind of people, living on the fringes of established Canaanite society. Other investigators, however, have discounted any connection between the Habiru and the Hebrews, pointing out that the two words cannot be linguistically related in spite of the fact that they have similar sounds. Furthermore, the social and political conditions described in the Amarna letters do not match the Israelite situation as found in the books of Joshua and Judges.

A verifiably accurate picture of early Israel's occupation of Canaan is incapable of being drawn at this time. But we can say certain things about the issue. It can be granted that the story as told in the book of Joshua is to a certain extent a theological idealization intended to affirm the fulfillment of God's promise of the land. Perhaps it never intended to provide a complete historical account, choosing only a few incidents of conquest to characterize the work of God.

On the other hand, history and archaeology, along with hints in the biblical text, combine to fill out our understanding of Israel at this time. Israel was certainly more diverse than scholars earlier had thought. It was a virtual melting pot of people. Certainly a core group traced their ancestry back to the patriarchs and matriarchs. And the nucleus of the occupation force came to Israel via Egypt. But other indigenous Canaanite social and ethnic groups aligned themselves with this nucleus for religious and political reasons, the Gibeonites among them. While the process of occupation begun under the leadership of Joshua achieved some victories that signaled complete control, the occupation efforts lasted a long time after his death and were accomplished with a combination of military confrontation and peaceful absorption. Certainly none of the above "purist" models alone explains the complex and lengthy process.

COVENANT CONSIDERATIONS (22–24)

The last three chapters of the book draw the Joshua era to a close. Joshua exhorts the tribes to remain faithful and engages them in covenant renewal.

JOSHUA'S FAREWELL

Toward the end of Joshua's life a conflict among the tribes arose, recorded in chapter 22, in which the transjordanian tribes of Reuben, Gad, and East–Manasseh fought against the Israelite tribes in Canaan. The conflict was religious in nature and almost provoked a full-scale civil war. The conflict had to do with the desire of those transjordanian tribes to have their own worship center, specifically an altar—yes, yet another pile of stones! The Canaan tribes believed that Yahweh could be worshiped only where the ark of the covenant was found; at this time it was Shiloh. The matter was settled only after those remote tribes agreed not to use the altar for sacrifice but only as a memorial to the work of

Yahweh. These are their words of dedication: "This is a witness among us that YHWH is God" (22:34).

Although a somewhat obscure incident, it nonetheless served at least two functions. First, it affirmed the religious centrality of the worship center that housed the ark of the covenant. Here it applied to Shiloh, but the principle later applied to Jerusalem. This principle was always important to the tradition of Deuteronomy. Second, it allowed for the possibility that Yahweh could still be honored elsewhere, even in the "foreign" territory of Transjordan. Those living in exile (when these stories were finally edited) certainly took comfort knowing that just because they were distant from the "Holy City," they were not necessarily distant from God.

The first five verses of chapter 22 and all of chapter 23 are heavily Deuteronomic in style and content. Chapter 23 contains the farewell speech of Joshua. Such speeches are characteristic of the Deuteronomic Historian. In the farewell speeches of Israel's great leaders, of course Moses, but also including Joshua, Samuel, and David, the theology of covenant is clearly articulated. Here in chapter 23 Joshua stresses the fulfillment of promise and encourages the people to remain faithful to the Torah of Moses. But he also sounds a strong note of warning. The Canaanites who were left in the land would threaten Israel's loyalty to Yahweh. If Israel strayed from complete covenant loyalty and worshiped the gods of the Canaanites, it would be removed from the land of promise.

These dire words of warning portend what actually happened to Israel resulting in the Assyrian destruction of the eighth century B.C.E., and to Judah in the Babylonian exile of the sixth century. But the words are not just there as an "I told you so." They contain the theology that would enable the Israelites to make sense out of what happened to them when they were dispossessed of the land. Punishments involving removal from the land are their own fault, and restoration would come with obedience.

COVENANT RENEWAL AT SHECHEM

Joshua called all the tribes to meet at Shechem. In a prophetic type of address, where he spoke for Yahweh in the first person, Joshua reviewed the history of Yahweh's care: I took Abraham from Mesopotamia, I gave him Isaac, I brought you out of Egypt, I gave you the land. This historical review is reminiscent of the historical prologue section of treaty documents. Indeed, Joshua seems to be holding a treaty-signing session here. He got down in writing the tribes' loyalty pledge to Yahweh, their overlord.

Then Joshua challenged the people to choose Yahweh and reject both their ancestral gods and all the gods of Canaan. The people answered, "Yahweh our God we will serve. Him we will obey." Joshua recorded the covenant in the book of the Torah of God and set up a stone as a memorial to the event. The stone monument would be a witness to the people's pledge to serve Yahweh. As throughout the book of Joshua, a monument serves as a lasting testimony to the faithfulness of Yahweh and the people's acknowledgment of God's goodness.

This covenant commitment event helps to explain how the Israelites found unity. Going back to our discussion of the nature of this early community, we recognize that early Israel was composed of many different groups. Some came from outside, descended from Abraham. Others were native to the area, such as Rahab and the Gibeonites. What did they have in common? How did they find unity? It was through a common commitment to Yahweh. This commitment was formalized in covenant and was recorded in the Deuteronomic literature. It defined the people's loyalty to Yahweh and to each other.

Concluding the book, we are told that Joshua died and the bones of Joseph, which the people had been carrying around since they left Egypt, were finally laid to rest at Shechem. Thus, the first momentous phase in the occupation of the land found closure and fulfillment.

OVERALL SHAPE OF THE BOOK OF JOSHUA

The book of Joshua contains stories and other material from many sources. It contains sagas of military confrontation, origin stories that explain phenomena familiar to Israelites of the monarchy (called etiological tales), lists of conquered kings, and lists of tribal territory. All of this material was organized to tell a story of lightning conquest, and it was all placed within the career of Joshua.

The book of Joshua in its final form consists of three main parts: the military campaigns, the tribal territories, and covenant considerations. The three parts connect logically.

Outline of the Book of Joshua

I. Military Campaigns (1–12)
    A. Yahweh commissions Joshua (1)
    B. Spying the land (2)
    C. Crossing the Jordan (3–4)
    D. Events at Gilgal (5)
    E. Military stories (6–12)
        1. Jericho (6)
        2. Ai (7–8)
        3. Southern city–states (9–10)
        4. Hazor (11)
        5. List of conquests (12)
II. Tribal Territories (13–21)
    A. Settlement of claims (13–17)
    B. Remainder of tribes (18–19)
    C. Cities of refuge (20)
    D. Levitical cities (21)
III. Covenant Considerations (22–24)
    A. Worship in Transjordan (22)
    B. Covenant address to leaders (23)
    C. Covenant renewal at Shechem (24)

The surface simplicity of the story masks an underlying literary and historical complexity, as we have seen.

Why was the conquest story told in this simplistic way? No doubt part of the reason has to do with historical memory and the creation of legends. Joshua was idealized and the sweep of victory was portrayed as absolute. But the picture also has to do with the troubled times during which the story of occupation was shaped. It was crafted during the time of Babylonian domination in the sixth century B.C.E., so the writers placed emphasis on possession of the land as the fulfillment of promise. They stressed the faithfulness of Yahweh to his word, for they, too, were looking to reclaim their ancestral homeland, to recover a home of their own.

To that end, the Deuteronomic Historian framed the book with a theology of promise. Chapters 1 and 23–24 form the interpretive framework of the book. The opening address of Yahweh and the closing address of Joshua confirm that occupation of the Promised Land by the Israelites was in fulfillment of a promise made to the ancestors. On this promise, projected into the future again by the exiles who heard this story, Israel based its hope.

Turning next to the book of Judges, we find that, due to the people's lack of faith, their grip on the Promised Land was quite shaky.

QUESTIONS FOR REVIEW

1. What were the major campaigns of the conquest?
2. What is holy war and what conquest stories or parts of stories illustrate the principles of holy war?
3. What are the major scholarly models of the occupation of Canaan by the Israelites?

4. In what ways was Joshua like his mentor, Moses? In what ways did he differ?
5. Where were monuments set up throughout Canaan in connection with conquest events? What lesson was each monument intended to teach?

QUESTIONS FOR DISCUSSION

1. What archaeological evidence lends support to the narrative of the conquest? What archaeological evidence seemingly contradicts the narrative? On the basis of these difficulties, what do you think the role of archaeology should be in biblical studies?

2. How does the perspective of the Deuteronomic Historian find expression in the book of Joshua? What Deuteronomic themes surface in Joshua?
3. How did the themes of the book of Joshua support the faith of later generations of Israelites?

FOR FURTHER STUDY

The following are two balanced commentaries on the book of Joshua.

Boling, Robert G., and G. Ernest Wright (1982). *Joshua*. Anchor Bible. Garden City, N.Y.: Doubleday. Emphasizes the history and archaeology of Israel.

Butler, Trent C. (1983). *Joshua*. Word Bible Commentary. Waco, Tex.: Word. Insightful, from an evangelical Christian perspective.

The book of Joshua raises many important historical and theological issues, including the theology of warfare, the historical accuracy of the Hebrew Bible, and the uses of archaeology. The following bibliography directs your attention to some helpful resources.

Literary and Theological Analysis

Auld, A. Graeme (1980). *Joshua, Moses and the Land: Tetrateuch-Pentateuch-Hexateuch in a Generation Since 1938*. Edinburgh : T. & T. Clark.

Hawk, L. Daniel (1991). *Every Promise Fulfilled: Contesting Plots in Joshua*. Literary Currents in Biblical Interpretation. Louisville, Ky.: Westminster/John Knox Press. Examines the interaction of two plot structures (obedience and disobedience; integrity and fragmentation) and interprets the data in terms of the desire for concordance and affirmation experienced by both the narrator and reader.

Wenham, Gordon J. (1971). "The Deuteronomic Theology of the Book of Joshua." *Journal of Biblical Literature* 90:140–56.

Archaeology of the Conquest

Bartlett, John R. (1982). *Jericho*. Cities of the Biblical World. Grand Rapids, Mich.: Eerdmans.

Stiebing, William (1989). *Out of the Desert? : Archaeology and the Exodus/Conquest Narratives*. Buffalo, N.Y.: Prometheus Books.

Warfare and Theology of Conquest

Craigie, Peter (1978). *The Problem of War in the Old Testament*. Grand Rapids, Mich.: Eerdmans.

Lind, Millar (1980). *Yahweh is a Warrior. The Theology of Warfare in Ancient Israel*. Scottsdale, Penn.: Herald Press.

Miller, Patrick D. (1973). *The Divine Warrior in Early Israel*. Cambridge: Harvard University Press.

Niditch, Susan (1992). *War in the Hebrew Bible. A Study in the Ethics of Violence*. New York: Orbis Books.

von Rad, Gerhard (1991). *Holy War in Ancient Israel*. Grand Rapids, Mich.: Eerdmans.

Williams, James G. (1991). *The Bible, Violence, and the Sacred. Liberation from the Myths of Sanctioned Violence*. San Francisco: Harper & Row.

Sociohistorical Theories of the Conquest

Coote, Robert B. (1990). *Early Israel: A New Horizon*. Minneapolis: Fortress Press.

Davies, Philip R. (1992). *In Search of "Ancient Israel."* JSOT Supplement Series, 148. Sheffield: Sheffield Academic Press.

Ramsey, George W. (1981). *The Quest for the Historical Israel*. Atlanta: John Knox Press.

Shanks, Hershel, William G. Dever, Baruch Halpern, and P. Kyle McCarter, Jr. (1992). *The Rise of Ancient Israel*. Symposium at the Smithsonian Institution, October 26, 1992. Washington, D.C.: Biblical Archaeology Society.

Thompson, Thomas L. (1992). *Early History of the Israelite People: from the Written and Archaeological Sources*. Studies in the history of the ancient Near East, 4. Leiden; New York : E. J. Brill.

WORKS CITED

Albright, William F. (1949; rev. ed. 1963). *The Biblical Period from Abraham to Ezra*. New York: Harper & Row.

Bimson, J. J. (1978). *Redating the Exodus and Conquest*. JSOT Supplement Series, 5. Sheffield: University of Sheffield.

Bimson, J. J. (1987). "Redating the Exodus." *Biblical Archaeology Review* 14:40–52.

Gottwald, Norman K. (1979). *The Tribes of Yahweh: A Sociology of the Religion of Liberated Israel, 1250–1050 B.C.E.* Maryknoll, N.Y.: Orbis Books.

Mendenhall, George E. (1962). "The Hebrew Conquest of Palestine." *Biblical Archaeologist* 25:66–87. Reprinted in *Biblical Archaeologist Reader 3* (1970):100–20.

Noth, Martin (1960). *The History of Israel*, rev. ed. New York: Harper & Brothers.

Weippert, Manfred (1971). *The Settlement of the Israelite Tribes in Palestine. A Critical Survey of Recent Scholarly Debate*. Studies in Biblical Theology, 2d series, 21. London: SCM Press.

Wood, Bryant G. (1990). "Did the Israelites Conquer Jericho?" *Biblical Archaeology Review* 16: 44–59.

Wright, G. Ernest (1962). *Biblical Archaeology*, rev. ed. Philadelphia: Westminster.

Yadin, Yigael (1972). *Hazor*. The Schweich Lectures, 1970. London: Oxford University Press.

JUDGES: SECURING THE LAND

Names and Terms to Remember

Deborah	Nazirite vow
Gideon	Philistines
judge	Samson

The book of Judges differs radically in style and character from the book of Joshua. The book of Joshua surges with excitement at the Israelite victory upon entering the Promised Land. By the end of that book Israel was secure in the land thanks to the faithful leadership of Joshua.

Come the era of the Judges and Israel is found cowering in the forests, hiding in the hills, afraid of being wiped out by Canaanites and other assorted bands of opponents. The book of Judges finds Israel in that transitional period after the great leadership of Moses and Joshua and before the coming era of the monarchy—and things are not going well.

The age of the Judges was a time of threat and danger (see Figure 7.1). Internally, Israel seemed to be losing the faith of its ancestors. Externally, other peoples were threatening Israel with extinction. Significant regional political developments were afoot as groups were searching for living room. The pressures of the age forced the disparate (and desperate) groups who identified with the God Yahweh to come together in a union that transcended tribal interests. It forced them to see that Israel could exist only as a federation of tribes helping each other. It prompted them to see that they could be held together in this federation only by their common faith in Yahweh.

WHAT IS A JUDGE?

The traditional name of the book is a bit misleading. The name *Judges* was taken from references to the main figures about whom tales are told. None of the figures is actually called a **judge**. The name was applied because the text says so-and-so "judged" Israel a certain number of years.

There are twelve so-called judges in the book. But they are not judicial figures such as the justices of the U.S. Supreme Court who sit in a courtroom behind a mahogany bench. While some of these ancient figures might have occasionally arbitrated disputes (Deborah, in particular), they possessed peculiar qualities of leadership for which they were termed *judges*. The exact reason *judges* applies remains somewhat unclear, yet it might be the case that they got the title because they promoted God's judgment on Israel's opposition. As in other passages of the Hebrew Bible, judging means standing up for the oppressed and delivering the afflicted rather than judicially applying a notion of equity. The judges might better be called *saviors* or *defenders*, in keeping with their historical function.

If the traditional date of the exodus is accepted (mid-thirteenth century B.C.E.), the tales of the judges would be set in the twelfth and eleventh centuries B.C.E. From the evidence we have at our disposal, this was, to say the least, an unsettled time in Canaan. The period began with the great international powers in stalemate and then in decline. Both the Egyptians and the Hittites wished to control Canaan because of the importance of its trade routes but were unable to do

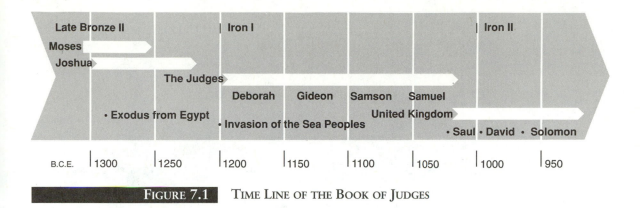

FIGURE 7.1   TIME LINE OF THE BOOK OF JUDGES

so. Canaan was not dominated by either of these powers, and this created a virtual free-for-all among the lesser peoples.

The most significant challenge came from a group called the Sea Peoples. They moved into the coastal plain of Canaan as part of a larger movement of peoples fleeing the Aegean. One of the groups of the Sea Peoples is called the **Philistines** in the Hebrew Bible.

They sought to dominate lands eastward from the Mediterranean coast toward the Jordan River. The Israelites, assuming some form of incursion model of conquest, arrived from the east and pushed west. Meanwhile, the indigenous population was not willing to stand for a wholesale takeover of its territory and found it had to defend itself. The book of Judges reflects the instability in the land at this time and paints a picture of various groups vying for supremacy (Figure 7.2).

PATTERN OF FAITH

Joshua's death was told in the book by his name. The first chapter of Judges is noteworthy for the tone it sets. While it tells of some continued successes of the Israelites after the death of Joshua, it also mentions certain failures of the Israelite conquest initiative. It seems that not all the territory of Canaan was taken or controlled by Joshua and his followers. Many Canaanites remained in the land. The narrator, as we will see, attributes this shortcoming to a lack of faith on the part of the generation that followed Joshua.

The following passage recounts the death of Joshua as the occasion to remark on his faithfulness, the faithfulness of the people, and the faithfulness of the elders.

2:6 Joshua sent the people away. Each one of the Israelites went to their inheritance to take possession of the land. 7 The people served YHWH all the days of Joshua's life, and all the days of the elders who outlived Joshua, those who had seen every great work which YHWH had done for Israel. 8 Joshua, son of Nun, the Servant of YHWH, died one hundred and ten years old. 9 They buried him within the borders of his inheritance, in

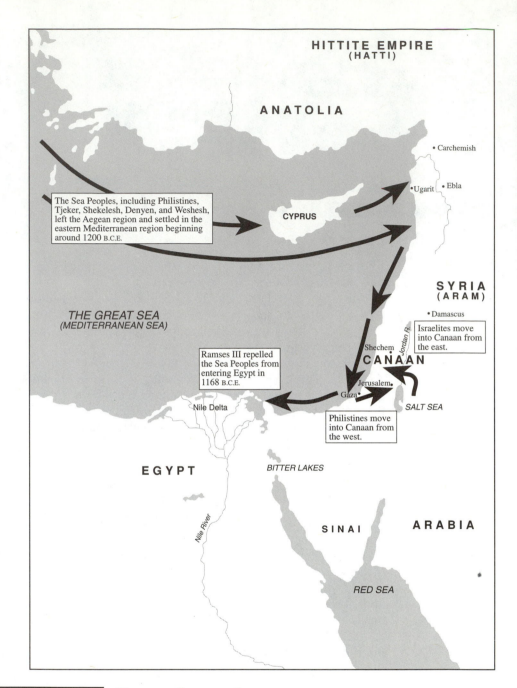

The Sea Peoples, including Philistines, Tjeker, Shekelesh, Denyen, and Weshesh, left the Aegean region and settled in the eastern Mediterranean region beginning around 1200 B.C.E.

Ramses III repelled the Sea Peoples from entering Egypt in 1168 B.C.E.

Israelites move into Canaan from the east.

Philistines move into Canaan from the west.

FIGURE 7.2   TWELFTH-CENTURY CANAAN

Timnath–Heres in the hill country of Ephraim north of Mt. Gaash. 10 That entire generation was gathered to their fathers. A new generation came after them who did not know YHWH or the work he had done for Israel.

This is the third time the Bible mentions the death of Joshua. The book of Joshua ended with it (see Joshua 24:29–30, which has virtually identical wording as 2:8–9) and the book of Judges began with it (see 1:1). It must have been viewed as a significant transition point for Israel. And his faithfulness sets in relief the next generation's lack of it.

The attention given to Joshua's faith can, in part, be explained because of his tribal affiliation. Joshua's burial place in Timnath indicates that he was from the tribe of Ephraim, which would become the heart of the Northern Kingdom. He comes from the home territory of the Deuteronomic circle of theologians who were responsible for writing down this history.

The mention in the text of "the new generation which did not know Yahweh," of course, does not bode well and suggests that something had gone awry. "Did not know" means more than lack of knowledge. "To know" is typical covenant terminology, indicating that the parties in the covenant relationship acknowledge their obligation. This is what the Israelites gave up. In their unfaithfulness they are like that first generation out of Egypt, except that the first exodus generation had the advantage of knowing the work of Yahweh firsthand.

> 2:11 The Israelites acted wickedly in the eyes of YHWH. They served the Baal gods. 12 They abandoned YHWH, the God of their fathers, the one who brought them out of the land of Egypt. They followed other gods, including the gods of the people living around them. They worshiped them and made YHWH angry. 13 They abandoned YHWH and served Baal and Ashtaroth. 14 The anger of YHWH erupted against Israel and he handed them over to marauders who plundered them, and he sold them to the enemies in their vicinity. They were not able to stand up against their enemies. 15 No matter what they tried to do, the power of YHWH was against them resulting in misfortune—just as YHWH had sworn to them—and they were in dire straits.

Note how the text identifies Yahweh as the God of the fathers and the one who delivered them from Egypt. Both descriptions recall God's early promises and his work in history.

Baal and Ashtaroth are a male god and female god, respectively. These figures and their characters are known especially from texts discovered at ancient Ugarit. They were worshiped because it was thought they were responsible for agricultural productivity.

The Israelites were attracted to the gods worshiped by indigenous Canaanites. The essential theological problem entailed by the worship of Canaanite gods was the implied abandonment of Yahweh. The covenant that bound Yahweh and Israel together demanded absolute and unwavering loyalty between these two parties. Worshiping another god was nothing less than a breach of covenant.

For punishment Yahweh withdrew his leadership as Divine Warrior. This resulted in Israel's total inability to gain the advantage over the other groups in Canaan.

> 2:16 YHWH raised up judges. They saved them from the power of the marauders. 17 Yet they did not even listen to their judges, but they whored

BAAL AND UGARIT

Texts from Ugarit, an ancient city discovered in 1929, contain tales of Baal and other Canaanite gods and goddesses (Figure 7.3). Though dated to the Late Bronze Age (1550–1200 B.C.E.), hence before the Hebrew Bible was written or Israel even existed, they contain important stories of gods and heroes who appear in various guises in the Hebrew Bible.

FIGURE 7.3   **BAAL FIGURINES FROM UGARIT**

The three major myth and epic cycles are translated in Coogan (1978). The following selection from the Baal cycle gives you the flavor of the texts. In this selection a divine supporter of Baal encourages him to be courageous against his enemy Yamm, the god of the sea.

"Let me tell you, Prince Baal,
let me repeat, Rider on the Coulds:
behold, your enemy, Baal,
behold, you will kill your enemy,
behold, you will annihilate your foes.
You will take your eternal kingship,
your dominion forever and ever."[1]

---

[1] Michael D. Coogan, *Stories from Ancient Canaan*. Philadelphia: Westminster Press, 1978, p. 88. On the relevance of Ugaritic studies to the Hebrew Bible, see Peter C. Craigie, *Ugarit and the Old Testament*. Grand Rapids, Mich.: Eerdmans, 1983.

after other gods and worshiped them. They quickly turned from the path on which their ancestors walked—heeding the commandments of YHWH. That is just what they did not do!

18 When YHWH raised up judges for them, YHWH was with the judge his whole life, so that he could deliver them from the power of their enemies. YHWH was moved to pity when they groaned on account of their persecutors and oppressors. 19 When the judge died, they reverted and turned out worse than their ancestors by following other gods, serving, and worshiping them. They did not abandon any of their practices or their ingrained ways. 20 So, the anger of YHWH erupted against Israel, and he thought, "Because this nation has broken the covenant to which I obligated their ancestors, and they have not obeyed my voice, 21 I will not continue to dispossess any of the nations Joshua left when he died." 22 In order to test Israel to see whether or not they would guard the path their ancestors guarded, 23 YHWH allowed to remain those nations he did not dispossess quickly, those over whom he had not given Joshua power.

These two paragraphs provide the schematic outline that virtually every judge story follows. When the Israelites were in trouble, God empowered a judge to rescue them. After the judge died, the Israelites reverted back to the worship of non-Yahweh gods. God again allowed a foreign group to dominate the Israelites as punishment (compare Figure 7.4). This cyclic pattern repeats itself each generation throughout the book of Judges: (1) apostasy, (2) oppression by an enemy, (3) cry for help, (4) judge sent to deliver them. As you read, note how the pattern articulated in this general introduction is related to the framework surrounding the tale of each individual judge.

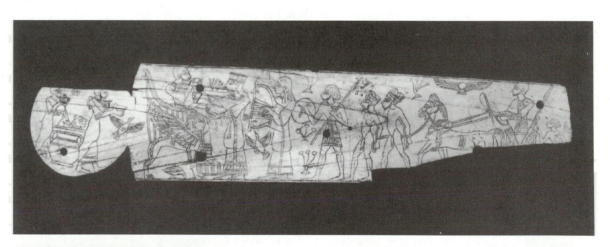

FIGURE 7.4 **MEGIDDO IVORY** This ivory plaque was found at Megiddo and dates to the time of the judges. The drawing depicts a Canaanite king seated on a throne in the shape of a winged sphinx. He is receiving an entourage returning from war that includes two bound captives.

In the following paragraph from the book of Judges, the unfaithfulness of the people is also used by the theologian–writer to explain why these foreign groups were still around when they should have been completely wiped out. They were kept around to be used as Yahweh's instrument to test the people.

> 3:1 These are the nations YHWH allowed to remain to test Israel (all those who did not know the wars of Canaan—2 it was only to teach the Israelite generations about war, only for those who had not experienced the wars): 3 the five Philistine lords, all the Canaanites, the Sidonians, the Hivites who live on Mt. Lebanon (from Mt. Baal-hermon to Mt. Lebo-hamath). 4 They were for the testing of Israel, to find out whether they would heed the commandments of YHWH which he commanded their ancestors through Moses. 5 The Israelites lived among the Canaanites, Hittites, Amorites, Perizzites, Hivites, and Jebusites. 6 They took their daughters as wives for themselves, and they gave their own daughters to their sons, and they served their gods.

The editor provided this theological framework so that the significance of the individual tales could be appreciated. Be alert to the elements of this theological introduction as you read the stories of the judges.

The parenthetic note about teaching the Israelites how to fight was probably added by the exilic Deuteronomic editor. One of his themes was teaching divine discipline through the rigors of warfare. This is also expressed in Judges 20.

JUDGE NARRATIVES

The core of the book of Judges is the collection of stories, as expected, about the judges themselves. Although there are twelve judges, they do not get equal treatment. Some are mentioned in only a few verses. Only a few get major treatment. Following biblical precedent, we will give in-depth treatment to Deborah, Gideon, and Samson.

DEBORAH (4–5)

The tale of Othniel follows immediately upon the theological narrative introduction. Othniel's saga (3:7–11) is very sketchy. It seems to serve as the "typical" tale, really only stating the cyclic pattern of apostasy and deliverance.

The story of Ehud, a left-handed judge from the tribe of Benjamin, comes next and contains a great deal more human interest. Described in vivid detail is Ehud's assassination of the Moabite king Eglon. He was so fat that when the dagger pierced his belly it disappeared into the fat and Ehud could not retrieve it.

The next story, the story of **Deborah** and Barak, begins with a description of the dire straits in which the Israelites found themselves.

> 4:1 Again the Israelites acted wickedly in YHWH's eyes. Ehud was dead. 2 YHWH gave them over to the control of Jabin, the Canaanite king who

ruled from Hazor, and Sisera his army general (he lived in Haroshet–hagoyim). 3 The Israelites cried out to YHWH, because Jabin had nine hundred iron chariots. He severely oppressed the Israelites for twenty years.

The hard times were prompted, as always in this book, by Israel's behavior. The particular offense is not specified, but based on the theological introduction we can assume it was unfaithfulness to Yahweh.

The oppressor was Jabin from Hazor. This places the conflict in northern Canaan. The mention of Hazor, as well as other places mentioned later in the story, position the action just to the west of the Sea of Galilee. A problem does arise with the mention of Jabin and Hazor. They were explicitly said to have been destroyed by Joshua in Joshua 11. How can this be explained? Maybe Jabin was not originally attached to this story and was for some reason inserted later. The reference to Jabin is found only in the introduction and conclusion to the Deborah–Barak tale (verses 1–3 and 23–24) and in the mention of a treaty (verse 17). The actual fighting is against Sisera.

After the stage-setting words, Deborah is introduced as a prophet who judged Israel in Ephraim. She was obviously a respected leader. In the mode of a prophet she delivered an oracle (a message from God) to Barak commanding him to organize troops from the tribes of Naphtali and Zebulun to fight Sisera on Mt. Tabor. Barak requested that Deborah accompany him. She agreed, but only after telling him that the coming victory would be credited to a woman. The story highlights the insecurity of Barak and the decisiveness and courage of Deborah.

> *4:6 She sent for Barak son of Abinoam from Qedesh in Naphtali and said to him, "Has YHWH, the God of Israel, not commanded you?—'Go, march to Mt. Tabor, and take ten thousand men from Naphtali and Zebulun with you. 7 I will march Sisera, Jabin's army commander, to you at the Kishon River, along with his chariots and his troops. I will hand them over to you.'" 8 Barak said to her, "Only if you go with me will I go. If you do not go with me, I will not go." 9 She said, "I will go with you. But you will get no glory this way. YHWH will sell out Sisera by the hand of a woman." Deborah got up and went with Barak to Qedesh.*

After the battle was joined, the Canaanite army was outmaneuvered, and Sisera fled the battle scene on foot. He found refuge in the tent of Jael, a one-time friend. Jael greeted him warmly, gave him drink and let him rest. But after Sisera fell asleep, she sneaked back into the tent and pounded a tent stake through Sisera's temple into the ground. The victory was celebrated in song. The text of the victory hymn, sometimes called the Song of Deborah, is found in Judges 5. Judging by the style of its language, Hebrew linguists tell us it is one of the oldest compositions in the Old Testament and was written very close to the event.

The tale of Deborah and Barak reveals many things about the period of the Judges. It illustrates how at various times, out of military necessity, individual tribes would join forces to combat a formidable enemy. But, as the Song of

Deborah indicates, not all the tribes always answered the call for help. Some refused. Israel as a confederacy was still dominated by regional interests. There was no national cohesion at this time.

The story also profiles the prophetic and military role female Israelites at times played in Israel. The courage of Deborah and Jael, and the credit for victory they received, sets in relief the deplorable lack of male initiative and leadership in Israel at the time of the Judges.

GIDEON (6–9)

The land rested for forty years after the victory over Sisera. Then the Israelites turned away from Yahweh. Again, the judge tale is framed with the editor's pattern of faith statements.

> *6:1 The Israelites acted wickedly in YHWH's eyes. YHWH gave them over to the control of Midian for seven years.*

The first stage of the pattern is thus stated. The Midianites were marauders who would descend on the more settled Israelites, foraging grain and stealing livestock.

> *6:6 Israel became very poor on account of Midian, and the Israelites cried out to YHWH.*

The Israelites realized that they did, in fact, need Yahweh. He responded by sending an angel to commission **Gideon**, who was from the tribe of Manasseh. The setting of this encounter is very revealing of the conditions in Israel generally and of the quality of Israel's leadership specifically. The angel confronted Gideon as Gideon was threshing wheat in a winepress. A winepress is a depression carved out of rock. Normally threshing is done on a hard surface near the top of a hill, to catch the breeze. Gideon was obviously in hiding. The angel's words of address can only be heard as ironic in this context when he says, "Yahweh is with you, you mighty warrior!"

Gideon's first act in Yahweh's cause was to vandalize the local shrine of Baal. During the night he and a few of his servants sneaked up to the worship center and pulled down the altar and its associated Asherah symbol. Again, the insecurity of Gideon comes to our attention. He did it at night because he was afraid someone might recognize and blame him. Only after the townspeople confronted him did he own up to his act and stand up publicly against Baal.

The Spirit of Yahweh empowered Gideon, and he mustered troops from the northern tribes to fight against the Midianites. But in another act of insecurity he asked Yahweh for a sign to signal whether or not he would find victory. He himself proposed the test of the wet sheepskin. He laid out a sheepskin overnight. If it was wet while the surrounding ground was dry, then he would take that as a sign of victory. It was so, but Gideon still wasn't sure. He asked for just the opposite the next night, and when it happened Gideon had no choice but to acknowledge that Yahweh was signaling victory and that he would have to get on with the campaign.

Gideon then assembled a fighting force. But like Gideon, they were reluctant warriors. When the soldiers were given the opportunity to return home rather than fight, 22,000 out of 32,000 decided to leave. God told Gideon that was still too many—he wanted to make clear that the victory came from God. So the army experienced further attrition after Gideon observed them drinking water from a spring. Only those who brought water hand to mouth rather than by lapping the water from the pool were enlisted for the battle. The story seems to dwell on the timidity and even incompetence of these early "warriors" on the way to making the point that Israel's fighting men were less than valiant defenders of the Israelite state.

Left with only three hundred men, Gideon devised a plan of attack that involved surprise and clever deception. He and his men surrounded the Midianite camp in the middle of the night. Armed with ram's horn trumpets, jars, and torches, on Gideon's signal they shocked the enemy out of sleep by smashing the jars, blowing the trumpets, and holding high the torches. Disoriented, confused, and seemingly outnumbered, the Midianites tried to flee. Gideon's three hundred gave chase and killed many of them. The chase became the occasion for the writer to illustrate the lack of cooperation, and even distrust, among the various tribes. The Ephraimites felt slighted because they had not been invited to the originating attack and only got to be a part of the mopping up. Then the Israelites in Transjordan at Succoth and Penuel refused to help Gideon.

What happens next relates to the ideology of covenant and kingship, a major concern of the Deuteronomic Historian. After he had killed the last kings of the Midianites, the Israelites begged Gideon to be their ruler. Although he took tribute from them—a share of the booty taken from the defeated Midianites—he refused to be king, saying, "Yahweh will rule over you." (8:23).

In the following story of Gideon's son Abimelech (whose name means "my father is king"), we have the record of an individual's aborted attempt to establish a dynasty. Abimelech came to kingship by killing the other seventy sons of Gideon, though overlooking the youngest, Jotham. Abimelech assumed control of Shechem and by various campaigns sought to control other villages. He died ignominiously after a defender dropped a millstone on his head. Perhaps written by an author critical of monarchy, the tale illustrates the violence-prone and typically self-important character of kings.

SAMSON (13–16)

Samson is one of the most colorful personalities in the Old Testament. He is a walking contradiction. Brash, bold, and impressively powerful, at one and the same time he is also naive and vulnerable. He is physically massive, yet spiritually infantile. The story of Samson is the last of the stories of the judges. As such, we could say that the editor is telling us something special. Samson epitomizes the age. And in Samson, we have a portrait of Israel in miniature.

The Deuteronomic editor introduces the story with an abbreviated version of his theological framework. There is no mention of the Israelites crying out for help or repenting.

13:1 The Israelites again did what was bad in YHWH's sight, and YHWH gave them into the hand of the Philistines for forty years.

Samson was born to a woman previously unable to have children. An angel of Yahweh delivered the announcement of conception and directed her to raise Samson in a special way. Both she, during pregnancy, and he throughout his life must refrain from alcoholic beverages and not eat anything unclean. From the moment of conception Samson must be devoted exclusively to Yahweh, a state or condition called the **Nazirite vow.**

By his lifestyle Samson inadvertently demonstrated that neither the Nazirite vow nor his Israelite identity meant anything to him. Against his parents' wishes he chose to marry a Philistine woman. One day while going to see her, a lion attacked him. The spirit of Yahweh came upon him and he bare-handedly killed the animal. When later he was traveling the same road to his wedding, he stopped to view the carcass of the lion. A swarm of bees had made a hive there, and he scraped some honey out and ate it. By Hebrew law that honey would have been considered unclean, having been in direct contact with a dead body.

The Samson story is one long record of the love–hate relationship between Samson and the Philistines. He is drawn to them, especially to their beautiful women. Yet every meeting becomes an occasion for him to kill more Philistines. For example, at his wedding he makes a wager using a riddle about the lion and the honey and loses. Payment of the bet was thirty sets of clothing. Samson handily killed thirty Philistines and stripped them of their garments to pay his debt.

Samson's nemesis was Delilah. Only one of many women with whom he consorted, she was ultimately his undoing. After three unsuccessful attempts, she finally got him to reveal the secret of his strength. Although Samson had enough clues to figure out that she would betray him, Samson unwittingly told her that if his hair was cut off, he would be vulnerable. She did just that while he was asleep. He woke up helpless and was captured by his foes. The Philistines blinded him and put him to work at hard labor. In prison his hair began to grow back.

During a festival he was brought to the temple of Dagon, the high god of the Philistines, for a command performance. While waiting in the wings he found two central supporting pillars. He prayed to Yahweh for a return of his powers—then toppled those pillars and brought down the stadium. Yahweh had not abandoned him, even though he had abandoned Yahweh. In dying, he killed more Philistines than ever before.

This is the stuff of legends. A great story, full of love and lust, violence and manly challenge. Yet surely the writer was doing more than telling a good story. He was mirroring Israel in the figure of Samson. Like Samson, Israel was powerful, even invincible when filled with the Spirit of Yahweh. But Samson, like Israel, was indifferent to his special pedigree—conceived through the special intervention of God and dedicated to him at birth. He lusted after more enticing companions. The women in Samson's life are surely symbols of the foreign gods who continually attracted the Israelites. They were blind after having betrayed the secret of their strength, but Yahweh never totally abandoned them. The time of the Judges was a time of political and religious insecurity. But the God of Israel would not abandon them.

PHILISTINE WARRIOR

The book of Judges ends with stories describing the state of tension that existed among the tribes. The tribe of Dan migrated from the coastal plain to the far north of Israel. And some tribes tried to wipe out Benjamin.

In addition to the people's lack of faith in Yahweh, the problem was lack of leadership. The moral condition of the nation deteriorated massively after the death of Joshua. The writer repeatedly uses the statement, "In those days there was no king in Israel . . . all the people did what was right in their own eyes" to characterize the problem.

This chaotic situation would soon change. Order and stability would come. The books of Samuel detail the rise of kingship in Israel.

OVERALL SHAPE OF THE BOOK OF JUDGES

The core of the book of Judges is a collection of stories told about Israel's legendary tribal leaders. The independent stories probably existed orally for a long time, transmitted from generation to generation in the vicinity where the particular judge at one time lived. Many of the stories have a setting in the north and were incorporated into the all-Israel story after the destruction of the Northern Kingdom.

Figure 7.5 locates the individual judges in the areas of their activity. Notice how no judge covered all Israel, but when all are accounted for, they cover virtually the entire spectrum of territories.

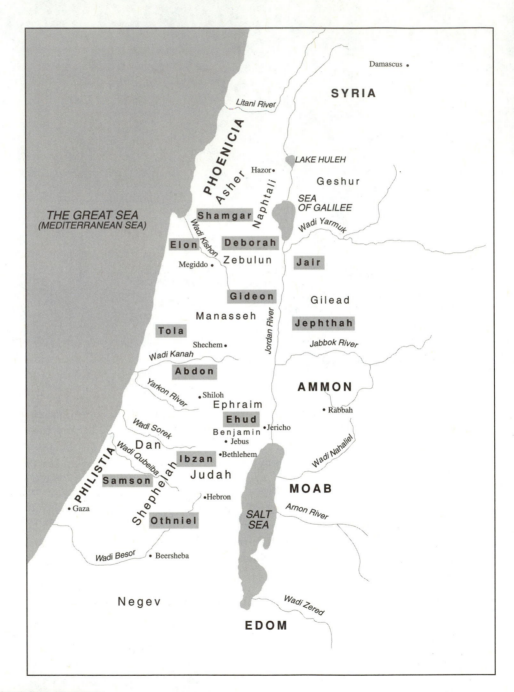

FIGURE 7.5   JUDGES OF ISRAEL

The chronology of the book suggests that the Deuteronomic Historian artificially chained the judge stories together to create the feeling of a continuous history such that each generation after the next fell away from Yahweh. If all the time indications are added together, the book spans exactly four hundred years. This is too exact to be an accident, and much too long to fit the archaeological and historical record. A reasonable estimate for the time span of the period of the judges is one hundred fifty years. Evidently, many of the judges actually lived and ruled contemporaneously. Further suggesting a certain artificiality, many of the judges judged for twenty, forty, or eighty years—or in biblical parlance, one-half, one, or two generations, respectively. Table 7.1 draws together the geographical and chronological data on the individual judges for easy reference.

TABLE 7.1 **LITERARY PARALLELS IN TOWER OF BABEL STORY**

Judge	Text	Home Territory	Area of Activity	Foe	Years of Oppression	Years Judged
Othniel	3:7–11	Judah?		Cushan-rishathaim king of Aram	8	40
Ehud	3:12–30	Benjamin	Hill country of Ephraim and Moab	Eglon king of Moab, Ammonites, Amalekites	18	80
Shamgar	3:31		Philistia	Philistines		
Deborah	4:1–5:31	Ephraim	Mt. Tabor, Naphtali, Zebulun	Sisera, Jabin king of Hazor, Canaanites	20	40
Gideon	6:1–9:57	Manasseh	Manasseh	Midianites, Amalekites, Kedemites	40	
Tola	10:1–2	Issachar	Ephraim			23
Jair	10:3–5	Gilead				22
Jephthah	10:6–12:7	Gilead		Ammonites	18	6
Ibzan	12:8–10	Bethlehem				7
Elon	12:11–12	Zebulun				10
Abdon	12:13–15	Ephraim				8
Samson	13:1–16:31	Dan	Philistia	Philistines	40	20
				Totals	144	256

The Deuteronomic Historian took up the judges' stories, gave them a theological introduction, and reshaped most of the individual stories to fit the cycle of disobedience outlined in the theological introduction. They were combined in such a way that the Israelites are pictured as continually forgetting Yahweh and falling into trouble. Thus, originally local stories were "universalized" into all-Israel tales and combined in linear fashion in order to say something in general about the entire nation and its faith tendencies.

Thus exposing the nation's corporate lack of faithfulness, the Deuteronomic Historian justified the need for a faithful king who would lead the people back to their God. The book of Samuel picks up the story at this point, recounting the rise of kingship. Note that the book of Ruth follows the book of Judges in many English versions, but you will not find a discussion of Ruth in the next chapter of our book. Ruth is not counted among the Former Prophets in the Hebrew Bible. Rather, it is one of the Five Scrolls, and we will treat it in chapter 16.

QUESTIONS FOR REVIEW

1. What is the theological framework of the book of Judges and how does this shape the way the individual tales of judges are told?

2. For Deborah, Gideon, and Samson, identify the foe and the way each judge achieved victory.

3. How is the book of Judges transitional between the era of Joshua and the rise of kingship?

4. How does the overall shape of the book of Judges, especially the cycle of disobedience through which the people go, reflect its theology of history?

QUESTIONS FOR DISCUSSION

1. Think about the character of the major judges. What was "wrong" with each of them? What do their flaws say about Israel at this time in its history? Do you think the judges were heroes or anti-heroes?

2. Reflect on the writer's perspective on women in these narratives, especially in relation to the Deborah story. Did the writer have a positive or a negative valuation of females in Israel?

3. The book of Judges presents clear evidence of the role of the editor in shaping the final product. What is the relationship between history-telling and history? Was the Deuteronomic Historian true or untrue to history in the way he shaped the book? What does it really mean to write history?

FOR FURTHER STUDY

Bal, Mieke (1988). *Death and Dissymmetry: The Politics of Coherence in the Book of Judges.* Chicago: University of Chicago Press.

Boling, Robert G. (1975). *Judges.* Anchor Bible. Garden City, N.Y.: Doubleday.

Klein, Lillian R. (1988). *The Triumph of Irony in the Book of Judges.* Bible and Literature Series, 14. Sheffield: JSOT Press.

Webb, Barry G. (1987). *The Book of Judges: An Integrated Reading.* Sheffield: JSOT Press.

Finkelstein, Israel (1988). *The Archaeology of the Israelite Settlement.* Leiden: E. J. Brill.

Deborah. Bal, Mieke (1988). *Murder and Difference: Genre, Gender, and Scholarship on Sisera's Death.* Bloomington: Indiana University Press.

Murray, D. F. (1979). "Narrative Structure and Technique in the Deborah and Barak Story." *Vetus Testamentum Supplement* 30: 155–89.

Samson. Crenshaw, James (1978). *Samson—A Secret Betrayed.* Atlanta: John Knox Press.

Exum, J. Cheryl (1981). "Aspects of Symmetry and Balance in the Samson Saga." *Journal for the Study of the Old Testament* 19: 3–29.

WORKS CITED

Coogan, Michael D. (1978). *Stories from Ancient Canaan.* Philadelphia: Westminster Press.

Craigie, Peter C. (1983). *Ugarit and the Old Testament.* Grand Rapids, Mich.: Eerdmans.

SAMUEL: RISE OF THE MONARCHY

Names and Terms to Remember

Abner	Elkanah	Michal
Absalom	Goliath	Mt. Gilboa
Amnon	Hannah	Nathan
anointing	Hebron	Philistines
Araunah	Hophni and Phineas	Samuel
ark of the covenant	Jebus	Saul
Bathsheba	Jerusalem	Shiloh
David	Joab	Tamar
Davidic covenant	Jonathan	
Eli	messiah / christos	

There is no compelling reason for these books to be called the books of Samuel. They were not written by Samuel, and they deal with Samuel only part of the time. The books might better be entitled "Kingship in Israel" or "The Rise of the Monarchy," because they deal with the development of that institution. In fact, this is very nearly what the books of Samuel and Kings are called in the Septuagint—"Kingdoms I, II, III, and IV."

Nonetheless, associating the content of these books with Samuel is not entirely inappropriate. Samuel is an important, even pivotal, figure. He guides Israel's transition to kingship and bridges the periods of the judges and the monarchy.

The Samuel material is configured as two books in English versions. Originally they were one. Ignoring the book division, the subject matter divides neatly into three main sections on the basis of the editor's transitional passages in 1 Samuel 13:1 and 2 Samuel 1:1. Each section focuses on a major historical figure—Samuel (1 Samuel 1–12), Saul (1 Samuel 13–31), and David (2 Samuel). All three figures were pivotal in the development of Israel's institution of kingship. The following outline of the books of Samuel encapsulates its structure.

Outline of the Books of Samuel

I. Samuel Cycle (1 Sam. 1–12)
  A. Samuel's birth, dedication, and early ministry 1:1–4:1a
  B. Travels of the ark 4:1b–7:17
  C. Search for a king 8:1–12:25
II. Saul Cycle (1 Sam. 13–31)
  A. Saul's disobedience 13:1–15:35
  B. Saul versus David 16:1–31:13
III. David Cycle (2 Sam. 1–24)
  A. David's rise to power 1:1–8:18
  B. Dynastic succession struggles 9:1–20:26
  C. David's last days 21:1–24:25

You might recall that we were primed for a treatment of the issue of kingship by the often-stated refrain of the book of Judges, "in those days there was no king in Israel; all the people did what was right in their own eyes." As a whole

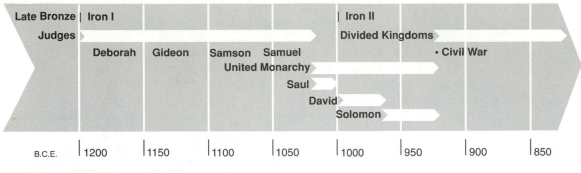

Late Bronze	Iron I					Iron II			
Judges						Divided Kingdoms			
	Deborah	Gideon	Samson	Samuel			• Civil War		
				United Monarchy					
					Saul				
					David				
					Solomon				

| B.C.E. | 1200 | 1150 | 1100 | 1050 | 1000 | 950 | 900 | 850 |

FIGURE 8.1   TIME LINE OF THE BOOKS OF SAMUEL

the books of Samuel treat the new institution of monarchy that emerged in Israel. They consider the rocky beginnings of monarchy, its early failures, and its golden age in David (see Figure 8.1).

If we place the leadership issues addressed in the books of Samuel within the context of the time the material was edited, we would have to observe that the question of leadership was especially urgent in the world of the Deuteronomic Historian. During the time of the Babylonian crisis and the exile, one of the reasons for the drastic decline of Israel was the perceived failure of political and religious leadership. If recovery was ever to happen, Israel would need strong leadership. They must have mulled over the questions long and hard—What shape should a new leadership take? Could a king extricate them? Would God again speak through Israelite leaders? Presumably the Deuteronomic Historian thought that reexamining the period of the development of kingship might provide some answers to these pressing questions, and additionally might provide some needed direction for any new leadership that might arise.

SAMUEL CYCLE (1 SAMUEL 1–12)

The first part of the books of Samuel deals with its namesake. It treats the birth and career of Israel's last judge figure, **Samuel**.

BIOGRAPHICAL SKETCH OF SAMUEL
Born to Hannah and Elkanah 1, 2
Grows up in the temple at Shiloh 3
Defeats Philistines at Mizpah 7
Anoints Saul as Israel's first king 9, 10
Delivers farewell speech 12
Rejects Saul 13, 15
Anoints David to be king in place of Saul 16
Dies and is buried at Ramah 25
Appears to Saul as a spirit 28

SAMUEL'S BIRTH, DEDICATION, AND EARLY MINISTRY (1:1–4:1A)

The story first treats the birth of Samuel. **Elkanah** was a pious man who had two wives. Peninnah had children but **Hannah** had none. It was commonly thought that sterility was a sign of God's disfavor. Hannah felt low and abandoned, yet she also had faith in God. During their annual pilgrimage to the central sanctuary at **Shiloh**, Hannah fervently asked Yahweh of Hosts, as he is called in these early chapters, for a son.

Eli was the high priest of the Shiloh temple. When he saw her praying, he mistakenly thought she was drunk, because he could only see her move her mouth and heard no sound; he could not recognize true piety when he saw it. Note how here and elsewhere one of the interests of the writer is to signal the ineffectiveness of Eli and his high priesthood.

God answered Hannah's prayer. She conceived, bore a son, and named him Samuel, meaning "God heard." In return for the gift of the child, Hannah later gave the child back to God by devoting him to divine service in the temple at Shiloh. Hannah prayed a prayer of thanksgiving at the dedication. A couple of the lines provide the flavor of the prayer:

> 2:1 *My heart rejoices in YHWH…because I rejoice in your victory. 4 The bows of the mighty are broken, but the feeble gird on strength. 6 YHWH kills and gives life, he brings down to Sheol and raises up, 7 YHWH makes poor and makes rich; he humbles, he also exalts. 8 He raises the poor up from the dust, he lifts the needy from the ashes to make them sit with princes.*

The prayer has a rich, poetic quality. Some scholars suggest that it once circulated as an independent poem. Maybe so, but what we notice is that it fits well here and was placed strategically to function as the theme of the books of Samuel. Often in works of literature and theology, the controlling theme is stated early in the work, and later stories develop that theme. Hannah's song, as this prayer has come to be called, voices a theme that resounds through the books of Samuel.[1] Yahweh raises up, and he pulls down. The humble are given honor and the proud are shamed. Pay special attention to the theme of the reversal of fortunes in the books of Samuel. The theme is typically worked out in an opposing pair of parties, one ascending and one descending.

The first instance of this theme working out in history is the reversal of Hannah's own station in life. Hannah was vindicated against arrogant Peninnah. Once barren, she now has a son, and a special one at that—one who now works in the holiest shrine in the land. Later, notice how Eli and his sons are contrasted with Hannah and Samuel, and how Saul and David later reverse positions. The Goliath and David pair is another instance of pride and a fall, and on the national level be alert to how the Philistines are set in contrast with the Israelites.

---

[1] With its celebration of how God gives life, Hannah's song models Mary's song of thanksgiving in the New Testament "Magnificat" in Luke 1:46–55.

Immediately after Hannah's Song we get a description of the sons of Eli and their priestly practices. They appropriated the sacrifices of the people in a self-serving way, taking the best for themselves. In contrast stands Samuel. Of all things to mention, we get a description of his clothing. He wears a totally unpretentious linen garment. His humility is implicitly contrasted with the presumptuousness of **Hophni** and **Phineas**. Eli was unable to control his sons, and as a result Yahweh was about to remove them from the priestly office. The juxtaposition of futures cannot be more starkly drawn than in 2:25–26.

> *2:25b Yet they would not listen to their father, for it was the will of Yahweh to kill them. 26 The boy Samuel continued to grow in stature and in favor with Yahweh and with the people.*

The Deuteronomic Historian, who was closely in touch with the prophetic tradition, frequently makes a point of how the course of history works out the prophetic word spoken by one of the prophets. An anonymous man of God came to Eli (2:27–36) and uttered the judgment word of God that Eli's family would be removed from priestly office and replaced by an unnamed "faithful priest." It would be anachronistic for the writer to state it here, but later the Deuteronomic Historian shows that by "faithful priest" he intended the dynastic priesthood of Zadok, which later supported the Davidic royal line. It is likely that Eli and the Shiloh priesthood are ancestors of the Abiathar priesthood, which was dispossessed when Abiathar lost out to Zadok. This account prefigures that change in clan privileges.

Samuel grew up in Shiloh and worked in the temple there. Although "the word of Yahweh was rare in those days, and visions were infrequent" (3:1), Yahweh appeared to Samuel in the middle of the night as he slept near the **ark of the covenant**. The message he received from Yahweh was the same as that delivered by the "man of God." Eli's family would be removed from office. From then on, the word of Yahweh was revealed to Samuel and he was recognized by everyone to be a prophet.

TRAVELS OF THE ARK 4:1B–7:17

The **Philistines** surface again as the main threat to Israel's existence. Facing the Philistines in battle at Aphek, the Israelites fetched the ark of the covenant from Shiloh thinking it would automatically give them victory. The Philistines proceeded to kill many Israelites, including Hophni and Phineas, and to capture the ark. When Eli heard about these events he died.

When the Philistines took the prize home, the ark wreaked havoc within their cities. After it was placed in the temple of their chief god, Dagon, it caused his statue to topple and its head to break off. Then physical illness broke out among the Philistines. They shuttled the ark among their cities until finally they decided to return it to the Israelites. It first arrived in Israelite territory at the town of Beth-shemesh. After seventy men died there because they peeked into the ark, the survivors sent it on to Kiriath-yearim, where it remained until David's day (Figure 8.2).

This account of the war with the Philistines interrupts the history of Samuel. He plays no role in it. The story appears to have been placed here to fulfill the judgment word of Eli's demise. It also demonstrates some things about the power of Israel's Yahweh. First, he refuses to be "used." He cannot be mechanically called on to perform for Israel's benefit, as they had attempted in battle at Aphek. Second, though apparently captured by the Philistines, Yahweh proves to be more powerful than their god Dagon, and Dagon even finds himself bowing down to Yahweh. Third, the Israelites had better respect him, or they will die, as did the men at Beth-shemesh.

Now Samuel returns to the story. He gathered the Israelites together at Mizpah and renewed their commitment to Yahweh. The Philistines fought them there but were defeated. In this part of the account (7:3–17) Samuel is described as Is-

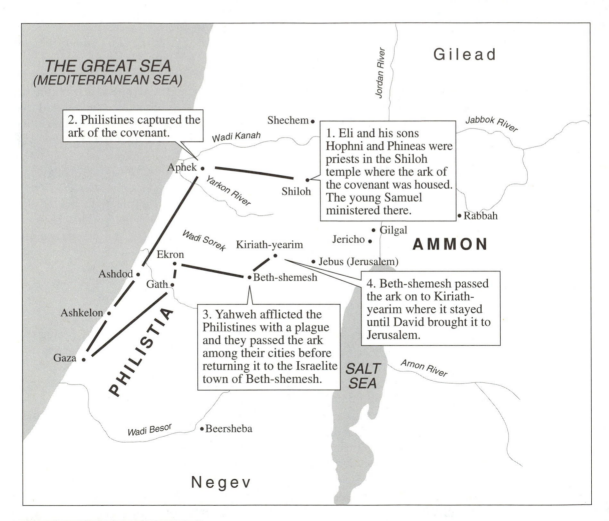

FIGURE 8.2   **TRAVELS OF THE ARK OF THE COVENANT**

rael's great savior and judge, after the model of the earlier judge heroes. He is talked about as if he is about to pass from the scene, and yet he will be a major force behind Israel for much of the remainder of First Samuel.

SEARCH FOR A KING (8–12)

How does a society manage to move from one leader to another and still retain stability? On whose authority does the next leader take office? Can a nation peacefully change its form of government? Israel faced these challenges when Samuel got old. Apparently, his sons were appreciated no more than Eli's sons, and the people did not want them to take over. The nation lobbied for a fundamental change. They demanded, "Appoint a king to rule us, like the other nations." (8:5)

This was radical and unheard of in Israel. The fundamental covenantal structure that had shaped Israel's life placed Yahweh in the position of the king, with Israel as his nation. The covenant federation founded at Shechem was based on this model. The people's demand for a human king appeared to be a rejection of that relationship. Samuel was deeply shaken by this as well as the apparent rejection of his leadership and his sons. But Yahweh counseled him that it was really a rejection of himself, not Samuel. Yahweh also instructed Samuel to go along with their demand.

Samuel warned them what a king would be like, drafting their sons and daughters to work for the crown, taxing them heavily, and in general making life difficult. This warning, not incidentally, is a fairly transparent prophetic critique of the monarchy as it actually came to be within Israel. Nobody could say they had not been forewarned!

Next we meet **Saul**. He is introduced as a tall, handsome man, the son of Kish from the tribe of Benjamin. Searching for some lost donkeys, he went to Samuel because of his reputation as a prophet. When Saul arrived, Samuel arranged a banquet in his honor, and afterward anointed him king. The ceremony of **anointing** involved pouring olive oil over the head of the person chosen by God. The oil may have been a symbol of the pouring out of the spirit of Yahweh. The person needed this empowerment by the spirit to carry out the responsibilities of office.

Although there is evidence that priests and prophets were anointed, the ceremony was especially used to designate kings. A person who had been authorized in this way was called an "anointed one." This is the translation of the Hebrew word *mashiach*, rendered **messiah** in English and **christos** in Greek, from which the title Christ was derived. Note that the designation *messiah* did not imply divinity in the Hebrew Bible. It was only a title attached to a divinely designated leader.

On his journey home Saul received proof that he was indeed Yahweh's anointed one. Passersby gave him gifts of bread and wine, presumably in recognition of his office, and he was overcome with ecstatic prophetic behavior, which was evidence that the spirit of Yahweh had in fact come upon him.

But Saul received a mixed review after Samuel formally presented him as Israel's first king. Some of the people assembled at Mizpah hailed him, while others grumbled, "How can he save us?" But shortly thereafter Saul silenced his detractors. When the Transjordanian Israelite town of Jabesh-gilead was besieged by the Ammonites, "the spirit of God came upon him powerfully." He put together an army and came to their rescue. Having seen proof of his leadership ability, the people gathered together at Gilgal and confirmed his kingship.

The time was right for Samuel to step down from national leadership and give way to Saul. Samuel took the occasion of the assembly at Gilgal to deliver a farewell speech (1 Samuel 12:6–25). He reminded the people of the nasty step they had taken—"the wickedness that you have done in the sight of Yahweh is great in demanding a king for yourselves." The farewell speech gave the writer the opportunity to encapsulate his theological perspective. So much of the theology of the Deuteronomic Historian comes out in big speeches. This particular address expresses the Deuteronomic critique of kingship once again.

> 12:14 *If you will fear Yahweh and serve him and heed his voice and not rebel against the commandment of Yahweh, and if both you and the king who rules over you follow Yahweh your God, it will be well. 15 But if you do not obey the voice of Yahweh, but rebel against the commandment of Yahweh, then the hand of Yahweh will be against you and your king.*

The king is not absolute. Both the king and the people must be subject to the law of God. The covenant and its demands take precedence over any rights of kingship.

Looking at this material as a whole, this set of stories is somewhat puzzling. On the one hand, as with this Samuel speech, the view of kingship is quite negative. A king is granted only grudgingly to the Israelites, and only with dire warnings. On the other hand, some passages reflect a positive appreciation of Saul, acknowledging that he was needed by Israel at this time. This situation has led many scholars to posit that chapters 8–12 originally contained two different sources, an antimonarchy one and a promonarchy one. Scholars have termed the promonarchy source the A source and the antimonarchy source the B source. They are intertwined in an alternating way, as if to say, "We like Saul and we need a king, but we really don't want one." Table 8.1 displays the texts alternating between these differing viewpoints.

TABLE 8.1   SOURCES IN SAMUEL

8:1–22	Samuel's warning against kingship	antimonarchy
9:1–10:16	Saul and his anointing	promonarchy
10:17–27	Another warning by Samuel	antimonarchy
11:1–15	Saul's victory over the Ammonites	promonarchy
12:1–25	Final warning by Samuel	antimonarchy

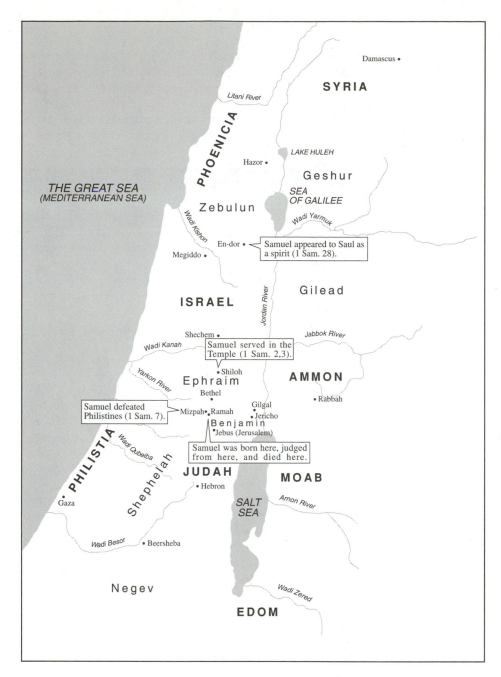

The map shows labeled locations:

Damascus •

SYRIA

Litani River

PHOENICIA

LAKE HULEH

Hazor •

*THE GREAT SEA
(MEDITERRANEAN SEA)*

Geshur

*SEA
OF GALILEE*

Zebulun

Wadi Kishon

Wadi Yarmuk

En-dor •

Samuel appeared to Saul as
a spirit (1 Sam. 28).

Megiddo •

Gilead

Jordan River

ISRAEL

Shechem •

Wadi Kanah

Jabbok River

Samuel served in the
Temple (1 Sam. 2,3).

Yarkon River

Ephraim

• Shiloh

AMMON

Bethel
•

Gilgal
•

• Rabbah

Samuel defeated
Philistines (1 Sam. 7).

Mizpah • • Ramah

• Jericho

Benjamin

• Jebus (Jerusalem)

PHILISTIA

Wadi Qubeiba

Samuel was born here, judged
from here, and died here.

Shephelah

JUDAH

MOAB

• Hebron

Gaza •

*SALT
SEA*

Arnon River

Wadi Besor

• Beersheba

Negev

Wadi Zered

EDOM

FIGURE 8.3   CAREER OF SAMUEL

The map in Figure 8.3 serves as a summary of the life of Samuel.

Samuel does not die until chapter 25. Yet the narrative focus changes at this point. Saul takes center stage as he assumes the leadership role in Israel.

SAUL CYCLE (1 SAMUEL 13–31)

The story of Saul is a tragic tale. Having risen to the position of king and been acclaimed by the people, he fell prey to the temptations of power. Although Samuel was supportive of him early on, he later turned away from Saul. From here on we will see an increasingly frustrated and ineffective Saul, and we will see the corresponding rise of **David**. Remember the theme of Hannah's song—how the mighty have fallen, but Yahweh exalts the lowly. It works out in the following cycle of narratives.

> ### BIOGRAPHICAL SKETCH OF SAUL
>
> Anointed king by Samuel and presented to Israel 9, 10
> Rescues Jabesh-gilead and is acclaimed king by Israel 11
> Disobeys Samuel by offering a sacrifice at Michmash 13
> Battles Philistines and orders Jonathan executed 14
> Rejected as king by Samuel 15
> Tries to kill David 19
> Pursues but never catches David; his life spared by David 23, 24, 26
> Dies on Mt. Gilboa in battle with the Philistines 31

SAUL'S DISOBEDIENCE (13–15)

Saul gathered the troops at Gilgal to fight against the Philistines. Samuel, in the role of army chaplain, was supposed to come and bless the troops. But when he did not show up on time, Saul went ahead and offered the ritual sacrifice. No sooner had the offering been ignited when Samuel appeared and condemned Saul for presuming to function as a priest. This is the first occasion Samuel indicated that Yahweh had rejected Saul and had chosen someone else to take his place as king.

Saul's tendency to make bad judgments (was it a sign that he was no longer in Yahweh's favor, or just a sign that kings tend to make bad decisions?) is seen in the next encounter with the Philistines. Saul's son **Jonathan** surprised a group of Philistines and thereby threw the entire Philistine army into a panic. The Israelites had the opportunity to completely wipe out the Philistines, except that Saul had foolishly decreed that the men should fast. This inappropriate abstention from food seems to signal a kind of misplaced religiosity on Saul's part. In any case, the Israelite warriors did not have the energy to pursue the Philistines to their death. Even worse, Jonathan had not heard about the fasting decree and unwittingly broke his father's command when he ate some wild honey. Saul would have executed Jonathan for disobedience had not Saul's own soldiers stopped him.

Later, Saul had the opportunity to eliminate Israel's old enemy, the Amalekites. Remember, they were the first ones ever to attack Israel, right after the Hebrews had left Egypt. But Saul did not follow the rule of holy war to completely eradicate the enemy and burn the remains. He took spoils of war and spared Agag, the Amalekite king. Samuel was furious when he found out. He summarily condemned Saul and proclaimed that Yahweh had rejected him as king. Then he himself killed Agag. Samuel completely disowned Saul and would not see him again—that is, until he came up from his grave to haunt Saul.

SAUL VERSUS DAVID (16–31)

Competition for high office is frequently the anvil of national history. The contest is evident on many levels in the books of Samuel: Eli versus Samuel, Samuel versus Saul, and now Saul versus David.

Both having rejected Saul, Samuel and Yahweh turned elsewhere for a new king. They went to a most unlikely place to find one, the insignificant village of Bethlehem in the southern tribe of Judah. Among the sons of Jesse, Yahweh passed by the elder sons and chose the youngest boy, David, to be king. This peculiar choice continues the countercultural ancestral tradition of passing the promise to the younger son: not Cain but Abel; not Ishmael but Isaac; not Esau but Jacob; not Reuben but Judah and Joseph; not Manasseh but Ephraim.

Samuel anointed David, and immediately the spirit of Yahweh came upon him. In the Hebrew Bible the spirit of God is the power God bestows on select individuals that enables them to perform their God-given task. As if the spirit could not simultaneously be on two people at once, in the next verse we are told that the spirit of Yahweh left Saul and in its place an evil spirit (also from Yahweh) took possession of him. In hopes of calming his troubled mind, Saul hired David to be the court musician. Skilled on the lyre (a type of harp), David comforted Saul, and Saul came to love him dearly.

Again the Philistines harassed the Israelites. This time they camped in the Elah valley near an Israelite garrison. Daily their champion warrior **Goliath** taunted the Israelites, trying to goad them into a fight. None of the Israelites took up the challenge, until one day David came by. He was delivering food to his brothers in the camp when he heard Goliath's challenge. David was astounded that none of the Israelites had the courage to face him. He immediately volunteered himself. Armed with only a slingshot and stones, he faced Goliath in single combat. His first shot struck Goliath in the forehead and knocked him unconscious. David ran over to him and cut off his head. This threw the Philistines into a panic, and the Israelites drove the Philistines away.

There was rejoicing, and women were singing in the streets, "Saul killed thousands, David killed ten thousands." Everyone, including Saul's own son Jonathan, was enamored with David—everyone except Saul himself. Saul was angered by the popularity of David. From then on he tried actively to eliminate David in one way or another. He tried to spear him in the palace, but David was too quick. He made him commander of the army, hoping he would die in battle, but David's popularity only grew as he won battle after battle.

In a plot to have the Philistines kill him, Saul offered David the honor of marrying one of his daughters and thereby officially joining the royal family. As always in the ancient world, a bride did not come freely. A bride price had to be paid to her parents. Saul stipulated the bride price to be one hundred Philistine foreskins. Saul was, of course, expecting David to get killed in the process. But David, always ready to do Saul one better, instead brought him two hundred. Saul had no choice but to give David his daughter **Michal** in marriage.

Frustrated and now obsessed with eliminating his rival, Saul planned outright to assassinate David. In an ironic turn, David was kept informed of Saul's plans by both Jonathan and Michal. Saul's own son and daughter betrayed him and took David's side, in effect acknowledging that he would be Israel's next king. The loyalty of Jonathan is remarkable, because by aiding David he was implicitly renouncing his own claim to the throne.

David found it necessary to flee. He found help and refuge wherever he could. The priest at Nob gave him provisions and later was killed for it by Saul's men. Those who refused to help, such as Nabal, paid the price. David also stayed for a time with the Philistines, cleverly making it look like he was on their side, while never really injuring Israelites. Twice while he was hiding in the Judean wilderness David had the opportunity to kill Saul, who was chasing him. Both times he held back out of respect for Saul's office. Each time the piety of David is set in contrast to the obsessive behavior of Saul.

Meanwhile, pressure from the Philistines continued to grow, driving the Israelites toward the Jordan River (Figure 8.4). Saul was hard pressed and tried to make a stand at Gilboa. He was at his wits' end as the time for battle approached. Samuel was dead. Pagan means of divination had been banned. He had no one to give him counsel, no one to bless the troops before the fight, and no one to assure him of the presence of Yahweh. Desperate for a word from Yahweh, Saul approached a professional diviner. In a seance-like encounter the spirit of Samuel appeared before him.

> 28:15 "Tell me what I should do." 16 Samuel said, "Why do you ask me? YHWH has turned from you and is now your enemy. 17 YHWH has done to you just what he spoke through me. YHWH has torn the kingdom out of your hand and has given it to your companion David 18 because you did not obey the voice of YHWH."

Looking for help, Saul received anything but a word of comfort. Samuel only confirmed his, and Yahweh's, earlier rejection of the benighted king.

Fulfilling the prophetic word of Samuel, the kingdom was taken away as Saul and his sons died in battle on **Mt. Gilboa**. When the Philistines came upon Saul's body, they beheaded him, stripped him of his armor, and hung his corpse on the wall of Beth-shean for all to see. Hearing of Saul's demise, the citizens of Jabesh-gilead, whom Saul earlier had rescued, bravely recovered his body, along with the bodies of his sons, and gave them respectful disposal.

The map in Figure 8.5 serves as a summary of the life of Saul.

DAVID CYCLE (2 SAMUEL 1–24)

The second book of Samuel deals with David's consolidation of power. He subsumed under his own authority all the territory of Judah and the northern tribes. For the first time all the tribes were united into a cohesive national entity.

FIGURE 8.4 **PHILISTINE ANTHROPOID COFFIN** This Philistine pottery coffin was found at Beth-shean and dates roughly to the time of Saul (twelfth–eleventh centuries B.C.E.). The coffin is the size of an adult. A body would have been slipped inside the coffin for burial. The removable lid bears a face, perhaps a likeness to the one interred inside. This coffin and other material evidence proves that Beth-shean was occupied by the Philistines at this time, attesting how far east they had penetrated and how dire the Philistine threat really was.

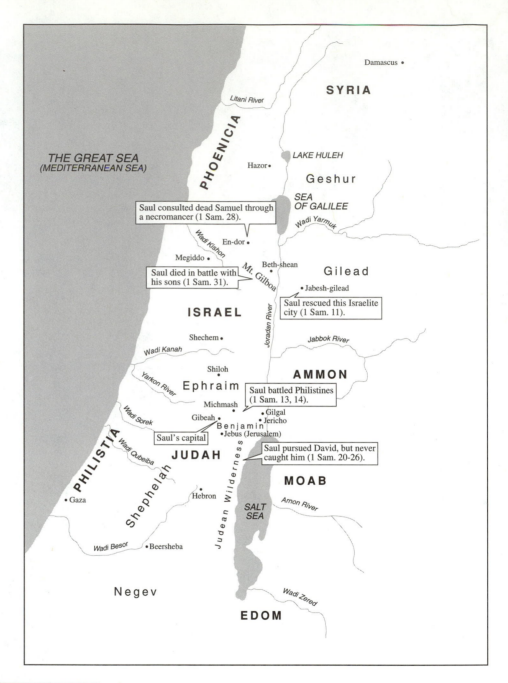

FIGURE 8.5   CAREER OF SAUL

The following text labels appear on the map:

Damascus

SYRIA

Litani River

PHOENICIA

THE GREAT SEA
(MEDITERRANEAN SEA)

LAKE HULEH

Hazor

Geshur

SEA
OF GALILEE

Saul consulted dead Samuel through
a necromancer (1 Sam. 28).

Wadi Yarmuk

Wadi Kishon

En-dor

Megiddo

Beth-shean

Gilead

Mt. Gilboa

Saul died in battle with
his sons (1 Sam. 31).

Jabesh-gilead

Saul rescued this Israelite
city (1 Sam. 11).

ISRAEL

Joradan River

Jabbok River

Shechem

Wadi Kanah

AMMON

Shiloh

Yarkon River

Ephraim

Saul battled Philistines
(1 Sam. 13, 14).

Michmash

Gilgal

Gibeah

Jericho

Benjamin

Wadi Sorek

Jebus (Jerusalem)

Saul's capital

PHILISTIA

Wadi Qubeiba

JUDAH

Judean Wilderness

Saul pursued David, but never
caught him (1 Sam. 20-26).

MOAB

Shephelah

Gaza

Hebron

SALT
SEA

Arnon River

Wadi Besor

Beersheba

Negev

Wadi Zered

EDOM

DAVID'S RISE TO POWER (2 SAMUEL 1–8)

Saul was mortally wounded and asked a soldier to finish him off. That soldier
ran to David, Saul's crown in hand, with what he thought would be news well

BIOGRAPHICAL SKETCH OF DAVID

Anointed king by Samuel 1 Sam. 16
Kills Goliath, the Philistine 17
Befriends Jonathan, Saul's son 18
Pursued by Saul, takes refuge in Philistia 18–30
Mourns the deaths of Saul and Jonathan 2 Sam. 1
Anointed king over Judah 2
Anointed king over Israel 5
Captures Jebus (Jerusalem) and makes it the capital 5
Brings ark of the covenant to Jerusalem 6
Given the Davidic covenant promises 7
Commits adultery with Bathsheba 11
Flees Jerusalem after Absalom's coup d'état 15
Builds an altar on Araunah's threshing floor 24
Dies and Solomon follows him as king 1 Kings 2

received. David was outraged that this man had finished off Saul, even though Saul realistically had no chance for survival. What do we see here? Do we see David turning as irrational as Saul? Is this the beginning of David's decline?

Probably not. David was genuinely pained that his one-time mentor, Saul, was dead. David's emotions come out in the sensitive and touching eulogy David delivered upon the deaths of Saul and Jonathan (2 Samuel 1:19–27). This poem, not coincidentally, picks up the theme of the books of Samuel first articulated in Hannah's Song—"How the mighty have fallen!" (See especially verses 19, 25, and 27.) Remember, the proud are humbled and the humble exalted.

Yet in addition, David's reaction reveals his political savvy. Contrary to the expected reaction, though Saul was his rival, he did not express his approval, nor would he condone in any way the death of Saul. He did nothing that could serve to alienate the loyal followers of Saul, which was virtually the entire entity of northern Israel. Even in this time of tragedy David kept the door open for the friends of Saul to join him in political union.

David went to Judah, his home tribe, to rally support now that Saul was dead. He set up his headquarters at **Hebron**, the regional capital of Judah. David ruled from Hebron for seven and a half years. Meanwhile in the north, Ishbaal[2] had been proclaimed king by **Abner**, the commander of Saul's army. The sides were drawn, the house of David against the house of Saul. David's power base got stronger; Ishbaal's got weaker. Seeing that the future lay with David, Abner (Ishbaal's commander) defected. This in turn provoked **Joab**, David's commander. Joab and Abner had earlier had a disagreement, and in addition, perhaps Joab felt insecure in his position as David's right-hand man. Joab secretly met Abner and killed him, thus getting rid of a serious rival.

David lamented Abner's death and blamed the treachery on Joab. Abner was well respected in northern Israel. Moreover, his presence in David's camp might

---

[2] The Hebrew text gives his name as Ishbosheth, which means "man of shame." Based on 1 Chronicles 8:33 and 9:39 we know the name originally to have been Ishbaal, meaning "man of Baal." The name was changed to eliminate the divine element Baal and at the same time to disparage this pretender to the throne.

have proved troublesome, yet none of the blame for his death fell on David. David was again sensitive to the feelings of Saul's loyalists and did not provoke their ill will.

Conditions in the north deteriorated completely. Ishbaal was attacked by two of his officers. They killed then decapitated him, carrying the head to David in Hebron as proof of their new loyalty to him. David, as we have come to expect, was not impressed; quite the opposite. He had those two traitors killed, again sending a signal that he did not condone violence done to the house of Saul.

Completely without direction or leadership, the tribes of the north asked David to become their king as well. With a covenant, David assumed kingship over both Judah and Israel, reigning over a united nation. David very wisely decided he must move his capital from Hebron. If left there it would seem he was favoring his ancestral tribe of Judah. David and his men attacked and occupied what was then called **Jebus,** to be identified with **Jerusalem.** David had it called "the city of David" to indicate it was directly under his command. He rid the surrounding territory of Philistines, providing greater security for his new capital city. Then, in an act of great piety and even greater political astuteness, he fetched the ark of God from Kiriath-yearim and brought it into Jerusalem. The great symbol of the tribal confederacy and focus of earlier religious devotion firmly established Jerusalem as the religious center of the newly united nation.

David had a desire to build a shrine for the ark in Jerusalem. **Nathan,** the Jerusalem royal court prophet, received word from Yahweh that David should not build Yahweh a house. With a divine double entente, Yahweh said that instead he would build a house for David, meaning a perpetual dynasty. Then, in what is termed the **Davidic covenant,** Yahweh pledged his enduring support for the line of David:

> 7:16 Your house and your kingdom will be established firmly forever before me. Your throne will be established forever.

Although Davidic kings might sin, Yahweh would never remove his support from them, as he once did with Saul. This promise is the foundation for messianic expectations in Judaism and Christianity. Yahweh promised he would never remove his support from the offspring of David. It implied, also, that there would be a divinely sponsored king over Israel forever.

David was at the peak of his career. Endorsed by Yahweh, loved by his people, he also managed to defeat Israel's inveterate enemies. Chapter 8 sums up his victories. He subdued the Philistines. Never again were they a threat to Israel. He defeated the Arameans, the Moabites, and the Edomites, giving Israel peace on every side. Verse 15 summarizes concisely the era of righteous rule David inaugurated. David ushered in a time of shalom, and it would be remembered as the golden age of Israel.

> 8:15 So David ruled over all Israel. David administered justice with equity to all his people.

As you might have suspected, things were almost too good to be true. Although David had the support of Yahweh and, indeed, of the entire nation, he became complacent, presumptuous, and ready for a fall. Remember the theme: the proud will be humbled and the humble exalted.

DYNASTIC SUCCESSION STRUGGLES (2 SAMUEL 9–20)

This portion of 2 Samuel, along with 1 Kings 1–2, details the family history of David as his sons fight with each other over who will follow David on the throne, hence *dynastic succession*. The narrative reads like a short story and may have been composed from court records. Scholars have variously termed this account the *succession narrative* and the *court history of David*.

By the way the writer introduces the **Bathsheba** story, the narrator signals that something bad had happened to David.

> 11:1 *In the spring of the year, the time when kings normally go out to do battle, David sent Joab with his officers and all Israel. They devastated the Ammonites and besieged Rabbah. But David remained in Jerusalem.*

David's troubles began when he neglected his royal responsibilities. Shirking his military duty—remember, it was his courage in facing Goliath that brought him national acclaim—it is no wonder that he got into trouble. David spied a beautiful woman from the roof of his house and asked her to the palace. Though married to Uriah, Bathsheba accepted David's invitation—who could refuse the king?—and David had an affair with her. Matters got complicated after it became apparent that she was pregnant even though her husband had been at the Ammonite battlefront with David's army. David tried to cover up his responsibility for the pregnancy by recalling Uriah in hopes that he would sleep with his wife. Uriah refused to enjoy the pleasures of home out of loyalty to his troops, certainly a sarcastic twist setting David's sin in relief.

David had Uriah killed and, with a grand kingly show of caring, he wed the widow. No doubt all Israel admired their sovereign for marrying Israel's newest widow, and one with child at that. David assumed he had managed to keep his sins of adultery and murder hidden, until Nathan exposed his guilt. This would be the test of Yahweh's commitment to David. Would Yahweh abandon him, as he had abandoned Saul when Saul sinned?

On analysis, David's sins were just as serious as Saul's, if not worse. For Saul's sins, Yahweh denied dynastic succession and removed his favor from the king. But Yahweh did not react the same way to David's sins. An inquisitive reader would want to know why.

David deserved to be removed from office, but Yahweh remained true to the spirit of the Davidic covenant. For the sake of the covenant promise David was allowed to remain on the throne. Yet David was not given blanket forgiveness without discipline. His punishment was this: The baby born to Bathsheba died. Furthermore, the sins of adultery and murder that he had committed in secret would be committed in public by his sons. Indeed, there is "poetic justice." David's own sins would be duplicated within his own family, yet in a more heinous way. Yahweh delivered the following judgment oracle through Nathan.

12:10 The sword shall not leave your house, because you have despised me, and have taken the wife of Uriah the Hittite to be your wife. 11 Thus says YHWH, I will raise up trouble against you from within your own house; and I will take your wives, and before your eyes give them to your neighbor. He shall lie with your wives in the full light of day. 12 You did it secretly, but I will do this thing in front of all Israel, and in the full light of day.

This prophetic word of punishment is the literary–theological agenda for the following narrative. We see how this punishment works out in the family of David as his sons vie for the right to follow him on the throne.

Amnon was the crown prince, the first in line for the throne. His particular sexual sin was that he was obsessively infatuated with his half-sister **Tamar**. One day feigning illness, he deceived her, trapped her, and then raped her. Then, as the ultimate act of rejection, he refused to acknowledge her in any way. Her full brother **Absalom** took revenge on Amnon two years later and killed him.

David deeply loved Absalom, but he had no choice except to punish him. He exiled Absalom and would not allow him to appear in Jerusalem. Absalom was a clever man, the consummate politician, much like his father. He was also very handsome. Eventually he was allowed to come as far as the city gate of Jerusalem, but no farther. There he endeared himself to the people. He intercepted citizens as they came looking for David's help. Instead, he offered his own services: no need to go to the king. In this way, the text says, "Absalom stole the hearts of the people of Israel."

Having won over the people, he made a run for the crown. First, he proclaimed himself king in Hebron, the place David first became king. Then, he gathered military support and attacked Jerusalem. Realizing he was powerless to resist, David fled into the Judean wilderness. Absalom took control of Jerusalem, and in a public display of power took David's concubines and slept with them on the roof of the palace, in full view of the citizenry. What David had done in secret, his son did in public.

Yet David was not totally without support. He left Hushai, one of his trusted counselors, behind. Hushai feigned support for Absalom, but in fact he was loyal to David and worked to frustrate Absalom's plans. He gave advice to Absalom that reversed the advice of Ahithophel, another royal counselor. Hushai's advice enabled David to make good his escape and eventually consolidate his strength. His advice rejected, Ahithophel went out and killed himself.

When finally Absalom mounted an attack on David in the wilderness, it was too late. Absalom's men were defeated, and he himself was killed by Joab, David's commander. Although almost incapacitated by grief, David returned to Jerusalem and resumed control.

DAVID'S LAST DAYS (2 SAMUEL 21–24)

These last chapters contain various materials pertaining to David and his rule but are not in any clear order, and they seem to be chronologically jumbled. There is poetic material written by David in chapter 22, which finds a virtual duplicate in Psalm 18. There is a list of David's warriors. And there is an account of David's sin in taking a census of the people, read by God as a sign of his lack

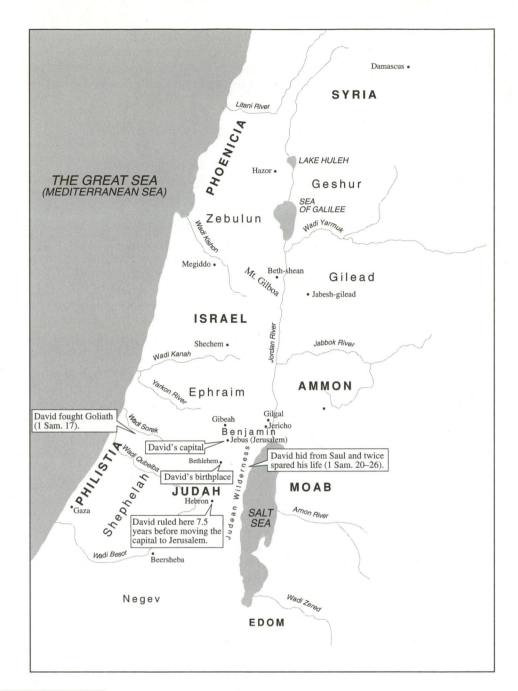

The Great Sea (Mediterranean Sea)

SYRIA

Damascus •

Litani River

PHOENICIA

LAKE HULEH

Hazor •

Geshur

SEA OF GALILEE

Zebulun

Wadi Kishon

Wadi Yarmuk

Megiddo •

Mt. Gilboa

Beth-shean •

Gilead

• Jabesh-gilead

ISRAEL

Shechem •

Jordan River

Jabbok River

Wadi Kanah

Yarkon River

Ephraim

AMMON

David fought Goliath (1 Sam. 17).

Wadi Sorek

Gibeah

Gilgal

Jericho

Benjamin

Jebus (Jerusalem)

David's capital

David hid from Saul and twice spared his life (1 Sam. 20–26).

PHILISTIA

Wadi Qubeiba

Bethlehem •

David's birthplace

Judean Wilderness

MOAB

Shephelah

JUDAH

Hebron •

SALT SEA

Arnon River

• Gaza

David ruled here 7.5 years before moving the capital to Jerusalem.

Wadi Besor

Beersheba •

Negev

Wadi Zered

EDOM

| FIGURE 8.6 | CAREER OF DAVID |

of faith. Instead of relying on Yahweh, he was counting the strength of his army. Yahweh punished him and the nation with a plague.

The book ends with David purchasing the property of **Araunah** and offering a sacrifice, which stopped the plague. The site of the altar, the so-called threshing floor of Araunah, became the site of the Jerusalem Temple. In its own way, the end of Samuel points ahead to the next momentous stage in the history of the monarchy, the reign of Solomon and the building of the Temple.

Figure 8.6 serves as a summary of the life of David.

OVERALL SHAPE OF THE BOOKS OF SAMUEL

The books of Samuel are a composition that went through various stages of development. They incorporate blocks of material that existed at one time separately, such as the Ark Narrative (1 Sam. 4:1–7:1), the story of Saul's rise (1 Sam. 9:1–11:15), the story of David's rise (1 Sam. 16–31), and the Succession Narrative (2 Sam. 9–20 and 1 Kings 1–2).

The rise of kingship is the central agenda of the books. The retention of the two sources on the monarchy, one positive and the other negative, allows the text to give a nuanced and realistic evaluation of the new institution. Kingship was part of the plan of God to deliver the people, but it also arose out of the people's disobedience and resulted from their turning away from the theocratic ideals of the Mosaic covenant.

An editor shaped the diverse materials into a linear history that incorporated a prophetic critique of the establishment of the monarchy. Within this history, Samuel was the main figure acting on God's behalf to monitor the kingship. The rise of kingship culminated in the divine covenant established with the house of David. And the lessons of David's career reinforced the need for absolute dependence on God, along with obedience to the Torah that would hold in check a king's impulse to exalt himself above the law.

On the literary plane, the book was cogently organized into three cycles of stories, each centering on a central player in the rise of kingship. The literary–theological theme that unites these cycles and reinforces the supremacy of divine justice is the one articulated in Hannah's Song: The proud will be humbled and the humble exalted.

The final stage of Samuel's editorial development came when this prophetic history was incorporated into the larger Deuteronomic History. This stage is marked by theological editorializing, including chapters such as 1 Samuel 8 and 1 Samuel 12, which reflect the Deuteronomic Historian's particular theological point of view.

QUESTIONS FOR REVIEW

1. What are the three cycles of stories in the books of Samuel?
2. What major national institution developed in the books of Samuel, and what theological struggle was associated with its establishment?
3. What literary–theological theme is articulated in Hannah's Song? List the many ways it works out concretely in Samuel.
4. What is the Davidic covenant? Why was it important?
5. What are the two conflicting views of kingship in Samuel?

QUESTIONS FOR DISCUSSION

1. What universal issues concerning national leadership surface in the books of Samuel? What perspectives on the issues are presented, and how may these perspectives provide guidance today?
2. Compare the careers of Saul and David. How were they alike and how were they different? What was the effect of the Davidic covenant on the course of David's life? What was its effect on the course of the nation?
3. The books of Samuel seem almost cynically preoccupied with the rise and fall of leadership. The proud will be humbled and the humble will be exalted. Do you think the author of Samuel is here writing a treatise on human nature and the politics of power? Do you think it is inevitable that powerful leaders become arrogant? Do you think it is unavoidable that power corrupts, and absolute power corrupts absolutely?

FOR FURTHER STUDY

Brueggemann, Walter (1990). *First and Second Samuel*. Interpretation Series. Louisville, Ky.: John Knox Press.

Eslinger, Lyle M. (1985). *Kingship of God in Crisis. A Close Reading of 2 Samuel 1–12*. Sheffield: JSOT Press.

Fokkelman, J. P. (1981). *Narrative Art and Poetry in the Books of Samuel, vol. I: King David*. Assen, Neth.: van Gorcum.

Frick, Frank S. (1985). *The Formation of the State in Ancient Israel. A Survey of Models and Theories*. The Social World of Biblical Antiquity Series, 4. Sheffield: JSOT Press.

Gunn, David M. (1980). *The Fate of King Saul: An Interpretation of a Biblical Story*. Sheffield: JSOT Press.

KINGS: A HISTORY OF THE KINGDOMS

Names and Terms to Remember

Adonijah	Jehoiachin	Rehoboam
Ahab	Jehoiakim	Sennacherib
Ahaz	Jehu	Shalmaneser V
Ahijah	Jeroboam	Solomon
Bathsheba	Jezebel	Tiglath-Pileser III
Elijah	Josiah	Zadok
Elisha	Nathan	Zedekiah
Hezekiah	Nebuchadnezzar	

Like the books of Samuel, the books of Kings were originally one. The story line of Kings continues the history of Israel's leadership that began in the books of Samuel. But Kings differs from Samuel in at least one feature: It does not have a small number of focal figures but instead traces the line of kings from David all the way to the exile.

Kings is a continuation of the Deuteronomic History, which (as its name implies) traces its pedigree all the way back to Deuteronomy. It shares a basic theological perspective with the other books of the DH. Its foundation is the covenant that united Yahweh and Israel and defined Israel's relationship to Yahweh. Central to the theology of the Deuteronomic Historian is a concern for the quality of Israel's religious life. If the people were faithful and loyal to Yahweh, then they would be protected and blessed by Yahweh. Otherwise, the nation would suffer.

The quality of Israel's devotion to Yahweh was measured by the exclusiveness of its religious focus. If Yahweh alone was worshiped, the people were judged faithful. If Yahweh was worshiped only in Jerusalem and in the prescribed manner, the people were judged loyal.

You should be especially struck by the theological judgments applied to the kings. It is not the king's effectiveness in domestic or international politics that the DH evaluates; it is the king's effectiveness as religious leader and model. Note how often the writer evaluates a king by whether he (rarely) "did right" or (most often) "did evil" in the eyes of Yahweh. Kings who rejected idolatry and promoted religious reform, such as **Josiah**, were approved. Kings who encouraged or even tolerated non-Yahwistic practices were denounced.

The DH's prejudice against the Northern Kingdom is especially obvious. No ruler from the north is given approval, regardless of his accomplishments. Nothing he does can be acceptable because Israel (as the Northern Kingdom was called) was established on religiously shaky ground. Jeroboam, its first king, broke with the divinely authorized Davidic dynasty and Jerusalem Temple and created alternate worship centers that employed golden calves as religious symbols. Because none of the following kings eliminated these centers, each is condemned. Ultimately, because of the golden calves at Dan and Bethel, the Northern Kingdom was destroyed.

We can divide the books of Kings into three sections based on historical content. The first section deals with the kingdom of Solomon, the second deals with the civil war and parallel histories of Israel and Judah, and the third deals with the history of Judah down to the Babylonian exile.

The following is a general outline of Kings, but be aware that it is not quite this straightforward. There are many insertions and digressions along the way.

Outline of the books of Kings

I. Solomon and the United Monarchy (1 Kings 1–11)
    A. Solomon secures the throne 1–2
    B. Solomon's wisdom 3–4
    C. Building the temple 5–8
    D. Solomon's downfall 9–11
II. Parallel Histories of Israel and Judah (1 Kings 12–2 Kings 17)
    A. Division of the kingdom 12–16
    B. Prophetic ministry of Elijah 1 Kings 17–2 Kings 2
    C. Prophetic ministry of Elisha 2–9
    D. Assyrian crisis 10–16
III. Judah to the Babylonian Exile (2 Kings 18–25)
    A. Hezekiah and Isaiah 18–20
    B. Josiah's Reform 21–23
    C. First conquest of Jerusalem 24
    D. Second conquest of Jerusalem 25

SOLOMON AND THE UNITED MONARCHY (1 KINGS 1–11)

A great deal of text is spent on the reign of **Solomon**. It is true that he ruled for a long time (961–921 B.C.E.), indeed, a "perfect" forty years. But more importantly in the mind of the Deuteronomic writer, the reign of Solomon is the first fulfillment of one of the important parts of the Davidic covenant articulated in 2 Samuel 7. During his tenure as king the great temple to Yahweh was built in Jerusalem (see Figure 9.1).

SOLOMON SECURES THE THRONE

These first two chapters relate how Solomon secured the right to follow David as king of all Israel.[1] David is an old man as the books of Kings begin. He was so frail that he needed a female companion to keep him warm at night, a beautiful young virgin named Abishag. **Adonijah** was the eldest remaining son and naturally expected to inherit the throne. He had the support of Joab and the priest Abiathar. Together they held a coronation ceremony in which Adonijah was proclaimed king.

But **Nathan**, the prophet who supported David, and others objected. They strongly promoted Solomon, a younger son, for the throne—continuing the tradi-

---

[1]Many scholars see 1 Kings 1–2 as the conclusion of an originally independent record called the Succession History or the Court History of David, comprising 2 Samuel 9–20 and 1 Kings 1–2. The appendices of 2 Samuel 21–24 break the continuity. The canonical ordering of books, however, positions these first chapters of Kings as the introduction to the history of Solomon's kingdom, rather than the conclusion of a history of succession.

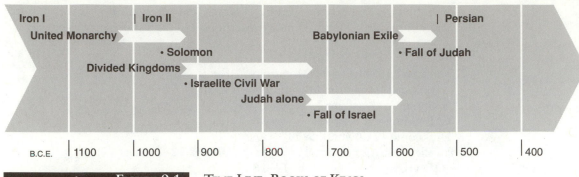

Iron I			Iron II					Persian
United Monarchy					Babylonian Exile			
		• Solomon				• Fall of Judah		
Divided Kingdoms								
		• Israelite Civil War						
		Judah alone						
			• Fall of Israel					

| B.C.E. | 1100 | 1000 | 900 | 800 | 700 | 600 | 500 | 400 |

FIGURE 9.1   TIME LINE: BOOKS OF KINGS

tion and biblical motif of the younger son supplanting the older.[2] Apparently, the process of the dynastic succession of the eldest had not yet been firmly established. Also siding with Solomon were **Bathsheba**, his mother, **Zadok**, another priest, and Benaiah, one of David's loyal commanders. They had the support of David and held their own coronation ceremony for Solomon. Evidently Solomon also had popular support and a stronger power base. Adonijah gave up his claim to the throne and asked Solomon for forgiveness.

When he was about to die, David counseled his son Solomon to remain faithful, using words reminiscent of Yahweh's charge to Joshua in Joshua 1, and recollecting the promise of the Davidic covenant, all heavily bearing the stamp of the Deuteronomic outlook.

> *2:2 I am about to go the way of all people. Be strong and courageous 3 and keep the will of YHWH your God, by walking in his ways and keeping his statutes, commandments, ordinances and testimonies as written in the torah of Moses, so that you may prosper in everything you do and wherever you go. 4 Then YHWH will affirm his word which he spoke concerning me: "If your heirs watch their way and walk before me in faithfulness, with all their heart and with all their soul, then you shall not fail to have a successor on the throne of Israel."*

Not one to give up easily, Adonijah made a veiled play for the throne after David died. Through Bathsheba he asked Solomon for permission to marry Abishag, David's former concubine. When Solomon heard the request he read into it a challenge to his power and accused Adonijah of treason. Apparently, if one possessed the king's harem, then he was *de facto* king. We might recall how this type of move telegraphed to all Jerusalem that Absalom was king—when he slept with David's wives on the roof of the palace. Solomon took this provocation seriously and put Adonijah to death. Shortly afterward, Joab, who had supported Adonijah's claim to kingship, was also executed.

---

[2]Think of Isaac supplanting Ishmael, Jacob over Esau, Ephraim over Manasseh, and David himself over his older brothers when Samuel came to find a king to replace Saul. Perhaps the reason the Yahwist was so interested in stories about divine preference for the younger son over the firstborn was just this need to justify the rise of Solomon to the throne over his older brother rivals.

Becomes king and secures the throne 1 Kings 1, 2
Receives wisdom from God 3
Builds a temple in Jerusalem for Yahweh 5–8
Visited by Queen of Sheba 10
Marries 700 wives and 300 concubines 11
Dies and is buried in Jerusalem 12

Furthermore, Abiathar, the priest who had sided with Adonijah, was exiled to Anathoth. In a Deuteronomic editorial note we are told that this last move fulfilled the prophetic word of condemnation voiced against the house of Eli (2:27, compare 1 Samuel 2–3).[3] Abiathar's support of Adonijah justified the expulsion of the house of Abiathar and their exile to Anathoth in favor of the priesthood of Zadok. The rights of priesthood in Jerusalem were jealously guarded, and this explains how the Zadokite priesthood came to power.

Having neutralized all potential rivals by either exile or execution, Solomon was secure on the throne. As the writer says, "The kingdom was firmly in the hand of Solomon" (2:46).

SOLOMON'S WISDOM (1 KINGS 3–4)

The beginning of Solomon's reign was auspicious. When Yahweh came to him in a dream at Gibeon offering to grant him his wish, Solomon could have asked for anything. Instead of choosing wealth, longevity, or political security he asked for the wisdom to discern good and evil so that he could rule God's people well. Gratified that Solomon had chosen so wisely (that's the wisdom of Solomon, isn't it?…he was wise enough to choose wisdom), Yahweh granted him "a wise and perceptive mind" (3:12) and provided the other suggestions as a bonus.

As so often happens in the literature of the Hebrew Bible, the next story provides proof of what had just been promised. In what is perhaps the most famous story involving Solomon, two women came to him looking for justice. Each had an infant, but by accident one of them had suffocated her child and had switched her dead baby with the living baby of the other woman. In the morning both laid claim to the living infant. Solomon cleverly cut through the conflicting claims in this way: He ordered a sword brought to the court and offered to give each woman half of the disputed child. As he had hoped, the real mother revealed herself when the compassionate one relinquished her claim in order to spare the life of the child.

Solomon's wisdom was celebrated far and near. Even the Queen of Sheba heard of his reputation and came to bask in his wisdom. Legend has it that he was considered wiser than anyone in the world at that time.

The text also tells us that in addition to judicious decision making he was renowned for composing 3,000 proverbs and 1,005 songs, and for analyzing

[3]This note may be especially enlightening if the contention of Friedman (1987) is correct, that the writer of Deuteronomy was Jeremiah. We know that Jeremiah hails from Anathoth, and the speculation is that he comes from the line of Abiathar, ultimately tracing its lineage to Eli of Shiloh.

flora and fauna in what appears to be an early scientific endeavor. By doing the latter, Solomon follows in the venerable tradition of Adam who, according to the Yahwist account of creation (which, not by accident, was likely written during Solomon's reign), called all the animals by name.

The writer tells us that Solomon set up twelve provincial districts for the purposes of administration and taxation. The boundaries of these districts did not conform to tribal boundaries. This appears to have been Solomon's attempt to sublimate tribal loyalties and create a sense of national purpose. But in so doing he seems to have created dissatisfaction that contributed to civil war shortly after his death. By placing the account of this change within the chapters reviewing his wisdom, the writer may have been suggesting that this administrative move was a manifestation of Solomon's wisdom. If so, his wisdom backfired.

The importance of the figure of Solomon for the tradition of wisdom in Israel will be examined at length in Part Three, "Writings."

BUILDING THE TEMPLE (1 KINGS 5–8)

Solomon set about building the temple in fulfillment of the terms of the covenant Yahweh made with David. He contracted Hiram of Tyre to supply the building materials and skilled craftsmen in return for food supplies. There were cost overruns, however, and Solomon ended up paying his bill to Hiram by deeding over territory in the north of Israel. This, of course, did not sit well with the people living there.

Nor did another policy. Solomon needed workers for the massive temple project, as well as for building his palace. Termed the *corvée*, or unpaid labor force, he conscripted Israelites and constrained them to provide manual labor, thereby further alienating his constituency. This reminded them of the bitter oppression of Pharaoh in Egypt before the exodus when the Hebrews were made to work on royal building projects.

The temple itself was a magnificent structure. Its walls were made of stone overlaid with wood paneling. There were two rooms within the sanctuary. The outer room housed an incense altar, lamps, and a table for ceremonial bread. The panels were decorated with carvings of flowers, trees, and cherubim. The inner room had perfectly symmetrical dimensions. It housed the ark of the covenant. The temple took seven years to build and was completed around 950 B.C.E.

The temple was the most sacred of Israel's buildings. Because it housed the ark of the covenant it was considered to be the location of Yahweh's presence among the people. This was expressed hymnically in the statement, "Yahweh sat enthroned between the cherubim" on the top of the ark. The ark was considered to be his throne and the inner sanctuary his throne room (see Figure 9.2).

The configuration of the temple complex, its decorations, and its various implements suggests that the temple was intended to symbolize the world over which Yahweh rules. The outer courtyard with its bowl of water represented the waters of chaos. The outer room of the temple with its pictures of plants and animals cut into the walls, the lights of heaven represented in the lampstands, depicted the physical world in microcosm. The inner sanctum, a perfect cube covered entirely with gold, with the ark throne flanked by cherubim, rep-

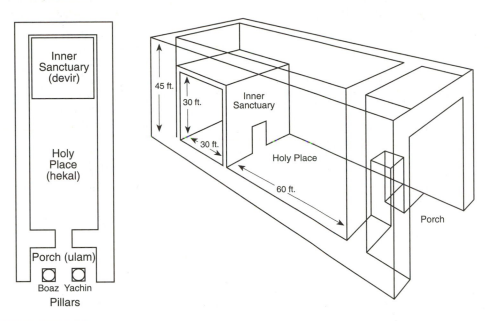

Top-Down View

Inner
Sanctuary
(devir)

Holy
Place
(hekal)

Porch (ulam)

Boaz Yachin
Pillars

Isometric View

45 ft.

30 ft.

30 ft.

Inner
Sanctuary

Holy Place

60 ft.

Porch

FIGURE 9.2   SOLOMON'S TEMPLE Solomon's temple follows the basic design layout of the Tabernacle (see chapter 3, "Exodus"). The inner sanctuary, termed the *Most Holy Place*, has perfectly symmetrical dimensions, befitting the dwelling place of God.[4]

resented the perfect heaven where Yahweh dwells, enthroned among the angels. The temple is a graphic symbol of the power and authority of Yahweh over his creation.

In addition to building the temple, Solomon also built an expansive (and very expensive) royal palace complex. It took twice as long to build as did the temple. This opulence further indebted the nation and ripened the growing dissatisfaction of the population.

SOLOMON'S DOWNFALL (1 KINGS 9–11)

In the evaluation of the Deuteronomic writer, none of this was as disastrous as the trouble caused by his harem.

> *11:1 King Solomon loved many foreign women, including the daughter of Pharaoh, and women from Moab, Ammon, Edom, Sidon and Hatti—2 from nations about which YHWH had said to the people of Israel, "You must not marry them, neither may they marry you, for they would surely turn your heart away after their gods." These women Solomon clung to in*

[4] For an explanation of temple architecture and architectural history, see Fritz (1987).

love. 3 He had seven hundred wives who were princesses, and three hun-
dred who were concubines. His wives turned away his heart.

What Solomon did here is not all that remarkable for his time, at least in principle. The fact that he had so many female retainers most certainly was not an
indication that he had an overly active sexual appetite. The 1,000 women were
rather a sign of the vast political contacts of the Solomonic administration in this
newly crafted Davidic empire. The wives Solomon took were a part of international arrangements, marriages for political and diplomatic purpose; treaties
with other nations and city–states were contracted through political marriages.

But the Deuteronomist interprets these marriages as the seeds of Israel's disintegration. Solomon was just too tolerant. He allowed these women to worship
their native gods and goddesses right there in Jerusalem. In so doing, Solomon
had compromised his loyalty to Yahweh. For this, God would soon strip a major
portion of the kingdom from the control of the house of David. This sets the
stage and gives the theological rationale for the division of the kingdom into two
separate nations.

PARALLEL HISTORIES OF ISRAEL AND JUDAH (1 KINGS 12–2 KINGS 17)

The second of the three main blocks of material in the books of Kings accounts
for the parallel histories of the two kingdoms that arose out of the civil war of
921 B.C.E. The Deuteronomist moves back and forth between Judah and Israel in
his treatment of history. The Deuteronomist introduces the kings of Judah using
a standard pattern of elements, including

1. the date the king took the throne relative to the reign of the king of Israel
2. the age at which he came to the throne
3. the name of the mother of the king (the queen mother)
4. a value judgment of the king relative to David, who was the standard of comparison

The Deuteronomist introduces the kings of Israel using a different standard
pattern of elements, including

1. the date the king took the throne relative to the reign of the king of Judah
2. the location of the capital city of Israel
3. the length of the reign
4. a negative evaluation of the king (applying to all kings except Shallum, who only reigned one month)

DIVISION OF THE KINGDOM (1 KINGS 12–16)

Solomon was able to keep the kingdom together during his lifetime, but trouble
was simmering. The seeds of dissatisfaction, primarily the cession of land in the

north, high public taxation, and the use of Israelites in forced labor, prompted those in the northern districts to cast elsewhere for leadership. They found it in the figure of **Jeroboam**.

Jeroboam, the son of Nebat, had been a foreman of one of Solomon's labor crews. Being an Ephraimite, he seems to have shared in northern dissatisfaction with the Davidic administration. With the prophetic support of **Ahijah** from Shiloh (located in the north, the religious center of the tribal federation during the period of the judges), Jeroboam organized resistance to Solomon. Solomon recognized him as the ringleader and sought to kill him, but Jeroboam survived.

After Solomon died, his son **Rehoboam** ascended the throne. He met with leaders from the north at Shechem, but the support of the population of the north was not forthcoming. Led by Jeroboam, the people demanded that Rehoboam humanize his policies and lighten the burden of taxation and government service. Rehoboam refused to change royal policy; in fact, encouraged by his closest counselors, with bravado he threatened to make the load even heavier. The northern delegation declared their independence.

> 12:16 *When all Israel saw that the king would not listen to them, the people answered the king, "What do we have to do with David?! We have no inheritance in the son of Jesse! To your tents, Israel! Take care of your own house now, David!"*

The Deuteronomist framed the conflict in terms of rival administrations and national ideologies. The northern territories refused to support Davidic rulers and Zion theology any longer. They had agreed to Davidic rule only after the house of Saul had let them down. Now they wanted out. The sympathies of the Deuteronomist are clearly with the Davidic line.

Rehoboam did not have the military power or strength of will to force them to accept his rule. And the kingdom, while spared a protracted and bloody civil war, for all intents and purposes now became two nations. The northern entity, consisting of ten tribes, kept the name Israel. As you read narratives that date to this period note that the term *Israel* designates the Northern Kingdom rather than the entire twelve-tribe nation. The southern kingdom of Judah was just Judah, the sole tribe that remained loyal to the leadership of the house of David. The twelfth tribe, Levi, did not have tribal territory. Instead, the Levites were found in both Israel and Judah.

An important order of business for Jeroboam was to consolidate his hold on Israel and give it a national identity. To that end he (re-)built Shechem and made it his capital. That site had all the associations of Israel's tribal beginnings, the good old days of the Joshua covenant.

Jeroboam had to put together a religious system independent of Judah. He was especially worried that his citizens would feel compelled to pilgrimage to Jerusalem to fulfill their religious obligations, as had become their practice under the Davidic administration. To counteract such a need, Jeroboam strategically located worship centers in his kingdom at its northern and southern boundaries, at Dan and Bethel respectively. Bethel, especially, had a long religious history, so this was not hard to do. You might recall that the forebears Abraham and Jacob had special connections with Bethel.[5]

The shape that the religious system of Israel assumed under Jeroboam called for special condemnation by the Deuteronomic writer. Jeroboam built golden calves as the centerpieces of these shrines (see Figure 9.3). The mere mention of these idols immediately recalls the fiasco at Mt. Sinai engineered by Aaron (see Exodus 32). Just as heinous in the eyes of the Deuteronomist, Jeroboam employed non-Levites as priests and set up a religious calendar with festivals that differed from those utilized in Jerusalem as specified in Deuteronomic legislation. For all of these transgressions, Israel, and Jeroboam himself, could not escape God's condemnation.

An unnamed "man of God from Judah," a prophetic figure of sorts (chapter 13), voiced Yahweh's dissatisfaction by condemning Jeroboam and the Bethel shrine. But in the end the Judean prophet was himself deceived by a Bethel holy man, resulting in his own execution by God. Clearly the message was this: Beware of the prophetic tricksters in the north, and stay away from Bethel. Although he reigned a healthy twenty-two years, Jeroboam was punished by the death of his son Abijah.

PROPHETIC MINISTRY OF ELIJAH (1 KINGS 17–2 KINGS 2)

The reign of **Ahab** of Israel is the setting for the prophetic activity of **Elijah**. The introduction of Ahab follows the standard Deuteronomic pattern of encapsulating the basic facts.

> *16:29 In the 38th year of King Asa of Judah, Ahab son of Omri began to reign over Israel. Ahab son of Omri reigned over Israel from Samaria for 22 years. 30 Ahab son of Omri did more bad things in the sight of YHWH than all who were before him. 31 And as if it were an insignificant thing for him just to continue committing the sins of Jeroboam son of Nebat, additionally he took Jezebel, daughter of King Ethbaal of the Sidonians, as his wife. He continued to serve Baal, and worshiped him.*

Typical of such summaries, the reign of the northern king, in this case Ahab, is matched with the reign of the king of Judah. The capital city is named Samaria; Ahab's father Omri moved the capital here, where it would remain for the term of Israel's existence. Note also the negative evaluation of Ahab, given in terms of continuing the idolatry of Jeroboam who set up the golden calves in Dan and Bethel. But Ahab went even further. He married **Jezebel**, who brazenly promoted the worship of Baal.

Like Solomon's marriages, Ahab's marriage to Jezebel was made for diplomatic reasons, to seal an alliance with the Phoenicians. But the Deuteronomist sees only the religious implications of this marriage. It was yet another sign of the deterioration of Israel's loyalty to Yahweh in favor of Baal.

[5] See chapter 2, "Genesis 12–50." Abraham built an altar near Bethel as he made his way to the Negev (Genesis 12:8), and Jacob had his dream of the stairway to heaven at that spot (Genesis 28:10–22), thus proving that it was a point of contact between heaven and humanity—hence, a suitable place for a sanctuary.

FIGURE 9.3   BAAL AND THE BULL   The bull was a symbol of virility and was associated with the storm god Baal in Syria and Palestine. The bull was probably considered to be Baal's mount or throne, as in this 8th-century B.C.E. relief of Hadad (another name for Baal) from Arslan-Tash in northern Syria. When Jeroboam employed the calf as a ritual object, he probably did not intend it to be the object of worship, but meant it to be the place Baal was enthroned.

The core of chapter 17 through 2 Kings 2 is a cycle of narratives revolving around the central figure of Elijah. Into this group of Elijah stories other material has been inserted, including the Micaiah account (chapter 22). The Elijah stories have been shaped to highlight the struggle between Yahweh's champion Elijah and the Israelite dynasty, which advocated the worship of Baal and Asherah.

The struggle between Yahweh and Baal was drawn up in such a way as to pit Yahweh against Baal on Baal's own turf. Baal was presumed to be the god who controlled agricultural fertility by providing the life-giving rains (see Figure 9.5). In Canaanite mythic texts he is called "the Rider on the Clouds." Logically then, Elijah declared a drought on the country. What better way to find out who really sends the rain?

Elijah himself found relief from the drought and attendant famine with a widow and her son in Zarephath. The irony in the story could not be more pointed. Zarephath is in the heartland of Jezebel's homeland, the territory of her patron god, Baal Melqart. There Elijah performed life-giving miracles to demonstrate the power of Yahweh. He provided unlimited food to this poor widow and even brought her dead son back to life.

Finally the issue was settled by a dramatic encounter. Elijah confronted 450 prophets of Baal in a contest to determine who sends the rain. The Baal prophets, assisted by some 400 prophets devoted to Asherah, tried to get the attention of their gods. Despite shouts and bodily mutilation, it was to no avail. In contrast,

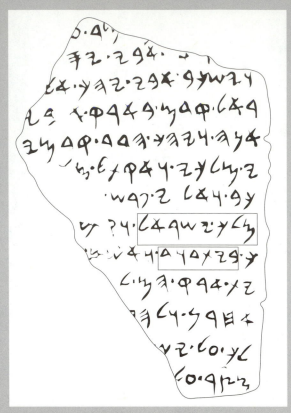

FIGURE 9.4 THE HOUSE OF DAVID INSCRIPTION

An inscription found at Tell Dan in northern Israel contains the first reference outside the Hebrew Bible to the dynasty of David. This fragmentary thirteen-line inscription written in early Aramaic and dating to the middle of the ninth century B.C.E. appears to celebrate the victory of the king of Aram in Damascus over a king in Israel. In it the phrases "king of Israel" (upper box) and "house of David" (lower box) are found.[6]

Elijah called on his God, who sent lightning down from heaven, devouring a well-drenched sacrifice and proving who really manages the storm. The citizenry who witnessed the outcome of the contest sided with Elijah and Yahweh and slew the prophets of Baal. Since they were sponsored by Jezebel, this upset her terribly, and she resolved to see Elijah dead.

Elijah fled to Mt. Horeb, a symbolic "forty-day" journey away. He returned to the site of Mosaic revelation, perhaps to reestablish contact with the God of the exodus. While there he awaited the revealing of God, expecting it to happen in storm, earthquake, or fire—the expected modes of theophany (divine appear-

[6] See Biran and Naveh (1993).

FIGURE 9.5 | **BAAL OF THE LIGHTNING**
This stone plaque, dating to the early second millennium B.C.E., was found at Ugarit. It depicts the Canaanite male deity Baal holding a lightning rod in his left hand. As the god of the storm he was thought to be responsible for providing rain and was worshiped to enhance agricultural productivity.

ance). Instead, God made his presence known in a barely audible whisper, the "still small voice" of the older English versions. Elijah was then assured that the cause of Yahweh was not dead in Israel, and that Elijah himself would oversee the demise of the house of Ahab.

To understand the logic of the text's organization, note how the next two chapters provide a characterization of Ahab with reasons enough for his elimination. Chapter 20 has nothing to do with Elijah, though unnamed prophets are part of the action. The text at first seems flattering in the way it describes Ahab's victory over the Syrians, but then condemns him because he failed to eliminate them totally when he had the chance. The story should remind you of Saul's similar failure to destroy the Amalekites when he had the chance. The text implies that Ahab must meet the same end as Saul.

Chapter 21 reveals the inner Ahab, the weak leader easily manipulated by his wife Jezebel. Ahab desired the property adjacent to the palace in Samaria. Its owner, Naboth, refused to sell family property. Jezebel arranged for Naboth to be falsely accused of a capital offense and executed. For this, Elijah condemned Ahab and declared that his dynasty would come to an end.

Ahab himself died in battle fighting the Ammonites, as the next chapter details. Chapter 22 is yet another chapter in which Elijah does not appear. Instead, another prophet, Micaiah, appears and foretells the death of Ahab. In contrast, about 400 prophets loyal to Ahab encouraged Ahab to fight with predictions of victory. Micaiah's was the lone voice in opposition, much like Elijah's. The description of Micaiah's meeting with God where he received the knowledge of Ahab's doom is especially intriguing, providing a glimpse of the divine council at work.

22:19 I saw YHWH sitting on his throne, with all the host of heaven flanking him right and left. 20 YHWH said, "Who will lure Ahab so that he will attack Ramoth-gilead and fall?" One said this and another that, 21 until a spirit came forward and stood before YHWH. "I will lure him." 22 "How?" YHWH asked. He replied, "I will go and be a lying spirit in the mouth of all his prophets." Then YHWH said, "You are to lure him, and you will succeed. Go and do it." 23 As you've seen, YHWH has put a lying spirit in the mouth of all these prophets of yours. YHWH has decreed disaster for you!

In other words, the true prophet has access to the throne room of Yahweh, where he receives true knowledge and historical insight. The true prophet gets his message straight from Yahweh. False prophets claim to be speaking for Yahweh when they are not.

Obviously still loyal to Baal, the dynasty of Ahab continues to fall under the condemnation of the Deuteronomic Historian in the continuing Elijah cycle. Elijah returns in 2 Kings 1. Here we find Ahaziah following his father Ahab as king over Israel. After Ahaziah fell through the roof of his palace he tried to send messengers to inquire of Baal-zebub (a local Baal god) whether he would live or die. Elijah intercepted the messengers and told them Ahaziah would most certainly die. Ahaziah tried to retaliate by sending soldiers to assassinate Elijah, but once again Elijah marshalled fire from heaven to destroy them.

Elijah departed from the scene in a spectacular way. While being followed by his disciple **Elisha,** he crossed the Jordan River and headed to the place in Transjordan where he would depart. While the exact location is left very vague, the implication might be that he went to the Mt. Nebo region to pass on, where Moses before him had died. Surely his other experiences, including the flight to Horeb (Sinai) and the miraculous crossing of the Jordan, are duplicates of Mosaic experiences.

As Elisha looked on, a chariot of fire engulfed Elijah and he was whisked into heaven in a whirlwind. It appears that the theophany itself transported Elijah to the Divine Council. As a result of this tradition, suggesting that Elijah did not die but is with God, significant expectations of Elijah's future return developed within Judaism and Christianity. It was believed that Elijah would someday come back to earth, and his arrival would signal the dawn of the Messianic era.[7]

---

[7] For texts that seem to connect Elijah with the future messiah, see Malachi 4:4–6, Sirach 48:9, and Mark 9:2–13 in the New Testament.

PROPHETIC MINISTRY OF ELISHA (2 KINGS 3–10)

The mantle of Elijah passed on to Elisha, his disciple, with all its attendant powers and responsibilities. Elisha was the legitimate successor to Elijah, as proven by Elisha's duplication of the Jordan River crossing miracle. The master–disciple relationship of Elijah to Elisha has more than a passing similarity to that of Moses and Joshua.

The Elisha cycle of stories has a different quality than the Elijah cycle. The Elisha cycle is much more occupied with miracles than it is with religious and political confrontation. Listing the miracles in the order of their occurrence:

1. Elisha changed undrinkable water to good
2. he directed two bears to maul some disrespectful children
3. he created an optical illusion that delivered the Moabites into the hands of Jehoshaphat of Judah
4. he multiplied a quantity of olive oil so a widow could pay off her debts (paralleling Elijah's miracle in Zarephath)
5. he resuscitated the son of the woman from Shunam (again duplicating one of Elijah's miracles)
6. he rescued some tainted stew
7. he fed 100 men with twenty loaves of bread
8. he cured Naaman of leprosy
9. he recovered an iron ax head from the Jordan River
10. he blinded the Syrian army and led them into captivity

All of these stories tend to glorify Elisha as a prophetic figure. Like Elijah, he was a northern prophet and represented that tradition.

Elisha was also involved in Israelite and even international politics. He supported Hazael to be king of Syria in place of Ben-hadad. This was in fulfillment of Yahweh's instructions to Elijah at Horeb (1 Kings 19). It might seem strange to see this Israelite prophet encouraging Hazael, who then went on to make war against Israel. But this is the Deuteronomist's way of showing how this Syrian pressure was planned by God as punishment for Israel's covenant breaking.

Elisha also supported **Jehu** in his coup d'état to overthrow the dynasty of Ahab. Again, this was punishment for the way Ahab and Jezebel promoted the worship of Baal and Asherah. Jehu's purge of the Ahab dynasty was swift and brutal. First, he went to Jezreel, the site of the royal retreat. He assassinated Joram, Ahab's son and king of Israel, along with his ally Ahaziah, king of Judah. Then he had Jezebel tossed out an upper-story window; landing on the pavement, she died. He continued to secure his position by assassinating the seventy sons of Ahab in Samaria the capital; he killed anyone closely associated with or even distantly related to Ahab, and capped it off with a massacre of the royally sponsored priests, prophets, and worshipers of Baal. It is no wonder that Hosea, a later prophet, recalled those times of infighting and ruthlessness as the "bloody business of Jezreel" (see Hosea 1:4). Though he acted by divine mandate, according to the Deuteronomic record of Kings, apparently this violent era was viewed with great disdain by other minds in Israel.

SHALMANESER III AND JEHU Jehu is one of the few Israelite kings mentioned by name in materials outside the Hebrew Bible. And he is the only one depicted in relief. The Black Obelisk of Shalmaneser III, a ninth century B.C.E. king of Assyria, is a carved basalt-rock standing monument that contains pictures and Assyrian inscriptions. In the center panel Shalmaneser is receiving tribute from "Jehu, son of Omri," who is on his hands and knees.

The house of Ahab was eliminated by divine decree and by Jehu. Jehu generally receives a good press in Kings, but he was not fully endorsed (after all, he was an Israelite king in a non-Davidic nation). He failed to eliminate the worship centers of the golden calves in Dan and Bethel. The familiar Deuteronomic refrain rounds out the account of Jehu: "But Jehu was not careful to observe the law of YHWH the God of Israel wholeheartedly; he did not turn from the sins into which Jeroboam led Israel" (10:31).

ASSYRIAN CRISIS (2 KINGS 11–17)

Meanwhile, the problems with the Ahab dynasty spilled over into Judah. Athaliah, of the line of Ahab, usurped the reins of government in Jerusalem and attempted to wipe out the dynasty of David. She turns out to have been the only ruling queen in Israel or Judah. The Jerusalemite priest Jehoiada succeeded in hiding the Davidide Joash, who was later restored to the throne in a bloodless coup.

Bouncing back and forth between Judah and Israel, chapters 11–15 quickly trace the careers of Joash (Judah 837–800), Jehoahaz (Israel 815–801), Jehoash (Israel 801–786), Amaziah (Judah 800–783), Jeroboam (usually termed Jeroboam II; Israel 786–746), and Uzziah, also called Azariah (Judah 783–742). Following in quick succession, the last kings of Israel, Zechariah, Shallum, Menahem, Pekahiah, and Pekah, cover only a few years (746–732), with whom Jotham of Judah (742–735) was roughly contemporaneous.

The writer occasionally pauses, usually only to detail the territory that one kingdom or the other lost to foreigners, or how a particular king broke the Mosaic covenant in some way, resulting in a typical Deuteronomic-styled condemnation. We have nothing in the nature of a complete political history of the kingdoms, only enough on which to form a theological evaluation of the king's disposition before God.

FIGURE 9.6 TIGLATH-PILESER III King Tiglath-Pileser III of Assyria effectively expanded the Assyrian empire into Syria and Canaan. He is pictured on this stone relief from the palace of Nimrud.

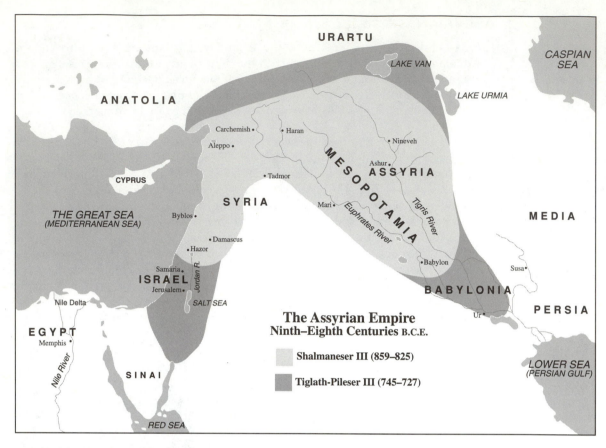

FIGURE 9.7   ASSYRIAN EMPIRE

The sins of Israel came home to roost in connection with an Assyrian movement into Canaan. First **Ahaz** (Judah 735–715) invited **Tiglath-Pileser III** of Assyria (745–727) to rescue him from a Syrian–Israelite joint venture to take Judah (see Figure 9.6). The result was the Assyrian capture of Damascus in 732. Ahaz himself was forced to pay tribute to Tiglath. These events form the background to Isaiah's Immanuel prophecy (see Isaiah 7–11).

Later, **Shalmaneser V** (726–722) reinforced Assyrian control and made Hoshea (Israel 732–724) his vassal. Judah under Ahaz more stubbornly held out. When Hoshea attempted to get Egyptian support against Assyria, Shalmaneser laid siege to Samaria, the capital of Israel. It fell in 722 after holding out for three years. Thus, the kingdom of Israel ceased to exist. The majority of the Israelite leadership elite was deported to other Assyrian-held territory. In their place the Assyrians moved other conquered peoples. The result was a mixture of ethnic groups and religious perspectives. The resulting population lacked corporate commitment to Yahweh or his covenant. These Samaritans, as they came to be called, would forever be suspect to those in the south who considered themselves more orthodox and obedient. The old rivalry between north and south continued, albeit on slightly altered grounds (Figure 9.7).

The voice of the Deuteronomist comes out especially clearly in chapter 17. He provides a comprehensive theological explanation for the demise of Israel. It was because they served other gods, worshiped idols, and ignored the commandments of Yahweh. Even Judah, while spared destruction, was not immune to criticism. The Deuteronomist seems to be sending out a warning. Do not depart from the way of covenant, or you, too, will be destroyed!

JUDAH TO THE BABYLONIAN EXILE (2 KINGS 18–25)

Only Judah, of all the original twelve tribes, was left. The remaining chapters of Kings form a record of reigns and events down to its destruction some one hundred plus years later.

HEZEKIAH AND ISAIAH (2 KINGS 18–20)

Hezekiah ruled Judah well (715–687) according to the Deuteronomist. Judged on the basis of his piety and religious reforms, he was one of the best kings of Judah.

During his reign, the Assyrian empire kept the pressure on Judah. **Sennacherib** attacked Jerusalem in 701 B.C.E. (Figure 9.8).

The Destruction of Sennacherib
by George Gordon, Lord Byron (1815)

I
The Assyrian came down like the wolf on the fold,
And his cohorts were gleaming in purple and gold;
And the sheen of their spears was like stars on the sea,
When the blue wave rolls nightly on deep Galilee.

II
Like the leaves of the forest when Summer is green,
That host with their banners at sunset were seen:
Like the leaves of the forest when Autumn hath blown,
That host on the morrow lay withered and strown.

III
For the angel of Death spread his wings on the blast,
And breathed in the face of the foe as he passed;
And the eyes of the sleepers waxed deadly and chill,
And their hearts but once heaved—and for ever grew still!

The account of this invasion in chapters 18–20 is closely paralleled by Isaiah 36–39. The outcome of this confrontation differed from that of the siege of Samaria. The Assyrian army departed after a disaster, attributed to the work of the angel of Yahweh, decimated the army and prompted them to leave Canaan.

According to the story, 185,000 soldiers died.[8] The biblical text hints that problems back home might have cooperated, forcing Sennacherib and his army to return to Assyria. Shortly after his return, Sennacherib was assassinated by two of his sons.

But the real deliverance was attributed to the piety of Hezekiah. When surrounded by Sennacherib's army he did not react in desperation as Ahaz did under similar circumstances, looking for outside military help. Hezekiah immediately brought the matter to his God. Hezekiah took the Assyrian letter demanding surrender into the Jerusalem temple, laid it out before Yahweh, and prayed for guidance. Isaiah delivered an oracle of salvation on behalf of Yahweh in response to Hezekiah's plea for help. Hezekiah becomes the model for appropriate response in time of national crisis.

Hezekiah was followed by Manasseh (687–642), a king as bad as Hezekiah was good. Although the Deuteronomist does not try, it would be difficult to explain how such a wicked king could reign so long if there is in fact a correlation between righteousness and blessing. Manasseh is spared no condemnation for rebuilding the Baal shrines that his father Hezekiah had eliminated. His breach of covenant was so serious that the ultimate blame for the destruction of Jerusalem was laid at his feet. His son Amon reigned only two years and was assassinated by opponents within his own court circle.

JOSIAH'S REFORM (2 KINGS 21–23)

After David, Josiah (640–609) was the best king Judah ever had. In 622 B.C.E., the eighteenth year of his reign, Josiah authorized and underwrote the restoration of the temple back to Yahwistic purpose after its disgraceful neglect under Manasseh and Amon. During the process of renovation Hilkiah, the high priest, came in possession of "the book of the law." Hilkiah gave it to Josiah's secretary Shaphan, who in turn read it to the king.

The experience was extremely disconcerting as the king heard words that seemed to spell doom for the nation because of their departure from the covenant. Huldah, a female prophet, interpreted the book to Josiah and the court, and comforted him with the word that he himself would not see the demise of the nation because of his own faith and acts of repentance.

Josiah was inspired to make further reforms throughout Judah and the territory to the north that Judah controlled. The various religious shrines to Baal, Asherah, astral deities, and numerous other abominations to Yahweh were all torn down. Worship of any kind could take place only in Jerusalem, and the Passover was celebrated for the first time in a long time.

The description of the reforms of Josiah inspired by the "book of the law," especially the elimination of all worship centers except Jerusalem, and the reference to the document as "the Book of the Covenant," make its identification as Deuteronomy quite sure. Deuteronomy is so closely associated with the reforms

[8] Again, these large numbers are troublesome. 185,000 men is a massive amount to lose in any campaign, dwarfing U.S. losses in the entire Vietnam War, when some 55,000 American soldiers were killed. Perhaps we should again resort to the alternate understanding of the term "thousand." As suggested elsewhere, it seems likely it designated a company of fighting men, a squad, so the text is saying 185 squads died in the camp.

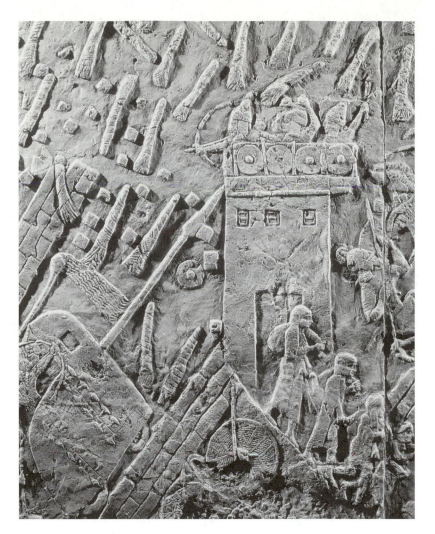

of Josiah that most scholars today grant that at least the core of the book received its final shape out of that historical context.

It must have come as a terrible shock, then, given his piety and devotion to Yahweh, that Josiah was killed in a battle attempting to stop the advance of the Egyptian army. Killed near Megiddo by Pharaoh Neco in 609 B.C.E., the supremely pious Davidic king seems to have fed an accumulating mythology about that place Megiddo. Mount Megiddo is *har megiddo* in Hebrew, from which Armageddon is derived. In apocalyptic thought Armageddon will be the site of the last great battle between the forces of good and the forces of evil. In the last days good will triumph.

FALL OF JERUSALEM (2 KINGS 24–25)

The Assyrian capital, Nineveh, fell to the onrushing Babylonians in 612 B.C.E. Jehoahaz, the successor to Josiah, was on the throne only three months before the Egyptians removed him. The combined forces of Egypt and Assyria were unable to neutralize Babylonia at Carchemish in 605. From then on, Judah became a vassal state to Babylonia (Figure 9.9).

Jehoiakim (609–598) followed Jehoahaz. When he withheld tribute from **Nebuchadnezzar**, the great Babylonian empire builder, Jerusalem was besieged. Jehoiakim was assassinated sometime during the onslaught and **Jehoiachin** replaced him. Hapless Jehoiachin was on the throne only three months until the city fell. He was naturally held responsible and was carted off to Babylon along with other Jerusalemite notables and officials, as well as the temple treasury.

Zedekiah (598–587) was installed as king of Jerusalem on the understanding that he would promote loyalty to the Babylonian overlords. When he rebelled, Nebuchadnezzar was compelled to return to Jerusalem to force compliance. Jerusalem was completely destroyed after an eighteen-month siege. Especially traumatic was the total destruction of the temple. The focus of Judah's religious life was gone.

Gedaliah was appointed governor of what became the province of Judea. But Jerusalem was in such a shambles that he administered the province from Mizpah. A sorry state, or province, it was. Only the least capable elements of the population were left in Judah. All those who had not been killed in the final conflagration of Jerusalem, the priesthood, members of the royal court, tradesmen, and craftsmen, were taken to Babylon, where they began a new life.

The book ends with a note of guarded optimism. Jehoiachin, Judah's Davidic king in exile, was freed from prison. According to our reckoning, it must have been around 560 B.C.E. He was treated with respect by Evil-merodach, king of Babylon, known in Babylonian records as Amel-marduk (562–560). Babylonian historical tablets record the payment of oil and barley rations to Yaukin (Jehoiachin) king of Iahudu (Judah).

For the faith of God's people, the most important point was that the Davidic line of Judah had not disappeared. There was still hope for the future. Thus, the Deuteronomic History ends negatively and positively. Judah had been destroyed, but God's community survived and might one day recover greatness through the messianic line.

OVERALL SHAPE OF THE BOOKS OF KINGS

The books of Kings contain clear indications that they were constructed, at least in part, using available written records and other materials. The writer drew upon a number of documents that he refers to by name but that are no longer available to us. He mentions "the book of the acts of Solomon" (1 Kings 11:41), "the book of the chronicles of the kings of Judah" (1 Kings 14:29), and "the book of the chronicles of the kings of Israel" (1 Kings 14:19). These must have been court records of some sort. In addition, the writer drew upon what were probably oral traditions of the prophets for the story cycles about Elijah and Elisha.

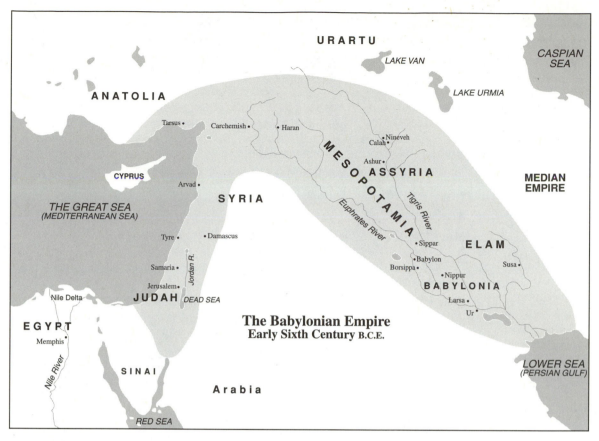

FIGURE 9.9 **BABYLONIAN EMPIRE**

The books of Kings are only an outline of the history from Solomon to the destruction of Jerusalem. Not attempting to be comprehensive, the writer used a principle of selection dictated by the lessons of history he wanted to teach. The history he told ends with the loss of the Promised Land and the forced exile of the people. The writer was intent on making clear that these tragic events were the result of the people's sins and were God's judgment on those sins.

Furthermore, the working out of God's judgment on disobedience fulfilled the word of God through his servants, the prophets. The prophets of Kings, including Nathan, Ahijah, Elijah, and Elisha, warned Israel and Judah of coming disaster. But the hearts of kings and people were hard. The historical process demonstrated the power of the word of God unleashed in the world.

Table 9.1 combines kings of Judah and Israel, and relevant international players in one place for easy reference. The names in bold print held special importance in our discussion of the books of Kings and should be remembered. This chart may be a helpful reference when we read the literature of the Latter Prophets, for whom keeping chronology straight can be a difficult matter.

TABLE 9.1   CHRONOLOGICAL TABLE OF KINGS AND EMPIRES

United Monarchy	Israel	Judah	Mesopotamia
Saul 1020–1000			
David 1000–961			
Solomon 961–922			
	Jeroboam 922–901	**Rehoboam** 922–915	
		Abijah 915–913	
	Nadab 901–900	Asa 913–873	
	Baasha 900–877		
	Elah 877–876	Jehoshaphat 873–849	
	Zimri 876		
	Omri 876–869		
	Ahab 869–850		Shalmaneser III 859–825 (Assyria)
	Ahaziah 850–849	Jehoram 849–842	
	Jehoram 849–842	Ahaziah 842	
	Jehu 842–815	Athaliah 842–837	
	Jehoahaz 815–801	Joash 837–800	
	J(eh)oash 801–786	Amaziah 800–783	
	Jeroboam II 786–746	Uzziah 783–742	
	Zechariah 746–745	Jotham 742–735	**Tiglath–Pileser III** 745–727 (Assyria)
	Shallum 745		
	Menahem 745–738		
	Pekahiah 738–737		
	Pekah 737–732	**Ahaz** 735–715	
	Hoshea 732–724		**Shalmaneser V** 726–722 (Assyria)
			Sargon II 721–705 (Assyria)
		Hezekiah 715–687	**Sennacherib** 704–681 (Assyria)
		Manasseh 687–642	
		Amon 642–640	
		Josiah 640–609	
		Jehoahaz 609	
		Jehoiakim 609–598	**Nebuchadnezzar** 605–562 (Babylonia)
		Jehoiachin 598–597	
		Zedekiah 597–587	

QUESTIONS FOR REVIEW

1. Briefly describe the course of Israel's history from the United Monarchy, through the division into two kingdoms, and down to the fall of each kingdom.
2. Why did the Deuteronomic writer criticize the Northern Kingdom more severely than Judah?

3. What prophetic figures appeared in the books of Kings, and what was their role within Israelite society?
4. What was the nature of the religious challenge facing Yahwism in Israel during the time of the kings?

QUESTIONS FOR DISCUSSION

1. Review the concept of the Davidic covenant (see chapter 8 on Samuel) and explain its relevance to the history of kingship.
2. What are the parallels between the prophetic ministries of Elijah and Elisha? What are the parallels between Elijah and Moses? Between Elijah and Jesus in the New Testament? What is the significance of par-

allels between the lives of significant biblical figures?
3. Compare and contrast the histories of Israel and Judah. What are the differing attitudes of the writer to the kingdoms? Although both kingdoms were destroyed by Mesopotamian empires, Judah survived in some form. Why did it survive? What lessons of history are to be learned from the disasters?

FOR FURTHER STUDY

Cogan, Mordechai, and Hayim Tadmor (1988). *II Kings*. Anchor Bible. Garden City, N.Y.: Doubleday. Strong orientation to Mesopotamian history and its biblical reflexes.

Cross, Frank M. (1973). "The Themes of the Books of Kings and the Structure of the Deuteronomistic History." In *Canaanite Myth and Hebrew Epic*. Cambridge, Mass.: Harvard University Press.

Hurowitz, Victor (1992). *I Have Built You an Exalted House: Temple Building in the Bible in Light of Mesopotamian and Northwest Semitic Writings*. JSOT Supplement Series, 115. Sheffield: JSOT Press. Places the Solomonic temple within its ancient historical and theological context.

Long, Burke (1984). *1 Kings: With an Introduction to Old Testament Historical Literature*. Forms of Old Testament Literature, 9. Grand Rapids, Mich.: Eerdmans. This and the following volume contain an exhaustive form-critical and literary

analysis of each text unit in the books of Kings.

Long, Burke (1991). *2 Kings*. Forms of Old Testament Literature, 10. Grand Rapids, Mich.: Eerdmans.

Nelson, Richard D. (1987). *First and Second Kings*. Interpretation, a Bible Commentary for Teaching and Preaching. Atlanta: John Knox Press. Oriented to literary analysis and the theological message of the text, with particular attention to Deuteronomic connections.

Rice, Gene (1990). *Nations Under God. A Commentary on the Book of 1 Kings*. International Theological Commentary. Grand Rapids, Mich.: Eerdmans. Provides theological reflection on the relevance of Kings to the modern world.

Wiseman, D. J. (1993). *1 & 2 Kings: An Introduction and Commentary*. Leicester, England; Downers Grove, Ill.: InterVarsity Press. A conservative Christian reading of Kings by a leading Assyriologist.

WORKS CITED

Biran, Avraham, and Joseph Naveh (1993). "An Aramaic Stele Fragment from Tel Dan." *Israel Exploration Journal*. 43/2–3: 81–98.

Friedman, Richard Elliott (1987). *Who Wrote the Bible?* Englewood Cliffs, N.J.: Prentice-Hall.

Fritz, Volkmar (1987). "Temple Architecture: What Can Archaeology Tell Us About Solomon's Temple?" *Biblical Archaeology Review*. 13/4: 38–49.

PROLOGUE TO THE LATTER PROPHETS

The second division of the Hebrew Bible, the Prophets, is itself subdivided into Former Prophets and Latter Prophets. As we have already seen, the Former Prophets consist of Joshua, Judges, Samuel, and Kings. They contain a running narrative account of the history of Israel from the time of the Canaanite conquest to the Babylonian exile.

The subdivision called the Latter Prophets, to which we now turn, deals with certain individuals in Israel who had a recognized social and spiritual role within Israel and who articulated a divine perspective on the events of their day. The Latter Prophets consists of four books: Isaiah, Jeremiah, Ezekiel, and the Book of the Twelve. The Book of the Twelve consists of twelve shorter works, Hosea through Malachi, by some people called the Minor Prophets. In the Hebrew Bible the Latter Prophets come between the Torah and the Writings, while in the Christian canon the Latter Prophets are, with some additions, the last grouping of books in the Old Testament. Note that Daniel is not included in the Latter Prophets in the Hebrew Bible, but rather is included in the Writings; the Christian Old Testament places Daniel after Ezekiel. The reasons for this will be discussed in chapter 17, "Daniel: Apocalyptic Literature."

The period of time covered by the Latter Prophets begins with the divided Israelite monarchy and continues into the postexilic era. Even though these books follow in canonical order the Former Prophets' account of Israelite history, most of the material must be placed chronologically *within* that history. It will take special effort on our part, but a necessary effort, to integrate these Latter Prophets into the time frame of the Former Prophets, especially the books of Kings.

PROPHETS AND PROPHETIC BOOKS

For virtually every prophet we can reconstruct a viable historical context. We know when he lived, where he lived, and to whom he prophesied. But the same cannot be said with the same level of certainty of the editorial history of the prophetic books. The books were not necessarily finalized during the lifetime of the prophets who gave their names to the books. It is important to distinguish the human prophets from the prophetic books attached to their names.

The prophetic books are not autobiographies. Most were not written by the named prophet himself. Most went through a lengthy process of composition, in many cases extending well after the lifetime of the prophet. Many times "schools" or prophetic interest groups that traced their outlook to a particular prophetic leader continued on after the death of the prophet and found their inspiration in the prophet. Many times it was they who were responsible for taking the message of the prophet and reapplying it to later circumstances. Frequently this will be reflected in the text itself. As you might well guess from our treatment of the books we have looked at so far, it will be important for us to pay attention to the literary and historical development of the book.

WHAT IS PROPHECY?

The first question we probably should ask ourselves is this: What is prophecy?

The answer must be sought in the literature and culture of ancient Israel, and our present Western culture might mislead us more than help us as we frame a response.

DEFINITION: PROPHECY (PROF'I SĒ), N. PL. —CIES.

1. The foretelling or prediction of what is to come. 2. That which is declared by a prophet, esp. divinely inspired prediction, instruction, or exhortation. 3. A divinely inspired utterance or revelation: oracular prophecies. 4. The action, function, or faculty of a prophet. (Random House Dictionary of the English Language).

This dictionary definition spells out the modern notion of prophecy, but it does not fully convey the nature of biblical prophecy.

The immediate association we tend to make with the words *prophet* and *prophecy* in the modern world is predicting the future. While we do not have as many people around who go by the name *prophet* as in the era of Israelite history, we do have plenty of people, some recognizably more reputable than others, who traffic in the future: economists, meteorologists, marketing consultants, futures traders, and astrologers, to name a few. Only a small number of prediction peddlers, so-called psychics, baldly attempt to foresee specific events—the Cassandras and Nostradamus's of old, and the Jeane Dixons of today.

But predicting the future was not the major component of the prophetic task in the Israelite world. The most basic function of biblical prophecy was to analyze then-contemporary political and social policies in light of Yahweh's straightforward demands of justice, loyalty, and faith in him. The prophet was most concerned that these moral and religious principles govern the corporate and personal lives of God's people. The closest analogies in our modern world to the biblical prophets of old might be leaders such as Martin Luther King, Jr., and Mahatma Gandhi, who each had a keen sense of the divine requirements for social justice, freedom, and human dignity.

Granted, biblical prophets would occasionally make predictions about the future course of events, yet they never did it to demonstrate how insightful or divinely inspired they were. So-called predictions were basically extrapolations from the current state of affairs into the future, based on their knowledge of what God demanded. If the people would not change their errant ways, then the future would hold nothing but trouble for them. If they repented, then the grim scenario would be averted.

Only in the distinctive type of literature called apocalyptic did future prediction take on a life of its own. While apocalyptic literature did have roots in classical prophecy, it eventually evolved into a distinct literary type.

What Is a Prophet?

A prophet was called a *navi* in the Hebrew Bible. The linguistic derivation of the term suggests it could be related to the Semitic verb "to call." A prophet is then either "one who calls out" or "one who is called." The first possibility, the active meaning, is analogous to the meaning of its Greek translation equivalent *prophetes*, "to speak before," from which our English term "prophet" was derived. The second possibility, the passive meaning, may be related to the initiation call to prophetic service. In this sense, a prophet is one called by God to deliver a message. The following evidence suggests that either understanding, the active or the passive, has cogency.

Prophecy: A Functional Definition

A branch of biblical scholarship called *form criticism* examines the language of the Hebrew Bible in an attempt to discover the original real-life type of situation for a way of speaking. The application of form criticism to prophetic literature has been especially productive.

Form critics have studied the phrase, "Thus says YHWH," which is widely used in many prophetic books. It prefaces a vast number of prophetic oracles, or divine statements communicated by the prophet. It is so frequent that it has been used to characterize the essential nature of the prophet's sense of identity and even of the general prophetic office. In an important study, Westermann (1967) demonstrated that the background of this phrase is the procedure of sending messages long distance in the ancient world. Typically, when a king wished to communicate with a distant client he would employ a messenger to commit the message to memory. After traveling to his destination, the messenger would recite the message as if he were the king himself speaking in the first person ("I"), prefacing his recitation with the phrase, "Thus says the king."

The use of the formula "Thus says Yahweh" by Israel's prophets suggests that they considered themselves divine messengers, having received the message directly from their Great King. This reconstruction of the prophet's sense of mission is supported by various prophets' descriptions of their calling to the prophetic task. Isaiah, Jeremiah, and Ezekiel each describe their experience of being in the presence of God, where each felt he was commissioned. Each received a message firsthand from Yahweh. Each was then sent to the people of God to deliver that message.

The prophets typically exhibited a strong sense of vocation in connection with their calling. The prophet is one who has been called (passive) and commissioned in the divine council. Then he was sent to call out (active) the message of the divine King. Often the prophets were reluctant to follow their calling because they knew how difficult the task would be. But they inevitably accepted the challenge in faith.

READING PROPHECY

Not meaning to scare anyone away, we must still be honest: Reading biblical prophecy is difficult—as difficult as it is rewarding. The difficulty stems from many features of the prophetic books, including the poetic form in which they were written and the need to know the historical settings of prophetic statements, most of which are not spelled out clearly.

Modern scholarship on biblical prophecy helps a great deal in clarifying the prophetic message. There are many things scholars look at when they examine the text of prophetic books, such as the following.

1. *Prophetic Genres*. The literature of the prophets contains a variety of types of speaking, including third-person narratives about the prophets, autobiographical sketches by the prophets themselves, poetically framed statements of salvation, laments, trust songs, praise songs, covenant lawsuits, and more. As we come across distinctive genres we will explain them. Form criticism has been especially effective in investigating the forms of prophetic speech and reconstructing early social settings out of which those ways of speaking make the most sense. The works of Westermann (1967, 1991) are pioneering and especially valuable in this regard. Also, the series published by Eerdmans titled *The Forms of the Old Testament Literature* has volumes covering the prophetic books.

2. *Social and Historical Setting*. Much of the activity of the prophets pertained to politics, both domestic and international. Biblical and extrabiblical documents have enabled scholarship to reconstruct the national and international settings that equip us to make sense out of the prophetic books. Recent anthropological analysis of prophecy, especially the work of Wilson (1980) and Gottwald (1985), has added further sophistication by placing the prophets within the social and class matrices of ancient Israel.

3. *Theological and Thematic Analysis*. Rather than being the mavericks of morality and spirituality earlier biblical scholars made them out to be, recent theological research has demonstrated that the prophets stand in continuity with Israel's covenantal traditions. There is evidence that some prophets made extensive use of earlier traditions, and some actually quote earlier sources as the basis for their own statements. All in all, there is a considerable network of interdependence linking prophet to prophet, and prophet to covenantal traditions.

As you read the literature of the Latter Prophets, remember to ask yourself the following questions:

1. When did this prophet live and work? What were the political and economic conditions at the time he ministered? Where did he prophesy?—It makes a big difference whether he was from Judah or Israel.

2. What prophetic speech type (genre) did the prophet use to make his preaching more effective? Why did he use this genre?

3. What historical and covenantal traditions, if any, did the prophet draw on as the basis of his prophetic preaching and ministry? Be especially alert to a prophet's use of the Moses–Exodus covenant, the David–Zion covenant, or any other allusions to prior historical traditions.

4. What message concerning the relationship between God and humankind did the prophet convey?

FOR FURTHER STUDY

The following books are general introductions to the Latter Prophets.

Blenkinsopp, Joseph (1983). *A History of Prophecy in Israel*. Philadelphia: Westminster Press.

Bright, John (1976). *Covenant and Promise. The Prophetic Understanding of the Future in Pre-Exilic Israel*. Philadelphia: Westminster Press.

Miller, John W. (1987). *Meet the Prophets. A Beginner's Guide to the Books of the Biblical Prophets*. New York/Mahwah: Paulist Press.

Sawyer, John F. A. (1993). *Prophecy and the Biblical Prophets*. Rev. ed. Oxford Bible Series. Oxford: Oxford University Press.

Winward, Stephen (1969). *A Guide to the Prophets*. Atlanta: John Knox Press.

Wood, Leon J. (1979). *The Prophets of Israel*. Grand Rapids, Mich.: Baker.

WORKS CITED

Gottwald, Norman K. (1985). *The Hebrew Bible. A Socio-Literary Introduction*. Philadelphia: Fortress Press.

Westermann, Claus (1967). *Basic Forms of Prophetic Speech*. Philadelphia: Fortress Press. The classic application of the form-critical method to biblical prophecy.

Westermann, Claus (1991). *Prophetic Oracles of Salvation in the Old Testament*. Louisville, Ky.: Westminster/John Knox Press.

Wilson, Robert R. (1980). *Prophecy and Society in Ancient Israel*. Philadelphia: Fortress Press.

Isaiah

10

Names and Terms to Remember

Ahaz	new exodus	Syro–Ephraimitic Crisis
Cyrus the Great	Second Isaiah	Third Isaiah
Hezekiah	(Deutero-Isaiah)	(Trito-Isaiah)
Immanuel	Sennacherib	Tiglath-Pileser III
Isaiah of Jerusalem	Servant of Yahweh	
(First Isaiah)	(Suffering Servant)	

The book of Isaiah provides a fine illustration of the growth of prophetic traditions. The entire book of Isaiah is attributed to Isaiah ben-Amoz (not to be confused with the prophet Amos) by the editorial superscription in 1:1. But in fact, the book contains prophetic material spanning more than two hundred years. A nucleus of material is attributable to **Isaiah of Jerusalem**, a citizen of Jerusalem in the eighth century B.C.E. But the remainder comes from the hands of a series of anonymous disciples (see 8:16, which mentions his followers) and prophets who saw themselves, or were seen by editors, as coming out of the Isaiah mold (see Figure 10.1).

The book of Isaiah is widely recognized to consist of three main collections, as the outline indicates.

Outline of the Book of Isaiah

I. Isaiah of Jerusalem: chapters 1–39 (eighth century)
    A. 1–12 Series of oracles, all but twelve by Isaiah of Jerusalem
    B. 13–23 Oracles against foreign nations, many composed after the eighth century
    C. 24–27 The Isaiah Apocalypse, from the Persian period
    D. 28–33 Prophecies by Isaiah
    E. 34–35 Late additions
    F. 36–39 Historical narrative section, parallel to 2 Kings 18–20
II. Second Isaiah: chapters 40–55 (mid-sixth century)
    A. 40–48 Concerning the fall of Babylon
    B. 49–55 The pursuit of justice
III. Third Isaiah: chapters 56–66 (late sixth century)

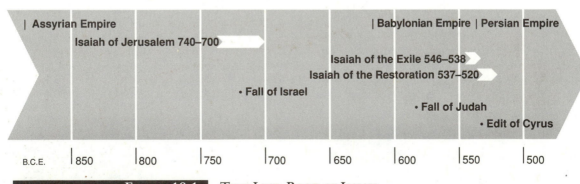

FIGURE 10.1   TIME LINE: BOOK OF ISAIAH

It would be an oversimplification to see a simple linear historical progression in the book of Isaiah from the preexilic period (chapters 1–39), to the exilic period (chapters 40–55), to the postexilic period (chapters 56–66). Later writers continued to rework earlier material and add to it, so even the first major section, which is largely attributed to the eighth-century prophet Isaiah of Jerusalem, contains postexilic material. Conversely, mostly postexilic Third Isaiah took up older prophetic sayings from the preexilic First Temple period and incorporated them into his material.

ISAIAH OF JERUSALEM—FIRST ISAIAH

The first major section of the book of Isaiah, chapters 1–39, contains a core of material attributable to Isaiah of Jerusalem. Chapters 1–11 are a series of prophetic judgment statements delivered by Isaiah and autobiographical accounts by Isaiah. Chapters 13–23 are oracles against foreign nations. Chapters 24–27 are the so-called Isaiah Apocalypse, a collection of sketches on apocalyptic themes such as universal judgment, the eschatological banquet, and heavenly signs. Chapters 28–32 are prophetic oracles datable to 715–701 B.C.E. concerning Judah and foreign policy. Chapters 34–35 appear to be postexilic additions that have affinities with chapters 40–66, and may have at one time served to bridge First and Second Isaiah. Chapters 36–39 are an historical appendix, paralleled in 2 Kings 18:13–20:19, dealing with Hezekiah and the Assyrian crisis.

Turning to Isaiah of Jerusalem, we will spend the most time on Isaiah 1–11, which are most securely connected with the prophet himself. These chapters apply to events surrounding the Assyrian crisis of the eighth century.

We do not know a lot of detail about the book's namesake, Isaiah, son of Amoz. We only know for sure that he began functioning as a prophet in Jerusalem in the latter half of the eighth century B.C.E. He appears to have been from Judah and generally had a high opinion of the Davidic dynasty, at least in principle. Gauging by the social circles in which he moved, he could very well have belonged to the Jerusalemite aristocracy.

Isaiah has a lot in common with the other, mostly earlier, prophets of the eighth century, Amos, Hosea, and Micah. It even seems likely that he was influenced to a degree by them. In material dating to the early years of his ministry, Isaiah's critique of official religion in contrast to the demands of social justice (1:12–17) sounds a great deal like Amos. The next section, chapters 2–4, contains material also like his predecessor's, condemning the aristocracy and high-society women, whose lifestyles imply disdain for the needs of the disadvantaged. Isaiah differs from Amos, of course, in targeting the ruling class of Jerusalem rather than that of Samaria.

Isaiah may also have been familiar with Hosea, judging by his description of faithless people as a harlot. Isaiah berates Jerusalem, describing it as a prostitute (1:21–26), and later uses images from the fertility cult to denounce Jerusalem, perhaps dependent on Hosea 10:1. Again, Isaiah takes metaphors earlier applied to the north and reapplies them to Judah.

Isaiah opposed the priestly and prophetic spokespersons who stood in the service of the royal court and its policies. He frequently equated them with the "smooth talkers" of the foreign nations, the diviners, soothsayers, and necromancers. He seems to have viewed himself differently, thinking of himself more as a teacher of Torah (5:24, 30:9) than as a prophet (Jensen 1973).

Unlike Amos and Hosea, Isaiah did not draw significantly from the resources of the Mosaic tradition of the exodus and settlement or the traditions of the Sinai covenant to give shape to his prophetic analysis. Isaiah's treasury was the complex of images and assurances dependent on Zion as the fortress of Yahweh (see the Zion poems in 2:2–4 and 4:2–6) and on the dynasty of David that administered Yahweh's rule on earth (Figure 10.2).

CALL OF ISAIAH (6)

The experience of initiation into the prophetic task can be referred to as the "call" of the prophet. In a call narrative the prophet describes his experience of being called into divine service. While each prophet's experience is unique in the details, there are some similarities. Most record the experience of standing in the presence of God and of being utterly frightened by the encounter. Most prophets felt ill equipped to perform the task of voicing the divine message, but God somehow enabled them to speak.

Isaiah's description of the call has a lot in common with Micaiah's experience of the divine council in 1 Kings 22. An experience of standing in the divine presence is also recorded by Ezekiel (chapter 1), and in a generalized way goes back to Moses' call experience at the Burning Bush (Exodus 3).

Out of this call experience, Isaiah became the messenger of the divine King, having been commissioned in the very throne room of the deity. This conception of the prophetic task provides the essential background to understanding the widespread prophetic formula that introduces oracles, the phrase, "Thus says YHWH," as explained in the "Prologue to the Latter Prophets."

Isaiah's call narrative is found in chapter 6.

1 In the year that King Uzziah died, I saw YHWH sitting on a throne, high and exalted. The hem of his robe filled the temple. 2 Seraphs attended him. Each had six wings: two to cover the face, two to cover the feet, and two to fly. 3 Each called to the other: "Holy, holy, holy is YHWH of hosts. The

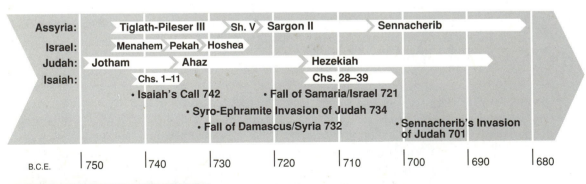

FIGURE 10.2 TIME LINE: ISAIAH OF JERUSALEM

whole earth is full of his glory." 4 The hinges on the thresholds shook from the voices of those heralds, and the house filled with smoke. 5 Then I said, "Woe is me! I am doomed, because I am a person of unclean lips, and I live among a people of unclean lips. Yet, how is it my eyes have seen the King, YHWH of hosts?" 6 Then one of the seraphs flew to me, holding a live coal that had been taken from the altar with a pair of tongs. 7 The seraph touched my mouth with it and said: "Because this has touched your lips, your guilt has departed and your sin is wiped out." 8 Then I heard the voice of YHWH saying, "Whom shall I send, and who will go for us?" And I said, "Here I am, send me!"

Isaiah's vision took place in the temple, either in reality or in Isaiah's imagination. If Isaiah was really there, this might suggest he was a priest. If only imagined, we cannot draw the same conclusion. The vision took place the year Uzziah died, making it 742 B.C.E. If this call vision marks the beginning of Isaiah's formal prophetic work, then it began in that year.

In Isaiah's call experience, Yahweh was envisioned as the Great King attended by the divine council. Called *seraphs* here, a word meaning "fiery ones," each member of the council had six wings. While foreign to our experience, the figures are on the analogy of the winged protector figures common in Mesopotamia (see Figure 10.3).

FIGURE 10.3   WINGED FIGURES These winged figures reflect an ancient Middle Eastern understanding of the divine world that included divine messengers, demons, and protector figures. The figure on the left is a four-winged demon god from Tel Halaf in Syria (9th century B.C.E.). The figure on the right is a winged sphinx from Samaria in Israel (9th century B.C.E.) carved in ivory.

With two wings, these Isaian seraphs flew. With two they covered their feet. These two are an enigma until we realize that *feet* is a euphemism (here as elsewhere in the Hebrew Bible) for genitals. They were guarding their nakedness in the presence of God. With two they covered their faces. As with humans, angels cannot look upon God and live. What is remarkable in this passage is that, while the seraphs cannot look upon God, the prophet Isaiah does, and yet he lives.

But in the direct presence of God Isaiah faced his total inadequacy. He cried out in fear because he recognized his impurity. To avert disaster a seraph took holy fire and burned away the uncleanness of his mouth. The object of cleaning being his mouth is consistent with the prophetic attention to the messenger function. Now qualified to serve, Isaiah volunteered to represent God to the people.

Isaiah refers to God as "Yahweh of hosts" here in this passage and frequently elsewhere. This divine title almost surely originated at Shiloh in the Northern Kingdom and is first attested during the Philistine wars. While Isaiah is clearly a Judean prophet, the use of this phrase links him, and Amos, who also uses it, with the prophetic holy war doctrine of the northern traditions. In like manner, the title "Holy One of Israel," not used here but frequently used elsewhere in Isaiah, was used outside Isaiah only by the earlier northern prophet Hosea (11:9). Not too much should be inferred from this, but it does appear that Isaiah was influenced by northern prophets.

SYRO–EPHRAIMITIC CRISIS AND IMMANUEL (7–8)

In the current arrangement of material, the autobiographical account of Isaiah's call, dated to 742 B.C.E., is followed by a third-person biographical narrative describing his counsel to **Ahaz** (king of Judah 735–715 B.C.E.) some eight years later in 734. At that time Ahaz faced a serious international problem. Judah had just been invaded by the Syrians and the Israelites (in the text, also called Ephraim). Ahaz was in a quandary over what to do. Should he give in and join a coalition the Syrians and Israelites were attempting to put together, or should he seek outside assistance against the **Syro–Ephraimitic** league?

Isaiah felt divinely compelled to give Ahaz advice. Meeting him in Jerusalem, Isaiah said, "Don't let your heart be afraid (7:4)." But Ahaz was not inclined to take the advice of the prophet. Apparently, Ahaz was more interested in the pressing political realities of his situation than in religious promises.

In an attempt further to encourage Ahaz, Isaiah gave him a sign or indicator of Yahweh's continued support of the dynasty. Ahaz was cavalier about this, too. He did not see the need for a sign, thereby, in the view of the writer, showing a deep callousness to the faith option. Now, the sign should not be understood as a magical act of some sort, but as more of an inspired interpretation of a natural happening. Isaiah's sign was this:

> 7:14 Look, the young woman is with child and shall bear a son, and shall name him Immanuel. 15 He shall eat curds and honey[1] by the time he knows how to refuse the evil and choose the good.

[1] "Curds and honey" may be an allusion to the "milk and honey" of the Promised Land, a positive allusion to security in the land derived from the conquest tradition. E. Hammershaimb, in "The Immanuel Sign" *Studia theologica* (1949–1951) 124–42, suggests parallels from Mesopotamian literature, where curds and honey are the food of royalty.

What follows is at least one plausible way to understand this text.[2] Isaiah, obviously being close to the royal court, knew that Ahaz's wife, the queen (here referred to as "the young woman"), was pregnant. Perhaps the text is suggesting Isaiah knew this even before Ahaz knew it himself. Isaiah is saying the queen would give birth to a son who would be concrete evidence of Yahweh's support of the Davidic line, evidence that the Davidic covenant was still in effect and that God was "with" them. The name **Immanuel** literally means "God is with us."

Concern for a crown prince was certainly a high priority of Judean kings, or, for that matter, of any king whatsoever. A son would be proof that the line would continue. A son would be evidence of God's direct intervention, as was perceived to be the case with so many births in the biblical text. Remember only Isaac, Jacob and Esau, and Samuel to recall the role of divine intervention in conceiving a child. In the context of the present crisis, the impending birth should be interpreted by Ahaz and all Judeans as a sign of God's favor. If we continue our line of interpretation, history reveals that the son born to Ahaz was **Hezekiah**.

Isaiah went on. Before this child would reach the age of puberty ("knowing how to refuse the evil and choose the good"), the threat posed by Syria and Israel would be gone. Indeed, as events worked out, Damascus of Syria was destroyed in 732 and Samaria of Israel in 721, just about the time Hezekiah, born around 734, was reaching puberty.[3]

The sign was intended to provide concrete evidence of God's care so that Ahaz would trust Yahweh rather than act rashly in a political way to counter the Syro–Ephraimite threat. However, contrary to Isaiah's advice to sit tight and trust Yahweh, Ahaz decided to take things into his own hands. He invited **Tiglath-Pileser III** and the Assyrians to help fend off the Syro–Ephraimitic league. They gladly accepted, and while Assyrian aid dissipated the immediate threat, Judah became an Assyrian client–state and remained such for about a century.

You might have noticed that the autobiographical chapter 6 is separated from biographical chapter 7 by about eight years. And chapter 7 is followed by another autobiographical piece, this one foretelling the coming of the Assyrians. We might want to ask why the material is arranged this way. More specifically, why is the biographical piece about Immanuel injected here? The answer has to do with the call narrative. Isaiah's burden of prophecy, as indicated by Yahweh in that account, would be to speak to a people who would hear but not listen, who would not repent to avert disaster.

> 6:9 "Go and say to this people: 'Keep listening, but do not comprehend.'
> 11 Then I said, 'How long, O YHWH?' And he said: 'Until cities lie waste
> without inhabitant, . . . 12 until YHWH sends everyone far away.'"

Ahaz's reaction to the counsel of Isaiah and his rejection of the Immanuel sign in chapter 7 demonstrated just the kind of callousness that Isaiah was told to

---

[2] The scenario developed here suggests that Hezekiah was the child to whom Isaiah is referring. Another plausible scenario is that the child is Isaiah's own son, perhaps the Maher-shalal-hash-baz referred to in chapter 8. For one development of this interpretation see H. Wolf, "A Solution to the Immanuel Prophecy in Isaiah 7:14–8:22" *Journal of Biblical Literature* 91 (1972) 449–56.

[3] The chronology of the life of Hezekiah is difficult to pin down due to contradictions within 2 Kings 18. We follow verse 13, which places the beginning of his reign at 715 B.C.E. making him 21 years of age when he ascended the throne, against 2 Kings 18:2, which puts his age at 25.

expect in that inaugural vision. The result was divine judgment. That came, as chapter 8 foresaw, when the forces of Assyria swept over Judah.

From these chapters, we see that Isaiah the prophet was heavily involved in Judean politics, close to the king, yet not a "yes-man." How should we understand the involvement of Isaiah in Judean political life?

ISAIAH AND JUDEAN POLITICS (9–11)

It appears that Isaiah was a member of the loyal opposition party that opposed Ahaz's policy of accommodation to the Assyrian empire. He also appears to be more of a parochial Judean traditionalist than Ahaz, preferring isolationism to involvement in international politics.

Isaiah and his party were at odds with royal policy during the reign of Ahaz. Although opposed to specific royal policies, Isaiah was still a staunch supporter in principle of the Davidic dynasty. The poems of chapters 9–11 express Isaiah's hopes attached to the Davidic heir. By their proximity to the Immanuel prophecy of chapter 7, they appear to express the profound expectations the prophet and the people had for a rebirth of national pride and status. Interpreted this way, they probably referred to Hezekiah.

Isaiah 9:2–7 could be interpreted as a coronation hymn in celebration of the crown prince Hezekiah's accession to the throne.

> 9:6 "For a child has been born to us, a son given to us. Authority rests on his shoulders. He will be called Wonderful Counselor, Mighty God, Everlasting Father, Prince of Peace. 7 His authority will continue to grow, and there will be everlasting peace for the throne of David and his kingdom. He will establish and sustain it with justice and with righteousness from now and into the future forever. The zeal of YHWH of hosts will do it."

With these words, made especially well known by Handel's oratorio *The Messiah*, Isaiah reflected the anticipation the people felt at the royal birth. Isaiah saw the ongoing tradition of Davidic kingship as the institution through which Yahweh would mediate peace and salvation to the people. Such high ideals no doubt fed popular expectations of prosperity and equity—ideals that Judah's actual kings hardly ever met. The people's disappointments, in turn, fed anticipation of yet a better Davidic king who would meet the ideal, an expectation that developed into the grand ideal of the coming Messiah.

ASSYRIAN INVASION (36–39)

Hezekiah succeeded his father, Ahaz, in 715 B.C.E. and inherited an independent but insecure Judah, one still threatened by Assyria. Shortly after taking the throne he instituted a policy of expansion. He sought to take Edomite territory to the south and Philistine territory to the west. He also looked to join an anti-Assyrian coalition that included Egypt. Isaiah sought to dissuade him, saying this could only lead to disaster (22:1–8, 12–14, 30:8–17).

Hezekiah instituted a policy of revolt against Assyria. This fired the wrath of **Sennacherib**, the Assyrian king (see Figure 10.4). In 701 he invaded Judah. However, by divine intervention, Yahweh demolished the Assyrian war machine and delivered Jerusalem. The text tells us that the angel of Yahweh killed 185,000 troops who were besieging Jerusalem. The tale, told in chapters 36–37, ended favorably when Sennacherib's decimated army withdrew. This was proof of the policy Isaiah promoted, and reaffirmed the power of Yahweh to protect Jerusalem and the Davidic empire.

Isaiah continued to provide counsel and support to Hezekiah. Later, Isaiah encouraged Hezekiah during a serious illness (chapter 38). Hezekiah was given added years of life due to his piety.

These last chapters of First Isaiah, along with 7–11, demonstrate the close connection between Isaiah and the king. Isaiah tried by various means to provide

FIGURE 10.4   **SENNACHERIB PRISM** This six-sided clay column chronicles the military campaigns of Sennacherib (704–681 B.C.E.) against Syria, Tyre, and Judah. It describes the 701 B.C.E. Assyrian siege of Jerusalem, including Sennacherib's claim that he made Hezekiah "a prisoner in Jerusalem, his royal residence, like a bird in a cage."

assurances, usually by means of signs, that Yahweh was supportive of royalty and the Davidic covenant.

Chapter 39, the last chapter of First Isaiah, contains Isaiah's rebuke of Hezekiah for allowing envoys of the Babylonian king Merodach-Baladan in to see the royal treasury. In a bit of foreshadowing, Isaiah predicted the Babylonian exile.

> 5 Then Isaiah said to Hezekiah, "Hear the word of YHWH of hosts: 6 Days are coming when everything in your house and everything your ancestors have accumulated up till today will be carried to Babylon. Nothing will remain, says YHWH."

This is a fitting, and no doubt editorially intentional, transition to Second Isaiah, which is set in the time of that exile.

ISAIAH OF THE EXILE—SECOND ISAIAH

Chapters 40–55 of the book of Isaiah most likely come from the hand of a prophet who lived during the Babylonian exile in the sixth century B.C.E.[4] Dated sometime within the period 546–538 B.C.E., they do not come from the hand of Isaiah of Jerusalem. We know virtually nothing about this prophet, not even his name. Scholars have taken to calling him **Second Isaiah**, or **Deutero-Isaiah** (meaning the same thing, only using a fancier term derived from Greek).

This prophet, though nameless, is one of the most inspiring of all time. And judging by the synthesis of traditions he was able to pull together, by his originality, and by the brilliance of his poetry, he was tremendously gifted. He drew from Israel's historic faith and reapplied it to the new setting of exile, giving the people reason for hope.

Second Isaiah consists almost entirely of poetic passages, with none of the narrative type material found in the first section of the book. Many scholars have tried to determine the boundaries of these poems, and the logic and flow of chapters 40–55 as a whole, with varying success. The most recognizable division within the text is between chapters 40–48 and 49–55. The first subsection addresses its audience as Jacob and Israel. It deals with the fall of Babylon and the **new exodus**. The second subsection addresses its audience as Zion and Jerusalem and deals with issues of justice among the listeners. Beyond this basic division though, little else is agreed upon.

So instead of trying to deal with compositional issues here and treating literary units in sequence, we will treat Second Isaiah thematically. The first theme taken up is the theme of a new exodus.

---

[4] Conservative Jewish and Christian scholars tend to maintain that all of the book of Isaiah was written by Isaiah of Jerusalem. They typically admit that these latter chapters apply to the situation of Babylonian exile but say they were written predictively by Isaiah in the eighth century. Some of the reasons mainstream scholarship believes chapters 40–55 were written in the sixth century are their reference to the destruction of Jerusalem as a past event (40:1–2), Babylonia as their present setting (43:14, 48:20), and Cyrus the Persian as their deliverer (44:28, 45:1–4).

NEW EXODUS (40)

Second Isaiah marks a dramatic change from the prophetic tone of the monarchy era voices of the likes of Amos and Jeremiah. Their words of judgment had by now come true. God had punished Israel and Judah completely (the "double punishment" in the text below) for their sins. Now things will be different. Second Isaiah has sometimes been called "The Book of Comfort" based on passages such as the following.

> 40:1 "Comfort, comfort my people!" says your God. 2 "Speak tenderly to Jerusalem and call out to her that her war time has ended, that her sin has been pardoned, that she has received double punishment from YHWH for all her sins." 6 A voice says, "Call out!" And I said, "What shall I call out?" "This—all flesh is grass. . . . 8 The grass withers, the flower fades, but God's word always will stand."

The anonymous prophet we call Second Isaiah, like his spiritual mentor Isaiah of Jerusalem, was conscious of his calling. This passage, the first one of Second Isaiah, is a bit difficult to sort out because of the different voices that speak, most of them without explicit identification. A number of scholars have reconstructed this text as a call narrative, and this makes some sense. Presupposing such a setting, the text would have the prophet being commissioned in the divine council to proclaim release from captivity. First, Yahweh issues the directive to comfort his people. Second, a member of the council ("a voice") looks for someone to go forth with the message. Then, the prophet speaks up to volunteer, requests the specific message he should bring ("What shall I call out?"), and receives it ("All flesh is grass").

An examination of the divine council's summons in verses 3–5 suggests that it is the announcement of the reappearance of Yahweh, a new theophany.

> 40:3 A voice calls out, "In the wilderness prepare the road for YHWH, make straight in the desert a highway for our God. 4 Every valley will be lifted up, and every mountain and hill will be flattened. The irregular ground will be level and the rough areas even. 5 The glory of YHWH will be revealed so all humanity will see it. It will happen because YHWH's mouth has spoken."

The destruction of Jerusalem by the Babylonians presupposed the withdrawal of Yahweh from that city. Some Judeans may have thought he had returned to the wilderness, his original home. Second Isaiah proclaims that the God of the wilderness will reveal himself, lead his people through the wilderness, and then bring them into the Promised Land once again.

Instead of a pathway through the Red Sea, there would be a straight and level highway right through the Arabian desert. This expressway would carry the people directly home. The exodus tradition once again becomes the basis for hope. The dynamic reuse of biblical traditions is nowhere more apparent than here in Second Isaiah. This prophet keeps coming back to the exodus theme to give shape to a hope for those currently in exile. He encourages them to have faith in a new exodus, this time from Babylonia rather than Egypt.

> *43:16 Thus says YHWH—the one who makes a path in the sea, a path through the raging water, 17 who brings down chariot and horse, army and soldier (they lie down, they cannot get up, they are snuffed out, put out like a wick)—18 "Remember not earlier events. Do not dwell on the past. 19 Indeed, I am doing a new thing. It is springing up right now, do you not see it coming? I will make a path through the wilderness, rivers in the desert."*

Note the details of the exodus tradition recalled in this passage: crossing the sea and the army of the enemy drowning in the sea. These recall the great salvation event at the Red Sea of the Mosaic age. Yet, in Second Isaiah's estimation, that Egyptian event will be nothing compared to the future exodus from Babylonia. Yahweh is the redeemer of Israel. If you read other portions of Second Isaiah, be alert to the numerous allusions made to Israel's earlier exodus experience, including the move from slavery to freedom, passing through the water, the miraculous providing of water and manna, and the conquest of the land.

In addition to the great exodus theme, Second Isaiah develops other significant themes.

CREATION-REDEMPTION

The book of Genesis is by no means the only place the Hebrew Bible talks about the creation of the world.

> *48:12 "Listen to me, Jacob; Israel whom I called! I am the one: I am the beginning (the first), I am also the end (the last). 13 My hand laid the foundation of the earth, my right hand extended the heavens. When I call them they stand at attention."*

The reason Second Isaiah talks about creation is to ground the redemptive capability of Yahweh in his power. Because he is the one who created the world, he is powerful enough to bring Israel out of captivity. In the following passage, Second Isaiah combines the creation myth with the expectation of redemption.

> *51:9 Rouse up, rouse up, put on strength, O arm of YHWH! Rouse up, as in the olden days of past generations! Was it not you who cut Rahab to pieces? Did you not pierce the Sea Monster? 10 Was it not you who dried up Sea, Great Deep? Did you not make the depths of Sea a road for the redeemed to cross? 11 Now, the redeemed of YHWH will return and come to Zion with singing. Eternal joy is on their head. They will obtain joy and gladness. Sorrow and sighing will leave.*

The terms Rahab[5], Sea Monster, Sea, and Great Deep, all synonymous, make reference to the waters of chaos. Their use here recalls the victory of Yahweh over the waters of chaos that led to the creation of the world (see Genesis 1; Levenson 1988). The victory was achieved by splitting Sea, similar to the way Marduk split Tiamat in half to create the world.

This myth was used to express the cosmic significance of the act of deliverance at the Red Sea. The splitting of the waters of the Red Sea (Exodus 14) became the splitting of Sea, a victory over the waters of chaos. Second Isaiah is saying that this type of powerful act of salvation would be repeated to return God's people to Zion.

SERVANT OF YAHWEH

Four poems in Second Isaiah speak of a servant figure, called the **servant of Yahweh**. For a long time scholars have seen these poems as related and have treated them together in the hope of coming up with a coherent picture of the servant figure. The first servant poem, 42:1–4, describes God's choice of the servant who will bring justice to the nations. The second poem, 49:1–6, describes in the servant's own words his experience of having been called by God to be a light to the nations. The reference in verse 3 to Israel is generally recognized as a late insertion intended to identify the servant with the nation. The third poem, 50:4–9, turns gloomy with a first-person description of how the servant was physically abused in the course of his mission. The last and longest servant poem, 52:13–53:12, except for the first few verses, is a third party's observation of the suffering of the servant. What follows is a fragment of the last servant poem.

> *53:4 Surely he has lifted our infirmities and carried our diseases. But we reckoned him stricken, struck down by God, and afflicted. 5 But he was wounded for our transgressions, crushed for our wrongs; upon him was inflicted the punishment that made us whole, and by his wounds we are healed.*

On the basis, especially, of this last poem, the servant of Yahweh figure has also come to be called the "suffering servant." The notion is a remarkable one. It appears to represent a transference from atonement by animal sacrifice, the traditional ritual means of atonement in Israel, to atonement by a human being's suffering. By his suffering, the servant of Yahweh receives God's punishment for the sins of the group.

Who was this servant? No one knows exactly who he was or how to interpret the figure in the poems. Some have suggested that the servant of Yahweh is a metaphor for Judah, which suffered terribly in the Babylonian exile (remember, this is the group Second Isaiah is directly addressing). By so doing Judah delivered healing to other nations in the form of a witness to the saving power of Yahweh.

[5] Spelled in Hebrew differently from the prostitute Rahab of Jericho, who assisted Joshua in the book of Joshua.

Others have suggested that the servant was an individual. Israel's prophetic figures were typically called "my servants, the prophets" and "servant of Yahweh." Moses is called this in Deuteronomy, and other prophets elsewhere. If the servant was a real prophetic figure, Jeremiah is a likely candidate. He was called by God (compare Jeremiah 1:5 and Isaiah 49:5). We know from Kings and the book of Jeremiah that he was socially outcast and physically abused. Besides Jeremiah, others have also been suggested, including Judah's king in exile, Jehoiachin, Second Isaiah himself (Whybray 1983), and Zerubbabel, the first governor of Judea after the exile.

Perhaps the very indefiniteness of the allusion, though, was Second Isaiah's intention. He may have had somebody real in mind as a model; but he may have been suggesting, by keeping the identification vague, that the way of selflessness and suffering is the way salvation comes in God's plan, and not by triumphant military might. By keeping the figure indefinite, such a figure is not just a historical curiosity, but a way of being for God's chosen and redeemed people.

CYRUS THE MESSIAH

Second Isaiah contains, among other things, a clear example of theological interpretation of history. **Cyrus the Great**, the Persian monarch who opposed the Babylonian empire, was viewed by the Judeans as their great deliverer. Second Isaiah even uses the term *messiah*, that is, "anointed one," to refer to him in order to indicate the divine initiative behind his mission.

> 44:24 *"I am YHWH, who made all things, . . . 28 who says of Cyrus, 'He is my shepherd, he shall carry out all my plans.'" 45:1 Thus says YHWH to his anointed one, to Cyrus, whose right hand I have grasped to subjugate nations before him, . . . 5 'I am YHWH, there is no other. Except for me there is no god. I equip you, though you do not know me.'"*

With eyes of faith, Second Isaiah interpreted the current events of his day as being ordained and directed by Yahweh, even down to the actions of their most likely political ally at that time. Second Isaiah clearly threw his support to Cyrus and promoted an anti-Babylonian policy. By 539 B.C.E. Cyrus was successful against the Babylonians.[6] And as it turned out (see the book of Ezra) Cyrus was kindly disposed toward the Judeans and even assisted the efforts of the Judeans who desired to return to Jerusalem and rebuild the temple there (see Figure 10.5).

Second Isaiah's willingness to identify Cyrus as *messiah* indicates a departure from the Jerusalemite theological tradition, which attached that term to the reigning king from the line of David. Second Isaiah seems not to put much stock in the Davidic line, nor does he look to it in hope. In fact, although there are numerous references to Zion and to Jerusalem, there are no references to David until 55:3.

---

[6] The references to Cyrus enable us to date Second Isaiah fairly reliably. From these Cyrus passages it is apparent that Cyrus was becoming known in Babylon for his military exploits. His first major victories were against Media in 550 B.C.E. and Lydia in 546 B.C.E. It was not until 539 B.C.E. that he defeated Babylon. The hope expressed by Second Isaiah, viewing Cyrus as Israel's deliverer, was no doubt then framed sometime within the decade between 550 and 539 B.C.E.

3b I will make with you an eternal covenant, my faithful Davidic-type lov-ing relationship. 4 See, I had made him a witness to the peoples, a leader and commander for the peoples. 5 See, you will call nations that you do not know, nations that you do not know will run to you.

Second Isaiah seems to be suggesting something quite remarkable. The loving covenantal arrangement God earlier had established with David would now be transferred to his people as a whole. The dynastic covenant would become a na-tional covenant. The people would complete the mission begun by David. In this way, Second Isaiah is claiming that the Davidic covenant had not been annulled. Rather, it had been democratized.

Much more could be said about Second Isaiah's writings. They are full of im-ages and promises of hope and restoration. However, now we turn to Third Isa-iah, which was written in that period when Judah was struggling to rebuild and realize those dreams fueled by Second Isaiah.

ISAIAH OF THE RESTORATION—THIRD ISAIAH

The last major chunk of Isaiah is called **Third** (or **Trito-**) **Isaiah**. It contains prophetic oracles coming from one or more of Second Isaiah's disciples. These oracles were addressed to the faithful and the not-so-faithful Judeans living in Jerusalem in the early postexilic period, that time when the people were strug-gling to reestablish a life in their homeland. This section of the book of Isaiah is datable to the period 538–520 B.C.E. Much of its message is intended to sustain the refugees recently returned from Babylonian captivity, who were discouraged and depressed by the difficulty of life back in Jerusalem. You can sense the des-perate need of the people in the following passage.

61:1 The Spirit of YHWH Elohim is upon me, because YHWH has anointed me to bring good news to the afflicted; he has sent me to shore up the broken spirited, to proclaim freedom to the captives, the opening of prison to those who are bound, 2 to proclaim the year of YHWH's favor, and the day of our God's vengeance.

As with Isaiah of Jerusalem and Second Isaiah, this prophet expressed his awareness of prophetic calling. Third Isaiah was drawn to minister to God's peo-ple, even to fire them up. He had a formidable job to do. Jerusalem was in ruins. The community, too, was morally fragmented. There was dissension between the Judeans who had never left, the so-called people of the land, and those who had returned from exile.

Third Isaiah may have attempted to encourage those struggling for faith in the absence of a temple and sacrifices. He assured them that God was present even if no building housed him.

66:1 Thus says YHWH: "Heaven is my throne, the earth my footstool. What house would you build for me, what place for me to rest? 2 All these things my hand has made, all these things are mine, says YHWH. But this is the one to whom I will pay attention: the one that is humble and unassuming and respects my word."

Third Isaiah, as you can see, is consistent with Second Isaiah in promoting the universal dimension of Yahweh's domain. Yahweh claims the entire world and would reveal his salvation to all people. Salvation had not yet arrived, but soon it would, and it would embrace all nations, not just Israel.

66:22 *"Just as the new heavens and the new earth which I am about to make shall stand before me, so shall your offspring and your name stand. 23 From new moon to new moon, from sabbath to sabbath, all flesh shall come to worship me," says YHWH.*

Through difficult times and dreadful conditions, Third Isaiah sought to keep the faith of the people alive (Figure 10.5).

OVERALL SHAPE OF THE BOOK OF ISAIAH

The book of Isaiah has undergone a complex process of compilation, expansion, and editorializing. The history of Isaiah scholarship has tended to emphasize the separation of the book into its three main sections, assigning the different portions to different historical periods and more or less just leaving them there. Much Isaiah scholarship has delineated the individual poetic units and has tried to establish the authorship of the units, with priority frequently given to genuine Isaiah of Jerusalem sections.

There have been few attempts to view the book as a whole, to try to construct the overall witness of the book. But we must keep in mind that somebody within the community of faith saw fit to put all this material together into one "book" under the heading "the words of Isaiah," and it was not just because they all fit conveniently onto one leather scroll. We have to ask ourselves, What gives the book its unity? What does the book as a whole have to say?

Clements (1982) argues that the destruction of Jerusalem in 587 B.C.E. is the clue to the editorial strategy that holds the book together. He argues that First Isaiah, while written primarily in reference to the Assyrian crisis of the eighth century, was edited during the Babylonian crisis and in its judgment oracles provided the prophetic explanation for the eventual fall of Jerusalem. Second and Third Isaiah were attached to First Isaiah by later scribes because they were motivated to balance prophetic judgment with prophetic promise. They were concerned to say that judgment is not the last word but is followed by restoration. This basic sequence of judgment followed by renewal is echoed in the books of Jeremiah and Ezekiel and appears to be a fundamental structure in the plan of God.

While acknowledging the critical analysis of the book into its component elements, Childs (1979) assesses the book of Isaiah from the point of view of the effect of its current shape, rather than for the purposes of a scholarly reconstruction. Childs points out that there are virtually no signals of the sixth-

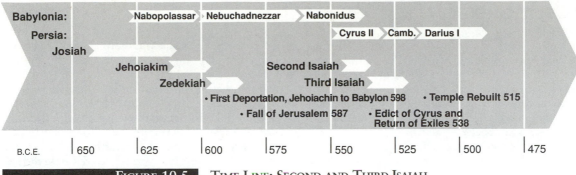

| Babylonia: | | Nabopolassar | Nebuchadnezzar | | Nabonidus | | | | | |
| Persia: | | | | | | Cyrus II | Camb. | Darius I | | |

Josiah

Jehoiakim

Zedekiah

Second Isaiah

Third Isaiah

• First Deportation, Jehoiachin to Babylon 598

• Temple Rebuilt 515

• Fall of Jerusalem 587

• Edict of Cyrus and
Return of Exiles 538

| B.C.E. | 650 | 625 | 600 | 575 | 550 | 525 | 500 | 475 |

FIGURE 10.5   TIME LINE: SECOND AND THIRD ISAIAH

century authorship of Second and Third Isaiah in a plain reading of chapters 40–66. The original setting of 40–66 is effectively disguised. In its current shape, the entire book is placed in the mouth of eighth-century Isaiah of Jerusalem: "These are the words of Isaiah, son of Amoz." In effect, this places both judgment and salvation within the eternal plan of God. For even before the destruction of Jerusalem and the Babylonian exile, as attested by 40–66, God intended to return his people to Judah. Even before destruction, he was planning ahead to their return.

The book then confirms the long-term saving Word of God.[7] God is faithful to his Word and trustworthy. God plans beyond judgment to forgiveness and reacceptance. Taken as a whole, the book of Isaiah is a witness to the good will and power of Israel's God, Yahweh.

QUESTIONS FOR REVIEW

1. What are the three main sections of the book of Isaiah, when was each written, and who was the audience for each section?
2. What happened at Isaiah's call to the ministry, and in what way does his call relate to his ministry?
3. Describe the political circumstances of the Syro–Ephraimitic crisis, and explain what Isaiah intended to do by giving Ahaz the Immanuel prophecy.
4. What are the main themes of Second Isaiah, and how do they relate to the Babylonian exile?
5. Describe the "servant of Yahweh" figure of Second Isaiah and explain his relevance to the experience of God's people in the sixth century B.C.E.

[7]Note the frequent references to the faithfulness of the Word of God (40:8, 44:26, 55:10–11).

QUESTIONS FOR DISCUSSION

1. Evaluate the advice Isaiah gave to Ahaz during the Syro–Ephraimitic crisis. Was it politically prudent? Was it realistic? Think about the role of religious faith in political decision making. Should national leaders make military and political decisions on the basis of divine promises of security and the advice of prophets?

2. What covenant traditions informed First, Second, and Third Isaiah, respectively? Did they draw from the same traditions? Some might suggest First Isaiah drew heavily from the Davidic covenant, and Second Isaiah from the exodus traditions. Are all traditions important all of the time, or are some more appropriate than others, depending on current political and spiritual conditions?

3. Read and study the four "servant of Yahweh" poems. The Christian tradition has identified the figure with Jesus of Nazareth. On what basis do you think Christians make this identification? To whom do you think the servant poems refer? Could the figure be messianic?

FOR FURTHER STUDY

There is no single outstanding commentary on the book of Isaiah. However, Clements (1980a) on First Isaiah is generally reliable. And Whybray (1983) is a clear verse-by-verse commentary on Second Isaiah, although he promotes a somewhat unorthodox interpretation of the servant. For historical and thematic issues, the other works of Clements are to be recommended.

Isaiah of Jerusalem. Childs, Brevard S. (1967). *Isaiah and the Assyrian Crisis.* Naperville, Ill.: Alec R. Allenson.

Clements, Ronald E. (1980a). *Isaiah 1–39.* New Century Bible. Grand Rapids, Mich.: Eerdmans.

Clements, Ronald E. (1980b). *Isaiah and the Deliverance of Jerusalem: A Study of the Interpretation of Prophecy in the Old Testament.* Sheffield: JSOT Press.

Daves, Eryl W. (1987). *Prophecy and Ethics: Isaiah and the Ethical Traditions of Israel.* Sheffield: JSOT Press.

Hayes, John H., and Stuart A. Irvine (1987). *Isaiah the Eighth-Century Prophet.* Nashville, Tenn.: Abingdon.

Irvine, Stuart A. (1990). *Isaiah, Ahaz and the Syro–Ephraimitic Crisis.* Atlanta: Scholars Press.

Oswalt, John N. (1986). *The Book of Isaiah. Chapters 1–39.* New International Commentary on the Old Testament. Grand Rapids, Mich.: Eerdmans.

Vriezen, Th. C. (1962). "Essentials of the Theology of Isaiah," pp. 128–46 in *Israel's Prophetic Heritage*, ed. B. W. Anderson and W. Harrelson. New York: Harper & Brothers.

Second and Third Isaiah. DeBoer, P. A. H. (1956). *Second Isaiah's Message.* OTS 11. Leiden: E. J. Brill.

Emmerson, Grace I. (1992). *Isaiah 56–66.* Old Testament Guides. Sheffield: Sheffield Academic Press. Claims the key to the interpretation of this block of Isaianic material is the nonfulfillment of Second Isaiah's promises. It contains a reinterpretation of Second Isaiah's message for the postexilic community.

Hanson, Paul D. (1975) *The Dawn of Apocalyptic. The Historical and Social Roots of Jewish Apocalyptic Eschatology.* Philadelphia: Fortress Press.

Melugin, Roy (1976). *The Formation of Isaiah 40–55.* Berlin, Germany: Walter de Gruyter.

North, Christopher R. (1956). *The Suffering Servant in Deutero-Isaiah. An Historical and Critical Study.* 2d ed. Oxford: Oxford University Press.

Stuhlmueller, Carroll (1970). *Creative Redemption in Deutero-Isaiah.* Rome: Biblical Institute Press.

Whybray, Ronald N. (1983). *The Second Isaiah.* Sheffield: JSOT Press. He suggests that Second Isaiah himself was the servant of Yahweh.

The Unity of Isaiah. Brueggeman, W. (1984). "Unity and Dynamic in the Isaiah Tradition." *JSOT* 29:89–107.

Clements, Ronald E. (1985). "Beyond Tradition History: Deutero-Isaianic Development of First Isaiah's Themes." *JSOT* 31:95–113.

WORKS CITED

Childs, Brevard S. (1979). *Introduction to the Old Testament as Scripture*. Philadelphia: Fortress Press.

Clements, Ronald E. (1982). "The Unity of the Book of Isaiah," *Interpretation* 36:117–29.

Jensen, Joseph (1973). *The Use of Torah by Isaiah: His Debate with the Wisdom Tradition*. Washington, D.C.: Catholic Biblical Association of America.

Levenson, Jon D. (1988). *Creation and the Persistence of Evil. The Jewish Drama of Divine Omnipotence*. San Francisco: Harper & Row.

Whybray, Ronald N. (1983). *The Second Isaiah*. Sheffield: JSOT Press. He suggests that Second Isaiah himself was the servant of Yahweh.

JEREMIAH

11

Names and Terms to Remember

Anathoth	Jehoiakim	new covenant
Baruch	Jeremiah	Zedekiah
Hananiah	Jeremiah's complaints	
Jehoiachin	Josiah	

Jeremiah, more so than any other Hebrew prophet, emerges from the biblical text with a full personality. While the other prophets are known almost solely through their messages, Jeremiah's character and personality comes out in his book through autobiography. In the past called "the weeping prophet," he passionately expressed his own feelings and laid bare his inner spiritual life. This makes Jeremiah unique among the prophets.

The book of Jeremiah seems to have had a complex literary history and consists of both prose narrative and poetic material. Three main types of sources underlie the book:

1. *Type A: Autobiography*. Naturally, this material is framed as Jeremiah's own speech. It is found mainly in chapters 1–25 and 46–51. Much of this material is poetic and is generally assumed to be closer to Jeremiah's own utterances than the following types.

2. *Type B: Biography*. This material is third-person stories about Jeremiah, probably written by **Baruch**, Jeremiah's personal secretary. These biographical episodes are found in chapters 19:1–20:6; 26–29, 36–44, and 45.

3. *Type C: Prose Sermons*. These show evidence of composition in the Deuteronomic style. That is, they contain the same vocabulary and style as the Deuteronomic school of theologians. Many have a common theme, namely, exposing the guilt of the people who have failed to heed prophetic warnings and have not repented. Included in this category are chapters 7:1–8:3, 11:1–14, 18:1–12, 21:1–10, 22:1–5, 25:1–11, and 34:8–22. As with Type A material, these sermons are framed as the direct speech of Jeremiah.

These components were combined to create the final form of the book. Unfortunately, the book lacks a clear organization; chronology was clearly not the determining principle. The date indications in the text jump back and forth, and the book does not follow a linear temporal order. Keep this in mind if you read the book in its entirety. It takes a special effort to orient the chapters within their historical context.

There is one obvious structural division in the book, and that comes after chapter 25. Most of the Type A autobiographical material is found in chapters 1–25, as well as most of the Type C material. Characteristic of passages from these chapters is the introductory phrase "the word of Yahweh came to me." On the other hand, from chapter 26 to the end, the prophetic introductory formula is mostly on the order of, "the word of Yahweh came to Jeremiah." This has led some scholars to make the suggestion that the second half of the book (chapters 26–52), in some form at least, comes from the hand of Baruch (see Figure 11.1).

The content of the entire book of Jeremiah spans about a fifty-year period, from the end of the seventh century B.C.E. to the middle of the sixth century. The

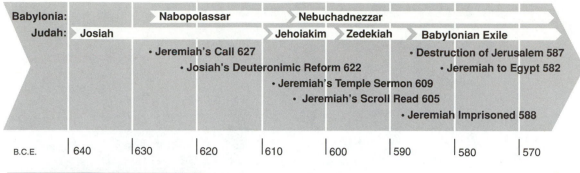

- Jeremiah's Call 627
- Josiah's Deuteronimic Reform 622
- Jeremiah's Temple Sermon 609
- Jeremiah's Scroll Read 605
- Destruction of Jerusalem 587
- Jeremiah to Egypt 582
- Jeremiah Imprisoned 588

B.C.E. |640 |630 |620 |610 |600 |590 |580 |570

FIGURE 11.1 TIME LINE: BOOK OF JEREMIAH

general historical situation taking us up to the beginning of the book of Jeremiah is as follows.

Israel (the Northern Kingdom) long ago had disappeared as an independent entity. Judah alone remained. Assyrian power and its sphere of influence was on the decline by the middle of the seventh century. Having previously been dominated by the Assyrians, Judah toward the end of this century enjoyed a bit of independence. By 628 under **Josiah**, Judah was politically free and economically prosperous, and had even begun expanding northward into former Israelite territory.

There was no longer any external pressure on Judah to pay allegiance to Assyrian deities, as was the case under Manasseh earlier in the century. Taking the opportunity political independence afforded, Josiah pressed for a return to indigenous Israelite religious practices and beliefs, namely Yahwism. The prophets Zephaniah and Jeremiah supported Josiah in this move to reform worship, which began in earnest in 622.

Our approach to the book of Jeremiah will step out of our typical canonical mode and instead treat the material chronologically. We will not try to reconstruct the editorial history of the text to understand its current canonical shape, but rather, more simply, we will look at texts in Jeremiah in temporal order, divided into periods based on the reigns of Judah's last kings.

EARLY YEARS (627–622 B.C.E.)

The beginning of Jeremiah's ministry occurred during the reign of Josiah. Josiah was the king of Judah from 640 B.C.E. until 609. The early years of Josiah's reign were a time of prosperity and political independence. In the evaluation of the Deuteronomic school, represented by the books of Kings, Josiah was a fine and faithful king.

Jeremiah became a prophet in 627 and continued during those years immediately preceding Josiah's reform movement. After the reform initiative in 622, Jeremiah was not heard from for about a decade. The reason, perhaps, is that Jeremiah felt Josiah had succeeded in doing what was necessary. Jeremiah resumed his prophetic ministry after the death of Josiah.

640	Josiah began to reign as king of Judah
627	Jeremiah began his ministry
622	Josiah initiated religious and political reform (Deuteronomic Reform)
609	Josiah died at Megiddo
	Jehoahaz (Shallum) made king; lasted three months
	Jehoiakim was installed king of Judah by the Egyptians
	Jeremiah delivered his Temple Sermon
605	Battle of Carchemish: Babylonia asserted its power over Egypt
	Jeremiah's scroll read before Jehoiakim, burned by Jehoiakim
598	Nebuchadnezzar laid siege to Jerusalem; First Deportation of refugees to Babylonia
	Jehoiakim died
	Jehoiachin became king, was taken to Babylon
	Zedekiah was installed king of Judah by Babylonians
	Jeremiah confronted Hananiah who broke the ox yoke
588	Jeremiah was imprisoned by Zedekiah
587	Destruction of Jerusalem
	Gedaliah appointed governor of Judea
582	Gedaliah assassinated
	Jeremiah traveled to Egypt
562	Jeremiah died in Egypt

The Jeremiah of the early years, which fall into the period from his call to 622, is represented by chapters 1–6. In them he has a lot in common with Amos and Micah. Like Amos, Jeremiah was concerned about social injustice and considered worship to be secondary to a lifestyle attentive to righteousness. Like Hosea, he personified Israel as an unfaithful wife (chapter 2) and longed for the days of the Exodus and the wilderness experience when Israel was thrown totally on the grace of God.

The book of Jeremiah begins with a Deuteronomic-style introduction that places Jeremiah within the context of Judah's history.

> 1:1 The words of Jeremiah son of Hilkiah, one of the priests in Anathoth in the land of Benjamin. 2 To him the word of YHWH came in the days of King Josiah son of Amon of Judah, beginning in the thirteenth year of his reign. 3 It also came in the days of King Jehoiakim son of Josiah of Judah until the end of the eleventh year of King Zedekiah son of Josiah of Judah, specifically, until the captivity of Jerusalem in the fifth month.

From this editorial introduction we learn that Jeremiah belonged to a priestly family from **Anathoth** in Benjamin. This is significant because it reveals one source of his antipathy to the Jerusalem priestly establishment. Admittedly we are dealing with a chain of evidence here, but this is how it goes.

When Solomon made his choice of priests back in the tenth century, he authorized Zadok as the legitimate family of priests and banished Abiathar to

Anathoth. Zadok was chosen over Abiathar because Zadok backed Solomon to be king, while Abiathar backed Adonijah. (See 1 Kings 2:26–27.) Since Anathoth was a very small village, it is reasonable to assume that Jeremiah was part of the Abiathar lineage. Although a priest, Jeremiah would have been denied the privilege of serving at the Jerusalem temple. All of this makes some sense of the negative stand Jeremiah took against the official temple in Jerusalem and the monarchy that had exiled his family. This begins to explain why he was treated as an outsider. That he got any kind of a hearing at all in the temple and royal court is amazing.

The editorial introduction further tells us that Jeremiah prophesied during the reigns of Josiah, **Jehoiakim,** and **Zedekiah,** all kings of Judah, right up until the captivity of Jerusalem in 587 B.C.E.

The only major disputed point in this introduction is the intent of verse 2, which states that "the word of YHWH came" to Jeremiah in the thirteenth year of Josiah's reign. Does this mean that this is the year Jeremiah was called to be a prophet, the year 627 B.C.E., or is this the year he was born? The question arises because the call narrative, which we examine next, suggests that Jeremiah was called to the prophetic ministry even before he was given birth.

Other prophets provide some accounting of how they came to the conclusion that God had called them to be prophets. Isaiah did it in his divine council vision account (Isaiah 6). Amos did it in a roundabout way in dialogue with Amaziah (Amos 7). Jeremiah did it too, and it was logically placed at the beginning of the book.

> *4 The word of YHWH came to me: 5 "Before I formed you in the womb I knew you, before you were born I set you apart—made you a prophet to the nations." 6 I replied: "But YHWH Elohim, I do not know how to speak. I am only a youngster." 7 YHWH replied: "Do not say 'I am only a youngster'—to all I send you, you must go, and what I command you, you must speak. 8 Do not be afraid of them. I will be with you delivering you."—says YHWH. 9 Then YHWH extended his hand and touched my mouth. YHWH said to me, "Now I have put my words in your mouth. 10 Today I have set you above nations and above kingdoms: to uproot and to break down, to destroy and to overturn, to build and to plant."*

Of whom does this remind you? An alert student of the Hebrew Bible would have to say "Moses." Jeremiah expressed the same reluctance as Moses to become a prophet. Jeremiah expressed the same kind of excuses as Moses, claiming a lack of qualifications. Jeremiah's hesitation dealt with the same problem, his mouth, as did Moses'. And in both cases Yahweh met the "mouth" objection: in Moses' case by providing Aaron as his "mouthpiece," and in Jeremiah's by placing the words right on his lips.

Of special importance in Jeremiah's call narrative is the articulation of his mission. It is repeated throughout the book. He will break kingdoms apart and plant kingdoms. It implies that as prophet, the authorized speaker of the word of Yahweh, he has the ability to destroy and to build. These extremes of destroying and building are another way of saying that this prophet's mission involved both judgment and renewal. And in that mission he had the protection of God. As we will see, he came to depend on that protection, and at times felt disillusioned when his enemies got to him.

If we survey chapter 1 to its end we find that Yahweh gave Jeremiah two signs to confirm his calling. In somewhat the same vein as Amos' visions, there are visual puns. First, Yahweh showed Jeremiah an almond tree, in Hebrew a *shaqed*. This became the occasion for Yahweh to say to Jeremiah, "I am watching—*shoqed*—over my word to see that it happens." Then Jeremiah saw a boiling cauldron tipping away from the north toward the south. Yahweh said, "Out of the north trouble is brewing." This is a foreshadowing of the political problems that lay ahead from the north, the direction from which Mesopotamian foes reached Palestine (see Figure 11.2).

DURING THE REIGN OF JEHOIAKIM (609–598 B.C.E.)

Josiah died in battle at Megiddo fighting Pharaoh Neco. He was succeeded by his son Jehoahaz (also called Shallum). Jehoahaz lasted only three months and was deported to Egypt, where he died. Jehoiakim succeeded his brother Jehoahaz and ruled until 598 B.C.E.

Jeremiah was active throughout the reign of Jehoiakim. He denounced the king and the people for their idolatry and injustice. Many of the prophecies of chapters 7–19, 25–26, and 35–36 are dated to this period. Perhaps Jeremiah's most notorious denunciation speech comes in chapter 7.

TEMPLE SERMON (7, 26)

Worship was central to Israel's religious life. A good deal of the Torah, as well as later writings, define proper worship. This includes the proper rituals, the authorized personnel, and the implements used in worship. Much of Samuel, Kings, and especially Chronicles deals with defining and justifying notions of formal religion by illustrating them out of the life of Israel and Judah. Most of the time this meant promoting a form of worship centered in Jerusalem on Mt. Zion.

Jeremiah was one of the few prophetic voices challenging the orthodoxy of Zionist theology, which to the religious and political establishment defined the "right" shape of worship. In his temple address, as recorded in chapter 7, he brought an opposing perspective to bear on the function of the temple and worship on Mt. Zion. From the parallel passage in Jeremiah 26 we learn that the sermon was given in 609 B.C.E. at the beginning of Jehoiakim's reign.

Jeremiah delivered these words in the temple courtyard.

> *2 Hear the word of YHWH, all you people of Judah who enter these gates to worship YHWH. 3 Thus says YHWH of Hosts, the Elohim of Israel: Reform your ways and your activity, and then I will let you live in this place. 4 Do not trust in these deceptive words—This is the temple of YHWH, the temple of YHWH, the temple of YHWH. 5 But if you reform your ways and your activity, genuinely act justly with each other, 6 do not oppress the resident-alien, the orphan or the widow, shed innocent blood here, or go after other gods (which can only hurt you), 7 then I will let you*

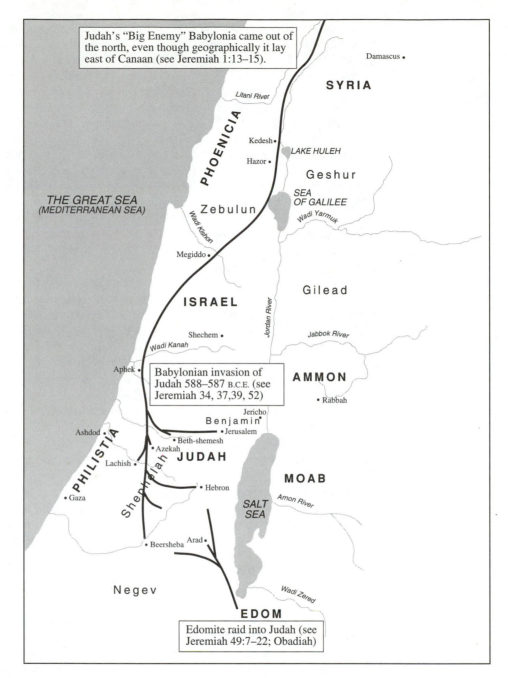

Judah's "Big Enemy" Babylonia came out of the north, even though geographically it lay east of Canaan (see Jeremiah 1:13–15).

DAMASCUS •

SYRIA

Litani River

PHOENICIA

Kedesh •
LAKE HULEH

Hazor •

Geshur

SEA OF GALILEE

Wadi Yarmuk

Zebulun

Wadi Kishon

THE GREAT SEA
(MEDITERRANEAN SEA)

Megiddo •

Gilead

ISRAEL

Jordan River

Shechem •

Jabbok River

Wadi Kanah

Aphek •

Babylonian invasion of Judah 588–587 B.C.E. (see Jeremiah 34, 37,39, 52)

AMMON

• Rabbah

Jericho
Benjamin •

Ashdod •

• Jerusalem

• Beth-shemesh
• Azekah

PHILISTIA

Lachish •

Shephelah

JUDAH

MOAB

• Hebron

SALT SEA

Arnon River

• Gaza

• Beersheba   Arad •

Negev

Wadi Zered

EDOM

Edomite raid into Judah (see Jeremiah 49:7–22; Obadiah)

FIGURE 11.2   OUT OF THE NORTH

live in this place, here in the land that I gave your parents in perpetuity a long time ago. 8 Right now you are putting your faith in misleading words (This is the temple of YHWH!) but to no avail. 9 Would you steal, murder, commit adultery, swear falsely, burn incense to Baal, go after other gods you do not know 10 and then come and stand before me in this temple, the one called by my name, and say 'We are safe'—only to keep on doing these travesties?! 11 Has this house, the one called by my name, become a den of thieves in your opinion? Right now it appears that way to me, says YHWH. 12 Then go now to my place that was once in Shiloh. That is where I first housed my name. See what I did to it as a result of the wickedness of my people Israel. 13 Now, because you have done these things, says YHWH (and though I spoke to you persistently you would not listen, when I called you you would not answer) 14 therefore I will do to the house now identified with me—the one in which you trust, the place I gave to you and to your ancestors—just what I did to Shiloh. 15 I will cast you out of my sight, just as I cast out your cousins, all the descendants of Ephraim.

It is rather easy to see why Jeremiah was not welcomed with a warm hug and a handshake after that speech. He roundly condemned the Judean people for putting their faith in the temple. But why?

Two reasons. First, Jeremiah claimed that the people were immoral, and given their immorality, nothing could save them, not even their sacred temple. Second, it seems the people viewed the temple almost superstitiously. They thought that the temple conferred automatic security. Official Jerusalemite theology claimed that Yahweh lived in the temple, and as long as he was there nothing tragic could ever affect Judah. Historical precedent backed them up in this belief. When Sennacherib surrounded Jerusalem in 701, Yahweh miraculously delivered the city, no doubt, they thought, because he lived there.

But Jeremiah brings up other historical precedent. He refers to the sanctuary city Shiloh of the judges period. Under Eli and Samuel it was the location of Yahweh's sanctuary. In spite of its unsurpassed importance at that time, it was unceremoniously destroyed—probably by the Philistines, though we do not know all the details.

Jeremiah countered that the only genuine security can come from their faith in Yahweh. They must commit themselves to him, and their faith had to be actualized in moral living and undivided loyalty to him. This is none other than the Mosaic prescription. In fact, the very vocabulary of the decalogue is evident here, especially in verse 9.

As was indicated in both the call narrative and the temple address, Jeremiah was thoroughly shaped by the Mosaic tradition. He has northern roots, perhaps Elohist connections—notice his reference to "the Elohim of Israel" in verse 3 and his reference to the descendants of Ephraim in verse 15. And the terminology of the sanctuary as "the place where my name dwells" sounds very Deuteronomic—the theological voice originally coming from the north.

Jeremiah was a dissenting voice in the "den of thieves," the temple courtyard, the heart of the Jerusalemite establishment. And he was pitting the Mosaic tradition against the dogma of Zionist–Davidic theology. He got quite a reaction. Although we do not hear any of it in chapter 7, we do get a full report later in the book.

Jeremiah 26 provides a narrative account of the temple sermon, providing interesting contextual details and the surrounding circumstances. Jeremiah's message is given only in summary, but the reaction to it is given in rich detail. When the priests and prophets heard Jeremiah's condemnation of the Jerusalem temple, they pressed the king's government to execute him. After all, he opposed everything they stood for. They considered it treason.

Jehoiakim's bureaucracy would have put him to death were it not for judicial precedent. In a prior age Micah (the same one as in the Book of the Twelve by that name) proclaimed destructive judgment on Jerusalem, just as Jeremiah was now doing. Hezekiah declined to execute him. The people took Micah seriously, repented, and Jerusalem was delivered. More on the sober side, another case was cited, this one of a certain prophet named Uriah, who was not so lucky. He was executed by Jehoiakim. And so we learn that the threat to Micah and Jeremiah was real.

This encounter between Jeremiah and the Judean establishment reveals two political and theological traditions in conflict. Both provided a way of reading God's relationship with his people and his work in history. One way, the Sinai–Mosaic track, stressed the people's covenant obligation. The other, the Zion–Davidic track, stressed Yahweh's commitment to Judah. This conflict of theologies would surface again.

The temple sermon raises two important theological questions that deserve consideration. First, Jeremiah argues that only if the people practice personal and corporate morality would God allow them to dwell in Palestine. But is such a perspective politically realistic? What is the relationship between moral behavior, of individuals and nations, and political destiny? It would seem that international political forces, in this case the Babylonians, controlled Judah's destiny. The assertion Jeremiah and other prophets make is this: Yahweh controls the destinies of all the nations, including Babylonia.

Second, Jeremiah seems to come down hard on temple rituals and sacrificial practices. What were Jeremiah's deepest attitudes toward formal worship practices—were they entirely useless? Did he issue a blanket condemnation of religious ritual or a conditional one? If conditional, under what circumstances is worship acceptable?

Both questions, the relation of morality and destiny, and the role of worship, raise enduring issues in biblical theology.

READING THE SCROLL (36)

Not surprisingly, Jeremiah was barred from entering the temple–palace compound after that temple sermon. But there was plenty he still wanted to say to the king and his council. Jeremiah directed his companion and secretary Baruch to take dictation. Writing on a scroll with pen and ink, Baruch recorded Jeremiah's urging to repent and warnings of Babylonian danger. The year was 605, the same year the Babylonians bested the Egyptians in battle at Carchemish north of Palestine.

Baruch first read the scroll to a receptive audience in the temple area. They took the message seriously but advised him not to deliver it to the king personally. Fearing reprisals and persecution, Baruch and Jeremiah went into hiding while others approached Jehoiakim to read him the scroll.

Jehoiakim was in his winter palace at the time. As the scroll was read a few columns at a time, the king stripped the columns off the scroll with a knife and burned them. In this way he and his associates demonstrated their contempt for Jeremiah. They obviously were not moved to faith by the message.

After Jeremiah heard what Jehoiakim had done with the scroll, he proceeded to dictate another one with even more messages. But this one he did not deliver to the king. In this series of events many scholars see evidence for the construction of the book of Jeremiah and perhaps even the point of transition from an oral to a written ministry. We can assume this second scroll was the core of the book of Jeremiah as we have it today.

DURING THE REIGN OF ZEDEKIAH (598–587 B.C.E.)

Jehoiakim died just three months before Jerusalem succumbed to the Babylonian siege. In his stead, **Jehoiachin** was placed on the throne. After Nebuchadnezzar of Babylon subdued Jerusalem in 598 he deported many of its citizens to Babylonia, including Jehoiachin. Zedekiah replaced Jehoiachin and ruled with the support of Nebuchadnezzar.

Jeremiah remained in Jerusalem and continued to prophesy after the deportation of Jehoiachin and the others. The words of chapters 24, 27–29, 32–34, and 37–39 come from the time of Zedekiah's reign.

FALSE PROPHECY (27–28)

The Babylonian kingdom of Nebuchadnezzar seemed vulnerable in 594 after a revolt within his army. This led many Judeans to think that their subjugation to the Babylonians might be near its end. Yahweh sent Jeremiah to Jerusalem to discourage such optimism. To reinforce his message he put an ox harness on his shoulders and declared that the yoke of Babylon would endure for a long while to come. He denounced the prophets who suggested otherwise.

> 27:14 *Do not listen to the talk of the prophets who say to you, "You will not serve the king of Babylon." For they are prophesying a lie to you. 15 I have not sent them, says YHWH; rather, they are prophesying falsely in my name.*

Jeremiah was obviously not the only voice giving counsel in Jerusalem. There were other prophets giving advice to Zedekiah and the royal court. One of them was **Hananiah**. When he saw Jeremiah wearing the yoke*bar* he tore it off his back and cracked it in half. He prophesied that within two years Yahweh of Hosts would break the yoke of Babylon, and Jehoiachin, along with all the stolen temple implements, would return to Jerusalem. Jeremiah said he wished it would be so, but maintained that the end of Babylonian domination was not yet at hand.

While the book does not record the reaction of the witnesses to the confrontation that took place in the temple courtyard, we can assume they must have been puzzled. Both prophets spoke in the name of Yahweh of Hosts, and both sounded like real prophets. We can be sure the people *wanted* to believe Hananiah; he had the more attractive message. But whom *should* they believe?

Jeremiah claimed that history favors the doomsayer, that is, himself, rather than the optimist.

> 28:8 *The prophets who preceded you and me from ancient times prophesied war, famine, and disease against many nations and powerful kingdoms. 9 As for the prophet who prophesies peace—only if the word of that prophet comes to pass will it be clear that YHWH has sent that prophet.*

Jeremiah was saying, if a prophet tells you what you want to hear, presume that he is not telling the truth. Only declare him to be a prophet if events prove him true. Otherwise, believe the worst, and you probably won't be disappointed.

LETTER TO THE EXILES (29)

The Judean refugees living in Babylonia were easy prey to the same false optimism as the citizenry in Jerusalem. Jeremiah was determined to debunk their illusions, as he had tried to do with the Jerusalemites. He sent a letter to the Jewish leadership in Babylonia telling them not to expect a speedy return to Judea. Instead, he said, build permanent homes in Babylonia, raise families, and get on with the business of life. He even said the refugees should promote the prosperity and peace of Babylonia, the kingdom of their oppression. Outrageous! If anything was treasonous, this was. Yet he was not all gloom and doom.

> 29:10 *When seventy years in Babylon are finished I will come to you and fulfill my promise to bring you back to this place. 11 I know the future I have in store for you, says YHWH, plans for prosperity and not for disaster, plans to give you a future and hope.*

Although the immediate future would entail the destruction of Jerusalem, there was always the "to build and to plant" of Jeremiah's message. Yet, it would not happen in the lifetime of the refugees. The seventy years Jeremiah mentions is the typical lifespan of an Israelite (see the "three score and ten years" of Psalm 90:10). Only after a lifetime of exile, presumably the passing of a generation, should the Judeans expect to return to their homeland.

NEW COVENANT (30–33)

While remembered mostly for his message of doom, Jeremiah's full mission, as defined at his calling, also included restoration: "to uproot and to break down, to destroy and to overturn, *to build and to plant*." Sometimes called "The Little Book of Comfort," chapters 30–33 contain Jeremiah's message of building and planting.

During the darkest days of the siege of Jerusalem in 588 B.C.E., Jeremiah had the opportunity to purchase some ancestral property in his hometown of Anathoth. With the Babylonians in control of the entire area, it would have seemed foolish for anyone to lay out good shekels to buy land. Yet that is exactly what Jeremiah did. His cousin Hanamel, from whom he bought it, must have thought Jeremiah an idiot. But by this act, Jeremiah was literally putting his money where his mouth was, affirming his deepest faith that Yahweh would not abandon his people or forever remove them from the Promised Land.

An additional expression of Jeremiah's faith, though this time mostly in prophetic poetry, comes in chapters 30–31 (see Bozak 1991). These chapters are undated, and scholars' opinions vary. Certain portions seem to echo the early chapters of Jeremiah, which date to the first years of his prophetic activity. But the overriding theme of restoration and rebuilding may suggest a setting immediately prior to the destruction of Jerusalem. Jeremiah was instructed to write down God's words as a testimony of their return.

> 30:3 For see, in the coming days, YHWH's word, I will restore the restoration of my people Israel and Judah, said YHWH, and I will bring about their restoration to the land which I gave to their fathers, and they will possess it.

Here, and in the remainder of these chapters, Jeremiah affirms the basics of the faith, including possession of the land of Palestine and the unity of Judah and Israel.

Jeremiah is rightly famous for articulating this faith in terms of a renewed covenant with Yahweh. Jeremiah 31:31–34 builds on the old covenant and adds new features.

> 31:31 See, in the coming days (YHWH's word) I will make a new covenant with the house of Israel and the house of Judah. 32 It will not be like the covenant which I made with their fathers when I took them by their hand to bring them out of the land of Egypt—my covenant which they broke, though I was their lord (YHWH's word). 33 Rather, this is the covenant I will make with the house of Israel after those days (YHWH's word): I will put my torah inside them, I will write it on their hearts. I will be their God, and they will be my people. 34 No longer will friends and relatives teach each other saying, "Know YHWH!" All of them will know me, from the least to the greatest of them (YHWH's word). I will forgive their faults, and their sins I will never remember.

In this remarkable passage, Jeremiah affirms the continuity of the Mosaic formulation of covenant. The allusions to the exodus are clear. The essential content of this **new covenant** will remain the same: the union of Yahweh and his people in a bond of unity. But the newness lies in the way the essence of the covenant will be internalized. Yahweh will put his torah inside them. Furthermore, in the future God will overlook breaches of covenant as he did not do in the past. Jeremiah is laying the groundwork for a restoration not just of Israel's homeland and institutions, but of the Israelites' fundamental relationship to God.

AFTER THE FALL OF JERUSALEM (587–582 B.C.E.)

The fall of Jerusalem in 587 B.C.E. fulfilled Jeremiah's predictions of doom. On the surface Jeremiah's foretelling of Babylonian victory made it appear he was sympathetic to the victors. Though captured with others at the fall of Jerusalem, he was later released and given permission to travel wherever he wished. He was in the good graces of the Babylonians.

The story of Jeremiah's last years is told in chapters 39–44. Jeremiah remained in Judah for a time. Gedaliah was appointed governor of Judah by the Babylonians. He was betrayed by rival Judeans because he cooperated with the Babylonians and was assassinated in 582. Following the death of Gedaliah, Jeremiah was forced to travel to Egypt with a group of refugees. While there he continued to prophesy until his death.

JEREMIAH'S COMPLAINTS

A distinctive feature of the book of Jeremiah is a set of autobiographical passages that provide insight into the prophet's inner feelings about God and his calling. Called the "Confessions of Jeremiah" by some scholars, they are really laments or complaints that Jeremiah addressed to God. These passages have similarities to the individual complaint psalms of the Psalter. **Jeremiah's complaints** are found in 11:18–12:6, 15:10–21, 17:14–18, 18:18–23, 20:7–13, and 20:14–18. In them he expressed his feelings of frustration in being a prophet. He claimed that his enemies within Judean political and prophetic circles seemed always to get the upper hand. He accused God of abandoning him, even though he had been promised support. The complaint in 20:7–13 is especially direct in its criticism of God.

> 7 YHWH, you have seduced me, and I fell for it, you have overpowered me, and you have won. I have become a perpetual laughable clown, everybody mocks me. 8 Whenever I speak up and cry out I feel compelled to shout, "Bloody murder!"

The language here is quite strong. Jeremiah goes so far as to say that God "seduced" him; in effect, raped him. Not only are his political opponents his enemies, God even seems so at times.

The reasons for Jeremiah's disillusionment are apparent. Jeremiah experienced mistreatment at the hands of the Jerusalem establishment. He was opposed by priests and prophets, as we saw in chapter 26. At various other times he was punished by royal officials when he seemed to be advocating the demise of the Judean monarchy. Pashur, a priest, beat Jeremiah and put him in stocks overnight after he heard Jeremiah preach the submission of Judah (20:1–6).

One especially notable incident happened right before the fall of Jerusalem, as told in chapters 37–38. When he tried to leave Jerusalem during the siege of 588 to travel to his home tribe of Benjamin on legitimate business, he was arrested and was accused of treason and inciting desertion. Court officials tried to kill him by dropping him into a cistern. Normally full of water, fortunately for Jeremiah only muck was in the hole. A friend at court pleaded his case with Zedekiah, who allowed him to be lifted out of the cistern.

These incidents indicate how Jeremiah suffered the consequences for his unpopular views. Although we have these examples of rough treatment, we cannot definitively connect his complaints with any specific one of them or attach them to any identifiable period in the life of Jeremiah. They could be general reflections on his prophetic calling or undated but specific reactions to personal experiences.

Only one of the complaints seems to be tied by editorial arrangement to a specific incident. The placement of chapter 20 implies that the complaint of 20:7–18 is a response to the physical beating that Jeremiah took from Pashur in the temple.

In spite of their general lack of context, the complaints of Jeremiah are theologically significant, even remarkable. They are amazing for the way they express Jeremiah's feelings of alienation, not only from fellow citizens, but also from God. Yet the frankness of Jeremiah in not hiding his feeling of betrayal from God, but facing God directly, is to be appreciated for its courage and honesty.

OVERALL SHAPE OF THE BOOK OF JEREMIAH

As we have seen, the final shape of the Book of Jeremiah is somewhat convoluted. The book was constructed out of a variety of materials, including autobiography, biography, and narratives showing signs of Deuteronomic reworking, and these were not always arranged in chronological order. In spite of the compositional problems, certain structural trends can be identified.

Chapters 1–25 stand out as a structural unit. They consist mostly of Jeremiah's own prophetic statements and include some autobiographical and biographical material. Perhaps this is what was contained on the scroll written down by Baruch.

Chapters 26–45, on the other hand, mostly contain biographical narratives about Jeremiah. Chapters 46–51 are judgment statements directed against Judah's enemies. And chapter 52, the final chapter, contains an account of the fall of Jerusalem, taken from 2 Kings 24:18–25:30.

One of the most interesting compositional issues concerns the book's purpose. This is related to its intended audience. Clearly the book in its final form was compiled after the destruction of Jerusalem in 587 B.C.E. The Babylonian invasion and its devastating results were proof positive of the truth of Jeremiah's prophetic gift. He had been right all along! Someone, apparently someone dominated by the Deuteronomic perspective of guilt and punishment, saw the truth in Jeremiah's life and teaching and fashioned his message into a form that could serve as preaching to the surviving refugees in exile (see Nicholson 1970). The core message was this: Yahweh had not abandoned his people. They had to be punished for their sins, but the covenant was still in effect. In fact it was a new covenant, new in the way God would relate to his people.

QUESTIONS FOR REVIEW

1. What were the main phases of Jeremiah's career in relation to the history of Judah? What was the basic thrust of Jeremiah's prophetic ministry before the destruction of Jerusalem, and what was its thrust after the destruction? In what way did his message change?

2. Jeremiah prophesied in Jerusalem but had family roots in Israel, in particular, Anathoth. How does his message reflect the regional tension that existed between north (Israel) and south (Judah and Jerusalem)?

3. What vocabulary and themes suggest that Jeremiah had a connection with the theological perspective of the Deuteronomic school?

4. How did Jeremiah both affirm the importance of the Mosaic formulation of God's covenant with his people and give it a new twist?

5. What are "Jeremiah's complaints," and what insight do they give you into the personal relationship of the prophet with God?

QUESTIONS FOR DISCUSSION

1. In propounding the "new covenant," Jeremiah stressed that God would forgive the Israelites their sins and renew his relationship with them. What do you think Jeremiah meant by forgiveness? Does God forget what the people have done? Or does he simply disregard? What do the people have to do to get this thing called forgiveness?

2. Jeremiah's autobiographical complaints contain frank indictments of God and the way he treated Jeremiah. Study these complaints again. Do you think Jeremiah had the right to call God into question? Do you think God actually misled Jeremiah at any point? Was God at fault? Can God be at fault? Should Jeremiah have been so frank and forthright with God?

FOR FURTHER STUDY

The premiere commentary on Jeremiah is the two-volume set in the Hermeneia series by Holladay.

Blank, Sheldon H. (1986). *Jeremiah*. Philadelphia: Westminster Press.

Carroll, Robert P. (1986). *Jeremiah*. Philadelphia: Westminster Press. A major commentary that treats the Jeremiah traditions with considerable skepticism. Views the prose material as the work of a postexilic Deuteronomic school, and the poetry as the work not of Jeremiah but of anonymous exilic prophets.

Holladay, William L. (1986). *Jeremiah 1: A Commentary on the Book of the Prophet Jeremiah, Chapters 1–25*. Hermeneia Series. Philadelphia: Fortress Press. A major commentary that treats both the prose and the poetic material of the book of Jeremiah as coming essentially from Jeremiah himself.

Holladay, William L. (1989). *Jeremiah 2: A Commentary on the Book of the Prophet Jeremiah, Chapters 26–52*. Hermeneia Series. Philadelphia: Fortress Press.

Holladay, William L. (1990). *Jeremiah: A Fresh Reading*. New York: Pilgrim Press. Based on a lifetime of study in Jeremiah, this makes Holladay's research more easily accessible to the general reader than his massive and more technical two-volume commentary.

McKane, William (1986). *The Book of Jeremiah*. Vol I. International Critical Commentary Series. Edinburgh: T. & T. Clark. He takes a mediating position between Holladay and Carroll. He credits the prose material to an exilic Deuteronomic writer and attributes the poetry to Jeremiah himself.

WORKS CITED

Bozak, Barbara (1991). *Life 'Anew.' A Literary–Theological Study of Jeremiah 30–31*. Analecta Biblical 122. Rome: Pontifical Biblical Institute.

Nicholson, E. W. (1970). *Preaching to the Exiles: A Study of the Prose Traditions in the Book of Jeremiah*. Oxford: Basil Blackwell.

EZEKIEL

12

Names and Terms to Remember

Ezekiel	Throne–Chariot
Glory of Yahweh	Zadok
Gog	

For the survivors, the destruction of Jerusalem and the Babylonian exile was as painful a loss as the death of a loved one. Psychologists tell us that those who experience great loss go through predictable stages of grief, including denial, anger, and acceptance. The surviving Judeans felt all these emotions. And **Ezekiel**, as God's prophetic "pastor," supported them through this process.

But he was a curious pastor by today's standards. His way of providing pastoral support was to expose the people's responsibility for the disaster that afflicted them and tell them that their only hope for recovery was to change. No warm fuzzies from Ezekiel. Yet through it all Ezekiel never abandoned God's people or saw their situation as hopeless.

Ezekiel endured the Babylonian exile with the people, then emerged on the far side to present a vision of what the survivors must do to rebuild an identity. Ezekiel was a key figure in the survival of a Judean identity, and he was a major transitional figure in the move from an Israelite religion to what became the religion of Judaism.

EZEKIEL AND THE EXILE

Ezekiel was taken to Babylonia in 598 B.C.E. in the first major deportation of Judeans to the land of their conquerors. It appears that he was taken in that early deportation because he was a priest. In all, almost five thousand Judeans were taken to Babylonia in that early displacement. Those taken were the leaders of the community, including royalty, scribes, counselors, craftsmen, and religious leaders.

Ezekiel stayed in Babylonia for his entire career, being a prophet until at least 571. He was unable to perform the traditional priestly functions in exile, which included offering sacrifices of atonement and guarding the holiness of the community. Still, his vocation shaped his perspective on virtually everything, including religious obligations and relationships to God.

Being a priest from Jerusalem meant that he was thoroughly familiar with the rituals and procedures of temple service. This familiarity is evident in his visions, many of which center on the temple.

A priestly orientation also meant he was profoundly shaped by the experience of serving in the presence of Yahweh in the temple. Priests referred to the divine presence by the term **glory of Yahweh**. It was believed that the presence of Yahweh in Jerusalem bestowed favor on the city and its people. Attentiveness to the divine presence dominated Ezekiel's experience.

Ezekiel was a contemporary of Jeremiah. Both were prophets immediately before and after the destruction of Jerusalem (see Figure 12.1).

The structure of the book of Ezekiel is fairly straightforward. It follows a chronological progression and has a topical arrangement within that chronologi-

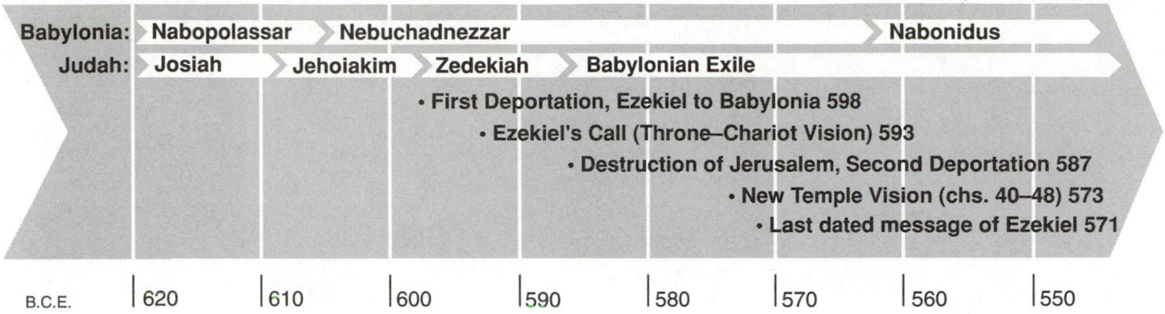

Babylonia:	Nabopolassar	Nebuchadnezzar				Nabonidus		
Judah:	Josiah	Jehoiakim	Zedekiah	Babylonian Exile				

• First Deportation, Ezekiel to Babylonia 598
• Ezekiel's Call (Throne–Chariot Vision) 593
• Destruction of Jerusalem, Second Deportation 587
• New Temple Vision (chs. 40–48) 573
• Last dated message of Ezekiel 571

B.C.E.	620	610	600	590	580	570	560	550

FIGURE 12.1   TIME LINE: BOOK OF EZEKIEL

cal framework. The book consists of two main parts, each with identifiable subsections. Although some scholars view the oracles against foreign nations as a separate main section, we include it in the "Hope and Restoration" section because the demise of the foreign nations is the precondition of Israel's restoration.

Outline of the Book of Ezekiel

I. Prophetic Warnings (before 587 B.C.E.): chapters 1–24
  A. Throne–chariot vision (1–3)
  B. Symbolic acts (4–7)
  C. Vision of a corrupted temple (8–11)
  D. Symbolic acts and allegories of disaster (12–24)
II. Hope and Restoration (after 587): chapters 25–48
  A. Oracles against foreign nations (25–32)
  B. Words of hope after the fall of Jerusalem (33–39)
  C. Vision of a restored temple (40–48)

The book of Ezekiel is much easier to follow than the book of Jeremiah because of its logical and chronological structure. It also has a certain thematic unity. At least three major issues interweave the book, surfacing in various ways.

First, Ezekiel gives considerable attention to the continued presence of God among his people, along with the reasons for God's withdrawal and conditions under which he would reappear. Second, Ezekiel probes the issue of moral responsibility for the religious and political failures of Judah. Third, although with less attention than the preceding two, Ezekiel examines the nature and legitimacy of religious and political leadership in Judah and in the restored community.

Be alert to these issues as we examine the book of Ezekiel.

PROPHETIC WARNINGS BEFORE 587 B.C.E. (1–24)

Chapters 1–24 contain Ezekiel's visions and prophetic pronouncements dating between 593 (the date of his initiating experience) and the fall of Jerusalem in

587. Much of the material was written in the first person as Ezekiel's autobiographical recollections.

The pervasive tone of the first half of the book is divine anger.

> *5:13 My anger will find completion, and I will vent my fury on them. And they will know that I, YHWH, have spoken out of my jealousy for them, when my fury finds completion on them: 14 "I will make you a desolation and an object of derision among the nations which surround you and among those who see you as they pass by."*

Yahweh was in a rage because the people had betrayed him.

THRONE-CHARIOT VISION (1-3)

The first chapter of the book is a description of Ezekiel's visionary encounter with God in Babylonia. This vision of God set the stage for Ezekiel's commission into the prophetic ministry. It occurred in 593 when Ezekiel was in Babylonia with fellow refugees who had been taken there in 598. This is the beginning of what Ezekiel saw in the vision.

> *1:4 Now, as I looked I saw a stormy wind come from the north, a huge cloud with fire flashing and shining around it, and in the middle of it something like amber, in the middle of the fire. 5 And in the middle of it was the likeness of four animals. This is their appearance: they had the likeness of a human.*

We note the following: The language of these verses, indeed the entire vision account, is highly descriptive, and the syntax is difficult. What is in the middle of what? How are the elements related? It's not at all clear. What we get are mostly impressions and images. Ezekiel saw a storm approaching from the north, it glowed from the inside, and strange hybrid creatures were in the middle of it.

If nothing else, what becomes clear is that Ezekiel experienced a theophany—an experience of standing in the presence of God. Although the language and the combination of images here are especially creative, it is clear that we are in the conceptual realm of the storm, cloud, and fire theophany we noticed in the divine-human encounters of Moses (Exodus 24), Elijah (1 Kings 19), Isaiah (Isaiah 6), and elsewhere (see Psalm 18).

Ezekiel's description of the theophany takes up an entire chapter. It becomes apparent that each of the four creatures had four faces (human, lion, ox, and eagle) and four wings (see Figure 12.2). The creatures with their wings appear to be hybrid angels, no doubt somehow related to the divine council of Yahweh, sometimes called the *cherubim*. Wheels attached to these creatures gave the "storm" its means of locomotion. Stretched out over the wings of these creatures was a *dome*—the same term that designated the "expanse" created on the second day, according to the Genesis 1 account of creation. Then Ezekiel saw a figure seated above the dome.

FIGURE 12.2 **WILLIAM BLAKE'S "EZEKIEL'S WHEELS"** Ezekiel's vision of God inspired this design by William Blake (circa 1803). In Babylonian captivity Ezekiel saw God approach him carried on the wings of four angelic beings, each with four faces. This vision expresses Ezekiel's confidence that God was present with his people even in distant Babylonia under the most difficult circumstances.

(Purchased 1890. Courtesy, Museum of Fine Arts, Boston.)

1:26 Above the dome over their heads I saw a sapphire-colored throne-like thing. Seated on this throne-like thing was something like a human. 27 And I saw something like amber with fire in the middle of it from its midsection up. From its midsection down I saw something like fire, and it was shining all around. 28 Like a rainbow on a rainy day, so was the sheen around it. It had an appearance similar to the glory of YHWH. I saw it and fell on my face. And I heard a voice speaking.

You can tell Ezekiel is struggling to articulate exactly what it is he saw. He struggled to give description to something the likes of which had never been seen before. Repeatedly he says, "I saw something like . . . " His uncertain descriptions perhaps reflect his incredulity in seeing what he finally realized he was seeing. It finally dawned on him that he was seeing some form of God himself on the throne. The New Revised Standard Version well expresses the tentativeness with which he states it: "This was the appearance of the likeness of the glory of the Lord."

Note that Ezekiel does not claim to see God directly but only his "glory." The glory of God is evidence of his presence, an aura of sorts, an apparition. This is priestly language (no surprise, since Ezekiel was a priest), used often to describe this presence of God. Among other things, "the glory of Yahweh" recalls the descriptions of God's appearance to the Israelites in the wilderness.

Taking the vision as a whole, Ezekiel seems to be describing a notion of great significance. In the vision Yahweh was seen to be traveling on a mobile throne, a version of the ark of the covenant, borne by special cherubs of the Divine Council. Normally thought to be permanently housed in the holiest room of the Jerusalem temple, now Yahweh on his throne was movable. In other words, Yahweh had wheels! He was not restricted to the territory of Judah but could travel abroad, even so far from home that he could be with his people in exile.

Yahweh came to Babylonia in his **throne–chariot** to commission Ezekiel to be a prophetic voice to the Judean refugees. Ezekiel was to be a watchman to the house of Israel. The metaphor used of his vocation is that of a sentinel standing on a tower, seeing the evidence of coming disaster and conveying God's warning to the people so they could prepare for trouble.

To equip him for his prophetic role, God handed Ezekiel a scroll on which were written words of woe. He ate the scroll, which curiously was sweet as

LATER INTERPRETATIONS OF THE THRONE–CHARIOT VISION

The throne–chariot vision had a mystical quality about it in a later Jewish context. A form of mysticism, called *merkavah* (after the Hebrew word for *chariot*) mysticism, developed in Medieval Judaism. The vision was considered so powerful that underage men were not allowed to read it.

A more radical interpretation of the vision appeared in the once widely popular (but really quite wacky) book by Erich von Däniken titled *Chariots of the Gods*. In the chapter "Was God an Astronaut?" he suggests that Ezekiel saw an extraterrestrial vehicle, an "unidentified flying object" (UFO). From out of this vehicle travelers from outer space gave Ezekiel "advice and directions for law and order, as well as hints for creating a proper civilization."

honey, rather than sour as expected. Having internalized the word of God, he was sent to deliver the message—never mind whether the people heeded the warning or not (that was not Ezekiel's responsibility). The experience of commissioning and the message he was to bring were so traumatic that Ezekiel was overwhelmed and remained unable to speak for seven days afterward.

Although imaginative in its handling of the details, Ezekiel's commissioning contains many of the standard elements of other prophetic call narratives. The most common elements are standing in the presence of God in his throne room, seeing God in the form of fire or brilliant light, and the equipping of the prophet's mouth to convey the word of God. Remember that a prophet was essentially a messenger who received a message directly from God and then delivered it to the target audience.

SYMBOLIC ACTS (4–7)

The burden of Ezekiel's prophetic career from 593 B.C.E. until 587 was to convince the Babylonian refugees that God was punishing them for their wickedness through the exile, and that instead of getting better, things first were going to get worse.

Ezekiel not only spoke words of warning, he also acted them out. He made a clay model of the city of Jerusalem and played out a siege of the city. Then he lay on the ground, first on his left side for 390 days and then on his right side for 40 days, to symbolize the captivity of the two kingdoms, Israel and Judah respectively. While on the ground he ate only small amounts of food to simulate siege rations.

Then he shaved his head with a sword and disposed of the hair in ways that symbolized the fate of Jerusalem after its fall. One-third he burned, one-third he struck with the sword, and one-third he scattered to the wind. A small wisp of hair he stitched up in the hem of his garment to symbolize the small remnant that would survive.

Lastly, Ezekiel faced in the direction of Palestine and announced the coming destruction of the nation of Israel and specifically its religious installations that promoted the worship of pagan fertility goddesses.

These signs have engendered scholarly discussion. Some take the bizarre nature of these acts as an indication that Ezekiel was psychologically troubled, and have tried to define his psychosis. Others observe that we are not told how his audience reacted, suggesting that he never really performed these acts, and that they are merely literary in character. Others stress the symbolic nature of these acts.

VISION OF A CORRUPTED TEMPLE (8–11)

In a vision dated to 592 B.C.E., Ezekiel was transported back to the temple in Jerusalem. There he witnessed a variety of improper activities. The religious leaders of Jerusalem were secretly worshiping foreign gods in the temple compound. Women were devoted to Tammuz, the Babylonian fertility god.

These activities were an outrage to Yahweh. In consequence, he got up to leave the temple. Ezekiel's description of Yahweh's departure utilizes the throne–chariot imagery of chapter 1. The "glory of Yahweh" mounted the cherub-driven vehicle. In stages Yahweh exited the temple, stopping at certain points, including the threshold of the temple and the east gate of the courtyard, as if reluctant to leave. Hovering over Jerusalem, then over the Mount of Olives east of the city, finally Yahweh was gone.

The people had driven away Yahweh by their corrupt practices. He would no longer be there to protect them. And they would be taken into captivity. This is the message that Ezekiel brought to the exiles: Jerusalem would fall as punishment from Yahweh.

But Ezekiel did not leave them without hope. Ezekiel assured his audience that Yahweh would not abandon them. Instead, he would gather them from among the nations of their exile and reaffirm his covenant with them.

> 11:19 I will give them one heart, and I will put a new spirit inside them. I will remove the heart of stone from their flesh and give them a heart of flesh. 20 Then they will follow my directives, and my laws they will obey and do them. They will be my people and I will be God to them.

In Hebrew anthropology the heart was not the seat of emotions but was the center of the will and the seat of rationality. A new heart and spirit, which Ezekiel cites here and elsewhere, indicates a new willingness to abide by the covenant. In words reminiscent of Jeremiah's new covenant (31:31–34), this talk of a new spirit and a transformed heart voices the hope that the people will undergo a spiritual transformation. Although the heart of the people would change, inspiring new devotion to keeping the covenant, the original intent of the Mosaic covenant remained the same: "They will be my people and I will be their God."

As a whole, this section (chapters 8–11) describes how false worship drove away the glory of Yahweh. The theme comes full circle at the end of the book of Ezekiel in an elaborate program of restoration, chapters 40–48. Specifically, in chapter 43 Ezekiel describes how true worship would bring the glory of Yahweh back to Jerusalem.

SYMBOLIC ACTS AND ALLEGORIES OF DISASTER (12–24)

Ezekiel took symbolic actions and drew numerous word pictures in an attempt to convince his compatriots that Jerusalem would fall and that they should not hold out for an early return from exile.

To symbolize the imminent fall of Jerusalem, Ezekiel packed his bags and in the middle of the night dug through a wall and hurried away as if to escape (chapter 12). In another image he compared Jerusalem to a vine that is no longer productive, so its branches can serve only as fuel for a fire (chapter 15).[1]

Chapter 16 contains an extended allegory of the history of Jerusalem. The main figure in the allegory is Jerusalem in the guise of a female who turns out to

---

[1] The imagery of the vine is also used by Isaiah (5:1–7) and Jeremiah (2:21), and also became a symbol for the New Testament church (Gospel of John 15:1–11).

be an unfaithful wife to Yahweh.[2] The allegory is developed in great detail. Jerusalem is first described as the daughter of an Amorite father and a Hittite mother. Abandoned by her parents, she was adopted by Yahweh, who cared for her and made her beautiful. But then she used her God-given advantages to entice and seduce foreigners. God, in turn, used those foreigners to punish his wife. But ultimately he did not disown her, restoring her instead to full status as wife in covenant with God. The allegory of Oholah and Oholibah in chapter 23 likewise describes the unfaithfulness of Israel and Judah in terms of women wed to Yahweh.

Ezekiel used extended images of eagles, trees, and vines to depict the uprooting of Judah and its kings in chapter 17. In chapter 18 Ezekiel addressed the issue of responsibility and blame. It seems Judeans were seeking to disown responsibility for the current state of affairs. They blamed their troubles with the Babylonians and the weakness of Judah on the sins of their fathers. The following proverb was widely quoted by the people to justify this analysis:[3]

18:2 *"The fathers have eaten sour grapes and the children's teeth are set on edge."*

Ezekiel denied the continuing validity and applicability of this proverb and instead asserted that Yahweh knows each person individually. All people would be judged on the basis of their own actions. All people should know that they get what they deserve—on the positive side, if they repent they can be delivered.

18:30 *Therefore I will judge you, house of Israel, each person according to his ways (the Lord YHWH's word). Turn and repent of all your offenses, and do not let them be a stumbling block leading to iniquity. 31 Toss away from you all your offenses by which you offend, and make for yourselves a new heart and new spirit. Why die, house of Israel?! 32 I do not relish the death of the dead (the Lord YHWH's word). Repent and live!*

This passage is subject to varying applications. Many commentators argue that here in Ezekiel we have one of the first evidences of individual moral identity as opposed to a corporate concept of identity, the first glimmerings of individualism. But this may be reading too much into it.

Joyce (1989) argues that Ezekiel was not affirming individual responsibility but was declaring that each *generation* makes its own moral choices and is not bound by either the sins or the merits of the preceding generation. Ezekiel in effect cuts the moral link between generations. And this cuts two ways. On the one hand, the past shortcomings of the parents do not predetermine that the children must be punished. On the other hand, the current generation can no longer use

---

[2] The literary comparison of Israel to a bride or wife is a common prophetic device in biblical literature. It was used by Hosea (chapters 1–3) and Jeremiah (chapter 2). The relationship of the man and woman in the Songs of Songs was taken by the rabbis as an extended metaphor for Yahweh's relationship to Israel.

[3] Jeremiah also cites this proverb (see 31:27–30) and says that while it may have been true in the past, in the days to come each person would be liable for his or her own sins.

the preceding generation for an excuse; it has to stand on its own moral two feet. Ezekiel told his generation, put aside your self-pity and fatalistic thinking. Take responsibility for change, and then there is hope.

Ezekiel continued to preach that ample opportunity for restoration would be given, if only the people would acknowledge their complicity and repent. But throughout this entire section Ezekiel was invariably pessimistic about Israel's interest in repenting. Ezekiel failed to see any good in Israel at all and viewed the people as base, ungrateful, and unfaithful.

After oracles and images assuring his audience of coming disaster, this section ends with its most powerful statement yet (chapter 24). Ezekiel's dearly beloved wife died, and this understandably plunged him into deepest grief. But, by God's instructions, he did not shed a tear or give sign of mourning. This stoicism stood as a sign of God's own resolve, as presumably God determined not to be overcome by sentiment and forgo the punishment. Ezekiel did not speak another word, and by implication, Yahweh himself was silent until Jerusalem had fallen.

HOPE AND RESTORATION AFTER 587 B.C.E. (25–48)

The second half of the book of Ezekiel, written after the destruction of Jerusalem in 587, promotes the territorial and spiritual restoration of Israel. Ezekiel tries to build the hope of the people and assures them that Judah will be restored and God will return to Jerusalem.

ORACLES AGAINST FOREIGN NATIONS (25–32)

A series of oracles against the oppressors of God's people is a common feature of prophetic books.[4] A set of such oracles of judgment is found in Ezekiel 25–32. The following nations and city–states come under verbal attack and condemnation: Ammon, Moab, Edom, Philistia, Tyre, Sidon, and Egypt. These were all entities in the immediate vicinity of Judah who took advantage of Judah's woes to increase their own spheres of influence (see Figure 12.3).

These judgment oracles served at least two theological functions for Ezekiel's audience in the exile. First, they reaffirmed God's justice. By all standards of judgment these nations were no better than Judah; indeed, they were less humane and more ungodly. Ultimately they would have to be punished by God, even though then they were being used by God to punish Judah. Second, their power and influence would have to be checked in order for Judah's political restoration to take place.

Tyre and Egypt are objects of special curse in this series of oracles against the nations. Tyre is condemned in three chapters (26–28) and Egypt in four (29–32). The lamentation over the king of Tyre (28:11–19) is especially interesting for its description of the king as primeval man in the Garden of Eden.

> *28:12 You were a perfect seal, full of wisdom, altogether beautiful. 13 You were in Eden, the Garden of God. Every precious stone covered you: car-*

---

[4] Compare Isaiah 13–23, Jeremiah 46–51, and the entire books of Obadiah and Nahum.

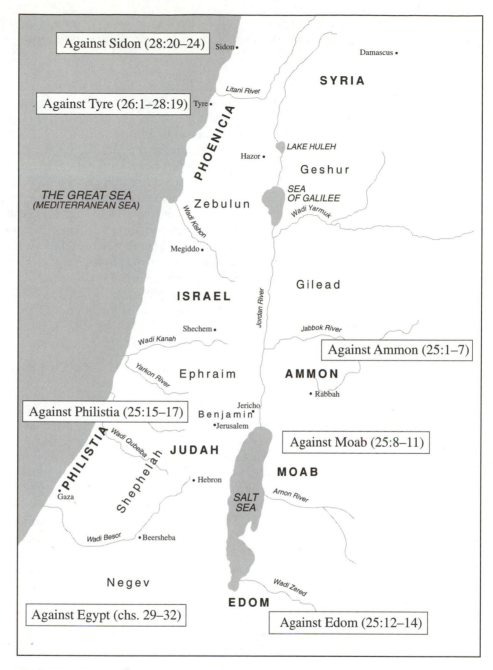

Against Sidon (28:20–24)

Sidon •

Damascus •

SYRIA

Litani River

Against Tyre (26:1–28:19)

Tyre •

P H O E N I C I A

LAKE HULEH

Hazor •

G e s h u r

SEA OF GALILEE

THE GREAT SEA (MEDITERRANEAN SEA)

Z e b u l u n

Wadi Kishon

Wadi Yarmuk

Megiddo •

ISRAEL

Gilead

Jordan River

Shechem •

Jabbok River

Against Ammon (25:1–7)

Wadi Kanah

E p h r a i m

AMMON

Yarkon River

• Rabbah

Against Philistia (25:15–17)

Jericho

Benjamin •

• Jerusalem

Against Moab (25:8–11)

P H I L I S T I A

Wadi Qubeiba

JUDAH

Shephelah

• Hebron

MOAB

• Gaza

SALT SEA

Arnon River

Wadi Besor

• Beersheba

N e g e v

Wadi Zered

Against Egypt (chs. 29–32)

EDOM

Against Edom (25:12–14)

FIGURE 12.3   EZEKIEL'S ORACLES AGAINST THE NATIONS

nelian, chrysolite, and amethyst . . . 14 With an anointed guardian cherub I placed you on the holy mountain of God. You walked among the shining stones. 15 You were blameless in your ways from the day I created you, until iniquity was found in you. 16. In connection with your far-reaching trading you became full of lawlessness, and you sinned. So I cast you down from the mountain of God, and the guardian cherub drove you from among the shining stones.

This description of beauty in the garden, expulsion, and the guardian angel recalls features of the creation story of Genesis 2–3. Though no serpent is involved in this story, sin is the reason for the expulsion, specifically the ruthlessness of the king of Tyre. Elements additional to the Genesis version are the location of the garden of Eden on the mountain of God and the business of the fiery, shining stones. Taken with Genesis 2–3, this story is corroborating evidence that primeval beginnings in Eden, followed by expulsion, were widely believed.

Ezekiel used the creation scenario to characterize the king of Tyre as an evil man who deserved his downfall. History tells us that Tyre held out against Nebuchadnezzar and the Babylonians for thirteen years. This gave many in Judah faint hope that they, too, might be able to hold out against Babylonia. But Tyre ultimately fell. Ezekiel used his lament over fallen Tyre to disabuse his fellow exiles of the notion that holding out against Babylonia would be successful. The reuse of the creation story in its application to Tyre is a fascinating example of the way the story was historicized. That is, the drama of creation was seen as a veiled account of historical events.

WORDS OF HOPE AFTER THE FALL OF JERUSALEM (33–39)

Chapters 33–39 contain oracles of restoration, written after the predicted final destruction of Jerusalem had become reality. In chapter 34 Ezekiel depicted the past rulers of Israel as negligent shepherds. In their place God would become the Good Shepherd who would rescue his sheep from disaster.[5] He would also restore the Davidic monarchy. Extending the shepherd metaphor, he says this.

34:23 I will establish one shepherd over them and he will shepherd them— my servant David. He will shepherd them and he will be their shepherd. 24 And I, YHWH, will be their God, and my servant David a prince among them.

Ezekiel never gave up hope in the rebirth of the Davidic rule. Jehoiachin was still alive and living in exile with Ezekiel. He remained the focus of the people's hope. The Judean refugees and those back in Palestine continued to look to the line of David for restoration of the nation. The mention of "one shepherd" expresses Ezekiel's hope that the two kingdoms, Israel and Judah, would once again be united. This reference to the line of David is one of the latest expressions of Davidic messianic expectation in prophetic literature.

But the reference to the Davidic leader as a prince rather than as king is somewhat puzzling. The use of this term is consistent with the restoration vision of chapters 40–48, where David is consistently referred to as prince. The question is this: Was this way of referring to David an expression of antimonarchic senti-

---

[5] The use of the shepherd motif in the New Testament Gospel of John 10:1–18 has affinities with this chapter from Ezekiel.

ment on Ezekiel's part, or was he just expressing the old covenant's theocratic ideals?[6] The issue of leadership, its shape and legitimacy, remained a major one throughout the exile and well into the period of restoration.

In chapter 36 Ezekiel reiterates the internal spiritual dimension of the restoration.

> 36:26 *I will give you a new heart, and a new spirit I will put inside you. I will remove the heart of stone from your body and give you a heart of flesh.*

This was earlier expressed in chapter 11, and some of the implications are drawn out in following verses. The ground itself would gain from this restoration. Grain would be abundant, and fruits and vegetables would abound. There would never be famine again. The people would be cleansed and forgiven, and even the land would reap the benefits.

Ezekiel's most powerful image of restoration is the vision of the valley of dry bones (chapter 37). Yahweh took Ezekiel in a vision to a vast valley filled with parched human bones. God told him to prophesy to these bones, to implore them to come to life. As he preached, the bones began to rattle and shake. They came together to make skeletons, then ligaments bound them together, and skin covered them. Ezekiel continued to preach, a spirit-wind infused the bodies, and they became alive.

AFRICAN-AMERICAN SPIRITUAL

The famous African-American spiritual "Dry Bones" derives from Ezekiel's valley full of bones vision.

Ezekiel cried them dry bones.
Now hear the word of the Lord.
Ezekiel connected them dry bones.
Now hear the word of the Lord.
Your toe bone connected to your
  foot bone.
Your foot bone connected to your
  ankle bone.
Your ankle bone connected to your
  leg bone.
Your leg bone connected to your
  thigh bone.
Your thigh bone connected to your
  hip bone.

Your hip bone connected to your
  back bone.
Your back bone connected to your
  shoulder bone.
Your shoulder bone connected to
  your neck bone.
Your neck bone connected to your
  head bone.
Now hear the word of the Lord.
Them bones gonna walk around.
Now hear the word of the Lord.

The dry bones were Israel of the exile, and Ezekiel foresaw the day when they would be reborn as a nation and returned to their land. It can also be taken as an affirmation of the life-giving potential of prophetic preaching. Above all, the

---

[6] Levenson (1976: 55–107) discusses this issue at length and argues that the use of prince rather than king is not a rejection of the institution of kingship.

word of God, accompanied by the spirit-wind of Yahweh, can bring the nation back to life.

The imagery of Ezekiel turns apocalyptic in chapters 38–39 as he describes a great battle. **Gog** of the land of Magog is evil incarnate, a caricature of all Israel's enemies combined. This enemy comes out of the north, seeking to wipe out Israel once and for all. But after a cataclysmic battle, described in great detail in these chapters, God's people are victorious. Israel will be vindicated for all time.

The exaggerated character of this account and its future setting have prompted some interpreters to read this as a prescription for the final battle of Armageddon. More probably, it was an imaginative rendition of the expected confrontation with the Babylonians, who had long been the nemesis of Israel. The more grandiose the battle, the more impressive would be Yahweh's (and Israel's) victory.

VISION OF A RESTORED TEMPLE (40–48)

Ezekiel, remember, was a priest as well as a prophet. His most elaborate depiction of restoration naturally involved that most sacred of areas, the temple complex in Jerusalem. In a vision dated to 573 B.C.E. (twenty-five years after the beginning of his exile and twenty years after his call vision) he was given a vision of the restoration of the nation. The plan for restoration placed the temple at the center of the nation both physically and spiritually. Placing the temple in the center allowed for the dwelling of Yahweh, consistently called the glory of Yahweh in Ezekiel, in the middle of the people.

Ezekiel's vision for the future included the following important features of the restoration program. A rebuilt temple would be located in the geographical center of the tribes, which would be arrayed around it symmetrically, three to a side. The rights and privileges of serving in the temple itself would be given exclusively to priests from the line of **Zadok** of the family of Aaron.

The ground would be revived. A river of fresh water would flow from under the temple and run all the way to the Salt Sea, in the process making the sea wholesome and the surrounding wilderness a paradise. Jerusalem would once again be the center of attention. Its name would be changed to *Yahweh is there* because he would again take up residence.

Overall, Ezekiel had a comprehensive vision of the need for holiness and how it would be accomplished. He had a priest's sense of the need for devotion and worship centering on the presence of Yahweh in the temple. He combined this with a prophet's attention to inward spiritual renewal and devotion. His combination of devotion, as defined by the Mosaic covenant, along with an openness to the work of the spirit of God, makes him a major figure in the emergence of Judaism.

OVERALL SHAPE OF THE BOOK OF EZEKIEL

The book of Ezekiel evidences a deliberate and well-considered overall structure. It is framed beginning and end by visions of the presence of God, the "glory of

Yahweh." The early visions of corruption in the Jerusalem temple are balanced by the ending vision of restoration.

The general chronological flow is evident. The oracles against the nations interrupt the flow of material applying to Judah. But there is a logic to their placement. The foreign nations come under God's judgment and must be subdued before Israel is restored. The book as a whole also shows an intentional movement from prophecies of woe before the disaster of 587 (chapters 1–24) to prophecies of hope after the disaster (chapters 25–48).

Much of the critical scholarship on the book of Ezekiel concentrates on discerning the origin of individual prophetic units. Zimmerli (1979, 1983) takes great pains to separate what he judges to be texts original to Ezekiel from the commentary provided by later writers and editors. He gives priority to the former.

Childs (1979) says that such a distinction—along with the differing valuations of the traditions that usually mean giving privilege to Ezekiel's own oracles—overlooks the most important point for the book. The so-called commentary additions were canonized along with Ezekiel's originals. The commentary is evidence of how the originals were heard and applied by the community of faith, and they, too, bear scriptural authority.

QUESTIONS FOR REVIEW

1. What are the two main sections of the book of Ezekiel, and what is the basic message of each section?

2. Describe Ezekiel's throne–chariot vision and how it relates to his call to be a prophet.

3. When was Ezekiel taken to Babylonia and how long did he stay there?

4. How did Ezekiel try to convince his companions in exile that Jerusalem was going to be destroyed? Why did he try so hard to convince them of this?

5. What visions did Ezekiel have that related to the temple in Jerusalem?

6. What does the vision of the valley of dry bones signify?

QUESTIONS FOR DISCUSSION

1. Ezekiel judged Israel to be guilty of willfully disregarding Yahweh. The first twenty-three chapters are an unmitigated declaration of Yahweh's condemnation. Clearly, Ezekiel had a demanding standard of human moral responsibility against which the people were judged. Ezekiel presumed that the people knew right from wrong but just failed to do the right thing. Is this an adequate view of the nature of human failure and sin? What factors, other than sheer lack of willpower to do good, may be involved? Also, how does Ezekiel compare with other Hebrew prophets on the topic of sin and divine retribution?

2. The book of Ezekiel has an extended treatment of the issue of individual responsibility in chapter 18. Consider the nature of Ezekiel's argument and the adequacy of a view that posits individual responsibility for human destiny. Do we get what we deserve? How does what we "get" relate to our past, including family history and social context? Do you think Ezekiel really posited a theological doctrine of individual responsibility, or may there have been a rhetorical or homiletical purpose behind his way of relating to this issue?

FOR FURTHER STUDY

The Exile. The following books outline the history of the Babylonian exile and summarize the theology of the major Hebrew thinkers of this period.

Ackroyd, Peter R. (1968). *Exile and Restoration. A Study of Hebrew Thought of the 6th Century* B.C. Philadelphia: Westminster Press.

Klein, R.W. (1979). *Israel in Exile: A Theological Interpretation*. Overtures to Biblical Theology, 6. Philadelphia: Fortress.

Raitt, Thomas A. (1977). *A Theology of Exile*. Philadelphia: Fortress.

The Book of Ezekiel. The magisterial commentary on Ezekiel is by Zimmerli, who has devoted virtually a lifetime to its study. A catalog of the form-critical components of Ezekiel can be found in Hals.

Blenkinsopp, Joseph (1990). *Ezekiel*. Interpretation Series. Louisville, Ky.: Westminster/John Knox.

Carley, Keith W. (1975). *Ezekiel Among the Prophets*. SBT, 2d. series, 31. London: SCM Press.

David, Ellen F. (1989). *Swallowing the Scroll: Textuality and the Dynamics of Discourse in Ezekiel's Prophecy*. JSOT Supplement Series, 78. Sheffield: JSOT.

Greenberg, Moshe (1983). *Ezekiel 1–20*. The Anchor Bible. Garden City, N.Y.: Doubleday.

Hals, Ronald M. (1989). *Ezekiel*. The Forms of the Old Testament Literature. Grand Rapids, Mich.: Eerdmans.

Tuell, Steven Shawn (1992). *The Law of the Temple in Ezekiel 40–48*. Harvard Semitic Monograph Series. Atlanta: Scholars Press. This study traces Ezekiel's temple vision to the early Judean Restoration of the Persian period, and argues for a postexilic dating of the Priestly Writer.

Zimmerli, Walter (1982). *I Am Yahweh*. Atlanta: John Knox Press.

Zimmerli, Walter (1979, 1983). *Ezekiel*. Two volumes. Hermeneia Series. Philadelphia: Fortress. A major commentary, strong in form-critical and tradition-historical analysis. Demonstrates how Ezekiel has close parallels to the priestly tradition of the Holiness Code (Leviticus 17–26).

WORKS CITED

Childs, Brevard S. (1979). *Introduction to the Old Testament as Scripture*. Philadelphia: Fortress Press.

Joyce, Paul M. (1989). *Divine Initiative and Human Response in Ezekiel*. JSOT Supplement, 51. Sheffield: JSOT. Argues that Ezekiel was not most concerned to affirm the moral independence of individual persons, but to affirm the moral autonomy and independence of generations that are not bound to repeat the sins of the past.

Levenson, Jon D. (1976). *Theology of the Program of Restoration of Ezekiel 40–48*. Harvard Semitic Monographs, 10. Missoula, Mont.: Scholars Press.

Zimmerli, Walter (1979, 1983). *Ezekiel*. Two volumes. Hermeneia Series. Philadelphia: Fortress.

. . . we are not satisfied, and we will not be satisfied

until justice rolls down like waters and righteousness

like a mighty stream. . . . I have a dream that one day

every valley shall be exalted, every hill and mountain

shall be made low, the rough places shall be made

plain, and the crooked places shall be made straight

and the glory of the Lord will be revealed and all flesh

shall see it together. . . .

Excerpted from Martin Luther King Jr.'s "I Have a Dream"
speech, delivered at the Lincoln Memorial at the climax of the
March on Washington on August 28, 1963.

THE TWELVE PROPHETS

Names and Terms to Remember

Amaziah	Hosea	Nahum
Amos	Jezreel	Nineveh
Bethel	Joel	Obadiah
Book of the Twelve Prophets	Jonah	Second Zechariah
Day of Yahweh	Joshua	theodicy
Edom	Lo-ammi	Zechariah
Gomer	Lo-ruhamah	Zephaniah
Habakkuk	Malachi	Zerubbabel
Haggai	Micah	

The **Book of the Twelve Prophets** is a collection of the following twelve prophetic books. In canonical order they are Hosea, Joel, Amos, Obadiah, Jonah, Micah, Nahum, Habakkuk, Zephaniah, Haggai, Zechariah, and Malachi.

These books have been grouped together since the earliest canonical collections. Augustine in the fourth century C.E. seems to have been the first to call them the *minor* prophets (*City of God* 18.29). Although it may sound pejorative, they were labeled minor only because they are shorter in length than the "major" Latter Prophets. To be called the "Minor Prophets," as is done in some faith communities still today, tends to relegate them to the shadows. As we will see, there are some gems in these books, and they are worthy of attention.

"MINOR" PROPHETS

The prophets Habakkuk and Amos
Are considerably less famous
Than Isaiah or Jeremiah.
It's not that they lack fire
(The curse of any minor prophet
Can send a miscreant to Tophet).
But when they exhort,
They do keep it short.[1]

The Twelve Prophets contain expressions of the highest ideals of justice and righteousness and some of the most vivid pictures of the love of God. In addition, they provide significant insights into the nature of prophecy in Israel and Judah, as well as insights into the history of Israel's religion.

As with the longer books of the Latter Prophets, we have to make a special effort to integrate these books into the chronology of Israel's history. These books dovetail with the historical time periods covered by the books of Kings and even go beyond them into the postexilic period of Judean restoration. Additional effort is needed to orient these twelve books because their canonical order within the Book of the Twelve Prophets is not their chronological order going from earliest to latest (see Figure 13.1).

[1] From *The Old Testament Made Easy* by Jeanne Steig, pictures by William Steig. Michael Di Capua Books. New York: Farrar, Straus, Giroux, 1990.

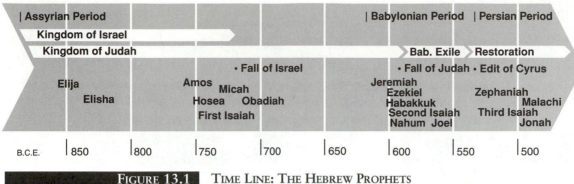

| | Assyrian Period | | | | | | Babylonian Period | Persian Period |

FIGURE 13.1   TIME LINE: THE HEBREW PROPHETS

Because the Book of the Twelve Prophets is not arranged in historical order, we will reorder them for our treatment, clustering them according to three major historical eras: the Assyrian period, the Babylonian period, and the Persian period.

BOOKS OF THE ASSYRIAN PERIOD: AMOS, HOSEA, AND MICAH

Israelite prophecy tended to coagulate around periods of political insecurity and crisis. The eighth century B.C.E. was just that for the Israelites and Judeans, largely because of the Assyrians. The Assyrians dominated international politics from the middle of the eighth century until the end of the seventh. Important dates for the end of the Assyrian Empire are 612 B.C.E., which marks the destruction of Nineveh by the Babylonians, and the battle of Carchemish in 605, which definitively established Babylonia as the major power in Mesopotamia (see Figure 13.2).

The earliest prophetic books of the Twelve Prophets originated at this time. **Amos, Hosea,** and **Micah** all date to the Assyrian Period. These books do not extensively deal with Assyria. Rather, they address the moral and spiritual condition of Israel and Judah in the middle of the eighth century B.C.E. (see Table 13.1).

The rise of the Assyrian Empire created foreign policy problems for Israel and Judah. These, in turn, had domestic ramifications. Prophecy was one response to the need for political and spiritual guidance in this period of crisis.

AMOS

Taken in chronological rather than canonical order, Amos is the earliest of all Hebrew prophets with books named after them. Amos was an older contemporary of Hosea and Isaiah. He prophesied sometime during the decade 760–750 B.C.E.

The book of Amos appears at first reading to be a collection of sayings with very little organization. But a close reading looking for connections reveals that

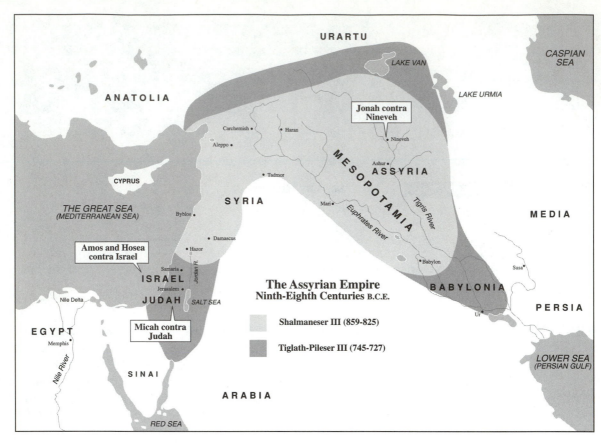

FIGURE 13.2   THE ASSYRIAN EMPIRE

there are identifiable groupings of material. The first group of similar material is the oracles against the nations (1:3–2:16), discrete units aimed one at a time at the nations of Syro–Palestine. Chapters 3–6 are a collection of various Amos sayings. Chapters 3, 4, and 5 all begin with the same phrase, "Hear this word . . . " This phrase may have provided the principle of organization for this subcollection. Chapters 7–9 are largely vision reports and so have a certain commonality.

There is strong evidence that the book of Amos grew in stages. Wolff (1977) has posited six stages in the literary formation of the book of Amos, beginning with words attributed to Amos himself and ending with editorial work in the postexilic period. Simplifying somewhat the work of Wolff, Coote (1981) has discerned three primary editorial stages in the book. The first stage, the Amos edition, contains Amos's words to eighth-century Israel. Among the passages included in this early stage are 2:6–8, 2:13–16, 3:9–12, 4:1–3, 5:1–3, 5:18–20, and 8:4–7. In the following two stages material was added by writers who felt they were speaking with an "Amos voice" in their own age.

The first words of the book were clearly written by an editor because they refer to Amos in the third person.

TABLE 13.1 KINGS AND PROPHETS OF THE ASSYRIAN PERIOD

Kings of Judah	Kings of Israel	Hebrew Prophets
Amaziah 800–783	Joash 802–786	
Uzziah 783–742	Jeroboam II 786–746	Amos c. 760–750
Jotham 742–735	Zechariah 746–745	Hosea c. 750–725
	Shallum 745	Isaiah of Jerusalem c. 740–700
	Menahem 745–737	
	Pekahiah 737–736	
Ahaz 735–715	Pekah 736–732	
Hezekiah 715–687	Hoshea 732–724	Micah c. 730

1:1 The words of Amos, one of the shepherds from Tekoa, which he saw concerning Israel during the reign of Uzziah, king of Judah, and Jeroboam son of Joash, king of Israel—two years before the earthquake. 2 He said, "Yahweh roars from Zion and thunders from Jerusalem; the shepherd's pastures dry up and the height of Carmel shrivels."

The very first words are, in effect, the title of the book: "The words of Amos." There is also the effort made to date the prophet by reference to the kings ruling in Judah and Israel. This kind of beginning is typical of a number of prophetic books, including Isaiah, Jeremiah, and Hosea.

The date indicators of this introduction place Amos in the middle of the eighth century. Uzziah reigned 783–742 and Jeroboam 786–746. The latter king is usually referred to as Jeroboam II to distinguish him from the first king of the Northern Kingdom.

This introduction goes further than that of most other prophetic books in making the time even more precise, specifying that the words of Amos date two years before the earthquake. The reference to the earthquake has been correlated with geological data obtained through field work. The archaeological excavation of Hazor evidenced in stratum VI a violent quake datable to the time of Jeroboam II (Yadin 1964).

From this introduction we learn a few things about Amos. He was from a little town in Judea called Tekoa and he was a shepherd. This has been interpreted by some to mean that he was poor, but this was not necessarily so. In addition, from 7:14 we learn that he was an agricultural worker, "a dresser of sycamore trees," and he strongly denied he was a professional prophet. Though not belonging to the prophetic guild, he was called to be a prophet directly by God.

Verse 2 contains the theme statement of the book. These, the first words of Amos in the book, describe an angry Yahweh. In roaring like a lion he laid waste the green pastures of Carmel. Note the geographical indicators, for they tell us a lot about Amos's theological and political perspective. Yahweh roars from

Jerusalem, the home of Davidic ideology, and condemns the heartland of the Northern Kingdom.

This raises an important issue concerning the perspective of Amos. It would appear, on first reading, that Amos was an advocate of Zion ideology. But this might depend on the attribution of these words. If they are Amos's, then perhaps yes. If they are an editor's words, shaping the book from a Judean and Davidic slant, then perhaps no. The one other passage in the book of Amos that reflects a strong Davidic bias is the last paragraph, 9:11–15. Here is a sample, with Yahweh speaking.

> *9:11 On that day I will restore David's fallen house. I will repair its gaping walls and restore its ruins. I will rebuild it as it was a long time ago.*

Clearly looking to the rebirth of the Davidic dynasty, these words are usually attributed to an editor later than Amos's day.

Turning to an examination of the book in terms of its major structural units, the first is 1:3–2:16. This section is a series of condemnatory statements aimed at the nations in Syro–Palestine in this order: Syria (Damascus), Philistia (Gaza), Phoenicia (Tyre), Edom, Ammon, Moab, Judah, and finally Israel (Figure 13.3).

Notice how the order of treatment crisscrosses Syro–Palestine—jumping over Israel, systematically dancing around it, until finally Amos hit the intended target: Israel itself. A sample, the oracle against Syria (1:3–5), gives us the flavor of Amos's language.

> *3 Thus says YHWH, "For three transgressions of Damascus, and for four, I will not revoke it (the punishment) on account of their threshing Gilead with iron threshing sledges. 4 I will send fire on the house of Hazael and it will devour the fortresses of Ben-hadad. 5 I will break the gate bars of Damascus and cut off the inhabitants from the Valley of Aven and the scepter-bearer from Beth-eden. The people of Aram will go to Kir in exile."*
> *Says YHWH.*

Speaking for God in the first person, Amos condemned Syria for dealing cruelly with the Israelites who lived in Gilead, that is, to the east of the Sea of Galilee. The king and his royal city would be destroyed because of their cruelty, and the population would be exiled to Kir, a place far in the east, near Elam.

The oracles continue with all of Israel's neighbors coming under God's condemnation one by one. The condemnation of Judah must have been especially sweet to the Israelites. They no doubt welcomed Amos's words and urged him on. Israel's enemies deserved what they got! It was a surprise, then, when Amos continued after Judah and exposed God's anger with Israel "because they sell the righteous for silver, and the needy for a pair of sandals" (2:6).

Amos is especially to be appreciated for his sensitivity to matters of social welfare in Israel. He spared no words in condemning the royalty and aristocracy of Israel, who abused the privilege of wealth and even used their authority to get richer at the expense of the poor.

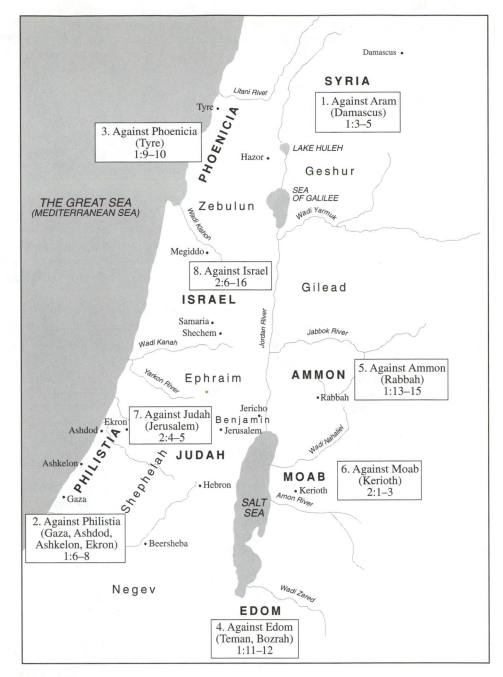

FIGURE 13.3 AMOS'S ORACLES AGAINST THE NATIONS

The next major unit, chapters 3–6, is another collection of oracles, but without the focus and structure of the first collection. The words from chapter 4 continue Amos's accusatory tone and strong condemnation of the Israelite ruling elite, in this case the wives of the aristocracy.

1 Hear this word, you cows of Bashan who are on Mount Samaria—you who oppress the poor, who crush the needy, who say to their husbands, "Bring us something to drink!" 2 YHWH has sworn by his holiness: the time is definitely coming when they will take you away with hooks, even the last of you with fishhooks. 3 You will leave through breaches in the wall, each of you going straight out, and you will be tossed into Harmon.

These words of Amos are direct and announce that punishment is inevitable and close. There is no hint that it can be avoided—the culprits will not be able to dodge the coming doom. Characteristic of this early stage, Amos does not seem to allow for repentance.

The socioeconomic background for these words is an Israelite elite enjoying an indulgent lifestyle at the expense of the disenfranchised peasants. Amos's announcement of punishment is so direct and certain that Coote (1981) argues Amos must have uttered these words around 745 when Tiglath-Pileser III, the Assyrian expansionist king, came to power and directly threatened Israel. This would account for the vividness and accuracy of the language describing Assyrian policies of capture and deportation.

In addition to castigating the rich ("you cows of Bashan") who callously oppressed the poor (4:1), Amos was critical of Israel's centers of religious worship, especially Bethel and Gilgal (4:4–5, 5:4–7).

5:21 I hate and despise your festivals; I do not take pleasure from your pious meetings. 22 Although you offer me burnt offerings and your grain offerings, I will not accept them. The peace offering of your choice animals I will not eye. 23 Away from me with the noise of your songs! The melody of your harps I will not hear. 24 Let justice roll down like water, righteousness like an eternally flowing stream.

Amos's call for social caring, "Let justice roll down like water!" are some of his most famous words. Amos took the religious concepts of justice and righteousness, which had primary application to the way God deals with his people, and applied them to social interaction.

In Amos's analysis, Israel was just going through the motions of worshiping God and observing proper rituals, thinking that this was the sum total of their obligation to God. In reality, God valued personal responsibility and community caring above formal worship. Amos here disparaged formal religion when its practicers used it to make themselves right with God in the absence of personal and corporate morality. His words should not be absolutized as a total prophetic condemnation of all formal worship. This is typical of Amos's unconditional language. It is a fine example of a blanket condemnation, in its context appropriate, but not meant by Amos to be generalized.

The last major section is chapters 7–9. These chapters contain five visions and a prophecy of restoration. The first four visions are similarly structured. Each begins with the sentence, "This is what my lord YHWH showed me." In each vision Amos saw something that indicated God was going to destroy Israel. In the first (7:1–3) he saw locusts devouring the produce of the land. In the second (7:4–6) he saw a fire consume the land. In both of these visions, after Amos cried out with concern for Israel, God changed his mind and withdrew the punishment.

In the third vision (7:7–9) Amos saw Yahweh with a plumb line in his hand. This vision is different from the prior two. It is not an image of destruction. Rather, Amos sees God holding a measuring device against which Israel was measured.

> 7:8b YHWH said, "I am putting a plumb line in the middle of my people Israel. I will never again overlook them. 9 The high places of Isaac will be made barren, and the holy places of Israel will be leveled. I will come against Jeroboam with a sword."

A plumb line is a construction worker's tool consisting of a weight attached to a string. The weighted string provides a true vertical (or plumb) standard against which other objects, such as masonry walls or door posts, can be built straight. Judged against true vertical, Israel was tilted and out of plumb. Religion was not doing it any good. Consequently, Israel's worship centers would be destroyed, especially the "high places," which had Canaanite Baalistic associations. And Jeroboam II, king of Israel, would be removed.

This, the third vision, is not followed directly by the fourth. Instead, a narrative was inserted recording a confrontation between Amos and **Amaziah**, a Bethel priest loyal to Jeroboam II. Amaziah was provoked by the preaching of Amos. In **Bethel**, the main Israelite worship center sponsored by the king, Amos proclaimed that Jeroboam would die and Israel would go into exile (7:11). Amaziah told Amos to go back to Judah where he came from.

This narrative breaks up the flow of the vision accounts, but the arrangement does have a certain editorial logic. The vision accounts condemned Israel for sinning, and especially the third vision account blamed Israelite sanctuaries. The Amos–Amaziah confrontation is evidence of the perversity of Israelite sanctuaries, condemned in the third vision, and evidence of Israelite hardness of heart. Whereas after the first two visions God relented of his planned punishment, there is no relenting in the third and fourth visions. This confrontation account demonstrates that there was no repentant spirit in Israel that could warrant a removal of God's planned destruction.

The fourth vision account, 8:1–3, was built around a visual–verbal pun. Amos saw a basket of summer fruit (Hebrew *qayits*). Yahweh said in explanation, "the end (Hebrew *qets*) of my people has arrived." What follows, almost until the end of the book, is a series of disaster descriptions: famine, mourning, violence, exile, death, and despair.

The last oracle, 9:11–15, contains an expectation for the rebirth of the Davidic dynasty and a delightful depiction of the glorious future awaiting the land and its people. The ground will be so productive harvesters will not be able to keep pace, and the people will enjoy peace and prosperity. This last unit is so radically different from the preceding words of Amos, concerning not Israel but the rebirth of the Judean Davidic dynasty, that it is usually attributed to someone other than Amos.

Why was it attached to the book as the final unit? Perhaps because otherwise the ending would be too depressing. In the view of the compiler of Amos in its canonical form, judgment had to be followed by salvation. Judgment could never be the last word. It was not fitting to end on a note of despair. The final form of the book strongly suggests that judgment followed by salvation was the complete message of God.

HOSEA

Hosea was placed first in the Book of the Twelve Prophets. We cannot be sure why. Perhaps because it is the longest book of the twelve. Perhaps because someone at one time mistakenly thought he was the earliest prophet of the twelve. The evidence of the book itself, however, indicates that Hosea prophesied a little later than Amos. Like Amos, he prophesied in the Northern Kingdom. Unlike Amos, he was a native of the north. In fact, Hosea was the only non-Judean literary prophet besides Jeremiah.

Hosea's northern origin probably put him in touch with the substantial northern prophetic tradition represented by Elijah, the Elohist traditions of the Pentateuch, and the traditions of Deuteronomy. This may account for Hosea's frequent allusions to the decalogue and the Sinai covenant traditions.

Historical indications in the text, including the editorial framework of the first verse, suggest that Hosea prophesied from 750 to 725 B.C.E. Jeroboam II was the king of Israel at the beginning of Hosea's prophetic activity, and after he died there was virtual anarchy in the Northern Kingdom until its destruction by Assyria in 721.

The final book was compiled much after the time of Hosea the prophet. The book has a discernible structure, falling into two basic parts. The first unit, chapters 1–3, is built around Hosea's ordeal of marrying a prostitute. This marriage functions as a living parable of husband Yahweh's relationship to Israel. The second unit, chapters 4–11, begins with the phrase, "Hear the word of YHWH" and consists largely of uncontextualized statements. It has no obvious thematic unity but consists of oracles of disaster and salvation. This alternation of disaster and salvation, even discernible to some extent in the first unit, provides a structuring principle to the book (see Table 13.2).

TABLE 13.2   OUTLINE OF HOSEA

	Disaster	Salvation
I. Chapters 1–3	1:2–9	1:10–2:1
	2:2–13	2:14–23
	3:1–4	3:5
II. Chapters 4–14	4:1–11:7	11:8–11
	11:12–14:1	14:2–9

The first chapter contains a third-person narrative describing Hosea's marriage to **Gomer.**

2 The beginning of YHWH's speaking through Hosea: YHWH said to Hosea, "Go, take for yourself a promiscuous woman and children from promiscuity, because the land is promiscuous with regard to YHWH." 3 He went and took Gomer, the daughter of Diblaim. She conceived and bore him a son. 4 YHWH said to him, "Call his name Jezreel, because in yet a little while I will avenge the blood of Jezreel on the house of Jehu, and I will put an end to the kingdom of the house of Israel. 5 In that day I will break the bow of Israel in the valley of Jezreel." 6 She conceived again and bore a daughter, and he said to him, "Call her name Lo-ruhamah, because I will no longer show mercy to the house of Israel. I will not forgive them. [7 But to the house of Judah I will show mercy, and I will save them, by YHWH Elohim, but I will not save them by bow, sword, warfare, horses or charioteers.] 8 She weaned Lo-ruhamah, conceived and bore a son. 9 He said, "Call his name Lo-ammi, because you are not my people, and I am 'Not I am' to you."

Gomer had three children. The text clearly indicates the first child was fathered by Hosea himself, but the second and third might have been children of "whoredom." In any case, the children serve as prophetic signs having to do with the northern kingdom of Israel.

The first child was named **Jezreel** (which in Hebrew sounds very close to Israel: *Yizreel* and *Yisrael*, respectively). "The blood of Jezreel" refers to Jehu's bloody coup d'état and slaughter of the house of Ahab. For these acts the monarchy would be punished.

The second child's name, **Lo-ruhamah,** means "Without mercy." The Hebrew word *rehem* (literally, "womb") to which it is related recalls descriptions of Yahweh as the merciful God of the covenant (see Exodus 33:19), the one who loves Israel with parental (a mother's?) love.

The third child's name, **Lo-ammi,** means "Not my people." This name is also related to covenant notions. The essence of God's covenant with Israel was this: "I will be your God, and you will be my people." The (anti-) covenant context is reinforced with the words "I am 'Not I am' to you." The Hebrew original of the phrase "Not I am" is *Lo-ehyeh,* and undoubtedly puns on the covenant name of God, Yahweh, whose name was revealed to Moses at the burning bush (Exodus 3) as "I am who I am," *ehyeh asher ehyeh* in Hebrew.

A major interpretive, indeed moral, issue regarding this account is whether or not Gomer was a known prostitute at the time of her marriage to Hosea. The command, "Go, take for yourself a wife of whoredom and have children of whoredom," as the New Revised Standard Version renders it, sounds like he was told to marry an out-and-out prostitute. If she was, then Yahweh was asking a very difficult thing of Hosea.

On the other hand, it is quite possible that the wording was affected by Hosea's experience and theology. The account was, of course, written after the fact. While at the time he may not have known she was a prostitute, in retrospect it is obvious she was. God in his providence must have known ahead of time her propensities; therefore, he had told Hosea to marry a prostitute.

Yet a third interpretive possibility is that Gomer was not unfaithful to the marriage bond as such, but that she was associated with Canaanite Baalistic bridal rites of initiation (Wolff 1965). The children were considered, metaphorically speaking, to be children of "whoredom" because conception was credited to Baal and not Yahweh.

Hosea was the first prophet to use his family life, and in particular his children, to make a theopolitical prophetic point. Prophesying shortly after him, Isaiah would do the same. Hosea's marriage to Gomer was a mirror of Yahweh's experience with Israel. Marriage was equated with the covenant God made with Israel in the wilderness.

Chapter 1 is a third-person account of Hosea's marriage. Chapter 3 is an autobiographical description of his marriage. In his own words, Hosea describes "purchasing" a prostitute. Some interpreters suggest this account temporally follows the story of chapter 1, with Hosea buying back his wife after an intervening period of unfaithfulness. Other interpreters view it as the same story of chapter 1, just retold in the first person.

> 1 YHWH said to me again, "Go, love a woman who has a lover and is a prostitute, just as YHWH loves the people of Israel—even though they turn to other gods and love raisin cakes." 2 So I bought her for fifteen shekels of silver and a homer of barley and a measure of wine. 3 And I said to her, "You must stay mine in the future; you must not play the prostitute. You must not have intercourse with a man, including me with you." 4 For the Israelites shall remain many days without a king or prince, without sacrifice or pillar, without ephod or teraphim. 5 Afterward the Israelites shall return and seek YHWH their God, and David their king. They shall come in fear to YHWH and to his goodness in the days to come.

Again, the relationship of man and woman is a mirror of Yahweh's relationship to Israel. The specified purchase price consisted of silver and grain, the usual offerings to a deity. After paying the price, Hosea's expectation was that the former prostitute, now his wife, would be pure.

Originally applying to the Israel (read Northern Kingdom) of Hosea's day, the description of the relationship was reapplied by a later writer in verses 4–5 to Judah. Brought to Judah after the fall of the north, the experience of Hosea became a lesson to the Southern Kingdom.

Abstinence from sexual intercourse was appropriated as a symbol of Judah's isolation, without king or sacred paraphernalia in Babylonian exile. Mention of the return pointed to the future in expectation of the return to power of the Davidic line. Although the people were wayward, days of blessing would return. Perhaps this prophetic material was shaped by Deuteronomic circles, as was so much other classical prophecy. In this case especially it would be natural for Deuteronomic theology to have an influence, given the similar northern origin of Hosea and Deuteronomy.

As has just been suggested, chapters 1 and 3 may be viewed as third-person and first-person renderings, respectively, of the same experience of marital betrayal and alienation. It seems, however, that the editor took chapter 3 and placed it as a historical continuation of chapter 1. Note the use of "again" in 3:1. Perhaps his intention in repeating the scandalous affair was to suggest the patience of Yahweh, who puts up with his people even as time after time they, like Hosea's wife, go running after forbidden gods. A recurring biblical theme was this: Generation after generation of Israelites forgetting their genuine husband, Yahweh, and seeking out the company of Baal and Asherah.

MICAH

Micah was a southerner, a Judean, as was Amos. Micah was a contemporary of Isaiah of Jerusalem, coming from a rural background, specifically from a town called Moresheth, which lay to the west of Jerusalem. Wolff (1981) argues that Micah was, in effect, a Moresheth city councilman who served as an advocate for his people, presenting their concerns to the rich and famous in Jerusalem. Micah is cited in Jeremiah 26 as an antiestablishment prophet who, nonetheless, was respected by the king.

The book of Micah consists of three units. Each of the three main sections opens with the call: "Hear!" Each has the same basic structure, alternating disaster and salvation, such as we saw in the book of Hosea (see Table 13.3). There is scholarly agreement that most of chapters 1–3 come from Micah, with the latter chapters coming from elsewhere.

The prophet Micah prophesied in the latter part of the eighth century during the rising threat of the Assyrian Empire. Except for one oracle that includes the Northern Kingdom in its purview (1:2–7), the bulk was directed against Judah. The oracle that predicts the demise of Samaria places the earliest words of Micah before 721. The explicit allusion to the Babylonian exile, as well as the repatriation hinted at in 4:9–10, indicates that the book went through the hands of editors as late as the postexilic period.

Micah's social criticism consists of a critique of the economic aristocrats, whose greed for homes and property had no bounds. Micah opposed the ritualistic righteousness of the pious (as did the other eighth-century prophets, especially Amos but also Hosea and Isaiah).

6:6 *"With what should I come before YHWH, and bow before God on high? Should I come before him with burnt offerings, year old calves? 7 Would YHWH be pleased with thousands of rams, ten thousand rivers of*

TABLE 13.3 OUTLINE OF MICAH

	Disaster	Salvation
I. Chapters 1–2	1:2–2:11	2:12–13
II. Chapters 3–5	3:1–12	4:1–5:15
III. Chapters 6–7	6:1–7:7	7:8–20

oil? Should I give my firstborn for my sin, the produce of my own body for my very own sin?"

8 He has told you, O Being, what is good, what YHWH requires of you: Do justice! Love kindness! Walk humbly with your God.

This passage appears to borrow from temple liturgies through which the worshiper sought entry into the presence of God (for a similar liturgy, see Psalm 24). The prophet Micah modified this genre and applied it to one's personal relationship with God.

The earnestness with which Micah pursued a critique of the opportunistic and heartless upper class suggests that he may have been one of the farmers who was threatened by the influential aristocracy (see 3:2–3). He probably belonged to that class called "the people of the land," conservative landowners who were distrustful of royal and religious bureaucrats who sought to control their lives.

The preaching of Micah might have contributed to the Deuteronomic reform movement in Judah (Blenkinsopp 1983). It advocated land reform but at the same time was supportive of the Davidic monarchy, as long as its kings remained true to Mosaic ideals (see Deut. 17:14–20).

Micah wrestled with the nature of prophecy and condemned prophets who worked for wages. Perhaps he was standing in critique of cult or royal prophets who were eager to please (see 3:5–6). The prophets he criticized produced the Official Zion Theology. Based on their belief in the divine election of the nation, the Davidic dynasty, and the city of Jerusalem, it defined a theology highly supportive of the establishment and designed to foster high morale and fierce loyalty and pride. Micah merely pointed out that a prophecy that supported this type of theology was prone to deceive the people by feeding their need for support and reassurance and by telling them exactly what they wanted to hear. When he says, "I am filled with power and justice and strength to declare to Jacob his transgression" (3:8), his challenge sounds very much like Amos's. In 3:11–12 he criticized the self-assured security of those who felt Zion and Jerusalem were inviolable.

But the book of Micah does not appear to completely reject Davidic ideology.

5:2 You, Bethlehem of the Ephrathites, small among the tribes of Judah— you will produce for me a ruler in Israel, one whose origin is venerable, from ancient times.

These words, with most of chapters 4–7, are usually attributed to a writer other than Micah. They put the book more in sympathy with the mainstream of Jerusalemite views by placing hope on the Davidic dynasty. Bethlehem was venerated because "David slept there." It was his birthplace.

BOOKS OF THE BABYLONIAN PERIOD: ZEPHANIAH, NAHUM, HABAKKUK, AND OBADIAH

Historians refer to this Babylonian period as the Neo-Babylonian period. It affected Judah roughly from 630 to 539 B.C.E. Nabopolassar extended Babylonian influence westward, eclipsing the Assyrians. Babylonian power began to grow until 605, when Nebuchadnezzar decisively established Babylonian supremacy at the battle of Carchemish. In 587 the Babylonians destroyed Judah and Jerusalem (see Figure 13.4). In 539 Babylon was conquered by Cyrus the Great of Persia, who incorporated Babylonian territory into his empire.

The prophets of the Babylonian period deal with the international crisis. The major issues surfacing in these books are the guilt of Judah, which was the reason God was punishing them, and the role of foreign powers in working out the punishment (see Table 13.4).

TABLE 13.4 KINGS AND PROPHETS OF THE BABYLONIAN PERIOD

Kings of Judah	Kings of Babylon	Hebrew Prophets
Manasseh 687–642		
Amon 642–640		Zephaniah c. 640–622
Josiah 640–609	Nabopolassar 626–605	Nahum c. 620, Jeremiah 627–562
Jehoahaz 609	Nebuchadnezzar 605–562	Habakkuk 608–598
Jehoiakim 609–598		
Jehoiachin 598		
Zedekiah 597–587		Ezekiel 593–571
Gedaliah	Amel-Marduk 562–560	Obadiah c. 587
	Neriglissar 560–556	
	Nabonidus 556–539	Second Isaiah 546–538

There is about a fifty-year gap between the prophets of the Assyrian period, Isaiah of Jerusalem being the last, and the cluster of prophecy in the Babylonian period. The dating of some of these books is uncertain, but Zephaniah may have been the first of the Babylonian era.

ZEPHANIAH

Zephaniah was a Judean prophet, possibly descended from the Davidic line, who was active during the reign of Josiah. His condemnation of the kinds of religious practices that were eliminated by the Josiah Reformation in 622 suggests that he prophesied before that time, somewhere between 640 and 622.

Typical of most other Judean prophets, Zephaniah's words cover these three main topics: condemnation of Judah and Jerusalem for religious sins, condemnation of foreign nations (including Philistia, Moab, Ammon, Ethiopia, and Assyria), and promises of salvation for God's people.

Zephaniah follows the lead of Amos and proclaims that the **Day of Yahweh** is coming. But it will be a sad day for God's people, and not a day on which they see victory.

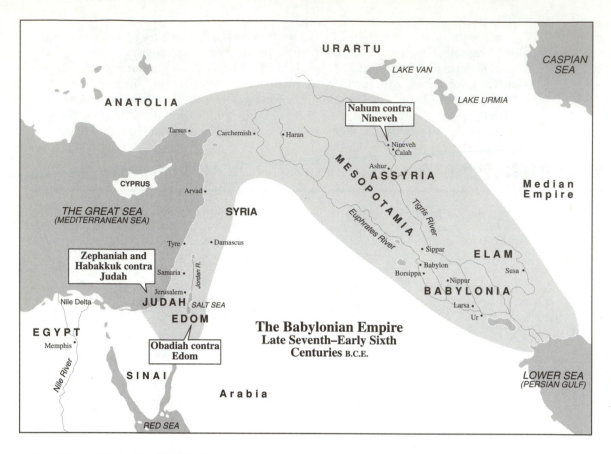

FIGURE 13.4   BABYLONIAN EMPIRE

1:14 The great day of YHWH is near, near and fast getting closer. The sound of the day of YHWH is harsh. On it the warrior screams. 15 A day of wrath will be that day: a day of trouble and anguish, a day of ruin and waste, a day of darkness and gloom, a day of cloud and thick darkness.

The people will see clouds and fire, effects that should signal the protective presence of God, but God would be active this time to punish them.

NAHUM

The book of **Nahum** is one thing only, an oracle denouncing **Nineveh**, the glorious capital city of the Assyrian domain. The book looks forward to the destruction of this city, which epitomized everything the Judeans hated about the Assyrians. Because the city was not destroyed until 612 B.C.E., the book that places its destruction in the future must have been before that time. Some scholars place it as early as 650 B.C.E., others just before the actual destruction of the city.

Nahum vividly depicts the battle of Nineveh in all its confusion and gore. The prophet seems eager to gloat—no wonder, after the decades of Assyrian tyranny and oppression under which Israel and Judah suffered. The basic theme of Nahum is this: Yahweh punishes any nation, in this case Assyria, that has exploited his people and treated them cruelly. Israel's enemies are God's enemies, and God is supreme, being even more powerful than the mightiest empires.

HABAKKUK

The prophet **Habakkuk** worked in Judah during the first part of the Babylonian crisis, from around 608 to 598. Virtually nothing is known about the prophet himself. The book essentially consists of two units. The first unit, chapters 1–2, is a dialogic give-and-take between Habakkuk and Yahweh. The second unit, chapter 3, is a hymn, much in the style of hymns in the book of Psalms, which anticipates the victory march of Yahweh, who would vindicate his people.

The first unit is remarkable for the frankness of its theological dialogue. Habakkuk questions God in an attempt to understand the morality of God's actions, specifically how God could use the evil Babylonians to punish his own covenant people, who presumably are not as bad as that nasty Nebuchadnezzar. The investigation of the morality of God's actions is referred to by the theological term **theodicy**. Habakkuk put it this way:

> 1:13 *Your eyes are too clean to countenance evil. You are not able to put up with wrongdoing. Why then do you put up with treacherous people, and are silent when the wicked devour those more righteous than they?*

Yahweh replied:

> 2:2 *Write down the vision, make it legible on clay tablets so that anyone in a hurry can read it. 3 For this vision is for a time yet to come. It deals with the end and will not deceive. If it seems to be delayed, just wait for it. It will definitely come, it will not be late. 4 Now the proud, his life is not virtuous. But the righteous, by his faithfulness will he have life.*

Although there are interpretive problems with verse 4, in essence God's answer seems to be this: Be patient, Habakkuk. This is the way I planned it. The proud, that is, the Babylonians, will meet their end eventually, and in the not too distant future. The righteous, that is, the Judeans, will survive if only they remain faithful to God.

The prophecy of Habakkuk affirms the sovereignty of God and that in the end the wicked would be punished and the righteous vindicated.

OBADIAH

The book of **Obadiah** is the shortest book in the Hebrew Bible. It is only one chapter long and consists of a single oracle against the country of **Edom**, which lay immediately to the southeast of Judah. We know virtually nothing about the prophet Obadiah, except that his name means "servant of Yahweh," a common Hebrew name.

The book of Obadiah is undated, but it is usually credited to the period immediately after the destruction of Jerusalem in 587 B.C.E. The theme of the oracle is divine condemnation of Edom because the Edomites took advantage of the Judeans when they were forced to leave Jerusalem. The Edomites even seem to have cooperated with the Babylonians in despoiling Judah at the time of the exile. Obadiah voices the words of Yahweh:

> *13 You should not have entered the gate of my people on the day of their tragedy. You of all people should not have gazed on his disaster on the day of his tragedy. You should not have looted his goods on the day of his tragedy.*

With nobody to stop them, Edomites encroached on Judean territory during the period of Judean exile. Obadiah makes reference to the Day of Yahweh as the time Edom would be punished by a vengeful God. He predicts a time when the exiles would return and Mt. Zion would again be glorious.

There was a long-standing antagonism between Israel and Edom. The antagonism was traced in the national epic all the way back to the rivalry between Jacob and Esau, who was the ancestor of the Edomites. Obadiah stands with Amos, Jeremiah, and Ezekiel as a prophetic voice condemning Edom. In fact, Obadiah and Jeremiah stand so closely together that portions of Jeremiah's oracle of judgment against Edom in 49:7–22 are found in Obadiah 1–9.

Jeremiah 49:14–16 (NRSV) 14 I have heard tidings from the LORD and a messenger has been sent among the nations: "Gather yourselves together and come against her, and rise up for battle!" 15 For I will make you least among the nations, despised by humankind. 16 The terror you inspire and the pride of your heart have deceived you, you who live in the clefts of the rock, who hold the height of the hill. Although you make your nest as high as the eagle's, from there I will bring you down, says the LORD.

Jeremiah 49:9 (NRSV) If grape-gatherers came to you, would they not leave gleanings? If thieves came by night, even they would pillage only what they wanted. 10 But as for me, I have stripped Esau bare, I have uncovered his hiding places.

Obadiah 1–4 (NRSV) 1 We have heard a report from the LORD, and a messenger has been sent among the nations: "Rise up! Let us rise against it for battle!" 2 I will surely make you least among the nations; you shall be utterly despised. 3 Your proud heart has deceived you, you that live in the clefts of the rock, whose dwelling is in the heights. You say in your heart, "Who will bring me down to the ground?" 4 Though you soar aloft like the eagle, though your nest is set among the stars, from there I will bring you down, says the LORD.

Obadiah 5 (NRSV) If thieves came to you, if plunderers by night—how you have been destroyed!—would they not steal only what they wanted? If grape-gatherers came to you, would they not leave gleanings? 6 How Esau has been pillaged, his treasures searched out!

Obadiah's version is a bit wordier perhaps, but either both draw on the same tradition, or Obadiah borrowed from Jeremiah.

BOOKS OF THE PERSIAN PERIOD: HAGGAI, ZECHARIAH, MALACHI, JOEL, AND JONAH

The Persian period extended from 539 to 332 B.C.E. The Persian Empire was founded by Cyrus the Great and superseded the Babylonian Empire. Cyrus was kind to the Judeans, both those who had remained in Palestine and those dispersed within his empire. He allowed any who wanted to return to Palestine to do so and even provided financial support (see Figure 13.5).

The prophetic books dating to the Persian period are largely concerned with reconstructing life after the devastation of the Babylonian exile. Many of these prophets were involved in rebuilding the Jerusalem temple and encouraging the

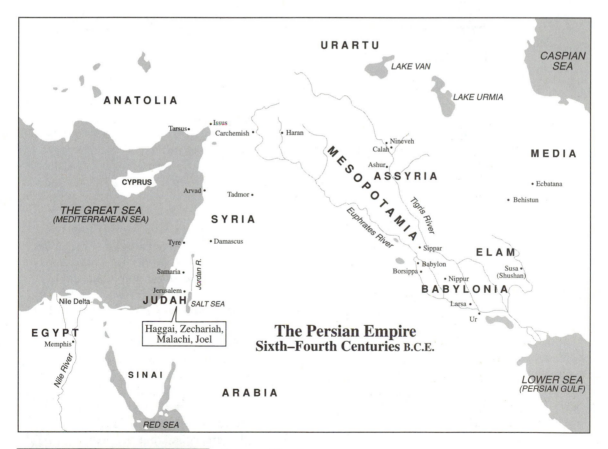

FIGURE 13.5 PERSIAN EMPIRE

people to support it. The prophets also helped to reshape the religious outlook of the survivors of the recent tragedy (see Table 13.5).

| TABLE 13.5 | KINGS AND PROPHETS OF THE PERSIAN PERIOD |

Jewish Leaders	Persian Kings	Hebrew Prophets
Sheshbazzar 538	Cyrus 550–530	
Zerubbabel c. 520	Cambyses 530–522	Third Isaiah 537–520
	Darius I 522–486	Haggai 520
		Zechariah 520–518
		Malachi c. 500–450
	Xerxes 486–465	Joel c. 400–350
Ezra c. 450	Artaxerxes I 465–424	Jonah c. 400?
Nehemiah c. 445		Second Zechariah c. 400

HAGGAI

Cyrus the Great allowed the Judean refugees to return to Judea, and he encouraged them to rebuild the temple in Jerusalem. Life was very difficult back in Judea, and the work, though begun shortly after 538, soon ground to a halt. **Haggai** was a major figure in Jerusalem encouraging the work to be completed. In 520 he gave five addresses, collected in the book of Haggai, which urged the Jewish leaders to assume responsibility for the project and finish it. The leaders at this time were **Zerubbabel,** the governor, and **Joshua,** the high priest. Addressing the people of Jerusalem, Haggai said,

> 1:2 *Thus says YHWH of hosts, "These people said, 'It is not yet time to rebuild YHWH's house.'" 3 The word of YHWH came through the prophet Haggai, 4 "Is it time for you to live in your paneled homes while this house remains in ruins?" . . . 9 "You have expected much but now it has come to little. When you brought it home, I blew it away. Why?" says YHWH of hosts. "Because my house lies in ruins, while all of you are concerned about your own homes."*

Evidently the people were busy reestablishing their own ways of life, putting off rebuilding the temple until they were doing well personally. Haggai demanded that the people reverse their priorities. First Yahweh's house must be rebuilt, and only after it was finished could the people expect to prosper. In large measure due to Haggai's encouragement, the temple was completed in 515.

Haggai expressed a Jerusalemite priestly perspective that the presence of Yahweh in Jerusalem was the precondition for the return of national prosperity and blessing. And Yahweh could not return until he had a dwelling place, the temple. In his last address to Zerubbabel (2:20–22) Haggai foresaw the demise of the other nations and the rise to power of Zerubbabel, who would be God's "signet ring."

ZECHARIAH

The prophet **Zechariah** was a contemporary of Haggai, and both were contemporaries of the leaders of the early Judean restoration, Zerubbabel and Joshua. Zechariah prophesied in Jerusalem from 520 to 518 B.C.E. Whereas the style of Haggai's prophecy was hortatory, Zechariah's prophecy took the shape of visions and dialogues with God.

The book of Zechariah divides into two main parts. The first unit, chapters 1–8, is usually attributed to the prophet Zechariah of the sixth century. The second unit, chapters 9–14, sometimes referred to as **Second Zechariah**, was written by an unnamed prophet (a situation much like that in the book of Isaiah) in the Greek period of the fourth and third centuries B.C.E.

Zechariah was concerned about the religious purity of the people and the morale of Jerusalem's leaders. To that end he attempted to inspire them. In eight visions Zechariah glimpsed the changes ahead. In the first vision he saw four horsemen patrolling the earth in anticipation of the punishment of the foreign nations and the return to power of Jerusalem. In the second he saw four horns representing world powers and four blacksmiths who would destroy those horns. In the third he saw a man measuring Jerusalem for the rebuilding of its walls, who was then told that the city would be huge, and Yahweh would be its protecting wall.

In the fourth vision Zechariah saw an unclean Joshua, the high priest, standing accused by Satan of being unfit for duty. Then he was confirmed by God and given the duties of the high priesthood. In the fifth he saw two olive trees, representing Zerubbabel and Joshua, who supplied a golden lamp stand that illuminated the world. In the sixth he saw a flying scroll containing the covenant laws. All fell under the judgment of the Torah. In the seventh he saw wickedness personified as a woman in a flying basket, which was removed to a distant land. In the eighth, forming an envelope structure with the first vision, he saw four horses patrolling the earth in anticipation of the messianic age.

The first unit closes on a highly positive note. Yahweh declared that he would return to Jerusalem, restore its greatness, and usher in a time of peace.

> 8:7 Thus says YHWH of hosts, "Now I am saving my people from the eastern territory and from the western territory. 8 I will bring them to live in Jerusalem. They will be my people and I will be their God, with faithfulness and righteousness.

Here Zechariah anticipates even further repatriations of the people. Jerusalem remained the holy city of the Jews and the ideal for the Jews of the dispersion was to return to Zion. Notice also how Zechariah uses the covenant phraseology to express hope: "They will be my people and I will be their God."

We note a couple of features of the prophecies of Zechariah. The book of Zechariah demonstrates a considerable awareness of past prophecy. Zechariah clearly sees himself as standing in a long line of prophetic tradition. The book begins by drawing connections.

> 1:4 *Do not be like your forebears, to whom earlier prophets preached, "Thus says YHWH of hosts, return from your evil ways and from your evil deeds." But they did not hear me, says YHWH. 5 Where are your forebears now? Do the prophets live forever? 6 But my words and my laws, which I commanded my servants the prophets, did they not overtake your forebears so that they repented and said, "YHWH of hosts has dealt with us according to our ways and deeds, just as he planned to do."*

Zechariah attests here to the power of the word of Yahweh spoken through the prophets. The tragedy of the exile was the result of the hardness of the ancestors' hearts and happened according to God's plan. This should be a warning to the current generation. Furthermore, standing as this does as the introduction to the visions, it reinforces the certainty of the prophetic word concerning the future.

Zechariah also shows his dependence on earlier prophecy by the way he adopts and adapts earlier prophetic images. Jeremiah's prophecy of the seventy years of captivity (chapter 29) was used in the first vision to designate the length of captivity. It also became the basis of Daniel's vision of seventy weeks of years (chapter 9). And the flying scroll of the sixth vision seems to derive from Ezekiel's scroll (chapters 2–3).

The oracles of the second unit of the book of Zechariah, chapters 9–14 (called Second Zechariah), echo familiar prophetic themes: the destruction of the foreign nations, the restoration of Israel, and the coming Day of Yahweh. Second Zechariah gives special attention to messianic leadership. He describes the triumphant king who comes on a donkey (chapter 9). The evil shepherds would be removed from office (chapters 11 and 13). The evil nations would be finally destroyed, and Jerusalem would become a holy place where Yahweh the king would dwell forever.

MALACHI

Nothing is known about the prophet **Malachi**. Based on an analysis of the themes of the book, it is supposed that he lived in the period 500–450 B.C.E. He complained about abuses in the Second Temple, which was completed in 515 B.C.E. Concern about foreign marriages (2:10–12) was a major issue in Ezra's day (around 450 B.C.E.).

The book of Malachi makes extensive use of the disputation literary form. That is, it frames its prophecies in a question-and-answer dialogic style. In chapters 1 and 2 Malachi examines the shortcomings of the priests in this disputation style.

> 1:6 *"A son honors a father, and a servant his master. I am a father. Where is my honor? If I am master, where is my respect?" says YHWH of hosts to you priests who despise my name. You say, "How have we despised your*

name?" 7 "By offering on my altar defiled food." You say, "How have we defiled you?" "By your saying that the table of YHWH is defileable. 8 If you offer for sacrifice something blind, is that not wrong? If you offer something lame or sick, is that not wrong? Offer it to your governor! Would he take it? Would he show you favor?" says YHWH of hosts.

Here the priests are exposed for dishonoring God with inferior animal sacrifices. Damaged animals were not acceptable for sacrifice. Being less valuable, they indicated less than total devotion.

Except for a few negative remarks about Edom, Malachi is concerned less with the foreign nations and more with the spiritual condition of the priesthood and the people. He anticipates a judgment day when the wicked would be destroyed and the righteous rewarded. The book closes with references to the two figures that epitomize the Torah and the prophets, thereby upholding the venerable covenant traditions of Israel.

4:4 Remember the torah of Moses my servant that I commanded him at Horeb for all Israel, the laws and rules. 5 Now, I am sending to you Elijah the prophet before the great and terrible Day of YHWH comes. 6 He will turn the heart of fathers to sons and the heart of sons to their fathers, so that I will not come and smite the land with utter destruction.

The expectation of the return of Elijah before the judgment day is here stated clearly. This has given rise to expectations within both Judaism and Christianity. Elijah has a place within the traditional Jewish celebration of the Passover yet today. And New Testament writers who addressed the career of John the Baptist viewed him as the realization of this expected return of Elijah.

The book of Malachi is the last book of the Twelve. It is not necessarily the last book chronologically, given the undefined setting of this book and our inability to nail down the chronology of some of the other books of the Twelve. Yet it was judged to be a fitting conclusion to the Book of the Twelve, probably because of its eschatological flavor.

JOEL

It is difficult to pin down the historical setting of the prophecies of **Joel**. Early readers must have thought him preexilic, hence his placement between Hosea and Amos. The book of Joel was placed before Amos, perhaps because of the correspondence between Joel 3:16, 18 and Amos 1:2, 9:13 and perhaps because Amos, like Joel, was alert to the coming Day of Yahweh.

The evidence for establishing a historical context for Joel is only inferential. Nothing is mentioned about the destruction of Jerusalem, perhaps suggesting a preexilic date and making him a contemporary of Jeremiah. But the absence of any reference to a king or to the Assyrians and Babylonians and an apparent reference to the dispersion all suggest a postexilic date. The general consensus is that Joel is to be placed somewhere in the period 400–350 B.C.E.

The central theme of the book of Joel is the notion of the Day of Yahweh, which gives the book as a whole its coherence. The book of Joel divides into two parts. The first part, chapters 1:1–2:27, centers on an elaborate vision of a locust plague, which is a way to warn of the coming judgment of God, called the Day of Yahweh. The second part, chapters 2:28–3:21, is a description of the blessings on Judah and Jerusalem with the coming Day of Yahweh and the corresponding punishment of the surrounding nations.

Joel has sometimes been called a "cult prophet." That is, he was supportive of the priesthood and the temple and perhaps was even a priest himself. He was concerned that offerings were not coming in as expected, in part because the land itself was not providing the produce, and in part because the people were not being generous. Consequently, the priests were unable to perform their duties.

> 1:9 *The grain offering and the drink offering are cut off from the house of YHWH. The priests mourn, the ministers of YHWH.*

This concern for the temple and its priests is more characteristic of postexilic prophets than preexilic. Compare Jeremiah, who argued against the complacency and self-servingness of the priests in the Jerusalem temple. Joel is more like Haggai and Malachi in his support of the temple.

Joel was a prophet of the judgment day. He called it the "Day of Yahweh" (1:15), as did Amos, but broadened the concept out into a comprehensive world historical event. Accepting the postexilic dating of Joel, the book is a study in the appropriation of earlier prophetic tradition, especially Amos, and the Day of Yahweh.

> 1:15 *Watch out for THE DAY! The Day of Yahweh is near. As destruction from Shaddai it comes.*

Here Joel uses the priestly designation of the God of the Ancestors, (El) Shaddai. But the God of the Ancestors has turned against Israel. The notion of the Day of Yahweh appears to come out of the Conquest tradition. It was Yahweh's day, the day when he demonstrated his power by destroying Israel's enemies. Times change. Now his power will be unleashed against Israel. But if the people take warning and repent, disaster can be averted.

The occasion for Joel's core prophecy most likely was the devastating locust plague described in 1:4. The only way to avert disaster is through a communal fast. The coming destruction is described as a locust plague, which became a metaphor for the devastating army that would do the actual work of punishing Israel.

Joel also foresaw the coming of a new age, a time of salvation.

> 2:28 *Then afterward, I will pour out my spirit on all flesh. Your sons and your daughters will prophesy, your old men will dream dreams, and your young men will see visions. 29 I will even pour out my spirit on male and female slaves in those days.*

The pouring out of God's spirit seems to continue the spirit theme expressed in Jeremiah and Ezekiel. In those books, God would give the people a new heart and a new spirit. Here, if we are dealing with the same general expectation, this new spirit would have its source in God.

The pouring out of the spirit in Joel has associations with prophetic anointing. The spirit would inspire dreams and visions. The remarkable aspect of the outpouring is its democratic range. Everyone, young and old, male and female, would receive the prophetic gift in the latter days.

Joel's interest in the future has been read as having apocalyptic characteristics:

> 2:30 *"I will show portents in the heavens and on earth, blood and fire and columns of smoke. 31 The sun will be turned to darkness, and the moon to blood, before the great and terrible day of Yahweh comes."*

The Day of Yahweh, in Joel's description, has cosmic associations. The fire and smoke we associate with an appearance of God, a theophany. The blood could connote many things, including the taking of life. The imagery here in Joel has an apocalyptic flavor. This, combined with Joel's "end of the world," or eschatological, interest, shows he has affinities with the full-fledged apocalyptic literature that proliferates in the late postexilic period.

JONAH

The book of **Jonah** is quite unlike any other book of the Twelve—in fact, quite unlike any other book in the Hebrew Bible. For one thing, it is a tale *about* a prophet, rather than a collection of utterances *by* him. No one really knows for sure when it was written, or where. And then, of course, there is this business of a fish swallowing the prophet, who survives and is vomited onto the shore. This is so wild, could it really have happened?

To address this and other issues we have to wrestle with the nature of the book. In particular, what is its genre, or literary type? Scholars have made many suggestions. Some scholars tend to argue for the historicity of the record, finding reasons to affirm that a fish could swallow a person live. Many others have read it as fiction, regarding it as didactic narrative, a novella, a short story, or even a satire of Jewish piety.

The main character in the book is Jonah. He is attested as a real figure by 2 Kings 14:25, which tells us that he was from Gath-hepher and that he was a prophet during the reign of the Israelite king Jeroboam II in the eighth century B.C.E. That would have made Jonah a contemporary of Amos, probably accounting for the juxtaposition of the two books in the Twelve. The book's date of composition, however, is uncertain. Many scholars place it in the postexilic period.

This is the story line. Yahweh directed Jonah to go to Nineveh, the capital city of the Assyrian Empire. Jonah went by boat in the opposite direction. Yahweh sent a storm to stop him. The sailors determined that Jonah was the cause of the storm. After considerable moral anguish, they threw Jonah overboard and the seas calmed.

Jonah was swallowed by a large fish. From the innards of the fish he addressed God with a hymn of thanksgiving for deliverance. The fish deposited Jonah on the coast. From there he proceeded to Nineveh, where he declared its doom. The people repented, and God withdrew the destruction he had devised for the city. Then Jonah became very angry. He resented God's mercy and left the city to pout and see if the city would really be spared (see Figure 13.6).

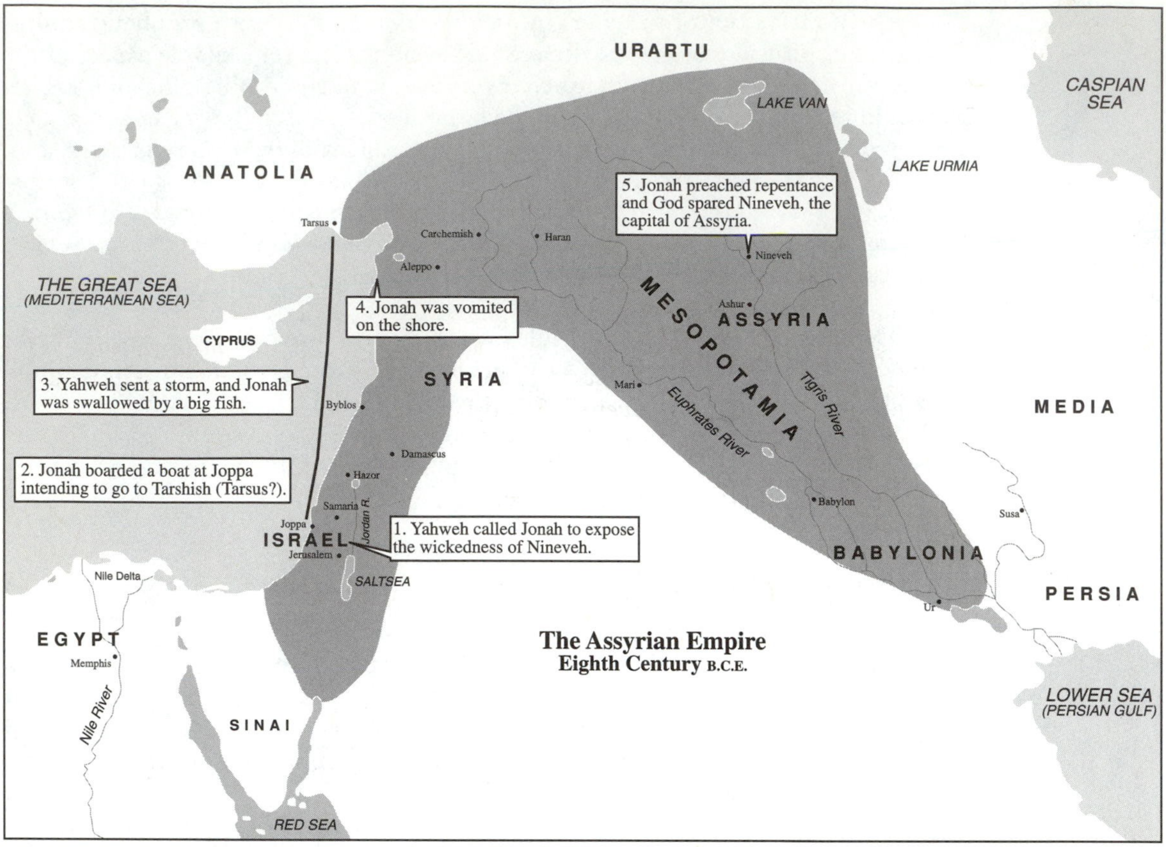
URARTU
LAKE VAN
CASPIAN SEA
LAKE URMIA
ANATOLIA
5. Jonah preached repentance and God spared Nineveh, the capital of Assyria.
Tarsus
Carchemish
Haran
Nineveh
Aleppo
THE GREAT SEA
(MEDITERRANEAN SEA)
4. Jonah was vomited on the shore.
MESOPOTAMIA
Ashur
ASSYRIA
CYPRUS
3. Yahweh sent a storm, and Jonah was swallowed by a big fish.
SYRIA
Mari
Tigris River
Euphrates River
MEDIA
Byblos
Damascus
2. Jonah boarded a boat at Joppa intending to go to Tarshish (Tarsus?).
Hazor
Samaria
Jordan R.
Babylon
Susa
Joppa
ISRAEL
1. Yahweh called Jonah to expose the wickedness of Nineveh.
Jerusalem
BABYLONIA
Nile Delta
SALTSEA
Ur
PERSIA
EGYPT
Memphis
The Assyrian Empire
Eighth Century B.C.E.
LOWER SEA
(PERSIAN GULF)
Nile River
SINAI
RED SEA

FIGURE 13.6 JONAH AND HIS TRAVELS

There in the desert God created a shade bush for Jonah and then removed it the next day. Jonah was overjoyed to have the bush, and the next day was absolutely distraught that it had died. Hidden somewhere in this was God's lesson to Jonah about his grace and mercy. Jonah should have been happy that Nineveh had not been destroyed; instead, he was disappointed.

The book of Jonah has been interpreted in a variety of different ways. The following are some of the interpretive angles that have been proposed.

- It is a snide commentary on prophetic calling, with hyperbole portraying the reluctance of professional prophets to follow the leading of God.
- It is a criticism of Israelite prophets, exposing their insincerity at preaching repentance, not really wanting to see it, and being disappointed (and taking it as personal failure) when destructive judgment is not meted out by God.
- It is an implicit criticism of the Jewish community, which was generally unwilling to respond to prophetic calls to repentance, in contrast with the willingness of Nineveh, including king, people, and even cattle, who responded immediately in faith.

- It is a criticism of an exclusionary Jewish belief in divine election, the belief that God was only concerned about his chosen people and no one else.
- It asserts God's freedom to change his mind.
- It is a treatment of true and false prophecy, claiming that the words of true prophets (Jonah in this case) do not always come true.

The point of the story is difficult to determine (if, in fact, there is only one intended point), especially in light of the indeterminate way the book ends—with a rhetorical question.

> *4:9 God said to Jonah, "Is it right for you to be angry about the bush?" He replied, "It is right for me to be angry, to death." 10 YHWH said, "You cared about the bush over which you did not labor or cause to grow, which between a night and a night came up and died. 11 Should I not care about the great city Nineveh, in which there are more than 120,000 people who do not know their right hand from their left, and many animals?"*

In light of the prophetic preoccupation with cursing foreign nations, God's concern for those notoriously nasty Assyrians is especially remarkable. Perhaps among other things, the book of Jonah is at least saying that God has the freedom to show mercy to the foreign nations if he wants to. The people of God have no right to be self-righteous or to hold an exclusivist claim on the love of God.

Drawing on the remarkable "God is slow to anger and abounding in love" tradition of the Torah (see Numbers 14:18), Jonah angrily threw back in the face of God his reputation for showing compassion.

> *4:2 "Is this not what I said while I was still back home? That is why I fled to Tarshish in the first place. I know that you are a gracious and merciful God, slow to anger, and abounding in love, and ready to relent from punishing."*

Jonah's sarcasm exposed his own pettiness and self-absorption, in contrast to God's love and concern for all people. God shows an amazing capacity to love, compared to humankind's legalism and tendency to hatred. This lesson seems to have been needed by the Jewish community of the postexilic period, when it was natural to be resentful of its neighbors and too easy to be preoccupied with itself. The self-criticism implicit in this book makes its inclusion in the canon especially remarkable.

OVERALL SHAPE OF THE BOOK OF THE TWELVE PROPHETS

Is the Book of the Twelve a unitary work in any sense? Were these twelve rather short books placed together on one scroll of sheepskin only for convenience? The first recorded reference to these books as the "Twelve Prophets" comes from the Wisdom of Ben Sirach in the second century B.C.E. So they have been grouped together for a long time. But why?

It is safe to say that each book has its own editorial integrity and canonical shape. Each can stand on its own. Yet the question we ask at this point is this: Do we gain anything from seeing these books as a collection? Might there have been a theological or literary reason in creating this collection and ordering it in this particular way?

Although nothing can be "proven," the answer seems to be yes. There is a rough chronological progression going from first to last in the Twelve. And there is unity within diversity. The books taken as a whole address the big issues of prophecy: namely, Israel's devotion to Yahweh, the responsibility of foreign nations to respect God's people, and the expectation that God will act in the future to vindicate his people and punish wickedness. The future held both punishment of the nations and vindication for Israel. Punishment occurred when in succession the empires of Assyria, Babylonia, and Persia were themselves eclipsed, and vindication occurred when the people of God survived. Through it all, Israel was the place where God's Torah was honored, if at times only half-heartedly.

The Book of the Twelve ends on a note of anticipation. Malachi affirmed the enduring relevance of the Torah of Moses and looked forward to the return on the Day of Yahweh of Elijah, who would decisively turn the hearts of the people back to God.

QUESTIONS FOR REVIEW

1. *Amos* What was Amos's attitude to issues of social justice, and how did he perceive the relationship between religious worship and community responsibility?

2. *Hosea* In what way was Hosea's personal life a lesson to Israel of its relationship to God?

3. *Micah* What social class conflict is evident in Micah, and how does it relate to covenant theologies?

4. *Zephaniah* What is the Day of Yahweh theme, employed in Zephaniah and also in Amos?

5. *Nahum* Why did Nahum condemn Nineveh?

6. *Habakkuk* What issue of God's justice did Habakkuk raise?

7. *Obadiah* Whom did Obadiah condemn for taking advantage of the plight of the Judeans?

8. *Haggai* How did Haggai explain the dismal conditions in Jerusalem after the return from Babylonian exile, and what must the people do to change this situation?

9. *Zechariah* How did Zechariah provide spiritual and moral support to the returned refugees in Jerusalem?

10. *Malachi* What did Malachi have to say about Elijah?

11. *Joel* What is the central theme of Joel and how is it related to locusts?

12. *Jonah* What are some possible interpretations of the book of Jonah, and which do you think best fits the book?

QUESTIONS FOR DISCUSSION

1. Is world history really the arena where God expresses his pleasures and displeasures with nations? Most of the twelve prophets, but especially Nahum, Habakkuk, and Obadiah, argued that Israel was "better" than this or that foreign nation. Habakkuk was upset that Judah was suffering at the hands of the Babylonians when Judah was more righteous than the Babylonians. Is there a divine national ranking system whereby we can say one nation is better than another in God's eyes? Is there a corporate morality that is judgable and that is judged by God, independent of personal morality?

2. Reflect on the vehement prophetic condemnations of the foreign nations. A couple of the Twelve deal only with judgment on foreign nations. Then reflect on the message of the book of Jonah with regard to Nineveh. What were the options with regard to God's justice in relation to God's mercy? Did God treat the foreign nations differently than he treated his own people? Was there a different standard of judgment? For what are they held accountable?

3. The twelve prophets—if not the namesakes themselves, then certainly their editors and compilers—were concerned to balance judgment with salvation. Do you think God's punishment is inevitable, or will there always be salvation in the end?

FOR FURTHER STUDY

The following are general introductions to the prophetic books of the Hebrew Bible and so include treatments of the Twelve Prophets.

Blenkinsopp, Joseph (1983). *A History of Prophecy in Israel*. Philadelphia: Westminster Press.

Miller, John W. (1987). *Meet the Prophets. A Beginner's Guide to the Books of the Biblical Prophets*. New York/Mahwah: Paulist Press.

Sawyer, John F. A. (1993). *Prophecy and the Biblical Prophets*. Rev. ed. Oxford: Oxford University Press.

Ward, James M. (1991). *Thus Says the Lord. The Message of the Prophets*. Nashville, Tenn.: Abingdon Press.

Winward, Stephen (1969). *A Guide to the Prophets*. Atlanta: John Knox Press.

Wood, Leon J. (1979). *The Prophets of Israel*. Grand Rapids, Mich.: Baker.

Amos. Barstad, Hans M. (1984). *The Religious Polemics of Amos*. VTS 34. Leiden: E. J. Brill.

Coote, Robert B. (1981). *Amos Among the Prophets: Composition and Theology*. Philadelphia: Fortress Press.

Crenshaw, James L. (1975). *Hymnic Affirmations of Divine Justice: The Doxologies of Amos and Related Texts in the Old Testament*. SBL Dissertation Series, 24. Missoula, Mont.: Scholars Press.

Paul, Shalom M. (1991). *Amos. A Commentary on the Book of Amos*. Hermeneia Series. Philadelphia: Fortress Press.

Polley, Max E. (1989). *Amos and the Davidic Empire. A Socio–Historical Approach*. Oxford: Oxford University Press.

Ward, James M. (1969). *Amos and Isaiah: Prophets of the Word of God*. Nashville, Tenn.: Abingdon Press.

Wolff, Hans W. (1973). *Amos the Prophet: The Man and His Background*. Philadelphia: Fortress Press.

Wolff, Hans W. (1977). *Joel and Amos*. Hermeneia Series. Philadelphia: Fortress Press.

Hosea. Brueggemann, Walter (1968). *Tradition for Crisis: A Study in Hosea*. Richmond, Va.: John Knox Press.

Emmerson, Grace I. (1984). *Hosea: An Israelite Prophet in Judean Perspective*. JSOT Supplement Series, 28. Sheffield: JSOT Press.

Wolff, Hans W. (1965). *Hosea*. Hermeneia Series. Philadelphia: Fortress Press.

Yee, Gale A. (1987). *Composition and Tradition in the Book of Hosea: A Redactional Critical Investigation*. SBL Dissertation Series, 102. Atlanta: Scholars Press.

Micah. Alfaro, Juan (1989). *Micah: Justice and Loyalty*. ITC. Grand Rapids, Mich.: Eerdmans.

Hagstrom, David G. (1988). *The Coherence of the Book of Micah: A Literary Analysis*. SBL Dissertation Series, 89. Atlanta: Scholars Press.

Hillers, Delbert (1984). *Micah*. Hermeneia Series. Philadelphia: Fortress Press.

Jeppesen, K. (1978). "New Aspects of Micah Research." *JSOT* 8:3–32.

Mays, James L. (1976). *Micah*. OTL. Philadelphia: Westminster Press.

Wolff, Hans W. (1981). *Micah the Prophet*. Philadelphia: Fortress Press.

Zephaniah. Kapelrud, Arvid S. (1975). *The Message of the Prophet Zephaniah: Morphology and Ideas*. Oslo: Universitetsforlaget.

Szeles, M. E. (1987). *Habakkuk and Zephaniah: Wrath and Mercy*. ITC. Grand Rapids, Mich.: Eerdmans.

Nahum. Baker, David. W. (1988). *Nahum, Habakkuk and Zephaniah*. TOTC. Leicester, Eng., and Downers Grove, Ill.: Inter-Varsity Press.

Coogins, Richard J., and S. P. Re'emi (1985). *Nahum, Obadiah, Esther: Israel Among the Nations*. ITC. Grand Rapids, Mich.: Eerdmans.

Mihelic, Joseph (1948). "The Concept of God in the Book of Nahum." *Interpretation* 2: 199–208.

Habakkuk. Gowan, Donald E. (1976). *The Triumph of Faith in Habakkuk*. Atlanta: John Knox Press.

Haak, Robert D. (1992). *Habakkuk: Translation and Commentary*. SVT 44. Leiden: E. J. Brill.

Obadiah. Allen, Leslie C. (1976). *The Books of Joel, Obadiah, Jonah and Micah*. NICOT. Grand Rapids, Mich.: Eerdmans.

Baker, David. W., T. Desmond Alexander, and Bruce K. Waltke (1988). *Obadiah, Jonah, Micah*. TOTC. Leicester, Eng., and Downers Grove, Ill.: Inter-Varsity Press.

Myers, Jacob M. (1971). "Edom and Judah in the 6th–5th Cents. B.C.," in *Near Eastern Studies in Honor of W. F. Albright*. Baltimore: Johns Hopkins University Press.

Wolff, Hans W. (1986). *Obadiah and Jonah*. Minneapolis: Augsburg.

Haggai. Baldwin, Joyce G. (1972). *Haggai, Zechariah, Malachi*. TOTC. Leicester, Eng., and Downers Grove, Ill.: Inter-Varsity Press.

Coggins, Richard J. (1987). *Haggai, Zechariah, Malachi*. Old Testament Guides. Sheffield: JSOT Press.

Meyers, Carol L., and Eric M. Meyers (1987). *Haggai; Zechariah 1–8*. AB. Garden City, N.Y.: Doubleday.

Petersen, David L. (1984). *Haggai and Zechariah 1–8*. Philadelphia: Westminster Press.

Stuhlmueller, Carroll (1988). *Haggai and Zechariah*. ITC Grand Rapids, Mich.: Eerdmans.

Verhoef, Pieter A. (1987). *The Books of Haggai and Malachi*. NICOT. Grand Rapids, Mich.: Eerdmans.

Wolff, Hans W. (1988). *Haggai*. Minneapolis: Augsburg Press.

Zechariah. See commentaries under Haggai above.

Malachi. Kaiser, Walter C. (1984). *Malachi: God's Unchanging Love*. Grand Rapids, Mich.: Baker.

Ogden, Graham S., and Richard R. Deutsch (1987). *Joel and Malachi: A Promise of Hope, A Call to Obedience*. ITC. Grand Rapids, Mich.: Eerdmans.

Joel. Ahlstrom, G. W. (1971). *Joel and the Temple Cult of Jerusalem*. SVT 21. Leiden: E. J. Brill.

Allen, Leslie C. (1976). *The Books of Joel, Obadiah, Jonah and Micah*. NICOT. Grand Rapids, Mich.: Eerdmans.

Hubbard, David A. (1989). *Joel and Amos*. TOTC. Leicester, Eng., and Downers Grove, Ill.: Inter-Varsity Press.

Prinsloo, Willem S. (1985). *The Theology of the Book of Joel*. BZAW 163. Berlin and New York: Walter de Gruyter.

Wolff, Hans W. (1977). *Joel and Amos*. Hermeneia Series. Philadelphia: Fortress Press.

Jonah. Ackerman, James S. (1981). "Satire and Symbolism in the Song of Jonah," in *Traditions in Transformation: Turning Points in Biblical Faith*, ed. Baruch Halpern and Jon D. Levenson. Winona Lake, Ind.: Eisenbrauns.

Day, John (1990). "Problems in the Interpretation of the Book of Jonah," in *In Quest of the Past. Studies on Israelite Religion, Literature and*

Prophetism, OTS 26, ed. A. S. Van der Woude. Leiden: E. J. Brill.

Fretheim, Terence E. (1977). *The Message of Jonah*. Minneapolis: Augsburg.

Lacocque, André, and Pierre-Emmanuel Lacocque. (1981). *The Jonah Complex*. Atlanta: John Knox Press.

Magonet, Jonathan (1983). *Form and Meaning: Studies in Literary Techniques in the Book of Jonah*. Sheffield: Sheffield Academic Press.

WORKS CITED

Blenkinsopp, Joseph (1983). *A History of Prophecy in Israel*. Philadelphia: Westminster Press.

Coote, Robert B. (1981). *Amos Among the Prophets: Composition and Theology*. Philadelphia: Fortress Press.

Wolff, Hans W. (1965). *Hosea*. Hermeneia Series. Philadelphia: Fortress Press.

Wolff, Hans W. (1977). *Joel and Amos*. Hermeneia Series. Philadelphia: Fortress Press.

Wolff, Hans W. (1981). *Micah the Prophet*. Philadelphia: Fortress Press.

Yadin, Yigael (1964). "Excavations at Hazor," in *The Biblical Archaeologist Reader 2*, ed. David Noel Freedman and Edward F. Campbell, Jr. Garden City, N.Y.: Doubleday.

EPILOGUE TO THE PROPHETS

THEOLOGICAL THEMES IN PROPHETIC LITERATURE

LITERARY AND HISTORICAL ISSUES IN PROPHETIC LITERATURE

Prophetic literature includes both Former and Latter Prophets. The books of the Former Prophets rehearse the history of Israel from the united monarchy to the Babylonian exile. They recount that history from a theological perspective, always attentive to divine initiative and divine purpose in history. The books of the Latter Prophets were oriented to the great prophetic personalities of Israel's history. They mostly contain collections of statements and pronouncements voiced by the prophets of Israel and Judah. Composed in poetic form, these books contain very little narrative description.

Having studied the individual prophetic books of the Former and Latter Prophets, we can now pull together some of the larger themes and issues that surfaced in the course of our readings.

THEOLOGICAL THEMES IN PROPHETIC LITERATURE

The literature of biblical prophecy is first of all theological literature. When we studied the individual books, we gave a great deal of attention to historical and literary matters, as is necessary in order to provide a context for reading. Yet we never lost sight of the message.

The following list pulls together many of the theological themes that appeared in prophetic literature. Use this list to recall the basic message of biblical prophecy and to focus your reading when you go back for further study.

1. *God in Israel's History*. The prophets believed implicitly that God controlled history. They believed that God had chosen Israel as his people, had formed an enduring relationship with them, and intended them to be his holy people forever. Because of this, everything that happened to Israel in history was a reflection of their relationship to God. If the people were faithful to Yahweh, they enjoyed freedom and prosperity. If they were unfaithful, God brought disaster on them in order to stir them to repentance. The Former Prophets demonstrate these biblical principles in the history of the monarchy. The Latter Prophets contain calls to repentance for averting or overcoming disaster. After disaster occurred, the prophets brought words of hope, knowing that God would never allow his people to disappear.

2. *Covenant Traditions*. The message of the prophets was rooted in the covenantal traditions of Israel. The covenants of Moses and David were especially influential. These traditions defined Israel's relationship to God. On the basis of the requirements laid out in these traditions, the prophets called the people back to faith. Prophets sometimes recalled Israel's covenantal roots to reaffirm the truth of God and to ground God's faithfulness. At other times they recalled those traditions to demonstrate how God was going to do something new and even more wonderful than what he had done in the past. In any case, the prophets carry on their ministry against the background of God's covenantal relationship with Israel. Reading prophetic literature in terms of its intertextual relationships with the Torah, where the records of those covenant traditions are found, can be very exciting.

3. *Ritual and Faith*. The prophets tried to shape the faith of the people so that they would think and act properly. Sometimes prophets were in conflict with institutional religion. Yet prophets never completely condemned religious ritual practices or formal worship. They only opposed such things when they served to promote religious self-satisfaction, complacency, and social injustice. In fact, some prophets were also priests, and all true prophets were informed by the best principles of Israel's priestly tradition, including the reality of sin and the need for sacrifice, purification, and holiness.

4. *Prophetic Calling and the Word of God*. Many prophets conveyed their understanding of the nature of prophetic calling and the task of prophecy in call narratives—Isaiah 6, 40; Jeremiah 1; Ezekiel 1–3; Amos 7. These narratives convey the personal conviction that motivated Israel's true prophets. They believed that God revealed his word to them and that God spoke through them. Furthermore, they believed that the word of God was not just divine information but had the power to drive and determine history. It also had the power to change personal lives and the lives of nations.

LITERARY AND HISTORICAL ISSUES IN PROPHETIC LITERATURE

In addition to the theological themes of prophetic literature listed above, the study of prophetic literature involves a number of literary and historical issues. The following list summarizes many of the issues that surfaced when we examined the prophetic books and should be kept in mind as you continue to study this literature.

1. *History and Prophecy*. We have seen that prophets spoke in history, and they tried to influence the course of history. It is important to remember to correlate the writing of prophets with the historical context in which they spoke, for only then does what they say make good sense.

2. *Formation of Prophetic Books*. Every one of the prophetic books of the Hebrew Bible shows signs of having been compiled over a period of time. Although this oversimplifies the process a bit, we can say that the core of each book goes back to the oracles and pronouncements of the named prophet. These oracles were then written down and organized into books. Some books reworked the original prophetic core more extensively than others. But each book is the result of a composing and editing process that sometimes took centuries to complete. The final shape of prophetic books bears witness to how the words of the Hebrew prophets were heard by later communities and how original prophetic pronouncements gave direction to later people.

3. *Deuteronomic Editing*. Although the character of the so-called Deuteronomic school is still being worked out by scholars, the telltale signs of its editorial work can be found in much of the prophetic literature. Its

theological perspective became a major filter for the telling of history and for the shape of theology.

4. *Social Setting of Prophecy*. Prophets did not operate in a social vacuum but were shaped by their sociohistorical situation. Each spoke out of his particular background, whether urban or agricultural, priestly or lay, wealthy or of moderate means. Each tended to be shaped by his region's theological traditions, whether northern or southern, Israelite or Judean.

Readers of biblical prophecy must keep all of these factors and issues in mind in order to understand prophetic literature properly.

WRITINGS

3

PROLOGUE TO THE WRITINGS

Names and Terms to Remember

apocalyptic literature	wisdom literature
Chronicler's history	Writings
Five Scrolls	

The third major division of the Hebrew Bible is the *Ketuvim* (the *k* of Tanak), otherwise called the **Writings**. The title *hagiographa* (*sacred writings* in Greek) has been applied to this division by Roman Catholics and some Protestant Christians. It contains a variety of materials, including songs, prayers, moral maxims, philosophical investigations, short stories, worship liturgies, and histories. Some of the individual books draw from material going back to Israel's early history, but all the books of the Writings in their final form date to the postexilic period. The Writings was the last of the three divisions of the Hebrew Bible to take shape, sometime late in the first century C.E.

The Writings will be treated in five chapters. The organization of our discussion follows the traditional order of books in the Hebrew canon (see Table 1).

The book of Psalms contains the collection of songs and prayers that Israel used as its voice to God. Proverbs and Job are grouped together in the category **wisdom literature**. The Song of Songs, Ruth, Lamentations, Ecclesiastes,

TABLE 1   THE WRITINGS

Textbook Chapter	Group	Biblical Book
14	Songs and Prayers	Psalms
15	Wisdom Literature	Proverbs
		Job
16	Five Scrolls	Song of Songs
		Ruth
		Lamentations
		Ecclesiastes
		Esther
17	Apocalyptic Literature	Daniel
18	Chronicler's History	Ezra
		Nehemiah
		1 and 2 Chronicles

and Esther are grouped together and called the **Five Scrolls**. Each was read during one of Israel's major festivals. Daniel is in a class by itself. Not a prophetic book in the traditional sense, it is visionary in a special way and is classed as **apocalyptic literature**. Finally, the books Ezra, Nehemiah, and Chronicles are historical literature. Together called the **Chronicler's history**, they retell Israel's early history and continue it down to the end to the fifth century B.C.E.

While the Hebrew Bible locates these books together at the end of the canon, English translations separate the books and distribute them among the books of the Prophets, often on the basis of chronology. For example, Ruth was placed between Judges and Samuel because the events recorded in the book are set in the period of the Judges. Esther was situated after Nehemiah because both books are set in the Persian period.

Some placements were made on the basis of literary judgments. Proverbs, Ecclesiastes, and Song of Songs are clustered together because it was thought all three were written by Solomon. Chronicles was placed after Kings because both are historical literature. Daniel was placed after Ezekiel because he was considered the fourth major prophet.

The associations and clusters in English versions make some sense but can often be faulted because they are based on misjudgments. For example, Daniel is quite unlike the literature of the Latter Prophets. It belongs to a different genre, apocalyptic literature, and is much later than mainstream prophecy. Ecclesiastes and the Song of Songs were not written by Solomon.

But more importantly, scattering the books throughout the Prophets dissipates the integrity of the collection. Together, the books of the Writings represent an important stage in the history of Israel and the development of their religion and society. Recognizing all these books as the products of postexilic Judaism enables us better to grasp the nature of that community. Even more, it enables us to understand the theological process, that is, how a faithful community saw itself in relationship to God as it wrestled with its changed circumstances and changing identity.

As we read the individual books of the Writings be alert to the many ways they draw from the literature of the Torah and the Prophets. They frequently allude to or quote passages that can be found in earlier writings. Recalling earlier traditions or prophecies became the occasion to affirm the faithfulness of God and to call the people back to faithfulness.

The Writings manifest the variety of ways the postexilic community responded to its traditions. Given the wealth of books and perspectives in the Writings, it is evident that there was no single literary response to the Torah and the Prophets. They reveal a vital, reflective community of faith that was wrestling with its theological past. The past was never of only antiquarian interest to them.

The Writings could be considered the record of a dialogue between the postexilic community and the traditions that had defined its faith to that point. In the Writings, the postexilic community wrestled with the meaning and application of the Torah and Prophets to (what was to them) the modern world. Times change, and in order for faith to be vital and current, traditions must be activated and applied in relevant ways. The Writings are evidence of such tradition activation and application.

None of this should suggest that the Writings are a rehashing of old traditions. They embody significant new departures. For example, wisdom literature, while having roots in the period of the united monarchy, presents a new way of analyzing the world. The genre of the short story, worked out in Ruth and Esther, is a new literary form that presents heroes of the faith as models to be emulated. The Song of Songs is poetry on the theme of human sexuality and love quite unlike anything that came before it. Even the Chronicler's retelling of Israelite history does it in a distinctively new way to meet the needs of the postexilic community.

Conversation is evident within the Writings, the dialogue of old formulations of the faith with new, the dialogue of the past with the present. That dialogue is mostly implicit but sometimes explicit. We will pay special attention to this dialogue in our treatment of the individual books. The fact of the dialogue tells us at least this much about the postexilic community: Religious tradition remained central to its life, and while it responded to tradition in various ways, the "Word of God" continued to speak powerfully.

Psalms: Songs and Prayers

Names and Terms to Remember

antithetic parallelism	hymn	Psalter
call to praise	invocation	stanza
climactic parallelism	lament	superscription
complaint	parallelism	synonymous parallelism
formal parallelism	petition	thanksgiving
form critique (form criticism)	praise	vow of praise

The book of Psalms exposes the pulsing heart of Israel. In it we find the life-blood of the faith of God's people. In it are Israel's songs of faith, expressing joy and confidence in God and God's chosen leaders. In it are Israel's prayers out of times of despair, tragedy, and alienation. By studying the book of Psalms we put ourselves in closest touch with the ebb and flow of the people's relationship to God. The book of Psalms served as the hymnbook and prayerbook of Israel from early times and remains the voice of God's people in contemporary Judaism and Christianity.

FIGURE 14.1   **ANCIENT MUSICIANS** An Assyrian soldier escorts three captive lyrists in this stone relief from the palace of Sennacherib (circa 700 B.C.E.). This scene is reminiscent of the sentiment of Psalm 137, "By the rivers of Babylon we sat down and wept when we remembered Zion. On willows there we hung up our harps. There our captors demanded we sing songs. But how could we sing Yahweh's songs in a foreign land?"

Our study of the psalms demands that we investigate both their form and their content. The psalms were written as poetry. If you open any English Bible and turn to the book of Psalms this would be immediately evident. English translations use the printing conventions of poetry in their presentation of the psalms: the lines are short and there is a lot of white space on the page. Understanding biblical poetry is essential to understanding the psalms.

BIBLICAL POETRY

The form of Israel's songs and prayers is defined by the general conventions of biblical poetry. In fact, a significant amount of Israel's literature in addition to the book of Psalms is in poetic form. For example, the book of Lamentations is a set of five poetic laments over the destruction of Jerusalem. A high percentage of the literature of the Latter Prophets is in poetic form. Even narrative literature contains occasional poetic insertions, such as the Blessing of Jacob (Genesis 49), the Song of the Sea (Exodus 15), and David's dirge on the death of Saul and Jonathan (2 Samuel 1).

What constitutes poetry in the Hebrew tradition? It is not a simple matter. Actually, a number of features taken together make for poetry. These features have to do with the nature of the language and imaginative imagery the poet used (Caird 1980) and the structures and forms into which the thoughts were poured (O'Connor 1980). Our brief treatment of biblical poetry will introduce the main levels where poetic features operate, as well as the tools and techniques available to the poet at each of these levels.

Figure 14.2 presents a diagram that may be used as a reference in our discussion of the levels of analysis.

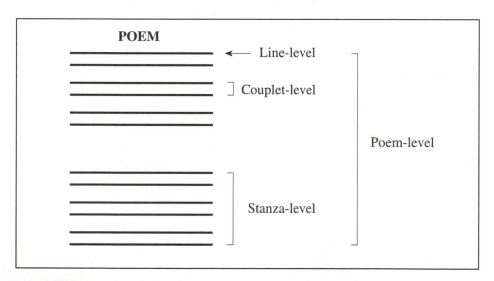

POEM

Line-level

Couplet-level

Poem-level

Stanza-level

FIGURE 14.2   BIBLICAL POETRY

LINE-LEVEL FEATURES

A single line of biblical poetry, sometimes called a *stich*, might or might not be a complete sentence. If it is not a complete sentence, then it is completed by the second line, and rarely by a third line. Whether or not a single line is a sentence, there are poetic features that operate on the line level.

Alliteration is the repetition of a consonantal sound in two or more words of a line. It is a sound device that can be perceived only in the original Hebrew version, for obvious reasons. In the following line notice the repetition of the underlined consonants *y*, *v*, and *d*, repeated in exactly that order.

> *yovad yom ivaled bo*
> *Perish the day on which I was born.*
> *(Job 3:3a)*

Alliteration can sometimes extend across multiple lines. In the following two couplets from Psalm 122 notice the repetition of the underlined sounds *sh* and *l*, with additional alliteration in *ayik* at the end of each couplet.

> *sha'alu shelom yerushalayim*
> *yishlayu ohavayik*
> *yehi sha lom bechelek*
> *shalvah be'armenotayik*
>
> *Entreat the peace of Jerusalem,*
> *May they prosper who love you.*
> *May peace be within your walls,*
> *Security within your towers.*
> *(Psalm 122:6–7)*

Paranomasia is a play on words, a verbal pun, that makes specialized use of alliteration. The poetry of prophecy contains examples of this device. Amos used it masterfully, as in the following line where *Gilgal* puns on *go into exile*.

> *ki hagilgal galoh yigleh*
> *For Gilgal will surely go into exile.*
> *(Amos 5:5)*

Also, when Amos saw a basket of summer fruit, *qayits*, he took this as a sign that the end, *qets*, was near (8:12). Paranomasia is used throughout the Hebrew Bible and is not restricted to poetry. Genesis 2:7 says God formed man, *adam*, out of the ground, *adamah*.

COUPLET-LEVEL FEATURES

A fundamental feature of Hebrew poetry is **parallelism**, the parallel structure of its lines. The basic building block of Hebrew poetry is the couplet (also called a *distich* or *bicolon*), which consists of two contiguous lines related to each other by form and by content. Usually each verse number in English versions of the psalms is a Hebrew poetic couplet, more rarely a triplet (also called a *tristich* or *tricolon*). Poetic analysts designate the two lines of a couplet the A-line and the B-line.

The exact formal relationship between the lines of a couplet has been difficult to specify. Hebrew poetry does not have rhythm and meter in the same sense as, for example, iambic pentameter verse in Western poetry. Rather, Hebrew poetry seems to be governed by a basic balance between the lines of a couplet (or triplet) whereby each line has the same number of word units. Most couplets have three major stressed word units in each line for a 3 + 3 pattern. In the following example, note that it often takes multiple English words to translate one Hebrew word.

> *Yahweh how-many-are my-foes*
> *1 + 1 + 1 = 3 A-line*
> *Multitudes are-rising-up against-me*
> *1 + 1 + 1 = 3 B-line*
> *(Psalm 3:2)*

Some couplets have unbalanced lines of 3 + 2 word units. Called lament meter (*qinah* in Hebrew), it predominates in the book of Lamentations and is frequently found elsewhere. Some analysts have sought to refine the notion of Hebrew poetic meter and suggest that parallelism occurs when each line of a couplet has virtually the same number of syllables (see Stuart 1976).

O'Connor (1980) suggests that parallelism is not constituted on the formal level by rhythm, meter, or line length, but by word devices such as alliteration, verbal repetition, and syntactic dependencies that bind poetic lines together into literary sense units. The problem with analyzing biblical parallelism is that everyone recognizes *that* it exists, but agreeing on exactly *how* it exists is another matter.

A widely used method of analysis classifies couplets by the meaning, or semantic, relationship of the two lines (Gray 1915, Geller 1979). Four basic types of relationship have been identified: synonymous, antithetic, formal, and climactic.

Synonymous parallelism is present when the notion of the A-line is repeated in the B-line.

> *Pay attention, my people, to my teaching,* A-line
> *Be attentive to the words of my mouth.* B-line
> *(Psalm 78:1)*

In **antithetic parallelism,** the notion of the A-line is stated in opposite terms in the B-line.

> *YHWH protects the way of the righteous,* A-line
> *But the way of the wicked will perish.* B-line
> *(Psalm 1:6)*

In **formal parallelism,** sometimes termed synthetic parallelism, the two lines have a formal relationship defined by rhythm or line length, but the A-line is semantically continued in the B-line. The couplet contains only one complete sentence, not two coordinated sentences as in the other types of parallelism. The two lines are parallel in form but not in content.

> Like a club, sword, or sharp arrow   A-line
> is one who bears false witness against a neighbor.   B-line
> (Proverbs 25:18)

Climactic parallelism combines synonymous and formal parallelism. The B-line echoes part of the A-line, then adds a phrase that develops the meaning and completes the sense.

> Accredit to YHWH, O Heavenly Ones,   A-line
> Accredit to YHWH glory and strength.   B-line
> (Psalm 29:1)

Formal parallelism exposes a basic problem with the broad notion of parallelism. Strictly speaking, formal parallelism is semantically nonparallel parallelism and so is not really genuine parallelism at all. Kugel (1981) challenges the traditional analysis of poetic parallelism and argues that the A- and B-lines of a poetic couplet are not typically synonymous in meaning. He claims that we should not really talk about semantic parallelism. Rather, the B-line was intended to be an expansion, elaboration, or seconding of the meaning of the A-line.

STANZA-LEVEL FEATURES

A **stanza**, sometimes called *strophe*, is a group of couplets that constitute a sense unit within a poem. It is the poetic equivalent of the paragraph. Stanzas can be recognized by features of form as well as content.

The transition from one stanza to the next can be marked by such things as changes in speaker or addressee, the use of words that signal logical or temporal transitions (such as *but* and *now*), and changes in verb forms from imperative to past tense.

Stanza structure is obvious when a repeated refrain is used within a psalm. In Psalms 42 and 43, which should be taken together as one psalm, the following refrain is found at 42:6, 42:12, and 43:5.

> My, how downcast you are, my soul,
> Upset within me!
> Put your hope in God.
> I will praise him yet—my savior and my God.

Parallelism can operate within stanzas to bind multiple couplets into a single thought unit. The individual couplets display their own internal parallelism and also have an external parallel relationship with each other.

> A-couplet   YHWH is my light and my salvation.   A-line
>   Of whom shall I be afraid?   B-line

<table>
<tr><td>*B-couplet*</td><td>*YHWH is the fortress of my life.*</td><td>*A-line*</td></tr>
<tr><td></td><td>*Of whom shall I be in fright?*</td><td>*B-line*</td></tr>
</table>

(Psalm 27:1)

Using refrains and external parallelism, literary sense units can extend beyond the limits of poetic couplets.

POEM-LEVEL FEATURES

Biblical poetry sometimes employs techniques on the level of the entire poem to bind couplets and stanzas into one composition. Some of these techniques involve alphabetic schemes in one form or another. Psalm 119 consists of twenty-two stanzas of eight couplets each. The first lines of each couplet of the first stanza begin with the Hebrew letter *aleph*, the first lines of each couplet of the second stanza begin with the letter *beth*, and so on for each of the twenty-two letters of the Hebrew alphabet.

Psalm 34 is an acrostic poem where the first verse begins with *aleph* and each succeeding verse begins with the next letter of the alphabet. Psalms 9 and 10 should be taken as a single poem by the evidence of the acrostic structure that starts in 9 and finds completion in 10.

In addition to the formal and structural features of Hebrew poetry at its various levels, numerous stylistic features lend a high literary quality to this type of writing.

LITERARY FEATURES

One of the notable features of biblical poetry, and poetry in general, is what we could call *compression*. That is, poetry packs the biggest thoughts into the least amount of words. This often means that a great deal is left to the reader's imagination and interpretative skill. The reader has to unpack poetic expressions to draw out their nuance and intent, and often a biblical poetic line can be rendered in many different ways. Serious study of biblical poetry (short of learning the Hebrew language and reading it in the original) demands gathering a variety of different English versions in order to compare translations. This reveals the variety of ways the poetic text could be interpreted and opens up possibilities of understanding.

In addition, the reader must be sensitive to the use of poetic language. Poetry often communicates through the creative and evocative use of language. Imagery can be used to help the reader visualize thoughts or feelings, as in the following verse.

Dogs surround me,
a group of evildoers encircles me.
(Psalm 22:17)

Imagery often takes the shape of *simile* or *metaphor*. Simile is more obvious than metaphor, because it uses the word *like* or *as* to introduce the comparison.

I am like a moth to Ephraim,
and like dry-rot to the house of Judah.
(Hosea 5:12)

Metaphor is less direct and more subtle, implying a comparison rather than introducing it with *like* or *as*. Psalm 18 uses metaphors to communicate the steadfastness of Yahweh to the psalmist.

YHWH is my rock and my fortress and my deliverer.
My God is my rock.
I take refuge in him.
My shield and the horn of my salvation, my stronghold.
(Psalm 18:3)

Many of the techniques found in narrative as well as in poetry, including anthropomorphism and personification, can be classified as specialized types of metaphor.

BOOK OF PSALMS

The book of Psalms, also called the **Psalter,** is an anthology of songs and prayers. It is not a book in the sense that one chapter logically follows the next. Instead, the individual psalms are like pearls on a necklace. The Psalter has less cohesion as a book than most other books of the Hebrew Bible. There is a staggering variety of psalm types. And the style of the psalms, going from one to the next, frequently changes dramatically. But this is not necessarily a weakness, and in fact may be a key to understanding the book as a whole, as we shall see.

AUTHORSHIP

As an anthology, the Psalter has a long history of development. Each of the 150 psalms in the collection has its own composition history. The individual psalms came from various places and times. Only after each psalm existed independently for a time were they gathered together into the Psalter.

Many psalms were addressed to Israel's God. But others were about (rather than to) God, the king, or the Torah. Consequently, there is no uniformity across the Psalter in who is being addressed or in who is speaking. For the most part we do not know who wrote particular psalms. The Psalms are commonly associated with David, the king of Israel, to the point that he is usually viewed in the popular mind as the author of the Psalter. This is not entirely correct. The association between David and the Psalms probably arose because he actually wrote some of the psalms, but also by general inference from the historical description of David as the star musician and poet laureate of the court of King Saul. In fact, the psalms themselves do not universally or unambiguously claim Davidic authorship.

Many psalms contain a label, called a **superscription,** that might contain musical directions, notes on how to perform the psalm, historical settings, and possibly suggestions of authorship.[1] Frequently found is the superscription *mizmor ledavid*, a Hebrew phrase sometimes rendered "A Psalm of David." While it might indicate Davidic authorship, it might otherwise indicate that the psalm was dedicated to David or belonged to a "David Collection." It remains an open question just what such a superscription means, but it is not necessarily the author's signature. It should also be noted that some superscriptions link particular psalms with the names Asaph, Korah, and Moses. Hence, if the *mizmor le-* phrase in a superscription does indicate authorship, many authors in addition to David are credited.

Perhaps we should not even talk about authorship in the traditional sense because it seems most of the Psalter consists of anonymous conventional poetry that developed within the community. The following discussion of speech forms and psalm types explains the conventional language of psalmic poetry.

SPEECH FORMS

Speech forms are recurring ways of speaking that can be identified and traced back to typical settings within the experience of the Israelites. The psalms employ a variety of conventional speech forms, and learning to recognize them will help us appreciate the range of the Psalter's ways of speaking to and about God.

- An **invocation** gets God's attention.

Give ear to my words, YHWH, pay attention to my groaning.
(5:1)

- **Praise** language expresses the greatness of God.

Your name, YHWH, lasts forever, your reputation, YHWH, through all generations.
(135:13)

Blessed be YHWH, for he has wonderfully demonstrated his steady love to me.
(31:21)

- **Complaint** language, also called **lament**, describes the psalmist's or the community's difficulty and often expresses feelings of abandonment.

Vindictive accusers confront me, they accuse me of things about which I know nothing. The good I did them they reimburse with evil.
(35:11–12)

---

[1] In many English versions the superscription is printed in different type from the rest of the psalm and is not given a verse number. Some versions, such as the New American Bible and the Tanakh (Jewish Publication Society), follow the Hebrew text more faithfully by giving the superscription a verse number, thereby counting it more deliberately as part of the text. Readers of different versions should note that this quirk of the versions can result in the same verse being numbered differently in different translations. In this textbook we follow the versification of Hebrew printed editions.

- A **petition** demands that God do something, perhaps intervene and give aid or forgive. Petition usually contains an imperative (and an exclamation point).

Arise, YHWH! Deliver me, my God!
(3:7)

Wash me completely of my crime, and clean me of my sin!
(51:2)

- A **call to praise** enlists fellow worshipers in acclaiming the wonders of God.

Praise YHWH!
Praise, servants of YHWH,
praise the name of YHWH!
(113:1)

- A **vow of praise** promises to credit God with the yet-to-be-experienced deliverance.

I will give you praise in the great assembly,
my vows I will fulfill before those who fear him.
(22:26)

I will enter your house with burnt offerings,
I will pay my vows to you,
what my lips spoke and mouth promised when I was in trouble.
(66:13–14)

These are just some of the modes of speech that can be found in the Psalter. These specific modes of speech have been combined in various ways in the psalms, often expressed with metaphoric language, to construct larger patterns. These speech form combinations are called *psalm types*.

PSALM TYPES

Much of modern scholarship on the psalms has not been done by historians trying to discover the authorship and literary history of the individual compositions. Rather, pioneered by Gunkel (1930), it has been done by scholars who have determined the real-life situations that gave rise to the psalms. They trace the conventional speech forms found in the psalms back to their earliest life settings. Called **form critique** (or *form criticism*), this approach has categorized the psalms according to a set of basic types, called *genres*.

Biblical research has developed a set of labels and genre classifications for the psalms. The following discussion presents these results in a simplified way using three major psalm types and a variety of minor types. Note that cataloging the psalms according to genre is not an exact science, and scholars sometimes differ among themselves when it comes to the analysis of certain psalms. Although scholars have established a certain set of psalm types, many individual psalms are not "pure" but, in fact, contain features from several different psalm types. We will look at psalm samples to identify the character of each type.

Complaint

Scholars call this psalm type a **lament**, but perhaps **complaint** communicates more immediately what this type of psalm expresses. The largest number of psalms in the Psalter fall under this heading. The heart of a complaint psalm is a description of the suffering of the psalmist and a plea for deliverance. Many complaint psalms also contain petitions and vows of praise. Frequently there is also a statement of confidence that God will come to the rescue. There are two subcategories of this psalm type, divided on the basis of whether an individual or a group is speaking.

An *individual complaint* can also be called an individual psalm of lament. About one-third of the psalms in the Psalter are of this type. Often included in this category are 3–7, 13, 17, 22, 25–28, 31, 35, 38–43, 69–71, 77, 86, 88, 102, 109, 120, 130, and 139–143.

Psalm 22 is a fine and emotionally moving representative of the individual complaint psalm type, especially notable within the Christian community because it was quoted by Jesus of Nazareth as he was being crucified. The psalmist begins with a complaint addressed to God (verses 2–12).

> 2 My God, my God, why have you abandoned me?
> Why are you so distant when I call for help, when I cry in pain?
> 3 My God, I call in the day time but you do not answer;
> at night, but I find no relief.
> 12 Do not stay far from me,
> for trouble is close,
> and there is no one else to help.

Next he moves to a vivid description of the trouble he experiences (13–19). Notice the highly metaphoric language he uses to describe his enemies and his own problems.

> 13 Many bulls surround me,
> fierce Bashan-bulls encircle me.
> 14 They open their mouths against me,
> ravaging and roaring lions that they are.
> 15 Like water my life is draining away,
> all my bones go soft.
> My heart has turned to wax,
> melting away inside me.

In the most unexpected move in the psalm, the writer offers an expression of confidence (20–26). He looks forward to the time he will have overcome his problems through the intervention of God.

22 Save me from the lion's mouth,
my puny life from the horns of wild bulls.
23 Then I will proclaim your name to the congregation,
in the community I will praise you.
26 I will offer praise in the great assembly,
my vows I will fulfill before those who fear God.

The psalm ends by encouraging everyone to praise God (27–32).

28 All the ends of the earth will worship and turn to YHWH,
all the families of nations will bow down before you.
29 For kingship belongs to YHWH,
the ruler over the nations.

The psalm moves from personal complaint to anticipation of salvation. The change comes when the psalmist makes a vow to give God the credit for helping him once his problem is overcome (verse 23). He will let everyone know that God is the one who made deliverance possible. The remarkable feature of this psalm, and ones like it, is the firm confidence the psalmist has that God will come to the rescue. In expressing this confidence, the complaint psalm actually becomes a thanksgiving psalm in advance.

A *group complaint* psalm follows the general outline of the individual complaint psalm but is the expression of the community as a whole. Generally included in this category are 12, 14, 44, 53, 58, 60, 74, 79, 80, 83, 85, 89, 90, 94, 106, 123, 126, and 137. Group complaint psalms, also called community psalms of lament, expressed the needs of the community when there was a large-scale crisis, perhaps a drought, enemy attack, or national tragedy of some other sort. Psalm 80 is typical of group complaint psalms. First, the psalmist seeks God's attention in the invocation (2). Then in the petition (4) he pleads for God to do something to help them.

2 Give ear, Shepherd of Israel,
you who lead Joseph like a flock,
you who are enthroned between the cherubim.
4 Restore us, God. Let your face shine, then we will be saved.

God is invoked as the Shepherd King who sits on his ark of the covenant throne among the divine council—the cherubim. The language of holy war is used in this psalm (signaled by "God of Hosts" in 5, 8, and elsewhere) as the expression of faith in God's power of military deliverance. This is followed by the complaint proper.

5 YHWH God of Hosts,
how long will you be angry with your people's petitions?...
8 You have let our neighbors fight over us,
and our enemies put us down.

After remembering God's past interest in them,

> *9 You brought us out of Egypt as if we were a vine;*
> *you drove out the nations and planted it.*

the psalmist goes back to petition for help, and concludes with an affirmation that they would praise God for it.

> *19b Give us life, and we will call out your name!*

Thanksgiving

The psalm of **thanksgiving** is the "flip side" of the psalm of complaint. Thanksgiving psalms are expressions of gratitude. Whereas the psalm of complaint anticipated God's deliverance, the psalm of thanksgiving was written after deliverance had been experienced. The psalmist thanks God for salvation.

The category of thanksgiving should be distinguished from the category of hymn, described later. A thanksgiving psalm expresses gratitude for an act of divine intervention in the life of the psalmist, whereas a hymn uses descriptive language to praise something about the character of God. Westermann (1981) calls thanksgivings "psalms of declarative praise" and calls hymns "psalms of descriptive praise." Thanksgiving psalms function to give public testimony to the caring nature of Yahweh and his will to save his people.

As with the complaint category, the thanksgiving category can be subdivided into two subgroups on the basis of who is speaking, an individual or the community.

The *individual thanksgiving* psalm complements the individual complaint psalm. In the individual complaint psalm, typically the psalmist asks for God's help and makes a vow of praise on its realization. In the thanksgiving psalm the psalmist makes good on his vow to praise God now that deliverance has come. Generally included in this category are 9–10, 11, 16, 30, 32, 34, 92, 116, and 138.

In typical thanksgiving psalm manner, Psalm 30 begins by recalling the adversity now past and then recounts the salvation.

> *3 YHWH my God, I cried to you for help,*
> *and you healed me.*
> *4 YHWH, you have brought me up from Sheol,*
> *you have returned me to life as opposed to those who have gone*
> *down to the underworld.*

The psalmist shares his joy by calling on the people of God to accredit the turnaround to God.

> *5 Sing praises to YHWH, you saints,*
> *and give thanks to his holy name!*

After recounting in more detail the story of his affliction and his rescue (7–13a), he concludes with his commitment to continue praising God.

13b YHWH my God, I will give thanks to you forever.

The *group thanksgiving* psalm was used on occasions of regional or national celebration. This type of psalm arose out of Israel's experience of victory and deliverance from foreign threats, as in Psalm 124.

1 If YHWH had not been on our side—
Let Israel say it!—
2 If YHWH had not been on our side
when our enemies attacked us,
3 then they would have swallowed us up alive.
6 Blessed be YHWH
who has not given us up as game to their teeth.

Not many psalms of this type found their way into the Psalter. Perhaps the reason is this: The Psalter was assembled in the postexilic period, at a time when Israel as a nation no longer experienced saving deeds of national scope. This being the case, communal psalms of thanksgiving became less relevant to their experience. Included in this category are 65–68, 75, 107, 115, 118, 124, 125, and 129.

Hymn

A **hymn** is a song in praise of God or in praise of something about God. It contains generalized praise language about God. It is not so much praise for what God has done to save (as in psalms of thanksgiving) as praise for who God is. Often included in this category are 33, 103, 104, 113, 117, 134–136, and 145–147. Psalm 113 is typical of the generalized mode of speaking.

1 Praise YHWH (Hebrew halleluyah*)!*
Praise, servants of YHWH,
praise the name of YHWH.
2 Blessed be the name of YHWH
from this time forward and forever!
3 From the rising of the sun to its setting
the name of YHWH should be praised!
4 YHWH is high above all nations,
and his glory above the heavens!

In addition to hymns of general praise, more specific subtypes can be identified, depending on what it is about Yahweh that is deemed worthy of praise.

A *creation hymn* finds reason to praise God for the wonder and magnificence of the natural world. Usually included in this category are 8, 19, 104, 139, and 148. Among creation hymns, Psalm 19 is notable for the way it conjoins the revelation of God's glory through creation with the revelation of God's will through

Torah. The first half of this psalm (1–6) deals with nature, as we see in the following sample.

> 2 *The heavens express the glory of God,*
> *and the expanse evidences his craftsmanship.*
> 3 *Daily it speaks volumes,*
> *nightly it declares knowledge.*

Although there are not many of them, hymns of *Yahweh's kingship* celebrate the rule of Yahweh. Included in this category are 47, 93, and 96–99. Most of these psalms begin with the shout "Yahweh is king!" alternately translated, "Yahweh reigns!" Another feature held in common by this group is the affirmation that Yahweh rules over the entire world. Psalm 93 is typical of this category.

> 1 *YHWH is king,*
> *he is majestically robed,*
> *YHWH is robed,*
> *he is clothed with strength.*
> *He has founded the world;*
> *it will never be moved.*
> 2 *Your throne was founded in the beginning,*
> *you are everlasting.*
> 3 *YHWH, the floods raised,*
> *the floods raised their voice,*
> *the floods lifted their roaring.*
> 4 *But more majestic than the thunder of powerful water,*
> *more majestic than sea waves,*
> *is YHWH, majestic on high.*

The threat to Yahweh's power is the primeval waters. Recall the mythological background to the Priestly story of creation. Yahweh triumphed at creation over the waters of chaos and demonstrated thereby his supremacy, here celebrated in hymnic praise.

Some scholars, on the basis of these psalms and Mesopotamian texts, attempt to reconstruct a festival of Yahweh's enthronement as king, yearly celebrated as the autumn new year observance (Mowinckel 1962). However, direct evidence within the Hebrew Bible for an Israelite festival that parallels the Babylonian new year's festival does not exist.

In Jewish traditions, the kingship of Yahweh psalms are messianic and forward-looking in anticipation of the decisive historical realization of the kingdom of God. In Christian traditions, they are eschatological and prefigured the coming of the messiah.

Mt. Zion was the location within Jerusalem of Yahweh's temple. As Yahweh's residence, it naturally became the object of hymnic praise, called *songs of Zion*. Generally included in this category are 46, 48, 76, 84, 87, and 122. Psalm 48 praises Zion with obvious hyperbole.

2 Great is YHWH and he must be praised profusely
in the city of our God.
His holy mountain,
3 beautiful in height, is the joy of the entire earth—
Mt. Zion, in the farthest north, the city of the great King.
4 Inside its fortress God has demonstrated he is a reliable defender.

In the ancient world, mountains were the dwelling places of high gods: Zeus on Mt. Olympus, Baal on Mt. Zaphon, and Yahweh on Mt. Sinai. As the Hebrew people moved from the Sinai to Canaan, the residence of their God moved to Mt. Zion within Jerusalem. Although geographically not overwhelming, Zion took on the mythic dimensions of divine mountain dwellings. It became a symbol of the presence and power of Israel's God and, consequently, Israel's absolute security.

Hymns to Israel's kings, sometimes called *royal psalms*, praise Israel's earthly kings as representatives of God. Generally included in this category are 2, 18, 20, 21, 45, 72, 89, 101, and 110. Although Israel never divinized its kings, still the kings were considered to be divinely appointed and stood in a special relationship to God. The dominant theology of Israel's monarchy, the Davidic covenant, was articulated in the Deuteronomic history. The Davidic covenant, as laid out in Nathan's oracle in 2 Samuel 7, is the object of praise in Psalm 89.

2 I proclaim that your loyalty is established for all time,
your faithfulness is as sure as the heavens.
3 You said, "I have made a covenant with my chosen one,
I have sworn to my servant David:
4 'I will establish your descendants forever, and build your throne through-
out all generations.'"

As part of the hymnbook of Israel, used especially in the postexilic period, royal psalms perpetuated the messianic ideal, namely, Israel's hope in the Davidic line to provide national leadership and resurrect an independent nation.

Minor Types

The following minor psalm types do not easily fit within the three main categories of complaint, thanksgiving, and hymn.

Torah psalms, including 1, 19:7–14, and 119, are hymns in praise of God's revelation in torah. At 176 verses, Psalm 119 is the longest chapter in the Hebrew Bible. In this psalm, as in the other torah psalms, the writer recommends a life of torah-keeping as the path to wellness.

1 Blessed are those whose way through life is blameless,
who walk in the torah of YHWH.
2 Blessed are those who keep his decrees,
who genuinely seek him.

The torah psalms, with their talk of blessing and torah observance, have a great deal in common with Deuteronomic theology.

Generally included in the category of *wisdom psalms* are 36, 37, 49, 73, 111, 112, 127, 128, and 133. They offer practical advice for living. Also, they operate with a black-and-white contrast between the wicked and the righteous. They hold these traits in common with the wisdom tradition of the book of Proverbs. Psalm 37 provides a clear example of this psalm type.

> *1 Do not be intimidated by the wicked,*
> *do not envy evildoers.*
> *2 For they will quickly dry up like grass,*
> *and wither like herbs.*
> *3 Trust in YHWH and do good,*
> *so you will dwell in the land and enjoy security.*

In their affirmation of God's blessing upon the righteous, they also have much in common with torah psalms.

A liturgy is a standardized format used in public worship or in a ritual. *Liturgy psalms* have survived for entering the temple (15, 24), temple celebration (68), priestly blessing (134), covenant renewal (50, 81), and ritualized condemnation of foreign gods (82, 115). Liturgies are those psalms that most obviously involved public performance, even if the exact shape of that performance remains unknown. Psalm 15 was a liturgy used for admission to the temple. The first verse was spoken by a priest or other official, the reply given by the pilgrim seeking entry.

> *1 YHWH, who may live in your tent?*
> *Who may dwell on your holy hill?*
> *2 Those who live morally and do what is right,*
> *who sincerely speak the truth.*

Songs of trust, also called songs of confidence, are found in both individual and community forms. Songs of trust are generalized expressions of faith in God, without having a specific backdrop of adversity. Generally included in this category are 11, 16, 23, 62, 63, 91, 121, and 131. Psalm 23 is the most famous song of trust.

> *1 YHWH is my shepherd,*
> *I lack nothing.*
> *2 He gives me rest in green fields,*
> *he brings me to peaceful waters.*
> *3 He refreshes me,*
> *he leads me down moral paths*
> *for the sake of his reputation.*

There is an almost bewildering variety of psalms in the Psalter, and a bewildering set of terms go along with them. But the variety and range of psalm types opens a window on the spiritual life of faithful Israel. In these psalms, which range over all the possible human emotions and ways of relating to God, we see that people of faith could bring any of their feelings and emotions to God. This observation may help us to grasp why the Psalter has continued to give God's people voice through the ages.

OVERALL SHAPE OF THE PSALTER

While many of the individual psalms were composed in the preexilic period, the collection of 150 psalms called the Psalter dates to the postexilic period. The Psalter is sometimes called the "Hymnbook of the Second Temple" because the compilation and final editing of the Psalter was completed within the lifetime of the temple rebuilt by Zerubbabel, probably sometime around 325–250 B.C.E., and because the individual psalms, if not the entire Psalter, were used in communal worship.[2]

On the way to compiling the Psalter from individual psalms there seem to have been stages to the collecting. Clusters of psalms can be identified having similarities of one sort or another. For example, Psalms 93–99 have to do with Yahweh as King, and 120–134 are all superscripted as Songs of Ascents. Virtual duplicates of certain psalms exist, which indicates that an independent psalm could find its way into separate subcollections of texts. For example, Psalms 14 and 53 are almost identical, the major difference being that Psalm 14 uses Yahweh as the name of God, and 53 uses Elohim. This squares with the first subcollection, 3–41, which as a whole uses Yahweh and probably originated as a collection in Judah, and 51–72, which as a whole uses Elohim and probably originated in Israel of the divided monarchy.

Table 14.1 labels the identifiable subcollections.

TABLE 14.1	SUBCOLLECTIONS OF PSALMS
3–41	Yahwistic Psalms of David
42–49	Psalms of Korah
51–72	Elohistic Psalms of David
73–83	Psalms of Asaph
84–88	Psalms of Korah
93–99	Psalms of Yahweh's Kingship
111–118	Halleluyah Thanksgiving Psalms
120–134	Songs of Ascents
146–150	Halleluyah Thanksgiving Psalms

[2] There is very little indication in the Psalter itself of the way the psalms were used in worship, apart from the superscriptions, which seem not to be original. Perhaps the obscure word *selah*, which concludes stanzas in certain psalms (for example, in 3 and 9), was a liturgical direction used in communal performance.

At some point the psalms were organized into five books: Book 1 (1–41), Book 2 (42–72), Book 3 (73–89), Book 4 (90–106), and Book 5 (107–150). Each book ends with a benediction (41:13; 72:18–20; 89:52; 106:48; 150 in its entirety). Division into five books perhaps emulates the structure of the Torah of Moses and was meant to suggest that this work contains the totality of Israel's response to God, just as the Torah contains the definitive revelation of God.

The Psalter in Hebrew is called *tehillim*, meaning praises. This on first thought seems a bit strange, since the single largest category of psalms is the complaint. Yet there is something especially important being stated through this label. Granted, there is a great deal of complaint, yet even in psalms of complaint the psalmist concludes with a vow to praise.[3] So, even though the present is a disaster, the psalmist is looking forward to the heights of salvation. Whether in the heights or the depths, the psalmist is intent on praise. At one and the same time then, the Psalter declares that complaint is authorized for the person of God, it is an allowable approach to God, and yet complaint will not, and must not, end there.

The psalms evidence the overwhelming confidence of the Israelite believer that God grants and sustains life. When there is trouble, God always comes to the rescue. Complaint and thanksgiving, lament and praise, these are the dominant poles of Israel's faith life. No matter where Israel happened to be on the spectrum of human experience, from adversity on the one extreme to prosperity on the other, there would be a psalm that could express its deepest fears and joys.

The psalms taken together contain the full range of human attitudes and responses to God. Delight, appreciation of the work of God, alienation, despair, cursing, compassion—it's all here. The collection certainly is saying that all of these human feelings and emotions are permitted within the fellowship of God's people. And they can be brought before God. They do not have to be hidden.

Furthermore, these psalms constituted Israel's manual of songs and prayers used for worship. This reinforces the reality that Israel lived its life in the presence of God. Remembering, questioning, praying, and praising were all done in the context of the community's worship. Worship was not isolated from real life but was the activity where real life was sorted out, where the people sought understanding, where life was affirmed, and where credit was given to the divine.

QUESTIONS FOR REVIEW

1. What is poetic parallelism in general, and what are the four types of parallelism that can be found in biblical poetry?

2. What are the three main psalm types, and what is the life experience out of which each arose?

3. Name and describe one poetic feature from each analytic level of a poem.

4. Taking complaint and thanksgiving psalm types as the most frequent and most basic, what is the basic theology of the Psalter?

[3] Psalms 39 and 88 are rare exceptions to the typical movement of complaint psalms from lament to praise. These two psalms contain unmitigated complaint, with apparently no salvation in view.

QUESTIONS FOR DISCUSSION

1. Apart from the book of Psalms, most of the Hebrew Bible is presented as God's revelation to Israel. The Torah was divine revelation mediated through Moses. Prophetic literature contained a divine perspective on history. The Psalter, on the other hand, contains the songs and prayers of Israel directed to God. Instead of "top down," they are "bottom up." In what sense, then, does the Psalter lay out the authoritative way in which God's people should approach him?

2. Why do you think Israel's songs and prayers were written in poetry? Why must we keep in mind that they are poetic? What effect does the fact that they are poetry have on the task of interpretation?

3. Considering the overall shape of the Psalter, what is the effect of having so many different types of psalms in one book? What does the variety in the psalmist's modes of speaking to God have to say about the way temple and church can, and perhaps should, speak to God?

FOR FURTHER STUDY

Biblical Poetry. Alter, Robert (1985). *The Art of Biblical Poetry.* New York: Basic Books.

Berlin, Adele (1985). *The Dynamics of Biblical Parallelism.* Bloomington: Indiana University Press.

Fisch, Harold (1988). *Poetry with a Purpose. Biblical Poetics and Interpretation.* Indiana Studies in Biblical Literature. Bloomington: Indiana University Press.

Kugel, James L. (1981). *The Idea of Biblical Poetry. Parallelism and Its History.* New Haven, Conn.: Yale University Press.

O'Connor, Michael (1980). *Hebrew Verse Structure.* Winona Lake, Ind.: Eisenbrauns.

Watson, Wilfred G. E. (1986). *Classical Hebrew Poetry. A Guide to its Techniques.* JSOT Supplement Series, 26. Sheffield: JSOT Press.

Book of Psalms. Anderson, Bernhard W. (1974). *Out of the Depths. The Psalms Speak for Us Today.* Philadelphia: Westminster Press. An easy-to-read introduction to the basic psalm genres.

Brueggemann, Walter (1991). *Abiding Astonishment: Psalms, Modernity, and the Making of History.* Literary Currents in Biblical Interpretation. Louisville, Ky.: Westminster/John Knox Press.

Guthrie, Harvey H. (1966). *Israel's Sacred Songs. A Study of Dominant Themes.* New York: The Seabury Press. Organizes the themes of the psalms under the following headings: God as Overlord, God as Cosmic King, God as Savior, God as Source of Wisdom, and Yahweh's Songs in an Alien Age.

Lewis, C. S. (1958). *Reflections on the Psalms.* New York and London: Harcourt, Brace, Jovanovich. Thought-provoking meditations based on the biblical psalms.

Mitchell, Stephen (1994). *A Book of Psalms. Selected & Adapted from the Hebrew.* New York: HarperCollins. Translations and adaptations of fifty psalms, recreating the music of Hebrew verse in contemporary language.

Westermann, Claus (1980). *The Psalms: Structure, Content & Message.* Minneapolis: Augsburg. Takes each of the major psalm types and examines their typical structure.

Westermann, Claus (1981). *Praise and Lament in the Psalms.* Atlanta: John Knox Press. An in-depth form-critical study of the two major modes of praying to God, thanksgiving and complaint.

WORKS CITED

Berlin, Adele (1985). *The Dynamics of Biblical Parallelism*. Bloomington: Indiana University Press.

Caird, G. B. (1980). *The Language and Imagery of the Bible*. Philadelphia: Westminster Press.

Geller, Stephen A. (1979). *Parallelism in Early Biblical Poetry*. Harvard Semitic Monographs, 20. Missoula, Mont.: Scholars Press.

Gray, George B. (1915; 1972). *The Forms of Hebrew Poetry*. Reprint. New York: KTAV.

Gunkel, Hermann (1967). *The Psalms: A Form-Critical Introduction*. Facet Books, 19. Philadelphia: Fortress Press. (original work published 1930)

Kugel, James L. (1981). *The Idea of Biblical Poetry. Parallelism and Its History*. New Haven, Conn.: Yale University Press.

Lowth, Robert (1753). *De sacra poesi Hebraeorum*.

O'Connor, Michael (1980). *Hebrew Verse Structure*. Winona Lake, Ind.: Eisenbrauns.

Mowinckel, Sigmund (1962). *The Psalms in Israel's Worship*. New York and Nashville, Tenn.: Abingdon.

Stuart, Douglas K. (1976). *Studies in Early Hebrew Meter*. Harvard Semitic Monographs, 13. Missoula, Mont.: Scholars Press.

Westermann, Claus (1981). *Praise and Lament in the Psalms*. Atlanta: John Knox Press.

Proverbs, Job: Wisdom Literature

15

Names and Terms to Remember

fear of Yahweh	proverb	the satan
Job	retribution theology	wisdom
personification	theodicy	wisdom literature

There is a big market today for advice on how to be a good person and how to get the most out of life. Self-help volumes frequently top the best-seller lists. Seminars on self-improvement and how to achieve success draw big crowds, such as Dale Carnegie's "How to Win Friends and Influence People." Dear Abby, Ann Landers, Heloise, and other syndicated newspaper columnists dole out practical, no-nonsense advice for life's problem situations. And, of course, dads and moms love to give advice . . . most frequently, it seems, when it's not wanted.

Every community finds ways to transmit its accumulated knowledge, sometimes through storytelling or through institutions of learning. In the old days, elders and sages passed on wisdom around the campfire or the kitchen table.

Parents taught their children by word and example. In the Hebrew tradition, no less than any other, parents were concerned to teach the next generation how to cope with life and be decent citizens.

INTRODUCTION TO WISDOM LITERATURE

Where and how such instruction took place in Hebrew culture, we are not sure. But a great deal of its content was eventually written down. Today scholars call it **wisdom literature**. The books containing wisdom took shape in the hope that they would provide direction to those who sought to live moral and productive lives. They were textbooks of a sort to those who were looking for help in how to live life: how to think, how to cope, indeed, how to succeed.

HAGAR THE HORRIBLE

Reprinted by permission of King Features Syndicate.

WISDOM: LITERATURE, TRADITION, OR WAY OF THINKING?

The notion of **wisdom** is difficult to define precisely. The terms *wisdom* and *wise* as used in the Hebrew Bible apply to human efforts to master the self, society, or the environment. A number of scholars have studied biblical wisdom and have tried to synthesize its essence into a short definition. Crenshaw (1969), for one, says wisdom is "the quest for self-understanding in terms of relationships with things, people, and the Creator."

Von Rad (1962) considered wisdom the "practical knowledge of the laws of life and of the world, based on experience." Much of the wisdom needed for a happy and successful life is gained by experience accumulated over the generations. Such wisdom is gained by astute observation and the search for patterns, especially the observation of the relation of cause and effect.

Wisdom is such a big and potentially amorphous notion that it might be helpful to make some distinctions. Scholars talk about wisdom *literature*, wisdom *thinking*, and the wisdom *tradition*.

Proverbs, Job, Ecclesiastes, and the wisdom psalms are generally considered the wisdom literature of the Hebrew Bible.[1] If we were to include deutero-canonical books, the Wisdom of Solomon and Sirach (short for the Wisdom of Jesus ben Sirach, also called Ecclesiasticus) would be added. The category *wisdom literature* is a literary designation. It is not a native Hebrew category, as far as we can tell, but only a scholar's category to give definition to a large body of literature that is present not only in the Hebrew Bible but also in Egyptian and Mesopotamian literature.

The books of wisdom literature share a number of characteristics, one of which is an interest in instruction or pedagogy. They deliberately intend to pass on the wisdom of right living and right thinking to the next generation. This is especially evident in the book of Proverbs and even in Ecclesiastes, though less obvious in the book of Job.

Wisdom literature cannot be easily defined by literary genre. Included within wisdom literature are proverbs, parables, discourses, songs and poetry, and many more. What unites these various materials is something bigger, an approach to reality and a theory of knowledge. The thought contained in wisdom literature approaches the world of experience through the power of human intellect, not through divine revelation, as is the case with much of the Torah and Prophets material.

Whybray (1974) views wisdom not so much in terms of the literature that gave it expression but as an intellectual tradition or way of thinking that was not restricted to any one class of people. He says wisdom is innate intelligence and "simply a natural endowment which some people possess in greater measure than others." He argues that within Israel (and more generally throughout the ancient world) the wisdom approach to life differed from the priestly, prophetic, and legal approaches. The wisdom approach utilized logic to master life.

[1] Ecclesiastes will be covered in chapter 16 because, in addition to being wisdom literature, it is also part of a collection called the Five Scrolls. The wisdom psalms were covered in chapter 14, "Psalms," under *Minor Types*.

The wisdom literature of the Hebrew Bible is evidence that there was a lively community of observers and thinkers, an intellectual class. The sages searched for the abiding principles of human behavior, sought the laws of the universe, pondered the nature of human life, and raised questions of ultimate meaning.

BASIC THEMES OF WISDOM LITERATURE

Wisdom literature deals with everyday life and experience. It might seem to have a secular flavor because it is based on human observation and reason, as distinct from divine revelation, as in the Torah and Prophets. But the very inclusion of wisdom literature into the canon makes clear that the division between secular and sacred is foreign to the Hebrew Bible. Human rationality and the truths it discovered were no less sanctioned by God than prophetic revelations.

Von Rad (1972) distills the basic theme of wisdom down to this: Wisdom is the search for order in creation and society. Behind the search for order is the belief that God created the world in an ordered and consistent way. The task of wisdom research is to discern this order and suggest ways human beings can align themselves with it. The wise person has the ability to discover this order and live in harmony with it. Seen in this way, wisdom has a lot in common with the modern academic disciplines of the natural and social sciences. Their job, broadly conceived, is to discover the laws of the world of nature and human society.

Crenshaw (1981) suggests that the dynamic tension between order and chaos is a fundamental concern to Israel's faith as a whole and was not limited just to the wisdom literature. In Israel's worldview, the ordered realm of God's creation is constantly being threatened by the forces of disorder and dissolution. The creation theology of wisdom literature affirms the divine order by finding it and recommending it, and thereby upholds the goodness and integrity of God.

Murphy (1983) argues that wisdom literature is not so much concerned with the so-called "natural order" as with human conduct. In other words, he says that it is not so much philosophical as ethical in its intent. Wisdom literature is the attempt to impose order on human life rather than to discover it.

TYPES OF WISDOM

Just so that we do not overgeneralize wisdom theology, Crenshaw (1969) uses four different labels to classify wisdom literature. *Nature wisdom* is based on observations of the real world that enable humankind to understand and coexist in harmony with it. This is represented by the onomastica (lists of names) of Mesopotamian wisdom literature and is a precursor to what the physical sciences do in classifying and analyzing flora and fauna. According to 1 Kings 4:33, Solomon "spoke of trees, from the cedar that is in the Lebanon to the hyssop that grows in the wall; he spoke of animals, birds, reptiles, and fish."

Practical wisdom analyzed the social order, the modern analogs being sociology and psychology. Practical wisdom, and probably nature wisdom, originated from the everyday life of the family and clan.

Judicial wisdom sought ways to adjudicate disputes, such as when Solomon settled the matter of the two women who both laid claim to the living child (1 Kings 3:16–28). This type of wisdom originated from the royal court.

Lastly, *theological wisdom*, sometimes called speculative wisdom, sought answers to deeply puzzling issues such as the explanation for human suffering and God's role in upholding justice among humankind. This type of wisdom Crenshaw attributes to professional scribes.

SETTING-IN-LIFE OF WISDOM

A great deal of scholarly research has gone into determining which areas of Israelite social and institutional life gave rise to wisdom thought. This is a significant question, because determining what type of people produced wisdom thinking and wisdom literature helps us understand how it was supposed to be used. Was it common folk wisdom originating out of the family? If so, it would tell us about everyday life and what the common people valued. Was it something produced professionally by "academic" wise men? Then it would be more a product of sages employed by the government and religious institutions, and served to reinforce and encourage the kinds of behavior they were interested in promoting. It is a question, at some level, of who set the ethical agenda and who determined basic ethical values, the home or the political arena.

Von Rad (1962) promoted the view that the wisdom tradition had a close connection with the royal court in Jerusalem. According to his sociological reconstruction, the monarchy of David and Solomon involved an intellectual as well as political revolution. A new way of thinking developed that attended less to cultic matters and tended to view the world more humanistically. This intellectual enlightenment was centered at the royal court, where professional scribes and sages promoted the new outlook.

Crenshaw (1976) has questioned whether there was such a radical turnabout with the rise of the monarchy. He suggests that many of the sayings of Proverbs could have originated in family and clan settings. Royal wise men did not make them up but may have been the first to collect them and write them down.

The connection between Solomon and wisdom, therefore, should not be understood in terms of authorship. Rather, Solomon should be considered the royal sponsor of the business of collecting and organizing family and clan wisdom. He is the one who took an official interest in it and made it the object of study and reflection.

WISDOM LITERATURE AND THE CANON

Wisdom literature was treated as the orphan of Israelite theology when the study of theology was dominated by a salvation-history paradigm.[2] The salvation-history approach located the central theological importance of the Hebrew Bible in the historical material of the Torah and the Prophets, which portrayed God directing historical events in order to provide salvation for his chosen people. Since wisdom literature did not directly deal with such matters and in fact seemed untheological when defined in those terms, it was sidelined as being of lesser importance.

[2] For an explanation and critique of the salvation-history approach and the biblical theology movement that championed it, see Brevard S. Childs, *Biblical Theology in Crisis* (Philadelphia: Westminster, 1970).

The salvation-history approach no longer dominates the study of biblical theology. One of the results is that wisdom literature is now more appreciated in its own right and as a reinforcement of other biblical traditions. In fact, many important points of contact with the Torah and the Prophets can now be recognized. Common interests are found in their creation theologies (compare Proverbs 8:22–31 and Job 28:20–28 with Genesis 1–2) and in their concern with education and the importance of instilling values in the hearts of Israel's youth (compare Proverbs 1–9 with Deuteronomy 6:20–25). Furthermore, wisdom literature's concern with faithfulness in worship activities, including offering sacrifices, making vows, and praying, shows its commonality with the formal religious regulations of the Torah (Perdue 1977).

The influence of prophetic theology is evident in wisdom literature's strong connection with the Solomonic tradition. Solomon, of course, is prominent in the book of Kings. Traditional wisdom, especially that expressed in Proverbs, correlates blessing with moral behavior. This theology of retribution has important points of contact with the Torah and the Prophets, especially with the Deuteronomic tradition.

Wisdom literature rests on a basic belief in the goodness of God's created order. This is one of the premises that gets it into certain theological binds, especially with the issue called **theodicy**. Literally, *theodicy* means "the justice of God" and is a label applied to the problem of reconciling the belief that God is a good god who controls the world he created and the fact of suffering and injustice in the natural world. In Israel's case, the issue of theodicy was occasioned most pointedly by the conflict between the Torah–Prophets worldview of a God-given order and the plight of the postexilic community, which suffered at the hands of unrighteous pagans. This issue is perhaps behind the theological discussion carried on in the book of Job.

Certainly within the various books of the wisdom literature, and then more broadly between Torah–Prophets and the wisdom literature, there is a lively theological conversation, perhaps even an argument, between theologies in conflict.

PROVERBS

Advertisers work hard and do plenty of market research to find just the right phrasing to impress their product on our minds. Sayings such as "It's the Real Thing" and "Just Do It!" have immediate associations for most of us. Likewise, insights into human behavior and prudent practice can frequently be distilled into short memorable sayings called maxims and aphorisms. Maxims in Ben Franklin's *Poor Richard's Almanac*, such as "a penny saved is a penny earned," are American cultural artifacts.

A **proverb**, much like a Ben Franklin maxim, is a short, memorable saying that encapsulates a truth about life. Proverbs are typically framed as matter-of-fact statements of the way things are. But really they are lessons about the way you should be. For example, the proverb, "One wise-of-heart keeps commandments; a muttering fool comes to ruin" (10:8), consists of declarative statements, not commands. Nonetheless, the command is obvious: Be a wise and moral person! Although such declarative statements comprise the bulk of proverbs, there are other types of statements in the book, including riddles, allegories, taunts, and autobiographical sketches (see 24:30–32).

Just as do many English maxims, biblical proverbs frequently contain a play on words or alliteration, at least in the original Hebrew. Most biblical proverbs take the form of couplets containing parallel members, called the A- and B-lines. See, for example, Proverbs 16:1.

The plans of the heart belong to humans,	A-line
The answer of the tongue comes from Yahweh.	B-line

Parallelism is typical of biblical poetry generally. Most Israelite prophecy was written in parallel style, as were all of the psalms.[3]

The book of Proverbs is an anthology, a collection of seven collections. Each of the seven consists of a set of short sayings. Only the first collection (chapters 1–9) and the last (chapter 31) have longer subunits with thematic continuity (for example, chapter 31 contains a poem about the ideal wife, 31:10–31) . Each collection of sayings is easily identifiable because it is introduced with its own title: The Proverbs of Solomon (1:1, 10:1, 25:1), The Sayings of the Wise (22:17, 24:23), The Words of Agur (30:1), and The Words of Lemuel (31:1). Although it has these seven collections, the book as a whole does not demonstrate any kind of logical movement or plot. Though we begin by examining the prologue, it will make the most sense for us to treat the book somewhat topically rather than strictly sequentially.

PROLOGUE OF THE BOOK OF PROVERBS

The first collection within the book of Proverbs is chapters 1–9. It serves as an introduction or prologue to the rest of the book. Chapters 10–31 are mostly just

---

[3] For a fuller treatment of parallelism and biblical poetry, see chapter 14, "Psalms."

PROVERBS FROM AROUND THE WORLD

Sumerian proverb
- Into an open mouth a fly will enter.

Arabic proverbs
- The camel never sees its own hump, but that of its brothers is always before its eyes.
- Three things cannot hide themselves: love, a mountain, and a man on a camel.
- A scholar is mightier than the knight.

Japanese proverb
- Even monkeys fall from trees.

Chinese fortune cookie proverbs from a Holland, Michigan restaurant
- Every excess becomes a vice.
- Genius does what it must, and talent does what it can.

Native American proverb
- There is nothing so eloquent as a rattlesnake's tail.

single-sentence proverbs in linear sequence, one after another in seemingly random order. The proverbial material of the first collection develops recognizable themes over chunks of text; we could call them "brief essays." The topics of these essays include a justification for studying wisdom, characterizations of wisdom and folly, and the role of wisdom in creating the world.

Of all the collections the prologue contains the most variety, and, compared to the remainder of the book, it contains more references to God. This had led some scholars, including McKane (1965) and Whybray (1965), to date the prologue later than the rest of the book and to say it was composed to form an introduction to the proverb collections of chapters 10–31. They operate on the assumption that early wisdom was secular, and only later was wisdom incorporated within a religious worldview.

Instruction in Wisdom

The purposes of proverbs are stated in 1:2–6. They are

> 2 For learning wisdom and discipline,
> for understanding insightful words;
> 3 for getting instruction in wise behavior,
> righteousness, justice, and impartiality;
> 4 for giving shrewdness to the unlearned,
> knowledge and discretion to the young—
> 5 Let the wise also hear and increase learning,
> and the sophisticated improve skill;

*6 for understanding proverb and puzzle,
words of the wise and their riddles.*

Note all the words referring to education: learning, understanding, instructing, teaching. The book of Proverbs is introduced as a textbook in wisdom. This paragraph is especially helpful because, as it recommends the book, it provides a number of terms which are at least partially synonymous with *wisdom*, enabling us to get a sense of the scope of this foundational notion. Here is a partial list of associations with *wisdom*: discipline, instruction, understanding, shrewdness, knowledge, discretion, learning, skill.

The prologue is framed as the instructions of parents to their son. Wisdom is the knowledge of the right way to live, and they give him guidance. "Hear, my son, your father's instruction, and do not reject your mother's teaching." (1:8). Though perhaps self-evident, it bears mentioning: Wisdom is something that can be taught and that can be learned. The son has a choice to make. Will he choose the practice of wisdom, or will he be a fool? It's up to him. Wisdom, unlike intelligence, is neither genetically determined nor a matter of divine endowment. It can, indeed must, be acquired.

Fear of Yahweh

A basic theme of Israelite wisdom is that the **fear of Yahweh** is the beginning of knowledge and wisdom. This affirmation is made in Proverbs 1:7, immediately after the purpose statement quoted above, and serves as that statement's culmination.

*The fear of YHWH is the beginning of knowledge;
wisdom and discipline fools despise.*

The phrase "wisdom and discipline" is also found in 2a and functions as a way to bind verses 2–7 together as the thematic introduction to the proverbs. This device is called an *inclusion*. Placed before the actual instructions, the "fear of Yahweh" statement serves as the basic postulate of the book. It conditions all that follows and serves as a reminder that even though wisdom's instruction has to do with matters of personal behavior, family responsibility, business ethics, and community loyalty, it is grounded in fear of God.

What is the intent of the phrase "fear of Yahweh"? The notion may have originated in that edge-of-death fear that Israelites felt in the presence of God, such as when they were gathered at Mt. Sinai after the exodus. But in a wisdom context fear is not to be understood as terror or fright. It refers to the deep awe and reverence for God one must have in order to live properly. One must always be aware that there is a God and that he holds people responsible for their actions. Knowing that Yahweh keeps account of behavior is a marvelous motivator to wise and proper action.

The truth that "the fear of Yahweh is the beginning of wisdom" is well-nigh universal in wisdom literature, found additionally in Proverbs 9:10 near the conclusion of the prologue, in Job 28:28, in Psalm 111:10 (a wisdom psalm), and in apocryphal Sirach 1:14.

Lady Wisdom and Mistress Folly

Throughout the prologue wisdom and its opposite are literarily made to look like real people, a device called **personification**. Wisdom is portrayed as a respectable and proper woman (1:20–33, 8:1–36, 9:1–6). Folly is pictured as a loose woman, ready to deceive the young man with sensuous pleasures and lead him to his death (7:6–27, 9:13–18). The description of Mistress Folly is so sexually explicit that it no doubt held fascination for the young man under instruction. Perhaps the literary device of personification was used to inject personal interest, just as modern advertisers use voluptuous women and sex to sell everything from toothpaste to pickup trucks.

There are a couple of further observations we can make about these personifications. Wisdom is a female!—a remarkable concession for a patriarchal society (see Newsom 1989). In part this was linguistically natural because the Hebrew word for wisdom, *hochmah*, is grammatically feminine in gender. Still, this literary personification develops the notion above and beyond the demands of grammar.

The personification of foolishness as a mistress or prostitute has features in common with prophetic literature, especially Hosea, Jeremiah, and Ezekiel, which characterizes the covenant unfaithfulness of Israel as whoring after other divine pretenders, such as Baal.

Possibly related to the positive portrayal of female figures in the prologue is the concluding chapter of the book. The poem in praise of the ideal woman (31:10–31) may be the flip side of the wisdom personification of the prologue.

> *A virtuous wife, who can find?*
> *Her worth is more precious than jewels.*
> *The heart of her husband trusts in her.*
> *Profit he will not lack.*
> *(31:10–11)*

This passage contains perhaps the most profuse positive valuation of women in the Hebrew Bible, at least women in their role as wives. The description recalls the positive picture of wisdom, personified as a woman, in chapters 8–9. There is the hint that the industrious wife is the incarnation of Lady Wisdom. All the ideal qualities of Lady Wisdom are read into the ideal wife. Or, if the prologue was, in fact, composed after chapters 10–31, perhaps the virtuous wife was the model for Ideal Wisdom! In either case, this poetic conclusion to the book of Proverbs concretizes the virtues of wisdom and recommends its practice.

Creation Theology

The most profound personification of wisdom occurs in 8:22–31. She describes herself as the first being Yahweh acquired or created, even before the physical world took shape. Wisdom was God's mastercrafter,[4] present with him through the entire process of world formation. The implication seems to be that wisdom was God's instrument or tool for creating his realm.

---

[4] Alternately translated "confidant" or "little child," it is not entirely clear what this term means, so we cannot base too much on it.

Yahweh founded the earth by wisdom,
he established the heavens by understanding,
the depths broke open by his knowledge,
and the clouds drop down the dew.
(3:19–20)

This association of wisdom with creation, combined with the priestly notion that God created the world by the word of his mouth ("And God said, 'Let there be . . .'"), ascribes a powerful role to wisdom. Some have suggested that this is the closest Yahweh comes to having a consort, or female companion, in the orthodox tradition (see Lang 1986). Creation by word and wisdom was picked up by the Christian writer John, who intentionally conjoined Jesus of Nazareth with creation, word, and wisdom when he started his gospel by saying, "In the beginning was the word, and the word was with God, and the word was God."

PRAGMATIC WISDOM

Folk wisdom often sounds contradictory, taken in the abstract. Take our "Look before you leap" and consider it alongside, "He who hesitates is lost." Likewise, the proverbial advice of Proverbs is specific to particular situations and cannot be applied without discretion. The collector of Proverbs recognized this and wryly made his point in 26:4–5.

Don't answer a fool according to his folly,
or you will be like a fool yourself.
Answer a fool according to his folly
or he will be a fool in his own opinion.

This underscores the pragmatic character of proverbial wisdom. It must be applied situationally. It is also pragmatic in the broader sense because those who follow the wise counsel of wisdom will profit from it and enjoy success in life.

RETRIBUTION THEOLOGY

The traditional wisdom of Proverbs divides humankind into two groups, the wise (equated with the righteous) and the foolish (the wicked).

Wise men store up knowledge,
but the nonsense of a fool draws ruin near.
(10:14)

Retribution theology maintains that God uncompromisingly and unfailingly punishes the wicked for their evil deeds and rewards the righteous with long life and prosperity. The book of Proverbs affirms retribution theology as strongly as Deuteronomy. It maintains the strict correlation between the practice of wisdom and earthly reward, contrasted with the foolish life that leads inexorably to tragedy and ruin.

The righteous will never be removed,
but the wicked will disappear from the land.
(10:30)

This basic theological perspective of the proverbs mentality will be challenged and refined in other biblical literature, including the book of Job.

INTERNATIONAL CONNECTIONS

Israel did not exist in political, religious, or intellectual isolation from its geographical neighbors. Intellectual and even direct literary contact is nowhere more evident than in Israel's book of Proverbs.

The book of Proverbs looks a great deal like the *instruction literature* that has survived from ancient Egypt. The Maxims of Ptahhotpe and The Teaching for Merikare are major Egyptian writings that contain advice and instruction of a father to his son (see Simpson 1973). They give practical advice on how to behave and act in business with different classes of people. Much has to do with being a good and effective public servant. So also the book of Proverbs is addressed to the son. The analogy with Egyptian instruction literature suggests that this material may be the court wisdom that was used to train the next generation for effective public service.

The Instruction of Amenemope has the most direct bearing on the book of Proverbs. Written in thirty chapters and probably dating to 1200 B.C.E., it has close parallels to many verses in Proverbs 22:17–24:22.

Proverbs	*Amenemope*[5]
22:17–18a Direct your ear and hear wise words. Set your heart to know them. For it is pleasant if you keep them in your inmost self.	*3,10 Give your ears and hear what is said, give your mind over to their interpretation: It is profitable to put them in your heart.*
22:20 Have I not written for you thirty counsels and teachings to teach you what is right and true.	*27,7 Mark for your self these thirty chapters: They please, they instruct, they are the foremost of all books.*
22:24 Do not make friends with people prone to anger. With the hotheaded person do not associate.	*11,12 Do not fraternize with the hot-tempered man, nor approach him to converse.*
23:1–2 When you sit down to eat with a ruler, observe what is before you. Put a knife to your throat if you have a big appetite.	*23,16 Look at the cup in front of you, and let it suffice your need.*

Bryce (1979) has done a thorough study of parallels between biblical and Egyptian wisdom literatures. He notes that there are varying degrees of dependence, from direct literary borrowing to "thought" borrowing; the latter is barely

[5] The translation is from Simpson (1973).

recognizable because it has been so seamlessly integrated. While there are differences in wording, Israelite parallels with Egyptian instruction sayings seem quite direct here in Proverbs. This could be direct literary borrowing, or it could signal that there was a common Middle Eastern wisdom culture with universal insights of which both literatures partook.

JOB

Within wisdom literature we begin to see a growing theological sophistication in later books, and the recognition that easy answers will not suffice. The book of Job is a frontal assault on the glib retribution categories of traditional wisdom as represented by the book of Proverbs. The book of Job investigates the nature of the moral order of the universe by examining the microcosm of the man Job. There is an obvious misfit between the world of doctrine and the world of experience. Doctrine says reward follows a moral life. But reality, in the case of Job, does not uphold that doctrine.

STRUCTURE OF THE BOOK OF JOB

The book of Job consists of a poetic core surrounded by a prose narrative framework. The prose framework relates the story of Job, including the tragedy that strikes him and his family. The poetic core contains the theological heart of the book, including the dialogues of Job and his friends and the appearance of Yahweh himself.

Outline of the Book of Job

I. Narrative Prologue: Job's tragedy (1–2)
II. Job's Lament (3)
III. Cycles of Dialogue (4–31)
   A. First Cycle (4–14)
   B. Second Cycle (15–21)
   C. Third Cycle (22–31)
IV. Speeches of Elihu (32–37)
V. Theophany (38–41)
VI. Narrative Epilogue: Job's reversal (42)

In the cycles of dialogue each of Job's friends, Eliphaz, Bildad, and Zophar, speaks in his turn, and Job responds to each.

STORY LINE

The basic story line is straightforward. Job is a moral and genuinely upstanding individual. He has considerable wealth and a fine family. When the divine council meets in heaven God expresses his pride in Job, but he is challenged by one called *the adversary*, otherwise known as **the satan**. This figure is the official heavenly "gadfly" whose task is to challenge Yahweh's relationship with hu-mankind.[6]

Yahweh first gives the adversary permission to remove all of Job's wealth and family, and then his physical health. Job is reduced to being a suffering outcast. Three friends appear at his side to give him counsel: Eliphaz, Bildad, and Zophar. In conversation with Job they attempt to make sense out of his plight.

But neither Job nor his friends resolve the conundrum of Job's suffering. Elihu, another counselor–friend appears, but does not seem to further the argument. Finally, Yahweh comes to Job in a terrifying theophany and commands Job's attention. He never answers Job's questions directly. Instead, he questions Job in a most intimidating way, seemingly belittling Job because he presumed to question the wisdom of God, who, after all, created the world. But in the end he vindicates Job. Yahweh reprimands Job's friends and requites Job with a new family and even greater wealth. The story line is relatively simple. The theological argumentation is not necessarily so.

THEOLOGICAL ARGUMENTS

One way to get at the meat of the book is to survey the positions of the main players. We hesitate to do this because so much of the argument is in the telling. The following summary should not be taken as a replacement for reading the book itself. Job is a remarkable treatise and contains some of the best poetry in the Hebrew Bible. It should be savored.

Eliphaz

He observes that no one is ever completely sinless.

> 4:7 Think about it. What innocent ever perished?
> Where were the upright destroyed?
> 8 I have seen that those who plow evil
> and sow trouble reap the same.
> 9 By God's blast they perish
> and by the heat of his anger they disappear.

Everyone can expect at least a little suffering in life. Job is relatively innocent, so he will not suffer permanently. He should be patient; his suffering will soon be over.

Bildad

He applies the theology of retribution relentlessly. He claims that Job's children must have been notable sinners to be treated so brutally by God. No doubt they died justifiably.

---

[6] Note here that *the satan* does not have a capital s because it is a title. The satan figure referred to in the book of Job is a member of the divine council and is not the devil of later Judaism and Christianity.

8:3 Can God get justice wrong?
Can Shaddai distort rightness?
4 If your children sinned against him,
he delivered them over to the consequences of their violation.

Since Job is still alive, claims Bildad, he must not be too bad a sinner.

Zophar

He claims that Job must be suffering for his own sin. Even though he does not admit it publicly, he must be a sinner.

11:4 You say, "My principles are pure,
and I am innocent before you."
5 But if God would speak
and talk to you himself,
6 and tell you the secrets of wisdom—
there are many nuances to wisdom—
know that God is exacting less than you deserve.

Job should honestly face his sin and ask God for mercy.

Elihu

Elihu speaks (chapters 32–37) after Job's other three friends have had their say. He says that suffering is the way God communicates with human beings. It is the way God reveals that we are sinners and that he considers sin a serious offense.

36:10 He opens their understanding by discipline,
and orders them to turn away from wickedness.
11 If they listen and obey,
they will end up with good days and pleasant years.

All four speakers maintain the theology of retribution in some way. Their approach is very much "top down." In other words, they hold a basic belief in retribution, and they try to square Job's experience with the theological principles they hold, rather than developing a theology out of human experience.

Job

Job has no potent response to his calamity. He argues with his friends and attacks their counterarguments. But ultimately he remains confounded. He just does not know how to handle his predicament.

Yet there are certain claims he maintains throughout, certain points he will not relinquish. He never gives in and admits personal guilt in the measure that would call forth such suffering. He often calls on God to reveal himself and state why he is afflicting Job so. He challenges God in what amounts to a lawsuit, much in the manner of the covenant lawsuit popular with the prophets, even though he recognizes that if God actually appeared he would be powerless to respond. This sentiment is amazingly prescient of what would soon happen.

Yahweh

Yahweh does not choose to respond to the arguments of Job and his friends, all of which have to do in some way with the theology of retribution. He quite ignores that business, curiously neither affirming retribution nor denying it. By God's bracketing the big question of retribution, the book is saying retribution is not the real issue. God does not conduct affairs on a strictly cause-and-effect basis.

Yet God does address Job's urgent plea that he at least show himself. He appeared in a storm theophany (chapters 38–41), but instead of answering Job's questions, he put Job on trial.

> 38:2 Who is this confusing the issue
> with nonsensical words?!
> 3 Brace yourself like a man.
> I will quiz you. You teach me!
> 4 Where were you when I laid the foundations of the earth?
> Tell me, if you really have such deep understanding!

Yahweh continues in this same vein, badgering the witness and impressing upon Job that he really knows nothing about how God created the world and runs it. Job finally admits that he spoke presumptuously in demanding that God justify his actions.

> 40:1 YHWH said to Job:
> 2 "Will one in need of discipline complain about Shaddai?
> Let the one accusing God answer!"
> 3 Then Job answered YHWH:
> "I am worth nothing. How can I respond to you?
> I am putting my hand over my mouth.
> I spoke once, but have no answer for you,
> Twice I spoke, but I will say no more."

By now Job seems properly contrite and put in his place. One might have expected Yahweh at this point to coddle Job or at least lay off him. Just the opposite happens. God launches into a second discourse designed further to impress Job with his omnipotence. He describes in great detail his creation and the harnessing of Behemoth and Leviathan. These creatures have been likened to the hippopotamus and crocodile, respectively, but the overblown language of their description suggests that God is really referring to the mythic monsters of chaos that he tamed and holds at bay.

Through the whole encounter God is absolutely overpowering. One might wonder why God felt he needed to react in such an intimidating way. Yet God does give Job satisfaction of sorts, first, in the very fact of his appearing, and second, by putting the issue of suffering in perspective. The important outcome is that God ultimately affirmed Job, in fact had never abandoned him, even though it had seemed so at the time to Job.

Job wanted to know why. But God would not tell him why. This effectively marginalizes the theology of retribution. The real issue is trust—will we simply trust God and "leave the driving to him"? Job becomes the model of the one who suffers, with all the self-doubt, indignation, impatience, and spiritual agony typical of those in great crisis.

CONCLUSIONS

The narrative conclusion of the book seems artificial and unsatisfying to many readers—though, perhaps, not for retribution theologians. In the end, Job's fortunes were restored. He was given sons and daughters to replace those he lost, and his former material wealth was doubled. Although Job was reduced to humble acceptance of the power of God, he was vindicated and was told to pray for his three friends who were in the wrong.

Yet the ending is far from satisfying. In one grand narrative stroke what we thought was the lesson of the book to this point seems to be undone. The lesson of the book seemed to be that there is no direct and necessary correlation between righteousness and material well-being. Do we now, at the last, see Job rewarded for being in the right? If so, the theology of retribution seems to be upheld after all: Job is in the end rewarded for his uprightness. It almost seems the profound lesson of the theophany (38–41) is deconstructed by the triteness of the "and they lived happily ever after" conclusion.

How can we deal with this? Literary approaches to the book abound, and many seem quite able to live with the moral ambiguity of the book. Whedbee (1977) interprets the book using categories of comedy and irony. Westermann (1977) reads it as if it were a biblical lament. Habel (1985) reads Job as an allegory of the people of Israel in the postexilic period experiencing suffering and alienation from God. Modern takeoffs on Job creatively wrestle with the issue and can be recommended for the way they suggest interpretive possibilities. These include Archibald MacLeish's *J.B.* (1956), Neil Simon's *God's Favorite* (1975), Robert A. Heinlein's *Job, A Comedy of Justice* (1984), and probably Kafka's *The Trial*.[7]

Many still take the book of Job as serious theological literature in the category of theodicy, a genre known from extrabiblical writings such as the Babylonian *Ludlul Bel Nemeqi* and the *Babylonian Theodicy* (see Lambert 1960). On this model, the book as a whole deals with the impenetrable character of the governance of God.

The ending is the writer's somewhat clumsy way of affirming the ultimate justice of God. Heaven was not an option at this stage of biblical religion as the place where rewards and punishments would be meted out. Everyone, whether good or bad, went to the same underworld, called *sheol*. Job's reward had to

---

[7] See Stuart Lasine's discussion in "Job and His Friends in the Modern World: Kafka's *The Trial*" in Perdue (1992).

come during his lifetime. The writer responsible for the final shape of the book was willing, it seems, to live with the tension of the freedom and sovereignty of God as expressed in the theophany, the validity, at least at some level, of the theology of retribution, and the reality of righteous suffering.

EPILOGUE TO WISDOM LITERATURE

How, then, should we construe this wonder of wisdom literature? Many things could be said. For one, it represents Israel's literary and theological attempt to get behind the phenomena of reality to the underlying truth. It asks the question *why*. Wisdom literature approaches reality without dependence on divine revelation, a priesthood, or a theology of history. It uses reason, everyday experience, and the power of deduction in its attempt to discern how the power of God manifests itself in the world of human affairs.

A further observation is this: Proverbs and Job represent an inner canonical dialogue on the theology of retribution. The book of Proverbs affirms it unreflectively and somewhat naively. Not to be too hard on Proverbs, this may be a function of its role in providing straightforward moral instruction. On the other hand, the book of Job is a frontal attack on overly simplistic retribution theology. It shows that the principle of retribution is not the only, or even the most important, factor at work in divine–human relations.

The theological dialogue on this issue continues in the book of Ecclesiastes, which we will examine in the next chapter. Ecclesiastes deflects attention away from retribution by deconstructing it. The reality of death levels all rewards and punishments anyway. Retribution is not the real issue; how you live life is.

The body of wisdom literature attests to a lively theological tradition of dialogue and development within the Hebrew Bible. Upon examination, the wisdom literature reveals a spiritual and intellectual tradition within Israel that was not afraid to ask bold and ultimate questions, that tried to make sense out of the diversity of evidences, and that resisted dogmatism in favor of intellectual honesty. The legitimacy of such theological discussion is affirmed by the very fact that these contrary voices were all included in the canon of Scripture. This recognition should encourage continuing the conversation.

QUESTIONS FOR REVIEW

1. Define the notion *biblical wisdom* and summarize the basic themes of the wisdom tradition.
2. What books constitute the biblical wisdom literature, and what is each of them about?
3. Where do proverbial sayings come from? What is the relationship of the book of Proverbs and the historical figure Solomon?

4. What is the *fear of Yahweh*, and how is it related to wisdom?
5. What was the purpose of the book of Proverbs?
6. Summarize the story line of the book of Job. Who was *the satan*? What was the basic argument of Job's three friends? What was Job's claim against their argument?

QUESTIONS FOR DISCUSSION

1. The wisdom tradition represents an empirical, evidential approach to understanding reality. How is the wisdom tradition like the modern scientific approach to the world? How does it differ?

2. The wisdom tradition claims that the fear of Yahweh is the beginning of knowledge and wisdom. Do you think this is true? Do you think that a basic knowledge of and respect for God is essential for understanding reality?

3. Consider the ending of the book of Job. How does the ending of the book relate to the issues raised in the dialogues? Are you satisfied with the ending of the book? Does the ending support or refute the argument of Job in the dialogues?

4. Does retribution theology adequately account for the human situation in the real world? Consider the retribution theology of the book of Proverbs in relation to the book of Job. Do you see two theologies in conflict? Is there a way to reconcile the two?

FOR FURTHER STUDY

Wisdom Literature in General. Clements, Ronald E. (1992). *Wisdom in Theology.* Grand Rapids, Mich.: Eerdmans. Relates biblical wisdom to the world, health, politics, the household, and the divine realm.

Crenshaw, James L. (1976). *Studies in Ancient Israelite Wisdom.* New York: KTAV. A collection of essays by leading scholars of wisdom.

Crenshaw, James L. (1981). *Old Testament Wisdom: An Introduction.* Atlanta: John Knox Press. A general introduction to the wisdom literature of the Old Testament, intended to function as an introductory textbook.

Humphreys, W. Lee (1985). *The Tragic Vision and the Hebrew Tradition.* Overtures to Biblical Theology, 18. Philadelphia: Fortress Press.

Morgan, Donn F. (1981). *Wisdom in the Old Testament Traditions.* Atlanta: John Knox Press. Looks for wisdom influence in the Hebrew Bible outside the wisdom literature.

Murphy, Roland (1981). *Wisdom Literature: Job, Proverbs, Ruth, Canticles, Ecclesiastes, Esther.* The Forms of the Old Testament Literature, 13. Grand Rapids, Mich.: Eerdmans.

Murphy, Roland (1983). *Wisdom Literature and Psalms.* Nashville, Tenn.: Abingdon.

Murphy, Roland (1990). *The Tree of Life: An Exploration of Biblical Wisdom Literature.* The Anchor Bible Reference Library. New York: Doubleday. A general introduction to the wisdom books, including Ben Sira (Sirach) and the Wisdom of Solomon.

Perdue, Leo G. (1977). *Wisdom and Cult.* SBL Dissertation Series, 30. Missoula, Mont.: Scholars Press. Examines the relationship between the wisdom and priestly traditions.

Perdue, Leo G., Bernard Brandon Scott, and William Johnston Wiseman, eds. (1993). *In Search of Wisdom: Essays in Memory of John G. Gammie.* Louisville, Ky.: Westminster/John Knox. A collection of essays.

von Rad, Gerhard (1972). *Wisdom in Israel.* Nashville, Tenn.: Abingdon.

Proverbs. Camp, Claudia (1985). *Wisdom and the Feminine in the Book of Proverbs.* Sheffield: Almond Press.

McKane, William (1970). *Proverbs: A New Approach.* Old Testament Library. Philadelphia: Westminster.

Whybray, Roger N. (1965). *Wisdom in Proverbs: The Concept of Wisdom in Proverbs 1–9.* Studies in Biblical Theology, 45. London: SCM Press. Contains a detailed examination of the form of proverbs and their purpose in educating the youth of Israel.

Whybray, Roger N. (1972). *The Book of Proverbs.* The Cambridge Bible Commentary. Cambridge: Cambridge University Press.

Job. Good, Edwin M. (1990). *In Turns of Tempest: A Rereading of Job, with a Translation.* Stanford, Calif.: Stanford University Press.

Gordis, Robert (1965). *The Book of God and Man: A Study of Job.* Chicago: University of Chicago Press.

Habel, Norman (1985). *Job.* Old Testament Library. Philadelphia: Westminster Press.

Penchansky, David (1992). *The Betrayal of God: Ideological Conflict in Job*. Literary Currents in Biblical Interpretation. Louisville, Ky.: Westminster/John Knox Press.

Perdue, Leo G. (1991). *Wisdom in Revolt. Metaphorical Theology in the Book of Job*. JSOT Supplement Series, 112; Bible and Literature Series, 29. Sheffield: Almond.

Zuckerman, Bruce (1991). *Job the Silent: A Study in Historical Counterpoint*. New York and Oxford: Oxford University Press.

WORKS CITED

Bryce, Glendon E. (1979). *A Legacy of Wisdom: The Egyptian Contribution to the Wisdom of Israel*. Lewisburg, Pa.: Bucknell University Press.

Crenshaw, James L. (1969). "Method in Determining Wisdom Influence upon 'Historical' Literature." *Journal of Biblical Literature* 88: 129–42.

Crenshaw, James L. (1976). "Prolegomenon," in *Studies in Ancient Israelite Wisdom*. New York: KTAV.

Crenshaw, James L. (1981). *Old Testament Wisdom: An Introduction*. Atlanta: John Knox Press.

Habel, Norman C. (1985). *The Book of Job: A Commentary*. Old Testament Library. Philadelphia: Westminster.

Heinlein, Robert A. (1984). *Job, A Comedy of Justice*. New York: Ballentine Books.

Lambert, W. G. (1960). *Babylonian Wisdom Literature*. Oxford: Oxford University Press.

Lang, Bernhard (1986). *Wisdom and the Book of Proverbs: An Israelite Goddess Redefined*. New York: Pilgrim Press.

MacLeish, Archibald (1956). *J. B.* Boston: Houghton Mifflin.

McKane, William (1965). *Prophets and Wise Men*. Studies in Biblical Theology. London: SCM Press.

Murphy, Roland (1983). *Wisdom Literature and Psalms*. Nashville, Tenn.: Abingdon.

Newsom, Carol A. (1989). "Woman and the Discourse of Patriarchal Wisdom: A Study of Provebs 1–9." In *Gender and Difference in Ancient Israel*, ed. Peggy L. Day. Philadelphia: Fortress Press.

Perdue, Leo G. (1977). *Wisdom and Cult*. SBL Dissertation Series, 30. Missoula, Mont.: Scholars Press.

Perdue, Leo G., and W. Clark Gilpin, eds. (1992). *The Voice from the Whirlwind: Interpreting the Book of Job*. Nashville, Tenn.: Abingdon.

Simon, Neil (1975). *God's Favorite: A New Comedy*. New York: Random House.

Simpson, William K., ed. (1973). *The Literature of Ancient Egypt: An Anthology of Stories, Instructions, and Poetry*. New Edition. New Haven, Conn., and London: Yale University Press.

von Rad, Gerhard (1962). *Old Testament Theology*. Vol. 1. New York: Harper & Row.

von Rad, Gerhard (1972). *Wisdom in Israel*. Nashville, Tenn.: Abingdon.

Westermann, Claus (1977). *The Structure of the Book of Job*. Philadelphia: Westminster.

Whedbee, J. William (1977). "The Comedy of Job." *Semeia* 7: 1–39.

Whybray, Roger N. (1965). *Wisdom in Proverbs: The Concept of Wisdom in Proverbs 1–9*. Studies in Biblical Theology, 45. London: SCM Press.

Whybray, Roger N. (1974). *The Intellectual Tradition in the Old Testament*. BZAW 135. New York and Berlin: Walter de Gruyter.

SONG OF SONGS, RUTH, LAMENTATIONS, ECCLESIASTES, ESTHER

The Five Scrolls

16

Names and Terms to Remember

acrostic	Esther	Purim
Ahasuerus	Five Scrolls	Qohelet
allegory	Haman	Ruth
Bethlehem	Mordecai	
Boaz	Naomi	

The five books discussed in this chapter are strange bedfellows. They hold little form or content in common. The Song of Songs is pulsing love poetry, Ruth is a romantic short story, Lamentations is a collection of dirges, Ecclesiastes is a philosophical treatise, and Esther is a historical novella.

We treat these five short books together because they were grouped together within the Writings section of the Hebrew Bible as the **Five Scrolls**, in Hebrew, the five *megillot*.[1] This group of five may have been in imitation of the five books of the Torah and the five books of the Psalter. In spite of their lack of commonality, there is a logic to the collection. Each of the books was used by the Jewish community in connection with a yearly commemoration.

- The Song of Songs was read at Passover (Hebrew *pesach*), which commemorated the exodus from Egypt. It marked the growing season and coincided with the beginning of the barley harvest.
- Ruth was read at the feast of weeks (Hebrew *shavuot*), also called Pentecost, which commemorated the giving of the law at Mt. Sinai. It was observed seven weeks after Passover and marked the end of the barley harvest.
- Lamentations was read on the ninth day of the month of Av (Hebrew *tishah be'av*), marking the exact date of the destruction of the first Jerusalem temple in 587 B.C.E. It was also used later to mourn the destruction of the Second Temple, destroyed in 70 C.E.
- Ecclesiastes was read at the feast of booths, also called tabernacles (Hebrew *sukkot*), which commemorated Israel's forty years in the wilderness. Celebrated in the fall, six months after Passover, it coincided with the grape harvest.
- Esther was read at the feast of Purim in late winter and marked the time of Jewish deliverance during the Persian period.

The order of individual books within the Five Scrolls correlates with their sequence within the yearly Jewish calendar.

SONG OF SONGS

Now for something completely different—unlike any biblical literature we have read to this point. The Song of Songs is the stuff of love, highly erotic human

---

[1] The grouping of these books into the Five Scrolls is attested in the earliest copies of the Hebrew Bible, upon which current editions are based. However, the earliest evidence for the order of biblical books is in the Babylonian Talmud (Baba Bathra 14b). It intersperses the Five Scrolls among other books as follows: Ruth, Psalms, Job, Proverbs, Ecclesiastes, Song of Songs, Lamentations, Daniel, Esther, Ezra-Nehemiah, Chronicles. This ordering reflects their presumed chronological order.

love. Readers disagree whether or not the book has a plot. It is certainly not a story on the order of Ruth or Esther. Exactly what it is—drama, a collection of wedding songs, or something else—remains under discussion. Whatever its genre, all agree it makes for great reading.

Three voices are distinguishable in the Song: a male lover, a female lover, and an independent group of observers called the daughters of Jerusalem. Some interpreters prefer to call the two main speakers the lover (the male) and the beloved (the female), but this implies one is active and the other passive, and the female is certainly not passive in these poems. Though less poetic, the terms *male lover* and *female lover* are more accurate.

The female lover is the first to speak.

Kiss me with the kisses of your mouth,
for your love is better than wine.
Your anointing oils are fragrant,
your name is sweet smelling oil.
So the maidens love you.
(1:2–3)

The male lover has just as rich an appreciation of his companion.

You are beautiful, my lover,
you are beautiful, your eyes are doves.
You are beautiful, my lover, really beautiful.
Our couch is rich,
the beams of our house are cedar,
the rafters cypress.
(1:15–17)

The daughters of Jerusalem, to whom the female lover addresses herself at times, seem to be her companions, sometimes encouraging her to rush into the relationship. The female lover more than once urges them to stop pushing her.

I implore you, O daughters of Jerusalem,
by the gazelles and wild does,
not to stir up or rouse love until it's ready!
(2:7; see also 3:5 and 8:4)

The male lover unceasingly praises her physical attributes but appears to get a little impatient for love. Throughout the poems he calls her by the endearing term *sister*.

A locked garden is my sister, my bride,
a locked garden, a sealed spring.
(4:12)

The imagery of the garden seems to give shape to their shared experience.

Female lover
Awake north wind,
come on south wind,
blow on my garden
so its fragrance wafts away.
Let my lover come to his garden
and eat its luscious fruit.
(4:16)

Male lover
I've come to my garden, my sister, my bride.
I've gathered my myrrh mixed with spices,
I've eaten my honeycomb with honey,
I've drunk my mixed wine and milk.
(5:1a)

Companions
Eat, lovers, and drink.
Be drunk with love.
(5:1b)

The book ends with a stirring affirmation of the ultimacy of love.

Set me as a seal on your heart,
a seal on your arm.
For love is strong as death,
passion fierce as Sheol.
Its flashes are fire flashes,

a blazing fire.
Mighty waters cannot quench love,
nor floods sweep it away.
If anyone would offer
all his wealth for love,
he would be laughed to scorn.
(8:6–7)

Sheol is the term referring to the underworld, the residence of the dead. Nothing can compare in power to love, and love even transcends death.

The Song is notable for its frank, and at times frankly erotic, love language. Many of the metaphors are at best thinly veiled allusions to human sexuality. Physical love and human sexuality are the source of deep satisfaction in the Song.

The book abounds with interpretive problems. For one, is the book to be read as having dramatic movement, or are the poems simply unconnected sketches? If simply poems, were they intended to be used in wedding ceremonies or celebrations? For another, is the male lover the same as the king, with *king* just love language, or is the king in competition with a country-boy lover?

However one finally decides to regard the *dramatis personae* of the book and dramatic movement (if any), the unmistakable message of the book is the depth and power of human love.

Although it is one of the five scrolls, the Song of Songs has connections with the wisdom tradition of the Hebrew Bible by virtue of its connection to Solomon. English versions tend to call this book the Song of Solomon, though in Hebrew it is the Song of Songs.[2] It received the title *Song of Solomon* because the first verse appends the words *li-shlomo* to the phrase *song of songs*. Depending on one's interpretation, *li-shlomo* can be either "by Solomon" or "for Solomon."[3] The Solomonic connection was made because Solomon is mentioned in chapters 3 and 8 (though not as author), and because 1 Kings 4:32 says he composed 1,005 songs.

Various theories of the origin of the poems have been suggested. Some of the songs may go back to the early monarchic period, though this cannot be proven. The songs have their closest affinity in the ancient period with Egyptian love songs (White 1978, Fox 1985).

Parallels with Syrian wedding songs in Arabic have been noted for centuries. Other scholars have suggested they may be related to ancient Mesopotamian and Canaanite ceremonies uniting divinities in marriage. Pope (1977) claims that the Song of Songs was associated with funeral feasts.

Interesting from a canonical perspective is how the biblical community of faith wrestled with the book. The transparent nature of the love talk in the Song of

---

[2] This phrase *song of songs* is the Hebrew way of stating the superlative; in other words, this is "the greatest song." Other similar constructions are "lord of lords" and "king of kings." Pope (1977) calls it "the sublime song."

[3] The same ambiguity exists in many psalm superscriptions, where psalms are either by or for David. See chapter 14, "Psalms."

The love of my sister is on yonder side
Of the stream in the midst of the fish.
A crocodile stands on the sandbank
Yet I go down into the water.
I venture across the current;
My courage is high upon the waters.
It is thy love which gives me strength;
For thou makest a water-spell for me.
When I see my sister coming,
Then my heart rejoices.
My arms are open wide to embrace her;
My heart is glad in its place.[4]

This Egyptian love song comes from the thirteenth century B.C.E. and contains the same interest in animal imagery as the love poems in the Song of Songs. Also, in both compositions, the female lover is referred to as *my sister*. Nowhere outside Israel is anything like this love poetry found, except in Egypt.

Songs has scandalized more than one reader. This was so much the case that the book had some difficulty finding its way into the canon of the Hebrew Bible. The problem was heightened because, like the book of Esther, the Song of Songs never makes reference to God. It was accepted only after rabbis viewed it as an **allegory** of the relationship between Yahweh and the people of Israel. An allegory is a story in which people, places, and things have a meaning quite different from and unrelated to their surface meaning. Later, Christian interpreters applied a similar allegorical reading, interpreting it as the love relationship between Christ and the church. This was the reigning interpretation of the Song during the Middle Ages (see Matter 1990).

The inclusion of the Song of Songs within the canon is at some level an affirmation of the essential created goodness of sex. Certainly through the history of the formation of the canon this posed problems. Perhaps the rabbinic and early Christian allegorizing was really just a rationalization for including this erotic poetry in the canon. They knew all along the goodness of human love and realized the importance of canonically affirming it.

RUTH

This book tells the story of **Ruth,** a heroine of faith. The book of Ruth is one of the best-loved pieces of literature in the Hebrew Bible, notable for its simplicity and directness.

---

[4] This poem was taken from *Documents from Old Testament Times*, ed. D. Winton Thomas (New York: Harper & Row, 1961).

The story of Ruth unfolds in four scenes, each corresponding to a chapter.

Scene 1. An Israelite family from **Bethlehem** in Judah was forced to move to Moab because of a famine. The irony of the text has this family from Bethlehem (this Hebrew name means *house of bread*) leave the supposed land of plenty to live in Moab. In Moab, the two sons, Machlon and Kilion, married Moabite women, Ruth and Orpah.

After a time in Moab, Elimelek, the father, and his two sons died. Only **Naomi**, the mother, and her two daughters-in-law survived. Naomi decided to return to Bethlehem, and urged her daughters-in-law, both Moabite, to remain in Moab and find security with their families there. Orpah chose to remain, but Ruth refused to part from her mother-in-law. Ruth demonstrated dogged loyalty.

> *1:16 Ruth said, "Do not urge me to leave you or quit following you! Where you go, I will go. Where you live, I will live. Your people will become my people, and your God my God. 17 Where you die, I will die. That is where I will be buried. May YHWH do thus and so to me, and even more, if even death separates me from you!"*

Ruth insisted on staying with Naomi. Verse 17 contains an oath formula ("May YHWH do thus and so to me . . . if") invoking divine backing for her pledge.

Together Naomi and Ruth entered Bethlehem, with Naomi bemoaning her situation to the women of the city who came out to meet them. The first scene ends with the narrator's comment that they had come to Bethlehem at the beginning of the barley harvest. Once again there is food in Bethlehem, no doubt hinting that Naomi and Ruth may find fullness back in Naomi's homeland, perhaps in more ways than one.

Scene 2. Ruth went to glean in the field of **Boaz**, who was a relative of Elimelek, Ruth's deceased father-in-law. Gleaning is the practice of scavenging a field for stalks left behind by the hired workers. There Boaz took an interest in her, noting especially her loyalty to Naomi in her time of trouble. At mealtime he shared his food with her, and he arranged for the workers to leave extra stalks behind for her. On returning home, Naomi noted Boaz's kindness, which continued through the harvest season.

Scene 3. Naomi urged Ruth to capitalize on Boaz's interest. During the harvest celebration, an overnight party held on the threshing floor near the new grain, Ruth secretly snuggled up to Boaz. She asked Boaz to spread his cloak over her, metaphorically to give her protection, but perhaps also to spend the night with her. Boaz was overwhelmed by her initiative and interpreted it as an additional sign of her loyalty to Naomi and her dead husband. Boaz promised to secure legal rights to claim her in marriage the next day and act as her "next-of-kin." The Hebrew term used here is *go'el*, which can also be translated *redeemer*.

Scene 4. Boaz went to the city gate in the morning. This is where all public business was conducted. Boaz brought the issue to a conclusion this way. He announced that Naomi was seeking to sell the property of Elimelek. Another man stood closer in family relationship to Elimelek than Boaz, and this unnamed man initially expressed interest in purchasing the property. Then Boaz added that the one buying the property was required to marry Ruth and raise up sons to her

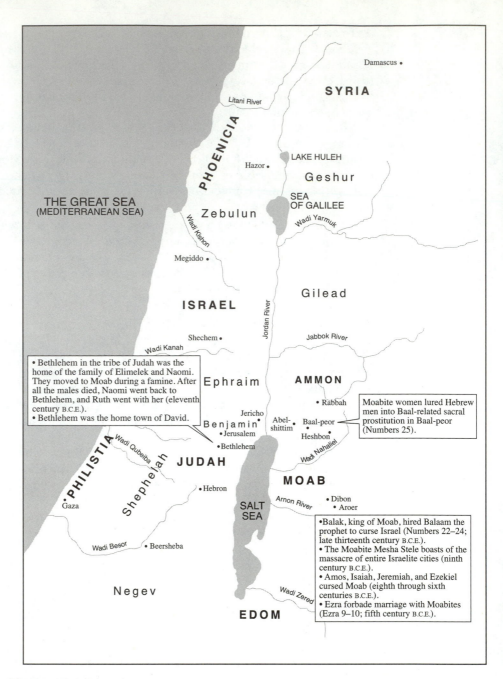

The following text labels appear within the map:

Damascus •

SYRIA

Litani River

PHOENICIA

LAKE HULEH

Hazor •

Geshur

SEA OF GALILEE

THE GREAT SEA (MEDITERRANEAN SEA)

Zebulun

Wadi Kishon

Wadi Yarmuk

Megiddo •

Gilead

Jordan River

ISRAEL

Shechem •

Jabbok River

Wadi Kanah

• Bethlehem in the tribe of Judah was the home of the family of Elimelek and Naomi. They moved to Moab during a famine. After all the males died, Naomi went back to Bethlehem, and Ruth went with her (eleventh century B.C.E.).
• Bethlehem was the home town of David.

Ephraim

AMMON

• Rabbah

Jericho •

Benjamin

Abel-shittim

Baal-peor

Moabite women lured Hebrew men into Baal-related sacral prostitution in Baal-peor (Numbers 25).

• Jerusalem

Heshbon •

• Bethlehem

Wadi Nahaliel

PHILISTIA

Wadi Qubeiba

JUDAH

Shephelah

MOAB

• Hebron

SALT SEA

Gaza

Arnon River

• Dibon

• Aroer

•Balak, king of Moab, hired Balaam the prophet to curse Israel (Numbers 22–24; late thirteenth century B.C.E.).
• The Moabite Mesha Stele boasts of the massacre of entire Israelite cities (ninth century B.C.E.).
• Amos, Isaiah, Jeremiah, and Ezekiel cursed Moab (eighth through sixth centuries B.C.E.).
• Ezra forbade marriage with Moabites (Ezra 9–10; fifth century B.C.E.).

Wadi Besor

• Beersheba

Negev

Wadi Zered

EDOM

FIGURE 16.1   JUDAH AND MOAB

dead husband. This other man withdrew his interest, and Boaz claimed the right to redeem.

The transaction was made official with a sandal-passing ceremony that transferred ownership from one party to another, and Boaz took Ruth to wife. In time

Ruth had a son, and Naomi was the first to rejoice. He was given the name Obed, and he became the father of Jesse, who was the father of David. Thus, Ruth, a Moabite foreigner, and Boaz became the great-grandparents of the greatest monarch of Israel.

This is a heartwarming story, as remarkable for its simplicity as for the excellence of its values. The story of Ruth is one of those rare Hebrew stories that on its most basic level was intended to be paradigmatic. That is, the characters are portrayed as models of virtue and goodness who should be emulated. Naomi is notable for the way she was concerned about the welfare of her daughter-in-law. Boaz, whose name means *strength* and was also the name of one of the pillars of the Jerusalem temple, went out of his way to show kindness to Ruth and provide for her protection.

Above all, Ruth displayed absolute loyalty to her mother-in-law and her adopted family, especially her dead husband. She was never motivated out of self-interest but faithfully sought to preserve the Elimelek estate. The book demonstrates that ordinary people will find peace and security when they behave unselfishly.

In addition, there are many other moral points that could be noted. Whether they were all intended by the writer cannot be proved. The main character of the story is Ruth, a female. She stands as yet another example of strong and influential women who influenced the course of Israelite history. Just as significantly, she was a foreigner, and a Moabite at that. The Moabites were hated by the Israelites through most of their history, but especially in the exilic and postexilic periods (see Figure 16.1). Yet this story demonstrates how a Moabite could possess the qualities of loyalty and piety and indeed could become part of the royal line of David.

The story of Ruth was set in the time of the judges, making her premonarchic. Because the book was set "in the days when the judges judged" (1:1) and provides background to the family of David, the early Greek version placed the book of Ruth between the books of Judges and Samuel, a practice followed by Christian versions of the Old Testament.

The actual time of the book's final composition is disputed, with Hals (1969) and Campbell (1975) advocating a date of composition in the early monarchical period. Most scholars today maintain a postexilic date. If this is the case, the book may have been intended as a countervoice to that of Ezra in fifth century B.C.E. Jerusalem. The Jewish community under Ezra took on a very nationalistic and religiously defined character. Foreigners were often unwelcome, and Ezra even made Jewish men who had Moabite wives divorce them.

The book of Ruth obviously presents a more appreciative evaluation of the Moabites, and perhaps foreigners in general, because it demonstrates that they could be loyal to Yahweh. Viewed in this way, the book of Ruth is a protest against excluding all non-natives from Judaism. Ruth projects a universalistic picture of Israel that includes non-Israelites. This openness is glimpsed occasionally in prophetic literature as, for example, in the Rahab story in Joshua, in the inclusiveness of Second and Third Isaiah, and in the book of Jonah—but nowhere more clearly than in the book of Ruth. The point is that foreigners can and sometimes do acknowledge Yahweh and can demonstrate loyalty to the people of Israel.

The tale of Ruth is self-contained and has a remarkable wholeness to it. But the book in its final form gives evidence of canonical transformation. The tale of

Ruth was given another purpose beyond that of modeling ideal people of God. The original story of Ruth was used to say something about David, even though David's line does not play any role whatsoever in the body of the story.

The story in its bare form was probably not about ancestors of David. It could stand alone without the concluding David notes. But the addition of 4:17b and the genealogy of 4:18–22 give the book an expanded meaning within the national epic. With these additions the book says that God was at work in the life of Naomi's family to provide for Israel's kingship needs. The genealogical additions do not add anything to the story line, but instead give the story an added context of significance as background to the royal family. Composed in the postexilic period from a preexisting Ruth tale, and given a Davidic context of interpretation, the book of Ruth is probably evidence for an intense interest in the royal messianic line in the late biblical period.

LAMENTATIONS

The book of Lamentations consists of five distinct poems, each in its own chapter. Each of the first four psalms is an alphabetic **acrostic** of one form or another. An acrostic utilizes the letters of the alphabet to develop a scheme. In the case of chapters 1–2, the first letter of each three-line stanza begins with the next letter of the Hebrew alphabet (twenty-two letters in all), so that the first triplet begins with a (*aleph* in Hebrew), the second with b (*beth*), and so forth. Chapter 4 consists of couplets rather than triplets in the same scheme. Chapter 3 consists of twenty-two triplets where each line of the triplet begins with the same letter of the alphabet in acrostic progression. Chapter 5 consists of twenty-two single lines without any observable alphabetic progression. Whatever the reason for the elaborate acrostic schemes, they do give evidence of the considerable poetic craftsmanship of the composer. They were not artlessly constructed.

Each of the five poems is a complaint psalm; as we saw in chapter 14, this is the dominant psalm type in the Psalter. Virtually all the lines of the first four lamentations were composed in the 3 + 2 *qinah* meter that typifies the lament style (see Garr 1983). Both individual and group complaint forms are found in Lamentations, with the voice changing unexpectedly from singular to plural throughout the poems. It is possible that when singular moves into plural, the singular still stands collectively for the group. The focus of attention in either case is on the desolation of Jerusalem.

> *How deserted sits the city, once full of people!*
> *She has become like a widow, once great among the nations!*
> *Once a princess among principalities, she has become a peasant.*
> *(1:1)*

The complaints were composed to lament the destruction of Jerusalem in 587 B.C.E. by the Babylonians. The destruction of the temple was the most devastating loss of all, for it meant the departure of Yahweh from their land. It appears from Jeremiah 41:5 that soon after the destruction of 587 people still came to the temple mount in Jerusalem to worship. Zechariah 7:1–7 and 8:19 suggest that fasts were held, perhaps as many as four a year, marking the destruction. The Lamentations were probably used on these occasions to mark the disaster. This traumatic moment in Israel's history is still observed today within the Jewish community as Tishah Be'av, the ninth day of the month of Av, falling somewhere between the end of July and the beginning of August.

Jeremiah has traditionally been identified as the author of Lamentations because of his personal complaints. For this reason the Christian canon has placed the book of Lamentations after the book of Jeremiah. In the Hebrew Bible it is included with the Writings. Jeremiah composed a lament upon the occasion of the death of Josiah (2 Chronicles 35:25), but there is no evidence he did the same thing over Jerusalem or that he composed Lamentations.

ECCLESIASTES

Ecclesiastes is usually included in the category of wisdom literature along with Proverbs and Job. However, because it is one of the five scrolls, we discuss it in this chapter. The style of its language, its vocabulary, and themes in common with Greek philosophy suggest that it dates to the second century B.C.E.

The theological conversation of Proverbs and Job concerning the relationship of human behavior and divine purpose continues in the book of Ecclesiastes. Like Job, it presents a challenge to traditional theology. The book of Ecclesiastes questions the purpose of human existence. It asks, What gives lasting meaning to life? If everyone only dies in the end, what is the meaningful difference between righteousness and wickedness? The seriousness with which the book probes this basic human issue makes it one of the most accessible, almost even "modern," pieces of biblical literature.[5]

PEANUTS Reprinted by permission of UFS, Inc.

[5] Books by Short (1973) and Ellul (1991) demonstrate the contemporary applicability of the book of Ecclesiastes.

Like Proverbs, Ecclesiastes approaches the world of experience looking for order and moral law. Using powers of observation and human reason, the writer attempts to put it all together in a meaningful way. But unlike the wisdom of Proverbs, Ecclesiastes fails to see an overall coherence or purposefulness. Sure, some things are predictable and make sense.

Sweet is the sleep of peasants, whether they eat a lot or a little.
But the abundance of the rich will not let them sleep.
(5:12)

There are regularities and predictable things.

For everything there is a season,
and a time for every matter under heaven:
a time to be born,
and a time to die;
a time to plant,
and a time to uproot what is planted.
(3:1–2)

But ultimately, life seems to have no meaning.

Everything is emptiness and a chasing after wind.
There is nothing to be gained under the sun.
(2:11)

The cynical wisdom of Ecclesiastes appears to challenge the neat and tidy world of proverbial wisdom. If there is no ultimate purpose to life, then why should you care whether you are wise or foolish, righteous or wicked?

The book of Ecclesiastes projects itself as the work of Solomon. Solomon is the "patron saint" of wisdom and he naturally gets the credit. And the reputation of Solomon as Israel's wealthiest and wisest king (whether, in fact, true or not doesn't matter) equips the supposed author to pursue the search for ultimate wisdom, unencumbered with limitations. If anyone had the means, time, talent, and opportunity to search for wisdom and find it, that person would be Solomon. But neither the introduction nor any other verse in Ecclesiastes makes the specific claim of Solomonic authorship. The speaker is simply referred to as **Qohelet** in the editorial introduction, "The words of Qohelet, the son of David, king in Jerusalem" (1:1).[6]

The book is royal autobiography and takes the form of reflections and reminiscence. It has been compared to the genre of royal journals found elsewhere (see Longman 1991). Qohelet's personal story is prefaced with a poem that clearly expresses the theme of the book as a whole and sets the mood.

---

[6] Qohelet is not a name but a title. Translators are not sure what it means or why the speaker of the book was called this. The word is related to the verb *to assemble*, accounting for its title *Ecclesiastes* in the Septuagint, meaning the "churchman" (related to the word *ekklesia*, "assembly, church"). The gender of the term *qohelet* is feminine, as is the gender of the Hebrew word *wisdom*—maybe not a coincidence.

2 Emptiness, Qohelet says, everything is emptiness.[7] 3 What do people gain from all the work they do under the sun? 4 A generation goes and a generation comes, yet the earth remains forever. 5 The sun rises and the sun sets, and rushes back to the place from which it rises again. 6 The wind blows south, then returns to the north, round and round goes the wind, on its rounds it circulates. 7 All streams flow to the sea, yet the sea does not fill up. 8 All matters are tiring, more than anyone can express. The eye is not satisfied with seeing, nor the ear filled with hearing. 9 What is is what will be, and what has been done is what will be done. There is nothing new under the sun. 10 Is there anything of which it can be said, "See this is new!"—It has already been, in eras before us. 11 The people of ages past are no longer remembered, nor will there be any remembrance of people yet to come by those who come after them.

The central thought of Ecclesiastes is contained in that first line "Emptiness, everything is emptiness." It is literally the beginning and the end of the book, found here in 1:2 and in 12:8. The circularity of the system perceived by Qohelet, the lack of directionality and goal, is reflected in the very structure of the book, which ends where it began.

Qohelet observes the circularity of nature, the endless cycle of birth, death, and rebirth. He sees regularity and predictability. But in seeing circularity he does not sense the beauty of a self-renewing system. Rather, he senses futility and purposelessness. The wisdom enterprise up until now had prided itself in discovering and articulating the order of nature, but that has turned into something quite different, a reason for despair.

Qohelet tells us how and why he arrived at this conclusion in chapters 1 and 2. With various experiments and investigations he sought to find the location of meaning. First he tried raw intellect. Applying his mind to know wisdom and folly, he only found that the attempt was an experiment in frustration.

Then he tried the opposite tack. He gave his life over to the pursuit of physical pleasure and personal satisfaction. He drank alcohol, built a magnificent home with palatial grounds, and accumulated precious metals, possessions, and a large staff of servants. Though in none of these did he find fulfillment, yet he felt there might be provisional satisfaction in these pursuits. His conclusion— "There is nothing better for mortals than to eat and drink, and find enjoyment in their work." (2:24)

The cause of Qohelet's frustration is the limited vantage point of humankind. The phrase "under the sun" occurs twenty-nine times in the book, usually in statements such as, "I saw under the sun that the race is not to the swift, nor the battle to the strong." (9:11) This may just be another way of saying "on earth," or it may serve to reinforce the limited perspective of humankind, being unable to transcend the human incapacity to see the whole. The writer puts it clearly in 3:11.

God made everything appropriate to its time. He has also done this—a sense of eternity he put in the heart of humankind, but without the ability to find out what God has done from the beginning to the end.

[7] The Hebrew term is *hevel*, which means *mist* or *vapor*.

The writer suspects that there is more to life than he or anyone else can figure out. God has planted in the human mind the notion of *eternity*, something that transcends human finiteness, yet has not equipped humans to grasp it. Because we are unable to transcend our limits, Qohelet counsels us to enjoy what God's creation has to offer in a positive way.

The book of Ecclesiastes frankly faces the limited capacity of the human spirit to create ultimate meaning. He does not deny that ultimate meaning exists, only that we can expect to find it. Yet all the while he does not come to the conclusion that there is no order. He affirms the reality and goodness of God (*Elohim*, never YHWH in the book). He affirms the continuing need to fear God.

Chapters 4–11 mostly contain rather traditional wisdom observations, generally on the order of what can be found in the book of Proverbs. He gives advice for coping in a world where meaningful activity is hard to find. Granted, all may be ultimately meaningless, yet even Qohelet understands that life must be lived and might even be enjoyed for what it does have to offer.

Yet many of his observations tend to highlight the unfortunate or even tragic side of human experience. Note how Qohelet appends a cynical commentary to an otherwise commonplace proverbial statement in 4:10.

> *The lover of money will not be satisfied with money;*
> *nor the lover of wealth with gain.*
> *This too is emptiness.*

Was Qohelet a heretic? For obvious reasons, the book of Ecclesiastes proved somewhat difficult to handle. It just does not contain the kind of upbeat, positive message that Jews wanted to hear. Yet the book was not just dismissed out of hand as the depressed (and depressing) ruminations of a tired old philosopher. There was truth in what Qohelet said, at least at some level. It probably rang true especially to Judeans who were looking to survive in a world dominated by Greek rule, where they felt at the mercy of higher political powers. They were unable to see God's larger purpose and felt unable to affect it significantly.

The Jewish community struggled with Ecclesiastes. Because of its somewhat troubling observations, they perceived the need to retrieve the book from heresy and give it an orthodox patina. The editorial history of the book gives evidence of their efforts. Although there has been considerable discussion concerning the structure and editorial shape of the book (see Wright 1968), there is a general consensus that the core of the book of Ecclesiastes is 1:2 through 12:8. To this was added the introduction that "Solomonized" the book and a series of two, perhaps three, conclusions.

Verses 9–11 of chapter 12 break with the style of the rest of the book, which is aphorism and autobiography, and were probably written by a devoted disciple of Qohelet. They affirm the wisdom of Qohelet and his effectiveness as a thinker and teacher.

> *9 In addition to being wise, Qohelet taught the people knowledge, and how to judge, study, and arrange many proverbs. 10 Qohelet looked for pleasing words and wrote truthful words plainly. 11 The sayings of the wise are like prods; like nails well set are the collected sayings of the one shepherd.*

Verses 13–14, on the other hand, were written by a theologian more conventional than Qohelet.

13 The end of the matter is this, all has been heard: Fear God, and keep his commandments. That is the whole duty of humankind. 14 For God will bring into judgment every deed, even every secret one, whether it is good or evil.

The editor got the final say (see Sheppard 1980). It is as if he was worried that Qohelet's investigation would lead to nihilism or denial of God. "Lest you be tempted to abandon the faith," he says, "fear God! Don't give up the faith, don't give up the demands of covenant! God still judges human actions. Lack of understanding is no excuse for immorality."

This concluding editorial is really quite remarkable. It attests the vitality of the faith of the postexilic community. It obviously accepted, even perhaps encouraged, the creative kinds of thinking that took Torah to the edge in their effort to apply Torah to their current circumstances. It took great effort—and the integration and synthesis were certainly not complete—yet room was made for theological thinking that stood on the verge of being unorthodox.

ESTHER

The book of Esther does not get the same unqualified reception by Jews and Christians as the book of Ruth, the other heroine tale. Not only does the book of Esther lack the standard religious features you come to expect in Hebrew literature—reference to the God of Israel, the covenant, Torah, and Jerusalem—it appears to condone certain baser human impulses such as violence, vengeance, and intrigue. Yet the book is part of the Hebrew canon. We will have to discover why.

The story of **Esther** is set in the Persian period, referred to by historians as the Achaemenid Empire (see Figure 16.2). The Persian monarch of the story is called **Ahasuerus**, otherwise known as Xerxes I, who ruled 486–465 B.C.E. The story is set in Susa, the winter palace, although Persepolis was the main capital of the empire.

The story begins with a description of a great feast. When Queen Vashti refused to be the main entertainment for the male guests, she was deposed. Ahasuerus organized a Miss Persia contest to replace her, and Esther won.

Esther was a Jewish orphan who had been cared for by her uncle **Mordecai**. Esther effectively concealed her Jewish identity from all at court. Mordecai, meanwhile, uncovered an assassination plot against Ahasuerus, and Esther told the king about it.

Meanwhile, the villainous prime minister **Haman** grew angry with Mordecai because Mordecai refused ever to bow down to him. Mordecai was loyal to the commandment not to bow down to anyone or anything except the God of Israel. Haman hatched a plot to kill Mordecai, as well as all Jews. An unthinking Ahasuerus went along with the plan.

When Mordecai heard about Haman's plan he asked Esther to do something about it. After all, she had access to the king and was in his good graces. At first,

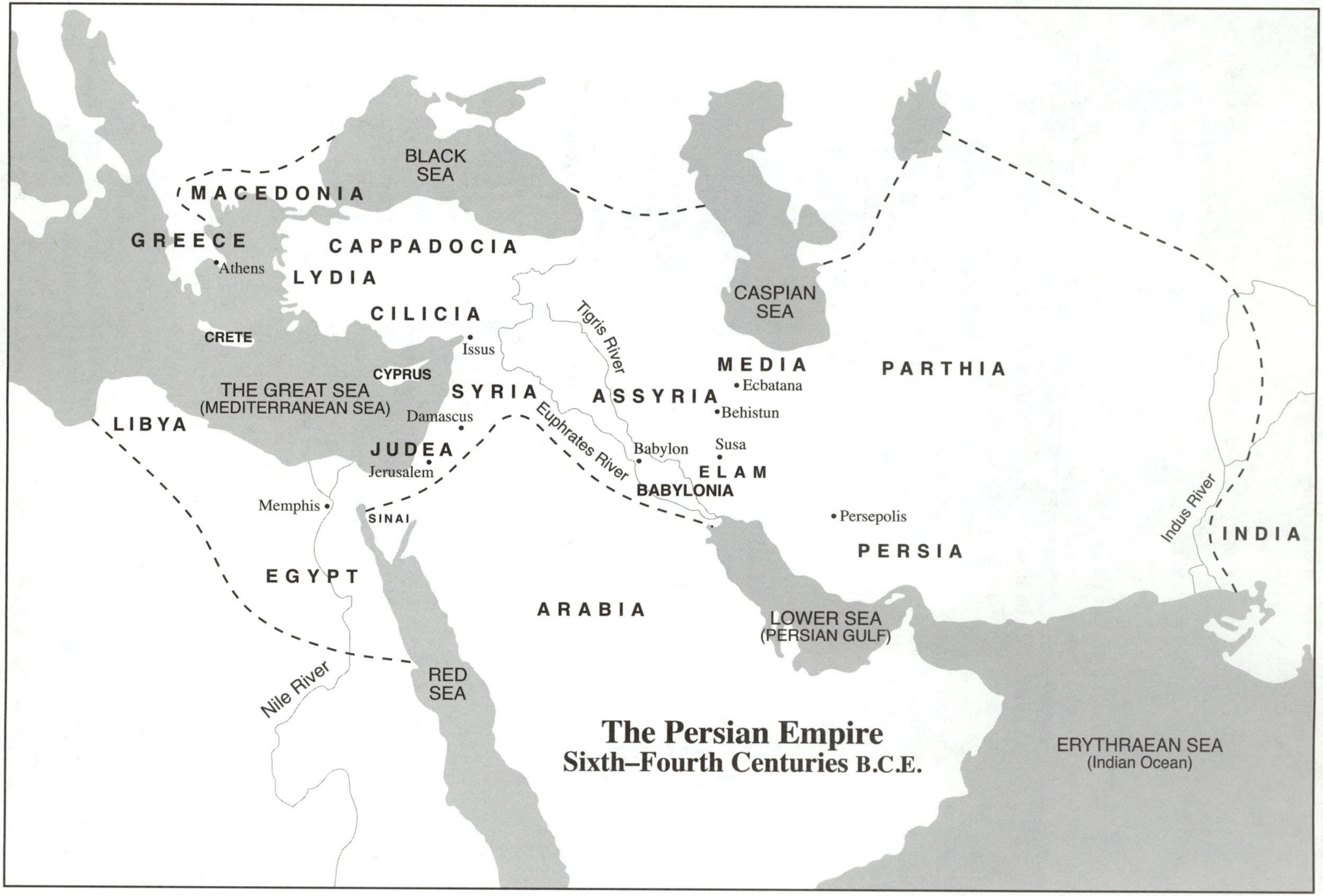

FIGURE 16.2   THE PERSIAN EMPIRE

Esther was reluctant to intervene, citing the danger of approaching the king un-invited. Mordecai prevailed upon Esther with this argument.

> 4:13 Do you think just because you live in the king's palace you will escape the fate of all the other Jews?! 14 If you keep silent at such a time as this, help and deliverance will come for the Jews from somewhere else, but you and your father's family will perish. Who knows? Maybe you have come to royal position for just such a time as this."

This is the closest the book ever comes to expressing any kind of theological sentiment—in this case, a general suggestion of divine providence and supernatural protection.

Esther approached the king and was granted an audience. She invited the king and Haman to a banquet. When Haman heard of the invitation he was delighted, but quickly became depressed after he witnessed Mordecai's insolence in refusing to bow after he left the palace. He decided to have Mordecai hanged.

That same day, Ahasuerus was reviewing the court records and came across the entry on Mordecai's report of the assassination attempt saving the king. After inquiry he found out Mordecai had never been honored for that. Haman just happened to be around at the time, so the king called him in and asked what kinds of things should be done to honor a faithful citizen. Thinking that the king had him in mind, Haman devised a wonderful ceremonial procession giving public acclaim to such a man. The king told him to arrange it. He was shocked when he found out that Mordecai was the one to be honored.

Afterward at the banquet, Esther pleaded for the lives of the Jewish people. Amazingly, the king revealed little awareness of the edict he himself had authorized.

> 7:5 King Ahasuerus said to Queen Esther, "Who is he, and where is he—the one who has presumed to do this?" 6 Esther said, "An antagonist and an enemy, this wicked Haman!"

Shocked (a bit dim-witted too, it seems), the king left the room. Haman fell on Esther's couch, pleading for his life. When the king came back and saw Haman on top of Esther, he thought Haman was making advances on his queen. The king was even more outraged and had Haman hanged on the gallows that Haman had built for Mordecai.

Esther and Mordecai convinced the king to issue an edict reversing the intended result of Haman's plan. Official letters were drafted and sent throughout the empire authorizing the Jews to defend themselves. They killed hundreds of their enemies in Susa and thousands elsewhere. A new respect for the Jews of the Diaspora developed, and many people became converts to Judaism.

The most basic significance of the book of Esther is this. It explains the origin of the Jewish celebration of **Purim**. This holiday came late in Jewish history and is not authorized by the Torah, so separate justification was needed. It was called Purim following the name of the divination device, the *pur* or lot (see 3:7) Haman used to determine the best day for the slaughter of the Jews.

Still celebrated by Jewish communities in February or March, it is a festival of freedom, remembering the time when Jews scattered around the world were given respect and recognition and the power to defend their own way of life. When it is observed today it can be a raucous affair. Adolescents are allowed to do things on Purim they could never get away with any other day. In celebration, the book of Esther is read in the synagogue, and whenever the name Haman is voiced, children shout, stamp their feet, and sound noisemakers. Special cookies called Haman's ears are eaten in disdain of the villain. Adults are supposed to drink so much wine that they can no longer tell the difference between "Blessed Mordecai" and "Accursed Haman."

As with the book of Ruth, there are other possible implications of the story. The book strongly suggests that the Jews must not forget their identity or think that they can somehow find safety by blending in. Mordecai pointed out to Esther that assimilating was not an option, and her position at court would not ultimately protect her. There is also the implication that the Jews must stick together, for only therein will they survive.

With Esther, we cannot fail to notice once again the importance of faithful women for the history of Israel. This story affirms the importance of a single courageous female character for the Jewish community. Indeed, its survival depended on her. The paradigmatic function of storytelling is again present, as Esther is projected as a positive role model for women of the faith.

The Hebrew Bible locates the book of Esther in the Writings as one of the Five Scrolls. The canonical tradition of the Christian Old Testament places it after Nehemiah, which makes it the last book in the collection of historical materials. This placement functions to assign a history-telling role to the book, as opposed to its storytelling role in the Hebrew Bible.

The book of Esther is a late book, obviously having been written after the reign of Ahasuerus (Xerxes I). The consensus is that it was written in the fourth or third century B.C.E. It had some trouble finding acceptance into the canon because of its lack of explicit "God talk." It has the distinction of being the only book of the Hebrew Bible not having attestation in at least a fragment among the Dead Sea Scrolls. The old Greek version of the Hebrew Bible (also known as the Septuagint) seems to have found it somewhat inadequate. It lengthened the book considerably by introducing prayers and petitions of Esther and Mordecai that refer explicitly to God.

Some scholars have suggested that the book has a pagan prehistory. For example, the name Mordecai could be derived from Marduk, the Babylonian high god, and Esther is linguistically related to Ishtar, a goddess. In this speculation, the story was originally related to the Babylonian New Year festival, and the plot was transformed along with the names to make a Jewish tale. Though unlikely, some such prehistory may at a far distant point underlie the book. But as it stands now, the book bears a recognizable historical and biblical setting.

The genealogical notes identifying Mordecai and Haman place the story within a larger biblical context. Mordecai is identified as a descendant of Kish from the tribe of Benjamin. This would make him a descendant of Saul. Haman is identified as a member of the Agag family and an Amalekite. The Amalekites were the prototypical enemies of the Israelites. They were the first to attack the

Hebrews after they left Egypt in the exodus. They also harassed the Israelites during the early monarchy. Saul's failure to eliminate Agag and the Amalekites was the cause of his demise. The book of Esther implies that Mordecai finally got the job done with the elimination of Haman.

The book of Esther is religiously nationalistic in focus. It has a definite "us" against "them" feel and deals with Haman's planned pogrom to eliminate Jews. The Jews, in Esther and Mordecai, proved themselves clever enough to overcome this threat. Jewish national and religious salvation involved the execution of Haman and community self-defense. In some ways this is a violent book. What, then, is the effect of having it in the Hebrew Bible? How can this be justified?

As Childs (1979) argues, the book itself shows evidence of wrestling with this issue. The letters of Mordecai and Esther contained in 9:20–32 appear to be additions. They change the tone of Purim considerably. They turn it from a time of slaughtering Jewish enemies to a time of celebration, gift-giving, and well-wishing. Through this canonical reinterpretation the original event became the occasion to celebrate Jewish identity and God's preservation of the Jews as a people.

Overall, the book exposes the serious threats God's people face when living in an alien and hostile culture. The book of Esther reveals that God directs affairs providentially to protect and deliver his people.

FIVE SCROLLS IN CANONICAL CONTEXT

The five books in this collection differ in many ways, including literary type and subject matter. They were grouped together primarily because they all relate to Jewish commemorative events. But we should ask if there is any further benefit, a thematic and theological bonus, in seeing them together as a collection.

If consensus reconstructions are accurate, all five of these books were compiled relatively late, in the exilic period of the sixth century B.C.E. or thereafter. These books should then be interpreted in light of the theological and sociological issues of that age, specifically the reformation of a Jewish community and the emergence of religious Judaism.

The book of Ruth may be viewed as a protest against a narrowly defined nationalism, and implicitly argues for a more inclusive community. The criterion for inclusion into the community should be not national affiliation but acceptance of the God of Israel. The book of Esther also addresses the issue of community, but from the opposite angle, that is, where Jews are the ones being excluded. It exposes the problems of religious intolerance and xenophobia from the view of the outsider. Esther portrays the ugliness of a society where Jews are systematically ostracized and abused. The book, at the same time, is empowering. The Jews of Esther are not helpless or ineffectual but are capable of defending themselves legally and physically. The story authorizes the postexilic Jewish community to affirm its identity in the face of racially and religiously based prejudice and discrimination.

The books of Ruth and Esther do not reflect the same community. They display different community attitudes, especially to the non-Israelite population.

They represent different challenges to pluralism. But both responses, by virtue of being included in the canon, represent legitimate responses.

The Song of Songs seems to present a different kind of social challenge. It stands, perhaps, as a protest against a world where the free expression of love is discouraged. Remember the abuse that the lovers suffered in the book. It is critical of a society that does not value true love and forces true lovers to give their love expression in secret. It is also critical of a dominating patriarchal society that attempts to manipulate female love and use it self-gratifyingly. The Song is startlingly progressive in the mutuality of the male–female relationship.

Ecclesiastes continues the late wisdom tradition's challenge to retribution theology. It presses the issue of divine governance by probing for the essential meaning of existence. While it does not deny the providence of God, it does seem to give up in frustration over its inability to penetrate to the purpose of God. If the book speaks not only on the personal level but also on the communal level, it expresses Israel's frustration at not knowing what God had in store for them historically. Only a backwater province within monstrous empires, they had lost a national sense of purpose.

Lamentations continues in the vein of challenge, if not protest. The very mode of complaint that is the genre of the book could be interpreted as a challenge to God. It demands to know why God treated his people so harshly and wants to know when he would restore them. Again, the community wrestles with God.

Perhaps it is no accident these voices gave expression through poetry and story instead of through prophetic genres. As poetry and story they might not so quickly give offense. Metaphoric poetry and heartwarming story can sometimes soften otherwise prickly lessons. In any case, they kept alive the theological discussion over the nature of the covenant community, especially the value of all members, indigenous-Israelite and non-Israelite alike, female and male alike. In all, these books were alternate voices, challenging voices, and critical voices that contested the dominant theologies of the Jews. Taken together, they highlight the need for foundational biblical and human values: loyalty, faithfulness, acceptance, security, freedom, and love.

QUESTIONS FOR REVIEW

1. *Song of Songs* What are the main ways that the Song of Songs can be interpreted?
2. *Ruth* Why is the fact that Ruth is a Moabite crucial to the story? How is this fact tied to the meaning and application of the story?
3. *Lamentations* What is the literary type of the poems in this book, and what historical event do they commemorate?

4. *Ecclesiastes* As speculative wisdom, with what theological issue does this book wrestle, and what are its conclusions?
5. *Esther* How did Mordecai convince Esther to intervene to save the Jews, and what was the outcome of her intervention?

QUESTIONS FOR DISCUSSION

1. As poetry in praise of human love and sexuality, how can the Song of Songs be reconciled with the high moral tone of the rest of biblical literature?

2. How are the books of Ruth and Esther alike? How do they differ? How does each face the issues of community identity and how to deal with foreigners? Are these still relevant issues in the modern world?

3. How does Ecclesiastes address the question of the meaning of life? How does his thinking compare to the spirit of the modern age? How did the editors of Ecclesiastes try to handle the potentially disturbing effect of the book? What adjectives would you use to describe the book and your reaction to it?

FOR FURTHER STUDY

Song of Songs. Falk, Marcia (1990). *The Song of Songs: A New Translation and Interpretation.* San Francisco: Harper & Row. Reads the song as thirty-one thematically and literarily related love poems in three voices.

Landy, Francis (1983). *Paradoxes of Paradise: Identity and Difference in the Song of Songs.* Sheffield: JSOT Press.

Murphy, Roland E. (1990). *The Song of Songs: A Commentary on the Book of Canticles or the Song of Songs.* Hermeneia Series. Minneapolis: Fortress Press.

Pope, Marvin H. (1977). *The Song of Songs.* Anchor Bible. Garden City, N.Y.: Doubleday.

Seerveld, Calvin (1967). *The Greatest Song. In Critique of Solomon.* Palos Heights, Ill.: Trinity Pennyasheet Press. The Song of Songs translated and arranged for oratio performance; renders it in dramatic fashion with Solomon viewed as a villain trying to come between the two lovers.

Tournay, Raymond Jacques (1988). *Word of God, Song of Love: A Commentary on the Song of Songs.* New York, N.Y., and Mahwah, N.J.: Paulist Press. Views the song both as an allegory of divine love and as a human love song.

Ruth. Atkinson, David (1983). *The Message of Ruth: The Wings of Refuge.* The Bible Speaks Today. Leicester, Eng. and Downers Grove, Ill.: Inter-Varsity Press.

Campbell, Edward F. (1975). *Ruth.* Anchor Bible. Garden City, N.Y.: Doubleday.

Darr, Katheryn Pfisterer (1991). *Far More Precious than Jewels: Perspectives on Biblical Women.* Gender and the Biblical Tradition Series. Louisville, Ky.: Westminster/John Knox Press. An introduction to traditional Jewish views of Ruth, Sarah, Hagar, and Esther.

Fewell, Danna Nolan, and David Miller Gunn (1990). *Compromising Redemption: Relating Characters in the Book of Ruth.* Literary Currents in Biblical Interpretation. Philadelphia: Westminster/John Knox Press.

Hals, Ronald (1969). *The Theology of the Book of Ruth.* Facet Books, 23. Philadelphia: Fortress Press.

Hubbard, Robert L., Jr. (1988). *The Book of Ruth.* New International Commentary on the Old Testament. Grand Rapids, Mich.: Eerdmans.

Sasson, Jack M. (1989). *Ruth: A New Translation with a Philological Commentary and a Formalist–Folklorist Interpretation.* 2d ed. Sheffield: JSOT Press.

Lamentations. Gottwald, Norman K. (1962). *Studies in the Book of Lamentations.* Studies in Biblical Theology, 1st Series, 14. London: SCM Press.

Hillers, Delbert R. (1972). *Lamentations.* Anchor Bible. Garden City, N.Y.: Doubleday.

Provan, Iain W. (1991). *Lamentations.* New Century Bible Commentary. Grand Rapids, Mich.: Eerdmans.

Ecclesiastes. Crenshaw, James L. (1987). *Ecclesiastes.* Old Testament Library. Philadelphia: Westminster Press.

Ellul, Jacques (1991). *Reason for Being. A Meditation on Ecclesiastes.* Grand Rapids, Mich.: Eerdmans.

Gordis, Robert (1951). *Koheleth: The Man and His World.* New York: Jewish Theological Seminary of America Press. A collection of essays on the literature and theology of Ecclesiastes.

Ogden, Graham (1987). *Qohelet.* Sheffield: JSOT Press.

Sperka, Joshua S. (1972). *Ecclesiastes: Stories to Live By*. New York: Bloch. A translation with stories from midrashic and talmudic literature illustrating each verse.

Esther. Berg, Sandra Beth (1979). *The Book of Esther*. SBL Dissertation Series, 44. Missoula, Mont.: Scholars Press.

Clines, David J. A. (1984). *The Esther Scroll: The Story of the Story*. JSOT Supplement Series, 30. Sheffield: JSOT Press.

Fox, Michael (1991). *Character and Ideology in the Book of Esther*. Columbia: University of South Carolina Press.

Talmon, Shemaryahu (1963). "Wisdom in the Book of Esther." *Vetus Testamentum* 13: 419–55.

WORKS CITED

Campbell, Edward F. (1975). *Ruth*. Anchor Bible. Garden City, N.Y.: Doubleday.

Childs, Brevard S. (1979). *Introduction to the Old Testament as Scripture*. Philadelphia: Fortress Press.

Ellul, Jacques (1991). *Reason for Being. A Meditation on Ecclesiastes*. Grand Rapids, Mich.: Eerdmans.

Fox, Michael V. (1985). *The Song of Songs and the Ancient Egyptian Love Songs*. Madison: University of Wisconsin Press.

Garr, W. Randall (1983). "The Qinah: A Study of Poetic Meter, Syntax and Style." *Zeitschrift für die Alttestamentliche Wissenschaft* 95: 54–74.

Hals, Ronald (1969). *The Theology of the Book of Ruth*. Facet Books, 23. Philadelphia: Fortress Press.

Longman, Tremper, III (1991). *Fictional Akkadian Autobiography: A Generic and Comparative Study*. Winona Lake, Ind.: Eisenbrauns.

Matter, E. Ann (1990). *The Voice of My Beloved: The Song of Songs in Western Medieval Christianity*. Philadelphia: University of Pennsylvania Press.

Pope, Marvin H. (1977). *The Song of Songs*. Anchor Bible. Garden City, N.Y.: Doubleday.

Sheppard, Gerald T. (1980). *Wisdom as a Hermeneutical Construct*. BZAW 151. Berlin and New York: Walter de Gruyter.

Short, Robert L. (1973). *A Time to Be Born—A Time to Die*. New York: Harper & Row. A collage of pictures suggesting the relevance of Ecclesiastes.

White, John Bradley (1978). *A Study of the Language of Love in the Song of Songs and Ancient Egyptian Poetry*. SBL Dissertation Series, 38. Missoula, Mont.: Scholars Press.

Wright, Addison G. (1968). "The Riddle of the Sphinx: The Structure of the Book of Qohelet." *Catholic Biblical Quarterly* 30: 313–34.

DANIEL: APOCALYPTIC LITERATURE

17

Names and Terms to Remember

Antiochus IV (Epiphanes)	dualism	Nebuchadnezzar
apocalypse	eschatology	prophetic eschatology
apocalyptic eschatology	Hasids	pseudonymity
apocalypticism	Hellenism	Son of Man
apocalyptic literature	kingdom of God	*vaticinia ex eventu*
Daniel		

ONCE BY THE PACIFIC

The shattered water made a misty din.
Great waves looked over others coming in,
And thought of doing something to the shore
That water never did to land before.
The clouds were low and hairy in the skies,
Like locks blown forward in the gleam of eyes.
You could not tell, and yet it looked as if
The shore was lucky in being backed by cliff,
The cliff in being backed by continent
It looked as if a night of dark intent
Was coming, and not only a night, an age.
Someone had better be prepared for rage.
There would be more than ocean-water broken
Before God's last Put out the Light *was spoken.*
—Robert Frost (1874–1963)

Will the world end some day? If so, will it be soon? Will it be in our lifetime? Will it end with a bang or with a whimper? These questions fascinate us and sometimes send shivers down our spines.

For decades the specter of global thermonuclear holocaust hung heavy over our heads. Even now, as the nuclear threat recedes somewhat, the peril of global ecological disaster provides another scary scenario for the end of the known world. Science, technology, and industrialization have put at our disposal numerous ways we can kill ourselves and take our planet with us.

Countless movies and novels provide imaginative, though not necessarily implausible, scenarios. An early end-time novel was Nevil Shute's *On the Beach* (1958), which presents a post–nuclear-war world. Stephen King's *The Stand* devises worldwide biological disaster. Walker Percy in most of his novels imagined a whimpering end to the civilized world. As for movies, *Dr. Strangelove, or how I learned to stop worrying and love the bomb*, is a comically absurd yet grim cinematic rendition of worldwide nuclear death. Movies like *Apocalypse Now* and *The Seventh Sign* all in some way envision the end.

End-time speculation is especially ripe at important transition points in history, as laid out nicely by Otto Friedrich in *The End of the World: A History* (1982). As we approach the end of the millennium, the year 2000, we approach one such breakpoint, and there seems to be heightened fascination with the end-time.

Certainly, an interest in the end of civilization has fueled a great deal of speculation, not a little of which has a religious flavor.

The Hebrew Bible has its own brand of end-time thinking. It is called **apocalyptic literature**.

APOCALYPTIC LITERATURE IN GENERAL

The adjective *apocalyptic* is a modern label for end-time literature. Ancient writers did not tag their own material "apocalyptic." Yet the term is apt; it derives from the ancient Greek verb *apokaluptein*, which means "to reveal, disclose, uncover." From this word we also get the noun **apocalypse**.

As we begin to deal with apocalyptic literature in its various dimensions it will be important to define some basic concepts. Hanson (1985) criticizes scholars for mixing apocalyptic categories dealing with form, concept, and sociology, and this is a good caution. *Apocalypse* designates a type of literature from the ancient world that contained a revelation of the future. Specifically, an apocalypse is a revelation initiated by God and delivered through a mediator (typically an angel) to a holy person; the revelation has to do with future events.

The Book of Daniel, but only in chapters 7–12, fits this formula. Other major works falling into the genre of apocalypse are the New Testament book of Revelation (in Greek its title is *apokalypsis*), 1 Enoch, 4 Ezra, and 2 Baruch. The first three gospels of the New Testament each contain an apocalyptic chapter (Matthew 24, Mark 13, Luke 24).

Apocalyptic literature is more than a literary phenomenon. It is associated with certain religious and sociological perspectives. The term **apocalypticism** applies to the thought world or world view of the community that gave rise to the literature. Most of the apocalypses were written during times of political persecution. They were intended to encourage perseverance by revealing the destruction of the wicked and the glorious future that awaited the faithful.

Scholars are interested in the sociology of apocalypticism. It is now generally recognized that literature is significantly shaped by the historical and sociological characteristics of the authoring community. Schmitals (1975) gives special attention to the developmental dimensions of what he calls the apocalyptic movement.

One of the main features of an apocalyptic community is its marginal status within the larger society. In its social, political, or economic alienation the community constructs an alternate universe where eventually it will triumph. This alternate universe comes to expression in apocalyptic literature.

Another important term associated with the study of apocalyptic literature is **eschatology**. Eschatology (derived from the Greek word for *end*) refers to the complex of religious beliefs that have to do with the end times. The eschatological perspective of biblical literature views history as moving to a final culmination defined by God and brought about primarily by his initiative.

Hanson also distinguishes **prophetic eschatology** and **apocalyptic eschatology**. Prophetic eschatology is more naturalistic in that it sees God using human agents and historical processes to bring about his purposes in history. Apocalyptic eschatology is more supernatural in that God breaks into history in cataclysmic ways to realize his goal. Human agency is only secondary to divine initiative.

General Characteristics of Apocalyptic Literature

Apocalyptic literature in the Hebrew–Greek tradition partakes of a common fund of characteristics. Not all apocalyptic literary works evidence all these characteristics, but they are representative of what you can expect to find.

Literary and Stylistic Characteristics

Being apocalypses, most of this literature is in the form of dreams or visions witnessed by a seer. The seer then describes the dream in the first-person "I."

Most apocalyptic works are anonymous: that is, we do not know exactly who wrote them. The books themselves claim to be the work of certain individuals, most of whom are legendary figures. Apocalyptic books have been ascribed to Adam, Enoch (see Genesis 5), Ezra, Moses, and many others. This phenomenon of ascribed authorship is technically called **pseudonymity** or pseudonomous authorship. The practice probably was designed to facilitate the acceptance of the work.

Most apocalyptic works also employ highly imaginative symbolic imagery. Strange hybrid animals are not unusual. Numbers are also used in a symbolic way. Secret code words, presumably understood by the intended audience but unclear to the uninitiated, are also used.

Many apocalypses contain a review of past history but frame it as if it were predictive prophecy. Predictive prophecy after the event (it's a lot easier that way) is called *vaticinia ex eventu*.

Outlook and Perspective

Apocalyptic literature has a more universal scope than other Hebrew literature. That is, the writer is interested in historical events beyond Israel—in fact, is more concerned with other nations than with Israel. He sees the other nations as under the control of Israel's God, who is determining their history to achieve God's own ends. Almost all apocalyptic literature shares the belief that God has determined the conclusion of history from the beginning.

Apocalyptic literature is ripe with dualisms. A **dualism** is a black-and-white way of looking at matters that does not allow for any gray. Apocalyptic literature's cosmic dualism construes the universe as heaven and earth, a two-storied world. The literature of Israel's monarchic period did not put much stock in a heaven, beyond referring to it as the residence of God. In apocalyptic literature heaven is the place where the most important events take place, including fierce wars between good and bad angels.

Temporal, or chronological, dualism divides the course of history into two eras. History as we know it is called "this age" and is dominated by the forces of godlessness and evil. Apocalyptic writers were obviously very pessimistic about the prospects for improvement in their time. They believed that God would bring this age to an end and would introduce "the age to come," where goodness would prevail.

A final dualism is ethical dualism—that is, a dualism of human action and character. In apocalyptic literature humankind is divided into two groups. One group, the large one made up of everybody else, is motivated by evil and violently opposes the smaller group of God-fearing, persecuted ones. At the culmination of history God will take the side of the latter and vindicate the cause of right. But until then only the worst can be expected by the righteous remnant. The smaller group, the apocalyptic community, believes that only they are in the right. They advocate a separatist policy, no doubt in response to the domination of the majority population that has marginalized them.

LITERARY PARENTAGE OF APOCALYPTIC LITERATURE

Only one book in the Hebrew Bible is generally classified as apocalyptic literature, and that is the book of Daniel. But that is not to say that Daniel is the only book that shows characteristics typical of apocalyptic literature. A good deal of scholarship has tried to uncover the parentage of apocalyptic literature.

Certain motifs characteristic of apocalyptic eschatology can be found in the myths of ancient Mesopotamia. Motifs of cosmic warfare pervade mythic material, such as the battle between the high gods and the sea monsters. The divine warrior motif is also present in biblical apocalyptic literature. The royal cult of Jerusalem may be the source of various warrior motifs in apocalyptic literature. Also, Persian dualism may have affected the development of apocalyptic ideology.

In addition to having affinities with literatures that predate the Hebrew Bible, some scholars suggest that apocalyptic literature has similarities with both the wisdom and the prophetic literatures of the Hebrew Bible. Von Rad argues that it has its origins in wisdom. Hanson (1975) traces the precursors of Jewish apocalyptic literature back to biblical prophecy. He dates the movement from prophetic eschatology to apocalyptic eschatology in the early postexilic period, roughly 538–500 B.C.E. The school of Second Isaiah contains a good deal of apocalyptic material in chapters 34–35, 40–55, 24–27, and 56–66. Apocalypticism seems to be in evidence then, but it really achieved prominence in the second century B.C.E. during the Hellenization program of **Antiochus IV**.

THE BOOK OF DANIEL

The book of Daniel can be divided more or less cleanly into two main parts based on content. The first part, chapters 1–6, contains six tales of Jewish heroism set in the late seventh and sixth centuries B.C.E. They are told in the third person and concern **Daniel** and his three friends, or Daniel alone, or the three friends alone. The second part, chapters 7–12, contains four apocalypses in the form of dream visions, which Daniel narrates in the first person (Figure 17.1).

Outline of Daniel

I. Tales of heroism (1–6)
  A. Daniel and his friends at the Babylonian court of Nebuchadnezzar (1)
  B. Daniel interprets the statue dream of Nebuchadnezzar (2)
  C. The three friends are placed in the furnace (3)
  D. Daniel interprets the tree dream of Nebuchadnezzar (4)

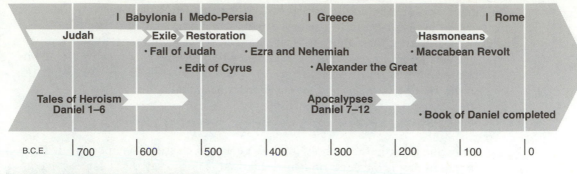

FIGURE 17.1   TIME LINE: BOOK OF DANIEL

E. Daniel interprets the handwriting on the wall of Belshazzar (5)
F. Daniel is placed in the lion's pit of Darius (6)
II. Apocalypses (7–12)
A. The four beasts and the Son of Man (7)
B. The ram and the goat (8)
C. Gabriel interprets Jeremiah's prophecy of the seventy weeks (9)
D. Vision of future history (10–12)

Only one feature of the book compromises this clean division. Daniel is one of two books in the Hebrew Bible that contain a substantial amount of text written in Aramaic rather than in Hebrew. (The other is Ezra.) The section of Daniel written in the Aramaic language, 2:4 through the end of chapter 7, spans the division based on form and content.

AUTHORSHIP ISSUE

The book of Daniel does not claim to have been written by Daniel. The first six chapters are a narrative about Daniel (and his friends), and while the final chapters contain Daniel's first-person dream accounts, they are introduced with third-person editorial frameworks.

Who exactly was this Daniel? We get conflicting signals. The first hero tale has Daniel being taken captive as a young man in 606 B.C.E. The story of Daniel in the lion's den in chapter 6 has a setting after 539, which would make Daniel an old man by this time. On the other hand, the book of Ezekiel (14:14 and 20, also 28:3), which was written around the time of the exile in 587, refers to Daniel in the same breath with Noah and Job—all exemplary righteous men. These references suggest that Daniel and these other two men were already well known and could stand as symbols of godliness. But how could Daniel be considered legendary to the preexilic Israelites if most of the stories told about him had not yet been written?

The Ugaritic texts from Syria come to the rescue. These texts, dating to the fourteenth century B.C.E. and written in a language close to Hebrew, contain an account of a Danel (close enough in spelling to our Daniel that they may be considered equivalent). This Danel was a notable, righteous Canaanite king who wanted to see justice done in his kingdom. This suggests that Danel/Daniel was a hero of the ancient world and that he was the model or namesake for our hero of Israel's exilic period. Or, . . . the Danel of Ezekiel fame has nothing to do with the Daniel of the book by that name.

Most scholars today hold the view that the book of Daniel contains stories about a legendary figure and his associates. The stories are set around the time of the Babylonian exile and may have been shaped originally at that time. But the apocalypses of chapters 7–12 betray a much later setting. The history they (fore-)tell culminates in the time of the Maccabees, specifically the years of Antiochus IV (167–164 B.C.E.). To be exact, the evidence strongly suggests that the latter half of the book was written around 165 B.C.E., shortly before the death of Antiochus in 163, and that the entire book was edited and finalized around that time. That would make Daniel the prime candidate for the latest book of the Hebrew Bible.

Various other stories about Daniel are found in apocryphal literature, called the "Additions to Daniel." Though not included in the canon, they attest to the continuing interest in this figure by the Jewish community.

TALES OF HEROISM (1–6)

The first six chapters contain some of the most popular and well-known stories in the Hebrew Bible. Shadrach, Meshach, and Abednego in the fiery furnace. Daniel in the lion's den. The handwriting on the wall. In addition to their popular appeal, the tales had a moral lesson, one of enduring importance. No matter what political and religious pressures urge you to conform to the dominant culture, don't give up your faith in Yahweh. God will surely take care of you and deliver you if you are faithful. And ultimately the evil kingdoms of this world will crumble before the Kingdom of God. This lesson is worked out in each of the tales.

Daniel 1 introduces the tales by describing Daniel and his three friends Hananiah, Mishael, and Azariah. Each was given a Babylonian name as part of the process of acculturating these young Jewish men into Babylonian society. Respectively they became Belteshazzar, Shadrach, Meshach, and Abednego. Interestingly, Daniel is referred to by his Hebrew name through most of the book, while the friends go by their Babylonian names. These young men were handsome and intelligent and were to be trained as Babylonian counselors, presumably in the expectation that they would serve **Nebuchadnezzar** as administrators in the Judean territories. The problem for these Jewish trainees was that eating at the Babylonian court would violate their dietary laws, called the laws of kosher. They were given a special reprieve by their overseer, and in spite of eating only simple kosher food, they turned out healthier than any other counselors. This proved that a person could keep religious laws even in a foreign land—a situation many Judeans faced after 587.

The next chapter describes a dream that Nebuchadnezzar had. He woke up and remembered that he had a fascinating dream, but he could not remember the details. Daniel came to the king's attention when it turned out that he was the only one who could bring the dream to Nebuchadnezzar's recollection and then interpret it. The dream's central image was a statue with a head of gold, chest and arms of silver, mid-section and thighs of bronze, legs of iron, and feet of iron and clay. A rock pulverized the statue and it blew away. The rock grew into a mountain that dominated the earth. Daniel's interpretation associated each of the four metals with an empire. These empires were destroyed and a kingdom set up by God took over in their place. As we will see, this statue dream has important parallels to the apocalypse of chapter 7, which also has a sequence of four empires eclipsed by the kingdom of God.

Chapters 3 and 6 are similar. By now Daniel and his friends had become important government officials, and they had acquired powerful political enemies. These rivals enacted certain religious requirements that they knew these Jews could not obey. First the three friends (3), then Daniel (6) were found guilty of refusing to worship anyone but Yahweh, and were to be executed. The friends were thrown into a well-stoked furnace but were delivered by God through an angel. And Daniel was thrown into a pit full of ravenous lions. He, too, was protected and survived. Both incidents prove again that God cares for the faithful.

Chapters 4 and 5 have a different twist. They reveal the arrogance of Babylonian power—first when Nebuchadnezzar brags about his kingdom and then when Belshazzar uses the sacred Jerusalem temple cups in a raucous feast. Nebuchadnezzar was removed from power until he came to his senses and acknowledged the supremacy of Yahweh. Belshazzar, on the other hand, was permanently deposed when Babylon was overthrown by the Medes. The message is clear: Yahweh will not put up with profane empires. He is ultimately in control and disposes of empires at will. This served to encourage faithful Jews by exposing the vulnerability of the pagan kingdoms that dominated them.

APOCALYPSES (7–12)

To understand the setting of the final portion of the book of Daniel it is necessary to summarize the history of the Maccabean period. The Maccabean conflict is the historical setting for the apocalypses as well as for the final compilation of the book.

Greek Rule and the Maccabean Revolt

Alexander the Great began his conquest of the eastern Mediterranean world in 332 B.C.E. By the time he died in 323, Greek control extended as far east as the Indus Valley. After his death, control of the empire was divided among his four generals, of whom only two are important for our purposes. Most of Mesopotamia went to Seleucus and became the Seleucid Empire. Syria, Palestine, and Egypt went to Ptolemy and became the Ptolemaic Empire. Palestine was roughly the dividing line between these two empires and for that reason became a matter of contention.

Palestine was under the control of the Ptolemaic Empire until around 200 B.C.E. The Greek way of life, with its compellingly attractive cultural institutions such as gymnasiums and theaters, Greek language and literature, refined manners, and colorful religion, was a serious temptation to the Jewish population and found not a few cultural converts. But during that time Judaism was still an acceptable and even thriving enterprise.

That changed when the Seleucid Empire extended its area of control to include Palestine. The Seleucid ruler Antiochus IV, nicknamed Epiphanes, ruled his empire from 175 to 164. He faced growing opposition to his rule throughout the Seleucid empire. He interpreted the movements toward independence as being in part inspired by local religious and cultural practices. He decided to eradicate everything that smacked of provincialism and impose, by force if necessary, a uniform Greek cultural expression, a process called Hellenization. He outlawed traditional Jewish commandments, including circumcision, dietary restrictions, and Sabbath observance, and made ownership of a Torah scroll a capital offense.

Antiochus IV took visible and outrageous actions to demonstrate royal disfavor of Judaism. He forced Jews to eat pork in violation of kosher regulations and even sacrificed a pig on the altar of burnt offering in the Jerusalem temple complex. Then he set up a statue of Zeus in the most holy place of the temple. Many Jews accommodated **Hellenism** and assimilated to a degree. Others opposed any sort of compromise. They were called **Hasids**, "faithful ones." The struggle between the Seleucids and the Hasids is told in 1 and 2 Maccabees.

Armed Jewish resistance broke out in 167, led by a provincial Jew named Mattathias and his sons. The most famous son is Judas Maccabee, "the hammer." They successfully waged a guerrilla campaign against the Seleucids, eventually resulting in the retaking of Jerusalem. They cleansed and restored the temple and resumed ritual activity as prescribed in the Torah. The temple was rededicated in 164 B.C.E. in an eight-day celebration called Hanukkah.

In apocalyptic literature's typically cryptic and veiled way, the apocalypses of Daniel 7–12 relate to the history of this period.

The Son of Man Apocalypse (7)

In this first apocalypse Daniel sees the **kingdom of God** overcome the kingdoms of this world.

> *7:1 In the first year of King Belshazzar of Babylon, Daniel saw a dream and his mind had a vision while he was in bed. Afterward he wrote down the dream. 2 Daniel related and said: "I saw the four winds stirring up the great sea in my nighttime vision. 3 Four great beasts came up out of the sea, each different from the others. 4 The first was like a lion and had eagle's wings. Then its wings were pulled off as I watched, and it was lifted up from the ground and made to stand on two feet like a human, and it was given a human mind."*

The narrative introduction to this first apocalypse introduces the dream vision. The year is 554 B.C.E., when Belshazzar ruled over Babylonia on behalf of Nabonidus. The great sea out of which the beasts arose recalls the mythic waters of chaos associated with evil, populated with dragons and monsters (see Isaiah 51:9–10 for another allusion to the waters of chaos). The stormy sea is a fitting image for the tumultuous affairs of the nations that threaten God's people. The lion represents Babylonia (see Figure 17.2).

FIGURE 17.2   WINGED LION   The winged lion is a known symbol of power, as in this winged lion of Ashurnasirpal (884–860 B.C.E.).

Daniel goes on to describe three other beasts, a bear standing for Media, a leopard for Persia, and a beast with ten horns so terrible it was unlike any natural creature standing for Greece. As he watched:

7:9 thrones were put in place, and an Ancient of Days took his throne, his clothing was white as snow, and the hair of his head was like pure wool; his throne was on fire and its wheels were burning. 10 A stream of fire is-

sued and flowed out from his presence. A thousand thousands served him, and ten thousand ten thousands stood attending him. The court sat in judgment and the books were opened.

The Almighty, described as a stately elder, is surrounded by the divine council. Called the Ancient of Days, he presided from his mobile fiery throne-chariot, recalling Ezekiel's throne–chariot vision and even Elijah's translation to heaven. Together they rendered judgment, and the terrible beast was destroyed by fire. Then another figure appeared, who received command of the earth.

7:13 As I watched the night visions, I saw one like a son of man coming with the clouds of heaven. He went to the Ancient of Days and was presented to him. 14 To him was given dominion, glory, and kingship. All people, nations, and languages would serve him. His dominion would be an everlasting dominion that would not disappear. His kingship would never be destroyed.

A humanlike **Son of Man** creature appeared, to whom was given complete control of the kingdom. In Daniel "a humanlike figure" typically refers to an angel, as in 8:15 and 9:21.[1] Following the description, Daniel is given the interpretation of these things by one of the members of the divine council. The humanlike figure is a symbol for the collective people of God, just as the individual beasts each stood for a nation. The "holy ones," as they are called, come to possess the kingdom of God for all time. The setting of this vision, as well as the detailed description of the fourth beast in verses 23–27, suggests that the term "holy ones" stands for the righteous Jews who were persecuted by Antiochus IV.

Most scholars believe the writer of the Daniel 7 wrote this apocalypse at the time of Antiochus's oppressive rule over Judea (175–164 B.C.E.). He was writing in the expectation that the Seleucid kingdom of the wicked Antiochus IV would come to an end, and then Israel would receive the power of the kingdom of God forever.

The Three Other Apocalypses (8–12)

The other apocalypses provide additional details about the rule of the wicked kingdoms. Chapter 8's tale of the ram and the goat allegorically relates the transition from Persian to Greek rule. It spends the most time on "the little horn," the code word throughout the book of Daniel for Antiochus IV. It tells of the desecration of the sanctuary and its reconsecration at Hanukkah.

Chapter 9 is an updating of Jeremiah's prophecy that Israel would be in captivity to Babylonia for seventy years (see Jeremiah 25:11–12 and 29:10). In

---

[1] This "one like a son of man" figure becomes a messianic individual in intertestamental literature and is a component in the identity of Jesus of Nazareth in the New Testament era.

Clearly the writer of the Daniel 7 apocalypse knew the tale of Nebuchadnezzar's dream in Daniel 2 and updated it to his time. The four metals of Nebuchadnezzar's dream correspond to the four beasts; the stone that becomes a mountain is the "one like a son of man," later the "holy ones."

The four-age scheme of world history can be found in other ancient literatures. The dynastic prophecy published by Grayson (1975) describes the fall of Assyria and the rise of Babylonia, the fall of Babylonia and the rise of Persia, then the fall of Persia and the rise of the Hellenistic monarchies. Also, the *Works and Days* of Hesiod divide history into four ages: gold, silver, bronze, and iron.

Daniel's apocalypse that period of domination is extended to seventy weeks of years, or 490 years. Thus, Daniel explains why Israel was never reestablished in power after the fall of Babylonia. The recovery still awaits the future.

The extended apocalypse of 10–12 in great but cryptic detail relates the conflict between the Ptolemies and Seleucids for control of Palestine. Included is a description of the great tribulation, which is introduced by the military campaigns of Antiochus IV. Typical of apocalyptic literature, these apocalypses were to be kept secret until the end of time, that is, the time of the great conflict therein predicted. This perpetuates the literary fiction that these materials were written long before the events themselves transpired, and that their meaning would only be revealed at the end.

MODERN APOCALYPTIC LITERATURE

Many conservative Christians lay great store in the apocalyptic material of Daniel, as well as other Old Testament and New Testament apocalyptic passages. Like pieces of a giant divine jigsaw puzzle, the biblical references are correlated with contemporary events to provide a "map" of the end of the world.

Genuinely creative, apocalyptic literature could be considered the ancient equivalent of our modern genre of science fiction for the way it tries to conceptualize and visualize the shape of the future. The book of Daniel reflects a new approach to dealing with historical experience. It extrapolates from the present and tries to imagine how the future might look, heavy on the imagination.

DANIEL IN CANONICAL CONTEXT

Daniel is classed with prophetic literature in the arrangement of books in most English Bible translations. But Daniel is obviously different from mainstream prophetic literature. The picture we get of Daniel in the book is that of a wise man, a diviner, a counselor to kings. He does not play the role of the prophet. In the Jewish canon, the book of Daniel was classed with the Writings in recognition of its unique qualities and also because the book is much later than the prophetic body of writings that was considered closed after around 400 B.C.E.

Childs (1979) raises an important canonical question concerning Daniel. How was Daniel heard by Jews in the post–Maccabean period? There would seem to be a problem insofar as the book of Daniel foretold the end of world history with the demise of Antiochus IV. Yet the world did not end in the way predicted. In fact, it did not end at all, as the writer expected it would. Some might interpret the book to be mistaken. So how could it still speak to a later age? And how could it be canonized?

Although the future that the book of Daniel imagined did not come to pass as he had envisioned it, it gave powerful expression to the need for vision and the need for some (imaginative) conceptualization of the future. The book is quite pessimistic about the ability of human structures to redeem the world. The kingdom comes by the intervention of God. Yet even this is profound testimony to the writer's deep hope in the power of God's rule and the ability of the faithful to cope and endure in a time of severe social and political crisis.

QUESTIONS FOR REVIEW

1. What is the difference between an *apocalypse* and *apocalyptic literature*?
2. What are the literary characteristics of apocalyptic literature?
3. What is the typical sociopolitical background out of which apocalyptic literature arises?

4. What are the two main sections of the book of Daniel, and what kind of literature is in each?
5. How is the book of Daniel related to the Maccabean era?

QUESTIONS FOR DISCUSSION

1. What books have you read or movies have you seen that deal with apocalyptic themes? How do they portray the future?
2. In what ways do we try to discern and control the future in our modern world? How do our methods compare to apocalyptic methods?

3. Can Daniel be studied to provide a roadmap for our future? What is the message of the book of Daniel for today?

FOR FURTHER STUDY

Apocalyptic Literature. Hanson, Paul D. (1987). *Old Testament Apocalyptic.* Interpreting Biblical Texts. Nashville, Tenn.: Abingdon Press.

Koch, Klaus (1972). *The Rediscovery of Apocalyptic.* London: SCM Press.

Reddish, Mitchell G., ed. (1990). *Apocalyptic Literature: A Reader.* Nashville, Tenn.: Abingdon.

Russell, D. S. (1964). *The Method and Message of Jewish Apocalyptic: 200 B.C.–A.D. 100.* Philadelphia: Westminster Press.

Schmitals, Walter (1975). *The Apocalyptic Movement.* Trans. John E. Steely. Nashville, Tenn.: Abingdon Press.

The Book of Daniel. Collins, John J. (1977). *The Apocalyptic Vision of the Book of Daniel.* Harvard Semitic Monographs 16. Missoula, Mont.: Scholars Press.

Fewell, Danna Nolan (1991). *Circle of Sovereignty. Plotting Politics in the Book of Daniel.* Nashville, Tenn.: Abingdon Press

Lacocque, Andre (1978). *The Book of Daniel.* Atlanta: John Knox Press.

Russell, D. S. (1989). *Daniel, An Active Volcano: Reflections on the Book of Daniel.* Louisville, Ky.: Westminster/John Knox Press.

Thompson, Henry O. (1992). *The Book of Daniel: A Bibliography.* Hamden, Conn.: Garland.

Postbiblical Apocalyptic Literature. Collins, John J. (1984). *The Apocalyptic Imagination: An Introduction to the Jewish Matrix of Christianity.* New York: Crossroad.

Rowland, Christopher (1982). *The Open Heaven: A Study of Apocalyptic in Judaism and Early Christianity.* New York: Crossroad.

Stone, Michael (1980). *Scriptures, Sects and Visions: A Profile of Judaism from Ezra to the Jewish Revolts.* Philadelphia: Fortress Press.

Modern Apocalypticism. Boyer, Paul (1992). *When Time Shall Be No More: Prophecy Belief in Modern American Culture.* Cambridge, Mass.: Harvard University Press. Beginning with a discussion of apocalyptic literature in Hebrew and Christian literature, this book traces the evolution of Christian millennialism, with special focus on the nature and significance of prophecy belief in the post–World War II era. It includes discussions of such topics of prophetic speculation as the atomic bomb, the Cold War, Israel, the Antichrist, ecological disaster, computer technology, and the rise of the European Economic Community.

WORKS CITED

Childs, Brevard S. (1979). *Introduction to the Old Testament as Scripture.* Philadelphia: Fortress Press.

Friedrich, Otto (1982). *The End of the World: A History.* New York: Coward, McCann & Geoghegan.

Grayson, A. K. (1975). *Babylonian Historical–Literary Texts.* Toronto: University of Toronto Press.

Hanson, Paul D. (1985). "Apocalyptic Literature." In *The Hebrew Bible and its Modern Interpreters.* Chico, Calif.: Scholars Press.

Hanson, Paul D. (1975; rev. ed. 1979). *The Dawn of Apocalyptic: The Historical and Sociological Roots of Jewish Apocalyptic Eschatology.* Philadelphia: Fortress Press.

King, Stephen (1978). *The Stand.* New York: Doubleday.

Schmitals, Walter (1975). *The Apocalyptic Movement.* Nashville, Tenn.: Abingdon Press.

Shute, Nevil (1958). *On the Beach.* New York: New American Library.

CHRONICLES, EZRA, NEHEMIAH: THE CHRONICLER'S HISTORY

18

Names and Terms to Remember

Chronicler's history	Jeshua	Sheshbazzar
Cyrus the Great	Nehemiah	Zerubbabel
Ezra	Second Temple	

God cannot alter the past, but historians can.
—Samuel Butler (1835–1902)

Progress, far from consisting in change, depends on retentiveness. . . .
Those who cannot remember the past are condemned to repeat it.
—George Santayana (1863–1952)

The stars are dead. The animals will not look:
We are left alone with our day, and the time is short,
and
History to the defeated
May say Alas but cannot help nor pardon.
—W. H. Auden (1907–1973)

The one who wins gets to write the history.
—Dennis Voskuil (1944–)

The writing of history, as all modern historians acknowledge, is not an entirely objective recording of facts. It is an interpretation of the past shaped by the present of the historian.

Furthermore, the one who has political power, which determines who gets heard, is more often than not the one who shapes written history. The priestly party, in the absence of the monarchy, emerged out of Judah's Babylonian exile firmly in control. They were the preservers and guardians of Israel's traditions and historical memory, and they shaped the period of Judean restoration. Consequently, biblical history in the postexilic period was written by the priests and Levites.

CHRONICLER'S HISTORY

We earlier studied the Pentateuch and the Former Prophets. These contain a history of God's people from creation to the Babylonian exile. Our current concern is with First and Second Chronicles, Ezra, and Nehemiah. They provide a history of equal scope but tell it in quite a different manner. They can be grouped together and called the **Chronicler's history** (or CH).

Some scholars dispute whether Chronicles, Ezra, and Nehemiah should be considered a single unified work produced by a single author, rather than two works, Chronicles and Ezra–Nehemiah. Their main focuses are not the same.

First and Second Chronicles emphasize David and the Prophets. A combined Ezra and Nehemiah emphasize Moses and the Torah.

On the other hand, they hold a number of features in common. The ending of Chronicles is the same as the beginning of Ezra, suggesting an overlap or connection of some sort. Both works abound in lists and genealogies. They also share technical vocabulary pertaining to the Levites and certain phrases that are infrequently found elsewhere, such as *house of God*. Both works are preoccupied with the temple in Jerusalem, the institutions of the priesthood, and Levitical functions.

The Chronicler's history has not been studied as intensively in biblical scholarship as the Torah and the Prophets, although this has been changing of late. The postexilic period is increasingly being seen as central to the development of the canon, and the writings of the postexilic period, including the CH, provide important clues as to how the canon was shaped.

The Chronicler's history had not been all that well studied due to certain historical prejudices in biblical scholarship. Earlier scholarship was obsessed with the drive to recover the earliest sources. This was thought to provide the best chance of recovering "what really happened." The CH is a comparatively late source, so it was neglected in favor of the Former Prophets. The Chronicler used Samuel and Kings as his main sources. He did not add much to them, and what he did add was late.

Students of the biblical text are taking a new look at the Chronicler's history. A study of how the Chronicler retold the history of Israel opens up a window on the beliefs and expectations of the postexilic community of the sixth and fifth centuries B.C.E. Relatively little textual material directly relates to the culture and history of this period, and the CH turns out to be one of the most important.

Furthermore, a comparison of the Chronicler's history and the Deuteronomic history provides an occasion to analyze how history writing is conditioned by particular historical and cultural contexts (see Table 18.1). The Deuteronomic history reflects a sixth-century exilic perspective, while the Chronicler's history reflects a late fifth-century postexilic perspective. The Chronicler's history used the Deuteronomic history as its main source and "repurposed" it to rebuild postexilic culture and religion along certain lines. Such recasting of history is sometimes called *revisionist history*.

TABLE 18.1 COMPARISON OF THE DEUTERONOMIC AND CHRONICLER'S HISTORIES

	DH	*CH*
Authorship	Northern Levites	Postexilic Levites
Date of Composition	550 B.C.E.	400–250 B.C.E.
Audience	Exilic community	Restored community
Theme	Reasons for God's judgment	Jerusalem temple, worship, Levites

SOURCES AND AUTHORSHIP

The Chronicler's history retells the story of God's people from Adam to Ezra. It makes obvious use of preexisting written sources. The sources include letters, lists, genealogies, and the block 1 Samuel 31–2 Kings 25 of the Deuteronomic history. The Chronicler also drew on the Torah, Judges, Ruth, Psalms, Isaiah, Jeremiah, Lamentations, and Zechariah. As would any good historian, the Chronicler cited his sources (though certainly not all of them). Unfortunately, most of the sources cited by the Chronicler, including "the records of the seer Samuel" and "the midrash on the Book of Kings," are unknown outside the Bible.

Some scholars date the composition of the Chronicler's history to the time of Ezra in the fifth century B.C.E., others to the fourth century, and still others place it in the Hellenistic period of the third century.

THEOLOGY

The Chronicler was mostly concerned with the Judean monarchy and the Jerusalem religious establishment. The Northern Kingdom of Israel is mentioned rarely and then only in passing. The Chronicler idealized the reigns of Solomon and Hezekiah and especially of David. David became the model of the godly monarch. He ruled obediently and established religious service as it was meant to be, with the temple, its priesthood, singers, prayers, rituals, and offerings.

Of course, to make such exalted claims about David, the historian had to exercise selective memory. Although the Chronicler's history of David was based on the books of Samuel, the Chronicler ignored narratives that put David in a bad light. Furthermore, he traced the establishment of important priestly and Levitic institutions back to David, although other historical evidence suggests this is unlikely. He grounded proper worship practices in the traditions of the past, mainly those of David's time, in order to give them validity.

The Chronicler's main focus in writing his history was the priesthood, the temple, and worship practices in Judea. All of history was viewed in terms of how it promoted these concerns. Kings were evaluated in terms of their disposition to temple and cult. And history moved to a climax at the time of Ezra and Nehemiah with the reestablishing of temple worship.

The Chronicler was a defender of the status quo and had no vision for a better political future. As long as Yahweh could be worshiped properly, seemingly all else was acceptable.

FIRST AND SECOND CHRONICLES

The two books of Chronicles were originally one book. Like the books of Samuel and Kings, they became two in printed editions. We will refer to combined First and Second Chronicles simply as *Chronicles*. Jewish tradition holds that most of Chronicles, along with the books of Ezra and Nehemiah, were written by **Ezra** the scribe and completed by **Nehemiah**. In Jewish tradition Ezra is venerated to a degree second only to Moses. Chronicles can be divided into two main parts on the basis of content: pre-monarchy history and the history of the Davidic monarchy.

PRE-MONARCHY HISTORY (1 CHRONICLES 1–10)

The first part of Chronicles retells history from Adam to Saul. Most of the story is told by means of lists of names and genealogies. Some of the genealogical lists extend all the way into the postexilic period by including individuals from that time, indicating that this material was finally edited in the postexilic period.

There is very little storytelling narrative in this first part of Chronicles. It is dominated by genealogies. Special attention was given to the names of priests and Levites. The genealogies focused on the tribe of Judah and its line of David, the tribe of Benjamin and its line of Saul, and the tribe of Levi. These comprised the nucleus of the Persian province of Jehud (Judea) in the postexilic period.

Genealogies serve different purposes within the biblical world (see Wilson 1977). Within the family they define privilege and responsibility, as with the first-born son over later born children and children of concubines. Within tribes they establish political and territorial claims, especially land ownership, and might also reflect military conscription lists. Within the religious sphere they establish membership in the priestly and Levitic classes. Membership determines who can and cannot hold priestly offices and who can acquire the privileges and responsibilities associated with them. All of these uses of genealogies are present in Chronicles.

HISTORY OF THE DAVIDIC MONARCHY (1 CHRONICLES 11–2 CHRONICLES 36)

This part of Chronicles covers the history of the Davidic monarchy from David to the Babylonian exile. It can be subdivided into three sections.

1. David's reign: 1 Chronicles 11–29
2. Solomon's reign: 2 Chronicles 1–9
3. Kings of Judah from Rehoboam to Cyrus's Edict of Return from Exile: 2 Chronicles 10–36.

The Chronicler used the books of Samuel and Kings from the Deuteronomic history as his main source in retelling the history of the Judean monarchy. About half of Chronicles comes from the books of Samuel and Kings.

David's Reign (1 Chronicles 11–29)

This section contains an extended account of the reign of David. In it there is no record of Saul's conflict with David. It begins with all Israel at Hebron asking David to be their king. This in itself is a recasting of the Samuel account, where first Judah acclaims David as king, followed seven years later by the remainder of the tribes. Throughout his account the Chronicler uses the phrase *all Israel* to promote a perception of the unity of God's people (see Williamson 1977).

The account continues with a description of David's capture of Jerusalem and his moving the ark of the covenant into the city. A comparison of how Samuel and Chronicles tell the story of the ark's trip to Jerusalem demonstrates how the Chronicler repurposed the older account to validate the essential role of the

Levites. 2 Samuel 6:1–11 is closely paralleled in 1 Chronicles 13:1–14, telling the story of the death of Uzzah when he touched the ark and the abandonment of the ark with Obed-edom. 2 Samuel moves directly to David's fetching the ark from Obed-edom and taking it to Jerusalem (2 Samuel 6:12–19). Before 1 Chronicles picks up the story at that point it inserts a lengthy account of the appointment of the Levites to carry the ark on to Jerusalem (1 Chronicles 15:1–24), including these words.

> *15:2 Then David said, "Carrying the ark of God is not allowed except by Levites, for YHWH chose them to carry the ark of YHWH and to minister to him forever." 3 David assembled all Israel at Jerusalem to bring up the ark of YHWH to the place he had prepared for it. 11 Then David summoned the priests Zadok and Abiathar, and the Levites Uriel, Asaiah, Joel, Shemaiah, Eliel, and Amminadab, 12 and said to them, "You are the heads of the families of the Levites. Sanctify yourselves, you and your brothers, so that you may bring up the ark of YHWH, the God of Israel, to the place I have prepared for it. 13 Because you did not carry it the first time, YHWH our God exploded in anger on us, because we did not seek out the rules for handling it." 14 So the priests and the Levites sanctified themselves to bring up the ark of YHWH, the God of Israel. 15 And the Levites carried the ark of God with the poles on their shoulders, as Moses had commanded according to the word of YHWH.*

Whereas no lesson was drawn from Uzzah's death in the Deuteronomic history's account, the Chronicler used this as the occasion to validate the special role of the Levites and to draw the lesson that only the Levites may handle the ark.

Generally speaking, the Chronicler's deviations from the Samuel–Kings account are noteworthy. The Chronicler omitted any reference to David's war against Saul and his alliance with the Philistines. He omitted the story of how David intimidated Nabal and then married Abigail. David's affair with Bathsheba was completely ignored. In one way or another all of these stories might put David in a bad light or tarnish his image, so they were conveniently left out.

On the other hand, the Chronicler added information not present in Samuel–Kings. David's extensive preparations for the building of the temple are detailed in 1 Chronicles 23–28. This effectively makes David the founder and sponsor of the Jerusalem temple. In contrast, the book of Kings attributes the entire process of temple building to Solomon.

An especially interesting retelling of history is found in the Chronicles account of David's census of the nation. Taking a census was an act of disobedience because it signaled a reliance on military forces rather than the power of God. The Samuel account implies that Yahweh incited David to take a census in order to have an occasion to punish the people.

2 Samuel 24	1 Chronicles 21
1 Again the anger of YHWH was inflamed against Israel, and he incited David against them, "Go, count the people of Israel and Judah."	1 Satan stood up against Israel and incited David to count the people of Israel.

In the Samuel account Yahweh is responsible for getting David into trouble. The Chronicler's account removes Yahweh and introduces Satan as the instigator. This reflects the growing interest in Satan in the late postexilic period and the Chronicler's concern to distance God as far away from evil as possible. The Chronicler probably would have chosen to omit this story altogether because of the picture it gives us of David, but retained it because the account goes on to describe how David secured the threshing floor of Araunah as the future site of the temple. Thus it still fit his overall purpose.

Solomon's Reign (2 Chronicles 1–9)

Most of this section is devoted to a description of the building and dedication of the Jerusalem temple, taken almost verbatim from the book of Kings. The Chronicler idealized Solomon just as he did David, by omitting the stories of the Deuteronomic history that could put him in a bad light, including the following.

- The bloody political struggle between Adonijah and Solomon that ended with Solomon's triumph (1 Kings 2:13–46a)
- Solomon's adjudication of the case of the two prostitutes and their babies (1 Kings 3:16–28)
- Solomon's wealth and power (1 Kings 4:22–34)
- Solomon's marriages to the multitude of foreign women and the building of shrines in Jerusalem to their foreign gods (1 Kings 11:1–13)
- Solomon's enemies and the prophecy of Ahijah (1 Kings 11:14–40)

The Chronicles account of Solomon in his role as temple builder adds details not found in the Kings account. In particular, it depicts Solomon as Bezalel, who was the architect of the tabernacle at the time of Moses. Bezalel is mentioned nowhere outside the book of Exodus except in the Solomon narrative of Chronicles. In their parallel roles both Bezalel and Solomon were designated for their tasks by God, came from the tribe of Judah, received the spirit of wisdom to complete their tasks, built a bronze altar for the sanctuary, and made the sanctuary furnishings. Solomon, as the new Bezalel and great temple builder, continued in the Mosaic sanctuary tradition.

Kings of Judah (2 Chronicles 10–36)

This section is devoted almost entirely to the kings of Judah after the division of the kingdoms. Virtually no mention is made of the Northern Kingdom. The Chronicler dwells on the role of the kings of Judah in promoting worship and proper ritual. When disaster finally came by way of the Babylonians, it was because certain kings failed in their religious duties.

The Chronicler's account supplements the Deuteronomic history on a couple of points. The reform program of Hezekiah, not detailed in Kings, is given extended attention in chapters 29–32. This includes an account of his temple cleansing and the celebration of the Passover. Also, Josiah's Passover celebration is given increased attention. All this accords with the Chronicler's interest in the right performance of religious ritual.

EZRA AND NEHEMIAH

The books of Ezra and Nehemiah are the main biblical sources for the return of the Jewish community from exile. Talmon (1987) calls Ezra and Nehemiah *biblical historiography* in the style of straightforward prose narration. They were compiled fairly close to the events they report and can be considered reliable historiography for the most part. They are generally considered to be two parts of one book.[1] The events described in Ezra–Nehemiah are the major moments in the rebuilding of a religious community after the time of Babylonian exile (see Figure 18.1).

The return from Babylonian exile, the process of rebuilding Jerusalem, and the restoration of Jewish community in Judea took place in four stages.

1. *538 B.C.E.* **Sheshbazzar** led a return after Cyrus the Great, king of Persia (550–530), gave permission. Temple rebuilding was begun, but due to economic hardship and local opposition it was not finished at that time.

2. *522 B.C.E.* **Zerubbabel** and **Jeshua,** the high priest, led a second group of Jews back to Palestine during the reign of Darius I (522–486). They succeeded in completing a temple in Jerusalem in 515.

3. *458 B.C.E.* **Ezra** led a group of Jews back to Palestine during the reign of Artaxerxes I (465–424) and reestablished adherence to Mosaic standards of law and religion.

4. *445 B.C.E.* **Nehemiah** organized the rebuilding of the walls of Jerusalem and returned religious and civil authority to the Levites.

The book of Ezra–Nehemiah is a single unit consisting of three identifiable sections, each centered around a significant leader of the restoration (see Figure 18.2).

The editorial history of Ezra–Nehemiah is difficult to sort out, and scholars disagree about the original order of the chapters. Though opinions vary, it is reasonable to suggest the book of Ezra–Nehemiah was completed around 400 B.C.E.

BOOK OF ZERUBBABEL (EZRA 1–6)

The first section of Ezra, termed the book of Zerubbabel, relates the history of the early returns from Babylonian exile. It covers the period from the end of exile in 538 to the completion of the rebuilt temple in 515. The book begins with a verbatim record of the decree of **Cyrus the Great** allowing the Judean refugees to return to Jerusalem.

1:2 Thus says King Cyrus of Persia, "YHWH the God of heaven has given me all the kingdoms of the earth. He has commanded me to build him a house in Jerusalem of Judah. 3 May God be with those of you who are his people. Go up to Jerusalem of Judah and build the house of YHWH the

---

[1] The Septuagint and the Babylonian Talmud refer only to the book of Ezra when citing both Ezra and Nehemiah, indicating they considered them one book.

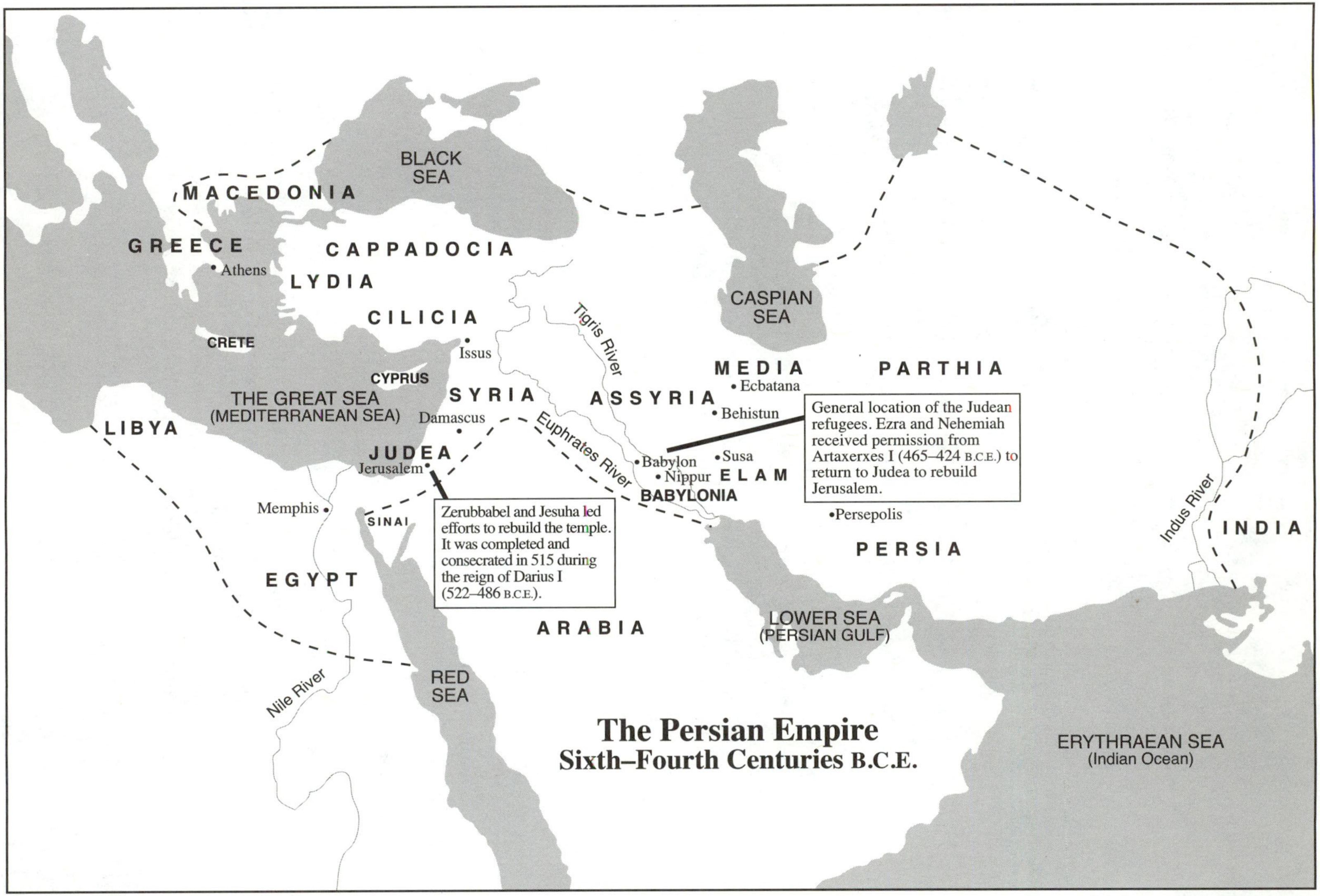

The Persian Empire Sixth–Fourth Centuries B.C.E.

General location of the Judean refugees. Ezra and Nehemiah received permission from Artaxerxes I (465–424 B.C.E.) to return to Judea to rebuild Jerusalem.

Zerubbabel and Jesuha led efforts to rebuild the temple. It was completed and consecrated in 515 during the reign of Darius I (522–486 B.C.E.).

INDIA

Indus River

ERYTHRAEAN SEA (Indian Ocean)

PARTHIA

MEDIA
•Ecbatana

CASPIAN SEA

•Behistun

ELAM
•Susa

PERSIA

•Persepolis

ASSYRIA
•Babylon •Nippur
BABYLONIA

LOWER SEA (PERSIAN GULF)

Tigris River

Euphrates River

ARABIA

SYRIA

•Issus

Damascus •

CILICIA

CYPRUS

JUDEA
Jerusalem•

SINAI

RED SEA

BLACK SEA

CAPPADOCIA

LYDIA

MACEDONIA

GREECE
•Athens

CRETE

THE GREAT SEA (MEDITERRANEAN SEA)

Memphis •

EGYPT

Nile River

LIBYA

FIGURE 18.1   THE PERSIAN EMPIRE

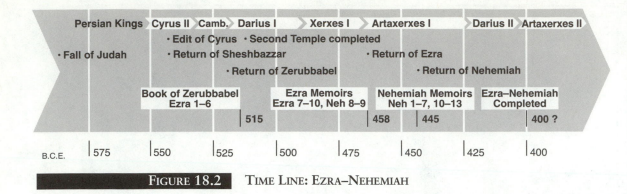

| Persian Kings | Cyrus II | Camb. | Darius I | Xerxes I | Artaxerxes I | Darius II | Artaxerxes II |

· Fall of Judah

· Edit of Cyrus · Second Temple completed
· Return of Sheshbazzar
· Return of Zerubbabel

· Return of Ezra
· Return of Nehemiah

Book of Zerubbabel
Ezra 1–6

Ezra Memoirs
Ezra 7–10, Neh 8–9

Nehemiah Memoirs
Neh 1–7, 10–13

Ezra–Nehemiah
Completed

515   458   445   400 ?

B.C.E.   575   550   525   500   475   450   425   400

FIGURE 18.2   TIME LINE: EZRA–NEHEMIAH

*God of Israel, the God who is in Jerusalem! 4 Let all who remain behind
assist the people of their place with silver, gold, goods, and livestock in addition to freewill offerings for the house of God in Jerusalem."*

This decree, issued in 538, authorized the rebuilding of the temple. Notice
how Cyrus, a Persian, talks as if he acknowledges Yahweh, the God of Israel,
and attributes to him the gift of his power. The fact that Cyrus authorized the
temple rebuilding becomes important later in the book when Samaritans from
the north and others opposed rebuilding activities in Jerusalem.

The first group of returned refugees was led by Sheshbazzar, who had been
appointed governor of Judea. He may have been the son of Jehoiachin, Judah's
king in exile. Sheshbazzar and the first group of returnees succeeded in re-laying
the foundations of the temple, but then the work broke off and remained unfin-
ished until the next return.

The most productive return was led by Zerubbabel, a leader from the line of
David, in 522 B.C.E. (Figure 18.3). The most significant event of this period was
the rebuilding of the temple in Jerusalem, called the **Second Temple**, the first
being the one built by Solomon. The Second Temple remained intact until it was
destroyed by the Romans in 70 C.E. Aided by Jeshua and the prophets Haggai
and Zechariah,[2] Zerubbabel motivated the people to complete the project begun
by Sheshbazzar. This section ends with an account of the dedication of the temple and the celebration of Passover.

EZRA MEMOIRS (EZRA 7–10, NEHEMIAH 8–9)

There is a gap of about sixty years between the events of the Book of Zerubbabel
and those of the Ezra Memoirs. Chapters 7–10 of the book of Ezra, along with
Nehemiah 8–9, which were misplaced, deal with Ezra the scribe.

Ezra was a priest descended from the line of Aaron through Zadok. He was
also a scribe and court official under the Persian king Artaxerxes I. He returned

[2] The history of this period may be supplemented with the books of Haggai and Zechariah (chapters 1–8).

DARIUS ON HIS THRONE Darius I (522–486 B.C.E.), seated on the throne, was the Persian king at the time of Zerubbabel's return. Behind him stands Prince Xerxes who followed him as king. The story of the book of Esther takes place during his reign.

to Judea from Babylon in 458 with another group of refugees.[3] Ezra had the full authorization of the Persian government to reestablish proper modes of Yahweh worship and adherence to the Torah of Moses.

In Ezra's analysis, one of the most serious problems among the Judeans was mixed marriages. In the interim, male Judeans had married Canaanite, Hittite, Ammonite, Moabite, and Egyptian women. Ezra saw this as a breach of the injunction to remain separate from non-Israelite people. Intermarriage promoted assimilation and was a threat to Yahwistic religion. Israel's theological historians had concluded that one of the biggest reasons for Israel's downfall was intermarriage with Canaanites that led to idolatry.

Ezra required the men to divorce their non-Jewish wives and expel them, along with any children of the marriage. It was a time of great anxiety and mourning, but the priests, Levites, and ordinary people who had married foreign women carried out the directive.

Ezra also rededicated the people to keeping the Torah (see Nehemiah 8–9). He assembled all Jewish adults in Jerusalem and read the Torah to them in Hebrew. However, because Hebrew was no longer the native tongue, having been replaced by Aramaic during the exile, there were translators who interpreted the text to the people as he read. Such an Aramaic translation of a Hebrew original

---

[3] There continues to be debate over the date of Ezra's mission. The seventh year of Artaxerxes I would be 458 B.C.E., the date we use. The problem is this: Ezra and Nehemiah do not seem to acknowledge each other, and they seem to work independently of each other, even though the straightforward reckoning of their dates puts them in Jerusalem at the same time. Consequently, some scholars place Ezra after Nehemiah and read *thirty*-seventh year of Artaxerxes, rather than seventh, placing the beginning of Ezra's mission in 427. Still others place Ezra in the reign of Artaxerxes II (404–358). Nehemiah 8:9 and 12:26, 36 place Ezra and Nehemiah in Jerusalem at the same time, though these are often judged to be late editorial insertions.

is called a *targum*. This is the first biblical attestation of the practice of Scripture translation from one language to another.

After the Torah was read and interpreted, the people celebrated the Festival of Booths, which is a commemoration of the wilderness wandering period of their early history. Then Ezra offered a prayer to God, recounting the history of God and his people from creation to that moment. This is not unlike other covenant renewal events, such as the ones under Moses (the entire book of Deuteronomy), Joshua (Joshua 24), and Samuel (1 Samuel 12). Such covenant renewal occasions were times of corporate reflection and rededication to the compact with Yahweh.

NEHEMIAH MEMOIRS (NEHEMIAH 1–7, 10–13)

This material deals with the history of Nehemiah. He was an official at the court of Artaxerxes I in Susa. He traveled to Jerusalem in 445 B.C.E. to be the governor of the Persian empire's province of Jehud, that is, Judea. His main job was to rebuild the external walls of Jerusalem. His work was opposed by Sanballat, leader of the Samaritans, and Tobiah, leader of the Ammonites. They saw this as a threat to their power in the region. On various occasions they tried to stop the work, and they tried to assassinate Nehemiah.

Nehemiah and his crew were able to complete the rebuilding of the walls in fifty-two days in spite of the opposition. These walls gave Jerusalem the protection and security its people needed. Nehemiah served twelve years as governor of the province and then returned to Babylon in 433.

Shortly afterward he went back to Jerusalem and instituted some important religious reforms. He closed the city on the Sabbath so that no trading could take place. He guaranteed that the Levites would receive their proper support, and, like Ezra, he forbade mixed marriages.

OVERALL SHAPE OF THE CHRONICLER'S HISTORY

In English Bibles the Chronicler's history immediately follows the Deuteronomic history, giving the work of the Chronicler the character of a historical supplement to the Deuteronomic history. In this ordering, Ezra and Nehemiah as separate books follow Chronicles.

Ezra, Nehemiah, and Chronicles are included in the division of the Writings in the Hebrew Bible. Curiously, even though chronologically Ezra and Nehemiah follow Chronicles, within the Writings they are placed before the books of Chronicles. Their placement at the very end is deliberate and was meant to suggest that they were a summary of the entire course of history of the people of God. Chronicles does in fact go from creation to the end of exile.

The Chronicler's history essentially parallels the coverage of the combined Pentateuch and Deuteronomic history. But why should there be two accounts of the same history in the Hebrew Bible? The fact that multiple versions of biblical history were retained affirms that each generation needs to rethink, reevaluate, and rewrite history and understand it in relation to present concerns. The Chronicler's history retold Israel's history with almost single-minded attention to worship institutions because at its moment in time the community needed the temple as the core of its rebuilding efforts, and the priests were the prime movers.

The Chronicler's history did not replace Deuteronomic history. Both are still valid. The Chronicler's history is evidence of a continuing historiographic tradition within the community of faith. In each generation the past needs to be reappropriated. The Chronicler's history is evidence of the value of studying history to understand the present. Studying the Chronicler's history enables us to see how retelling history in Israel grounded the identity of the Jews.

The tradition of retelling history continued even beyond the canon of the Hebrew Bible, some of it continuing to be connected with the figure of Ezra. The apocryphal book 1 Esdras appears to be a newer, or at least a different, edition of material from 2 Chronicles, Ezra, and Nehemiah. Later, the *Antiquities* of Josephus and the *Biblical Antiquities* of Pseudo-Philo also retold the history of the Jewish people.

Finally, the Chronicler's history, including Ezra and Nehemiah, is notable for its focus on two heroes of the faith from the Torah and the Prophets. Chronicles focuses on David (and the Davidic monarchy) in his role in the development of the temple, and Ezra–Nehemiah focuses on the importance of Moses and the Torah for community rebuilding. This is a witness for the continuing vitality of these founding fathers.

The role of Ezra in reading and reinterpreting the Torah for the fifth century Jewish community has canonical implications. It demonstrates that the Mosaic Torah continued to provide the foundation for the faith of Israel, even though it needed reinterpretation and updating. The reappropriation of Torah demonstrates its ongoing vitality and adaptability. Ezra's role has been considered so significant for the development of the canon that he has been considered by some the final compiler of the Pentateuch, in addition to having had a role in the formation of the Chronicler's history. Yet today Ezra is considered the "father of Judaism."

QUESTIONS FOR REVIEW

1. What books constitute the Chronicler's history? Why are they grouped together under this heading?
2. What was the Chronicler's reading of David, and why was he so prominent in the Chronicler's history?
3. What were the stages in the Jewish return to Jerusalem and the restoration of Jewish community life there?
4. How did Ezra deal with the problem of intermarriage?
5. What did Nehemiah do to ensure the security of the Jews?

QUESTIONS FOR DISCUSSION

1. Compare the Deuteronomic history with the Chronicler's history. For what purpose did each give an account of Israel's history? To what end might Jews today retell the history of ancient Israel? Why might Christians retell that history? Why might Muslims?

2. Why was the rebuilding of the temple so important for reestablishing a viable Jewish community in Jerusalem? Why was the restoration of the Jews at this time so dependent on religious institutions and worship?

3. Do you think it is important to study history? What does the inclusion in the Hebrew Bible of both the Deuteronomic history and the Chronicler's history suggest about the purpose of studying history? What are the dangers of not studying history?

FOR FURTHER STUDY

Newsome, James D. (1986). *A Synoptic Harmony of Samuel, Kings, and Chronicles: With Related Passages from Psalms, Isaiah, Jeremiah, and Ezra.* Grand Rapids, Mich.: Baker. Places in parallel format primarily those passages from Chronicles that match passages from Samuel and Kings. This is extremely useful for analyzing the omissions and additions of the Chronicler as a way of determining his perspective and interests.

Stern, Ephraim (1982). *Material Culture of the Land of the Bible in the Persian Period 538–332 B.C.* Warminster, Eng.: Aris and Phillips.

1 and 2 Chronicles. Ackroyd, Peter R. (1991). *The Chronicler in His Age.* JSOT Supplement Series, 101. Sheffield: JSOT Press.

Noth, Martin (1987). *The Chronicler's History.* Trans. H. G. M. Williamson. JSOT Supplement Series, 50. Sheffield: JSOT Press.

Talmon, Shemaryahu (1987). "1 and 2 Chronicles." In *The Literary Guide to the Bible.* Ed. Robert Alter and Frank Kermode. Cambridge, Mass.: Harvard University Press. Focuses on issues of literary structure and composition.

Williamson, H. G. M. (1982). *1 and 2 Chronicles.* The New Century Bible Commentary. Grand Rapids, Mich.: Eerdmans.

Ezra–Nehemiah. Blenkinsopp, Joseph (1988). *Ezra–Nehemiah: A Commentary.* Old Testament Library. Philadelphia: Westminster Press.

Fensham, F. Charles (1982). *The Books of Ezra and Nehemiah.* The New International Commentary on the Old Testament. Grand Rapids, Mich.: Eerdmans.

Talmon, Shemaryahu (1987). "Ezra and Nehemiah." In *The Literary Guide to the Bible.* Ed. Robert Alter and Frank Kermode. Cambridge, Mass.: Harvard University Press.

Throntveit, Mark A. (1992). *Ezra–Nehemiah.* Interpretation Series. Louisville, Ky.: John Knox Press.

WORKS CITED

Talmon, Shemaryahu (1987). "Ezra and Nehemiah." In *The Literary Guide to the Bible.* Ed. Robert Alter and Frank Kermode. Cambridge, Mass.: Harvard University Press.

Williamson, H. G. M. (1977). *Israel in the Books of Chronicles.* Cambridge: Cambridge University Press.

Wilson, Robert R. (1977). *Genealogy and History in the Biblical World.* New Haven, Conn., and London: Yale University Press.

EPILOGUE TO THE WRITINGS

The Writings contain an almost bewildering variety of voices emanating out of the larger Jewish community. While many of the books contain material from the preexilic period, they were shaped in the postexilic period. These books present the perspectives and concerns of postexilic Judaism as it was reshaping the religion of Israel for changed sociohistorical conditions.

The individual books of the Writings stand as witnesses of what was deeply important to the postexilic Jewish community. The Psalter affirms the continuing centrality of prayer and worship for sustaining the community of faith. As the songbook and prayer book of God's people, it displays the full range of feelings and emotions that are proper for worshipers to bring to God. The preponderance of complaint psalms in the Psalter is testimony to the people's pain but, in the complaint psalm's typical move to thanksgiving, also testimony to their hope in God.

Wisdom literature supplies a set of principles and values that would sustain the postexilic community. It reaffirms, in its own way, the principles of reward and retribution. At the same time it honestly faces the enigmas and apparent contradictions in that view of God's role in human existence. It also provides a "philosophy of life" that stands as an alternative to the philosophies of the dominant cultures among which they lived. Furthermore, when the demise of Davidic kingship and the absence of prophecy put the postexilic community in a

crisis of leadership, wisdom literature recommended new models of community leadership in the figures of the sage and the *saddiq*, or righteous one, of the wisdom circles.

The Five Scrolls as a group affirm the importance of remembering formative moments in a nation's history. Some of the festivals associated with the scrolls can be related to seasonal and agricultural breakpoints, such as the return of spring and the harvest. But they became occasions for the community to remember foundational events in their past. The Song of Songs was read at Passover, marking the exodus from Egypt. Ruth was read at the harvest Festival of Weeks, a time of remembering the giving of the Torah at Mt. Sinai.

Individually, the books of the Five Scrolls address important community issues. The Ruth and Esther short stories reveal how the Jewish community wrestled with identity and survival issues. Who can be a member of the community? Can outsiders, epitomized by Ruth the Moabite, be full-fledged members? How shall we survive within a threatening and hostile empire? Will God take care of us, as he did through Esther and Mordecai?

The Song of Songs deals with the most elemental, and most essential, human virtue—love. It probes love openly and honestly and affirms that genuine love can be realized only when there is full mutuality in personal relationships. The earliest readings of the book in Jewish and Christian communities must be taken seriously. Those interpretations see the book transcending the topic of human love and view it as the most powerful literary monument in the canon to the covenantal relationship of God and his people.

Ecclesiastes represents the wisdom tradition moving to its logical conclusion. It displays a wisdom enterprise turning in on itself when it asks, What is the purpose of life under the sun? It reveals the frustration of human intellect in the absence of a piety that provides a context for life. Ecclesiastes both affirms the legitimacy of human wisdom and warns that by itself it is not enough.

Lamentations recalls the destruction of the temple in 587 B.C.E. and mourns the loss of Israel's central institution. It stands as a memorial to the importance of the human responsibility to remain faithful and the reality of God's judgment. It was Israel's unfaithfulness that occasioned the fall of Jerusalem. But the impact of the Jewish yearly commemoration of this tragedy goes well beyond breast-beating and mourning. It is a witness to the grace of God that enabled his people to emerge out of destruction and, though scarred and chastened, to flourish.

Written during a time of national crisis, the apocalyptic literature of Daniel provides the vision of a triumphant conclusion to the historical process. The great ungodly empires will one day fall, and the kingdom of God will prevail. The legends of Daniel and his friends' heroism were an encouragement to the Jews to remain courageous in the meantime, while their faith was being challenged.

Lastly, the historical literature of the Chronicler demonstrates the value and importance of studying the past. The postexilic community, in spite of all the changes it had undergone, still found itself in continuity with God's people of preceding eras. Seeing this continuity enabled them to affirm that they still stood in covenant with God and that the covenant endures.

The Chronicler's selective retelling of Israel's history highlights the centrality of the temple and its attendants, as well as the importance of the Davidic dynasty. In this way the Chronicler's history proposes that any hope of renewal must be centered on a divinely empowered Davidic messianic kingdom centered around God's holy temple. By tracing the origins of the Second Temple and their priestly institutions back to the time of David and Solomon, they were able with confidence to use them as the basis of community life.

Taken as a body of literature, the Writings demonstrate the persistence and adaptability of Jewish religious faith. In creative ways the community remained true to its traditions yet found ways to adapt those traditions to meet contemporary challenges.

The forward to the book of Ecclesiasticus, written in the second century B.C.E., refers three times to "the law, the prophets, and the later authors" (or "the rest of the books"). This suggests that the Jewish community had by this time settled on a three-part division of books that together made its canon. The first two parts correspond to the books we have covered in the Torah and the Prophets. The third part, the Writings, was more fluid and open-ended, and probably remained such well into the first century C.E.

The fact that the Writings eventually did become part of the fixed Jewish and Christian canon is quite significant. As we have seen, the Writings consistently appropriate the traditions of Israel and wrestle with them in light of contemporary challenges. The canonization of the Writings is implicitly an affirmation and authorization of such theological conversation and dialogue within the community of faith. It is an acknowledgment that theological reflection is at the heart of the faith community.

God's requirements are always the same. Yet what God expects changes from age to age. God's people are always the same. Yet God's people change with changing conditions. The Writings are evidence of the continuing vitality and relevance of God's earliest and continuing revelation to humankind, and the need for God's people to continually reexamine and reapply it, from generation to generation.

FOR FURTHER STUDY

Childs, Brevard S. (1992). *Biblical Theology of the Old and New Testaments: Theological Reflection on the Christian Bible*. Minneapolis: Fortress Press. Treats the two testaments in mutual relationship and exposes their theological continuities and discontinuities.

Goldingay, John (1987). *Theological Diversity and the Authority of the Old Testament*. Grand Rapids, Mich.: Eerdmans. Deals with the diversity of theological voices within the Old Testament in light of the need to have the Bible speak with a single authoritative voice.

Levenson, Jon D. (1993). *The Hebrew Bible, the Old Testament, and Historical Criticism: Jews and Christians in Biblical Studies*. Louisville, Ky.: Westminster/John Knox Press. A collection of Levenson's essays, written from a Jewish perspective, that examine the relationship between Jewish and Christian interpretive communities, the role of modern biblical criticism, and the canon.

Morgan, Donn F. (1990). *Between Text and Community: The "Writings" in Canonical Interpretation*. Minneapolis: Augsburg/Fortress Press. A study of how the books of the Writings represent a re-appropriation and application of the Torah and the Prophets.

Sanders James A. (1987). *From Sacred Story to Sacred Text: Canon as Paradigm*. Philadelphia: Fortress Press. A collection of Sanders' essays on the development of the canon of the Hebrew Bible.

CONCLUSION

After the Hebrew Bible

HISTORICAL SKETCH

    PERSIAN PERIOD

    GREEK PERIOD

    HASMONEAN PERIOD

    ROMAN PERIOD

APOCRYPHA AND PSEUDEPIGRAPHA

    APOCRYPHA

PSEUDEPIGRAPHA

DEAD SEA SCROLLS

    BIBLICAL MANUSCRIPTS

    ORIGINAL DOCUMENTS

NEW TESTAMENT

RABBINIC LITERATURE

Names and Terms to Remember

apocrypha	Judas the Maccabee	pseudepigrapha
Christians/Christianity	Maccabean revolt	Qumran
Dead Sea Scrolls	Mishnah	Rabbinic Judaism
Dispersion/Diaspora	New Testament	Sadducees
halakah	Oral Torah/Written	Talmud
Hasmonean dynasty	Torah	targum
Hellenism	Palestinian Judaism	Zealots
Jesus of Nazareth	Pharisees	

The Hebrew Bible eventually became an established body of literature. Often called the Torah, it was the core document of Judaism. The religion of Judaism had strong ties with Israelite religion and in its specific form developed out of the experiences of the Babylonian exile and the efforts to reconstruct a Judean community.

The Jewish communities of faith did not stop producing books with the close of the Hebrew Bible. They continued to produce a variety of literatures. Most Jewish post–Hebrew-Bible documents show strong theological and literary ties with the Hebrew Bible. They demonstrate that the traditions and beliefs expressed in the Hebrew Bible retained their vitality and continued to be foundational to later communities of faith. By the creative ways they interpreted and reapplied elements of the Hebrew Bible they display a vital and continuing interest in Torah. The documents stand to a degree in continuity with the traditions of the Hebrew Bible, and they stand to a degree in discontinuity.

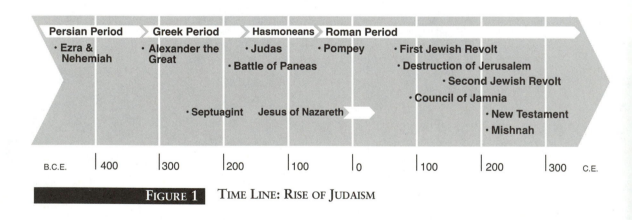

FIGURE 1   TIME LINE: RISE OF JUDAISM

HISTORICAL SKETCH

PERSIAN PERIOD (539–332 B.C.E.)

After the demise of the Babylonian empire, the Persians, first led by Cyrus, controlled the ancient Middle East. During this time Judaism began to develop and accommodate to its new surroundings through the guidance of the prophets Haggai, Zechariah, and Malachi, and the leadership of Ezra and Nehemiah. Strong

Jewish communities developed both in Palestine and throughout the Persian Empire at places such as Babylon, Susa, and even Egypt. The Judaism that developed outside Palestine is called the **Dispersion**, also termed the **Diaspora**. The character of this type of Judaism often differed markedly from that of **Palestinian Judaism** in that it was more open to influences from the non-Jewish culture around it. Palestinian Judaism was more conservative and traditional as defined by the Hebrew Bible.

GREEK PERIOD (332–164 B.C.E.)

The period of Persian control of the ancient Middle East came to an end when Alexander the Great successfully campaigned and brought that area under Greek control. Greek influence was strong and comprehensive. The Greek language displaced Aramaic as the language of the empire. Greek literature, philosophy, and forms of civic life transformed the ancient world.

Alexander allowed the Jews to observe their own ritual laws and traditions and was generally kindly disposed to them. This lenient policy of "live and let live" continued through the period of Ptolemaic control of Judea. This changed when control of Palestine passed from the dynasty of Ptolemy to the dynasty of Seleucus in 198 B.C.E. The Seleucids, especially Antiochus IV, attempted to force **Hellenism** on the Jews of Palestine, often with extreme cruelty.

Many Jews "modernized" and went along with the change. But others resisted and refused to give up their Jewishness as traditionally defined. Led by **Judas the Maccabee**, they revolted and defeated the Syrian Greek Seleucids in a series of battles.

HASMONEAN PERIOD (164–63 B.C.E.)

Judas and his militant followers secured the political independence of Judea and established a sovereign Jewish state in the middle of the Greek empire. The ruling house founded by Judas, son of Mattathias, and his brothers continued to 63 B.C.E. and was called the **Hasmonean dynasty**.

ROMAN PERIOD (63 B.C.E.–325 C.E.)

In the year 63 B.C.E. the Roman general Pompey captured Jerusalem, and the territories of Palestine were incorporated into the larger Roman empire. Local government was first entrusted to local princes, of whom Herod the Great was one. Herod was the ruler of greater Palestine at the time of the birth of Jesus. Later, procurators appointed by Roman emperors were placed in charge of smaller Palestinian territories.

During the period of Roman rule Judaism developed variations on the basic theme of the Hebrew Bible. The **Zealots**, a militant form of Judaism traceable to the Maccabees, campaigned militarily for Jewish national independence—a resurrection of the great Israelite monarchy. The **Sadducees** advocated an exclusively Torah-based form of religion and continued the ritual forms of the priesthood. The Essenes, often associated with the **Dead Sea Scrolls**, advocated an ascetic form of Judaism devoted to Torah rather than ritual sacrifice, and eagerly anticipated the dawn of the messianic age. The Jewish group later called **Christians** believed that the messianic age had been inaugurated through the life, death, and resurrection of their leader, **Jesus of Nazareth**. The **Pharisees**, perhaps the Jewish group that accommodated the most to the Greco–Roman world, practiced a dynamic faith that actively tried to translate Mosaic and prophetic religion to life in the modern world. Of all the traditional Jewish groups, not surprisingly it was Pharisaic Judaism that survived the disasters of the first and second Jewish Revolts (66–73 C.E. and 132–135 C.E.), along, of course, with Christianity.

APOCRYPHA AND PSEUDEPIGRAPHA

Many Jewish books were composed between 200 B.C.E. and 100 C.E. Written in Hebrew, Aramaic, or Greek, the books include wisdom literature, history, short stories, and apocalyptic literature. Some of the books were widely used by Jews of this period, especially the Jews of the Dispersion. None of the books, however, became part of the official Jewish collection of scriptures.

APOCRYPHA

Being part of the Greek and Latin translation tradition of the Bible, the books now called by scholars the **apocrypha** (meaning *hidden books*) include fifteen compositions. Twelve of them remain part of the canon of the Catholic church. During the Protestant Reformation these books were removed from the canon and are not now part of the official Bible of Protestant churches. In the face of Protestant opposition to the inclusion of the apocryphal books, the Roman Catholic Council of Trent, held in 1546, reaffirmed their official status and called them the *deuterocanonical* books. The following is a list of the books of the Protestant apocrypha. An asterisk marks the apocryphal books that are not canonical for Roman Catholics.

*1 Esdras (=Roman Catholic 3 Esdras or Greek Ezra)
*2 Esdras (= Roman Catholic 4 Esdras or Ezra Apocalypse)
Tobit
Judith
Additions to the Book of Esther
Wisdom of Solomon
Ecclesiasticus, or the Wisdom of Jesus the Son of Sirach
Baruch
Letter of Jeremiah
Prayer of Azariah and the Song of the Three Young Men
Susanna
Bel and the Dragon
*Prayer of Manasseh
1 Maccabees
2 Maccabees

The apocryphal books contain a wealth of evidence for the character of Judaism both in Palestine and in the Dispersion during the post–Hebrew Bible period. A small sampling of the apocrypha should display how these books continue the literary and theological traditions of the Hebrew Bible while at the same time adding their own twists.

The book of Ecclesiasticus stands in the tradition of Hebrew wisdom literature. It was written in Hebrew between 200 and 175 B.C.E. by a sage who lived in Jerusalem. He was thoroughly immersed in Torah, the priesthood and temple, and worshiping God. As a shrewd observer of life in Palestine, especially the pressures on Jews to become more "modern" after the model of Greek culture, he set about urging his fellows to remain true to their religious traditions. It seems he wrote his book to be a collection of wisdom and learning that could serve the Jews as a guide for living, making unnecessary a move to Greek philosophy.

> 2:10 Look to generations of long ago and see: Who believed in YHWH and came to shame? 11 Or who stood in fear of him and was abandoned? Or who called on him and he ignored him? 12 For compassionate and merciful is YHWH. He forgives sins and saves in time of trouble.

Ecclesiasticus is very much like the book of Proverbs in the way it contains aphorisms and maxims and aims to give moral guidance.

> 4:21 My son, watch your time well; guard yourself from evil, and to yourself bring no shame.
> 6:5 A sweet mouth multiplies love, and gracious lips inspire peace.

The two books of Maccabees contain accounts of the events surrounding the attempted suppression of Judaism in Palestine in the second century B.C.E. 1 Maccabees was written around 100 B.C.E. by a Palestinian Jew who remains nameless. In describing the deliverance of the Jews through the family of Mattathias, he models his accounts of these heroes on Israel's ancient champions—the Judges, Samuel, and David.

The dominating conflict at the center of 1 Maccabees is between the representatives of Greek culture, the Seleucids under the direction of their king Antiochus Epiphanes, and adherents of traditional Jewish culture. The conflict came to a head when Antiochus deliberately vandalized the temple in Jerusalem and made it a capital offense to practice Judaism.

> 1:54 The king set up the outrageous abomination upon the altar of burnt offerings, and in surrounding Judean cities they built pagan altars. 55 They also burnt incense at the doors of houses and in the streets. 56 Any Torah scrolls they found they tore up and burned. 57 Whoever was found in possession of a scroll of the covenant and whoever observed the Torah was condemned to death by royal decree. 60 Women who had allowed the circumcision of their children were put to death, as per the decree, 61 with the babies hung from their necks. Their families and those who had done the circumcising were also killed.

The events recorded here occurred in December of 167 B.C.E. Antiochus erected a statue of Zeus in the holiest part of the temple and slaughtered pigs in sacrifice. He deliberately provoked the Jews and tried to goad them into giving up their religion. It did not work.

The family of a pious Jew named Mattathias, led especially by his zealous son Judas, nicknamed *the Maccabee* (probably meaning "the hammer"), instigated a revolt of Torah-observant Jews. The **Maccabean revolt** was bloody and determined, and after more than three years of struggle it succeeded in displacing the Hellenizing forces from the temple mount. After ritually purifying the temple and fighting further battles, the family of Mattathias established local Jewish rule again over a Jewish–Palestinian state. This rule lasted until 63 B.C.E., when the Roman empire took control of Palestine.

Pseudepigrapha

The **pseudepigrapha** come from the same general time period as the apocrypha. The term *pseudepigrapha* literally means "pseudonymous writings" where typically the text is falsely attributed to a character from the Hebrew Bible. The pseudepigrapha are writings that were never part of the official scriptures of Judaism or Christianity. The following is a list of Jewish pseudepigraphical books whose core was composed before the destruction of Jerusalem in 70 C.E.

1 Enoch (or Ethiopic Enoch)
2 Enoch (or Slavonic Enoch)
2 Baruch (or Syriac Baruch)
3 Maccabees
4 Maccabees
Apocalypse of Elijah
Ascension of Isaiah
Jubilees
Letter of Aristeas
Life of Adam and Eve (or Apocalypse of Moses)
Lives of the Prophets
Psalms of Solomon
Sibylline Oracles
Testament of Job
Testament of Moses (or Assumption of Moses)
Testaments of the Twelve Patriarchs

The book of 1 Enoch was one of the most widely read and circulated books of the pseudepigrapha. It has been found in multiple copies among the Dead Sea Scrolls. It was even quoted in the book of Jude (verses 14–15) in the New Testament. The figure of Enoch comes from Genesis 5:24, where he was said to have walked with God. Being supremely righteous in an unrighteous age, he was taken directly into heaven. Because of his peculiar position before God, so the legend goes, God transmitted to Enoch special revelation about the nature of the world and about the end times. 1 Enoch is one of the best examples of the apocalyptic literature that was wildly popular during this period.

1 Enoch contains a story about the rebellion of the angels in primeval times and their subsequent judgment. The story takes Genesis 6:1–4 as its point of departure but adds a significant amount of detail.

> 6:1 *And it came to pass when the children of men had multiplied that in those days were born unto them beautiful and comely daughters. 2 And the angels, the children of the heaven, saw and lusted after them, and said to one another: "Come, let us choose us wives from among the children of men and beget us children." 3 And Semjaza, who was their leader, said unto them: "I fear ye will not indeed agree to do this deed, and I alone shall have to pay the penalty of a great sin." 4 And they all answered him and said: "Let us all swear an oath, and all bind ourselves by mutual imprecations not to abandon this plan but to do this thing." 5 Then sware [sic] they all together and bound themselves by mutual imprecations upon it. 6 And they were in all two hundred.*
>
> 7:1 *And all the others together with them took unto themselves wives, and each chose for himself one, and they began to go in unto them and to defile themselves with them, and they taught them charms and enchantments, and the cutting of roots, and made them acquainted with plants. 2 And they became pregnant, and they bare great giants, whose height was three thousand ells: 3 Who consumed all the acquisitions of men. (Charles 1913)*

The discussion of the Genesis 6:1–4 passage in the first chapter of our textbook noted that the identification of the "sons of God" is not obvious from the biblical text. Some readers have interpreted the sons of God to have been the line of Seth. But evidence from the use of the phrase *sons of God* elsewhere in the Hebrew Bible strongly suggests that the writer had angels in mind.

Here in 1 Enoch there is no doubt how the phrase was interpreted: It is clearly "angels, the children of the heaven." The writer understands the story to be the description of how evil angels corrupted the human race. Of special interest is how the writer elaborated on the Genesis core story. He notes how beautiful these human women were and adds that the angels were motivated by sexual lust. The story goes on to describe how the bad angels were policed by the good angels, Michael, Uriel, Raphael, and Gabriel. The bad angels were bound, taken prisoner, and eventually destroyed.

DEAD SEA SCROLLS

The Dead Sea Scrolls are probably the most famous archaeological discovery of the modern world. Their fame is the product of the serendipitous nature of the find, the scholarly circumstances surrounding their publication, and their potential for illuminating the texts and history of Judaism and Christianity.

The texts date roughly to the period 150 B.C.E.–70 C.E. Most of the scrolls were found in caves in the vicinity of an ancient ruins called **Qumran**, near the northwestern shore of the Dead Sea (see Figure 2). The nature of the ruins, the identity of the people who lived there, and even the identity of the people who

FIGURE 2 **QUMRAN CAVE 4** Qumran Cave 4, one of many caves in the vicinity, is the location where fragments of approximately 580 different manuscripts were discovered in 1954.

wrote the scrolls are still topics of hot debate. The scholarly consensus that the texts were written by a Judaic group called the Essenes who also lived at Qumran is increasingly disputed and under discussion.

The Dead Sea Scrolls manuscripts include copies of all the books of the Hebrew Bible except the book of Esther. Copies of some of the apocryphal books were found. In addition, there are numerous writings never before known.

BIBLICAL MANUSCRIPTS

The biblical manuscripts provide evidence for the process by which books of the Hebrew Bible were passed on by copyists. Before the Dead Sea Scrolls discovery, the earliest copies of the Hebrew Bible dated to the tenth century C.E. With the Dead Sea Scrolls we now have copies dated to the third and second centuries B.C.E.—bringing us more than 1,000 years closer to the originals.

Some of the Dead Sea Scrolls biblical manuscripts provide copies that seem more accurately to reflect the original biblical text. They have provided helpful evidence to modern translators, and some of the most recent modern-language versions of the Hebrew Bible have made use of these texts. For example, the New Revised

Standard version of 1 Samuel 10 adds an entire paragraph, about seventy-one words (in the English translation) not found in the traditional Hebrew Bible.

ORIGINAL DOCUMENTS

Many Dead Sea Scrolls texts are original, at least never before known. The Temple Scroll, twenty-eight feet long, deals with the structure of the temple and its furniture, ritual service, and rules for sacrifices and observing the Sabbath and seasonal feasts. The Community Rule appears to contain the constitution of the Dead Sea Scrolls community. Dated to around 100 B.C.E., it contains a discourse about truth and falsehood, rules for membership, a disciplinary code, and the expectations of the leader of the group called the "teacher of righteousness."

According to a Dead Sea Scrolls belief called *dualism*, the world was governed by two forces, good and evil, described here in the Community Rule.

> III *He has created man to govern the world, and has appointed for him two spirits in which to walk until the time of His visitation: the spirits of truth and falsehood. Those born of truth spring from a fountain of light, but those born of falsehood spring from a source of darkness. All the children of righteousness are ruled by the Prince of Light and walk in the ways of light, but all the children of falsehood are ruled by the Angel of Darkness and walk in the way of darkness. (Vermes 1987)*

The Dead Sea Scrolls community had an "us and them" view of the world. They believed humankind is dominated by two spirits and consists of two camps, the "sons of light" and the "sons of darkness." The two will finally face off in an end-times battle, described in the War Rule. The forces of light will ultimately prevail, and God's people will be vindicated.

Most Dead Sea Scrolls texts have a close relationship to the Hebrew Bible. The various texts used in worship contain direct quotations from the Hebrew Bible. The Dead Sea Scrolls community had its own hymnbook, largely composed using phrases and lines out of the biblical Psalms. Some manuscripts are commentaries on biblical texts, mostly prophetic texts from the Hebrew Bible. Called *pesharim*, these commentaries reveal how this community read the Hebrew Bible. Their basic interpretive principles were these: Everything in the Hebrew Bible applied to their own day, and, in particular, the prophetic texts predicted events in their generation. They firmly believed that the prophetic predictions of the Hebrew Bible were being fulfilled in their own experience.

The prophecy of Habakkuk of the Hebrew Bible was written out of the sixth century B.C.E. Babylonian crisis. Essentially the prophet Habakkuk was questioning how God could use the wicked Babylonian empire to punish his more righteous covenant people of Judah. The Pesher on Habakkuk applied this directly to the conflict they faced with the Romans and the (in their view) corrupted factions of Judaism. The commentary on Habakkuk proceeds by quoting the biblical text and then expounding it.

> *But the righteous shall live by his faith (Habakkuk 2:4b).*
> *Interpreted, this concerns all those who observe the Law in the House of*

Judah, whom God will deliver from the House of Judgment because of their suffering and because of their faith in the Teacher of Righteousness. (Vermes 1987)

The original text of Habakkuk seems to be saying that the righteous Israelite would find deliverance from disaster by personal faith in God, not through membership in the community or the faith of the fathers. The Habakkuk Commentary reinterprets this and says Torah-observing Jews will be delivered through suffering and their trust in their community leader, called the Teacher of Righteousness—quite a different twist to that text.

NEW TESTAMENT

Christianity began as a Jewish movement in the first century C.E. Followers of Jesus of Nazareth became convinced after his death and reported resurrection that he was the Messiah that the Hebrew Bible had described and that Judaism awaited. The **New Testament** is a collection of writings developed by members of this messianic movement. These writings include narrations of the life of Jesus and moral instruction to his followers.

Because most of the earliest followers of Jesus were Jewish, many of the writings naturally have thematic continuity with the Hebrew Bible. Some of the writings argue that Jesus fulfills Jewish expectations, while others highlight his uniqueness. Whatever the case, the New Testament cannot be understood apart from its grounding in the Hebrew Bible. In fact, the Hebrew Bible *was* the one and only Bible of the earliest Christians. The earliest New Testament books date to the middle of the first century, years after the death of Jesus. The last New Testament books date to the late first century or early second century.

The collection of all the books that now constitute the New Testament was, for all practical purposes, closed by the end of the second century C.E. The collection took on the name New Testament, or New Covenant, to communicate both the essential continuity and the significant discontinuity with the text of the Old Covenant, the Old Testament, the Hebrew Bible.

As does the Hebrew Bible, the New Testament contains a great variety of literary types. It encompasses narratives on the career of Jesus called gospels, a history of the earliest church, letters from early leaders to congregations and individuals around the Mediterranean, and an apocalyptic-style description of an end time of tribulation. The following is a categorized list of the twenty-seven books of the New Testament in their traditional order.

Gospels:
    The Gospel according to Matthew
    The Gospel according to Mark
    The Gospel according to Luke
    The Gospel according to John
History:
    Acts of the Apostles

Letters (also called Epistles):
    Paul's Letter to the Romans
    Paul's First and Second Letters to the Corinthians
    Paul's Letter to the Galatians
    Paul's Letter to the Ephesians
    Paul's Letter to the Philippians
    Paul's Letter to the Colossians
    Paul's First and Second Letters to the Thessalonaians
    Paul's First and Second Letters to Timothy
    Paul's Letter to Titus
    Letter to the Hebrews
    Letter of James
    First and Second Letters of Peter
    First, Second, and Third Letters of John
    Letter of Jude
Apocalyptic Literature:
    The Revelation of John

The following excerpts, one from each of the four types, are intended to display how the New Testament has continuity with the Hebrew Bible, and also show how the earliest Christian writers argued that some special act of fulfillment and consummation had occurred through the Jesus event.

A gospel, of which there are four in the New Testament, reflects on the events of the life of Jesus that evidenced his character and mission from God. The gospels as books are not biographies of the life of Jesus but are arguments for identifying him as the son of God and the Messiah.

The gospel according to Mark is probably the earliest of the four gospels, quite likely written before the destruction of Jerusalem in 70 C.E. Mark 15 describes the trial, crucifixion, death, and burial of Jesus. The essential claim of the earliest Jewish Christians was that Jesus was the Jewish Messiah. In fact, their very name derives from this claim: the word *christ*, from which the terms *Christian* and *Christianity* derive, comes from the Greek word *christos*, which means "anointed one," the same meaning as Hebrew *meshiach*—messiah. Throughout chapter 15 Mark ironically highlights Jesus' messiahship by recounting the nonperception and the downright denial of Jesus' kingship by Jews and Romans.

15:25 It was nine o'clock in the morning when they crucified him. 26 The inscription of the charge against him read, "The King of the Jews." 27 And with him they crucified two bandits, one on his right and one on his left. 29 Those who passed by derided him, shaking their heads and saying, "Aha! You who would destroy the temple and build it in three days, 30 save yourself, and come down from the cross!" 31 In the same way the chief priests, along with the scribes, were also mocking him among themselves and saying, "He saved others; he cannot save himself. 32 Let the Messiah, the King of Israel, come down from the cross now, so that we may see and believe." (NRSV)

A messiah in the tradition of the Hebrew Bible and Judaism was a kingly figure endowed by God with power to rule over a political kingdom. Jesus did not fit that mold, yet his followers still proclaimed him Messiah. They could do this only by redefining the nature of the Kingdom of God to be a spiritual and moral kingdom.

The Acts of the Apostles describe the missionary work of Jesus' followers and the founding of Christian churches. Often Luke, the writer of a gospel and this book, draws connections to the Hebrew Bible as a way to authenticate this new movement. His description of the Pentecost event and his record of Peter's sermon on that occasion are replete with connections to the Hebrew Bible. For example, his description of the distribution of the Holy Spirit recalls the storm and fire of biblical theophanies.

> *2:1 When the day of Pentecost had come, they were all together in one place. 2 And suddenly from heaven there came a sound like the rush of a violent wind, and it filled the entire house where they were sitting. 3 Divided tongues, as of fire, appeared among them, and a tongue rested on each of them. 4 All of them were filled with the Holy Spirit and began to speak in other languages, as the Spirit gave them ability. (NRSV)*

The Jewish festival of Pentecost (also called the Feast of Weeks) marks the end of the grain harvest. It coincides with that day, seven weeks after Passover, on which, according to Jewish tradition, the Torah was given. The Spirit of God arrived with a wind storm and was evident in licks of fire. Storm and fire were the visible evidences of God's presence in the narratives of the Hebrew Bible, including the Burning Bush episode of Moses and Elijah's transfer to heaven via the fire chariot. The birth of the church, as Pentecost is usually deemed, was thus construed as the natural outgrowth of the Torah of God and its harvest.

The Letter of Paul to the Galatians, written sometime in the 50s C.E., deals with the critical question of whether or not Gentile Christians must conform to traditional Jewish laws. Essentially Paul said no. But in order to justify his position he had to reinterpret the traditional definition of Jewish identity.

> *3:1 You foolish Galatians! Who has bewitched you? It was before your eyes that Jesus Christ was publicly exhibited as crucified! 2 The only thing I want to learn from you is this: Did you receive the Spirit by doing the works of the law or by believing what you heard? . . .*
> *6 Just as Abraham "believed God and it was reckoned to him as righteousness," 7 so, you see, those who believe are the descendants of Abraham. 8 And the scripture, foreseeing that God would justify the Gentiles by faith, declared the gospel beforehand to Abraham, saying, "All the Gentiles shall be blessed in you." 9 For this reason, those who believe are blessed with Abraham who believed. (NRSV)*

Paul quotes Genesis 15:6 to certify that inclusion in the covenant community is made possible by believing in God, not by obeying the Torah. This also warrants extending the bounds of the covenant community to non-Jews.

The Revelation of John closes the New Testament collection of books. Literally named the *Apocalypse*, it has affinities to apocalyptic literature of the Old Testament and Intertestamental periods such as the second half of Daniel and Enoch. The book uses a great deal of symbolism involving numbers, hybrid beasts, seals, and bowls. Due to the veiled nature of its symbolism and other factors, it is subject to widely varying interpretations.

The Revelation purports to be a vision given to John that discloses events of the end time of history. Times of warfare and conflict are described until the ultimate victory of God is achieved. Then the universe would be remade, recalling the words of Isaiah 65–66, into a "new heavens and a new earth." The last words of the Revelation also draw from creation imagery, as if to say that the new world would be a remake of the Garden of Eden in Genesis.

> *22:1 Then the angel showed me the river of the water of life, bright as crystal, flowing from the throne of God and of the Lamb 2 through the middle of the street of the city (i.e., the New Jerusalem). On either side of the river is the tree of life with its twelve kinds of fruit, producing its fruit each month; and the leaves of the tree are for the healing of the nations. 3 Nothing accursed will be found there any more. But the throne of God and of the Lamb will be in it, and his servants will worship him; 4 they will see his face, and his name will be on their foreheads. 5 And there will be no more night; they need no light of lamp or sun, for the Lord God will be their light, and they will reign forever and ever. (NRSV)*

Some clear points of contact with Hebrew Bible creation motifs are the tree of life, the river, not curse but only blessing, the light that comes from God without a sun, and perhaps even the use of the divine designation "Yahweh Elohim" (the Lord God) that was used consistently in Genesis 2–3. The Revelation provides a satisfying closure to the Christian Bible by returning the believer to the beauty of God's perfect creation.

RABBINIC LITERATURE

The specific type of Judaism associated with the Pharisees had its roots in the Maccabean period. Pharisaic Judaism became a dominant force by the first century C.E. It was the only Jewish religious group, apart from Christianity, that survived the disaster of the First Jewish Revolt. It lived on in what has come to be called **Rabbinic Judaism**.

One valuable source of insights into the nature of Rabbinic Judaism is its translation of the Bible. As the Hebrew language receded from active use in Jewish communities and Aramaic took its place, the Hebrew Bible was translated into the common tongue. An Aramaic translation of a Hebrew Bible original is called a **targum**. Targums from various regional Jewish communities have survived, and they can tell us a great deal about how the Hebrew Bible was understood. More often paraphrases rather than literal translations, they reveal what the Bible meant to them.

Pharisaic Judaism was in every way closely tied to the Hebrew Bible. The Bible was the focus of religious devotion. Reading the Torah was the heart of synagogue services and thoroughly shaped Jewish liturgy.

The Hebrew Bible was called the **Written Torah** in this tradition to distinguish it from the **Oral Torah**. The Oral Torah consisted of interpretations and applications of the Hebrew Bible. The Written and Oral Torahs together became the authoritative guide for life and belief within the Jewish community. The accumulation of text and interpretation came to be called **halakah,** from the Hebrew verb "to walk," because this literature provided the torah of walking in righteousness. Judaism defined a Torah-centered nation, and the community became known as "the people of the book."

The wealth of Oral Torah that was generated by generations of Jewish scholars and teachers, called rabbis, was collected and organized into tractates in the second century C.E. by Judah the Prince and is called the **Mishnah**. The process of reapplying Torah to life in the community did not stop with the finalization of the Mishnah. The **Talmud** contains yet another set of interpretations of Torah for the Jewish community.

The following excerpt from tractate Berakoth of the Mishnah communicates the flavor of Oral Torah. This paragraph contains a discussion of when the Shema should be recited each day. The Shema is the Jewish prayer derived from Deuteronomy 6 that became the basic creed of Judaism.

> *1:1 From what time in the evening may the Shemá be recited? From the time when the priests enter [the Temple] to eat of their Heave-offering until the end of the first watch. So R. Eliezer. But the Sages say: Until midnight. Rabban Gamaliel says: Until the rise of dawn. His sons once returned [after midnight] from a wedding feast. They said to him, "We have not recited the Shemá." He said to them, "If the dawn has not risen ye are [still] bound to recite it. Moreover, wheresoever the Sages prescribe 'Until midnight' the duty of fulfilment lasts until the rise of dawn." The duty of burning the fat pieces and the members [of the animal offerings] lasts until the rise of dawn; and for all [offerings] that must be consumed "the same day," the duty lasts until the rise of dawn. Why then have the Sages said: Until midnight? To keep man far from transgression. (Danby 1933)*

This discussion provides an example of the Rabbinic Jewish practice of "making a hedge around torah." That is to say, laws were often applied more strictly than was dictated by the original statement of the law in the Hebrew Bible. This was done so that a person might break the new application of the law and yet not break the original law itself.

There is a much richer body of Jewish interpretive literature from this period than our brief discussion could communicate. In addition to the translations of the Hebrew Bible and halakah there developed a vast collection of commentaries on biblical books and often delightful retellings of biblical stories that communicated moral lessons.

This storehouse of literature from the variety of communities that together constituted Judaism, including the Pharisees, Essenes, and Christians, reveals to us the vitality and longevity of the Hebrew Bible. It provided the foundation for life and practice in these centuries. It demonstrates how the text of scripture provided a certain stable set of core beliefs and moral norms and yet within itself allowed for continual reinterpretation and reapplication to account for changing social and historical conditions. Stability and adaptability, continuity and change—the Hebrew Bible reveals itself to be a remarkable book that formed communities and enabled them to survive, even thrive, in a challenging world.

FOR FURTHER STUDY

Cohen, Shaye J. D. (1987). *From the Maccabees to the Mishnah*. Philadelphia: Westminster Press. A social and literary history of Judaism from the second century B.C.E. through the first century C.E.

McNamara, Michael (1983). *Intertestamental Literature*. Wilmington, Del.: Michael Glazier. Another sampler of literature roughly from 200 B.C.E to 200 C.E. It is organized by type of literature or source of origin, using such categories as "apocalyptic literature" and "literature of Hellenistic Judaism."

Nickelsburg, George W. E., and Michael E. Stone (1983). *Faith and Piety in Early Judaism. Texts and Documents*. Philadelphia: Fortress Press. An anthology of texts with brief literary and historical explanations drawn from the apocrypha, pseudepigrapha, Dead Sea Scrolls, the works of Philo and Josephus, the New Testament, and the literature of Rabbinic Judaism. Organized by topics such as piety, deliverance, and wisdom, this is a handy sampler of texts "after the Hebrew Bible."

The following resources apply specifically to individual literatures from this period.

Apocrypha and Pseudepigrapha. Some editions of the Bible contain the apocrypha. Roman Catholic translations of Scripture, such as the New American Bible, intersperse these books among the books of the Hebrew Bible. Other versions and editions, such as the New Oxford Annotated Bible based on the New Revised Standard Version, collect all the apocryphal books in one place and situate them between the Old Testament and the New Testament.

Charlesworth, James H. (1983–1985). *The Old Testament Pseudepigrapha. Volume 1: Apocalyptic Literature and Testaments; Volume 2: Expansions of the "Old Testament" and Other Legends, Wisdom and Philosophical Literature, Prayers, Psalms, and Odes, Fragments of Lost Judeo–Hellenistic Works*. Garden City, N.Y.: Doubleday. This is the standard edition of the texts of the apocrypha and pseudepigrapha in English translation.

Nickelsburg, George W. E. (1981). *Jewish Literature Between the Bible and the Mishnah. A Historical and Literary Introduction*. Philadelphia: Fortress Press. This volume summarizes the content of the apocryphal and pseudepigraphical books and provides historical background and literary analysis.

Dead Sea Scrolls. Vermes, Geza (1987). *The Dead Sea Scrolls in English*. London: Penguin. Third revised and augmented edition, including the Temple Scroll and other recently published manuscripts. This is the most up-to-date and affordable edition of the scrolls. Introductory chapters summarize the history of the Dead Sea Scrolls community and the beliefs of their authors.

New Testament. The books of the New Testament are found in all but Jewish editions of the Bible. Books describing the literature and history of the New Testament abound. One such volume is by David L. Barr (1995). *The New Testament Story. An Introduction*, Second Edition. Belmont, Calif.: Wadsworth.

Rabbinic Literature. Danby, Herbert (1933). *The Mishnah*. London: Oxford University Press. The core text of Rabbinic Judaism is the Mishnah. This is an authoritative translation. The expansion on the Mishnah, called the Talmud, can be found in Isidore Epstein, (1935–1948). *The Babylonian Talmud*. London: Soncino Press.

Bowker, John (1969). *The Targums and Rabbinic Literature. An Introduction to Jewish Interpretations of Scripture*. Cambridge: Cambridge Uni-

versity Press. This volume contains a detailed explanation of the various types of classical rabbinic literature that interpret the Hebrew Bible, along with samples of Targum Pseudo-Jonathan on Genesis in English translation.

WORKS CITED

Charles, R. M. (1913). *The Apocrypha and Pseudepigrapha of The Old Testament in English*. Volume II: Pseudepigrapha. Oxford: Oxford University Press.

Danby, Herbert (1933). *The Mishnah*. London: Oxford University Press.

Vermes, Geza (1987). *The Dead Sea Scrolls in English*. London: Penguin.

GLOSSARY OF NAMES AND TERMS

A.D. Abbreviation of *anno domini*, Latin for "year of the Lord." See C.E.

Aaron The brother of Moses, Israel's first high priest.

Abel The second son of Adam and Eve; he was murdered by his brother Cain.

Abner The commander of Saul's army; he was killed by Joab.

Abraham (Abram; adj. Abrahamic) The first father (patriarch) of Israel; first called Abram; God made a covenant with him in which God promised to make him a great nation; Isaac was his son by Sarah, and Ishmael was his son by Hagar.

Abraham cycle Genesis 12–25; a collection of stories focused on Abraham.

Abrahamic covenant The covenant Yahweh made with Abraham, sealed by circumcision.

Absalom A son of David who murdered his half-brother Amnon, took the throne from David, and was killed by Joab.

Absolute law Also called apodictic law, it is law stated in an unconditional manner without qualifying clauses; absolute law is distinguished from case law.

Achan A contemporary of Joshua who kept spoil from the conquest of Jericho, was held responsible for Israel's defeat at Ai, and was executed by the Israelites.

Acrostic A series of poetic lines or verses whose initial letters form the alphabet, a word, or a regular pattern, as in Lamentations 1–4 and Psalms 111, 112, and 119.

Adam The first male God created; he and his mate, Eve, disobeyed God and were expelled from the Garden of Eden.

Adonijah A son of David who was executed by Solomon.

Adultery Having sexual relations with someone other than one's husband or wife.

Aetiology A story giving an explanation of the origin of a name, a place, or a custom.

Aggada(h) See Haggada(h).

Ahab (869–850) King of Israel, married to Jezebel, whose Baalistic practices were opposed by the northern prophet Elijah.

Ahasuerus The king of Persia during the time of Esther, identified as Xerxes I (486–465).

Ahaz (735–715) The king of Judah at the time Isaiah was a prophet.

Ahijah An Israelite prophet who encouraged Jeroboam to rebel against Solomon's administration.

Ai A Canaanite city conquered by Joshua and the Israelites.

Akkadian The Semitic language of Mesopotamia; Assyrian and Babylonian are dialects.

Allegory A literary device in which characters and events stand for abstract ideas, principles, or forces, so that the literal sense has or suggests a parallel, deeper, symbolic sense.

Almighty (Hebrew *shaddai*) A name of God that connotes his power and strength.

Altar A raised platform, made of undressed stones, dirt, metal, or wood, on which incense or sacrifices are offered.

Amaziah Priest of Bethel loyal to Jeroboam II; opposed Amos's preaching and presence in the Northern Kingdom.

Am ha'aretz (pl. *ammey ha'aretz*; Hebrew for "people of the land") A term used in the Hebrew Bible for citizens, or some particular class of citizens; in rabbinic literature, for persons or groups that dissented from or were uninstructed in rabbinic halaka and rigorous purity and tithing norms; it sometimes signifies the unlearned, sometimes is used condescendingly (boor); it was also used of the broad mass of Jewish people of the first century C.E., who cannot be categorized into any of the subgroups of the time.

Amnon Son of David who raped his half-sister Tamar and was killed by Absalom.

Amoraim Jewish teachers from the period 200 to 500 C.E. whose work culminated in the Talmud.

Amos One of the Twelve Prophets; eighth-century prophet from Tekoa in Judah who preached to the Northern Kingdom emphasizing social justice and the coming Day of Yahweh.

Amphictyony Greek term for a religio-political federation whose common focus is a sanctuary dedicated to God; an association of neighboring states or tribes in ancient Greece that banded together for common interest and protection; this model has sometimes been used to describe the tribal confederation in the period of the judges (prior to Saul and David) in ancient Israel.

Anathoth The hometown of Jeremiah in the tribal territory of Benjamin.

Ancestors In Old Testament study this refers to the forebears of the nation of Israel; the patriarchs and matriarchs of the Hebrews, usually Abraham and Sarah, Isaac and Rebekah, Jacob and Rachel and Leah, and sometimes the twelve sons of Jacob.

Ancestral story The accounts in Genesis 12–50 that pertain to the ancestors of the Israelites.

Anoint To pour oil over the head; this was part of a ritual of designation by which priests and kings were initiated into office; an "anointed one" (Hebrew *meshiach*) was a divinely designated leader.

Anthropomorphism (adj. anthropomorphic) A Greek term for the attribution of human behavior or characteristics to inanimate objects, animals, natural phenomena, or deity; with regard to deity, anthropomorphism became a point of theological discussion in Judaism, Christianity, and Islam.

Antiochus IV Epiphanes (175–163) Seleucid king who persecuted the Jews of Judea during the Maccabean period.

Antithetic parallelism Type of poetic parallelism where the second line of a poetic couplet is the opposite of the first line.

Apocalypse (adj. apocalyptic; Greek for "revelation") An "unveiling" of something hidden; apocalyptic literature is a genre of literature (attested in Jewish, Christian, and Muslim traditions) in which the author claims to reveal the future and to show how the divine plan will be worked out in history, often expressing it in vivid symbolism; the final book of the Christian New Testament is sometimes called (in accord with its Greek title) "the Apocalypse" (it is also known as "the book of Revelation").

Apocalyptic eschatology The view of the end times expressed in apocalyptic literature.

Apocalyptic literature Old Testament, intertestamental Jewish and early Christian literature that consists predominantly of apocalypses; this literature is often pseudepigraphical; Daniel 7–12 is apocalyptic literature.

Apocalypticism The thought world or worldview of the community that gave rise to apocalyptic literature.

Apocrypha (adj. apocryphal; from Greek for "to hide, to uncover") It is used in a technical sense to refer to certain Jewish books written in the Hellenistic–Roman period that came to be included in the Old Greek Jewish scriptures (and thus in the Eastern Christian biblical canon) and in the Latin Vulgate Roman Catholic canon, but not in the Jewish or Protestant biblical canons; they are called deutero-canonical books in the Roman Catholic tradition.

Apodictic law See Absolute law.

Apsu The god of the freshwater ocean in the Enuma Elish, the Babylonian creation story.

Aqedah (Hebrew for "binding" [of Isaac]) The Jewish biblical account of God's command to Abraham to offer his son Isaac as a sacrifice (Genesis 22).

Aram (Aramea, Aram-naharaim, Padan-Aram) The territory north and east of Palestine where Abraham's ancestors had settled and from where the wives of Isaac and Jacob came; roughly the region of modern northern Syria and northwestern Iraq.

Aramaic A language in the same family as Hebrew, used in Daniel 2:4–7:28; Ezra 4:8–6:18 and 7:12–26; and Jeremiah 10:11; its square script replaced the Old Hebrew script in Hebrew manuscripts before the Christian Era.

Araunah The owner of a threshing floor in Jerusalem (Jebus) where David built an altar; David bought the threshing floor and Solomon built the temple there (2 Samuel 24).

Archaeology The science of unearthing sites containing remains of ancient habitation, with the goal of learning everything such sites have to offer about culture, society, ecology, intellectual life, and religion; modern archaeology employs the tools of history, anthropology, geology, and biology to recover the hidden past.

Ark of the covenant A gold-overlayed wooden chest with two cherubim on the lid that stored the tablets of the covenant; it was housed first in the tabernacle, then in the Most Holy Place room of the Jerusalem temple; it was the location of God's presence within Israel.

Armageddon Derived from Hebrew "mountain of Megiddo," it is the site of the final battle between God and the forces of evil in apocalyptic thought.

Atone (n. atonement) To make right with God by satisfying the penalty for breaking relationship; in the Old Testament this was done through offering sacrifices to God. See Yom Kippur (Day of Atonement).

Atrahasis epic A Babylonian story that recounts the creation of humankind.

Av (sometimes spelled *Ab*) A month in the Jewish calendar; the 9th of Av is a day of mourning for the destruction of the Jerusalem temple in 587 B.C.E. and again in 70 C.E.

B.C.E./C.E. Abbreviations meaning "before the common era" and "common era"; theologically neutral replacements for the traditional designations B.C. ("before Christ") and A.D. ("year of the Lord").

Baal Word meaning "lord, master" (in Modern Hebrew, "husband") that was applied to the chief god of Canaan; various locations in Canaan had their patron Baal gods, for example, Baal of Peor and Baal of Hermon.

Babel See Tower of Babel and Babylon.

Babylon The capital city of Babylonia in southern Mesopotamia; the Babylonians led by Nebuchadnezzar destroyed Jerusalem in 587 B.C.E. and took Judeans into Babylonian exile; called Babel in Genesis 11.

Babylonian exile. See Exile.

Balaam A thirteenth-century B.C.E. Mesopotamian seer–prophet who was hired by Balak of Moab to curse the Israelites but ended up blessing them instead.

Balak King of Moab who opposed Moses and the Israelites.

Baruch Jeremiah's scribe, perhaps responsible for composing and editing the latter half of the book of Jeremiah.

Bathsheba The wife of Uriah who committed adultery with David; she later became his wife and the mother of Solomon.

Ben (Hebrew for "son, son of"; Aramaic *bar*) Used frequently in "patronymics" (naming by identity of father); Rabbi Akiba ben Joseph means Akiba son of Joseph.

Benjamin The twelfth son of Jacob, the younger brother of Joseph; Rachel was his mother; he was the ancestor of the tribe of Benjamin.

Berakah (Hebrew for "blessing") In Judaism, an offering of thankfulness that praises God for a benefit conferred or a great event experienced.

Berit (also spelled *brit*; Hebrew for "covenant") Used in Judaism especially for the special relationship believed to exist between God and the Jewish people.

Bethel A city that became a center of Israelite worship; literally means "house of El."

Bethlehem A city in the tribe of Judah, hometown of David; literally means "house of bread."

Bible (adj. biblical; from Greek *biblos*, "book") The designation normally used for the Hebrew Bible plus the Christian New Testament; in classical Roman Catholic and Greek Orthodox Christianity it designates the Hebrew Bible plus the Apocrypha plus the New Testament.

Birthright The special inheritance rights of the firstborn son giving him claim to the bulk of the ancestral property.

Bless (n. blessing) To show favor to; to ask God to show favor.

Boaz A wealthy Israelite who lived in Bethlehem; he married Ruth and became an ancestor of David.

Book of the Covenant Also called the Covenant Code, Exodus 20:22–23:33; a collection of Israelite laws.

Book of the Twelve Sometimes called the minor prophets, a collection of twelve short prophetic books in the Latter Prophets; also called the Twelve Prophets.

Burning bush The bush out of which Yahweh spoke to Moses in the Sinai to reveal God's identity (Exodus 3).

C.E. "Common Era"; an attempt to use a neutral term for the period traditionally labeled A.D. (*anno domini* or "year of the Lord") by Christians; thus, 1995 C.E. is identical to A.D. 1995. See also B.C.E.

Cain The first son of Adam and Eve; he murdered his brother Abel.

Caleb One of the twelve spies Joshua sent into Canaan; of the generation that left Egypt in the Exodus, only he and Joshua were allowed to enter Canaan.

Calendar Judaism follows a lunar calendar adjusted every three years or so to the solar cycle (by adding a second 12th month)—thus "lunisolar"; the oldest Jewish annual observances are Passover/pesah, Shevuot, Yom Kippur, and Sukkot; other ancient celebrations include Rosh Hashanah, Simhat Torah, Hannukah, and Purim; in general, Christianity operates on a "solar" calendar based on the relationship between the sun and the earth (365.25 days per year); the main Christian observances are Easter, Pentecost, and Christmas.

Call narrative An account found in some historical and prophetic books that records the prophet's experience of being called into prophetic ministry; the call was usually issued in the presence of God.

Call to praise A speech type found in certain biblical psalms where the psalmist enjoins others to join him in praising God.

Canaan The geographical territory between the Mediterranean coast and the Jordan River that was claimed and occupied by the Hebrews; also called the Promised Land.

Canon The authorized collection of material constituting the sacred writings of a religious community; the material is believed to have special, usually divine, authority; the Hebrew Bible is the canon of the Jewish community; the Old and New Testaments (respectively with and without the Apocrypha) are the canon of the Roman Catholic and Protestant Christian communities.

Canon criticism (sometimes called *canon critique*) A type of biblical study that places emphasis on the final form of the text as normative for Judaism and Christianity.

Canonization The process whereby a religious community defined the body of texts it considered authoritative for its life and belief.

Case law Legal sayings with modifying clauses often in the *if . . . then* form: "If this is the situation . . . then this is the penalty"; also called casuistic law, this type of legal formulation contrasts with absolute law.

Casuistic law See Case law.

Catholic (from Greek for "universal, worldwide") A self-designation used in early Christianity to suggest universality over against factionalism; thence, it became a technical name for the Western, Roman Catholic church.

Centralization of worship A theme of the Deuteronomist whereby proper worship could be performed only in the city God designated, presumably Jerusalem.

Chaos The disordered state of unformed matter that existed before the universe was ordered; biblical and ancient Middle Eastern origin stories thought of chaos as an unruly cosmic ocean.

Charismatic Gifted, filled with the divine, with divinely given powers, or with God's spirit. This state may be linked with ecstasy or trance, which is reported to have been experienced by the early prophets and by Saul, the first king.

Cherub (Hebrew pl. *cherubim*) An angelic being, in appearance something like a human but with wings; they were mythical celestial winged creatures prominent in Temple decoration; cherubim were considered God's ruling council, also called the host of heaven.

Chiasmus (adj. chiastic) A literary device in which, for emphasis, the second part of a text is parallel to the first, but in reverse, for example, ABBA, ABCBA.

Christ (from Greek *christos*, "anointed one"; Greek translation of Hebrew *meshiach*) Applied to Jesus/Joshua of Nazareth by his followers as a title, but soon came to be treated as a sort of second name. See Messiah.

Christians/Christianity The followers of Jesus of Nazareth who believe him to be the Jewish messiah (*christos*) of God; Christianity is the collective body of Christians who believe the teachings of Jesus of Nazareth.

Christos The Greek word for "anointed one." Also see Christ.

Chronicle An annal or account of events in the order in which they occurred.

Chronicler Writer of the books of Chronicles; generally considered to be a later interpreter of the history of Judah.

Chronicler's history The books of the Writings considered to be a postexilic retelling of Israel's history intended to profile the role of the house of David; consists of the biblical books First and Second Chronicles, Ezra, and Nehemiah.

Church (from Greek *ekklesia*, "summoned group"; compare "ecclesiastical") The designation traditionally used for a specifically Christian assembly or body of people, and thus also the building or location in which the assembled people meet, and by extension also the specific organized subgroup within Christianity (e.g., Catholic, Protestant, or Methodist); similar to synagogue and *kahal* in Judaism.

Circumcise (n. circumcision) To cut off the loose fold of skin at the end of the penis; circumcision was the ritual attached to the covenant God made with Abraham; in Judaism, it is ritually performed when a boy is eight days old in a ceremony called *brit milah*, which indicates that the ritual establishes a covenant between God and the individual; in Islam, it is performed at the age of puberty.

Cities of refuge Six cities designated in Mosaic law for those who accidentally killed someone.

Classical Judaism The form of Judaism that has survived as traditional throughout the centuries.

Clean animals Animals that were approved for ritual sacrifices.

Climactic parallelism The type of poetic parallelism where the second line of a poetic couplet echoes part of the first line and adds a phrase to it, thereby extending and completing its sense.

Code of Hammurabi A Mesopotamian law code associated with the eighteenth-century B.C.E. Old Babylonian monarch Hammurabi; it has similarities to the biblical Book of the Covenant.

Colon A single line of poetry, sometimes called a *stich* or *stichos*.

Commandments (Hebrew *mitzvot*; sing., *mitzvah*) Orders given by God; God gave Ten Commandments as the core of the covenant on Mt. Sinai, and a multitude of other moral and cultic laws; according to rabbinic Jewish tradition, there are 613 religious commandments referred to in the Torah (and elaborated upon by the rabbinic sages); of these, 248 are positive commandments and 365 are negative; the numbers respectively symbolize the fact that divine service must be expressed through all one's bodily parts during all the days of the year; in general, a *mitzvah* refers to any act of religious duty or obligation; more colloquially, a *mitzvah* refers to a "good deed."

Commentary A discussion of a book of the Bible that treats linguistic, literary, historical, and theological aspects of its meaning. See the Bibliography of this text.

Complaint (sometimes called *lament*) A literary type that expresses the pain and alienation of the writer and asks God for help; complaints are found in psalmic and prophetic literature.

Concordance An alphabetical listing of all the important words in a text and their textual locations; a useful tool for studying biblical themes. See the Bibliography of this text.

Concubine A woman who belonged to a man but did not have the full rights of a wife; she was frequently acquired as spoils in war, and her main function was to bear sons for the man.

Consecrate (n. consecration) To set aside or dedicate to God's use.

Cosmogony A theory or model of the origin and evolution of the physical universe; ancient creation stories, such as Genesis 1–2 and the Enuma Elish, are cosmogonies.

Cosmology A model of the structure of the physical universe; the Israelites viewed the world as an inhabitable region surrounded by water.

Covenant (Hebrew *berit* or *brit*) A pact or formal agreement between two parties in which there are mutual obligations and expectations; covenant is used as a metaphor of God's relationship with his people. The major covenants in the Old Testament are God's covenant with Abraham (Genesis 15) and the Sinai/Moses covenant (Exodus 19–24) between God and Israel. The Priestly writer used a succession of covenants to track the development of salvation history; in Judaism, the covenant is a major theological concept referring to the eternal bond between God and the people of Israel grounded in God's gracious and steadfast concern (Hebrew *chesed*) that calls for the nation's obedience to the divine commandments (*mitzvot*) and instruction (*torah*). For Christianity (e.g. Paul), God has made a "new covenant" (rendered as *new testament* in older English) with the followers of Jesus in the last times, superseding the "old covenant" (thus, *old testament*) with Moses at Sinai (see Jeremiah 31:31–34).

Covenant Code See Book of the Covenant.

Creation What has been brought into being; the Hebrew Bible attributes the creation of the world to Israel's God; the classic descriptions of creation are found in Genesis 1 and 2, but there are many other allusions to creation found in Israel's Psalms and in prophetic literature.

Criticism When used in biblical scholarship in such phrases as *biblical criticism*, *higher criticism*, and *form criticism*, it means evaluating evidence to arrive at a reasoned judgment concerning the matter under investigation; it does not imply that the reader is taking a negative or "criticizing" position over against the Bible; our textbook suggests that *critique* may be a better term to use.

Cubit A biblical unit of measurement, the distance from elbow to fingertip—approximately 18 inches, or half a meter.

Cult The formal organization and practice of worship, usually associated with a sanctuary and involving a regular cycle of sacrifices, prayers, and hymns under the direction of priests and other leaders; when used in biblical studies the term is descriptive and does not imply anything dark, devilish, false, or unseemly, as is often the case in modern uses of the term.

Curse To ask God to bring something tragic or disastrous on someone or something else; the opposite of blessing; as a noun, it is the description of the bad thing that will happen, as in the curses and blessing of the law.

Cycle As in *Abraham cycle*, *Jacob cycle*, and *Joseph cycle*, the term refers to a collection of stories centered or "cycling" around a single individual.

Cyrus (550–530) Persian monarch, sometimes called Cyrus the Great, who founded the Medo-Persian empire in the sixth century B.C.E. and allowed the Judean refugees to return to their homeland after the Babylonian exile.

D The acronym for the Deuteronomist source of the Torah/Pentateuch, written in the seventh century B.C.E.

Dan A son of Jacob, and one of the twelve tribes of Israel.

Daniel A Judean who was taken into Babylonian captivity by Nebuchadnezzar; a Jewish hero, he is the main character in the book of Daniel.

David The son of Jesse, anointed by Samuel to become king in place of Saul; he killed Goliath; his sons Amnon, Absalom, Adonijah, and Solomon fought to follow him on the throne; he is associated with the biblical psalms and is credited with politically and militarily uniting the ancient Israelite confederation into a centralized kingdom with Jerusalem as its capital; he created the largest empire Israel ever knew; David is said to have planned for the Temple that his son and successor, Solomon, built.

Davidic covenant A covenant God made with David pledging that the family of David would provide kings to rule over Israel in perpetuity (2 Samuel 7).

Day of atonement (Hebrew *yom kippur*) The one day each year when special sacrifices were made by the high priest for the sins of the people; only on this day the high priest entered the Most Holy Place of the temple to sprinkle blood on the ark of the covenant to reconcile Israel with God (Leviticus 16).

Day of Yahweh Also termed the Day of the LORD, the day God battles his enemies; derives from the holy war tradition and was cited by Amos, Joel, Obadiah, and Zephaniah.

Dead Sea Scrolls A collection of scrolls dating to the first century B.C.E. found in caves near the Dead Sea; they are generally thought to be linked with the settlement at Qumran and with a Jewish religious group called the Essenes.

Deborah The judge of Israel who engineered victory over Canaanites (Judges 4–5).

Decalogue (Greek for "ten words") Refers to laws collected into a group of ten; *The* Decalogue is the Ten Commandments received by Moses on Mt. Sinai (Exodus 20:1–17 and Deuteronomy 5:1–21); the cultic decalogue is found in Exodus 34.

Demythologize The process of interpreting a myth in nonmythic language to express its meaning without clinging to its mythic form.

Deutero-canonical Pertains to writings regarded as Scripture by some (particularly by Christian groups) but not contained in the Hebrew Bible. Also see Apocrypha and Pseudepigrapha.

Deuteronomic history (abbreviated DH; sometimes called the Deuteronom*istic* history) The body of material that consists of the introduction to Deuteronomy (chapters 1–4) and Joshua, Judges, Samuel, and Kings; it is an extended review of Israel's history from the conquest under Joshua through the destruction of 587 B.C.E. written from the perspective of principles found in the book of Deuteronomy.

Deuteronomic reform A reform of Judah's religious institutions carried out by Josiah in the seventh century B.C.E.; the book of Deuteronomy is closely associated with this initiative.

Deuteronomist (abbreviated D) The writer or school of writers responsible for the book of Deuteronomy, the fifth book of the Torah/Pentateuch.

Deuteronomy The fifth book of the Torah/Pentateuch; many modern scholars consider it to be part or all of a scroll found during a reform of the temple and its institutions carried out by Josiah in 622 B.C.E.

DH (sometimes *DtrH*) The acronym for the Deuteronomic history. See Deuteronomic history.

Diaspora (Greek for "scattering") The technical term for the dispersion of the Jewish people, a process that began after defeats in 721 and 587 B.C.E. and resulted in the growth of sizable Jewish communities outside Palestine; the terms *diaspora* and *dispersion* are often used to refer to the Jewish communities living among the Gentiles outside the "holy land" of Canaan/Israel/Palestine.

Dietary laws See Kosher.

Divine Council Consisted of the "sons of God," a council of angels that surrounded God and served as his deliberative assembly.

Divine warrior The notion that God is a warrior fighting on behalf of his people. See also Holy War.

Documentary hypothesis Scholarly hypothesis suggesting that the Torah/Pentateuch was not the work of one author, such as Moses, but is a composition based on four documents from different periods: J (the Yahwist) from about 950 B.C.E., E (the Elohist) from about 850, D (Deuteronomy) from about 620, and P (the Priestly document) from about 550–450. J and E were combined around 720, D was added about a century later, and P about a century after that, giving final shape to the Torah.

Dualism The belief that there are two elemental forces in the universe, Good and Evil; apocalypticism typically holds a dualistic view of the world.

E The acronym for the Elohist source.

Early Judaism Also sometimes called "formative," "proto-," "middle," and even "late" Judaism; refers to Judaism in the intertestamental period (and slightly later) as a development from the religion of ancient Israel, but prior to the emergence of its classical, rabbinic form in the early centuries C.E.

Eden The Garden of Eden was the place God located the first created humans, Adam and Eve (Genesis 2–3).

Edom A territory south of Judah, the location of the Edomites, the descendants of Esau.

El The Semitic word for God, found alone or compounded with other terms as names of God (El Shaddai, El Elyon, etc.); often found as the theophoric element in personal and place names (Elijah, Bethel, etc.).

Election A term used theologically in Judaism to indicate God's choice of Israel to receive the covenant—a choice based not on the superiority or previous accomplishments of the people but on God's graciousness (see covenant); in Christianity, the concept of election was applied to the "new Israel" of Jesus' followers in the last times.

Eli The high priest at Shiloh with whom Samuel ministered in his early years.

Elijah An Israelite prophet during the reign of Ahab; he defeated the prophets of Baal at Mt. Carmel and was taken to heaven in a firestorm.

Elisha The prophet who succeeded Elijah in the Northern Kingdom of Israel.

Elkanah An Ephraimite, the husband of Hannah and the father of Samuel.

Elohim A Hebrew word meaning God; Israel's most general way of referring to its deity; the Elohist portions of the Pentateuch refer to God with this term.

Elohist (also called the Elohist source; abbreviated E) The name given to a reconstructed source underlying Pentateuchal narratives; it is characterized by the use of the divine name Elohim.

Enuma Elish A Babylonian story of creation, featuring Apsu, Tiamat, and Marduk.

Ephod A linen apron worn by a priest over his robe.

Ephraim One of Joseph's two sons; he became the ancestor of one of the tribes of Israel; the name Ephraim was often used as a designation of the ten northern tribes after the division of the kingdoms.

Eponym A supposed ancestor (eponymous ancestor) whose name is the same as, or related to, the name of a later group, tribe, or nation.

Eretz Yisrael/**Israel** (Hebrew for "land of Israel") In Jewish thought, the special term for the Palestinian area believed to have been promised to the Jewish people by God in the ancient covenant.

Esau The first son of Isaac and Rebekah, the twin of Jacob; he was the ancestor of the Edomites.

Eschatology (adj. eschatological; from Greek *eschaton*, "last" or "the end-time") Refers in general to what is expected to take place in the "last times" (from the inquirer's perspective); thus the study of the ultimate destiny or purpose of humankind and the world, how and when the end will occur, what the end or last period of history or existence will be like. See also Apocalypse and Apocalyptic literature.

Essenes A Jewish group that lived in retreat in the wilderness of Judea between the first century B.C.E. and the first C.E., according to Josephus, Pliny the elder, and Philo. See also Dead Sea Scrolls and Qumran.

Esther A Jewish heroine of the diaspora who became queen of Persia under Xerxes I; she secured the safety of the Jews when they were threatened with genocide; her story is told in the book that carries her name.

Etiology (sometimes spelled *aetiology*; from Greek for "cause, origin") A term used to describe or label stories (etiological tales) that claim to explain the reason for something being (or being called) what it is; for example, in the old Jewish creation story (Genesis 2:23), woman (*ishshah*) is given that name because she has been taken out of (the side or rib of) "man" (*ish*).

Eve The first female God created; mated to Adam, her name means "life."

Ex nihilo A Latin phrase meaning "from nothing" that some theologians apply to the biblical story of creation; Genesis 1, as well as other Old Testament allusions to creation, suggests that God created the world out of water.

Exegesis (from Greek for "interpretation") The process of drawing out meaning from a text; interpreting a text in its literary and historical context.

Exile (also called the Babylonian exile) The Babylonian exile was the period in the middle of the sixth century B.C.E. when Judeans were taken as captives to Babylonia and resettled there; it officially ended in 539 B.C.E., but many Judeans nonetheless remained there.

Exodus (from Greek for "to exit, go out") The term refers to the event of the Israelites leaving Egypt and to the biblical book that tells of that event, the second book of the Torah; the release from Egyptian captivity and the exodus from Egypt were led by Moses, probably in the thirteenth century B.C.E. See Passover.

Ezekiel A priest taken to Babylonia who became a prophet to the community of Judean refugees living there in the sixth century B.C.E.; also, the prophetic book associated with this prophet.

Ezra A priest and teacher of the Torah; he led a group of Jewish refugees back to Judea from Babylonia in the fifth century B.C.E.

Fear of Yahweh A deep respect and reverence of God; an important theme in the Elohist fragments and in the wisdom literature.

Five Scrolls (sometimes called the *Five Megillot*) A subgroup of books within the Writings section of the Hebrew Bible consisting of the Song of Songs, Ruth, Lamentations, Ecclesiastes, and Esther; each book or scroll is associated with a festival occasion in the life of Israel.

Flood The watery inundation during the time of Noah that destroyed all life on earth, except for Noah and the representative sample of created things that survived in the ark (Genesis 6–9).

Form criticism (also called *form critique*) The analysis of literary units to discover the typical formal structures and patterns behind the current text in an attempt to recover the original sociological setting or "setting in life" (German *Sitz im Leben*) of that form of literature.

Formal parallelism (sometimes called *synthetic parallelism*) The type of poetic parallelism where the second line of a poetic couplet completes the thought of the first line.

Former Prophets The technical name for the books of Joshua, Judges, Samuel, and Kings—possibly because it was assumed that prophets had written them.

Galilee The northern part of Palestine, specifically the territories north and west of the Sea of Galilee.

Galut (Hebrew for "exile") The term refers to the various expulsions of Jews from the ancestral homeland; over time, it came to express the broader notion of Jewish homelessness and state of being aliens; thus, colloquially, "to be in *galut*" means to live in the diaspora and also to be in a state of physical and even spiritual alienation.

Gemara (Hebrew for "completion") Popularly applied to the Jewish Talmud as a whole, to discussions by rabbinic teachers on Mishnah, and to decisions reached in these discussions; in a more restricted sense, it applies to the work of the generations of the

Amoraim from the third through the fifth centuries C.E. in "completing" Mishnah to produce the Talmuds.

Genealogy A list or family tree of ancestors or descendants; the Priestly history and the Chronicler's history contain extensive genealogies.

Generation A group of people born and living at about the same time, usually reckoned as forty years in the Old Testament; grandparents, parents, and children are three generations.

Genre The term used by literary critics as the equivalent of "type of literature"; the basic genres found in the Hebrew Bible are prose and poetry, with many different subtypes including song, hymn, story, saying, speech, law, genealogy, saga, and history.

Gentiles (Hebrew *goyyim*) In pre-Christian times, non-Jewish peoples; thereafter, non-Jewish and non-Christian (roughly synonymous with *pagan*).

Gibeon A village north of Jerusalem that tricked Joshua and the Israelites into making a treaty with them.

Gideon A judge who delivered the Israelites from the tyranny of the Midianites.

Gilgal A village near Jericho where the Israelites first stopped after they entered the Promised Land.

Gilgamesh epic A Babylonian epic centering on Gilgamesh, ancient king of Uruk; the eleventh tablet of this epic contains a story of a flood that has parallels to the biblical story of Noah and the ark.

Glory of Yahweh The revelation of God's being, nature, and presence to humankind, often through physical or meteorological phenomena.

God The supreme divine being, called Elohim by the Israelites, who was also known as Yahweh.

Gog An eschatological figure, a personification of evil, that battled God's forces in Ezekiel 38–39.

Golden calf A statue constructed by Aaron at Mt. Sinai that the Israelites worshiped; Jeroboam, first king of Israel, built golden calf shrines at Bethel and Dan.

Goliath The Philistine giant who was killed by David.

Gomer The wife of Hosea the prophet who turned out to be unfaithful to their marriage.

Goshen The territory in the eastern Nile delta of Egypt where Joseph settled the family of Jacob.

Grace An undeserved gift or favor; the undeserved attention, forgiveness, kindness, and mercy that God gives.

Habakkuk One of the Twelve Prophets; a sixth-century Judean prophet who sought to understand God's purpose in sending the Babylonians to punish Judah.

Habiru (sometimes spelled *'Apiru*) An Akkadian term denoting persons or groups who were social and political outlaws from established society; existing in the ancient Middle East in the second and first millennia B.C.E., they appear as slaves, merchants, mercenary soldiers, bandits, and outlaws; some scholars link the term to the word *Hebrew*.

Hagar The servant of Sarah and one of Abraham's wives; the mother of Ishmael, who was driven away from the family by Sarah.

Haggada(h) (adj. haggadic; Hebrew for "telling, narration"; sometimes spelled *aggada[h]*) Jewish term for nonhalakic (nonlegal) matter, especially in Talmud and Midrash; it includes folklore, legend, theology, scriptural interpretations, biography, etc.; in a general sense, in classical Jewish literature and discussion, what is not halaka (legal subject matter) is (h)aggada; technically, "the Haggada(h)" is a liturgical manual about the exodus from Egypt in the time of Moses used in the Jewish Passover Seder.

Haggai A prophet who encouraged the Israelites to rebuild the temple after a return from the exile in Babylonia in the sixth century B.C.E.

Halaka(h) (adj. halakic; Hebrew for "going," i.e., how we go about our daily lives) Deals with practical guidance, rules, and expectations in Judaism; any normative Jewish law, custom, practice, or rite—or the entire complex; halaka is law established or custom ratified by authoritative rabbinic jurists and teachers; colloquially, if something is deemed halakic, it is considered proper and normative behavior.

Ham One of the sons of Noah; he abused his father and Canaan, his son, was cursed for it.

Haman The wicked opponent of Mordecai and the Jews in the book of Esther.

Hananiah The Judean prophet who challenged Jeremiah over the issue of the yoke of Babylon.

Hannah The wife of Elkanah and mother of Samuel; she prayed for a son; after Samuel was born she dedicated him to God's service at Shiloh.

Hanukka(h) (Hebrew for "dedication") The Jewish festival of lights that commemorates the rededication of the Jerusalem temple to more traditional modes of Jewish worship by Judah the Maccabee around 164 B.C.E. after its desecration in the time of the Seleucid king Antiochus IV Epiphanes.

Hasid (pl. *hasidism*; Hebrew for "pious one") The term may refer to Jews in various periods: (1) a group that resisted the policies of Antiochus IV Epiphanes in the second century B.C.E. at the start of the Maccabean revolt; (2) pietists in the thirteenth century C.E.; (3) followers of the movement of Hasidism founded in the eighteenth century C.E. by Baal Shem Tov.

Hasmonaean Dynasty Hasmon is the family name of the Maccabees, so the Maccabaean rulers are often referred to as Hasmonaean; the Hasmonaeans included the Maccabees and the high priests and kings who ruled Judea from 142 to 63 B.C.E.

Hazor A city in northern Canaan that resisted the Israelites but was conquered by Joshua.

Hebrew The language of the Old Testament Israelites and the language in which most of the Old Testament/Hebrew Bible was written.

Hebrew Bible The collection of twenty-four books constituting the Old Testament according to the arrangement of the Jewish canon; it can also be referred to as the Tanak; originally written in Hebrew and Aramaic, it is the written canon of Judaism and the first section of the canon of Christianity.

Hebrews Another name for Israelites, usually used in reference to them before they settled in the Promised Land.

Hebron A major city in Judah, the place from which David first ruled; Abraham and many other ancestors were buried here.

Hellenism (adj. hellenistic; Greek for "Greekish") The civilization that spread from Greece through much of the ancient world from 333 (Alexander the Great) to 63 (dominance of Rome) B.C.E.; as a result, many elements of Greek culture (names, language, philosophy, athletics, architecture, etc.) penetrated the ancient Middle East.

Hellenistic Pertaining to Greek culture as disseminated by the conquests of Alexander the Great and the rule of his successors.

Hellenization The process of becoming enculturated by the ideals of Hellenism.

Hermeneutics (from Greek for "to interpret, translate"; hence, "science of interpretation") It denotes the strategy of interpreting texts to enable them to be applied to circumstances contemporary with the interpreter; the term is often used with reference to the study of Jewish and Christian scriptures.

Hexateuch The first six books of the Hebrew Bible; there may be an underlying assumption that these belong together historically.

Hezekiah (715–687) A king of Judah; he restored the temple, reinstituted proper worship, and received God's help against the Assyrians.

High priest The chief religious official in Israel; he offered the most important sacrifices to God on behalf of the people.

Hillel Often called by the title "the Elder"; probably a Babylonian, Hillel was an important sage of the early Jewish period in Palestine around the turn of the era. His teachings convey the Pharisaic ideal through many epigrams on humility and peace (found in *Sayings of the Fathers* 1–2) and were fundamental in shaping the Pharisaic traditions and modes of interpretation. In rabbinic lore, Hillel is famous for a negative formulation of the "golden rule" (recited to a non-Jew): "What is hateful to you do not do to your fellow man. That is the whole Torah, the rest is commentary. Go and learn it"; his style of legal reasoning is continued by his disciples, known as Beit Hillel ("House/School of Hillel"), and is typically contrasted with that of Shammai (a contemporary) and his school.

Historiography The reconstruction of the past based on a critical examination of ancient materials.

Holiness Code Chapters 17–27 of Leviticus, which detail the laws for ensuring, protecting, and promoting holiness (sacredness, separateness).

Holy (adj. holiness) To set apart for God; to belong to God; to be pure.

Holy Spirit (sometimes termed the "Holy Ghost") In Judaism, the presence of God as evidenced in the speech of the prophets and other divine manifestations; in Christianity, understood more generally as the active, guiding presence of God in the church and its members.

Holy war War authorized by God and led by him; Old Testament holy war called for the complete slaughter of the enemy and the dedication of all spoils to God. See Divine warrior.

Hophni He and Phineas were two sons of Eli, the high priest at Shiloh; they died in battle at Aphek–Ebenezer fighting the Philistines.

Horeb The term used in the Elohist and Deuteronomist sources to designate the location where God delivered the commandments and covenant to the Israelites through Moses, apparently the equivalent of Mt. Sinai.

Hosea One of the Twelve Prophets; an eighth-century Israelite prophet who exposed the people's lack of faith in Yahweh.

Hyksos Derived from Egyptian for "rulers of foreign countries," these Semitic rulers of Egypt from 1750–1550 B.C.E. were probably the people in control of Egypt during the sojourn of Joseph and Jacob's descendants.

Hymn A song praising God, the king, Zion, or Torah that contains a description of why the object of praise is wonderful.

Iconography The expression of religious principles or doctrines using pictorial or symbolic images or icons; icons may serve as visual metaphors; a faith that favors this type of expression is called *iconic*.

Image of God Phrase deriving from Genesis 1:26–7; God created humankind in his own image.

Immanuel (sometimes spelled *Emmanuel*) The figure in Isaiah's prophecy (chapter 7), which means "God is with us."

Incense A component in rituals of worship; spices burned on an altar or in a censer to make a sweet-smelling smoke.

Intertestamental period The period in which early Judaism developed, between about 400 B.C.E. (the traditional end date for the Old Testament/Hebrew Bible) and the first century C.E. (the composition of the Christian New Testament); the Jewish intertestamental literature includes the Apocrypha (mostly preserved in Greek) and the Pseudepigrapha (works from this period ascribed to ancient authors like Enoch, the ancestors, and Moses).

Invocation The formula used at the beginning of many psalms that appeals to God and asks him to listen.

Isaac The son of Abraham and Sarah who inherited the ancestral promises; he married Rebekah and was the father of Esau and Jacob.

Isaiah A prophet in Jerusalem in the eighth century B.C.E.; also, the prophetic book that contains the words of Isaiah of Jerusalem, Second Isaiah, and Third Isaiah.

Ishmael The son of Abraham and Hagar; he was not the son of the promise; he and his mother were expelled by Sarah and Abraham.

Israel A secondary name for Jacob; the name of the ten northern tribes who formed the "kingdom of Israel" (alternatives are *Ephraim* and *Samaria*), destroyed in 721 B.C.E.; also used as the name of the Twelve Tribes and for the whole territory occupied by the Israelites, Canaan. Historically, Jews have continued to regard themselves as the true continuation of the ancient Israelite national–religious community; in modern times, it also refers to the political state of Israel. Christians came to consider themselves to be the "true" Israel, thus, also a continuation of the ancient traditions.

J The acronym for the Yahwist source of the Pentateuch.

Jacob The second son of Isaac and Rebekah; he was the twin brother of Esau. His name was changed to *Israel* after he wrestled with God at the Jabbok River; he became the recipient of the ancestral promises, and his twelve sons became the tribes of Israel.

Jacob cycle The narratives of Genesis 25:19–35:29, which revolve around the ancestor Jacob.

Japheth One of the sons of Noah, blessed because with Shem he covered his father's nakedness.

Jebus The Canaanite city conquered by David and made his capital, Jerusalem.

Jehoiachin King of Judah for only three months in 598 B.C.E., he was taken captive to Babylon.

Jehoiakim (609–598) One of the last kings of Judah.

Jehovah An early and mistaken attempt to represent the special Hebrew name for deity, YHWH; a more probable reconstruction of the divine name is Yahweh.

Jehu (843–815) King of Israel who was instrumental in engineering the demise of the house of Ahab.

Jeremiah A prophet in Judah during the Babylonian crisis (late seventh and early sixth centuries B.C.E.); he was persecuted because of his unpopular prophetic statements, including a prediction of the fall of Jerusalem; also, the prophetic book containing his oracles and narratives about him.

Jeremiah's complaints Portions of the book of Jeremiah that express Jeremiah's frustrations and doubts concerning his prophetic calling.

Jericho The first city in Canaan conquered by Joshua and the Israelites.

Jeroboam (922–901) An administrator in Solomon's court who rebelled and became the first king of the northern kingdom of Israel; he built non-Yahwistic shrines in the cities of Dan and Bethel. A king of Israel in the eighth century B.C.E. also held this name and is sometimes referred to as Jeroboam II.

Jerusalem The political and religious capital of Israel when it was united, then of the southern kingdom of Judah; David captured Jebus and made it his capital city, the City of David. Mt Zion is the ridge in Jerusalem on which the royal palace and temple were built; Jerusalem is where Jesus/Joshua was crucified and resurrected.

Jeshua Another spelling of Joshua; Jeshua was the high priest of Judea in the sixth century B.C.E. during the time of Zerubbabel, Haggai, and Zechariah.

Jesus of Nazareth/Joshua (*Jesus* is the Greek attempt to transliterate the Semitic name "Joshua") The Palestinian popular figure from the first century C.E. whose death and resurrection as God's Messiah/Christ became foundational for an early Jewish subgroup known as the Nazarenes, from which Christianity ultimately developed as a separate religion.

Jethro Father of Zipporah and father-in-law of Moses, also called Reuel.

Jew The term applied to the people of God after the Babylonian exile; it is derived from the Hebrew/Aramaic term for Judeans, *jehudi*.

Jezebel The Phoenician wife of Ahab who promoted Baal worship in Israel and opposed Elijah the prophet.

Jezreel A Israelite royal city of the Omride dynasty, the place where Jehu executed Jezebel; it became a byword for Jehu's cruelty, and Hosea named his son Jezreel to signal God's judgment.

Joab David's military commander.

Job A righteous man whom God tested by disaster and personal suffering; in the end God restored his wealth and family; the book of Job, considered a work of wisdom literature, contains the story.

Joel One of the Twelve Prophets; date uncertain but perhaps of the fourth century, a prophet who preached the Day of Yahweh and the pouring out of Yahweh's spirit on everyone.

Jonah An eighth-century B.C.E. Israelite prophet who was called to preach to the Assyrians in Nineveh; the book of Jonah is one of the twelve books of the minor prophets.

Jonathan A son of king Saul, he had a special relationship with David; he was killed by the Philistines on Mt. Gilboa.

Jordan The river that flows from the Sea of Galilee to the Dead Sea; it is the border between Canaan and Transjordan.

Joseph Son of Jacob by Rachel; brother of Benjamin; he was sold into slavery by his brothers and became a high official within the Egyptian government; his sons Ephraim and Manasseh became tribes within Israel.

Joseph cycle The collection of stories centered on Joseph, son of Jacob, contained in Genesis 37–50.

Josephus (also known as Flavius Josephus) The Jewish general and author in the latter part of the first century C.E. who wrote a massive history (*Antiquities*) of the Jews and a detailed treatment of the Jewish revolt against Rome in 66–73 C.E.

Joshua Moses' aide during the wilderness sojourn; after the death of Moses he led the Hebrews into the Promised Land; another figure was called Joshua (sometimes Jeshua), the high priest of the Jerusalem community that rebuilt the temple.

Josiah (640–609) King of Judah who reformed Judean religion and died in battle at Megiddo.

Josiah's reform The religious reform of 622 B.C.E. initiated by Josiah, king of Judah, after the book of the covenant was found in the Jerusalem temple; it is sometimes called the Deuteronomic reform because the book appears to have been an early form of Deuteronomy.

Jubilee (from Hebrew *yovel*, "ram's-horn trumpet") Every fiftieth year was a jubilee (the year following seven-times-seven years, or seven weeks of years); special arrangements during this year were designed to aid the poor and dispossessed.

Judah Jacob's fourth son, he was the ancestor of the tribe of Judah; Judah became the name of the southern kingdom after the northern ten tribes separated from Judah and Benjamin.

Judah the Prince (also known as Judah Hanasi) Head of the rabbinic Jewish community in Palestine around 200 C.E.; credited with publication of the Mishnah.

Judaism From the Hebrew name of the ancestor Judah, whose name also came to designate the tribe and tribal district in which Jerusalem was located; thus, the inhabitants of Judah and members of the tribe of Judah come to be called "Judahites" or, in short form, "Jews"; the religious outlook, beliefs, and practices associated with these people comes to be called "Judaism," and has varying characteristics at different times and places, such as early Judaism and rabbinic Judaism.

Judas the Maccabee A second-century B.C.E. Judean who led the Jewish Maccabean revolt against the Hellenistic Seleucid occupation of Jerusalem and Judea.

Judge In the period of the Judges, a person who held off Israel's enemies—for example, Ehud, Deborah, Gideon, and Samson.

Judges The period of the Judges was between the conquest and the Davidic monarchy when Israelite tribes were settling the land of Canaan; the book of Judges contains the stories of the individual judges.

Kasher, kashrut See Kosher.

Ketuvim (Hebrew for "Writings") The last of the three main divisions of the Hebrew Bible (the *k* of Tanak), including Psalms, Proverbs, Job, the Five Megilloth or Five Scrolls (Song of Songs, Ruth, Lamentations, Ecclesiastes, Esther), Daniel, Ezra, Nehemiah, and Chronicles.

Kingdom of God The realm where God rules; the state of the world in which God's will is fulfilled; expected to be brought into being at the end of time when the Messiah returns.

Kosher (Hebrew, *kasher*, *kashrut* for "proper, ritually correct") Kosher refers to ritually correct Jewish dietary practices. Traditional Jewish dietary laws are based on biblical legislation; only land animals that chew the cud and have split hooves (sheep, beef; not pigs, camels) are permitted and must be slaughtered in a special way; further, meat products may not be eaten with milk products or immediately thereafter. Of sea creatures, only those (fish) having fins and scales are permitted; fowl is considered a meat food and also has to be slaughtered in a special manner.

Laban Rebekah's brother and Jacob's uncle who lived in Aram; Jacob became wealthy there and married his daughters Rachel and Leah.

Lament A cry of pain and grief; in the study of the Psalms, the lament, also called a complaint, is the literary type that expresses a cry of help, either of an individual or the community.

Latter Prophets The technical name for the collection of prophetic writings comprising the books of the three "major" prophets (Isaiah, Jeremiah, Ezekiel) and those of the twelve "minor" (or shorter) prophets, collectively called the Book of the Twelve.

Law See Commandments, Halaka, Oral torah, Ten commandments, Torah.

Leah Daughter of Laban, the first wife of Jacob who had six sons and one daughter.

Legend A general term denoting stories about heroes, usually from the distant past, whose primary intent is not historical accuracy but entertainment, illustration, and instruction; some scholars consider certain of the ancestral accounts in Genesis, some stories of Moses in Exodus, as well as some stories about Elijah and Elisha, to be legends.

Levirate marriage (from Latin *levir* for Hebrew *yabam*, "brother-in-law") A biblical system of marriage in which the *levir* marries his brother's widow (see Deuteronomy 25:5–10).

Levite One descended from Levi, son of Jacob; a member of the tribe of Levi. The Levites took care of the temple but could not serve as priests; only Levites from the family of Aaron could become priests.

Literary criticism (sometimes called *literary critique*) A critical, but not necessarily criticizing or judgmental, examination of a piece of literature that seeks to determine the type of literature it is, as well as its conventions, stylistic techniques, structure, and strategies; in older scholarship, it may mean source criticism.

Liturgy (adj. liturgical) Rites of public worship, usually institutionalized in temple, synagogue, or church tradition.

Lo-ammi A child of Gomer, the wife of the prophet Hosea; the name means "not my people."

LORD (Hebrew *adonay*) This term (note the use of small capital letters) substitutes for God's Hebrew personal name, Yahweh, in most modern translations of the Hebrew Bible.

Lo-ruhamah A child of Gomer, the wife of the prophet Hosea; the name means "no mercy."

Lot The nephew of Abraham who accompanied him to Canaan.

Lots A mechanical means of divination, perhaps similar to dice or drawing straws, that was used to determine God's decision in certain matters; used in the phrase *to cast lots*.

LXX The abbreviation for the Septuagint, the Greek translation of the Hebrew scriptures done in the last centuries B.C.E.

Maccabaean From the period of Judas Maccabaeus (Judah Maccabee) and his brothers, second century B.C.E.

Maccabean revolt The second-century B.C.E. Jewish revolt against Antiochus IV led by the family of Mattathias, including his son Judas the Maccabee, described in 1 Maccabees.

Malachi One of the Twelve Prophets; date uncertain but probably of the fifth century, a prophet who foresaw the return of Elijah.

Manna The food God provided to the Hebrews while they sojourned in the wilderness for forty years.

Marduk The chief god of the Babylonians and patron god of Babylon; he is the hero-god of the Enuma Elish.

Masoretes, Masoretic text (Hebrew for "transmitters," derived from Hebrew *masorah*, "tradition") The Masoretes were rabbis in ninth-century C.E. Palestine who sought to preserve the traditional text of the Bible (hence called the Masoretic text), which is still used in contemporary synagogues; the Masoretes were scholars who encouraged Bible study and attempted to achieve uniformity by establishing rules for correcting the text in matters of spelling, grammar, and pronunciation; they introduced vowel signs, accents (pointing), and marginal notes (*masora*).

Matriarch (from Latin for "first mother") A term used to refer to female ancestors such as Sarah, Rebekah, Rachel, and Leah.

Matzah Jewish unleavened bread used at Passover.

Megillah (pl. *megillot*; Hebrew for "scroll") Usually refers to the biblical scroll of Esther read on the festival of Purim.

Menorah The multi-armed lamp or candelabrum that was used in the tabernacle and temple; a nine-branched menorah is used at Hannukah, while the seven-branched was used in the ancient Temple.

Mesopotamia (from Greek for "between the rivers") The land defined by the Tigris and Euphrates rivers, this is the location of the birth of civilization and the origin of the Israelites; the Israelites interacted with Mesopotamian people throughout their history.

Messiah (from Hebrew *meshiach*; "anointed one"; equivalent to Greek *christos*) Ancient priests and kings (and sometimes prophets) of Israel were anointed with oil; in early Judaism, the term came to mean a royal descendant of the dynasty of David and redeemer figure who would restore the united kingdom of Israel and Judah and usher in an age of peace, justice, and plenty. The messianic age was believed by some Jews to be a time of perfection of human institutions; others believed it to be a time of radical new beginnings, a new heaven and earth, after divine judgment and destruction. The title came to be applied to Jesus/Joshua of Nazareth by his followers, who were soon called *Christians* in Greek and Latin usage.

Mezuzah (pl. *mezuzot*; Hebrew for "doorpost") A parchment scroll with selected Torah verses (Deuteronomy 6:4–9; 11:13–21) placed in a container and affixed to the exterior doorposts (at the right side of the entrance) of observant Jewish homes (see Deuteronomy 6:1–4) and sometimes also to interior doorposts of rooms; the word *shaddai*, "Almighty," usually is inscribed on the container.

Micah One of the Twelve Prophets; an eighth-century Judean prophet who advocated justice for all people.

Michal A daughter of Saul, given in marriage to David; she criticized David's behavior and he refused thereafter to have relations with her.

Midian Territory south of Canaan, of uncertain exact location; perhaps in the Sinai peninsula or western Arabia. Moses' father-in-law Jethro was a priest of Midian; the Midianites afflicted the Israelites during the time of the Judges.

Midrash (pl. *midrashim*; from Hebrew *darash*, "to inquire," whence it comes to mean "exposition" of scripture) The term refers to the "commentary" literature developed in classical Judaism that attempts to interpret Jewish scriptures in a thorough manner. Literary Midrash may focus either on halaka, directing the Jew to specific patterns of religious practice, or on (h)aggada, dealing with theological ideas, ethical teachings, popular philosophy, imaginative exposition, legend, allegory, animal fables, etc.—that is, whatever is not halaka.

Midwife A nurse who helped with the birth of a baby; Shiphrah and Puah were Hebrew midwives who refused to cooperate in Pharaoh's scheme to kill male children.

Millennium (from Latin for "thousand"; adj. millenarian) A thousand-year period; *millenarian* has to do with the expected millennium, or thousand-year reign, of Christ prophesied in the New Testament book of Revelation ("the Apocalypse"), a time in which the world would be brought to perfection; millenarian movements often grow up around predictions that this perfect time is about to begin. See also Apocalypse and Eschatology.

Miriam The sister of Moses and Aaron; she led the Israelites in worship after the crossing of the Red Sea.

Mishnah (Hebrew for "repetition, teaching") A thematic compilation of legal material, in particular, a compilation by Rabbi Judah Hanasi ("the Prince") of laws based ultimately on principles laid down in the Torah; produced aound 200 C.E., it became the most authoritative collection of oral torah. The code is divided into six major units and sixty-three minor ones; the work is the authoritative legal tradition of the early sages and is the basis of the legal discussions of the Talmud.

Mitzvah (pl. *mitzvot*; Hebrew for "commandment, obligation") A ritual or ethical duty or act of obedience to God's will. See also Commandments.

Moab A territory or country located in Transjordan, to the east of the land of Israel; a frequent enemy of the Israelites.

Monarchy Any state ruled or headed by a monarch; Israel and Judah were ruled by monarchies during the period of the kingdoms.

Monolatry The worship of one god while recognizing the existence of others; some scholars describe the religion of Israel as monolatry before the time of the prophets.

Monotheism The belief that there is only one God, and that no other gods even exist. It is unlikely that Israel early in her history construed reality in this way; rather, it seems that they only went so far as to claim Yahweh as their God, the god of Israel, leaving the question of the existence of other gods to later theologians and prophets.

Mordecai The uncle of Esther who looked after her and urged her to do everything in her power to effect the deliverance of the Jews throughout the Persian empire.

Mosaic covenant The covenant Yahweh mediated through Moses, including the Ten Commandments and rules for serving God.

Moses The leader of the Hebrews at the time of the Exodus from Egypt (thirteenth century B.C.E.); he led the people of Israel out of Egyptian bondage; God revealed the Torah to him on Mt. Sinai. He is also described as the first Hebrew prophet; throughout Jewish history he is the exalted man of faith and religious leader without peer.

Mt. Gilboa The location south of the Sea of Galilee where Saul and his sons died while fighting the Philistines.

Mt. Sinai The mountain in the Sinai peninsula where God communicated with Moses and revealed the covenant and Ten Commandments.

Mt. Zion. See Zion.

Myth A story, a theme, an object, or a character regarded as embodying an aspect of a culture; the creation stories in Genesis 1–3 may be called myths, not in the sense that they are factually false, but because they embody core beliefs of Israelite culture.

Nadab and Abihu These two sons of Aaron offered "strange fire" to God, for which they both died.

Nahum One of the Twelve Prophets; a late seventh-century Judean prophet who announced the coming destruction of Nineveh, the capital of the Assyrian empire.

Naomi The Israelite mother-in-law of Ruth.

Nathan David's court prophet who mediated the Davidic covenant and exposed David's transgressions.

Navi (sometimes spelled *nabi*; pl. *neviim*) Term for "prophet" in ancient Israel. See Nevi'im.

Nazirite A person dedicated by a strict vow to do special work for God; elements of the vow could include not cutting hair and refraining from alcohol; Samson lived under a Nazirite vow.

Nebuchadnezzar (605–562) Monarch of the Neo-Babylonian empire who invaded Judah and destroyed Jerusalem in 587.

Nehemiah The Jewish cupbearer of Artaxerxes of Persia in the fifth century B.C.E.; appointed governor of Judea, he rebuilt the walls of Jerusalem after the Babylonian exile.

Nevi'im (sometimes spelled *nebi'im*; Hebrew for "prophets") The second main division of the Hebrew Bible, comprising the Former and the Latter Prophets; the *n* of Tanak. See Tanak.

New covenant A theme of the prophet Jeremiah based on the Mosaic covenant; God would renew the covenant with his people and write it on their hearts.

New exodus A theme of the prophet Second Isaiah based on the exodus from Egypt led by Moses; Second Isaiah anticipated the release of Judean refugees from Babylonian exile in a new act of divine deliverance.

New Testament (abbreviated NT) The collection of Christian canonical writings that together with the Old Testament/Hebrew Bible constitute the Christian Bible. See Apocrypha.

Nineveh The capital city of the Assyrian empire, located on the Tigris river.

Noah He built a boat and survived the Flood with his family and representatives of the animal world; God made a covenant with him promising never again to destroy the world with a flood.

Noahic covenant The covenant God made with Noah promising he would never again send a flood to destroy the world; God signaled the covenant with the rainbow.

Obadiah One of the Twelve Prophets; a sixth-century Judean prophet who condemned Edom for its cruel treatment of conquered Judah.

Offering Something given to God as an act of worship, often animals and grains; the offering of animals made right the relationship between God and the worshiper.

Old Testament (abbreviated OT) The name of the Hebrew Bible used in the Christian community; it presupposes that there is a New Testament. The term *testament* goes back to *testamentum*, the Latin equivalent for the Hebrew word *covenant*. For most Protestant Christians, the Old Testament is identical to the Hebrew Bible; for classical Roman Catholic and Greek Orthodox Christianity, the Old Testament also includes the Apocrypha.

Oracle A statement originating with God, delivered by a prophet, and directed to an audience.

Oral torah (also called *oral law*) In traditional Jewish pharisaic/rabbinic thought, God revealed instructions for living through both the written scriptures and through a parallel process of orally transmitted traditions; these oral applications of the Torah for contemporary situations later took written form in the Mishnah and other Jewish literature. The Jewish belief in both a written and an oral torah is known as "the dual Torah"; critics of this approach within Judaism include the Sadducees and the Karaites.

Oral tradition Material passed down through generations by word of mouth before taking fixed written form.

Original sin In classical Christian thought, the fundamental state of sinfulness and guilt, inherited from the first man Adam, that infects all of humanity but can be removed through depending on Christ.

Orthodox (from Greek for "correct opinion/outlook," as opposed to heterodox or heretical) The judgment that a position is "orthodox" depends on what are accepted as the operative "rules" or authorities at the time; over the course of history, the term "orthodox" has come to denote the dominant surviving forms that have proved themselves to be "traditional" or "classical" or "mainstream" (e.g., rabbinic Judaism; the Roman Catholic and Greek Orthodox Christian churches).

OT See Old Testament.

P The acronym for the Priestly source of the Torah/Pentateuch.

Palestine (Greek form of "Philistine," for the seacoast population encountered by early geographers) An ancient designation for the area between Syria (to the north) and Egypt (to the south), between the Mediterranean Sea and the River Jordan; Canaan; roughly, modern Israel.

Palestinian Judaism The postbiblical form of Judaism that developed in Palestine, distinct from Hellenistic Judaism.

Paraenesis (adj. paraenetic) A sermon or exhortation; Deuteronomy has a paraenetic style.

Parallelism The literary form pervasive in biblical poetry whereby the first line (the A-line) of a couplet is in some way mirrored or doubled in the second line (the B-line).

Passover (Hebrew *pesach*) The major Jewish spring holiday (with agricultural aspects) also known as *hag hamatzot*, "festival of unleavened bread," commemorating the exodus or deliverance of the Hebrew people from Egypt (see Exodus 12–13); the festival lasts eight days, during which Jews refrain from eating all leavened foods and products; a special ritual meal (called the Seder) is prepared, and a traditional narrative (called the Haggadah), supplemented by hymns and songs, marks the event.

Patriarch (from Latin for "first father") The father and ruler of a family; the head of a tribe.

Patriarchs A common designation for the early founding figures of ancient Semitic tradition (before Moses) such as Abraham, Isaac, Jacob, and the twelve tribal figureheads of Israel (Judah, Benjamin, etc.); the patriarchs and matriarchs together are called the forebears or *ancestors* of Israel.

Pentateuch (from Greek for "five scroll jars" it comes to mean "five books/scrolls"; adj. Pentateuchal) Refers to the first five books of the Hebrew Bible traditionally attributed to Moses that together comprise the Torah (the *t* of Tanak): Genesis, Exodus, Leviticus, Numbers, and Deuteronomy; known in Jewish tradition as *Torat Mosheh*, the teaching of Moses.

Pentecost (Greek for "fiftieth [day]") A Jewish feast celebrated fifty days after Passover marking the first fruits of the agricultural year. See Shavuot.

Personification The literary device of portraying an idea or non-human object as a human being.

Perushim (Hebrew for "Pharisees") See Pharisees.

Pesach (Hebrew for "passover") The festival recalling the escape from Egypt in the exodus. See Passover.

Petition A speech form used especially in biblical psalms whereby the psalmist pleads with God for help, deliverance, or forgiveness.

Pharaoh Egyptian term for "great house" that became the generic term for a king of Egypt.

Pharisees (from Hebrew *perushim*, "separatists"; adj. pharisaic) The name given to a group or movement in early Judaism, the origin and nature of which is unclear; many scholars identify them with the later sages and rabbis who taught the oral and written torah. According to Josephus and the New Testament, the Pharisees believed in the immortality of souls and resurrection of the dead, in a balance between predestination and free will, in angels as active divine agents, and in authoritative oral law. In the early Christian materials, Pharisees are often depicted as leading opponents of Jesus/Joshua and his followers, and are often linked with "scribes" but distinguished from the Sadducees.

Philistia Beginning in the twelfth century B.C.E., the territory on the southern Canaanite coastal plain where the Philistines lived.

Philistine An inhabitant of Philistia; the Philistines were the most significant external threat to the Israelites during the time of the Judges and the early monarchy.

Philo Judeus "The Jew" of Alexandria; Greek speaking (and writing) prolific Jewish author in the first century C.E., he provides extensive evidence for Jewish thought in the Greco-Roman ("hellenistic") world outside of Palestine.

Phineas See Hophni.

Phylactery (pl. phylacteries; Greek for "protector") See Tefillin.

Praise (Hebrew *hallelujah* means "Praise Yahweh!") A speech form used extensively in the psalms whereby the psalmist extols the greatness of God.

Priest (Hebrew *kohen*) A functionary usually associated, in antiquity, with temples and their rites; a priest offered sacrifices and prayers to God on behalf of the people. In Israel, only Aaronic Levites could be legitimate priests; in classical Christianity, the office of priest was developed in connection with celebration of the mass and eucharist, and with celibacy as an important qualification especially in Roman Catholicism.

Priestly code The body of legislation in the Pentateuch that comes from the Priestly source.

Priestly source (abbreviated P) A literary source used in the composition of the Torah/Pentateuch; it probably was composed in Babylonia in the sixth century B.C.E.

Primeval story The account of earliest events found in Genesis 1–11.

Primogeniture The state of being the firstborn or eldest child of the same parents; the right of the eldest child, especially the eldest son, to inherit the entire estate of one or both parents; this is an important theme in the Torah/Pentateuch relating to Ishmael and Isaac, Jacob and Esau, and Joseph and his brothers.

Profane To make a holy thing impure by treating it with disrespect or irreverence.

Promised Land Phrase used with a religious and covenantal connotation that designates the territory west of the Jordan River, for the most part coextensive with Canaan.

Prophecy A message from God that a prophet delivers to the people.

Prophesy The act of delivering a prophetic message of God to the people.

Prophet (from Greek for "to speak for, to speak forth") Designation given to accepted spokespersons of God (or their opposites, "false prophets"); a person who speaks in the name of God.

Prophetic eschatology The perspective on the goal and end of history held by Old Testament prophets.

Prophets A designation for the second main section of the Hebrew Bible, called the *Nevi'im*; the *n* of Tanak. See Tanak.

Prostitute A person who allows the use of his or her body for sexual relations in exchange for compensation; Israel was metaphorically compared to a prostitute when it worshiped Baal gods.

Proto-Judaism See Early Judaism.

Proverb A short, pithy saying in frequent and widespread use that expresses a basic truth or practical precept; the book of Proverbs is one of the Writings and is classified as wisdom literature.

Psalter The book of the writings that contains 150 psalms.

Pseudepigrapha (adj. pseudepigraphical; from Greek *pseudos*, "deceit, untruth," and *epigraphe*, "writing, inscription") Intertestamental apocryphal writings purporting to be by somebody (usually a famous historical or legendary figure) who is not the author, such as Adam/Eve, Enoch, Abraham, Moses, Isaiah, Ezra, etc.; the term is sometimes used generically for deutero-canonical writings not in the Apocrypha.

Pseudonymity The practice of ascribing a work to someone, often a notable from the past, who was not the actual author.

Purim (from Hebrew for "lots") A Jewish festival commemorating the deliverance of Jews in Persia who were threatened with genocide, as described in the book of Esther; held in late winter (between Hanukkah and Passover) on the 14th of Adar. See Megillah.

Qohelet (Hebrew term related to the word *qahal*, "gathering, congregation"; translated *ekklesiastes* in Greek) The Hebrew name of the book of Ecclesiastes; the term used of the purported writer of the book of Ecclesiastes.

Qumran (Khirbet Qumran) The site near the northwest corner of the Dead Sea in modern Israel (west bank) where the main bulk of the Jewish "Dead Sea Scrolls" were discovered beginning in 1947; the "Qumran community" that apparently produced the scrolls seems to have flourished from the third century B.C.E. to the first century C.E. and is usually identified with the Jewish Essenes.

Rabbi (adj. rabbinic; Hebrew for "my master") An authorized teacher of the classical Jewish tradition after the fall of the second temple in 70 C.E.; traditionally, rabbis serve as the legal and spiritual guides of their congregations and communities. See Oral torah.

Rabbinic Judaism The Judaism associated with the Pharisees that survived the Jewish revolts against Rome to become the dominant shape of Judaism.

Rachel The daughter of Laban, most loved wife of Jacob, and mother of Joseph and Benjamin.

Ramses II (1290–1224) According to most historians, the king of Egypt at the time of the Hebrews' exodus (thirteenth century B.C.E.).

Rebekah (sometimes spelled *Rebecca*) The sister of Laban, Isaac's wife, mother of Esau and Jacob.

Redaction criticism (sometimes called *redaction critique*) The analysis of a book of the Hebrew Bible to determine the contribution of the editor (called the *redactor*) as he compiled and edited the book from older sources.

Redactor (n. redaction) A synonym for editor of a composite work, the one responsible for choosing and combining source materials into one coherent literary work; redaction is the editorial work of the redactor.

Redeem (Hebrew *go'el*, "redeemer"; n. redemption) To free from captivity or domination by paying a ransom; to buy back.

Rehoboam (922–915 B.C.E.) The son of Solomon who became the first king of Judah after the division of the kingdoms.

Resident alien Also called a *sojourner*, a person who lives in a country but does not hold citizenship; the Old Testament specifies certain rights for resident aliens.

Resurrection The idea that dead persons who have found favor with God will ultimately (in eschatological times) be raised from the dead with restored bodily form.

Retribution theology Punishment for doing wrong; the theology of retribution as found in Deuteronomic theology and in wisdom literature holds that God punishes people for their bad deeds.

Reuel The name of Moses' father-in-law; in some texts he is called Jethro.

Rhetorical criticism (sometimes called *rhetorical critique*) The analysis of a text on the basis of its rhetorical devices; it is similar to literary criticism.

Righteous (n. righteousness) To be one who does what is right; to be in a right relationship with God.

Rosh Hashanah (Hebrew for "beginning of the year") Jewish New Year celebration in the fall of the year, the month of Tishri.

Rosh Hodesh (Hebrew for "beginning of a lunar month") The New Moon Festival.

Royal grant covenant A type of covenant employed by monarchs that essentially consisted of a grant or gift to a faithful underling.

Ruth The Moabite widow who followed her mother-in-law Naomi back to Bethlehem; she married Boaz and was an ancestor of David.

Sabbath (from Hebrew *shabbat*, "to cease, rest") The seventh day of the week, a day of rest and worship; it extends from sunset Friday to sunset Saturday; it was the sign of the Mosaic covenant, and became especially important as an identifier of Jewishness beginning in the Babylonian exile.

Sackcloth A rough cloth, usually woven from goats' hair; clothing made from sackcloth was worn during mourning rituals as a sign of grief and sorrow.

Sacred Applies to holy things, things set apart for God in a special way; sacred is the opposite of profane.

Sacrifice (verb, to offer a sacrifice; noun, an offering given to God to atone for the sins of the people or to establish fellowship with God) Though there are many specific types of sacrifices, typically a sacrificial animal was slaughtered and burned on an altar and its blood was splattered on the altar.

Saddiq (Hebrew for "righteous one"; sometimes spelled *tsaddik* or *zaddik*) A righteous person, the ideal Israelite characterized by wisdom and piety; the spiritual leader of the modern Hasidim is the Saddiq, popularly known as *rebbe*.

Sadducees A group of Jewish leaders, many of them priests, who ruled during the late Second Temple period; Sadducees supported priestly authority and rejected traditions not directly grounded in the Torah/Pentateuch, such as the concept of life after death; they ceased to exist when the temple was destroyed in 70 C.E.

Saga A long, prose narrative having an episodic structure developed around stereotyped themes or object; sagas abound in the primeval and ancestral collections of Genesis.

Samaria Built as the capital of Israel, the northern kingdom, in the ninth century B.C.E.; fell in 721 B.C.E., after which leading members were deported; exiles from elsewhere were settled here and mixed with the Israelites who remained; their descendants are known as Samaritans.

Samaritans Residents of the district of Samaria north of Judah and a subgroup in early Judaism; they are said to have recognized only the Torah/Pentateuch as Scripture and Mt. Gerizim as the sacred center rather than Jerusalem; there was ongoing hostility between Samaritans and Judahites; Samaritan communities exist to the present.

Samson An Israelite judge and strongman who harassed Philistines during the period of the Judges.

Samuel The last judge of Israel and the first prophet, he was also a priest; the son of Hannah and Elkanah, he succeeded Eli as priest, anointing first Saul and then David to be king.

Sanctify (n. sanctification) To make holy.

Sanhedrin (from Greek for "assembly" [of persons seated together]) A legislative and judicial body from the period of early Judaism and into rabbinic times, traditionally composed of seventy-one members. See also Synagogue, Church.

Sapiential (From Latin *sapiens*, "to be wise") Containing or exhibiting wisdom; characterized by wisdom.

Sarah The wife of Abraham; first called Sarai, she was barren until God enabled conception and Isaac was born in her old age.

Satan (from Hebrew for "accuser") In the Old Testament *The Satan* was a member of the Divine Council who challenged God, especially in the books of Job and Zechariah.

Saul (1020–1000) The first king of Israel, he was anointed by Samuel but was later deposed because of disobedience.

Scribe (sometimes called an *amanuensis*, the Greek term for "scribe") A person trained in literacy who copied letters and books, and sometimes trained in the legal tradition; Baruch was Jeremiah's scribe; Ezra was a Jewish-Persian scribe.

Scriptures General designation for canonical or biblical writings.

Second Isaiah (sometimes called *Deutero-Isaiah*) The anonymous author of the book of Isaiah, chapters 40–55.

Second temple The Jerusalem temple rebuilt by Zerubbabel and completed in 515 B.C.E. that stood until it was destroyed by the Romans in 70 C.E.; the first temple was the one built by Solomon, which stood until 587 B.C.E.

Second Zechariah The latter portion (chapters 9–14) of the book of Zechariah dating to the Greek period.

Seder (pl. *sedarim*; Hebrew for "order") The traditional Jewish evening service and opening of the celebration of Passover, which includes special food symbols and narratives; the order of the service is highly regulated, and the traditional narrative is known as the Passover Haggadah.

Seleucid The dynasty of Seleucus, a general of Alexander the Great, that ruled Syria and Asia Minor after Alexander's death. Seleucid rule in Palestine was ended by the Maccabees in the second century B.C.E.

Semitic Pertaining to a race, language, or culture linked to the line of Shem (see Genesis 10); Semitic languages include Hebrew, Aramaic, Arabic, and Akkadian.

Sennacherib (704–681) Monarch of the Neo-Assyrian empire who besieged Hezekiah's Jerusalem in 701.

Septuagint The Greek translation of the Old Testament, consisting of the books of the Hebrew Bible and some deutero-canonical books, now know as the Apocrypha; traditionally dated to the reign of Ptolemy II (285–246), it is abbreviated LXX because it supposedly was translated by about seventy Jewish scholars.

Servant of Yahweh The otherwise anonymous figure of the book of Isaiah (Second Isaiah), who delivered God's people through suffering, variously identified by interpreters as Jeremiah, Zerubbabel, Israel, and Jesus of Nazareth.

Shabbat (Hebrew for "rest") See Sabbath.

Shalmaneser V (726–722) The monarch of the Neo-Assyrian empire who laid siege to Samaria, capital of Israel, thus preparing the way for Israel's destruction.

Shalom Hebrew word for "peace, wholeness, completeness."

Shavuot (sometimes spelled *shabuot*; Hebrew for "weeks"; Pentecost) Observed fifty days after Passover (*pesach*), the day the first sheaf of grain was offered to the priest; it celebrates the harvest and the giving of the Torah; also known as Festival of First Fruits.

Shechem City in central Israel that was the capital of the tribal confederacy during the time of Joshua and the Judges.

Shekel A unit of measure by weight, often used as a monetary designation.

Shem One of the three sons of Noah, he was chosen for special blessing; he was an ancestor of Abraham.

Shema (Hebrew imperative, "Hear!") Title of the Great Commandment, the fundamental, monotheistic statement of Judaism, found in Deut. 6:4 ("Hear, O Israel, the Lord is our God, the Lord is One"); this statement affirms the unity of God and is recited daily in the liturgy (along with Deuteronomy 6:5–9, 11:13–21; Numbers 15:37–41; and other passages) and customarily before sleep at night; this proclamation also climaxes special liturgies (such as Yom Kippur) and is central to the confessional before death and the ritual of martyrdom; the Shema is inscribed on the mezuzah and the tefillin; in public services, it is recited in unison.

Sheol The shadowy underworld to which the departed spirits of the dead go.

Sheshbazzar A prince of Judah who led the first return of Judean refugees from Babylonian exile in 538 B.C.E.

Shiloh The city in central Israel that contained a sanctuary during the time of Eli and Samuel where the ark of the covenant was housed.

Shofar A ram's-horn trumpet; in Jewish worship, a ram's horn sounded at Rosh Hashanah morning worship and at the conclusion of Yom Kippur, as well as other times in that period during the fall.

Sin Transgression or offense against God's laws or wishes; more generally in Christian belief, a continuing state of estrangement from God. See also Original sin.

Sinai The desert region south of Canaan and east of Egypt.

Sitz im Leben A German phrase meaning "setting in life," generally referring to the context of a tradition or ritual.

Sojourn A temporary stay, a brief period of residence; Israel's wilderness sojourn in the Sinai after the exodus lasted forty years.

Solomon (961–922) The son of David and Bathsheba who became the king of united Israel after David; he was renowned for his wisdom; he built the temple of Yahweh in Jerusalem.

Son of Man A phrase found in Daniel 7 that refers to a divine authority figure who has the appearance of a human being; it is also the phrase simply meaning "fellow" used by God throughout the book of Ezekiel to refer to the prophet.

Soul (Hebrew *nefesh*) In the Old Testament this refers to the whole person, including body, psyche, and spiritual identity.

Source criticism (source critique) The analysis of the Hebrew Bible to determine its underlying literary sources. See Documentary hypothesis.

Stanza One of the divisions of a poem, composed of two or more lines, usually characterized by a common pattern of meter, rhyme, and number of lines.

Sukkot (Hebrew for "booths, tabernacles") A seven-day Jewish fall festival beginning on Tishri 15 commemorating the *sukkot* where Israel lived in the wilderness after the exodus; also known as *hag ha'asiph*, the Festival of Ingathering (of the harvest).

Sumer (Sumerians) An ancient region in southern Mesopotamia that contained a number of cities and city–states, some of which were founded as early as 5000 B.C.E.

Superscription The psalm label that may contain musical directions, performance notes, historical setting, and an ascription of authorship.

Suzerain A master or overlord who ruled and protected his vassal clients and to whom they owed allegiance.

Suzerainty treaty (also called *suzerainty covenant*) A formal treaty drawn up to specify the terms of the relationship between a conquered and now client state and the dominating suzerain state.

Synagogue (Greek for "gathering") A place for meeting together that arose after the Babylonian exile; the central institution of Jewish communal worship and study since antiquity, and by extension, a term used for the place of gathering; the structure of such buildings has changed, though in all cases the ark containing the Torah scrolls faces the ancient temple site in Jerusalem.

Syncretism (Greek for "draw together, combine") Synthesis of variegated religious beliefs derived from more than one religion.

Synonymous parallelism A type of poetic parallelism in which the notion of the first line of a couplet is repeated or seconded in the second line.

Syro-Ephraimitic crisis The political crisis of 734–733 B.C.E. when Syria and Israel (also called Ephraim) attacked Jerusalem; the context of the Immanuel prophecy of Isaiah.

Tabernacles, Festival/Feast of See Sukkot.

Talmud (Hebrew for "study, learning") Rabbinic Judaism produced two Talmuds: the one known as "Babylonian" is the most famous in the Western world and was completed around the fifth century C.E.; the other, known as the "Palestinian" or "Jerusalem" Talmud, was edited perhaps in the early fourth century C.E. Both have as their common core the Mishnah collection of the Tannaim, to which were added commentary and discussion (Gemara) by the Amoraim (teachers) of the respective locales; *gemara,* thus, has also become a colloquial, generic term for the Talmud and its study.

Tamar The daughter-in-law of Judah (Genesis 38); the daughter of David (2 Samuel 13).

Tanak (sometimes spelled *Tanakh*) A relatively modern name for the Hebrew Bible; the acronym is composed of the first letters of the three parts of the Hebrew Bible, the Torah (Law), the Nevi'im (Prophets), and the Ketuvim (Writings).

Tanna (Hebrew for "repeater, reciter"; adj. tannaitic, pl. tannaim) A Jewish sage from the period of Hillel (around the turn of the era) to the compilation of the Mishnah (200 C.E.), distinguished from later Amoraim. Tannaim were primarily scholars and teachers; the Mishnah, Tosefta, and halakic Midrashim were among their literary achievements.

Targum (Hebrew for "translation, interpretation") Generally used to designate Aramaic translations of the Hebrew Bible; the Septuagint is, in a sense, Greek Targums.

Tefillin (Aramaic term usually translated as *phylacteries*) Box-like accessories that accompany prayer, worn by Jewish adult males at the weekday morning services; the boxes have leather thongs attached and contain scriptural excerpts; one box (with four sections) is placed on the head, the other (with one section) is placed (customarily) on the left arm, near the heart. The biblical passages emphasize the unity of God and the duty to love God and be mindful of him with "all one's heart and mind" (for example, Exodus 13:1–10, 11–16; Deuteronomy 6:4–9; 11:13–21). See also Shema.

Tell (sometimes spelled *tel*) A mound that contains the ruined remains of a human settlement; each layer or level, called a *stratum*, represents a particular historical period.

Temple A place of worship. In the ancient world, temples were the centers of outward religious life, places at which public religious observances were normally conducted by the priestly professionals. In Israel there were many temples in various locations, but the temple in Jerusalem built by Solomon eventually became the central and only authorized place to worship Yahweh; first built by King Solomon around 950 B.C.E., it was destroyed by the Babylonian king Nebuchadnezzar in 587 B.C.E. and rebuilt about seventy years later; it was destroyed by the Romans in 70 C.E. The site of the ancient Jewish temple is now occupied, in part, by the golden domed Mosque of Omar; in recent times, "temple" has come to be used synonymously with synagogue in some Jewish usage.

Ten Commandments Also called the decalogue; the "ten words" God delivered through Moses that became the heart of the Mosaic covenant; they are found in two versions, Exodus 20:1–17 and Deuteronomy 5:1–21.

Tent of meeting A simple form of the tabernacle used as the place Moses met God during the period of the wilderness sojourn.

Tetragrammaton (Greek for "four lettered [name]") See YHWH.

Tetrateuch The first four books of the Hebrew Bible, Genesis through Numbers; the use of this term implies that these belong together historically as a literary unit.

Textual criticism The study of the earliest texts and early translations of the Hebrew Bible to establish the form of the text that most closely approximates the original text, called the *autograph*; no autograph of any book of the Hebrew Bible has ever been discovered.

Thanksgiving To give thanks to God for his favors; in the study of the Psalms this is a major literary type of psalm that thanks God for individual or corporate deliverance.

Theocracy (adj. theocratic; Greek for "rule of God") A constitution in which God is regarded as ruler or sovereign.

Theodicy (Greek for "justice of God") A term that denotes the issue of God's justice in relation to the problem of human suffering, used often in discussions of the book of Job relating to the attempt to justify God in the face of evil.

Theophany (Greek for "appearance of God") A manifestation or appearance of the divine; for example, when God appears in the burning bush to Moses.

Theophoric An element in a proper name that derives from a name for God; for example, Daniel contains the theophoric component *El*.

Third Isaiah The third main section of the book of Isaiah (chapters 56–66), which dates to the sixth-century period of the restoration of Jerusalem.

Throne-chariot The vehicle carrying Yahweh that the prophet Ezekiel saw while in Babylonia during the exile.

Tiamat The female saltwater ocean goddess who fought Marduk; out of her body were created heaven and earth. The Babylonian name "Tiamat" is related to the Hebrew word for "deep waters," *tehom*.

Tiglath-Pileser III (745–727) Monarch of the Neo-Assyrian empire at the time of Isaiah and the Syro-Ephraimite war.

Toledot (sometimes spelled *toledoth*; Hebrew for "generations") The ten "generations" used in Genesis as a way of structuring the history told in the book.

Torah (Hebrew for "teaching, instruction, direction") In general, Torah refers to study of the whole gamut of Jewish tradition or to some aspect thereof; in its special sense, "the Torah" refers to the "five books of Moses", the first main division of the Hebrew Bible; it is the *t* of Tanak. See Pentateuch and Tanak.

Tradition Teachings and practices that have been handed down as standard and authoritative.

Tradition criticism (sometimes called *tradition critique, tradition history,* or the *traditio-historical method*) The analysis of the Hebrew Bible to uncover possible oral strands underlying the final form of the text; or, the study of the origins and development of a particular biblical theme—for example, the covenant relationship between Yahweh and Israel.

Transjordan The territory east of the Jordan River and west of the Arabian desert; the Israelite tribes Reuben, Gad, and East Manasseh settled there.

Treaty An agreement between two parties; the suzerain–vassal treaties of the ancient Middle East were the model for the covenant relationship God established with the Hebrews at Mt. Sinai.

Twelve, Book of the Sometimes called the minor prophets, a collection of twelve short prophetic books in the Latter Prophets.

Twelve Prophets The twelve prophets whose namesake books constitute the Book of the Twelve; the collection of books of these prophets is included in the Latter Prophets.

Twelve Tribes An ideal form of social and political organization that was believed to characterize early Israel before the monarchy; each tribe was traced back to an ancestor who was one of the sons of Jacob; in fact, the various lists of the tribes in the Hebrew Bible vary—some tribes vanished or were absorbed by others, and other tribes divided into distinct subunits.

Type-scene A typical conventionally structured story.

Typology A form of (usually biblical) interpretation wherein a person, event, or institution is viewed as foreshadowing a later one; for example, for Christian interpreters, Abraham's intended sacrifice of Isaac (Genesis 22) is seen as a "type" of the sacrificial death of Christ.

Unleavened bread (Hebrew *matzah*; pl. *matzot*) Bread baked without leaven or yeast; the festival of unleavened bread, *matzot*, was celebrated in connection with Passover.

Ur An ancient Sumerian and Babylonian city on the Euphrates river in southern Mesopotamia; the home of Abraham before he left for Canaan.

Vassal A servant or slave; an underling who is dependent on an overlord for protection. A vassal received the use of land and military protection from a lord and in return owed the lord loyalty, obedience, and a portion of the crops as payment.

Vaticinia ex eventu A Latin phrase meaning "prophecy from the results" or "prophecy after the event;" it is used in reference to prophecy that has been composed after the events it predicts.

Vow of praise A speech form found in the Psalms where the psalmist promises to credit God with deliverance once it happens.

Vulgate The translation of the Bible into Latin done by the Christian scholar, Jerome, in the late fourth and early fifth centuries C.E.

Wilderness wanderings (also called the *wilderness sojourn*) The forty-year period after the Exodus from Egypt when the Israelites lived in the Sinai peninsula before they entered the Promised Land.

Wisdom A comprehensive term used in reference to the distinctive wisdom literature and wisdom outlook of Israelite, Mesopotamian, and Egyptian cultures; suggests a perspective on understanding the world dominated by the use of reason, a search for order, and teaching moral behavior.

Wisdom literature In the Hebrew Bible, those books of a predominantly didactic (Proverbs) or philosophical (Job, Ecclesiastes) cast; in the Apocrypha, Ecclesiasticus and the Wisdom of Solomon belong to the didactic tradition of wisdom literature.

Writings The third main division of the Hebrew Bible, the *ketuvim*; it is the *k* of Tanak.

Written torah (also called *written law*) See Oral torah.

Yahwist The author of the narrative source in the Torah/Pentateuch that favors the use of the divine name Yahweh. See Yahwist source.

Yahwist source (abbreviated J) A reconstructed literary source lying behind the Torah/Pentateuch, written around 950 B.C.E. in Judah.

YHWH (Yahweh) The sacred name of God in the Hebrew Bible; also known as the *tetragrammaton*. Since Hebrew was written without vowels in ancient times, the four consonants YHWH contain no clue to their original pronunciation; they are generally rendered Yahweh in contemporary scholarship. In traditional Judaism, the name is not pronounced, but *Adonay* ("Lord") or something similar is substituted; in most English versions of the Bible the tetragrammaton is represented by "LORD" (or less frequently, "Jehovah").

Yom Kippur (Hebrew for "Day of Atonement") Annual day of fasting, penitence, and atonement, occurring in the fall on Tishri 10 (just after Rosh Hashanah); the most solemn and important occasion of the Jewish religious year.

Zadok A descendant of Aaron, he was a priest at David's court; he supported Solomon's succession, so his descendants had rights to the chief-priestly duties in the temple.

Zealot Someone zealous for the Torah; in particular, a member of a Jewish group founded, perhaps, by Judas the Galilean in 6 C.E., made up of dedicated political activists that militarily opposed Greek, then Roman, rule in Palestine.

Zechariah A prophet and priest who returned to Jerusalem after Babylonian exile and encouraged the Jews to rebuild the temple; the book of Zechariah contains postexilic visions and divine oracles.

Zedekiah (597–587) The last king of Judah.

Zephaniah One of the Twelve Prophets; a seventh-century Judean prophet who proclaimed the coming Day of Yahweh.

Zerubbabel A member of the royal Davidic line, an heir to the throne of Judah who led a return from Babylonian captivity in the sixth century B.C.E.; he was appointed governor of Judea by Cyrus, king of Persia.

Ziggurat (from Akkadian *ziqquratu*, "pinnacle, mountain top") Of Sumerian origin, a Mesopotamian pyramidal staged-temple tower; the tower of Babel was one.

Zion (also called Mt. Zion) The hill on which the city of Jerusalem first stood. David's royal palace and the temple of Yahweh were both located on Mt. Zion; later Zion was used to refer to the entire city of Jerusalem. Already in biblical times it began to symbolize the national homeland (see, for example, Psalm 137:1–6); in this latter sense, it served as a focus for Jewish national-religious hopes of renewal over the centuries.

Zipporah Wife of Moses, mother of Gershom, dauther of Jethro/Reuel.

BIBLIOGRAPHY

BIBLE VERSIONS

STUDY BIBLES

CONCORDANCES

BIBLE DICTIONARIES AND ENCYCLOPEDIAS

ELECTRONIC RESOURCES

BIBLIOGRAPHIC AIDS

JOURNALS AND PERIODICALS

ARCHAEOLOGY, GEOGRAPHY, AND MAP STUDY

METHODS IN BIBLICAL STUDIES

BIBLICAL COMMENTARIES

THEOLOGY OF THE OLD TESTAMENT/HEBREW BIBLE

HISTORY OF ISRAEL

ANCIENT TEXTS RELATED TO THE OLD TESTAMENT

HISTORY AND CULTURE OF THE ANCIENT WORLD

Each chapter of *Reading the Old Testament* contains bibliographic suggestions **For Further Study**. The following classified bibliography indicates additional resources for studying the historical and literary background of the Old Testament. This bibliography also introduces the main kinds of tools that are accessible to nonspecialists. While sometimes challenging, they generally do not presuppose a knowledge of the Hebrew language. This bibliography does not presume to be exhaustive, but merely indicates starting places for further study.

BIBLE VERSIONS
English translations of the Old Testament/Hebrew Bible come in many "flavors." Some are more literal, which is to say they closely follow the linguistic structure of the original

Hebrew text. Others are less literal and follow the principle of dynamic equivalence, which means they translate the biblical text with equivalent ideas but not necessarily with equivalent vocabulary. Listed in order of publication date, the following are widely used English translations, or *versions,* as they are sometimes called.

The Torah: A New Translation of the Holy Scriptures according to the Masoretic Text (1963). Philadelphia: Jewish Publication Society.

The New English Bible (1970). London: Oxford University Press; New York: Cambridge University Press.

The New American Bible (1971). Camden, N. J.: Thomas Nelson.

New American Standard Bible (1971). La Habra, Calif.: Foundation Press Publications, publisher for the Lockman Foundation.

The Living Bible, Paraphrased (1971). Wheaton, Ill.: Tyndale House.

Good News Bible: The Bible in Today's English Version (1976). New York: American Bible Society.

The Holy Bible, New International Version (1978). Grand Rapids, Mich.: Zondervan.

The Holy Bible, New King James Version (1982). Nashville, Tenn.: Thomas Nelson. This is based on the Authorized Version of 1611, commonly called the King James Bible.

Tanakh: A New Translation of the Holy Scriptures According to the Traditional Hebrew Text (1985). Philadelphia: Jewish Publication Society.

The New Jerusalem Bible (1985). Garden City, N.Y.: Doubleday.

The Holy Bible: New Revised Standard Version (1989). New York: Oxford University Press.

The Revised English Bible with the Apocrypha (1989). New Rochelle, N.Y. : Oxford University Press; Cambridge University Press.

Parallel Bibles combine two or more Bible translations into one volume. They display the versions in parallel columns, facilitating comparison of the translations and helping to identify problem areas in the biblical text.

The Comparative Study Bible: A Parallel Bible Presenting the New International Version, New American Standard Bible, Amplified Bible, and King James Version (1984). Grand Rapids, Mich.: Zondervan.

The Complete Parallel Bible: Containing the Old and New Testaments with the Apocryphal/Deuterocanonical Books: New Revised Standard Version, Revised English Bible, New American Bible, New Jerusalem Bible (1993). New York: Oxford University Press.

The following resources evaluate various translations and narrate the history of translating the Bible into English.

Ackroyd, P. R., and C. F. Evans, eds. (1963–1970). *The Cambridge History of the Bible.* 3 vols. Cambridge: Cambridge University Press.

Bailey, Lloyd R. (1982). *The Word of God: A Guide to English Versions of the Bible.* Atlanta, Ga.: John Knox Press.

Bruce, F. F. (1970). *The English Bible: A History of Translations from the Earliest English Versions to the New English Bible.* New York: Oxford University Press.

Minkoff, Harvey (1988). "Problems of Translations: Concern for the Text Versus Concern for the Reader." *Bible Review* IV(4): 34–40.

STUDY BIBLES

Many publishers have combined modern English translations of the Bible with reading aids. Called study Bibles, they are helpful resources for use in introductory courses and personal Bible study. Typical reading aids include content outlines of the individual biblical books, historical and literary introductions to sections and books, explanatory notes to ideas and vocabulary, and maps. Some study bibles include dictionaries, glossaries, and concordances. Readers should note that the study aids embody interpretations of the biblical text and reflect the perspective of the editors. Choice of a study Bible for personal or class use will depend on one's choice of which translation to use and with which perspective one is most comfortable.

Barker, Kenneth, ed. (1985). *The NIV Study Bible*. Grand Rapids, Mich.: Zondervan Bible Publishers. Based on the New International version.

Scofield, C.I., ed. (1989). *The New Scofield Study Bible: New King James Version: with introductions and outlines, annotations, subject chain references, in-text maps, subject indexes, and concordance*. Nashville, Tenn.: T. Nelson Publishers. From a dispensationalist perspective.

Senior, Donald, ed. (1990). *The Catholic Study Bible*. New York and Oxford: Oxford University Press.

Metzger, Bruce M., and Murphy, Roland E., eds. (1991). *The New Oxford Annotated Bible with the Apocryphal/Deuterocanonical Books*. New York: Oxford University Press. Based on the New Revised Standard version.

Suggs, M. Jack, Sakenfeld, Katharine Doob, and Mueller, James R., eds. (1992). *The Oxford Study Bible: Revised English Bible with the Apocrypha*. New York: Oxford University Press.

Meeks, Wayne, ed. (1993). *The HarperCollins Study Bible: New Revised Standard Version, with the Apocraphal/Deuterocanonical Books*. San Francisco: HarperSanFrancisco.

CONCORDANCES

A biblical concordance contains an alphabetical listing of all significant words in the Bible, along with the locations of their occurrence. Such a tool is essential for doing an inductive study of a biblical theme or topic. Because the Bible exists in distinctive English translations, concordances are based on specific English versions. Lloyd R. Bailey explains the use of a concordance in "What a Concordance Can Do for You: The Bible Word by Word" (1984) in *Biblical Archaeology Review* X(6): 60–67.

Strong, James, ed. (1977; originally published in 1890). *Strong's Exhaustive Concordance of the Bible: With brief dictionaries of the Hebrew and Greek words of the original with references to the English words*. Nashville, Tenn.: Thomas Nelson. Based on the King James version.

Thomas, Robert L., ed. (1981). *New American Standard Exhaustive Concordance of the Bible*. Nashville, Tenn.: A. J. Holman.

Goodrick, Edward W., and John R. Kohlenberger III, eds. (1990). *The NIV Exhaustive Concordance*. Grand Rapids, Mich.: Zondervan.

Kohlenberger, John R. III, ed. (1991). *The NRSV Concordance Unabridged Including the Apocryphal/Deuterocanonical Books*. Grand Rapids, Mich.: Zondervan.

BIBLE DICTIONARIES AND ENCYCLOPEDIAS

Dictionaries and encyclopedias are good places to start when investigating a biblical theme or topic. Entries are arranged alphabetically, and most articles have their own bibliographies. Theological dictionaries contain thematic studies of theologically significant terms. A survey and evaluation of Bible dictionaries can be found in Walter Harrelson (1986), "What Is a Good Bible Dictionary?" *Biblical Archaeology Review* XII(6): 54–61.

Achtemeier, Paul J., ed. (1985). *Harper's Bible Dictionary*. San Francisco: Harper & Row.

Botterweck, G. J., and H. Ringgren, eds. (1974–). *Theological Dictionary of the Old Testament*. Grand Rapids, Mich.: Eerdmans. The entries are arranged alphabetically by

Hebrew word, so this may not be easily used by beginning students, yet the articles are authoritative and contain significant bibliographies.

Bromiley, Geoffrey W., ed. (1979). *The International Standard Bible Encyclopedia*. 4 vols. Grand Rapids, Mich.: Eerdmans.

Buttrick, George A., ed. (1962, 1976). *The Interpreter's Dictionary of the Bible: An Illustrated Encyclopedia*. 5 vols. Nashville, Tenn.: Abingdon.

Elwell, Walter A., ed. (1988). *Baker Encyclopedia of the Bible*. 2 vols. Grand Rapids, Mich.: Baker.

Encyclopaedia Judaica (1971–72). Jerusalem. A comprehensive encyclopedia of Judaism, including the biblical periods.

Freedman, David Noel, ed. (1992). *Anchor Bible Dictionary*. 6 vols. New York: Doubleday.

Metzger, Bruce M., and Michael D. Coogan, eds. (1993). *The Oxford Companion to the Bible*. Oxford; New York: Oxford University Press.

Wigoder, Geoffrey, ed. (1989). *The Encyclopedia of Judaism*. New York: Macmillan.

ELECTRONIC RESOURCES

There are two types of electronic resources for Bible study and research: those that reside on your own personal computer and those you access through the Internet. Personal computer resources include electronic forms of the Bible with concordance features, atlases, and hypertext networks.

BibleWindows includes KJV and RSV texts, as well as the Hebrew Bible, Greek New Testament, Septuagint, and Vulgate. For use on IBM-PC systems. Cedar Hill, Texas: Silver Mountain Software.

BibleWorks for Windows has a range of texts including KJV, ASV, and RSV. For use on IBM-PC systems. Seattle, Wash.: Hermeneutika.

BibleSource for DOS and Windows provides search facilities for a variety of texts including NIV, KJV, NASB, and the Hebrew and Greek texts, each available as an add-on module. For use on IBM-PC systems. Grand Rapids, Mich.: Zondervan.

Logos Bible Study Software for Windows has a base package that includes the KJV text with Strong's numbers, NIV text, and Strong's enhanced dictionary. Add-on modules include NKJV and NRSV texts, Hebrew text, and Greek text. For use on IBM-PC systems. Oak Harbor, Wash.: Logos Research Systems, Inc.

macBible is a modular system with NIV, KJV, NASB, NRSV, Hebrew Old Testament, Greek New Testament, and Septuagint texts available. For use on Apple Macintosh systems. Grand Rapids, Mich.: Zondervan.

TheWORD has a variety of Bible software, including different types of search programs, dictionaries, KJV, NKJV, NRSV, Hebrew, and Greek Bibles. For use on IBM-PC systems. Irving, Texas: WordSoft Software.

The Internet provides access to research resources useful in biblical studies. For example, one can access libraries to do searches of their collections, join electronic discussion groups related to biblical studies, and retrieve documents related to the Bible.

The following Internet conferences are of relevance to Old Testament/Hebrew Bible studies.

ANE-L for the Ancient Near East. Address: ane@oi.uchicago.edu

Ioudaios for first-century Judaism. Address: listserv@yorkvm1.bitnet

J-Seminar for Jewish law and the Bible. Address: listserv@israel.nysernet.org

OT-Hebrew for Hebrew Old Testament. Address: ot-hebrew-request@virginia.edu

A bibliography and guide to electronic resources relevant to religious studies in general, including biblical studies, can be found in a document published electronically called

"The Electric Mystic's Guide to the Internet" (1992) by Michael Strangelove. It can be downloaded from panda1.uottawa.ca (137.122.6.16) in the directory /pub/religion/ as the file electric-mystics-guide-v1.zip (zipped WordPerfect 5.1 text) or as the file electric-mystics-guide-v1.txt (low ascii text). Volume 3, which discusses electronic academic conferences and journals, is also available there.

BIBLIOGRAPHIC AIDS

Bibliographic aids will not themselves help you better understand the Old Testament/Hebrew Bible. Rather, they will help you locate research materials that will. The following volumes are indexes to publications in biblical studies.

Book List. Published once each year by the Society for Old Testament Study, Sheffield, Eng., this contains reviews of recently published books in Old Testament studies.

Elenchus bibliographicus biblicus of Biblica. Rome: Pontifical Biblical Institute Press. An index of periodical literature on biblical books.

Epp, Eldon Jay, ed. (1988–). *Critical Review of Books in Religion*. Atlanta, Ga.: Scholars Press. An annual volume that contains book reviews in Old Testament and Judaism, as well as other areas in religion and theology.

Hupper, William G., ed. (1987–). *Index to English Periodical Literature on the Old Testament and Ancient Near Eastern Studies*. American Theological Library Association Bibliography Series, no. 21. Metuchen, N.J.: Scarecrow Press.

Internationale Zeitschriftenschau für Bibelwissenschaft und Grenzgebiete. International Review of Biblical Studies. Revue Internationale des Études Bibliques. Düsseldorf: Patmos Verlag, 1951/52–. A classified bibliography of periodical articles and chapters in multiauthored books.

Langevin, Paul-Emile, ed. (1972–). *Bibliographie biblique. Biblical bibliography. Biblische Bibliographie. Bibliografia biblica. Bibliografía bíblica*. 3 vols. Quibec: Presses de l'Université Laval. An index of periodical and monographic literature classified by biblical book, chapter, and verse, and by theme.

Old Testament Abstracts. Published by the Catholic Biblical Association, this tool comes out three times a year (three issues make one volume). Each issue contains a listing and brief description of virtually every article published in scholarly journals on an Old Testament topic for the preceding review period (about one-third of a year). They are classified by topics and by books of the Old Testament. The third issue of each volume contains cumulative indexes for the entire volume and includes an index of Bible passages.

The following volumes are research guides for Old Testament study.

Brisman, Shimeon (1977). *A History and Guide to Judaic Bibliography*. Cincinnati, Ohio: Hebrew Union College Press. Describes Hebraic and Judaic bibliographies, including subject bibliographies, bibliographic periodicals, and indexes.

Danker, Frederick W. (1993). *Multipurpose Tools for Bible Study*. Rev. ed. Minneapolis: Augsburg/Fortress.

Fitzmyer, Joseph A. (1990). *An Introductory Bibliography for the Study of Scripture*. 3d ed. Rome: Pontifical Biblical Institute.

Zannoni, Arthur E. (1992). *The Old Testament: A Bibliography*. Collegeville, Minn.: Liturgical Press.

Religion Index One: Periodicals (1977–), *Religion Index Two: Multi-Author Works* (1976–), and *Index to Book Reviews in Religion* (1986–) are produced by the American Theological Library Association (Chicago) and cover biblical studies as well as the field of religion more broadly. All three indexes are currently available on CD-ROM.

JOURNALS AND PERIODICALS

Scholars who do research on the Old Testament/Hebrew Bible publish their results in professional journals so others can make use of their findings. Most journals also contain reviews of recently published scholarly books. The following periodicals related to the Old Testament are those most commonly found in college, university, and seminary libraries.

Journal for the Study of the Old Testament, as well as its New Testament counterpart, *Journal for the Study of the New Testament*, contains articles that mostly address literary and theological issues. *Journal of Biblical Literature* contains articles on both Old and New Testament and some Judaic literature. The articles tend to be somewhat technical and can cover literary, linguistic, theological, and historical issues. In the same vein but often more technical are *Vetus Testamentum* and *Biblica*. *The Catholic Biblical Quarterly* contains scholarly articles on both Old and New Testaments. *Zeitschrift für die alttestamentliche Wissenschaft*, translatable as *Journal for Old Testament Science*, is published in Germany but often contains articles in English. *Biblical Archaeology Review* is a periodical meant for a nonspecialist audience rather than a journal for scholars. It is "glossy" with full-color photographs and illustrations and contains articles that explain the significance of recent archaeological finds. Though not a technical journal and sometimes bordering on the sensationalistic, most of its articles are written by scholar-specialists. The companion periodical, *Bible Review*, contains interpretive articles covering biblical themes and texts.

ARCHAEOLOGY, GEOGRAPHY, AND MAP STUDY

A knowledge of geography in relation to history is essential for understanding biblical events. Collections of maps and studies of historical geography are collected in atlases and related works.

Aharoni, Yohanan (1979). *The Land of the Bible: A Historical Geography*. 2d ed. Philadelphia: Westminster..

Aharoni, Yohanan (1982). *The Archaeology of the Land of Israel*. Philadelphia: Westminster.

Aharoni, Yohanan, and Michael Avi-Yonah (1993). *The Macmillan Bible Atlas*. 3d ed. New York: Macmillan. A text-oriented atlas with maps keyed to specific narratives, providing geographical background to selected biblical stories.

Beitzel, Barry (1987). *The Moody Atlas of Bible Lands*. Chicago: Moody Press.

Gilbert, Martin (1976). *Jewish History Atlas*. 2nd ed. London: Weidenfeld and Nicolson.

Lance, H. Darrell (1981). *The Old Testament and the Archaeologist*. Philadelphia: Fortress.

Laney, J. Carl (1988). *Baker's Concise Bible Atlas: A Geographical Survey of Bible History*. Grand Rapids, Mich.: Baker.

May, Herbert G. (1985). *Oxford Bible Atlas*. 3d ed. London and New York: Oxford University Press.

Mazar, Amihai (1992). *Archaeology of the Land of the Bible, 10,000–586 B.C.E.* New York: Doubleday.

Pritchard, James B., ed. (1987). *The Times Atlas of the Bible*. New York: Times Books.

Pritchard, James B. (1991). *The Harper Atlas of the Bible*. San Francisco: HarperCollins.

Rasmussen, Carl (1989). *The Zondervan NIV Atlas of the Bible*. Grand Rapids, Mich.: Zondervan.

Stern, Ephraim, ed. (1993). *The New Encyclopedia of Archaeological Excavations in the Holy Land*. 4 vols. Jerusalem: Israel Exploration Society & Carta; New York: Simon & Schuster.

METHODS IN BIBLICAL STUDIES

The following books provide general introductions to biblical criticism and interpretive methodologies.

Barton, John (1984). *Reading the Old Testament: Method in Biblical Study*. Philadelphia: Westminster.

Coggins, R. J., and J. L. Houlden, eds. (1990). *Dictionary of Biblical Interpretation*. London: SCM Press ; Philadelphia: Trinity Press International.

Goldingay, John (1990). *Approaches to Old Testament Interpretation*. Rev. ed. Downers Grove, Ill.: InterVarsity.

Hayes, John H., and Carl R. Holladay (1987). *Biblical Exegesis: A Beginner's Handbook*. Rev. ed. Atlanta, Ga.: John Knox.

Knight, Douglas A., and Gene M. Tucker, eds. (1985). *The Hebrew Bible and Its Modern Interpreters*. Philadelphia: Fortress.

McKenzie, Steven L., and Stephen R. Haynes (1993). *To Each Its Own Meaning: An Introduction to Biblical Criticisms and Their Applications*. Louisville, Ky.: Westminster/John Knox.

Morgan, Robert, and John Barton (1988). *Biblical Interpretation*. New York: Oxford University Press.

Soulen, Richard N. (1981). *Handbook of Biblical Criticism*. 2d ed. Atlanta, Ga.: John Knox.

Stuart, Douglas (1984). *Old Testament Exegesis: A Primer for Students and Pastors*. 2d ed. Philadelphia: Westminster.

The following books provide more elaborate treatments of specific methods and interpretive approaches.

LITERARY CRITICISM

Note that there are two distinctly different types of so-called literary criticism of the Hebrew Bible. An older method discerns the underlying literary sources of biblical documents and is sometimes called source criticism (see Habel, below). A newer method of literary analysis, sometimes called new literary criticism, examines biblical texts to elucidate their literary features, such as plot, structure, and artistic devices (see especially Alter and Powell, below).

Alter, Robert (1981). *The Art of Biblical Narrative*. New York: Basic Books. A very influential book that engages in a close reading of biblical texts, mostly from Genesis, in the mode of the "new criticism."

Alter, Robert (1992). *The World of Biblical Literature*. New York: Harper and Row.

Alter, Robert, and Frank Kermode, eds. (1987). *The Literary Guide to the Bible*. Cambridge: Harvard University Press. A collection of essays written by a variety of scholars that attempts to provide a literary synthesis of all the books of the Old and New Testaments.

Exum, Cheryl J., and David J. A. Clines, eds. (1993). *The New Literary Criticism and the Hebrew Bible*. Sheffield, Eng.: JSOT Press.

Gabel, John B., and Charles B. Wheeler (1990). *The Bible as Literature: An Introduction*. 2d ed. New York: Oxford University Press.

Habel, Norman C. (1971). *Literary Criticism of the Old Testament*. Philadelphia: Fortress.

Longman, Tremper, III. (1987). *Literary Approaches to Biblical Interpretation*. Grand Rapids, Mich.: Zondervan.

Minor, Mark (1992). *Literary-Critical Approaches to the Bible: An Annotated Bibliography*. West Cornwall, Conn.: Locust Hill Press.

Powell, Mark Allan (1990). *What is Narrative Criticism?* Minneapolis: Fortress.

Powell, Mark Allan (1992). *The Bible and Modern Literary Criticism: A Critical Assessment and Annotated Bibliography*. New York: Greenwood Press.

Preminger, Alex, and Edward L. Greenstein, eds. (1986). *The Hebrew Bible in Literary Criticism*. New York: Ungar.

Ryken, Leland, and Tremper Longman III, eds. (1993). *A Complete Literary Guide to the Bible*. Grand Rapids, Mich.: Zondervan.

FORM-CRITICISM

Koch, Klaus (1969). *The Growth of the Biblical Tradition: The Form-Critical Method*. New York: Charles Scribner's Sons.

Lohfink, Gerhard (1979). *The Bible: Now I Get It! A Form-Critical Handbook*. Garden City, N.Y.: Doubleday.

Tucker, Gene M. (1971). *Form Criticism of the Old Testament*. Philadelphia: Fortress.

The series *The Forms of the Old Testament Literature* published by Eerdmans is a multivolume form-critical examination of the Hebrew Bible book by book.

TRADITION-HISTORY

Jeppesen, Knud, and Benedikt Otzen, eds. (1984). *The Productions of Time. Tradition History in Old Testament Scholarship*. Sheffield, Eng.: Almond Press.

Knight, Douglas K., ed. (1977). *Tradition and Theology in the Old Testament*. Philadelphia: Fortress.

Rast, Walter E. (1972). *Tradition History and the Old Testament*. Philadelphia: Fortress.

CANON CRITICISM

Central to our study of the Hebrew Bible has been an awareness of the dynamics of the relationship between the biblical text and the community that produced it (and was shaped by early forms of it). Brevard Childs and James Sanders are two important figures in the development of a perspective that sees this relationship as vital to understanding the Old Testament/Hebrew Bible, an approach sometimes called *canon criticism*. A growing body of literature comes out of this perspective, though certainly not all the authors cited below would necessarily want to be identified with the approach of canon criticism, strictly speaking. What follows is a bibliography of some of the more important and accessible works dealing broadly with this approach, both advocating it and critiquing it.

Barr, James (1983). *Holy Scripture: Canon, Authority, Criticism*. Philadelphia: Westminster Press. A thoroughgoing critique of the canonical approach.

Barton, John (1988). *Oracles of God: Perceptions of Ancient Prophecy in Israel after the Exile*. New York: Oxford University Press. Deals with the canon and how prophets and prophecy were perceived after the exile.

Beckwith, R. (1985). *The Old Testament Canon of the New Testament Church*. Grand Rapids, Mich.: Eerdmans. Describes the canon as it existed in the first century C.E. Suggests that the canon of Jesus was the same as the canon of Protestantism.

Childs, Brevard S. (1970). *Biblical Theology in Crisis*. Philadelphia: Westminster. A critique of the biblical theology movement, with a sketch of a new canonical approach.

Childs, Brevard S. (1979). *Introduction to the Old Testament as Scripture*. Philadelphia: Fortress. A massive work containing an outline of a canonical reading of each book of the Old Testament.

Childs, Brevard S. (1985). *Old Testament Theology in a Canonical Context*. Philadelphia: Fortress. Short chapters on theological concepts from a canonical perspective.

Childs, Brevard S. (1993). *Biblical Theology of the Old and New Testaments: Theological Reflection on the Christian Bible*. Minneapolis: Fortress.

Fishbane, Michael (1985). *Biblical Interpretation in Ancient Israel*. Oxford: Clarendon Press. A technical examination of inner biblical exegesis; that is, how certain texts of the Hebrew Bible either quote or allude to earlier traditions, and reshape those traditions.

Kugel, James L., and Rowan A. Greer (1986). *Early Biblical Interpretation*. Philadelphia: Westminster.

Leiman, Sid Z. (1976). *The Canonization of Hebrew Scripture: The Talmudic and Midrashic Evidence*. Hamden, Conn.: Archon. Differs with the old view that the Jamnia conference was the occasion of canonization.

Levenson, Jon (1993). *The Hebrew Bible, The Old Testament, and Historical Criticism. Jews and Christians in Biblical Studies*. Louisville, Ky.: Westminster/John Knox. Focuses on the relationship between Judaism and Christianity, and the community responsible for the canonization, preservation, and interpretation of the Hebrew Bible.

Sanders, James A. (1972). *Torah and Canon*. Philadelphia: Fortress Press.

Sanders, James A. (1984). *Canon and Community: A Guide to Canonical Criticism*. Philadelphia: Fortress.

Sanders, James A. (1987). *From Sacred Story to Sacred Text*. Philadelphia: Fortress Press. Sander's collected writings on the canon.

Tucker, Gene M., David L. Petersen, and Robert R. Wilson, eds. (1988). *Canon, Theology, and Old Testament Interpretation*. Philadelphia: Fortress Press. A collection of essays applying the canonical approach.

SOCIOLOGICAL ANALYSIS

Kirkpatrick, P. G. (1988). *The Old Testament and Folklore Study*. JSOT Supplement Series 62. Sheffield, Eng.: JSOT Press.

Matthews, Victor H. (1991). *Manners and Customs in the Bible*. Peabody, Mass.: Hendrickson.

Matthews, Victor H., and Don C. Benjamin (1993). *Social World of Ancient Israel 1250–587 B.C.E.* Peabody, Mass.: Hendrickson.

Niditch, Susan (1993). *Folklore and the Hebrew Bible*. Minneapolis: Fortress.

Wilson, Robert R. (1984). *Sociological Approaches to the Old Testament*. Philadelphia: Fortress.

Wright, Christopher J. H. (1990). *God's People in God's Land: Family, Land, and Property in the Old Testament*. Grand Rapids, Mich.: Eerdmans.

FEMINIST INTERPRETATION

Laffey, Alice L. (1988). *An Introduction to the Old Testament: A Feminist Perspective*. Philadelphia: Fortress. Surveys the Old Testament with a special interest in stories and issues that have a particular focus on feminist issues.

Meyers, Carol L. (1988). *Discovering Eve: Ancient Israelite Women in Context*. New York: Oxford University Press.

Newsom, Carol A., and Sharon H. Ringe, eds. (1992). *The Women's Bible Commentary*. Louisville, Ky.: Westminster/John Knox. A one-volume commentary on the Old and New Testaments that is especially attentive to features in the biblical text that bear on women's issues.

BIBLICAL COMMENTARIES

A Bible commentary typically covers a book of the Bible chapter by chapter and verse by verse. It explains difficulties in the text and interprets the meaning. Commentaries are a good place to start if you are asked to write an interpretive paper on a biblical passage.

The following one-volume commentaries treat all the books of the Bible, Old and New Testaments combined.

Brown, Raymond E., ed. (1968). *The Jerome Biblical Commentary*. Englewood Cliffs, N. J.: Prentice-Hall Roman Catholic.

Elwell, W.A., ed. (1989). *Evangelical Commentary on the Bible*. Grand Rapids, Mich.: Baker. Evangelical Protestant.

Mays, James L., ed. (1988). *Harpers' Bible Commentary*. San Francisco: Harper & Row. American higher-critical scholarship.

Many major publishers have sponsored biblical commentary projects. Typically, individual volumes are devoted to a single book of the Bible. Within a commentary series a host of different writers are responsible for the volumes, but there is usually a common perspective or purpose that all the volumes share.

Ackroyd, Peter et al., eds. (1961–). *Old Testament Library*. Philadelphia: Westminster. American and German works in the critical tradition.

Ackroyd, Peter A., R.C. Leaney, and J.W. Packer, eds. (1971–1979). *The Cambridge Bible Commentary*. Cambridge University Press. British critical scholarship, based on the New English Bible.

Albright, William F., and David N. Freedman, eds. (1964–). *The Anchor Bible*. Garden City, N.Y.: Doubleday. Mainstream American higher-critical scholarship.

Cross, Frank M. et al., eds. (1974–). *Hermeneia*. Philadelphia: Fortress. Technical, higher-critical, many volumes are translations of outstanding German commentaries.

Gibson, J.C.L., ed. (1981–). *The Daily Study Bible*. Philadelphia: Westminster. Generally conservative, mainly British scholars.

Harrison, R.K., ed. (1976–). *New International Commentary on the Old Testament*. Grand Rapids, Mich.: Eerdmans. Evangelical Protestant, scholarly yet readable.

Mays, James L., ed. (1982–). *Interpretation*. Atlanta, Ga.: John Knox. Moderately critical, the volumes emphasize contemporary connections.

Motyer, J.A., ed. (1976–). *The Bible Speaks Today*. Downers Grove, Ill.: InterVarsity Press. British Evangelical Christian.

Sarna, Nahum, ed. (1989–). *Jewish Publication Society Torah Commentary*. Philadelphia: Jewish Publication Society. Modern Jewish scholarship.

Stuhlmueller, Carroll, and Martin McNamara, eds. (1981–). *Old Testament Message. A Biblical-Theological Commentary*. Wilmington, Del.: Michael Glazier. Roman Catholic.

Watts, John D.W., ed. (1983–). *Word Biblical Commentary*. Waco, Texas: Word. Evangelical Christian.

Our textbook includes bibliographies for the individual books of the Old Testament/Hebrew Bible at the end of each chapter. Outstanding commentaries on the individual books are included there. A complete bibliography of commentaries on the Old Testament would be unmanageable here. For help in locating commentaries, see the following books, which contain listings of commentaries as well as evaluations of individual volumes.

Childs, Brevard S. (1977). *Old Testament Books for Pastor and Teacher*. Philadelphia: Westminster.

Goldingay, John (1981). *Old Testament Commentary Survey*. 2d ed. Madison, Wis.: Theological Students Fellowship.

Guides to Biblical Scholarship: Old Testament Guides (1983–). Sheffield, Eng.: JSOT Press. These research guides to individual biblical books contain surveys of commentaries as well as discussions of major interpretive issues.

Longman, Tremper III (1991). *Old Testament Commentary Survey*. Grand Rapids, Mich.: Baker.

THEOLOGY OF THE OLD TESTAMENT/HEBREW BIBLE

Clements, R. E. (1976). *Old Testament Theology: A Fresh Approach*. Atlanta, Ga.: John Knox. Modern British scholarship.

Hasel, Gerhard (1982). *Old Testament Theology: Basic Issues in the Current Debate*. 3d ed. Grand Rapids, Mich.: Eerdmans.

Hayes, John H., and Frederick Prussner (1985). *Old Testament Theology: Its History and Development*. Atlanta, Ga.: John Knox. A history of the discipline of Old Testament theology.

Levenson, Jon (1985). *Sinai and Zion: An Entry into the Jewish Bible*. San Francisco: Harper & Row. Jewish theological approach.

Martens, Elmer A. (1981). *God's Design: A Focus on Old Testament Theology*. Grand Rapids, Mich.: Baker. Evangelical Christian.

Ollenburger, Ben C., Elmer A. Martens, and Gerhard F. Hasel, eds. (1992). *The Flowering of Old Testament Theology: A Reader in Twentieth-Century Old Testament Theology, 1930–1990*. Winona Lake, Ind.: Eisenbrauns. Classic essays from major Old Testament theologians.

Rad, Gerhard von (1962–65). *Old Testament Theology*. 2 vols. The tradition-historical approach at its best.

Smith, Ralph L. (1993). *Old Testament Theology: Its History, Method, and Message*. Nashville, Tenn.: Broadman & Holman. Evangelical Christian.

Westermann, Claus (1982). *Elements of Old Testament Theology*. Atlanta, Ga.: John Knox. Contemporary German Christian scholarship.

HISTORY OF ISRAEL

Ahlstrom, Gosta (1993). *The History of Ancient Palestine*. Minneapolis: Augsburg/Fortress.

Bright, John (1981). *A History of Israel*. 3d ed. Philadelphia: Westminster. Stands in the American tradition of biblical scholarship associated with W. F. Albright and G. E. Wright; takes an optimistic view of the Hebrew Bible's historical accuracy and scholars' ability to reconstruct history.

Coote, Robert B. (1990). *Early Israel: A New Horizon*. Minneapolis: Augsburg/Fortress.

Hayes, John H., and J. Maxwell Miller (1986). *A History of Ancient Israel and Judah*. Philadelphia: Westminster.

Hayes, John H., and J. Maxwell Miller, eds. (1990). *Israelite and Judean History*. London: SCM Press; Philadelphia: Trinity Press International.

Herrmann, Siegfried (1975). *A History of Israel in Old Testament Times*. Philadelphia: Fortress.

Krentz, Edgar (1975). *The Historical-Critical Method*. Philadelphia: Fortress.

Miller, J. Maxwell (1976). *The Old Testament and the Historian*. Philadelphia: Fortress.

Shanks, Herschel, ed. (1988). *Ancient Israel: A Short History from Abraham to the Roman Destruction of the Temple*. Washington, D.C.: Biblical Archaeology Society.

ANCIENT TEXTS RELATED TO THE OLD TESTAMENT

Many ancient texts from Mesopotamia, Asia Minor, and Egypt are useful for providing background information for bibical studies. Many of these texts have been discovered only recently as a result of archaeological excavations. The texts provide various kinds of illumination. Some texts provide historical information that supplements our knowledge of biblical history. Some texts have literary parallels to biblical texts and can help us understand literary genres. Some texts help us reconstruct the religion and culture of ancient peoples with whom the Israelites had contact.

Beyerlin, Walter, ed. (1978). *Near Eastern Religious Texts Relating to the Old Testament.* Philadelphia: Westminster.

Dalley, Stephanie (1989). *Myths from Mesopotamia: Creation, The Flood, Gilgamesh, and others.* New York: Oxford University Press.

Foster, Benjamin R. (1993). *Before the Muses: An Anthology of Akkadian Literature.* 2 vols. Bethesda, Md.: CDL Press.

Jacobsen, Thorkild (1987). *The Harps That Once . . . Sumerian Poetry in Translation.* New Haven, Conn.: Yale University Press.

Lichtheim, Miriam (1973–1980). *Ancient Egyptian Literature: A Book of Readings.* 3 vols. Berkeley: University of California Press.

Matthews, Victor H., and Don C. Benjamin (1991). *Old Testament Parallels: Laws and Stories from the Ancient Near East.* New York: Paulist Press.

Pritchard, James B., ed. (1969). *Ancient Near Eastern Texts Relating to the Old Testament.* 3d ed. with Supplement. Princeton, N.J.: Princeton University Press. Also available in two paperback volumes, *The Ancient Near East Volume I* (1958) and *Volume II* (1975). This is the standard collection of ancient documents in translation that bear on biblical interpretation.

Simpson, William K., ed. (1972). *The Literature of Ancient Egypt: An Anthology of Stories, Instructions, and Poetry.* New Haven, Conn.: Yale University Press. Groups the documents by literary type.

Smelik, Klaas A. D. (1991). *Writings from Ancient Israel: A Handbook of Historical and Religious Documents.* Louisville, Ky.: Westminster/John Knox Press. Translation and commentary of significant Palestinian inscriptions that enlarge our understanding of the biblical period.

Thomas, D. Winton, ed. (1958). *Documents from Old Testament Times.* London and New York: T. Nelson.

HISTORY AND CULTURE OF THE ANCIENT WORLD

Bottéro, J. (1992). *Mesopotamia: Writing, Reasoning, and the Gods.* Chicago: University of Chicago Press.

Cambridge Ancient History (1970–). 8 vols. 3d ed. London: Cambridge University Press.

Dandamaev, M. A., and V. G. Lukonin (1989). *The Culture and Social Institutions of Ancient Iran.* Cambridge: Cambridge University Press.

Hallo, William W., and William K. Simpson (1971). *The Ancient Near East: A History.* New York: Harcourt, Brace, Jovanovich.

Jacobsen, Thorkild (1976). *The Treasures of Darkness: A History of Mesopotamian Religion.* New Haven, Conn.: Yale University Press.

Kramer, Samuel Noah (1963). *The Sumerians.* Chicago: University of Chicago Press.

Oppenheim, A. Leo (1977). *Ancient Mesopotamia: Portrait of a Dead Civilization.* 2d ed. Chicago: University of Chicago Press.

Roaf, Michael, and N. Postgate, eds. (1990). *Cultural Atlas of Mesopotamia and the Ancient Near East.* New York and Oxford: Facts on File. Richly illustrated with photographs and charts to visualize the material culture and history of the ancient world.

Roux, Georges (1980). *Ancient Iraq.* 2d ed. Baltimore: Johns Hopkins University Press.

Saggs, H. W. F. (1989). *Civilization before Greece and Rome.* New Haven, Conn.: Yale University Press.

Soden, Wolfram von (1993). *Introduction to the Ancient World. The Background of the Ancient Orient.* Grand Rapids, Mich.: Eerdmans. Focuses on the cultures of Sumer, Babylonia, and Assyria from earliest times to the period of Hellenization. Covers the history of language and systems of writing, the state and society, nutrition and agriculture, artisanry, and trade and commerce.

Wiseman, D. J., ed. (1973). *Peoples of Old Testament Times.* Oxford: Clarendon Press. A collection of essays on the peoples who interacted with Israel during the Old Testament period.

ABBREVIATIONS

AB	Anchor Bible
ABRL	Anchor Bible Reference Library
ANET	J. Pritchard, ed., *Ancient Near Eastern Texts Relating to the Old Testament* (Princeton University Press)
ASV	American Standard Version
B.C.E.	Before the Common Era
BAR	*Biblical Archaeology Review*
BZAW	Beihefte zur *Zeitschrift für die alttestamentliche Wissenschaft*
c.	circa, "about," used to indicate an approximate date
C.E.	Common Era
ITC	International Theological Commentary
JSOT	*Journal for the Study of the Old Testament*
KJV	King James Version
NASV	New American Standard Version
NEB	New English Bible
NICOT	New International Commentary on the Old Testament
NIV	New International Version
NRSV	New Revised Standard Version
NT	New Testament
OBT	Overtures to Biblical Theology
OT	Old Testament
OTS	Oudtestamentische Studien
SBL	Society of Biblical Literature
SJLA	Studies in Judaism and Late Antiquity
SVT	Supplements to *Vetus Testamentum*
TC	Torah Commentary
TOTC	Tyndale Old Testament Commentary
ZAW	*Zeitschrift für die alttestamentliche Wissenschaft*

INDEX OF BIBLICAL PASSAGES

Index of Names and Terms

Judah, 15, 27, 103, 104, 259, 279
Judaism, 342
Judas Maccabee, 19, 477, 507
Judge, 232
Judgement day, 381
Judges, 13, 231–247
  map, 244
  time line, 233
Judicial wisdom, 426
Justice, 366

Kadesh, 157, 211
Kafka, Franz, 439
Kaufmann, Yehezkel, 196
Ketuvim, 397
ketuvim, 3
King, 470
Kingdom of God, 415, 477
Kings, 272–294
  time line, 274
Kingship, 241, 250, 255, 256
Kingu, 63, 64
Kiriath-yearim, 253, 264
Kish, 462
Kline, Meredith, 178
Korah, 152, 160, 409
Kosher, 151, 475
Kugel, James L., 406

Laban, 90
Lachish, 291
Lady Wisdom, 432
Lambert, W. G., 69, 439
Lamech, 46, 48
Lament, 409, 411
Lament meter, 405
Lamentations, 454, 455
Lampstand, 142
Land, theme of, 100
Lang, Bernhard, 433
Lasine, Stuart, 439
Latter Prophets, 204, 298
Law, 3
Law, book of the, 290
Law of retaliation, 140
Leadership, 251
Letter to the exiles, 335
Levenson, Jon, 317, 353
Levi, tribe of, 152, 153, 279
Leviathan, 43, 65, 438
Levine, Baruch, 153
Levite(s), 29, 30, 138, 153, 156, 221, 490
Leviticus, 148–156
lex talionis, 140
Life, tree of, 152
Literary criticism, 7–8
Literary history, 10
Literary sources, time line, 32

Liturgy psalms, 417
Lo-ammi, 369
Lo-ruhamah, 369
Longman, Tremper, 456
LORD, 14, 25
Lord's Supper, 122, 136
Lot(s), 216, 461
Lotan, 43
Ludlul Bel Nemeqi, 439
LXX, 4

Maccabean revolt, 476, 510
MacLeish, Archibald, 439
Magog, 354
Maher-shalal-hash-baz, 311
Malachi, 380
Manasseh, 17, 274, 290, 327
Manna, 157, 213
Marduk, 51, 62–65, 462
Marriage, 42
mashiach, 255
Matriarchs, 12
Mattathias, 509
Matter, E. Ann, 450
Maxims of Ptahhotpe, 434
McKane, William, 430
Medad, 158
Medo-Persian empire, 11
Megiddo, 291, 330
Megiddo ivory, 237
Mendenhall, George, 178, 223
Menorah, 142
Merneptah, 126
Merneptah stele, 126
Merodach–baladan, 314
Meshach, 475
meshiach, 515
Mesopotamia, 8, 11, 39
  map, 41
Mesopotamian law collections, 139
Messengers, 192
Messiah, 19, 255, 312, 318, 415, 515, 516
Messianic era, 284
Metaphor, 407, 408
Micah, 333, 361, 371, 372
Micaiah, 281, 284
Michal, 259
Michelangelo, 167
Midian, 117
Midianites, 240
Migration model, 223
Milgrom, Jacob, 153, 154
Military conquest model, 223
Millard, A. R., 61
Millennium, 7
Minor Prophets, 298, 360

Miriam, 125, 159
Mishnah, 518
Mistress Folly, 432
Mixed marriages, 495
mizmor ledavid, 409
Mizpah, 254, 255, 292
Moab, 49, 452, 541
Monotheism, 168
Mordecai, 459
Moresheth, 371
Mosaic authorship, 25
Mosaic covenant, 96
Mosaic tradition, 332
Moses, 13, 25, 96, 114, 128, 135, 152, 192, 210, 318, 329, 409
Moses, book of, 25
Mount Moriah, 86
Mountain of Elohim, 191
Mowinckel, Sigmund, 415
Mt. Ebal, 217
Mt. Gerazim, 217
Mt. Gilboa, 260
Mt. Horeb, 282
Mt. Nebo, 210, 284
Mt. Olympus, 51
Mt. Saphon, 51
Mt. Sinai, 13, 51, 96, 114, 166, 169
Mt. Zion, 169, 330, 415
Murphy, Roland, 426
Musicians, 402

Naboth, 283
Nadab, 135, 137, 152
Nahum, 374
Nakedness, 43, 44
Name, 73, 79
Naomi, 451
Nathan, 15, 264, 265, 273
Nature wisdom, 426
Naveh, Joseph, 282
Nazirite vow, 156, 242
Nebuchadnezzar, 17, 292, 334, 352, 373, 375, 475
Neco, 291, 330
Nehemiah, 19, 492, 496
  memoirs, 496, 497
nevi'im, 3
New covenant, 335, 336
New exodus, 314
New spirit, 382
New Testament, 25, 514
Newsom, Carol A., 432
Nicholson, Ernest W., 176, 338
Nineveh, 292, 374, 383
Noah's insobriety, 48
Noah, 48, 70, 72, 92
Noahic covenant, 92
Normalcy, 150, 151
Northern Kingdom, 16

Noth, Martin, 26, 196, 205, 223
Numbers, 156–161

O'Connor, Michael J., 403, 405
Offspring, theme of, 100
Oholah, 349
Oholibah, 349
Old Epic, 30
Old Testament, 2
  books of, 5–6
  survey of history, 10–20
  time line, 11
Oracle, 239
Oracles against foreign nations, 350, 351, 362, 365
Oral Torah, 2, 518
Oral tradition, 4
Order, 426, 428, 456
Original sin, 46
Othniel, 238

P, 31
Paddan-aram, 90
Palestinian Judaism, 507
Paradise, 39
Parallelism, 404
  antithetic, 405
  climactic, 405
  synonymous, 405
  synthetic, 405
Paranomasia, 404
Pashur, 337
Passover, 13, 121, 155, 171, 175, 213, 381, 446, 491, 494, 516
Passover seder, 122
Patriarchs, 12
Peniel, 91
Peninnah, 252
Pentateuch, 24, 198, 497
  documentary hypothesis, 25
Pentecost, 171, 446, 516
Penuel, 91
People of God, 173
People of the land, 372
Peor, 161
Percy, Walker, 470
Perdue, Leo G., 428
Persian Empire, map, 377, 460, 493
Personification, 408, 432
pesach, 446
pesharim, 513
Petition, 410
Pharisees, 19, 508
Pharoah, 103, 115
Philistines, 14, 49, 233, 242, 243, 253, 258, 261
Philo, 25

Thanksgiving, 413
   group, 414
   individual, 413
Thematic analysis, 301
Theocracy, 180, 255, 353
Theodicy, 375, 428
Theological analysis, 301
Theology of retribution,
   438, 440
Theology, 9
Theophany, 82, 127, 129,
   134, 282, 344, 383,
   436
Third Isaiah, 319
Thomas, D. Winton, 450
Throne-chariot, 344, 346
Tiamat, 54, 62, 63, 65
Tigay, Jeffrey, 69
Tiglath-Pileser III, 287,
   288, 311, 366
Tigris River, 11, 39
tishah be'av, 446, 455
Tobiah, 496
toledot, 66, 97, 106
Torah, 3, 4, 19, 24–33,
   186–198, 495
   book of the, 175
   terms for, 24
   time line, 197
Torah psalms, 416
Tower of Babel, 49–52,
   72, 78
Tradition history, 26
Transjordan, 90, 211
Tree of knowledge, 40
Tri-level concept of the
   cosmos, 132

Tribal federation, 255
Tribal territories, map, 222
Tricolon, 404
Tristich, 404
Trito-Isaiah, 319
Twelve Prophets, 360
Tyre, 352

Ugarit, 43, 236
Ugaritic texts, 474
Unclean, 150
Underworld, 439, 449
United Kingdom, 14
Unleavened bread, 122
Ur, 12
Uriah, 265
Urim and Thummim, 152
Utnapishtim, 70

Valley of dry bones, 353
Van Seters, John, 32
vaticinia ex eventu, 472
Vine, 348
Vision of a restored temple,
   354
Visions, 83, 192
von Rad, 172, 175, 198,
   206, 425, 426, 427
Voskuil, Dennis, 486
Vow of praise, 410, 419

Warfare, 215
Waters of chaos, 54, 415,
   477
Weinfeld, Moshe, 176
Weippert, Manfred, 223

Wenham, Gordon, 149
Westermann, Claus, 190,
   301, 413, 439
Whedbee, J. William, 439
White, John Bradley, 449
Whybray, Roger N., 33,
   318, 425, 430
Wilderness, 211
Wilderness journey, 125
   map, 158
Williamson, H. G. M., 489
Wilson, Robert R., 70,
   301, 489
Winged figures, 309
Winged lion, 478
Wisdom, 425
   literature, 397, 424–428,
      501
   of Solomon, 275, 425
   psalms, 417
   tradition, 425
Wolf, H., 311
Wolff, Hans W., 206, 362,
   370, 371
Woman, 40
Wood, Bryant G., 216
Word of God, 31, 195, 322
Worship, 114, 174, 497
   centralization of, 169
Wright, G. Ernest, 223,
   458
Writings, 3, 4, 397–399,
   501–503
Written Torah, 2, 518

Xerxes I, 459

Yadin, Yigael, 219, 363
Yahweh, 14, 25, 51
yahweh, 120
Yahweh of hosts, 310
Yahweh's kingship, 415
Yahwist source, 26, 27, 32,
   38, 65, 123, 186–190
Yahwist-Elohist edition, 30
Year of Jubilee, 155
yester hara, 46
yester hatov, 46
YHWH, 14, 25, 93
YHWH Elohim, 39, 43
YHWH's servant, 211
Yisrael, 369
Yizreel, 369
Yom Kippur, 156

Zadok, 15, 253, 274, 275,
   328, 354, 494
Zarephath, 281
Zealots, 20, 507
Zechariah 9, 379, 380, 494
Zedekiah, 17, 292, 329,
   334
Zephaniah, 327, 373
Zerubbabel, 19, 318, 378,
   379, 418, 492, 494
Zeus, 51
Ziggurat, 51, 52
Zimmerli, Walter, 355
Zion, 308, 318
Zion theology, 279, 330,
   372
Zipporah, 114
Zophar, 435, 437